PALOS HEIGHTS PUBLIC LIBRARY

W9-AVP-981

APR 2 3 2019

Rick Steves®

SICILY

EST. PHL 1944 | PALOS HEIGHTS
PUBLIC LIBRARY

Rick Steves & Sarah Murdoch
with Alfio Di Mauro

CONTENTS

Welcome to Rick Steves' Europe

Travel is intensified living—maximum thrills per minute and one of the last great sources of legal adventure. Travel is freedom. It's recess, and we need it.

I discovered a passion for European travel as a teen and have been sharing it ever since—through my tours, public television and radio shows, and travel guide-books. Over the years, I've taught thousands of travelers how to best enjoy Europe's blockbuster sights—and experience "Back Door" discoveries that most tourists miss.

Written with my talented co-author, Sarah Murdoch, this book offers you a balanced mix of Sicily's lively cities and cozy towns, from bustling Catania to sleepy Cefalù. And it's selective: Rather than listing dozens of archaeo-logical sites, we recommend only the best ones. Our self-guided museum tours and city walks give insight into the island's history and today's living, breathing culture.

We advocate traveling simply and smartly. Take advantage of our money- and time-saving tips on sight-seeing, transportation, and more. Try local, characteristic alternatives to expensive hotels and restaurants. In many ways, spending more money only builds a thicker wall between you and what you traveled so far to see.

We visit Sicily to experience it—to become temporary locals. Thoughtful travel engages us with the world, as we learn to appreciate other cultures and new ways to measure quality of life.

Judging from the positive feedback we receive from readers, this book will help you enjoy a fun, affordable, and rewarding vacation—whether it's your first trip or your tenth.

Buon viaggio! Happy travels!

Rick Steves

SICILY

Sicily is a fertile mix of geology and culture. Eruptions from its volcano, a glowing sun, generations of hard work, and wave after wave of civilizations storming through over the centuries—they all come together here, giving visitors a full-bodied travel experience that engages all the senses.

If Italy is one of the most dramatic, flamboyant places in Europe, Sicily is its distilled and intensified sibling—pure passion set in wild beauty. To those who have traveled in other parts of Italy, Sicily may feel similar—but it's not the same. The beauty is more rugged, the food is more flavorful, and the highs and lows of human history are more extreme. Coming to this island requires not only patience and a sense of adventure, but a willingness to be open to its seductions.

Sicily floats just off the toe of Italy's boot, like a soccer ball about to be kicked. At about 9,900 square miles, the island can be driven end to end in three hours—a journey that traverses a variety of landscapes, climates, and cultures. This is the only place I can think of where you can marvel at a well-preserved Greek temple, wander through Carthaginian ruins, listen to the Arab-influenced sales pitches of market vendors, dine on African couscous, and admire the glittering mosaics of a Norman cathedral...all in a single day.

Western Sicily is home to Palermo, the busy capital. Ringed by mountains and citrus groves, the once-elegant city has a 19th-century center spiced with fragments of Arab and Norman buildings from a thousand years ago. Nearby

Twilight Palermo, cradled by mountains; eye-catching ceramics in Erice

is the magnificent Norman cathedral at Monreale. Outside Palermo, this region is quiet and untamed—and often wet and windy—with rolling hills punctuated by jagged mountains and aquamarine waters lapping at windmill-sprinkled salt flats. On the southwest coast is Agrigento, home to an amazing ensemble of cliff-hanging Greek temples.

Things get drier as you move inland, with rolling fields of wheat. In the island's arid midsection, dusty medieval hill towns crown peaks scattered along dry riverbeds. Burrowed here, in the middle of nowhere, is the ancient, mosaic-rich Villa Romana del Casale.

Sicily's sunny eastern side is dominated by Europe's most active volcano, Mount Etna. From her smoking peak, the mountain slopes gently down to the southeast coast. Surrounding Etna are thriving cities (earthy Catania, historic Siracusa, and resorty Taormina), ancient wonders, and a tropical natural beauty. This side of the island bustles with shopping centers, factories, urban sprawl, and traffic. To the south, deep valleys and rolling green hills lead to a sunny coast strewn with ancient artifacts and wide sandy beaches.

Sicily's location at the center of the Mediterranean made it a strategic base for successive waves of long-ago invaders—each conquest leaving a mark on the culture and

A Sweet Trip Through Sicily

Typical Italian desserts, such as tiramisu and biscotti, are lightly sweetened and made with little butter. But Sicilian sweets pull out all the stops—they're packed with calories and sugary goodness.

The difference in desserts stems from 200-plus years of Arab occupation. When the Arabs arrived in 827, they brought date palms, oranges, lemons, almonds, ginger, and most important, sugar. New farming techniques, such as irrigation, made it possible to cultivate these delicacies—which thrived. Today's Sicilian desserts owe their sweetness to this Arabic heritage.

Most pastries are made with some combination of sugar, almonds, citrus, and ricotta. Every town has a *pasticceria* crafting the local version of each sweet, and many desserts have funny names and backstories (like the *minnuzze*, or breasts, of Sant'Agata—a round spongy cake topped with a cherry). Sicilian sweets are eaten any time of day, not just after a meal. A typical breakfast is a sweet one, with cakes, cookies, and pies, all washed down with a cappuccino.

Pasta di mandorla is an almond cookie. Made with almond flour, sugar, and egg whites, this basic recipe comes in many variations, usually named for the shape: little pyramids (*tette delle monache*, "nuns' breasts"), wavy wafers (*foglie da té*, "tea leaves"), or clumps of dough dropped roughly in the pan (*brutti e buoni*, "ugly but good").

Cassata is a classic, colorful, sugar-bomb cake. The simplest *cassata* is a crust filled with lightly sweetened ricotta. More elaborate ▶▶▶

Authentic Sicilian pastries include cassata *cake, the cherry–topped "breasts of Sant'Agata," and almond cookies stuffed with pistachios.*

▶▶▶ versions can have a base of liquor-infused cake, topped with sweet ricotta cheese and chocolate chips, then crowned with a layer of neon green marzipan and a sugar glaze.

Gelato is found all over Sicily, with local varieties such as *pecorino* (sheep's milk), *fichi d'india* (prickly pears), and *cassata*, a gelato version of the cake.

Sicilians also enjoy a lighter, more refreshing frozen treat called **granita.** Similar to a slushie, it's served only during the warmer months (April-Oct). Traditional flavors are *mandorla* (almond), *limone* (lemon), and *gelsi* (mulberry), but you'll find many others. Sicilians enjoy a *granita* for breakfast, topped with whipped cream. For a truly local treat, order your *granita* with a warm brioche bun to use as a scoop.

Cannoli are the most famous Sicilian sweet. A crispy fried pastry tube is filled with sweetened ricotta, then dusted with powdered sugar. The ends can be dipped in nuts, chocolate chips, or candied fruit, depending on the local style. The mark of a high-quality *cannolo* is one that's filled right when you order it—otherwise, the shell gets soggy and loses its crunch.

Choosing a Sicilian sweet from a pastry case can be a challenge, as they are all beautiful and enticing. If you can't decide, ask for *un piatto misto*, a mixed tray of shop selections. ◼❘

Gelato on soft brioche is Sicily's version of an ice cream sandwich (top). Granita mixed with spirits makes a slushy cocktail (middle). Take the cannoli, but only if they're filled at the last moment (bottom).

landscape. And that too has had an effect on Sicily's regional differences.

Carthaginians from North Africa used the west side of the island a trading base. Meanwhile, the Greeks settled the east side. Ancient ruins lie just beneath the surface all along this coast—remnants of Greek colonies that grew to surpass their homeland in splendor. Today, a cultural divide still remains. The west has traditionally been poorer and more rural, and the east more affluent and cosmopolitan.

The people of Sicily are warm and treat visitors almost as a curiosity. Although English is spotty outside of big cities, that's never a barrier to conversation, as most Sicilians speak more with their hands than with words.

Sicilians live outdoors, flooding piazzas and outside café tables. Early evening is the time for the ritual *passeggiata* promenade up and down the main drag. Sit in the town square and soak in the atmosphere, eavesdropping on the spirited conversations. Most people are talking about the same thing: food.

While food may be an art form in Italy, it's more like a religion in Sicily. Even if you know Italian food well, Sicilian cuisine will surprise you with its complexity—a legacy of its multicultural background. Sicily grows everything from citrus to nuts to tomatoes, and feeds the rest of Italy with its harvests. Produce is fresh, cheap, and plentiful—and sold at markets that more closely resemble an Arab souk than a European marketplace.

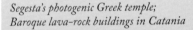

Segesta's photogenic Greek temple; Baroque lava-rock buildings in Catania

9

Taormina, in Mount Etna's shadow; locals celebrating one of Sicily's many religious processions

Family has always been the thread that holds this cultural tapestry together. Several generations often live in close proximity. Most Sicilians can say they reside within a few miles of where their great-grandparents lived. Sundays are set aside for family, with a big lunch or a drive in the country.

Sicily, like Italy, is almost entirely Roman Catholic. Attendance at Mass has sharply declined in the past 20 years, but that hasn't dampened a spirited participation in religious festivals. Every city has a patron saint who is celebrated effusively with processions, fireworks, and of course, eating.

Sicily lags behind mainland Italy in terms of modernization, but is quickly catching up. Some travelers are put off by the chaotic traffic, broken infrastructure, garbage, and graffiti. Public transit is spotty, opening hours change without notice, and Wi-Fi works when it wants to. Things won't go the way you expect, and "island time" is firmly in effect.

Rather than seeing these as problems, use them as an invitation to enjoy *il dolce far niente* ("the sweetness of doing nothing"), and surrender to the island's charms. Slow your pace, linger over a glass of wine, and breathe the sea air. Embrace, rather than resist the chaos, and open yourself up to the wonders of a place that lives by its own rules.

Sicily's Top Destinations

Mamma mia! There's so much to see in Sicily and so little time. This overview breaks Sicily's top destinations into must-see sights (to help first-time travelers plan their trip) and worth-it sights (for those with extra time or special interests). I've also suggested a minimum number of days to allow per destination.

MUST-SEE DESTINATIONS

Sicily's top cities show off the historical and cultural diversity of the island. For the best quick visit, focusing on these two destinations will give you a sampler platter of ancient Greek, Arab, Norman, and late Baroque Sicily, set against a modern backdrop.

▲▲▲Palermo (1-2 days)
Sicily's sprawling capital is gritty on its face, but its colorful markets and bustling shopping streets signal a fun-loving city in regeneration. Top activities include eating your way through the thriving Ballarò or Capo street markets, touring the massive Teatro Massimo, marveling at glittering mosaics at the Palatine Chapel or La Martorana Church, visiting the eerie Capuchin Crypt, and simply exploring the city's maze of back streets.

▲▲▲Siracusa (1-2 days)
Once the greatest ancient Greek city on Sicily, today's Siracusa centers around the lovely, historic island of Ortigia, boasting shabby-chic lanes, a grand Baroque piazza, and a lazy seafront promenade, plus a charming puppet museum/theater and a unique cathedral built on the skeleton of an ancient temple. Even the drab, urban, mainland part of town is worth a visit for its ancient sites, archaeological museum, spooky catacombs, and modern church.

Opposite: Byzantine mosaics of Monreale
This page: Palermo back street, Siracusa beach, Ballarò street market, and Siracusa's Puppet Museum

Opposite: Inlaid mosaic columns of Monreale's cloister

This page: Monreale Cathedral, mosaic floor at Villa Romana del Casale, picturesque Cefalù hugging the coast, and a golden sunset in Trapani

WORTH-IT DESTINATIONS

You can weave any of these destinations—rated ▲ or ▲▲—into your itinerary. It's easiest to add destinations based on proximity (if you're going to Palermo, Cefalù is next door), but some out-of-the-way places can merit the journey, depending on your time and interests.

▲▲Monreale Cathedral (half-day)

An easy side trip from Palermo, this hilltop cathedral is known for its well-preserved interior, wallpapered with golden Byzantine mosaics, and an adjoining Benedictine monastery.

▲▲Cefalù (1 day)

This fishing-turned-beach-bum village, an hour from Palermo, has a charming old town center with a Norman cathedral, fine seafood options, and an inviting, sandy beach.

▲Trapani & the West Coast (1-2 days)

The laid-back port town of Trapani, famous for its nearby salt flats, makes an easy home base for day trips to the hilltop village of Erice, fishing island of Favignana, Carthaginian ruins at Mozia, and ancient ruins of Segesta and Selinunte.

▲▲Agrigento (1 day)

This town, on the southern coast, is home to Sicily's premier ancient attraction: the Greek ruins at the Valley of the Temples, with a fine archaeological museum nearby.

▲▲Villa Romana del Casale (half-day)

Deep in the middle of the island, this remote palace ruin has the largest collection of Roman mosaics ever found in situ—with 32,000 exquisite square feet detailing wild animal hunts, myths, and chariot races.

▲▲Ragusa & the Southeast (1-2 days)

The southeastern corner of Sicily is packed with rolling hills and picturesque towns—the finest being Ragusa, with higgledy-piggledy stone homes blanketing two adjacent hilltops. From here, Modica (famous for chocolate), the valley village of Scicli, the scenic southern coastline, and the showcase Baroque city of Noto are within reach.

▲Catania (half-day)

Sicily's second city and the de facto capital of the east, workaday Catania is most useful as a transportation hub. Still, its rejuvenated Baroque city center is worth a visit for its splashy fish market, hidden Roman theater, and rare-in-Italy WWII museum.

▲▲Mount Etna (1 day)

The most active volcano in Europe is also the top tourist sight in Sicily. Activities include hikes in a lunar landscape, a visit to the steaming summit, and tours and tastings at up-and-coming wineries on its north slope.

▲Taormina (1 day)

Perched cliffside overlooking the sea, this cushy resort town with a Grand Tour vibe offers enjoyable views of Mount Etna, a dramatic Greek-Roman Theater, easy access to the island's east side, and the chance to rub shoulders with high-end tourists.

Catania fish market; a view of stair-stepped Ragusa

Planning Your Trip

To plan your trip, you'll need to design your itinerary—choosing where and when to go, how you'll travel, and how many days to spend at each destination. For my best advice on sightseeing, accommodations, restaurants, and transportation, see the Practicalities chapter.

DESIGNING AN ITINERARY

As you read this book and learn your options...

Choose your top destinations.

My recommended itineraries (see the next page) give you an idea of how much you can reasonably see in one or two weeks, but you can adapt the plans to fit your own interests and time frame.

City lovers could spend three or four days in Palermo, taking in the 19th-century atmosphere, exploring the churches and many interesting museums, and day-tripping to nearby sights. Wine connoisseurs could spend several days in the countryside (especially along the slopes of Mount Etna) sampling regional vintages. And beach bums could easily lose a week idling on the sandy beaches at Cefalù.

Decide when to go.

Sicily is one of the few European destinations that is open year-round. March through June and October are ideal, with few crowds, lots of festivals, and mild weather. The days leading up to Easter are full of celebrations, and

Sicily's Best Two-Week Trip by Car

To get the most from your time in Sicily, it's best to have a car. This two-week itinerary covers the island's top sights.

Day	Plan	Sleep in
1	Fly into Palermo, begin sightseeing there	Palermo
2	Sightsee Palermo; side-trip to Monreale	Palermo
3	Pick up car, visit Segesta en route to Trapani	Trapani
4	Day-trip to Mozia and the salt flats, and up to Erice	Trapani
5	Morning drive to Agrigento to tour the Valley of the Temples	Agrigento
6	Morning drive to Villa Romana del Casale, sightsee there, then afternoon drive to Ragusa	Ragusa
7	Follow my southeast Sicily countryside drive (with stops in Scicli and Modica)	Ragusa
8	Morning drive to Noto, then to Siracusa; start sightseeing there	Siracusa
9	Sightsee Siracusa	Siracusa
10	Drive north, choosing between Catania (fish market and WWII museum) or Mount Etna (volcanic sights and wineries); end your day in Taormina	Taormina
11	Vacation from your vacation in Taormina (or day-trip to Etna wineries)	Taormina
12	Morning drive to Cefalù, afternoon on the beach	Cefalù
13	Return to Palermo, drop off car, fly out of Palermo	

Tips: To avoid driving in intense Palermo, pick up your rental car from the airport as you leave town. With extra time, spend more days in Palermo and include both Catania and Mount Etna.

With Less Time: To pare this itinerary down to one week, from Palermo (2 nights) head directly to Agrigento (1 night) and the Valley of the Temples. From Agrigento, visit Villa Romana del Casale on the way to Siracusa (2 nights). Then drive north, sightseeing at Catania or Mount Etna along the way to Taormina (2 nights). The next day, drive to Catania, where you can drop the car and fly elsewhere.

Sicily's Best One-Week Trip by Bus and Train

If you're relying on public transportation, it's wise to group over-nights in big cities and day-trip from there.

Day	Plan	Sleep in
1	Fly into Palermo, begin sightseeing there	Palermo
2	Sightsee Palermo; side-trip to Monreale	Palermo
3	Day-trip to beachy Cefalù (1 hour by train) or the Valley of the Temples in Agrigento (2 hours by bus)	Palermo
4	Morning in Palermo, afternoon bus to Siracusa (3.5 hours)	Siracusa
5	Sightsee Siracusa	Siracusa
6	Morning in Siracusa, afternoon train to Taormina (2 hours)	Taormina
7	Join an excursion tour to Mount Etna or take it easy in Taormina	Taormina
8	Bus to Catania Airport (1.5 hours) and fly out from there	

With More Time: You can stretch out this itinerary by doing any of the following: overnight in Cefalù (train); add Trapani (bus); spend a night or two in Catania (train/bus); or relax in Ragusa for a night or two (train), with a side trip (by bus) to Noto.

The vertical Baroque city of Modica, best known for its chocolate; the salt flats near Mozia, with its medieval windmills

worth planning around. July and August are hot and can be crowded—especially at beaches and resorts. September is the busiest (and most expensive) month. Note that even at its liveliest, the island is far less crowded than the big, mainland Italian cities.

In the off-season (roughly Nov-Feb), Sicily can be chilly (temperatures in the 40s and snow at high altitudes), but you'll have the island to yourself. Bring plenty of layers, and be prepared for cooler inside temperatures, as Sicilians don't heat their houses the way Americans do. Expect shorter hours, more lunchtime breaks at sights, and fewer activities. Stick to bigger cities, as remote areas shut down.

For temperature specifics, see the climate chart in the appendix.

Connect the dots.

Link your destinations into a logical route. Determine which cities you'll fly into and out of. Catania in the east and Palermo are the biggest airports. Begin your search for transatlantic flights at Kayak.com.

Decide if you'll travel by car or public transportation, or a combination. A car is particularly helpful for exploring west and southeast Sicily (where public transportation can be sparse) but is useless in big cities (park it). Trains connect some cities, but not all. Long-distance buses fill in the gaps, but few run on Sundays and holidays.

Trip Costs Per Person

Run a reality check on your dream trip. You'll have major transportation costs in addition to daily expenses.

Flight: A round-trip flight from the US to Palermo costs about $1,000-2,000, depending on where you fly from and when.

Public Transportation: For a two-week trip, allow $75 for buses and trains. In some cases, a short flight can be cheaper than taking the train.

Car Rental: Allow roughly $250 per week, not including tolls, gas, parking, and insurance (theft insurance is mandatory in Italy).

AVERAGE DAILY EXPENSES PER PERSON

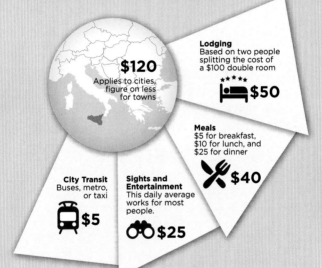

$120
Applies to cities, figure on less for towns

Lodging
Based on two people splitting the cost of a $100 double room
★★★★
$50

Meals
$5 for breakfast, $10 for lunch, and $25 for dinner
$40

City Transit
Buses, metro, or taxi
$5

Sights and Entertainment
This daily average works for most people.
$25

Budget Tips

You can cut my suggested average daily expenses by taking advantage of the deals you'll find throughout Sicily and mentioned in this book.

Avid sightseers buy combo-tickets or passes that cover multiple museums. If a town doesn't offer deals, visit only the sights you most want to see, and seek out free sights and experiences (people-watching counts).

Some businesses—especially hotels and walking-tour companies—offer discounts to my readers (look for the RS% symbol in the listings in this book).

Book your rooms directly with the hotel. Some hotels offer a discount if you pay ▶▶▶

Rick Steves Sicily

▶▶▶ in cash and/or stay three or more nights (check online or ask).

Rooms cost less outside of peak season (July–Sept). And even seniors can sleep cheap in hostels (some have double rooms) for about $20 per person. Or check Airbnb-type sites for deals.

It's no hardship to eat cheap in Sicily. You can get tasty, inexpensive meals at bars, markets, or take-away counters. Cultivate the art of picnicking in atmospheric settings.

When you splurge, choose an experience you'll always remember, such as a food tour or a boat ride. Minimize souvenir shopping—how will you get it all home? Focus instead on collecting wonderful memories. ■

A vineyard near Catania, a wine bar (enoteca) featuring typical Sicilian drinks, and a welcoming hotel staff in Palermo

To determine approximate drive times between your destinations, consult the driving chart in the Practicalities chapter. Bus and train travel times are given in this book (in the "Connections" sections per chapter); for schedules, confirm bus travel locally and see Trenitalia.com for trains. To go beyond Sicily, check budget intra-European flights at Skycanner.com.

Write out a day-by-day itinerary.

Figure out how many destinations fit comfortably in your time frame. Don't overdo it—few travelers wish they'd hurried more. Allow enough days per stop (see estimates in "Sicily's Top Destinations," earlier). Minimize one-night stands. It can be worth taking an afternoon drive or bus ride to settle into a town for two consecu-tive nights—and gain a full day for sightseeing. Allot sufficient time for transportation; whether you travel by train, bus, or car, it'll take a half-day to get between most destinations.

Staying in a home base (like Taormina) and making day trips can be more time-efficient than changing locations and hotels.

Take sight closures into account. Avoid visiting a town on the one day a week its must-see sights are closed. Check if any holidays or festivals fall during your trip—these at-tract crowds and can close sights (for the latest, visit Italy's tourist website, www.italia.it).

Give yourself some slack. Every trip, and every trav-eler, needs downtime for doing laundry, picnic shopping, people-watching, and so on. Pace yourself. Assume you will return.

BEFORE YOU GO

You'll have a smoother trip if you tackle a few things ahead of time. For more information on these topics, see the Practicalities chapter, and check RickSteves.com for helpful travel tips and talks.

Make sure your passport is valid. If it's due to expire within six months of your ticketed date of return, you need to renew it. Allow up to six weeks to renew or get a passport (www.travel.state.gov).

Arrange your transportation. Book your international flights. Figure out your local transportation options: If renting a car, reserve it before you go. (If relying on trains and buses, buy tickets in Sicily.) If traveling beyond Sicily, book any cheap European flights you'll need. (You can wing it once you're there, but it may cost more.) Drivers: Consider bringing an International Driving Permit (sold at AAA offices in the US, www.aaa.com) along with your license.

Book rooms well in advance, especially if your trip falls during peak season or any major holidays or festivals.

Hire local guides in advance. Reserve ahead by email; popular guides can get booked up.

Consider travel insurance. Compare the cost of the insurance to the cost of your potential loss. Check whether your existing insurance (health, homeowners, or renters) covers you and your possessions overseas.

Call your bank. Alert your bank that you'll be using your debit and credit cards in Europe. Ask about transaction fees, and get the PIN number for your credit card. You don't need to bring euros for your trip; you can withdraw euros from cash machines in Europe.

Use your smartphone smartly. Sign up for an international service plan to reduce your costs, or rely on Wi-Fi in Europe instead. Download any apps you'll want on the road, such as maps, translation, transit schedules, and Rick Steves Audio Europe (see sidebar).

Pack light. You'll walk with your luggage more than you think. Bring a single carry-on bag and a daypack. Use the packing checklist in the appendix as a guide.

∩ Stick a Guidebook in Your Ear!

My Rick Steves Audio Europe app makes it easy to download audio content to enhance your trip. Enjoy my audio tours of many of Europe's top destinations and a library of insightful travel interviews from my public radio show with experts from Sicily and around the globe. The app and all of its content are entirely free. (And new content is added about twice a year.) You can download the app via Apple's App Store, Google Play, or Amazon's Appstore. For more info, see www.ricksteves.com/audioeurope.

Travel Smart

Sicily can fray nerves with its carefree approach to time and rules. If you have a positive attitude, equip yourself with good information (this book), and expect to travel smart, you will.

Read—and reread—this book. To have an "A" trip, be an "A" student. Note opening hours of sights, closed days, and any crowd-beating tips (but in Sicily, make sure to confirm hours locally). Check the latest at RickSteves.com/update.

Be your own tour guide. As you travel, get up-to-date info on sights, reserve tickets and tours, reconfirm hotels and travel arrangements, and check transit connections. Visit local tourist information offices (TIs). Upon arrival in a new town, lay the groundwork for a smooth departure; confirm the road, bus, or train you'll take when you leave.

Outsmart thieves. Pickpockets abound in crowded places where tourists congregate. Treat commotions as smokescreens for theft. Keep your cash, credit cards, and passport secure in a money belt tucked under your clothes; carry only a day's spending money in your front pocket. Don't set valuable items down on counters or café tabletops, where they can be quickly stolen or easily forgotten.

Minimize potential loss. Keep expensive gear to a minimum. Bring photocopies or take photos of important documents (passport and cards) to aid in replacement if they're lost or stolen. Back up photos and files frequently.

Beat the summer heat. If you wilt easily, choose a hotel with air-conditioning, start your day early, take a midday siesta, and resume your sightseeing later. Churches offer a cool haven (though dress modestly—no shorts or bare shoulders).

Take frequent *granita* breaks. Join the *passeggiata*, when locals stroll in the cool of the evening.

Guard your time and energy. Taking a taxi can be a good value if it saves you a long wait for a cheap bus or an exhausting walk across town. To avoid long lines, follow my crowd-beating tips, such as sightseeing early or late. For example, visiting Villa Romana del Casale early will let you enjoy the mosaics with fewer crowds on its narrow catwalks.

Be flexible. Even if you have a well-planned itinerary, expect changes, strikes, closures, sore feet, bad weather, and so on. Your Plan B could turn out to be even better.

Attempt the language. Many Sicilians—especially in the tourist trade and in cities—speak English, but if you learn

Taormina's main drag entices at night (top). Don't be afraid to negotiate at a market—it's a Sicilian sport (left).

even just a few phrases of Italian, you'll get more smiles and make more friends. Practice the survival phrases in the appendix of this book, and even better, bring a phrase book.

Connect with the culture. Interacting with locals carbonates your experience. Enjoy the friendliness of the Sicilian people. Ask questions; most locals are happy to point you in their idea of the right direction. Set up your own quest for the best *arancine* (fried rice balls). When an opportunity pops up, make it a habit to say yes.

Sicily...here you come!

PALERMO

Misunderstood, underrated Palermo may be Sicily's most delightful surprise. For years, its touristic reputation was tarnished: gritty, run-down, polluted, traffic-clogged, crime-ridden, and synonymous with Mafia violence. But those days are long gone. Over the last decade or so, the city has revitalized itself with new museums, gentrified neighborhoods, pedestrianized streets, and upscale shops and hotels. The attitude towards the Mafia has also changed, and its influence has significantly diminished. Today, travelers are surprised by how much Palermo (pop. 680,000) entertains them with striking architecture, a cosmopolitan vibe, and a fun-loving energy—while still maintaining the wonderful edge that makes travel in Sicily such a treat.

While other parts of the island are known for their ancient sites, Palermo only really began to thrive under Arab rule (9th-11th century), when it became an impressive metropolis. The Norman invaders took note and claimed Palermo as their capital. And since then, with each successive wave of rulers, Palermo has remained Sicily's leading city—layered with fascinating artifacts of each era.

Spend a day (or two) exploring Palermo's wide, lively, endearingly potholed streets. Dodge motor scooters on "pedestrianized" lanes as you visit great museums (art, archaeology, aristocratic villas, marionettes, and more). Tour some of Italy's most exuberantly decorated churches, and rub shoulders with the *palermitani* (as the locals are known) at one of the city's famous landmarks (the Quattro Canti intersection, or the nearby Fountain of Shame). Commune with the dearly departed at the thought-provoking Capuchin crypt, and ogle stunning golden mosaics.

Palermo is also home to Italy's most vivid street markets. Make

Palermo's History

Like much of Sicily, Palermo has a complicated history of domination. But unlike much of the island, it doesn't have Greek roots. The city was founded in the eighth century BC by Phoenician traders, near the natural harbor between two rivers.

Although the town was never conquered by the Greeks, it adopted a Greek name, Panormus (meaning "all port"), because it was a critical trading center for the mostly Greek island. Palermo's prized location—with its excellent port and the fertility of the thriving valley behind it—attracted a parade of successive invaders.

Palermo was a small settlement until the Arabs arrived (in AD 827) and put it on the map by making it the capital of the island. Under Arab rule, Palermo flourished and became one of Europe's leading cities. With a population of 100,000, it was the second-largest city in Europe (only Córdoba was bigger). During those times, Palermo had an estimated 300 mosques. Eventually the city covered up its rivers to allow expansion. (For more on the important Arab period in Palermo, see the "Arab Palermo" sidebar, later in this chapter.)

Then came the Normans, who arrived in the late 11th century. The Normans were originally Vikings, settling first in northern France, and then conquering England, southern Italy, and finally Sicily. The first Norman king of Sicily, Roger II (r. 1130-1154), found a multicultural island ruled by Arabs. Rather than impose his own culture and Roman Catholic religion, he allowed the ethnic groups to stay—each continuing in their traditional businesses: the Arabs as master engineers and craftsmen, the Byzantine Greeks as teachers, and the Jews in finance and trade. This tolerant attitude, allowing each community to play to its strengths, led to a period of economic prosperity that ushered in a golden age for Sicily.

Norman rule was followed by a series of other overlords: the Holy Roman Empire (1189-1250), French Angevins (1250-1282), Spanish Aragons and Bourbons (1282-1860), and, finally, a unified Italy (the Risorgimento of the 1860s). And, as throughout Sicily, each period of rule left its mark on Palermo. But Palermo's colonial heritage has been a blessing in disguise. Today's city is a wonderful patchwork of architecture, works of art, traditions, dialects, and delightful food cultures.

a point to wander amidst a cacophony of musical sales pitches and let yourself be tempted by some of Italy's best street food. If spleen sandwiches and boiled octopus are just too much, stick to the saffron-scented *arancine* rice balls and other deep-fried goodies. And be sure to look up—otherwise you'll miss the city's spectacular setting, facing the sea, and filling the mouth of a lush valley tucked between dramatic mountains.

Palermo can feel a bit like Naples when it comes to "organized chaos." As a pedestrian, the traffic is chaotic (keep your head on a swivel). And even the city's prettiest public spaces are rough around the edges. But Palermo's decaying elegance is one of the reasons I like it so much. Don't be afraid to fully experience Palermo. Let its grime get under your fingernails. While a few timid travelers may run screaming, most dive in, fall in love with this warts-and-all city, and leave wanting more.

PLANNING YOUR TIME

On a quick visit, Palermo deserves at least one very full day. But of all the destinations in this book, Palermo is the one most deserving of additional time.

While crowds are generally not a concern in Palermo, the exception is the Palatine Chapel—where lines can be long with cruise-ship groups. You'll save time by visiting either first thing in the morning or at the end of the day.

Palermo in One Day

On Sundays, when the Norman Palace and the Palatine Chapel close early, rearrange this plan to arrive at the chapel when it opens.

Morning: Tour the Teatro Massimo, then follow my self-guided walking tour of the city's historic core. Finish in time for a street-food lunch at Ballarò Market (where grazing also counts as sightseeing).

Afternoon: After lunch, visit the macabre Capuchin Crypt. On your way back into town, visit the cathedral and the Palatine Chapel in the Norman Palace, arriving late in the day to avoid long lines (pay attention to last entry times). Note that the Palatine Chapel is skippable if you're heading to the similar but more impressive Monreale Cathedral.

Evening: Join the locals for the *passeggiata* or an *aperitivo* before heading to dinner. Or catch a puppet show or live performance (concerts, theater, dance) at Teatro Massimo or another venue.

With More Time

A second (or third or fourth) day gives you time to side-trip to see the stunning interior of Monreale Cathedral, the beach town of Cefalù, the mountaintop Sanctuary of Santa Rosalia, and/or the beachy burg of Mondello. Or there's plenty more to do in Palermo, including more market browsing, a street-food tour, and seeing additional sights in town.

Orientation to Palermo

The city center is ringed by an eyesore blight of suburbs—especially to the north—hastily erected and cheaply built by the Mafia in the postwar years. Fortunately, the tourists' Palermo is its fairly compact city center; you can walk briskly from one end to the other in 20 to 30 minutes. This zone is bounded by the Norman Palace to the west, Teatro Politeama to the north, the main Stazione Centrale train station to the south, and the harbor to the east.

Downtown Palermo is built on a predictable grid street plan, but within its quadrants, the side streets can spin around in confusing curlicues. It can be doubly confusing to get oriented because tourist maps tend to show the city the way locals think of it: with the harbor—which is actually to the east—at the top. (This book's maps, however, show north on top).

The intersection called **Quattro Canti**—"Four Corners," for its quartet of sculpted facades—is considered the center of the city. (Just around the corner are other major landmarks—the Fountain of Shame and the three stunning churches on Piazza Bellini.) Quattro Canti is where two big streets meet: The north-south **Via Maqueda** is the pedestrian-only shopping and strolling hotspot, passing in front of Teatro Massimo. And the east-west **Via Vittorio Emanuele** leads west to the cathedral and Norman Palace, and east past a thriving restaurant zone to the harbor.

Quattro Canti is also the point from which the city core is divided into four medieval quadrants—called *mandamenti*—which locals and savvy visitors use as a shorthand for navigating the city: the northeast quadrant is Castellammare (better known as the **Vucciria**), the southeast is the district known as **La Kalsa,** the northwest is **Capo,** and the southwest is Albergheria (also known as **Ballarò**).

A few blocks east of Via Maqueda is **Via Roma,** the main traffic artery through the center. It runs from the main train station in the south to Teatro Politeama in the north, parallel to Via Maqueda.

While most Palermo sightseeing is easily done on foot, there are a few outlying sights—such as the Capuchin Crypt, the Sanctuary of Santa Rosalia, the beach resort of Mondello, and (covered in the next chapter) the Monreale Cathedral. While each of these is reachable, up to a point, by public transit, it can be efficient to hire a taxi for a few hours to link these (or hire a private driver—see "Getting Around Palermo," later).

TOURIST INFORMATION

Palermo's main TI sits just below the Church of San Cataldo on Via Maqueda. It has bus schedules and current sightseeing information

(Mon-Fri 8:30-18:30, Sat from 9:30, closed Sun, Via Maqueda 191, tel. 091-740-8021, https://turismo.comune.palermo.it). You can also find a TI desk at Teatro Massimo and TI kiosks at Teatro Politeama, the port, and in the beach town of Mondello (generally open Mon-Fri 8:30-13:30, closed Sat-Sun).

ARRIVAL IN PALERMO

For details on arriving by plane or boat, see "Palermo Connections" at the end of this chapter.

By Train: Palermo's main train station—Stazione Centrale—is at the southern edge of the central core, facing straight up Via Roma. Inside the station are basic eateries and predictable services; pay WCs are near track 1, and a luggage-storage office is near track 3. The main building also has ticket desks and machines, and a tobacco shop that sells local city bus tickets. With your back to the tracks, walk straight out the front door of the station to exit onto Piazza Giulio Cesare, where you'll find city buses, taxis, and (on the right) buses to the airport. Via Roma and the center of town is straight ahead; it's about a 15-minute walk to Quattro Canti. A taxi to most of my recommended hotels should cost around €10—but only catch a taxi where you see an official, orange *TAXI* sign. You can also take bus #102 or #124 straight up the Via Roma artery (buses leave from stop directly in front of the station; for details, see "Getting Around Palermo," later).

By Bus: Palermo's main bus terminal clings alongside the central station's train tracks (along track 1). Leaving your bus, follow the tracks (past a bus ticket office) into the main part of the train station; walk straight through the station and out the front door, then follow the directions above. Taxis often wait near arriving buses.

To get *to* the bus station, first go inside the train station, then bear left, alongside the outer platform of track 1 (follow the blue line in the pavement; look for *terminal bus*). First, you'll pass the bus ticket office, where each company operates its own sales window (the main operators here are Sais, www.saisautolinee.it; Interbus/Segesta/Etna Trasporti, www.interbus.it; and Salemi, www.autoservizisalemi.it). Just beyond that, buses line up in their numbered stalls.

By Car: Driving in Palermo makes no sense for the sightseer. Traffic moves in anything but a straight line; lights, signs, and laws are flagrantly ignored; buzzing motor scooters swarm everywhere; and double- or triple-parking while blocking traffic is common. I'd skip the stress and pick up your rental car at the airport when you leave town. If you do decide to drive in Palermo, be aware that the town center has a *Zona Traffico Limitato* (ZTL), or limited traffic zone, to reduce emissions and congestion. To drive within the

PALERMO

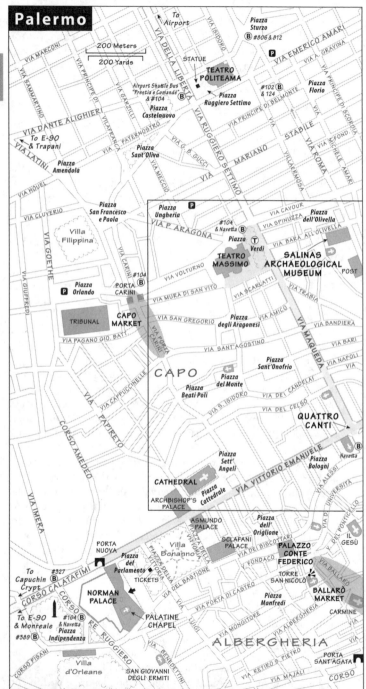

PALERMO

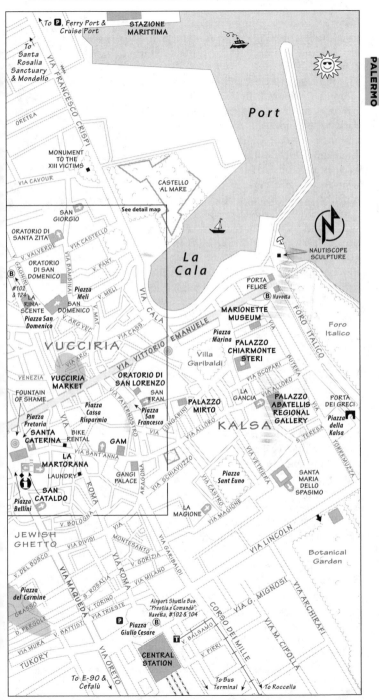

PALERMO

historic core during the week, you must purchase and activate a ZTL pass (for details,
see "Palermo Connections," at the end of the
chapter).

Parking spots inside the ZTL are scarce
(around €2/hour, €10-15/day). The easiest
parking option is in a secured underground
parking lot under the courthouse, near the
entrance to the Capo Market (Vittorio
Emanuele Orlando 49). Other underground
garages are a bit farther out: several options
near Teatro Politeama, such as Parking Tu-
minello on the corner of Via Roma and Via
Amari; and at Piazzale Ungheria. An easy

surface parking lot is at the port, at the end of Via Amari (€15/day).

HELPFUL HINTS

Safety Tips: While Palermo is generally safe, your wallet may not
be—particularly near the train station, at Ballarò Market,
and near the cruise port. As in any other big Italian city, use
common sense, wear a money belt, and be very careful with
your day bag. Secure your mobile phone and don't wear flashy
jewelry. Crowded street markets with lots of distractions are
common territory for thieves.

Bike Rental: Centrally located **Social Bike,** near Quattro Canti,
rents regular and electric bikes (€3/hour, €6/hour for electric,
daily 9:30-18:30, Discesa dei Giudici 21, mobile 328-284-
3734, www.socialbikepalermo.com).

Laundry: Il Pinguino has self-service washing machines on the
main drag (Mon-Sat 8:30-13:00 & 15:30-19:00, closed Sun,
Via Roma 154, mobile 380-341-9074).

Parking "Help": If you have a car and must park it on the street,
local men may "assist" you in finding street parking. It's smart
to give them a euro or two, as they make it their business to
"keep an eye on your car." Sadly, if you don't pay the local
man sitting on a chair nearby, there's a chance your car will be
robbed or damaged while you're sightseeing. It's also possible
they'll just pocket the money and disappear.

Best Views: Many Palermo sights (including the cathedral, the
Church of Santa Caterina, and the Teatro Massimo) offer a
"rooftop visit" for a few euros extra. While any of these can
give a nice overview of the city, doing all of them is redundant—pick one (the cathedral is probably best). For a free
view (mostly over the Piazza San Domenico), ride up to the
top-floor cafeteria at the La Rinascente department store (Via
Roma 289).

PALERMO

GETTING AROUND PALERMO

For most visitors, the best way to see Palermo is by foot. The streets of Via Maqueda and Via Vittorio Emanuele are nominally pedestrianized (but keep an eye out for bikes, scooters, and occasional cars) and enjoyable to stroll. Taxis and buses connect outlying sights.

Tuk-tuks and horse-drawn carriages loiter in the tourist zones to fleece unsuspecting visitors. Their scam is to quote a price up-front, but later claim that price is per person. If you are tempted by either of these services, be very clear with the driver before you get in; €30 per hour seems to be the fair base rate.

By Bus

Palermo's local bus company is AMAT. Single tickets are valid for 1.5 hours, including transfers; you can buy one at a newsstand or tobacco shop for €1.40, and sometimes on board for €1.80. Ask for *biglietto autobus* (beel-YEH-toh OW-toh-boos). A 24-hour ticket costs €3.50. All tickets must be validated in the yellow machines on the bus (www.amat.pa.it).

Bus stops are indicated by large *fermata* signs. The sign lists all stops on each route, with an arrow indicating the direction. A red dot is next to the name of the stop you're at. The frequency of bus departures is listed to the side, but rarely reflects reality. When your bus approaches, be sure to wave to the driver so they know to stop for you.

Bus hubs in the center include Stazione Centrale (for buses headed south, stop is in front of the train station); Piazza Indipendenza (west, stop is in front of the Norman Palace—from here buses fan out to the Capuchin Crypt and Monreale); and Piazza Ruggiero Settimo (north, in front of Teatro Politeama).

Most useful for travelers are buses #102 and #124, which stop all along Via Roma between Stazione Centrale and Teatro Politeama (including at Via Lattarini near Via Vittorio Emanuele and at the post office). Bus #104 links the Norman Palace, Capo Market, Teatro Massimo, and Teatro Politeama.

Free Shuttle Bus: An electric minibus (painted white, orange, and blue and labeled *Navetta*) runs around the historic center of Palermo; though it's designed for locals, visitors are welcome to hop on (no tickets needed, runs every 30 Sicilian minutes, less frequent Sun and holidays). It does a handy, one-way, clockwise loop past major landmarks in the city center, stopping at the following places in this order: the train station (in front), Piazza Indipendenza and the Norman Palace, Teatro Massimo (north side, near the taxi stand), and the harbor area at Piazza Marina, where it takes a break. Finally it runs back through the center of town to Quattro Canti. Because it's a one-way loop, it's much handier for

Palermo at a Glance

▲▲**Church of Santa Caterina** Sicilian Baroque architecture at its most extravagant. **Hours:** Mon-Sat 9:30-13:00 & 15:30-19:00, Sun 9:30-13:30; Nov-March daily 9:30-13:30. See page 56.

▲▲**Church of La Martorana** Oldest Byzantine-Norman mosaics in Sicily. **Hours:** Mon-Sat 9:30-13:00 & 15:30-17:30, Sun 9:00-10:30. See page 57.

▲▲**Teatro Massimo** Landmark Art Nouveau opera house—the largest in Italy. **Hours:** Daily 9:30-18:00. See page 59.

▲▲**Palatine Chapel and Norman Palace** Glittering mosaic-clad chapel inside Europe's oldest royal residence. **Hours:** Mon-Sat 8:15-17:40, Sun until 13:00 (chapel closed Sun 9:45-11:30). See page 63.

▲▲**Capuchin Crypt** Fascinating, albeit morbid, collection of embalmed bodies. **Hours:** Daily 9:00-13:00 & 15:00-18:00. See page 74.

▲▲**Sanctuary of Santa Rosalia** Mountaintop shrine dedicated to the patron saint of Palermo. **Hours:** Daily 7:30-19:30. See page 77.

▲▲**Il Ballarò Market** Palermo's oldest and most authentic street market. **Hours:** Generally open Mon-Sat 6:00-14:00, closed Sun. See page 73.

▲▲**Oratory of San Lorenzo** Playful Baroque space and site of notorious theft of Caravaggio masterpiece. **Hours:** Daily 10:00-18:00. See page 50.

getting, say, from the station to the Norman Palace than vice-versa. These shuttles can be crammed, so they work best if you're patient and not in a hurry. As with all public buses in Palermo, watch for pickpockets. You may even find it enjoyable to simply hop on and joy ride through the kaleidoscopic wonder of Sicily's biggest and liveliest city.

By Taxi

Palermo is a fine taxi town—especially when it's hot. You'll find taxis at orange-signed *TAXI* stands, usually near major attractions such as Teatro Massimo or the Norman Palace. If you can't find a taxi stand, ask someone at a bar or tobacco shop to call one for you. A typical ride in the city—say, from Teatro Massimo or the train

▲**Church of San Cataldo** Time-warp church with interesting mix of Arab and Norman architecture. **Hours:** Daily 9:00-19:00. See page 58.

▲**Salinas Regional Archaeological Museum** Limited but top-notch collection of ancient Greek, Roman, and Carthaginian art. **Hours:** Tue-Sat 9:30-19:00, Sun until 14:00, closed Mon. See page 59.

▲**Palermo Cathedral** City's favorite church with a wild mix of architectural styles. **Hours:** Mon-Sat 7:00-19:00, Sun 8:00-13:00 & 16:00-19:00. See page 62.

▲**Palazzo Chiaramonte Steri** Palace that also served as a prison for victims of the Spanish Inquisition. **Hours:** Tue-Sun 10:00-19:00, closed Mon. See page 68.

▲**Regional Art Gallery at Palazzo Abatellis** Palermo's top art museum, with Antonello da Messina masterpiece. **Hours:** Tue-Fri 9:00-19:00, Sat-Sun until 13:30, closed Mon. See page 69.

▲**Palazzo Mirto** Intimate peek at faded home of Sicilian aristocrats. **Hours:** Tue-Sat 9:00-18:00, Sun until 13:00, closed Mon. See page 70.

▲**Palazzo Conte Federico** Tour of elegant palace with an aristocrat as your guide. **Hours:** Thu-Tue 11:00-16:00, closed Wed. See page 72.

▲**Il Capo Market** Classic street market in city center. **Hours:** Generally open Mon-Sat 6:00-14:00, closed Sun. See page 74.

station to the Norman Palace—should run about €10. Make sure the meter is running—or, if you're going somewhere more distant, agree to a fixed price and have the driver write down the amount before you get in the cab. Taxis can be hired hourly (about €30/hour, €120/half-day), and most drivers can suggest a nice sightseeing itinerary for a fixed price. Avoid hawkers at tourist destinations offering rides—stick to official taxis (tel. 091-6878, www. radiotaxitrinacria.it).

By Private Driver
Salvatore "Sal" Coppola and his team of English-speaking drivers offer a handy way to reach sights near Palermo. They can take you to outlying sights around Palermo, such as Monreale and the

beaches of Mondello (€280/about 8 hours for up to 3 people); or farther afield, on side-trips to Cefalù, or to Segesta and Erice near Trapani (€350/8 hours). Sal also offers help tracking down your Sicilian roots in the countryside near Palermo, and runs multiday tours around Sicily (ask for prices for larger groups or custom trips, mobile 339-466-1233, www.insightsicily.it, salcop@libero.it).

Tours in Palermo

Bus Tours

City Sightseeing's hop-on, hop-off buses run generic tours with recorded narrations in two loops—one that hits most of the highlights with an occasional extension to Monreale, and another that hits lesser sights. This can be a low-stress, if expensive, way to get to Monreale (€20/24 hours on either route, April-Oct runs every 30 minutes 9:30-17:00, fewer departures off-season, Monreale bus departs from Piazza Indipendenza in front of the Norman Palace, tel. 055-901-938, www.city-sightseeing.it). Those arriving in Palermo on a cruise will find this ideal, as it picks up at the port.

Cheapskates can see many of the sights by riding the **free shuttle bus** *(navetta)* that loops around the city center (see "By Bus," earlier).

Bike Tours

Social Bike offers bike tours around the city in places that buses can't go. Their three-hour Palermo Old Town tour glides by the major sights and includes street food stops (€40); they also have longer rides into the outskirts (Discesa dei Giudici 21, mobile 328-284-3734, www.socialbikepalermo.com, Chiara and Anthony).

Walking Tour

Domenico Aronica, a professional photographer and guide, leads easygoing walking tours around the back streets of Palermo with entertaining commentary sprinkled with dad jokes. His tour varies each day and usually includes a stop for street food (€30, most days at 9:20, 3.5 hours, maximum 12 people, reservations required, mobile 347-133-6788, www.palermowalkingtour.com, domenico@domenicoaronica.com).

Local Guides

Jacqueline Alio is a tour guide and author, raised in the US, who has returned to her homeland to share her passion for Sicily. Her tours make the complex history of Palermo accessible, and her depth of knowledge works well for novices and historians alike (€120/2 hours, €180/half-day, www.palermoguide.net, aliojaqueline@gmail.com).

Andrea Masi is an archaeologist who grew up in England

and calls both places home. His strength is the archaeological areas of Sicily, such as Mozia and Segesta, but he also guides in the Palermo area (€150/half-day, mobile 339-440-9377, www. masitourguidesicily.com, masiandrea63@libero.it).

Food Tours

Streaty Food Tours provides a combination of nibbles and history on its entertaining tours. Marco and his colleagues will take you on a four-hour walk, sampling street food and delving into areas that a typical tourist might miss. This is a great way to spend time exploring Palermo with an energetic local (€35-40, maximum 12 people, www.streaty.com, info@streaty.com).

Market Tour and Cooking Class

Duchess Nicoletta, who rents apartments in her palace (see page 89), is also a well-known chef offering cooking courses. She'll lead you on a tour of a local market, then return to her palace for cooking instruction and lunch (€160/person, 5 hours including palace tour and lunch, usually Fri-Sat at 10:00—confirm ahead, mobile 333-316-5432, www.butera28.it, info@cookingwiththeduchess. com).

Palermo City Walk

On this self-guided walk, we'll loop from Teatro Massimo through the historic core of the city, exploring back streets and checking out churches. It's best to do the walk in the morning; if you finish by lunchtime, you can head to the Ballarò or Capo markets for street food (closed Sun). While this walk could be done without stops in an hour, there are several sightseeing opportunities en route; the most worthwhile stops (Teatro Massimo at the beginning, three churches on Piazza Bellini at the end) add another two to three hours.

❶ Teatro Massimo

Close to the heart of Palermo and its people, Italy's largest opera house (and Europe's third-largest, rated ▲▲) fills Piazza Verdi in a dramatic, Neoclas-  sical fashion. Started in 1875, soon after the Risorgimento united Italy and civic pride was at a peak, the massive theater took 22 years to build and became a symbol of the up-and-coming city as a magnet for arts and culture.

PALERMO

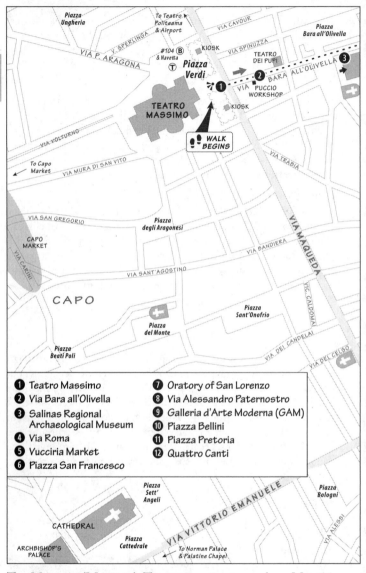

1. Teatro Massimo
2. Via Bara all'Olivella
3. Salinas Regional Archaeological Museum
4. Via Roma
5. Vucciria Market
6. Piazza San Francesco
7. Oratory of San Lorenzo
8. Via Alessandro Paternostro
9. Galleria d'Arte Moderna (GAM)
10. Piazza Bellini
11. Piazza Pretoria
12. Quattro Canti

The Massimo (Maximus) Theater was inaugurated on May 16, 1897 with a performance of *Falstaff*, the last opera written by then-80-year-old Giuseppe Verdi, to whom this square was dedicated.

True to its name, Teatro Massimo has a footprint of nearly two acres, half of which houses the massive backstage. While it may not appear so at ground level, this is also one of the tallest buildings in Palermo, accommodating a towering fly-space used to house scenery (hidden behind the pediment and dome).

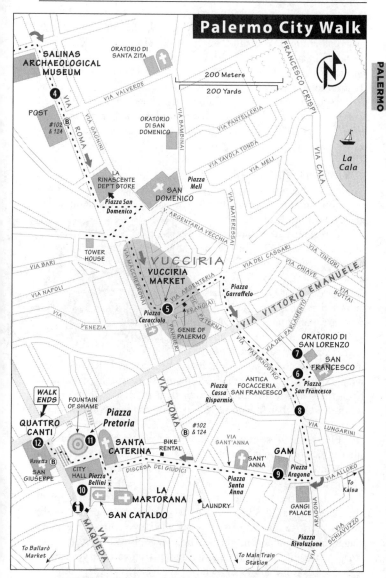

Palermo City Walk

If the grand front staircase looks familiar, you might remember it from the final scene of the *Godfather* trilogy. The two elegant **kiosks** on either side of the piazza facing the opera house were the original ticket booths.

While the exterior is stern Neoclassicism, the interior is a frillier and more playful Art Nouveau (called Liberty Style in Italy). **Performances** run virtually year-round, and tickets can be affordable (tickets sometimes available day-of-show, box office open Tue-Sun 9:30-18:00, closed Mon, tel. 091-605-3267, www. teatromassimo.it). You can duck into the **lobby** (to the left of the grand staircase) anytime the box office is open for a peek at the decor, to stop by the TI desk, or to have coffee at the Caffè del Teatro (open until 24:00).

Especially if you're not attending a performance, it's well worth joining a **30-minute guided tour** (described on page 59).

• *With the grand staircase at your back, walk straight across the street and jog slightly right to head up the lane called....*

❷ Via Bara all'Olivella

Enjoy a stroll along this little street, which is filled with small arti- san shops and touristy restaurants. Along the way, check out a few vignettes of local culture.

While Palermo may turn off some visitors with dirty and broken streets, remember to look up—where you'll see an entirely different city. Balconies (adorned with flowers or laun- dry) are common here. Older residents sit on them and chat with friends in adjacent build- ings, or talk to passersby on the street. Some balconies come wrapped in "privacy curtains"—allowing skirt-wearing women to hang their laundry while protecting their modesty. Conventional wisdom is that there are no secrets in Sicily, as there are always eyes on the street.

On the right, stop in at #60, and say *ciao* to **Signore Puccio.** He runs a workshop where he makes small, inlaid-wood art pieces and paints a variety of traditional handicrafts, such as colorful pa- pier-mâché boxes and nativity scenes.

A bit farther, on the left at #95, is the **Teatro dei Pupi** of the Cuticchio family. This Sicilian art form uses puppets on rods, unlike marionettes, which are controlled by strings. The plays staged by the puppeteers reenact fictional episodes from the epic story of the life of Charlemagne and his chivalrous yet merci- less knights (€10, shows most days April-Oct, weekdays often at 10:00, schedule posted on theater door, tel. 091-323-400, www. figlidartecuticchio.com).

Just beyond, on the right at #42 (labeled *torniere*), peek inside to watch a wood craftsman at work on the lathe, fabricating candle- sticks and reproduction parts for antique furniture.

Continue down Via Bara all'Olivella until you reach Piazza Bara all'Olivella. The building on the right is the ❸ **Salinas Re-**

gional Archaeological Museum, with one of Sicily's best archaeological collections (described later, under "Sights in Palermo").

• *Continue straight along the side of the museum. At the corner, turn right onto...*

❹ Via Roma

Opened in 1865 to celebrate the newly unified kingdom of Italy, this street throbs with cars, buses, and shoppers. This is the last artery still open to traffic through downtown Palermo, as the city has pedestrianized the other two major streets, Via Maqueda and Via Vittorio Emanuele. Traffic congestion has increased dramatically in Sicily in the past few years, as more people buy cars. To minimize traffic, the city recently created a limited traffic zone (ZTL)—charging a fee to drive in the city center—and added a free electric shuttle bus that circulates around the historic core.

The huge building on the right, dominating the street, is the main **post office,** built in the 1930s. This austere, imposing fascist

style of architecture was favored by Mussolini. Using materials and architectural language reminiscent of ancient Rome, Mussolini's architecture-as-propaganda sends one message: You are small. Individualism is eclipsed by the all-powerful state.

Cross the street, take in the scope of the post office, and then continue up the street; you'll find a sleek, blocky building on the left: **La Rinascente.** This is the Italian version of Nordstrom. Admire their high-fashion window displays, and step inside if you're in the mood for a bit of air-conditioning. If you're hungry, their top-floor terrace food court offers great views as well as sushi, pizza, and a mozzarella bar (daily 9:00-20:30, food court open until 23:00—entrance on Piazza San Domenico).

Continuing beyond La Rinascente, you'll reach Piazza San Domenico. Dominating the square is the huge Baroque **Church of San Domenico**—the city's second-largest. If it's open, step inside (free, Mon-Sat 8:30-16:00, Sun open only for Mass). This

very long church is bigger than it looks from the outside. The aisles are lined with tombs of famous Sicilians.

On the right aisle, about three-quarters of the way down, look for the tomb of Giovanni Falcone, marked *Magistrato—Eroe della Lotta alla Mafia* ("Magistrate—hero of the fight against the Mafia"). A Sicilian judge and prosecutor, Falcone led efforts to crack down on the Mafia, first in Palermo and later in Rome. After winning a series of convictions against Mafia leaders, Falcone, his wife, and several police officers were killed by a Mafia bomb in 1992. Falcone's death, intended to assert Mafia power, instead helped to turn public opinion against this social scourge. (For more on the Mafia in Sicily, see the sidebar on page 48.)

In the back-right corner is the elaborate float of the Virgin of the Holy Rosary, which is carried on people's backs through town each year. This is a tradition you'll see all over Sicily, where these religious processions are a fixture of life. Mary carries Jesus on a cloud of angels, as San Domenico (St. Dominic) kneels nearby.

Back out on Piazza San Domenico, with your back to the church, pass through the square and (carefully) cross Via Roma to Via Bandiera, and continue about 50 yards up the street. On the left at #14, you can see a Spanish Gothic **tower house,** the Palazzo Alliata di Pietratagliata, built in 1573. Even though Palermo has a long history, the majority of buildings you see today are Baroque, dating from the 1600s and 1700s, when the city was renovated by prosperous noble families. Prior to that (back when leading families needed to provide their own security), most of the city was made up of stone tower houses like this one.

• *Head back across the street, step back into the square, and turn right— facing the lane with the sign overhead reading* La Vucciria. *Before leaving Piazza San Domenico, consider a snack break at the recommended Bar Lucchese (on your left), well known for quality* granita, gelato, *and* spremuta—*fresh orange juice.*

When you're ready, head down Via Maccheronai (the "Street of the Pasta Makers") and wind your way through the stalls of the...

❺ La Vucciria Market

Browse the shops and stalls of Palermo's oldest marketplace (dead on Sunday). While this small market falls conveniently along the route of this walk, it pales in comparison to Palermo's biggies (Ballarò and Capo), which are much busier and more sprawling. The Vucciria Market (likely named for the French

boucherie—butcher) is less about the vendors, and all about experiences.

Exploring, you can find butchers, household goods, produce, fish, and deli meats and cheeses. At #30 (after the first set of stalls, on the right), a knife store sharpens knives the old-fashioned way, with the *arrotino* whetting stone.

Several blocks down, on the left at #9, saunter into **Taverna Azzurra** and sidle up to the bar for a quick glass of wine with the local characters. This gritty dive bar cultivates a clientele that's an oddly harmonious mix of blue-collar locals and gregarious tourists.

Walk to the square at the end of the street, **Piazza Caracciolo,** and notice what isn't there: market stalls. This once-sprawling market—which used to spill onto adjacent streets and squares—is getting quieter every year. Modern supermarkets are new in Palermo, and the competition has hit the traditional markets hard. Many stalls are disappearing, and being replaced by cocktail bars and cheap restaurants. This ragtag space is transforming into a handy one-stop shop for Palermo's famous street food—from boiled octopus *(polpo bollito)* and spleen sandwiches *(pani ca' meusa),* to less adventurous dishes like grilled meats, *arancine* (fried rice balls), and chickpea fritters *(panelle).* For more on your options here, see page 94. If you come back here in the evening, you'll find the Vucciria entering its next evolution—as a nightlife hotspot.

From the small fountain in the middle of the square, turn left and head down Via Argenteria Nuova ("New Street of the Silver Shop"). After a short block, step into the tiny piazza on the right to see the statue of the **Genie of Palermo** (in a niche in the wall on your right). This is a common symbol of the city, with a snake biting its chest and sucking its blood—a commentary on

foreign domination. If you keep an eye out, you'll find other genies around Palermo.

Back on the main street, you are now walking above the subterranean Kemonia River, which once defined one side of Palermo.

The next piazza is named for the water that flows under your feet—**Piazza Garraffello,** from the Arab *gharraf,* meaning "water in abundance." Survey the damaged buildings here, especially the one on the left. This area—located close to the strategic port—was heavily bombed by Allies during World War II, and today many buildings still await reconstruction. The money received from the Marshall Plan was not used as it should have been to restore the

PALERMO

The Mafia

Many travelers' first introduction to Sicily is *The Godfather,* the 1972 drama about the fictional Corleone family and the Sicilian crime syndicate known as the Mafia. While the Mafia still exists, it no longer holds sway over the island, and the violence that erupted in the 1970s and 80s is long past.

The origins of the Mafia—which referred to itself as Cosa Nostra ("Our Thing")—are murky, but probably date back to the transition out of feudalism after the unification of Italy in the 1860s. The nobility were no longer in control, but the fledgling Italian state did not have the resources to impose the rule of law in far-flung Sicily. After generations of colonial rule, Sicilians found that they couldn't rely on the government to protect them.

Instead, they looked to people they knew for help. In rural areas, clans formed to provide protection from theft of valuable livestock and fruit. But before long, these "security guards" became a racket in cahoots with the thieves. The clans looted and dominated the people they "protected," and ensured silence with threats. Without anyone to challenge them, the Mafia clans grew stronger and moved into politics, consolidating power by requiring the people under their "protection" to vote for Mafia-controlled candidates.

That system came to a halt under Mussolini, Italy's fascist dictator (r. 1922-1943). Mussolini brutally crushed the Sicilian Mafia in the 1920s, imposing national government control—and driving some crime bosses to America. But after the Allied invasion in 1943 and the fall of the fascist government, chaos reigned in Sicily. The Allies looked for local help to control the island—and opened the door to the return of the Mafia clans. Corrupt politicians channeled Marshall Plan reconstruction funds to Mafia-run companies, which explains the ugly, cheaply built postwar housing surrounding Palermo (much of the money simply disappeared).

The Mafia had a successful M.O.: They'd show up at a business owner's shop and request a tribute, called a *pizzo.* Sometimes they'd say that someone in the community needed help, and they were simply passing the hat. Any refusal to pay would result in physical intimidation, injury, arson, or even murder. And nothing was discussed—the Mafia ruthlessly enforced a code of

historic center, but instead funded cheap, sketchy apartment blocks on Palermo's outskirts.

• *From here, take the first right down Via Alessandro Paternostro and enjoy the stroll along one of Palermo's most characteristic streets, lined with innovative boutiques (for details, see "Shopping in Palermo," later). Carry on straight until you reach...*

silence, called the *omertà*. Their dominance continued into the 1980s, reaching a violent frenzy as drug trafficking and turf wars mixed with politics. Those who openly opposed the Mafia were threatened or murdered.

The tide turned in the early 1990s, beginning with the convictions of several high-profile Mafia leaders. In 1992, the two leading anti-Mafia judges, Giovanni Falcone and Paolo Borsellino, were murdered. A year later, a popular anti-Mafia priest, Giuseppe "Pino" Puglisi, was assassinated at point-blank range. But rather than strengthen the Mafia, the brazen murders fueled a growing resistance. Small acts, like shopkeepers refusing to pay the *pizzo*, emboldened the public. The *omertà* broke down and people started to report what they knew. One by one, crime families were taken down, some with claws deep in the Italian government. Today, the Mafia still exists, but is less active on the neighborhood level. However, organized crime remains big business: Criminal gangs operate on a worldwide scale, dealing in drugs, weapons, fraud, cybercrime, and human trafficking.

The typical visitor to Sicily will never directly encounter the Mafia, but will see monuments recalling events leading to its fall

from power. The tombs of Father Puglisi and Giovanni Falcone are inside Palermo Cathedral and the Church of San Domenico, respectively. The council room in City Hall (which you can ask to see) is lined with plaques dedicated to victims of the Mafia. On the road to the airport are pillars marking the sites of the Falcone and Borsellino assassinations. The facade of the Nautical Institute has an evocative mural honoring Falcone and Borsellino (facing the marina on Via Cala). And on Piazza Marina is a memorial plaque for Joe Petrosino, an American policeman assassinated on that spot in 1909 while gathering information against the Sicilian Mafia in the US.

❻ Piazza San Francesco

You've now crossed from the Vucciria into the Kalsa district. This neighborhood—even closer to the port—was also hit hard during WWII bombings, and the wealthier residents moved out, leaving this a poor and dangerous area. But recently, this district has been at the heart of the city's regeneration, and now the Kalsa is full of trendy boutiques and restaurants.

This beautiful square is one of the district's finest, where you'll find the famous, recommended Antica Focacceria San Francesco (a good place for a snack) and, opposite, a church also named for St. Francis. In a town with a Baroque facade on every corner, the Romanesque simplicity of the **Church of San Francesco d'Assisi** is a delightful surprise.

Franciscans arrived in Palermo in 1224, two years before St. Francis' death, and built this church in 1255. Later remodeled in Baroque style, it was damaged by WWII bombs—triggering a restoration process that brought the church back to its original design. If it's open, step inside (irregular hours, likely 7:30-12:00 & 15:30-19:00, may close in the afternoon). It's typical of Franciscan churches: large but less decorated, in keeping with the order's philosophy of poverty and simplicity. Notice the elegant Renaissance arch of the Mastrantonio Chapel (third on the left)—one of only a few Renaissance sculptures in the city.

• *Back outside, facing the church, follow the small brown signs for the Oratorio di San Lorenzo (to the left).*

❼ Oratory of San Lorenzo

Tucked away about 50 yards down the street, the Oratory of San Lorenzo (Oratorio di San Lorenzo) is well worth a quick visit—it warrants ▲▲. An *oratorio* was a service organization—a kind of medieval Rotary Club—designed to provide social work not provided by governments. They were Christian, proud, and competitive. Each was funded by a guild, neighborhood-based, and had its own *oratorio* like this one—a meeting/worship hall/headquarters.

Cost and Hours: €3, daily 10:00–18:00, Via Immacolatella 5, tel. 091-611-8168, www.amicimuseisiciliani.it.

Visiting the Oratory: Enter the garden patio, buy a ticket, then cross over to the oratory. Stepping inside, you'll be immersed in a luxurious and exquisite Baroque world. The Baroque style of art and architecture, common throughout Italy in the 17th and 18th centuries, is known for its exuberance and playful decoration; Sicilian Baroque—like Sicily itself—goes a step further, adding drama and intensity.

The patron saint of this brotherhood was San Lorenzo (St. Lawrence), who was martyred. As you enter, look high on the right to see him being grilled to death. Throughout the space, look for other symbolic grills (for example, in the center of the floor). Notice also the mischievous cupids. Find joyful—if occasionally painful—examples of their juvenile love of life. The decor is stucco (lightweight plasterwork over a frame, made to look like carved stone). The family that decorated this space, the Serpottas, is famous in Sicily for developing a technique (called *allustratura*) that made the plaster so shiny that it looked like fine marble. And driving all this artistic exuberance was the spirit of competition between the brotherhoods·of various *oratorios*.

The **Nativity altarpiece** is a reproduction. The original, by Caravaggio, hung here for over 350 years. It was stolen on October 17, 1969 and has never been recovered. Someone slipped in with a knife, cut it out of its frame, rolled it up, and vanished. The brazen theft of this venerated religious artwork was symbolic for Palermo, as it signaled the depth of depravity in a city under Mafia control. More than 4,000 pieces of art were stolen from churches in the 1960s, and many of them were never found.

Today, the priceless Caravaggio—unsalable on the legitimate art market—is probably in some criminal's basement. This reproduction, *Nativity 2.0,* was installed here in 2015 and inaugurated by the president of Italy—whose brother was assassinated by the Mafia. But the case isn't closed, and this theft remains in the top 10 on the FBI's list of unsolved art crimes.

• *Head back to Piazza San Francesco and stand facing the popular* focacceria. *Turn left to continue down...*

❽ Via Alessandro Paternostro

With its sturdy paving stones, bulky balconies, and delightful boutiques, Via Alessandro Paternostro is one of Palermo's most appealing residential streets. Movies often film here. And it's a great place for browsing craft shops—the best of which are marked with the logo of the local artisan association, ALAB (see "Shopping in Palermo," later).

After a few blocks, turn right at Piazza Aragona, a wide medieval street with more fun-to-browse little shops. At the far end of the square, the big stone palace houses the ❾ **Galleria d'Arte Moderna (GAM),** featuring mostly Sicilian artists from the 19th and 20th centuries (for details, see "Sights in Palermo," later).

Head straight up Via Alloro, with GAM on your right. You'll soon reach the facade of the ultra-Baroque **Church of Sant'Anna,** which faces a lovely square with lively cocktail bars (a fun place to hang out after dark). At the next corner, before the busy street, look on your right for the **street sign** for *Via Lattarini* (from the Arab *attariin,* or grocery vendor)—one of the few surviving that's still written in three languages: Italian, Hebrew, and Arabic.

• *Cross busy Via Roma and continue straight uphill, past a row of inviting bars. You'll pop out at a church-ringed square.*

⑩ Piazza Bellini: Palermo's Trio of Churches

This tiny square is surrounded by three of the city's most famous churches. On your right as you enter the square, up the stairs, is

Santa Caterina—with a boisterous Baroque interior that's a feast for the eyes. Across the square, up on a little plateau, are two other churches: On the left is **La Martorana,** with gorgeous gilded mosaics. And on the right is little **San Cataldo,** with its Arab architecture. Take time to tour these three, then head for the next stop (for details on visiting each church, see the listings under "Sights in Palermo," later).

• *Standing in the middle of Piazza Bellini, face the Church of Santa Caterina and take the little alley on its left side to...*

⑪ Piazza Pretoria

At the center of this piazza is the Fontana Pretoria, better known as the **Fountain of Shame.** While fountains like this one may

seem "typically Italian," they are actually quite rare in Sicily. The Renaissance never really took hold in Sicily, and this is one of the few Renaissance works in the city. The fountain, made of Carrara marble, was originally crafted in 1555 for the Tuscan villa of a Spanish viceroy. It was sold to the city of Palermo by the viceroy's son, who had become Palermo's governor. His workers broke the fountain down to about 640 pieces and rebuilt it in front of the City Hall. (Locals note the irony that one of their most famous landmarks is the least *palermitano* thing about their city.)

This fountain's gathering of statues includes gods, goddesses, and grotesques on several levels. If the gates are open, go in and walk around it.

The nickname "Fountain of Shame" comes from the nude figures—considered quite racy in conservative Sicily. To make things worse, the fountain was assembled right under the windows of the Dominican convent of Santa Caterina (notice the adjacent dome). Local folklore claims that the nuns tried dressing the figures, but to

Arab Palermo

Palermo has ancient roots going back to the Phoenicians, but it wasn't a major city until the arrival in AD 827 of the Arabs—the first inhabitants who really spurred the city's development. Sicily's Arabs were from the Fatimid dynasty, whose caliphate stretched along the North African coast and beyond. They ruled Sicily for more than 200 years, taking what was a Byzantine colony and reinventing it, making the most of its strategic location and fertile soil. The Arabs brought new crops like citrus, nuts, sugar, dates, and cotton, and were marvels at water engineering, turning dry areas into farmland. Considered the most modern of its time, Arab culture was admired for its commitment to education and for its advances in mathematics, medicine, and astronomy.

Palermo also benefitted from the Arabs' urban planning skills. The city was enlarged as the two rivers surrounding it, the Papireto and Kemonia, were channeled underground. With the newly formed land, the Kalsa district was laid out with wide streets and gardens, some of which still exist. Palermo became one of the largest and most modern cities in Europe; at the turn of the millennium, it was considered the jewel of the Mediterranean.

In the 11th century, the Normans came from northern France to conquer and re-Christianize Sicily. They succeeded—but were so impressed that they chose to keep the Arab community and incorporate their skills into the new kingdom. Arab mathematics, cartography, and architecture merged with the Norman culture, bringing on a Golden Age. The 1200s were the heyday of "Arab-Norman" art and architecture, a unique hybrid of two distinct cultures sharing one island.

Arabian influence can still be found today throughout the city. The architecture of Palermo Cathedral, San Cataldo Church, the Norman Palace, and other buildings of the Norman era incorporate Arab decoration and engineering. And their influence can be found in the sweet shops and in the sing-song of the merchants in the Ballarò and Capo markets, which began as Arab souks.

no avail. Eventually, they slipped out of their convent—chisel and hammer in hand—and chipped away some of the offending parts. The iron fence was added in the 19th century to prevent further "remodeling."

The **City Hall** (Palazzo Pretorio) flies four flags: the blue EU flag, the red, white, and green Italian flag, the Sicilian flag with the Trinacria symbol (see the sidebar, later), and the red-and-yellow flag of Palermo. Below the flags stands the imperial eagle—the symbol of Palermo since the reign of Frederick II. And up at the top of the building is a statue of Santa Rosalia, the city's patron saint (for more on Rosalia, see the sidebar on page 79). The bell to the left of the flags used to announce city assemblies. Don't be surprised to find *polizia* in riot gear loitering, as people usually gather here for protests. If you ask politely, you can often peek at the city council chambers, with its walls covered in plaques dedicated to victims of Mafia assassinations.

• *Go down the steps to Via Maqueda and turn right. At the intersection, look around at the four fancy facades.*

⓬ Quattro Canti ("Four Corners")

The Quattro Canti, or "Four Corners," is the heart of the city of Palermo. This intersection of Via Maqueda and Via Vittorio Emanuele divides the city into its four major historical neighborhoods. Officially named Piazza Vigliena, the intersection's four concave corner facades create a great example of the Sicilian delight in Baroque architecture. It was built under Spanish (Bourbon) rule to lure nobles to move from country villas into urban townhouses, in an effort to revitalize the city.

Starting from the bottom, Quattro Canti's three levels of statues represent the four seasons, each one personified as a woman  (from a young maiden for Spring, to an elderly woman for Winter); Spanish kings (Charles V, Philip II, III, IV—a reminder of the colonial overlords this island has endured); and four patron saints of Palermo (Cristina, Ninfa, Oliva, and Agata). Wondering why Santa Rosalia, the adored local saint, didn't make it to the Final Four? Quattro Canti was finished before she became the city's patron saint. (To make up for it, they added a statue of Rosalia—higher than any of these—on top of the City Hall building, in the square we just left.) The fountains at the bases of the four facades are still used as watering troughs for thirsty horses hauling tourists on carriage rides around town.

After "reading" the Quattro Canti vertically, scan it horizontally, noticing the complete circle created by the four seasons: Spring (holding flowers; she's on your left, as you enter the square), Summer (holding fruit), Fall (holding pinecones), and Winter (with a flame). Baroque architects often hide a trick in their buildings—some sort of optical illusion. In this case, the contrast of sunlight and shadows *(chiaroscuri)* on the facades at this intersection changes progressively as the sun moves across the sky. As you pass through this intersection at different times of the day, notice how the light shifts: starting in the early morning with Spring,

The Trinacria

The Trinacria, or Triskeles, is the ancient symbol of the island.

Although there are variations, it typically shows a face in the center with three disjointed legs bent around it. Often it is portrayed with wings on the sides as ears, and shafts of wheat sprouting from the center. Two pairs of tangled snakes, above the head and below the chin, create a hissing headdress.

The face is often referred to as Medusa, one of the three Gorgons, who with her two sisters had the power of turning enemies into stone with a single glance. Because of this, the symbol could be a reference to the stone-creating mama herself, Mount Etna. The first existing example of the symbol is found on a bowl dating from the seventh century BC (now in the archaeological museum at Agrigento's Valley of the Temples), but the symbol itself is very likely much older. It is possible that early colonists, intent on keeping the fertile island for themselves, used this scary symbol to ward off superstitious Greek settlers.

The wheat shafts represent the fertility of the island, as Greek myths claimed that wheat grew wild here. The three legs are likely a representation of the three corners of the island, which links to the name "Trinacria," meaning three promontories.

The symbol has become the centerpiece of the Sicilian flag, which features the Trinacria on a red-and-yellow background split diagonally: red symbolizing the bloodshed of the many invasions and yellow symbolizing the sun.

then moving clockwise as the day goes on, until illuminating Winter just before sunset. That's why Quattro Canti is also called the "Theater of the Sun."

Notice the elegant lampposts that ring the square. On the base of each lamppost you'll find a face with three legs surrounding it. This is the symbol of Sicily, the Trinacria, which has represented the island for more than 3,000 years. On our walk today we've seen the fragments of many civilizations that have arrived and departed, but the Trinacria remains, watching over her island from flags, pottery, and decorative elements like these.

• Our city orientation walk is over. From here, you have several excellent options for further exploring. From where you entered, you could continue straight up the lovely, mostly traffic-free Via Maqueda. In about 10 minutes, you'll reach the **Teatro Massimo**—where we began our walk.

The **Capo Market,** *a great stop for lunch, is a few minutes' walk behind the theater.*

Or, from where you entered, you could turn 90 degrees to the left and head up Via Vittorio Emanuele. In about eight minutes, you'll reach the **Palermo Cathedral;** *then, about eight minutes past that, is the* **Norman Palace,** *with its mosaic-encrusted Palatine Chapel. Or to reach the* **Ballarò Market,** *go back the way you came on Via Maqueda (passing the Fountain of Shame on your left). After two blocks, follow signs on the right to* Mercato Ballarò *and* Palazzo Conte Federico *on Via del Ponticello.*

All of these sights are described in the next section. You're in the center of Palermo life. Enjoy!

Sights in Palermo

CHURCHES ON PIAZZA BELLINI

This trio of glorious churches—facing each other across Piazza Bellini—are just a few steps from the Quattro Canti intersection and the Fountain of Shame.

Discount Deal: These three churches (and a few other, lesser religious sights in Palermo) are part of a group called *Il Circuto del Sacro.* If you have a ticket for any one of these, show it to get a significant discount at any other.

▲▲Church of Santa Caterina

Baroque—a hyperdecorative architectural style from the 1600s and 1700s—is at its most colorful and exuberant extreme in Sicily, as demonstrated in this church. Santa Caterina's simple exterior hides an explosive Sicilian Baroque interior, a riot of *marmi mischi e tramischi* (mixed and remixed) marble inlay decoration.

Cost and Hours: €2; Mon-Sat 9:30-13:00 & 15:30-19:00, Sun 9:30-13:30; Nov-March daily 9:30-13:30.

Visiting the Church: For all the details, borrow the English handout at the entrance. But here's a quick tour: The first square column on the right shows a three-dimensional depiction of the story of Jonah, where the ship and the whale's mouth appear ready to jump right out of the wall. Scenes on other columns are nearly as dynamic—look for Abraham about to slay his son, Isaac.

This marble inlay technique was popular in Florence during the Renaissance, later making its way down to Sicily. It's a type of mosaic, but rather than using small tiles, larger slabs are pieced together like a puzzle—taking advantage of the marble's color and pattern to heighten the design.

Walking farther down the nave—toward the over-the-top altar area—consider the history of this church, dedicated to Saint Catherine of Alexandria. This was the church of a prestigious convent, active until the early 2000s. In noble families of the past, the first-born daughter was given a dowry and strate- gically married off. Sub- sequent daughters, who lacked funds to marry into aristocracy, were instead "married to Christ" and sent to convents.

Posh families sent their spare daughters here to Santa Caterina, giv- ing a handsome donation for acceptance in this exclusive convent. The funds were used to take good care of the sisters...and to enrich the decor of their church.

Look up and find the golden screens. The families of the nuns could come for Mass on special days, and while they were not al- lowed to meet face to face, the sisters could observe from the hid- den upper galleries.

This convent was famous for making sweets. Find the door to the giant lazy Susan on the right near the altar, where orders and money were put, and sweets popped out without the cloistered nuns making any contact with the public. Sweets are sold in the cloister.

The convent cloister is often open for tours on the weekends; check the entrance facing Piazza Pretoria for details.

▲▲Church of La Martorana

This church (officially called Santa Maria dell'Ammiraglio) is a jewel box slathered in Byzantine-Norman mosaics—the oldest in Sicily.

Cost and Hours: €2, Mon-Sat 9:30-13:00 & 15:30-17:30, Sun 9:00-10:30, mobile 345-828-8231.

Visiting the Church: The core of the church dates from the 12th century. But that's not what you see when you first enter. Over the centuries, the original church was enlarged, with a Baroque extension at the front and back. (Since the standard-issue frilly Ba- roque altar dominates your view as you enter, it's easy to look right past the church's Norman highlights.)

In the first side chapel on the left is a mosaic of a man kneeling before Mary. This is George of Antioch, who commissioned the church in the 12th century. In a similar altar on the right, you'll find his boss, King Roger II, being crowned by Christ himself, mixing religious and political themes.

Now walk slowly up the nave. Look up at the ceiling decor, and you can't miss where you step from the Baroque extension into the gilded mosaic-clad original core of the church. Looking down, you'll notice the floor changes at the same point.

On the underside of the arch just before the cupola are scenes from Mary's life: On the left, a sweet Nativity scene, and on the

right, the Dormition of the Virgin. Based on the belief that Mary didn't "die," but rather went into a deep, peaceful sleep before ascending to heaven, this subject is rare in Italian Catholic churches—but common in Greek Orthodox ones. Although always devoted to the Greek Orthodox rite, in 1937 the church was officially handed over by the fascist government to the Albanian Orthodox community, who still celebrate their liturgy here today. Notice that the seats of the pews can be flipped up—in Eastern Orthodox worship services, the congregation stands rather than sits.

Continue deeper into the old church, appreciating other glittering mosaics. Standing under the main dome, look up to see Jesus as he's typically depicted in Eastern Orthodox churches: Christ Pantocrator ("All Ruling").

Exploring the rest of the church, think of this: Sicilians associate La Martorana with marzipan. In the past, nuns from the adjacent Benedictine convent (founded in the 12th century by Eloisa Martorana) raised funds making and selling fruit-shaped marzipan. That convent is long gone, but the traditional candies called "Frutta Martorana" live on in every sweet shop in town.

▲Church of San Cataldo

While built around the same time as its neighbor La Martorana, the architectural contrast between the two churches is striking.

Sicily was transitioning from Arab to Norman rule in the 12th century, and this church blends both styles of architecture. The solid Norman walls are lightened with the three round, red, Arab-inspired domes on top. Although the interior is plain, it will make you feel like you've gone back in time 900 years.

Cost and Hours: €2.50, daily 9:00-19:00, may be closed in the afternoon on Sun and off-season, Piazza Bellini 3, tel. 091-607-7111.

OTHER SIGHTS IN THE CITY CENTER

These are listed roughly in the order you'll reach them on my self-guided "Palermo City Walk," earlier.

▲▲Teatro Massimo

Palermo has two landmark theaters. Teatro Massimo—closer to the center and with the more impressive interior—can be seen on a concise, interesting 30-minute tour. (The theater's history and exterior are described earlier, at the beginning of my "Palermo City Walk.") On the tour, an English-speaking guide will lead you through the Liberty Style (Italian Art Nouveau) in-

terior—beginning with a detailed wooden model of the theater, which the architect used to win the commission. Then, stepping into the impressively huge auditorium, understand the forgotten elegance and importance of Palermo in the past. The auditorium boasts near perfect acoustics thanks to the horseshoe shape of the seats and mahogany wood used for the construction of the boxes, which naturally amplifies the sound. Very modern for its day, the theater even has an early form of climate control: the 11 fresco panels in the ceiling, arranged like the petals of a daisy, can be raised to let out hot air. From the auditorium, you'll head up to the royal box (with the best seats—and acoustics—in the house), then visit the Pompeiian Room, a domed lounge modeled after the frescoes from that ancient Roman city.

Cost and Hours: €8 tour, tours run daily 9:30-18:00, last tour at 17:30; enter through the door to the left of the grand staircase and ask about the next English tour; tel. 091-605-3267, www.teatromassimo.it. It's €20 for a tour that includes the rooftop terrace, but the views from here don't warrant the high price.

▲Salinas Regional Archaeological Museum
(Museo Archeologico Regionale Antonino Salinas)

Palermo's beleaguered archaeological museum has been a work in progress for years. While its complete collection is top-notch, only the lower floor is currently open to the public. Even so, it's worth a visit to see the sculptural fragments taken from Selinunte, a major Greek archaeological site on the southern coast.

Cost and Hours: €3; Tue-Sat 9:30-19:00, Sun until 14:00, closed Mon, last entry one hour before closing; Piazza Olivella 24, tel. 091-611-6805, www.regione.sicilia.it/bbccaa/salinas.

Visiting the Museum: Entering the museum, you'll pass through a serene little courtyard with a fountain and turtles, then step into a second, larger courtyard. Turn left and circle the exhibits clockwise.

The exquisite **Bronze Ram** is a rare Greek sculpture that decorated the palace of the tyrants of Siracusa in the third century BC. The detail of the fur and accuracy of the body are remarkable, but that it exists at all is what makes it special—most Greek bronzes were melted down for their valuable material.

Next is a series of small rooms displaying artifacts from nearby archaeological sites. In the first room are two large caskets, the **Sarcophagi of Cannita.** These tombs of Carthaginians were discovered near Palermo, at the ancient city of Solunto. It's rare to be in the presence of Carthaginian artifacts. Little survives from that culture because the Romans did their best to wipe out all signs of their great enemy (for more, see the sidebar on page 176).

Continue around the courtyard and find the **Torso of the Stagnone**—another Carthaginian piece, from the sixth century BC, discovered in the salt flats near Marsala. It displays some Egyptian characteristics (such as the clothing). Continuing along the courtyard rooms, you'll find Roman sculpture, Greek kraters (red-and-black vases), and small pieces of ancient jewelry.

At the end of the courtyard, you'll find the wing dedicated to the ancient Greek colony of **Selinunte** (including a model of the site). Perched on the southwest tip of the island of Sicily, Selinunte was one of the most important Greek cities, destroyed by the Carthaginians and still in ruins. Although it's the largest archaeological park in Sicily (described on page 184—a handy stopover on your way from Trapani to Agrigento), and the temple ruins are impressive, there's virtually no art displayed on-site—most of the sculptural remains are in this museum.

In the courtyard are pieces of the temple on top of life-size schematic drawings, giving you a feel for the scale of the site. Circling the rooms of artifacts, look for painted fragments. One large room is dedicated to the finest pieces from the site—the **metopes.** These bas-relief sculptural groups were used to decorate the upper bands that ran around the great temples, like a strip

of stories. Keep in mind that Greek temples were colorfully painted, so the statues would have been even more lifelike.

The rooms beyond the metopes contain smaller artifacts from Selinunte, such as pottery and devotional items. Considering that Selinunte was just one of Sicily's great Greek cities, you'll get a sense of the grandeur of Magna Graecia, or "Great Greece."

GAM (Galleria d'Arte Moderna)

In Italy, "modern" is a relative term. This art collection—mostly Sicilian artists from the 19th through early 20th century—may not sport any names familiar to Americans. But it's beautifully presented in a fine Spanish Gothic palazzo, and fans of Romanticism, Neoclassicism, and Impressionism enjoy seeing how those movements found expression in Sicily—including landscapes that give a flavor of the island in the past.

Cost and Hours: €7; Tue-Sun 9:30-18:30, closed Mon, last entry one hour before closing; slow but decent audioguide-€4, Via Sant'Anna 21, tel. 091-843-1605, www.gampalermo.it.

Eating: The museum's **$** café is more modern than the art collection and serves light lunch options (free entry, Tue-Sun 9:30-18:30, closed Mon, tel. 091-843-1605).

Visiting the Museum: The permanent exhibit begins on the ground floor. You'll see lots of fleshy nudes, epic historical scenes, Neoclassical sculpture, and misty landscapes. Then, in the adjoining cloister, head up the stairs to continue through the permanent collection: realism (genre scenes), expressive portraits, and more landscapes from around Sicily. Then climb up one more flight of stairs for a look at Sicilian Modernism. The treasure of the collection is Franz Von Stuck's *Il Peccato (The Sin)*, reminiscent of Gustav Klimt's work. From there, explore a world of pointillism, Cubism, Expressionism, and works by the "Group of Four" (Gruppo di Quattro).

WEST END OF DOWNTOWN

To reach these sights, head west from the main Quattro Canti intersection along the mostly traffic-free Via Vittorio Emanuele.

▲Palermo Cathedral (Cattedrale Metropolitana della Santa Vergine Maria Assunta)

Palermo's cathedral is a crazy quilt of architectural styles and patterns. Much like the city itself, it was added to and changed with each new ruling power. While the city has no lack of interesting churches, the cathedral is most dear to the locals, as it houses the bones of their celebrated patron, Santa Rosalia. Because it's free to enter, the cathedral is often jammed with cruise-ship crowds.

Cost and Hours: Cathedral—free, royal tombs—€1.50; Mon-Sat 7:00-19:00, Sun 8:00-13:00 & 16:00-19:00; Via Vittorio Emanuele, tel. 091-334-373, www.cattedrale.palermo.it. You can pay €5 to climb to the rooftop (Mon-Sat 9:00-17:30, closed Sun and in bad weather).

Background: When the Norman kings took over Sicily in the 1100s, they had a mission from the pope to consolidate the power of the western Roman church. Palermo was a melting pot—with Muslims, Jews, and Eastern Orthodox Christians—so building this new, bigger cathedral on the site of an older one was a political statement. Beginning in 1168, a powerful cardinal oversaw its construction, following an ambitious plan that was meant to intimidate the new young king, William II. But William had the last laugh when he diverted funds to building Monreale, an even more grandiose cathedral in the nearby hills. While Monreale was finished within a matter of decades (and is more impressive to visit today—see the Monreale Cathedral chapter), Palermo's underfunded cathedral project limped along for centuries, changing in style depending on the period. (For more on these two cathedrals, see the sidebar on page 105.)

Visiting the Cathedral: From the **exterior,** your eyes are drawn to wild graphic patterns—such as the crenellated fringe at the top of the walls, and the geometric tracery over the side door. These features are typical of the Byzantine-Norman style that was born in 12th-century Sicily, when the geometrical, fortified-church architecture of the Normans blended with the decorative Arabic style that preceded them.

The **portico** of the church—over the side door—dates from Spanish rule in the 1400s, in Gothic-Catalan style. Look for a carving on the farthest column to the left, which has inscribed verses from the Quran in Arabic—likely recycled from a mosque—and the entire structure is capped by a (much later) Sicilian Baroque dome.

Now step **inside.** The drab Neoclassical interior (renovated this way in 1801), full of somber Baroque side chapels, is a jarring contrast to the wild exterior. Head to the nave, turn right, stroll toward the altar, and try to imagine this space before its remodel. It would have had soaring Gothic arches, wallpapered with shining gold mosaics.

Near the altar, locate the brass line inlaid in the floor, illustrated with signs of the zodiac. This **meridian line** acts as a solar calendar. A small hole in the dome above allows in sunlight that pinpoints the zodiac, and therefore the month.

To the right of the main altar, a massive silver altar houses the bones of Palermo's patron saint, **Santa Rosalia.** During the plague of 1624, the saint appeared in a dream and revealed her resting place on nearby Monte Pellegrino. Once her bones were brought back to Palermo, the plague ended. Rosalia has delivered miracles to locals ever since. (For more on Rosalia, see the sidebar on page 79.) Palermo's other four patron saints—who don't command nearly the devotion of Rosalia—are squeezed into one crowded chapel, on the right aisle, about halfway down.

Opposite the church entrance and a bit toward the front is a modern altar celebrating another miracle worker, **Father Giuseppe Puglisi.** This priest served in Palermo's poor neighborhoods in the 1980s, and focused his ministry on vulnerable kids, encouraging them to stay away from the Mafia. His anti-Mafia stance led to his assassination on his birthday in 1993. The guilt-ridden assassins eventually turned themselves in, becoming Mafia informants.

Puglisi's death ignited local fury and helped to bring about the end of Mafia domination in the city. Notice how Father Puglisi is depicted: always smiling and happy, and with oversized hands (representing his hard work to serve his community). Considered a martyr and believed to be the last person killed by the local Mafia, Father Puglisi was beatified by the pope in 2013.

Before you exit, at the back of the church near the entrance door, a screened-off section houses mildly interesting **royal tombs,** most with elaborate canopies (requires admission—skip it).

▲▲Palatine Chapel (Cappella Palatina) and Norman Palace (Palazzo Normanni)

This sprawling palace (sometimes called the Palazzo Reale, "Royal Palace") has been home to the various rulers of Sicily since the ninth century. On weekdays, a visit includes the somewhat interesting royal apartments, where Sicily's regional assembly meets. But the main reason to visit is the sumptuous Palatine Chapel, a unique cross-cultural work of architecture from the 1100s. While the cathedral at Monreale is much bigger and displays more im-

pressive mosaics, if you won't make it out there, or if you prefer to see mosaics close up, you won't be disappointed by the elegance of the Norman-Byzantine mosaics here. Because the chapel is included in every cruise-ship excursion for Palermo, expect crowds (and consider skipping it if you're also going to Monreale).

Cost: €12 Fri-Mon (when apartments are open), €10 Tue-Thu (no apartments), audioguide-€5.

Hours: Mon-Sat 8:15-17:40, Sun until 13:00; chapel closed Sun 9:45-11:30, apartments open Fri-Mon only; last entry 45 minutes before closing.

Information: Tel. 091-626-2833, www.federicosecondo.org.

Getting There: The Norman Palace sits at the west end of Via Vittorio Emanuele, about a 15-minute **walk** from the main Quattro Canti intersection (past the cathedral). Walking up Via Vittorio Emanuele, you'll head toward the Porta Nuova—a gigantic decorative gateway that sticks out from the side of the palace, spanning the street. Before the gate, you'll pass a park, Villa Bonanno, on your left. Take a left at the next street, which is called Piazza della Vittoria. Halfway down the street you'll find the ticket kiosk. The entrance to the palace is opposite the kiosk, up a few steps, in Piazza del Parlamento.

If you don't want to walk, you can take the free *Navetta* **shuttle bus** that circulates around central Palermo, stopping at the train station, Teatro Massimo, Quattro Canti, and other central spots, and dropping off at Piazza Indipendenza and Via del Bastione (close to the entrance of the Norman Palace). A **taxi** from the station to the palace is about €10.

Crowd-Beating Tips: The Palatine Chapel is tiny, and only a few dozen people can enter at a time. Big cruise excursion and noisy student groups often create long waits for much of the day (peaking in the late morning). Try visiting first thing in the morning or in the late afternoon.

Services: Pay WCs are available on the corner right after security (coins only), and free WCs are located on the opposite side of the palace, just outside the gate.

Background: This palace, the oldest royal residence in Eu-

rope, was the seat of the Arab emirs, who began it in the ninth century—building it upon original Carthaginian foundations from the fifth century BC. Palermo was not the largest city on the island when the Arabs arrived, but over their two centuries of rule, they built Palermo into a capital, with sprawling palaces and gardens. Upon arriving in the late 11th century, the Normans were impressed with the city they found, and decided to adapt what was already there—making the Arab palace their own royal seat, and adding onto it. Other rulers who succeeded the Normans also made it their governmental seat. In the 1500s, the Spanish Bourbon governors who ruled the island moved in and added opulent royal apartments, which today house the Sicilian Regional Assembly—the modern version of a traditional parliament that dates all the way back to Norman times. (Sicily and Iceland have little in common, but both claim to have the "world's oldest parliament." I'll leave that title to the historians.) While Sicily is fully part of Italy, it's the only Italian region allowed to operate a "parliament," with a greater degree of self-rule than other regions.

Visiting the Palace: Before heading inside, look up and scan the building's eclectic **exterior.** You'll see a patchwork of architectural styles suggesting traces of each culture that shaped this building.

After buying your ticket, pass through security and the bookshop, following signs marked *percorso.* Enter the main court-

yard of the palace, Cortile Maqueda, and walk straight ahead, then climb the grand staircase on the opposite side, following signs to *Cappella Palatina.* On the first landing, you'll see the Palatine Chapel entry queue on the left. The royal apartments are up another flight of stairs. (If the apartments are open, and the chapel line is long, try touring the royal chambers first while waiting for the chapel line to die down.)

Palatine Chapel: While waiting in line, get ready for the glittering glass mosaics you're about to see by learning about the king who commissioned them: Roger II (r. 1130-1154), a cousin of William the Conqueror, who ruled over a complicated island. Yet somehow, he was able to honor each culture (see the "Palermo's History" sidebar, near the beginning of this chapter). In 1132, he commissioned a chapel to be built inside the royal residence, using architects and craftsmen from the different communities. That's why you'll find a mix of Norman, Byzantine, and Arab artistic traditions, architecture, and craftsmanship.

Upon entering the chapel, let your eyes adjust to the low light. The artistic style is eastern, coming from Constantinople (today's Istanbul), but the craft is rooted in ancient Roman mosaic tradition. The mosaic artists were Byzantine Greeks, and many of the motifs and imagery in this Catholic chapel are Eastern Orthodox. For example, over the altar, rather than Christ on the cross, you'll find Christ Pantocrator—the typical representation of the Eastern Orthodox Christ.

The **architecture** of the chapel is simple and boxy, in the Norman tradition—a rectangular, basilica-style structure with heavy walls and small windows. The arches supporting the nave are in the Arab-style high horseshoe shape. The lower walls have abstract, geometric designs, also coming from Arab artists. Muslim artists were forbidden from representing the human form, so they excelled at colorful patterns. Look for decorative Arabic writing hidden in the decoration and the stylized palm trees between the mosaic panels. The most unusual feature is the decorated ceiling, covered in wooden *muqarnas*—stalactite-like decorations seen in traditional Islamic architecture. Usually a church with *muqarnas* has been converted from a mosque, but this is the only original church in Europe to have a ceiling with this type of Muslim decoration.

The chapel's **mosaics** are set up to be read like a book. In the dome above the altar, Christ Pantocrator ("All Ruling") appears as a multiracial mascot: Jesus' nose and lips are straight like a Byzantine Greek, his eyebrows and mustache are brown as an Arab's, and his hair is blond and his eyes are light hazel in color, like the Normans. He was not just an icon, but the symbol of the melting-pot Norman kingdom in Sicily.

Flanking Jesus are domes featuring Peter (left, white beard) and Paul (right, balding). The stories of each of these saints' lives fill the walls of both side aisles. Higher up and farther down the central nave are stories of the Old Testament, beginning with the Creation in the top-right corner (to find the beginning of the story, look for the lands of the earth being cut up like a pie). Facing the high altar, in the back of the church, is another Christ Pantocrator, again flanked by Peter and Paul. Amazingly, 95 percent of the mosaics in the chapel are original.

A recent restoration found more evidence that Roger II was a tolerant and inclusive king. Hidden in the decoration was an inscription in Arabic reading "Roger is the chosen one of Allah," next to lines of the Quran. This is a truly remarkable statement about a Catholic French Norman knight who was sent by the pope to reclaim the island from the Arabs; it shows the respect he must have earned from the Sicilian people.

Royal Apartments: The Sicilian Regional Assembly is in session Tuesdays, Wednesdays, and Thursdays. On other days, it's possible to head up one more flight of stairs to see the rooms where they meet.

At the top of the stairs, walk through the hall to the first room, the "Stanza da Ercole" or Hercules room. This is where the Sicilian assembly meets and makes decisions for the island. If the

scenes on the wall are any indication, getting Sicilians to agree to anything must be the 13th Labor of Hercules.

In the first room you'll find large portraits of governors from the centuries of Spanish domination. Continuing to the left, the rooms that follow are each decorated in a different style, matching the tastes of the last Bourbons who lived here. You'll pass through a blue "Pompeii-style" room, painted to mimic the frescoes discovered when Pompeii was first uncovered in the 1700s. The adjacent room is in Chinese style. A Bourbon princess, Maria Carolina (the sister of Marie Antoinette), designed this room to show off her collection of Chinese porcelain.

At the end of the series of rooms is the Tower of the Winds, the only one of the original towers open to the public. While there used to be four towers, only two remain—and the other one houses the office of the president of Sicily. This tower's elegant mosaic decoration is similar to that of the Palatine Chapel, but shows off exotic animals and abstract, glittering patterns. The final rooms are plain but display large-scale paintings of Sicilian scenery from the 19th century. Stop for a moment and admire these pastoral scenes. Fix them in your mind so you can think back on them later in your trip, when you're enjoying similar views—in person—around Sicily.

IN LA KALSA, NEAR THE HARBOR

These sights cluster in the eastern end of central Palermo, just before the harbor, in the neighborhood called La Kalsa. Most are close to the delightful park called Villa Garibaldi—a fenced, shady retreat with inviting benches under gigantic trees.

▲Inquisition Cells at Palazzo Chiaramonte Steri

Palazzo Chiaramonte was the former home of the powerful Chiaramonte family during the Middle Ages (this is a famous name in Sicily—you'll find it all over the island). In 1392, the head of the family, Andrea Chiaramonte, refused to surrender to the Spanish Aragonese, and was beheaded in the piazza in front of his home, ending the family line. The Spanish mounted his head on the palace wall and moved in, basing their administration here.

During the Spanish Inquisition of the 1600s, the stables were converted into jail cells for those awaiting trial (the Inquisition hit Sicily hard, expelling many of its ethnic minorities and ending the period of religious tolerance). On the included guided tour, you'll see those cells (covered in drawings by prisoners) and learn about the story of the Inquisition.

Cost and Hours: €8 for mandatory one-hour guided tour, open Tue-Sun 10:00-19:00, closed Mon, multilingual tours depart hourly—check at the ticket office for the next departure, last tour departs one hour before closing, Piazza Marina 61, tel. 091-2389-3788.

Visiting the Palazzo: On the tour, you'll see about a half-dozen original cells, plus one that has been restored. The cells are elaborately decorated with line drawings, writing, and some carvings by bored prisoners waiting for an uncertain fate. As art supplies weren't readily available, prisoners used bodily fluids and dirt to paint the walls. Many of the drawings are religious, praying for a favorite saint to intercede on their behalf. Some drawings are more imaginary, but

The Fading Sicilian Aristocracy

Prior to the mid-19th century, Sicily was ruled under a feudal system. Wealthy noble families had large land holdings in the countryside and hired peasants to work the land; income from the estates supported the lifestyles of the noble and famous. Palermo is full of palaces built by those families, but today many are dilapidated and deserted. So, what happened?

In the mid-1800s, the fever of nationalism fell over Europe, and a call to unite the Italian peninsula was answered by the Risorgimento—the unification of Italy. A civil war swept from Sicily to Piedmont, and the foreign powers controlling Italy were deposed. The country was at last united under a common flag, with a new king.

As the old regimes ended, so did the social order. Lands from noble families were "redistributed" to the workers, and the upper classes began a long decline. The famous book *The Leopard (Il Gattopardo),* by the Sicilian author Giuseppe Tomasi di Lampedusa, documents this shift. With its nostalgia for a lost time, it's a Sicilian *Gone with the Wind.* World War II and Mussolini exacerbated the situation, as the monarchy was abolished and Palermo's city center was damaged by Allied bombs. Many of the noble families ran out of money and luck, and abandoned their palaces for good.

These days, a few noble descendants remain, hanging on to their palaces as best they can. Many look for ways to support their heritage, sometimes by welcoming tourists into their homes. (As a local "princess" in Palermo says, you can't eat a title.) One of my favorite places to sneak a glimpse of the aristocratic life is at the Palazzo Conte Federico in the Ballarò neighborhood. You can also tour Palazzo Mirto, which is a government-owned museum and less personal. And in Ragusa, you can tour the similar Palazzo Arezzo di Trifiletti (see page 243).

all tell a little about who the prisoners were. Keep an eye out for writing in Shakespearean English: Palermo was a trade capital, and foreigners were occasionally rounded up for an "interview."

▲Regional Art Gallery at Palazzo Abatellis

Built at the end of the 15th century for the magistrate of Palermo, Francesco Abatellis, this fine Spanish-Gothic palazzo, badly damaged during World War II, has housed Palermo's major art museum since 1954. While the building itself is basic, its treasures are impressive. The museum is dedicated primarily to Gothic and Renaissance art, although it also has a gallery of Baroque paintings.

Cost and Hours: €8, €10 combo-ticket with Palazzo Mirto; Tue-Fri 9:00-19:00, Sat-Sun until 13:30, closed Mon; Via Al-

PALERMO

loro 4, tel. 091-623-0011, www.regione.sicilia.it/beniculturali/palazzoabatellis.

Visiting the Museum: After getting your ticket, head diagonally across the courtyard to the entrance. The first large room displays one of the museum's highlights: *Triumph of Death,* a mysterious fresco by an unknown artist. It represents the Bubonic Plague as a skeletal knight on a white horse striking down clergy and nobles with laser-like precision. It's not complete, because it was detached from the walls of the former hospital of Palermo, Palazzo Sclafani. While a grim image for a hospital, it was fitting, as medieval hospitals were usually places you didn't walk out of.

Continuing through the small door to the right, the next few galleries display Renaissance sculpture. In the first room, you'll find the gracious bust of **Eleanor of Aragon,** a masterpiece by Francesco Laurana. In the next room you'll see several Madonna with Child statues; notice the *Madonna del Neve* proudly breastfeeding bambino Jesus. Note that the sculptures in this room show traces of their original Renaissance paint job.

Exiting back into the small courtyard and taking the stairs to the left, you'll arrive in the painting galleries. As you wind your way through Baroque canvases, you'll come to the most famous work in the collection: *Annunciation of the Virgin* by Antonello da Messina. Unlike most depictions of the Annunciation, here there's no angel—just Mary at her desk with her book. Mary's gesture is an artistic shorthand that this is an Annunciation scene. We can imagine the angel standing somewhere outside of the painting. The darkness in the background, contrasted with Mary's light skin and the thoughtful expression on her face, draw us in and make us wonder what she's thinking. Da Messina is the most famous Renaissance artist from Sicily, and one of the first to paint in oil. His oil technique was considered cutting-edge for his time, but perhaps the bigger advance was the psychological tension this image created. (For more about Antonello da Messina, see the sidebar on page 131.)

▲Palazzo Mirto

With all of the crumbling buildings in the city, it may be hard to believe that once Palermo was an elegant, fancy capital full of palaces. Palazzo Mirto is one of the very few homes open to visitors interested in experiencing the long-gone noble lifestyle of the past.

Although it's now somewhat faded, a visit here leaves you wondering about what other treasures the city's battered exteriors conceal.

Cost and Hours: €6, €10 combo-ticket with Palazzo Abatellis; Tue-Sat 9:00-18:00, Sun until 13:00, closed Mon; Via Merlo 2, tel. 091-616-4751.

Visiting the Palazzo: Built between 1300 and 1800, this was the home of the Filangeri family. Nobles with a long and complicated history, they lived here until their last descendant willed the house to the Sicilian government in 1983. Before you enter, ask the ticket desk for the English explanation booklet.

Upstairs, on the main floor *(piano nobile),* you'll pass through elegant state rooms with tapestries, frescoes, chandeliers, and period furniture. Peek in the

door of the small room in the middle of the house, which is painted to look like a Chinese pagoda—a very popular style of decoration in the late 1700s. The state room in the center of the palace hosted grand balls. Imagine the adjacent courtyard, with its seashell-grotto fountain, filled with revelers in ball gowns and tuxedos.

When you complete the loop, head up one more flight of stairs. The upper floor was the family's private quarters, and although not as opulent as the *piano nobile*, it tells a more intimate story of those who lived in the home. Family photos and personal effects from the last resident are scattered on well-worn furniture.

On the way out, don't miss the dusty, antique horse-carriage collection in the stables, and the kitchen (the doorway to the left of the entry), which had a revolving dumbwaiter system that ensured servants and residents would never cross paths.

International Museum of Marionettes
(Museo Antonio Pasqualino)

The Sicilian puppet tradition is alive and well. This compact, nicely presented mu-

seum displays puppets from cultures around the world, with TV screens showing the puppets in action. It's all in Italian, with a paltry English handout, but the puppets are easy to appreciate. The culmination of the tour is a huge hall where dozens and dozens of vintage marionettes hang on racks, ready for their next performance. Their theater presents *spectaccoli* (puppet shows) in an airy space surrounded by the collection. For more on the Sicilian art of puppetry, see page 303.

Cost and Hours: Museum—€5, Tue-Sat 10:00-18:00, Sun-Mon until 14:00; puppet show—€10, typically performed every Fri April-Oct, sometimes also Tue, daily in summer—check schedule online; Piazzetta Pasqualino 5, tel. 091-328-060, www.museodellemarionette.it.

Palermo Botanical Garden (Orto Botanico)

This botanical garden is one of the oldest in the Mediterranean, and is an active research garden for the University of Palermo. Considering Palermo's mild climate, it grows one of the most diverse collections in Europe, with more than 12,000 species from all over the world, including citrus, water lilies, bamboos, and an ancient fig tree. Though it's a little shabby and unkempt, a walk through this peaceful garden will delight the avid horticulturalist and soothe everyone else with the scent of orange blossoms.

Cost and Hours: €6, daily 9:00-20:00, closes earlier off-season, Via Lincoln 2, tel. 091-238-91236, www.ortobotanico.unipa.it.

IN BALLARÒ
▲Palazzo Conte Federico

This elegant and extremely lived-in mansion, built upon the Carthaginian city wall, offers a rare opportunity to get a personal glimpse into Sicilian aristocratic life. Count Federico's family has lived here for centuries, but now that the perks of nobility no longer pay the bills, the family has opened its doors to the paying public. The current count (Alessandro) is a vintage race-car enthusiast happy to show off some of his favorite toys; most tours  are led by one of his sons (Nicolò or Andreas). The countess, Alwine, is from Salzburg and fills her home with both joy and a respect for the family's illustrious history.

Cost and Hours: €10 for tour; Thu-Tue 11:00-16:00, closed Wed; 45-minute tour in English and Italian, reservations not necessary—just show up before the top of the hour; near the Ballarò Market at Piazza Conte Federico 2—from Quattro Canti, take Via

Maqueda toward Piazza Bellini and watch for signs on the right; tel. 091-651-1881, www.contefederico.com.

MARKETS

Sicily has some of the best street markets in Europe, and Palermo has two of the most famous. The island—the garden patch of

Italy—offers a wealth of produce, from ripe tomatoes to purple eggplants to comically long zucchinis to fragrant citrus. But markets aren't just for greengrocers—you'll also see fishmongers, butchers, spices, herbs, and everyday items like clothing and housewares. As you stroll the narrow lanes of a Palermo market—your senses assaulted by sights, smells, and sounds—you'll enjoy an almost Arabian vibe, echoing the rise of Palermo 1,200 years ago. Vendors here still maintain the tradition of calling out to passersby in a sing-song way, like an auctioneer. Street food carts are scattered among the stalls, selling *panelle* (chickpea fritters), *sfincione* (fluffy pizza with anchovies), and lots of other eats (see the street food sidebar under "Eating in Palermo," later).

Hours: Palermo's markets are generally open Mon-Sat 6:00-14:00 (with some stalls—especially imperishable items—staying open later), closed Sun.

Market Tips: Join in the fun by buying some olives, cheese, or fruit. Food is sold by the kilo (2.2 pounds), and a tenth of a kilo is called an *etto*. If you're buying cheese, cold cuts, or a snack sold by weight, *un etto* (about a quarter-pound) or *due etti* (roughly a half-pound) is a standard amount for a picnic. *Attenzione!* Don't touch the food on display. Vendors here consider themselves artists in their trade, so ask for what you want and tell them how and when you plan to eat it; they'll select a fruit or vegetable at the correct degree of ripeness.

▲▲Il Ballarò Market

Of all the street markets in Palermo, Ballarò is the oldest, most authentic, and liveliest, stretching from Piazza Ballarò (a few blocks east of Palermo Cathedral) to the train station. A thousand years ago, when Palermo was

still bounded by its now-underground rivers, this market was here with its singing merchants. The market's neighborhood is multi-ethnic and unpolished, with immigrant families squatting in dilapidated buildings a few steps off the main shopping street...an authentic slice of Palermo. It's best to wear sturdy shoes on the broken pavement. While a visit here is not dangerous, pay close attention to your belongings.

▲Il Capo Market

More central and less colorful than Ballarò, the Capo Market (from the Latin *caput*, "head"), winds its way behind Teatro Massimo, with the main entrance at Porta Carini. The market features food on its main street and mostly household goods on side streets. Similar merchants—fabric sellers, cleaning suppliers, clothing shops—tend to cluster together.

La Vucciria Market

Described on my "Palermo City Walk," earlier, the waning Vucciria Market used to be the city's beating heart. Now you'll find

a smattering of butchers, fruit and veggie vendors, antiques, and some fun street life. While it's no longer a classic Palermo street market, it still has one of the city's best street food scenes. And the Vucciria neighborhood—especially Piazza Caracciolo—is a charming, youthful, bohemian, and often boisterous hangout after dark.

AWAY FROM THE CENTER

▲▲Capuchin Crypt (Catacombe dei Cappuccini)

Perhaps Palermo's quirkiest sight is the crypt of its Capuchin monastery. The Capuchins, monks known for their brown robes (and the namesake of cappuccino), are a branch of the Franciscan order. Capuchins have a passion for reminding people of their mortality, called *memento mori* (a Latin phrase that translates to "remember that you will die"). Generally, when their brothers passed away, the Capuchins put their bones on display to send the macabre message: "What you are, we once were; and what we are, you will be." In

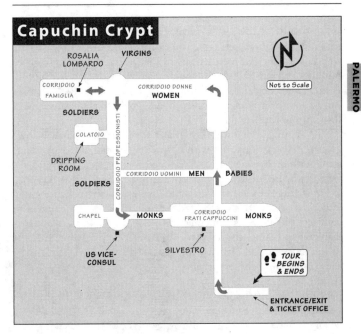

Capuchin Crypt

ROSALIA LOMBARDO — VIRGINS

CORRIDOIO FAMIGLIA

CORRIDOIO DONNE — WOMEN

Not to Scale

SOLDIERS

COLATOIO

DRIPPING ROOM

CORRIDOIO PROFESSIONISTI

CORRIDOIO UOMINI — MEN — BABIES

SOLDIERS

CHAPEL — MONKS

CORRIDOIO FRATI CAPPUCCINI — MONKS

US VICE-CONSUL

SILVESTRO

TOUR BEGINS & ENDS

ENTRANCE/EXIT & TICKET OFFICE

other words, live a noble life, and put yourself right with God while you still have time...because your time will come, and soon.

The monks of Palermo have taken this tradition a step further: Rather than just saving bones, they preserved the bodies. Later, the monks realized they could charge wealthy parishioners for the privilege of being mummified, which became a fashionable way to leave this life. By 1887, the practice had become forbidden except in special cases, and about 4,000 bodies had been collected

in their crypt. Today, the public is welcome to wander the halls of this collection of fully clothed and remarkably preserved bodies.

Cost and Hours: €3, daily 9:00-13:00 & 15:00-18:00; out of respect for these bodies without souls, photography is not allowed—but plenty of postcards are on sale; Piazza dei Cappuccini 1, tel. 091-652-7389, www.palermocatacombs.com.

Getting There: It's on the western edge of Palermo, about a mile and a half from Quattro Canti. To **walk,** first head to Piazza Indipendenza, behind the Norman Palace; then walk up Corso Calatafimi (with the Norman Palace at your back, it's the busy street at one o'clock). After several blocks, turn right on Via Pindemonte, which dead-ends at the crypt. You can also take **bus** #327 from the stop behind the Norman Palace on Piazza Indipendenza, ride 10 minutes, and get off at the Cappuccini stop (runs every 25 minutes). A **taxi** from central Palermo to the crypt costs about €15. **Drivers** can park in front (officially free, though you'll likely have to give a few coins to the "attendant").

Warning: This morbid site isn't for everyone—it's a below-ground crypt jam-packed with corpses in various states of decay, some with disturbing expressions, and only one exit. That said, it's well-lit and not nearly as musty and spooky as you might expect.

Visiting the Crypt: The visit follows a counterclockwise route. The oldest body, Brother Silvestro from 1599, is immediately to your left and above as you enter.
Look up and down the hallways to the left and right, filled with the Capuchin brothers them-selves (Corridoio Frati Cap-puccini). These bodies were originally buried elsewhere, but when a new crypt was built, their tomb was opened, and the brothers were found to be almost
perfectly preserved. This miracle was the inspiration for preserving and displaying the dead in this space.

Continuing straight ahead, you'll enter the Corridoio Uomi-ni (the hall of the men). Throughout the crypt, you'll notice that mouths gape open in what's called the "scream of death"—due to the gradual deterioration of the jaw muscles. Partway along this hallway, look for a small alcove on the right with the bodies of babies and small children.

Continue all the way to the end of the men's hall and turn left into the Corridoio Donne (hall of the women). All of the women are lying down, dressed in their Sunday best, with their heads all turned to greet you. A few more babies are also mixed in. At the next junction, you'll find anoth-er alcove on the right, dedicated to virgins (Cappella Vergini).

In the dead-end hallway ahead (Corridoio Famiglia), each alcove contains a family group. In the middle of the hall is the modern metal casket with the crypt's most famous body: two-year-old Rosalia Lombardo. She's dubbed *La Bella Addormentata* (Sleeping Beauty) by locals, who have been waiting for her to wake up since the 1920s. Although the Capuchin's practice of embalming was forbidden by this time, they made an exception for her grieving parents. Her body was studied recently by *National Geographic*, which provided this sealed case to stop any deterioration.

Returning to the main path, you'll pass the bodies of men of different professions (Corridoio Professionisti). Watch on the right for the small doorway marked *Colatoio*—the dripping room, where monks drained the body and cleaned the skin with vinegar and herbs. When the body was properly dried out (and stench-free), families brought clothing and did their dead loved ones' hair, and the body was put on display. The exact process used to preserve the bodies is unknown, but a recent CAT-scan of the most well-preserved body, the last to be embalmed, revealed that the internal organs are as equally well preserved as the facial skin and hair.

Continue down the hall; you'll pass a hall on your left lined with bodies of priests (Preti). Keep going straight, and at the end of the hall, turn right, walk up four steps, and look left to find the long casket with a glass cover, which houses the only American, Giovanni Paterniti, the vice-consul for the United States, who died here in Palermo in 1911.

Now head along the final hall, back to where you entered, and go in peace...for now.

BEYOND PALERMO

Several worthwhile destinations are within day-trip distance of Palermo, including the cathedral at Monreale, the beach town of Cefalù (both described in later chapters), and a pair of sights to the north of town, around Monte Pellegrino. The German writer Goethe called this hill, which towers over Palermo, "the most beautiful promontory in the world."

▲▲Sanctuary of Santa Rosalia

On top of Monte Pellegrino sits the Sanctuary of Santa Rosalia, the patron saint of Palermo. While a bit of a trek, it's a worthwhile pilgrimage for those who can make time for it. And the sanctuary—burrowed into a rock face with dripping walls and reverent locals—is a unique and powerful sight. A visit here with the right mindset will help you appreciate why locals say that, in their pantheon of saints, there is Santa Rosalia...then everyone else.

Hours: Free, daily 7:30-19:30, Nov-March until 18:30, tel. 091-540-326, www.santuariosantarosalia.it, kindly custodian Don Getano Ceravolo.

Getting There: The chapel perches on a mountaintop four miles north of Palermo's city center (but the drive is twice that far, thanks to many switchbacks). The journey to the top of Monte Pellegrino is scenic, with sprawling views over busy Palermo, the mountains, and the sea. **Bus #812** departs from the stop in the middle of Piazza Sturzo, a block behind Teatro Politeama (departs every 1.5 hours—more on Sundays, trip takes about 45 minutes depending on traffic). **Drivers** go north along the port, then head out of town on Via Montepellegrino, which becomes Via Isaac Rabìn. Reaching the base of the hill, bear right and follow Via Pietro Bonanno as it switchbacks steeply all the way to the top (figure at least 30 minutes' drive, depending on traffic). As you twist up the steep switchbacks, consider that many devout *palermitani* make this trek on foot from the city center each year in mid-July.

Visiting the Sanctuary: This church and convent were built on the place where Rosalia's bones were discovered. But the facade is just...a facade. Once inside, the roof cuts away to the open sky and the church blends into a dramatic cave, complete with dripping rock formations.

In this entryway—before passing through the gate of the church itself—you'll see a staggering variety of **votive** items, offered as thanks to Rosalia by those who pray to her for help. On the left wall hang hundreds of little silver plaques, some shaped like body parts—left by people who have recovered from illness or Vespa accidents. On the right is a pile of more modern ex-voto items, such as wedding dresses and baby clothing, surrounding the gigantic anchor of a ship that survived a rough journey in the seas near Palermo.

Now step into the **church interior.** The altar on the left houses an ivory sculpture of the saint (in the glass enclosure below)—

PALERMO

Santa Rosalia

Rosalia—whose name comes from the words for "rose" and "lily" (signifying beauty and purity)—was a Norman noblewoman and possibly the niece of King William II. According to tradition, 15-year-old Rosalia refused her arranged marriage to a nobleman and decided to dedicate herself to Christ. She lived out her life as a hermit on Monte Pellegrino, where she died in 1166. During the plague of 1624, Santa Rosalia appeared to a local hunter and told him where to find her remains. He discovered the bones in a cave (now the sanctuary) on July 14 and brought them down into the city...and the plague ended. Santa Rosalia is the most venerated saint in Palermo. She's also the patron saint of epidemics—and of volcanoes and fires (fitting for this volcanic island).

Thanks to Rosalia, July 14 and 15 are the most festive days of the year in Palermo. The mayor kicks things off by placing flowers at the Quattro Canti intersection (while the public either cheers or—more often—jeers, depending on the mayor's current popularity). Then the crowd marches down to the harborfront, where they watch fireworks and eat the traditional food of the feast of Santa Rosalia: snails. (Snails, which live in solitude in a little "house" they carry on their backs, are a common symbol for hermits.) After the celebration, everyone walks home—empty snail shells crunching underfoot. The festivities also include a long, laborious pilgrimage—by foot—from the city center to the Sanctuary of Santa Rosalia, high atop Monte Pellegrino.

though her actual bones are in Palermo Cathedral. The metal channels attached to the cave ceiling seem artistic, even surreal, but they're entirely practical—they're an elaborate system for channeling dripping water, which is believed to have miraculous properties. You can follow the water from the ceiling, across the top of the altar, and down into the holy water fonts.

This sanctuary is a powerful place for the faithful. People come to drink the water or rub it on troubled body parts. According to the sanctuary's custodian, even skeptical doctors have been healed here. It's poignant to simply step back and observe the steady stream of visitors who come to pay their respects and to thank Santa Rosalia for her help.

Connecting to Mondello: Drivers wanting to combine Santa

Rosalia with the alluring beach town of Mondello may find a shortcut road open: Carry on down the mountain road past Santa Rosalia, and you may be able to twist directly down to Mondello (with stunning views as you approach). However, sometimes this road is closed (especially off-season) due to rock slides, in which case you'll need to retrace your steps and loop around the bottom of the mountain—the seaside road is pleasant and avoids congested city streets.

▲Mondello

A favorite summer resort on the other side of Monte Pellegrino, Mondello is a popular hangout for families, teens, and tourists who are tired of city congestion.  Crystal clear blue waters and a crescent of soft, sandy beach beckon sun worshippers. The town offers turn-of-the-century boardwalk atmosphere, a cancan line of Liberty Style (Italian Art Nouveau) villas, and beautiful views along the coast—and occasionally all the way to Mount Etna. This area was originally a swamp, which was drained to create a beach community (with the help of Belgian engineers—notice the Belgian and Italian flags on the main pier). In the 1910s, this was *the* place for aristocrats to build their seaside villas. Overcrowded in summer and dead in the winter, Mondello is perfect on a warm spring or fall day.

Getting There: You can reach Mondello via bus #806 from Piazza Sturzo, behind the Teatro Politeama (4/hour, takes about 40 minutes). Mondello is about a 20-minute drive from downtown Palermo (if there's no traffic).

Eating: For a seafood treat, stop at **$$ Da Calogero** for *polpo bollito* (freshly chopped boiled octopus) eaten while standing on the sidewalk (Via Torre di Mondello 22, tel. 091-684-1333), or sit down at one of the many al fresco eateries ringing the piazza. For a splashy meal, the old-time bathing pavilion houses **$$$$ Alle Terrazze,** a pricey restaurant with killer views (closed Tue, tel. 091-626-2903).

Shopping in Palermo

Palermo has a variety of shopping experiences—from gritty street markets, to inviting artisanal shops, to the typical big-city department store.

Artisanal Crafts: The Kalsa district—near the port—has the

Sicilian Souvenirs

Palermo is a great place to find Sicilian handicrafts and gifty edibles to take home.

Pottery shops sell typical, colorful wares—hand-painted with bright colors and intricate designs. A popular pottery item is the "Head of the Moor" flower vase, described on page 372. Sicily's pottery capital is Caltagirone, in the middle of the island; you'll see work from that town sold everywhere.

The island's symbol, the three-legged **Trinacria,** is featured on pottery, flags, T-shirts, and magnets. The island's triangular shape is another popular subject for handicrafts, from wallets to trivets. You'll see traditional Sicilian **puppets** for sale, in varying sizes and priced according to their detail and workmanship.

A wide variety of **jewelry** is also available, from modern styles to pieces shaped like Sicilian symbols: the shape of the island, the Trinacria, traditional horse carts, and puppets. Men may want to pick up a *coppola*—a woven cap with a brim, traditionally worn by older men as a work hat.

Sicilian **wines** are excellent and generally affordable; Nero d'Avola is the most typical, but there are many unique local varieties in each part of the island. For more on Sicilian wines, see page 441. Also consider Sicily's high-quality **olive oil,** produced in the south, near Castelvetrano.

Canned **tuna** was invented in the western part of the island, and real Sicilian tuna packed in olive oil is a culinary treat. While it's not possible to take home cannoli, which are perishable, other sweets have excellent shelf life. **Almond cookies** stay fresh for months and make a great gift; they have different names in every city—look for *mandorla* in the name.

city's most appealing assortment of one-off craft boutiques. Around 50 artisan shops in the city center have formed the Associazione Liberi Artigiani-Artisti Balarm (www.alabpalermo. it); their shops are marked with an orange *ALAB* logo—watch for it as you window shop in the old center. If you like what you see, look for a free map locating all of ALAB's shops across Sicily.

Via Alessandro Paternostro is lined with creative boutiques selling leather bags, clothes, accessories, ceramics, and books. If you follow this from Via Vittorio Emanuele south, you'll enjoy one of Palermo's most atmospheric walking streets (also covered on my "Palermo City Walk"). Eventually you'll spill out onto the skinny

Piazza Aragona, with a cluster of fine shops, including **Elena & Fabrizio** (handmade leather accessories) and **LaboRiuso** (creative, youthful jewelry and accessories). Turning left at Piazza Aragona, along **Via Alloro,** you'll find a few more interesting shops.

Food: Sicilian sweets, particularly cookies and marzipan fruit, have a long shelf life. Cafés and sweet shops all over the city sell boxes of colorful sweets, including stalls at the Ballarò Market. Near Teatro Politeama, **I Peccatucci di Mamma Andrea** sells a seasonal variety of sweets, jams, and cakes that are beautifully packaged (Via Principe Scordia 67).

Department Stores and Big Chains: La Rinascente is the pick for a major department store fix in the very center, selling clothes and upscale housewares. Their top floor food hall has a terrace with views over Palermo (daily 9:30-20:30, food hall until 23:00). Beyond that, the most popular shopping area is between Teatro Massimo and Teatro Politeama, along **Via Ruggiero Settimo,** which hosts big-name retailers like H&M, Benetton, and OVS. **Antica Sartoria** sells clothing and jewelry with traditional Southern Italian motifs (Via Ruggiero Settimo 28). The Italian bookstore chain **Feltrinelli** also has a branch near Teatro Massimo that sells some English books and accessories for book lovers (Via Cavour 133). Higher-end shops are in the new part of town, just past Teatro Politeama on **Via della Libertà.**

Street Markets: The street markets of Capo, Ballarò, and Vucciria mostly sell food, but they do have sections of cheap clothing and household goods. Via Bandiera, near Piazza San Domenico, has a small clothing market (Mon-Sat 7:00-14:00, closed Sun).

Antiques: A weekly antiquarian market pops up in Piazza Marina in the Kalsa, selling furniture, jewelry, books, and all sorts of flea-market treasures (Sat-Sun 10:00-14:00).

Nightlife in Palermo

Palermo has become a hotbed for events and nightlife in recent years. Music, food, and art festivals happen frequently from May through October. Two websites (in Italian) keep updated schedules of upcoming events: www.palermotoday.it and www.balarm.it.

LOW-IMPACT NIGHTLIFE

Passeggiata: The evening *passeggiata* gets underway about 17:30 and lasts well into dinnertime. The best places to stroll and people-watch are **Via Maqueda** (the traffic-free zone stretching north from Quattro Canti to the Teatro Massimo) or **Via Vittorio Emanuele** (the restaurant-lined street between Quattro Canti and the harbor). Following the route of my "Palermo City Walk" in the evening lets you mix and mingle with the locals for a memorable experience.

Aperitivo: As in other parts of Italy, Palermo has a thriving *aperitivo* scene (Italian happy hour). In the early evening hours, buying an *aperitivo* at any bar will net you some free nibbles. Some bars even offer a small, complimentary buffet—ask before you order. Some bars offer *apericena* (a pun combining *aperitivo* and the word for "dinner"). Several of the places described under the "Lively Nightlife Areas," below, offer *aperitivo* nibbles if you arrive at the right time.

Theater: Teatro Massimo is the home of opera in Palermo, but also hosts concerts, dance, and special events such as literature readings. There are performances every month except August, and events almost every day in May and June. Summer performances take place outside of the theater, typically at Teatro di Verdura on the outskirts of the city, but tickets can be booked through Teatro Massimo. For evening performances, Sicilians tend to dress up. Same-day tickets are often available (tel. 091-605-3580, www. teatromassimo.it). The city's second grand theater, a few blocks north—**Teatro Politeama**—is another fine venue, and home to the Sicilian Symphony Orchestra, which performs from October through May (www.orchestrasinfonicasiciliana.it).

Summer Classical Music: From July through early September, **Palermo Classica** hosts music events across the city in memorable venues, such as Palazzo Chiaramonte Steri (tel. 091-332-208, www.palermoclassica.it).

Concerts: Santa Maria dello Spasimo, an unfinished church near the harbor, is an evocative venue for occasional live performances. In the 16th century, funds earmarked for completing the church were diverted to defending Palermo from Ottoman pirates. Without a roof, and with a stage where the altar should be, today the unfinished church hosts an eclectic lineup of open-air performances, including rock bands, jazz, and tango concerts. Check the calendar on www.palermotoday.it to see if anything's on during your visit (closed Mon, Via dello Spasimo 15).

LIVELY NIGHTLIFE AREAS

To sample Palermo after hours, wander through the city's core and connect a few lively squares that are a magnet for young and old. For locations, see the "Palermo Restaurants" map, later.

Piazza Rivoluzione: This colorful square, tucked a short walk from Via Roma and north of the train station, is a delightful place to hang out. Early in the evening, it hums with a happy *aperitivo* scene, where locals and visitors nurse €5 cocktails and munch a free little spread of light food while watching the gurgling "Genie of Palermo" fountain. Later, it becomes a boisterous nightlife zone. Anchoring the scene at #5, **Qvivi** has a rock-n-roll vibe, pleasing to backpackers and backpackers-at-heart. At #1, **Cavu** is a more sophisticated wine bar serving a large platter of snacks with a drink (€10/person). And at #35, **Zammù** is a relaxed cocktail bar. Also facing the square is **Pizzeria Ka Mancia,** handy for a bite outside of *aperitivo* time.

Piazza Aragona and Nearby: A block away from Piazza Rivoluzione, this square is a mellower scene—better by day—ringed by

artisan shops and easy cafés. The main watering hole here, **New Art 108,** has abundant outdoor tables and a long list of drinks. Two short blocks west, Piazza Santa Anna is enlivened by a couple of popular bars, including the thriving **Monkey Pub,** with an energetic local crowd spilling out into the square.

Via Alessandro Paternostro: The street heading north from Piazza Aragona is lined with a variety of bars and cafés that are lively after hours. Most of the action clusters around Piazza San Francesco (with the famous recommended Antica Focacceria). The trendiest spot is **Bar Garibaldi** (at #46), where you'll find Palermo's most painfully fashionable hipsters sipping drinks in a faux-nautical, faux-Risorgimento setting. On the other (north) side of Piazza San Francesco are the more old-school **Colletti** (#77) and the hip **Goccio** cocktail bar (#79). This up-and-coming area is changing fast—stroll here to see what's new.

Vucciria Market and Nearby: This area has bars with music and a fun, youthful scene after dark. A bohemian crowd spills from

the bars into the cobbled lanes on nice nights. Several spots on Piazza Caracciolo have open-air grills. Order your raw meat at the counter and watch it cook. Notice the oversized plume of smoke that pours out of some of the hissing grills. Vendors wipe down their grills with fat to generate extra smoke—not for the flavor, but as a sort of advertisement. The tangle of streets from Vucciria to Piazza Marina is hopping with a constantly changing scene of new and trendy bars and cafés. The recommended **Franco ù Vastiddaru** street food shop on Via Vittorio Emanuele is an epicenter for late-night eats and drinks.

A bit farther away is **Piazzetta della Canna,** deep in some seedy-feeling back streets a five-minute walk west of Via Maqueda. This younger-skewing scene fills a little square under big trees with shared tables of happy drinkers, ringed by mostly interchange-able bars. This scene doesn't really get rolling until later, and often comes with live music.

Near Teatro Massimo: In this neighborhood, locals hit **Bot-tiglieria Massimo** before and after dinner for a drink and conver-sation (daily 10:00-very late, Via Salvatore Spinuzza 59). This area is called the "Champagneria," which is filled with lively drinking spots open late, some with live music.

And to reach a very local-feeling, traffic-free street with some appealing spots for the *aperitivo* happy hour, walk a few short blocks north of the Teatro Massimo to **Via Principe di Belmonte.** In this workaday, urban-feeling area are several fine bars and cafés with generous outdoor seating, including the recommended **An-tico Caffè Spinnato.** This is a nice place to sip a drink and people-watch before dinner.

Sleeping in Palermo

Palermo is a busy, noisy, crazy city full of fun and excitement... which are not characteristics you want in a hotel room. Considering

how affordable Palermo is in comparison to other big Italian cities, it's smart to splurge a little here, and pick a hotel with some extra comforts. That said, some of Palermo's smaller, boutique B&Bs are a great value, offering hotelesque quality at *pensione* prices.

For some travelers, short-term, Airbnb-type rentals can be a good alternative; search for places in my recommended hotel neighbor-hoods. Parking here is tricky—which is why I recommend picking up your car on departure (if you must drive in Palermo, ask your hotel for parking advice, and be sure to get a ZTL pass—described later, under "Palermo Connections."

I rank accommodations from ¢ budget to **$$$** splurge. To get the best deal, contact my family-run accommodations directly by phone or email. When you book direct, the owner avoids a roughly 20 percent commission and may be able to offer you a discount. Book your accommodations well in advance if you'll be traveling during peak season or if your trip coincides with a major holiday or festival (see the appendix). For more information on rates and deals, making reservations, finding a short-term rental, and more, see the "Sleeping" section in the Practicalities chapter.

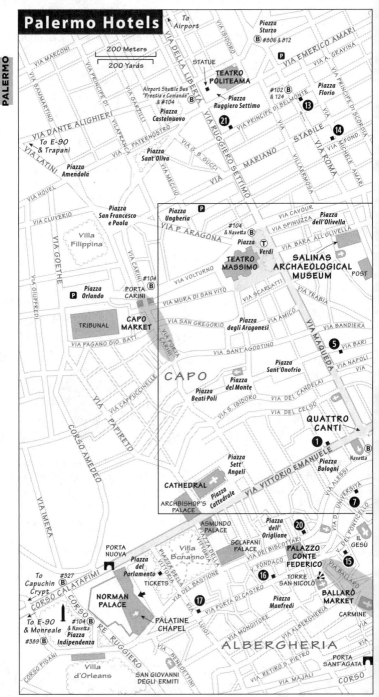

Palermo Hotels

PALERMO

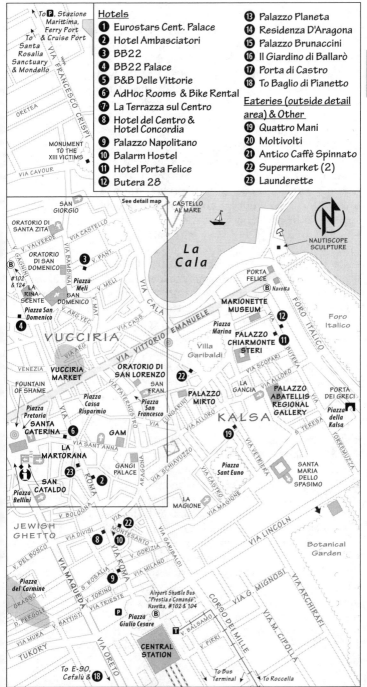

Hotels
1. Eurostars Cent. Palace
2. Hotel Ambasciatori
3. BB22
4. BB22 Palace
5. B&B Delle Vittorie
6. AdHoc Rooms & Bike Rental
7. La Terrazza sul Centro
8. Hotel del Centro & Hotel Concordia
9. Palazzo Napolitano
10. Balarm Hostel
11. Hotel Porta Felice
12. Butera 28
13. Palazzo Planeta
14. Residenza D'Aragona
15. Palazzo Brunaccini
16. Il Giardino di Ballarò
17. Porta di Castro
18. To Baglio di Pianetto

Eateries (outside detail area) & Other
19. Quattro Mani
20. Moltivolti
21. Antico Caffè Spinnato
22. Supermarket (2)
23. Launderette

CENTRAL PALERMO

$$$ Eurostars Centrale Palace is indeed central, just steps from Quattro Canti, within easy walking distance to the main sights. Housed in a large former noble palace, this is a great spot to relive the elegance of the belle époque in style. The 104 well-appointed—if worn—rooms are quiet, and a few have small terraces (abundant breakfast, air-con, elevator, rooftop restaurant, Via Vittorio Emanuele 327, tel. 091-8539, www.eurostarscentralepalace.com, info@eurostarscentralepalace.com).

$$$ Hotel Ambasciatori, right along Via Roma, has fine rooms with stately furniture and wood floors. The top-floor terrace has stunning views of the Palermo skyline (air-con, elevator, good restaurant, Via Roma 111, tel. 091-616-6881, www.ambasciatorihotelpalermo.com, booking@ambasciatorihotelpalermo.com, Aida).

$$$ BB22 is tucked away on a quiet lane behind San Domenico, like a hidden city retreat. The seven rooms have a trendy, shabby-chic appeal in neutral tones. **BB22 Palace,** run by BB22, is in a palazzo just off Via Roma. While not as cozy as BB22, the rooms are upscale and quiet, with white walls and simple but tasteful furnishings. For families, they offer a larger apartment (air-con, family rooms, small terrace, Via Pantelleria 22, tel. 091-326-214, www.bb22.it, info@bb22.it, Emmanuela).

$$ B&B Delle Vittorie is a boutique bed-and-breakfast shoehorned into a palazzo just off Via Maqueda. Its six rooms are clean and modern, with thoughtful touches. The breakfast room looks out onto a curious empty courtyard, built by the fascist government to display its victories...that never happened (air-con, elevator, Via Bari 52, tel. 091-335-453, www.bbdellevittorie.it, info@bbdellevittorie.it).

$ AdHoc Rooms is run by energetic Natalia and sweet but mostly silent Luca, with five bright, modern, comfortable rooms. Every room has a theme—music, library, superheroes—and the colorful communal kitchen looks out over a shared terrace just a stone's throw from Piazza Bellini and the Fountain of Shame. This place offers an ideal combination of good value, hospitality, and unbeatable location (air-con, lots of stairs, Discesa dei Giudici 15, mobile 393-929-0900, www.adhocrooms.it, info@adhocrooms.it).

$ La Terrazza sul Centro, warmly run by Barbara and Emiliano, has eight clean, modern rooms in a great location next to the university, just a few steps from Quattro Canti. Although there's no elevator and the area is pretty lively, the peaceful view terrace makes a good tradeoff (air-con, Via dell'Università 20, mobile 392-310-6267, www.laterrazzasulcentro.it, info@laterrazzasulcentro.it).

$ Hotel del Centro offers classic elegance at a budget price. Their 27 rooms have high ceilings and original 19th-century details, but there are also modern conveniences (RS%—use code "ricksteves," air-con, elevator, Via Roma 72, tel. 091-617-0376, www.hoteldelcentro.it, info@hoteldelcentro.it, Giuseppe).

$ Hotel Concordia, a floor above Hotel del Centro, is a simple, clean place with welcoming warmth a short walk from the train station. Friendly Dario mans the desk at his family's hotel, renting 12 colorful, good-value rooms (family rooms, air-con, elevator, Via Roma 72, mobile 324-091-7996, www.hotelconcordiapalermo.it, info@hotelconcordiapalermo.it).

$ Palazzo Napolitano, just steps from the train station along busy Via Roma, has four spacious rooms in an elegant turn-of-the-century palace. The rooms combine antique architecture with sleek, modern furniture (air-con, elevator, Via Roma 28, mobile 392-279-0688, https://palazzo-napolitano.webnode.it, b.bpalazzonapolitano@gmail.com).

¢ Balarm Hostel, run by friendly Massimo, is an efficient, clean, and friendly option for the traveler on a shoestring. The 40 beds are in mixed gender or female-only rooms, and include breakfast and a communal kitchen, all for about the price of a pizza dinner (air-con, laundry room, Via Roma 41, mobile 392-152-9769, www.balarmhostel.it, info@balarmhostel.it).

LA KALSA
$$ Hotel Porta Felice, near the harbor, has a modern, masculine feel with a professional staff. The 33 rooms are decorated with leather and wood, and some have hot tubs (air-con, elevator, Via Butera 45, tel. 091-617-5678, www.hotelportafelice.it, info@hotelportafelice.it).

$$ Butera 28 is an actual palace, still lived in by the duke and duchess, relatives of the famous author of *The Leopard*. Duchess Nicoletta rents out 12 rambling apartments scattered around the palazzo, all filled with antique furniture, colorful tiles, and the ambience of bygone Sicily. A tour of their private apartments is included in your stay. Nicoletta also offers cooking classes, see page 41 (no breakfast, air-con, Via Butera 28, mobile 333-316-5432, www.butera28.it, info@butera28.it).

NORTH OF THE CENTER
While not as central or characteristic, this area, near Teatro Politeama, has easier access to parking and more modern conveniences.

$$$ Palazzo Planeta rents seven apartments in a classy palazzo near a lively district. The elegantly furnished units have cozy living areas, kitchens, and washing machines. The property is run by a winery, so you'll find complimentary wine and olive oil stocked in the kitchen (air-con, elevator, no breakfast, Via Principe Belmonte 68, tel. 0925-195-5460, www.planetaestate.it, palazzoplaneta@ planeta.it).

$ Residenza D'Aragona, tucked down a quiet side street off Via Roma, is a cross between a boutique hotel and an apartment complex. Each giant room has a bedroom, bath, and living room with a tiny kitchenette. Although the concierge is rarely around, this is ideal for families or longer stays (air-con, elevator, Via Ottavio D'Aragona 25, tel. 091-662-2222, www.residenzadaragona. it, info@residenzadaragona.it).

BALLARÒ

The neighborhood surrounding Palermo's most lively market can be noisy during the day and intimidating at night. But those who don't mind a more colorful area will find it central and a good value. When you first arrive, stick to the main streets: From Via Maqueda (heading south from Quattro Canti, or north from the train station), angle into the Ballarò area on the tourist-friendly Via del Ponticello, passing the big Il Gesù church. Better yet, splurge for a taxi to take you right to your hotel's front door. (Forging a different path—or simply following a mapping app—could take you through some rougher parts of the Ballarò.)

$$$ Palazzo Brunaccini, set in a hidden courtyard in the Ballarò chaos, is surprisingly peaceful and elegant. The 18 rooms are spacious and spotless, with all the comforts, including high-end mattresses. As the neighborhood can seem a little scruffy, enter from Vicolo S. Michele Arcangelo to avoid loiterers (air-con, elevator, Piazzetta Brunaccini 9, tel. 091-586-904, www. palazzobrunaccini.it, info@palazzobrunaccini.it, Adrianna).

$$ Il Giardino di Ballarò is another quiet gem, tucked into a building surrounding a small garden and sun terrace. The modern, creatively decorated common spaces feel like a friend's home, and the 10 rooms are comfy (air-con, Via Porta di Castro 75, tel. 091-212-215, www.ilgiardinodiballaro.it, info@ilgiardinodiballaro.it).

$ Porta di Castro—at the western edge of the Ballarò, near the Norman Palace—is perfect for artsy, eclectic types who like their cities gritty and their hotels full of character. Alessandro is a collector, and his 15 rooms in a converted church showcase his collections. Every room has interesting furniture and features one of his 40 vintage Vespas (family rooms, air-con, elevator, Via Porta di Castro 223, tel. 091-702-5564, www.bebportadicastro.it, bebportadicastro@gmail.com).

NEAR PALERMO

$$$ Baglio di Pianetto is about 13 miles south of central Palermo, set among scenic, rocky hills. This winery and hotel is an oasis of classy pastoral calm. The 13 rooms are large and well furnished, and the restaurant serves locally sourced food to match their impressive wines. If you have a car, prefer countryside silence, and don't mind commuting to Palermo, this is a pleasant option (good-value half-pension deals available, air-con, elevator, large swimming pool, on Via Francia in Santa Cristina Gela, tel. 091-857-0148, www.bagliodipianetto.it, agrirelais@bagliodipianetta.it).

Eating in Palermo

The mix of cultures that contributed to the makeup of today's Palermo also created a vibrant food scene. Fish is the main ingredient here, but also look for local veggies, North African ingredients like couscous, and anything made with ricotta. Dishes *alla Palermitana* usually mean they are topped with breadcrumbs (yesterday's scraps of bread were an affordable substitute for those, who couldn't afford grated cheese).

I rank eateries from **$** budget to **$$$$** splurge. For even more advice on eating in Sicily, including details on ordering, dining, and tipping in restaurants, the types of eateries you'll encounter, and Sicilian cuisine and beverages, see the "Eating" section of the Practicalities chapter.

The restaurants listed here are popular with both locals and visitors; it's smart to book ahead, especially in high season, and as you approach the weekend.

PALERMO'S STREET FOOD SCENE

One of the most memorable ways to eat in Palermo is also one of the cheapest: street food. Fearless eaters will head to the Capo or Ballarò markets and simply try a nibble from each cart, with choices ranging from sesame bread to veal penis. To make things easier, join a street food tour, such as the one offered by Streaty (see "Tours in Palermo," earlier).

Lunch or Dinner at Vucciria Market: To sample a smorgasbord of classic Palermo street food in a graffiti-slathered square, make your way to Piazza Caracciolo in the heart of the Vucciria Market. While this was once a thriving market (like Ballarò or Capo), most of its meat, fish,

PALERMO

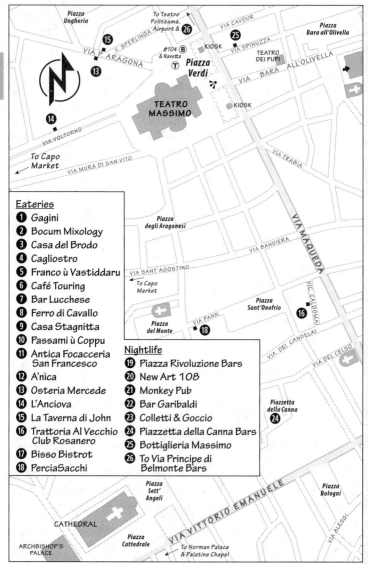

Eateries
1 Gagini
2 Bocum Mixology
3 Casa del Brodo
4 Cagliostro
5 Franco ù Vastiddaru
6 Café Touring
7 Bar Lucchese
8 Ferro di Cavallo
9 Casa Stagnitta
10 Passami ù Coppu
11 Antica Focacceria San Francesco
12 A'nìca
13 Osteria Mercede
14 L'Anciova
15 La Taverna di John
16 Trattoria Al Vecchio Club Rosanero
17 Bisso Bistrot
18 PerciaSacchi

Nightlife
19 Piazza Rivoluzione Bars
20 New Art 108
21 Monkey Pub
22 Bar Garibaldi
23 Colletti & Goccio
24 Piazzetta della Canna Bars
25 Bottiglieria Massimo
26 To Via Principe di Belmonte Bars

and produce vendors have moved elsewhere. But taking their place is an array of ramshackle food stands and cocktail bars. While it's open for lunch and dinner, it's particularly lively after hours, when this transforms into one of Palermo's trendiest nightlife spots. Take a spin around to consider your options: a classic cart selling *pani ca' meusa* (spleen sandwiches), an octopus man serving up *polpo bollito*, a fry stand selling *panelle* and *cazzilli*, and a sizzling grill with *stigghiola*, *mangia e bevi*, and other meaty choices (see sidebar, next

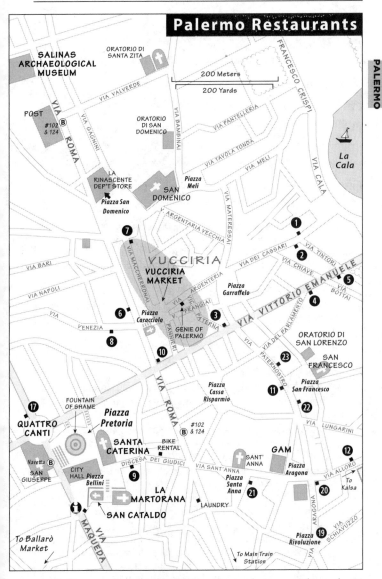

Palermo Restaurants

SALINAS ARCHAEOLOGICAL MUSEUM
ORATORIO DI SANTA ZITA
200 Meters
200 Yards
POST #102 & 124 B
VIA ROMA
VIA GAGGINI
VIA VALVERDE
VIA BAMBINAI
ORATORIO DI SAN DOMENICO
VIA PANTELLERIA
VIA TAVOLA TONDA
VIA MELI
FRANCESCO CRISPI
VIA CALA
La Cala
LA RINASCENTE DEP'T STORE
Piazza San Domenico
SAN DOMENICO
Piazza Meli
VIA MATERASSAI
V. ARGENTARIA VECCHIA
❼ VUCCIRIA
VUCCIRIA MARKET
Piazza Garraffello
VIA DEI CASSARI
VIA CHIAVE
❶
❷ VIA TINTORI
VIA BOTTAI ❺
VIA VITTORIO EMANUELE
VIA BARI
VIA NAPOLI
VIA VENEZIA
❻
❽
Piazza Caracciola
VIA ARGENTERIA
VIA FRANGIAI
VIA PATERNA
GENIE OF PALERMO
❸
❹
ORATORIO DI SAN LORENZO
VIA DEL PARLAMENTO
VIA PATERNOSTRO
SAN FRANCESCO
❿
VIA ROMA
Piazza Cassa Risparmio
❷❸
Piazza San Francesco
❶❶
❷❷
VIA LUNGARINI
FOUNTAIN OF SHAME
Piazza Pretoria
❶❼
QUATTRO CANTI
SANTA CATERINA
#102 & 124 B
BIKE RENTAL
GAM
Piazza Aragona
❶❷ VIA ALLORO
To Kalsa
Navetta B
SAN GIUSEPPE
CITY HALL
Piazza Bellini
DISCESA DEI GIUDICI
VIA SANT'ANNA
SANT' ANNA
❾
LA MARTORANA
SAN CATALDO
VIA MAQUEDA
Piazza Santa Anna
❷❶
LAUNDRY
❷❶
VIA ARAGONA
❷⓿
VIA SCHIAVUZZO
Piazza Rivoluzione
❶❾
ℹ
To Ballarò Market
To Main Train Station

page). Once you've got your food, pull up a chair at a rickety plastic table near the fountain in the middle of the square. Palermo street food doesn't get more adventurous, or accessible, than this.

Lunch at Ballarò or Capo Markets: These two sprawling markets have vendors similar to those at Vucciria, but they are more spread out among a larger area—tucked amid butchers, fishmongers, knockoff CDs and DVDs, clothing, and housewares. I'd walk through the market to survey your choices, then circle back

PALERMO

Sicilian Street Food

Palermo, with its strong street-food culture, is considered a capital for finger foods in Europe. The quintessential street-food experience is to hopscotch between vendors at one of the city's street markets. Prices are affordable (any of the items below shouldn't cost more than €1-2). Don't be intimidated—just point to what you want and dig in.

Arancina (plural *arancine*): A breaded, deep-fried rice ball filled with meat sauce or other ingredients. Traditionally, Palermo's *arancine* are flavored with vivid yellow saffron and contain no tomatoes. (Catania and mainland Italy call this dish *arancino* and add tomato to the filling—two things a proud local would never be caught dead doing.)

Cazzilli and **crocché:** Potato croquettes, usually filled with mashed potato, parsley, and mint. *Cazzilli* are a smaller version of *crocché.*

Frittola: Leftover cow parts, like cartilage and bone, fried up and assembled into a chewy meat fluff. It's the ultimate for the adventurous eater, and is usually found only at market carts (and sells out quickly).

Mangia e bevi: Thin strips of pork around green onion

Panelle: Deep-fried chickpea fritters. *Panelle* and *cazzilli* are often served together.

Pani ca' meusa (or **pane can milza**): Boiled spleen, lung, and other veal organ meat, served on a roll. It can be dressed with cheese *(maritatu),* or without *(schiettu).*

Polpo bollito: Octopus (large or small) that's been boiled in salty water, then chopped up and spritzed with lemon

Rascatura: A mix of leftover *panelle* and *cazzilli* with some onion and lemon, refried into little pieces of greasy goodness

Sfincione: Fluffy pizza, topped with tomato (and sometimes anchovy and cheese), sold on carts by the greasy slice. It doesn't look appetizing in the cart's display case, but the vendor will grill it on a hidden oven. (All the *sfincione* stands you see around Palermo are supplied by the same bakery. Since it takes Sundays off, you won't see *sfincione* on Mondays.)

Stigghiole: Lamb intestines wrapped around green onions. They may not sound appetizing, but they smell and taste great and are easy to find—just look for the grills spewing smoke. For something a bit more tame, look for *mangia e bevi* (described above). Often, other meats are also available to throw on the grill.

to the ones that appeal—assembling a moveable feast. Most food stands at the Ballarò and Capo markets are only open at lunchtime and closed Sunday.

Off the Street: In the neighborhood eating sections next, I've included several eateries that serve essentially the same food you'll find at the grungy markets, but in a more sane and sanitized setting—less fun but perhaps a little more convenient. Good choices include the Antica Focacceria San Francesco, Franco ù Vastiddaru, Café Touring, and Passami ù Coppu.

ON AND NEAR VIA VITTORIO EMANUELE

To quickly survey several good dining options, walk down Via Vittorio Emanuele—lined with cheap street food, high-end gourmet restaurants, trendy hotspots, and everything in between.

$$$$ Gagini, set in a former sculpture workshop, has a candlelit interior and attentive staff. The carefully prepared dishes are beautifully presented, even if the portions are small. With attention to detail and a fine wine list, this is my pick for a fancy celebration dinner—reserve ahead. Sit inside, under the massive stone vaults, or out on the back-streets sidewalk (€60-75 fixed-priced meals, daily 13:00-15:00 & 20:00-23:30, a block from Via Vittorio Emanuele at Via dei Cassari 35, tel. 091-589-918, www.gaginirestaurant.com).

Across the street and run by the same people is the charming **$$$ Bocum Mixology** cocktail bar, with creative drinks, wine, light bites, and wine-crate stools—a great place for a pre- or post-dinner drink, or while waiting for a table to open up (Wed-Mon 18:00-24:00, closed Tue, Via dei Cassari 6, tel. 091-332-009).

$$$ Casa del Brodo, a Palermo institution, is an old-school place for a reliably good meal. While it's just steps from the noisy Vuccria Market scene, it feels sedate and sophisticated, with photos of celebrity diners hanging on the walls. Their antipasto bar lets you pack a small plate with veggies for a set price, but you're there for the *brodo,* a clear broth with tortellini that's warmed bellies for generations (Wed-Mon 12:30-15:00 & 19:30-23:00, closed Tue, Via Vittorio Emanuele 175, tel. 091-321-655).

$$ Cagliostro is dressy yet casual. Brightly lit under high ceilings, it's run by three brothers and their dad. Pack into their tight dining room for an accessible menu of both Sicilian and crowd-pleasing mainland Italian and international dishes (plenty of fish), or simply burgers and pizza. As it can be crowded with groups, reservations are wise (Thu-Tue 12:15-15:00 & 19:00-23:00, closed Wed, Via Vittorio Emanuele 150, tel. 091-332-818, www.ledeliziedicagliostro.it).

$ Franco ù Vastiddaru bustles day and night, slinging out typical Palermo street food dishes such as *panelle e cazzilli* and *pani* *ca' meusa*. Choose the deep-fried snack of your dreams for takeaway from the window, or pull up a plastic lawn chair in the piazza out front (daily 9:00-24:00, Via Vittorio Emanuele 102, tel. 091-325-987).

ON AND NEAR VIA ROMA

Via Roma—Palermo's busy north-south thoroughfare—is less atmospheric and has simpler and more functional eateries.

$ Café Touring is a venerable café handy for a hot drink, snack, or light meal. It's well known for good *arancine* and cannoli (daily 6:30-23:00, at corner of Via Roma and Via Venezia, Via Roma 252, tel. 091-616-7242).

$ Bar Lucchese, on Piazza San Domenico, is a classic old café with a fine selection of gelato and *granita* (daily 8:00-24:00, Piazza San Domenico 11).

$ Ferro di Cavallo ("The Horseshoe") is an old-time eatery, serving simple dishes at basic prices since 1944 (Mon-Sat 12:00-14:45 & 19:00-22:45, closed Sun, Via Venezia 20, tel. 091-331-835).

$ Casa Stagnitta is a longstanding, respected coffee roaster with a fancy coffee bar attached. You can try different varieties of coffee from the menu, then pop in the shop to watch the roasting in action. Better than the coffee, though, is their pistachio *granita* and the lovely outdoor seating. This is particularly handy for a break near the Fountain of Shame and Piazza Bellini churches (Mon-Sat 8:00-19:00, closed Sun, Discesa dei Giudici 46, tel. 091-617-2819).

$ Passami ù Coppu sells little cones of fried bits from their lengthy menu at the busy intersection of Via Roma and Via Vittorio Emanuele. Pay at the register and pick up your paper cones from the "Sweet" or "Savory" window (Mon-Fri 8:00-23:00, Sat-Sun 9:30-24:00, Via Roma 195, tel. 091-584-498).

Groceries: A huge and handy **Lidl** supermarket sits on Via Roma, between the train station and city center (daily 8:00-22:00, Via Roma 59).

LA KALSA

This area is closer to the port.

$$$ Quattro Mani focuses on quality, with thoughtful twists on classic dishes. The interior—spacious, sparsely decorated, under high vaults—is a little plain. But chef Chiara's flavorful, seasonal menu is the draw. Try the fried artichokes if they are *in stagione*. It's smart to reserve ahead (Tue-Sun 19:00-23:30, also open for lunch Fri-Sun 12:30-14:30, closed Mon; Via Francesco Riso 3—for location see the "Palermo Hotels" map, earlier; tel. 091-616-5046, www.ristorantequattromani.com).

PALERMO

$ Antica Focacceria San Francesco has a vintage photo-op storefront with a long history (since 1834). It's such a venerable Palermo institution that it has spun off a chain of imitators—causing the original to lose a bit of its cachet. Still, it's a great spot to grab some local food on a characteristic square. The main part of the shop has counter service for street food—including *pani ca'*  *meusa* (spleen sandwiches), fried goodies (*arancine, panelle,* and *cazzilli*), *sfincione* (Sicilian pizza), and more. They also have table service (at higher prices) out front, on one of the city's most atmospheric squares (daily 11:00-23:00, Via Alessandro Paternostro 58, tel. 091-320-264).

$$ A'nìca is a trendy, modern pizzeria buried in a characteristic corner of the Kalsa. The interior is clean, white, and modern, but I prefer the seating out on the terrace. While the creative pizzas are a favorite, they also have pricier pastas and *secondi,* plus €10 lunch salads (daily 12:00-15:00 & 19:00-23:00, Via Alloro 135, tel. 091-982-6011).

Groceries: Carrefour is a large supermarket hidden in the Kalsa, just in front of Palazzo Mirto (daily 8:00-21:00, Salita Partanna 1, tel. 091-611-0322).

BALLARÒ

$ Moltivolti is a restaurant and community center in the Ballarò neighborhood with a mission to bring the diverse ethnic groups of the area together. Their menu features Sicilian and African dishes, served in a colorful communal atmosphere (daily 9:00-23:00; Via Giuseppe Mario Puglia 21—for location see the "Palermo Hotels" map, earlier; tel. 091-271-0285, www.moltivolti.org).

NEAR TEATRO MASSIMO

$$$ Osteria Mercede specializes in fish and seafood, served in an unpretentious nautical dining room (no outdoor seating). Chef Helios Gnoffo gained notoriety when he won a contest on a popular Italian cooking show (Tue-Sun 12:30-15:00 & 19:00-23:00, closed Mon, Via Pignatelli Aragona 52, tel. 091-332-243).

$$ L'Anciova has a cozy, inviting interior, and the well-priced menu has a nice selection of pastas and pizzas made in a wood-fired oven (Tue-Sun 19:45-23:00, closed Mon, Via Volturno 41, mobile 366-150-0881).

$ La Taverna di John is an unpretentious, rollicking pizzeria packed with families enjoying friendly service, good-value pizzas and salads, and each other's company (daily 19:30-23:30, Via Sperlinga 57, tel. 091-334-678).

$ Antico Caffè Spinnato, set on a wide, pleasant shopping street a few minutes' walk past the Teatro Massimo, is a classic spot for a coffee, cocktail, or light lunch (they also have fine *arancine*). Belly up to the bar for a quick snack or linger at their outdoor tables (daily 7:00-24:00, Via Principe di Belmonte 107—for location see "Palermo Hotels" map earlier, tel. 091-749-5104).

NEAR VIA MAQUEDA

Via Maqueda, stretching north from Quattro Canti to Teatro Massimo, is lined mostly with low-end chain junk food—handy for a quick bite, but hardly ideal for a good meal. However, a few more enticing places lie just west of Via Maqueda, in a characteristic (and somewhat run-down) maze of streets.

$ Trattoria Al Vecchio Club Rosanero, a seriously local restaurant, is dedicated to the only thing the people here love more than Santa Rosalia—their soccer club. Diners discuss and watch sports while slurping up the special of the day. The menu offers basic comfort food at prices that will make you do a double take (Mon-Sat 12:00-15:00, also open for dinner Thu-Sat 20:00-23:00, closed Sun, Vicolo Caldomai 18, mobile 349-409-6880).

$$ Bisso Bistrot, filling a former bookstore (still marked *Libreria Dante*) tucked just behind one of the Quattro Canti fountains, is a trendy spot for traditional Sicilian dishes in a homey, Old World interior (Mon-Sat 9:00-23:30, closed Sun, Via Maqueda 172a, mobile 328-131-4595).

$$$ PerciaSacchi, on a gritty street a few minutes' walk from the main drag, offers an enticing menu of updated, well-executed Sicilian dishes. The interior is nondescript, but the outdoor terrace seating is inviting (Tue-Sun 12:30-15:00 & 19:30-23:30, closed Mon, Via del Monte di Pietà 5, tel. 091-612-3960).

Palermo Connections

BY PLANE
Falcone-Borsellino Airport

Palermo's small and easy-to-manage Falcone-Borsellino (a.k.a. Punta Raisi) Airport is located on the coast, 20 miles northwest of Palermo and surrounded by dramatic landscape (airport code: PMO, tel. 800-541-880, www.gesap.it). Note that if you are arriving on an international connection (for example, you flew in from the US with a change in Rome), your bags may appear on a separate carousel. Look for the international baggage claim (www.gesap.it).

Connecting the Airport to the City Center: You can link the airport and Palermo by train, bus, taxi, or shared taxi.

Trains run on a new track between the airport and Palermo's main train station, Stazione Centrale (€5.90 one-way, confirm schedule locally, www.trenitalia.com). At the airport, after exiting the arrivals area, take the stairs or escalator down to reach the tracks. Buy your ticket from machines to the right before boarding the train (2/hour, runs 7:27-21:42, :27 departure takes 75 minutes, :42 departure makes fewer stops and takes one hour). Most sights and hotels are walkable from the train station—or take a taxi or bus the rest of the way (see "Arrival in Palermo" at the beginning of this chapter.) Trains *to* the airport from Stazione Centrale generally depart from track 10 (2/hour, runs 5:00-20:05, :05 departure takes 75 minutes, :35 departure takes one hour).

Shuttle buses (Prestia e Comandè) can drop you at either end of the main axis of the city: at Piazza Ruggiero Settimo (near Teatro Politeama, at the north end of the center) or Stazione Centrale (main train station, the last stop, at the south end of the center). Exiting the airport, buses are to the far right, beyond the end of the terminal. You'll load your luggage under the bus before boarding, but keep smaller bags and valuables with you (€6.30, buy ticket from driver or at desk in airport lobby, 2/hour, runs 5:00-24:30, takes about 50 minutes depending on traffic, tel. 091-586-351, www.prestiaecomande.it).

Taxis are twice as fast and eight times the cost. Take only official taxis, waiting at the taxi stand. The fare to central Palermo should be about €40-55, depending on the day, time, or mood of the driver. Negotiate, ask several drivers the price, be firm, and set a *prezzo fisso* (fixed price) rather than the metered price. Have the driver write down the price before you depart. To be sure there will be no other charges added later, ask, *"É tutto?"* (Is that everything?).

Shared minivan taxis are a compromise between a bus and a taxi, running the same route as the bus with minivans for up to eight people. They line up to the right of the exit, just before the bus parking. Drivers wait to gather a group (minimum of five) and drop at the same downtown points as the public bus: at Teatro Politeama and at the main train station. You driver may be willing to drop you halfway along Via Roma—ask when you board. Compared to the bus, these leave more frequently and are slightly faster (€7).

BY BUS

Long-distance buses arrive and depart from the north side of the train station, alongside track 1 (for details, see "Arrival in Palermo—By Bus" at the beginning of this chapter). Purchase bus tickets from the small ticket office near the bus stalls, or from the driver. Large luggage is stored beneath the bus; for efficient loading, they may ask for your destination.

There are three main bus operators in Palermo: **Sais** (www.saisautolinee.it), **Interbus/Segesta/Etna Trasporti** (www.interbus.it), and **Salemi** (www.autoservizisalemi.it). Since these websites are only in Italian, it's smart to ask your hotelier or the tourist information office for help confirming schedules. Fewer buses depart on Saturdays, and very few on Sundays.

From Palermo by Bus to: Catania (hourly, 3 hours, Sais), **Trapani** (hourly, 2 hours, Segesta), **Siracusa** (2/day direct, 3.5 hours, Etna Trasporti; more with a change in Catania), **Piazza Armerina** (near Villa Romana del Casale, 5/day, 2 hours, Sais), **Ragusa** (4/day, 4 hours, run by AST, www.aziendasicilianatrasporti.it). You'll need to change in Catania to reach **Taormina** (hourly, 4 hours, Sais to Catania, then Etna Trasporti to Taormina). The bus to **Agri-**

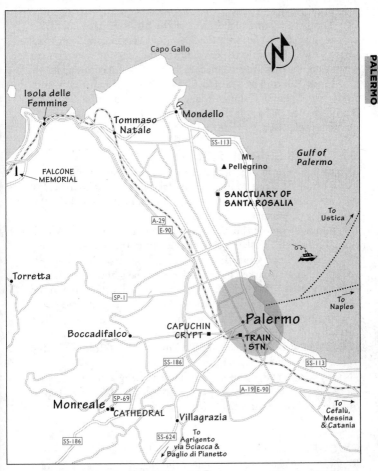

gento is run by Cuffaro (7/day, 2 hours, www.cuffaro.info) but the train may be better. Sais runs a few buses to **Cefalù,** but the train is far easier and more frequent (see below).

For mainland Italy, Sais and Salemi run daily overnight buses to several destinations, including **Rome** (12 hours) and **Milan** (18 hours).

BY TRAIN

Train connections leave from Stazione Centrale, at the southern end of the city center (for details on arriving by train and station services, see "Arrival in Palermo—By Train" at the beginning of this chapter). Sicily's train network is sparse; buses are often more efficient and frequent. Many cities, particularly in the west, have no train service at all. Note: There is no train service from Palermo to Trapani.

Trains to the mainland cross at the Strait of Messina. Train cars are loaded on a ferry for the 20-minute crossing, allowing passengers to walk around the ferry during the crossing. Once on the other side, the cars are reconnected to the rails and continue north.

From Palermo by Train to: Cefalù (hourly, 1 hour), **Agrigento** (hourly, 2 hours), **Catania** (6/day, 3 hours), **Taormina** (7/day, 4.5 hours, change in Messina), **Rome** (2/day, 11.5 hours; 2/night, 13 hours), **Naples** (2/day, 9 hours, 1/night, 10.5 hours).

BY CRUISE SHIP OR FERRY

Two companies run overnight ferries between Palermo and Naples, leaving from Stazione Marittima and taking about 10 hours: **GNV** (tel. 010-209-4591, www.gnv.it) and **Tirrenia** (toll tel. 199-303-040, www.tirrenia.it).

Ships dock near the city center at Palermo's Stazione Marittima, a reasonable walk or quick taxi ride from the sightseeing core. If you arrive here, from the busy harborfront road, head up Via Emerico Amari (marked by the pillar with the stone eagle on top). Carry on about 10 minutes along Via Amari; reaching the grand square in front of the Teatro Politeama, turn left and head down Via Ruggiero Settimo, which later becomes Via Maqueda. Follow this a few more blocks to the Teatro Massimo and the start of my self-guided walk. Allow about 20-30 minutes total from your ship to the heart of the city.

If taking a taxi, be aware that those meeting arriving ships are more likely to overcharge; it's better to walk farther into town to find a more honest cabbie. The trip to the city center should cost no more than €15.

BY CAR

Rental car agencies are located near the port and at the main train station. However, driving in Palermo is stressful, and parking is limited and expensive. For many, a better plan is to enjoy Palermo car-free, then return to the airport to pick up a car for further Sicilian adventures. That way, your first Sicilian driving experience will be on a highway with light traffic, rather than in the thick of an urban jungle.

ZTL Pass Tips: If you do need to drive into the historic core of Palermo, you'll have to purchase and register a ZTL pass (€5/day). Hotels and parking garages can usually help with this, but here are the basics: After parking your car, buy a ZTL pass either from the parking garage or at a tobacco shop. Scratch off the PIN and text it—along with your license plate number—to the number on the back of the pass (English instructions). If staying multiple days, you'll need to register a new ZTL pass each day. You can also

buy a pass or register your PIN online (https://ztl.comune.palermo.
it, but not user-friendly).

Route Tips for Drivers

Leaving Palermo, your goal is to make your way through the
snarled traffic to the ring road. For most destinations, you'll aim
for the E-90 highway that runs north-to-south along the western
edge of the city center.

Going north on E-90 takes you to the **airport** (in about 30
minutes once leaving downtown), near which the road becomes the
A-29 expressway to **Segesta** (1 hour from Palermo), then **Trapani**
(1.5 hours from Palermo).

Heading south/east on E-90 takes you toward **Catania** (2.5
hours from Palermo), along autostrada A-19—which serves as the
island's spine. To reach **Siracusa** (3.5 hours), head first to Catania,
then south to Siracusa.

To reach **Cefalù** (1 hour east of Palermo), begin by heading
south/east on E-90. Don't turn off when the road forks onto the
A-19 toward Catania; instead, stay on E-90, following the coast.
This is also a good plan if you're heading to **Messina** (3 hours from
Palermo) or even **Taormina** (3.5 hours from Palermo)—while it
may be slightly faster to zip to Catania on the autostrada, then head
north, it's more scenic to follow the coastal E-90 tollway past Cefalù, then turn south on E-45 at Messina.

Finally, to reach **Agrigento** (2 hours from Palermo), you won't
get on the E-90 highway—instead, you'll head south from downtown toward Sciacca (on the south coast), then head east from
there.

MONREALE CATHEDRAL

Duomo de Monreale

Situated on the slopes of a mountain six miles west of Palermo is one of Sicily's most important sights: the stunning Norman cathedral of Monreale. Built between 1174 and 1189, it's an amalgamation of Byzantine, Norman, and Arab elements in a Romanesque building—reflecting the intermingling cultures and religious tolerance of that period. While the exterior, with its elaborate stonework, and the cloister, with its decorated capitals, are both notable, the stars of the show are the intricate golden mosaics completely covering the church interior. Illustrating Bible stories, they form the largest cycle of Byzantine mosaics in Italy.

The cathedral's mountainous location once held an Arab manor house. The Norman kings used it as a private hunting reserve, and built a palazzo, Mons Regalis ("Royal Mountain")—the origin of "Monreale." William II, Sicily's last Norman king, chose this site for a magnificent cathedral, a Benedictine monastery, and a palace for his newly minted archbishop. Over time, a village grew around the cathedral; modern Monreale has a population of over 30,000. Although the original Norman palace and part of the monastery are long gone, the cathedral and cloister are well-preserved and make an easy side trip from Palermo.

GETTING THERE

By Public Bus: From Palermo, AMAT **bus #389** departs from Piazza Indipendenza, behind the Norman Palace (€1.40, €1.80 if purchased on board, hourly, 30 minutes, see schedule at www.amat.pa.it). The bus drops you in Monreale at a roundabout below the cathedral complex. From there, you'll hike about 10 minutes

Dueling Cathedrals: The Rivalry of Monreale and Palermo

The story of Monreale's construction begins with a legend.

While out hunting, young King William II stopped for a siesta under a tree. The Virgin Mary appeared to him in a dream, and revealed the location of a treasure hidden by his father. There was one condition: The fortune must be spent entirely on the construction of a basilica dedicated to the Virgin.

In reality, Monreale Cathedral was built for political reasons. A former tutor of William II, an Englishman known as Walter of the Mill, worked the system to become the archbishop of Palermo—according to some, "less by election than by violent intrusion." Walter had the support of much of the nobility, but his arrogance soured his relationship with the pope. King William, a supporter of the pope, sought to curb Walter's growing power—in a hurry. William needed his own archbishop. So he built this impressive church and abbey, and gave them to the Benedictine monks. The abbot was named to a new position—archbishop of Monreale—making Monreale a cathedral. Constructed in just 15 years, the grandiose church became Sicily's second archbishopric, despite being just six miles from the cathedral in downtown Palermo.

Monreale Cathedral was consecrated in 1189, and its diocese was endowed with large parcels of land throughout the province of Palermo. Monreale quickly overshadowed Walter's diocese as the most influential in the kingdom, effectively stopping Walter in his tracks. But later that year, William II died suddenly at age 36—without an heir. William left Sicily with a grand cathedral, but his lack of a successor also spelled the end of the island's Norman Golden Age.

uphill on Via d'Acquisito to reach the church. *Attenzione!* Pickpockets love this bus.

By Hop-On, Hop-Off Bus: The **City Sightseeing** tour bus from Palermo combines narrated sightseeing with transport (see page 40 for details).

By Taxi: A one-way ride from downtown Palermo to the cathedral door takes about 30 minutes (roughly €30, negotiate and confirm price in advance—traffic jams are common and can be costly).

By Car: It's a 30-minute drive to Monreale from Palermo. Head west from central Palermo on Corso Calatafimi (SS-186).

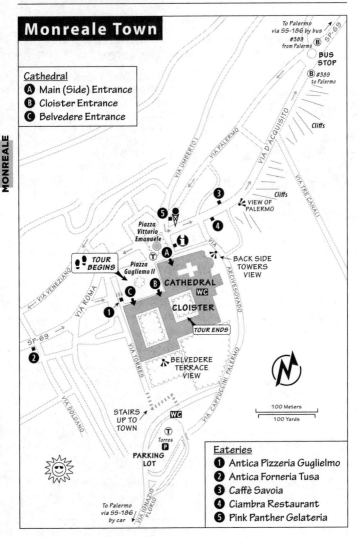

Monreale Town

Cathedral
- **A** Main (Side) Entrance
- **B** Cloister Entrance
- **C** Belvedere Entrance

To Palermo
via SS-186 by bus
#389
from Palermo

BUS STOP

B #389 to Palermo

Cliffs

VIA D'ACQUISITO

VIA TRE CANALI

VIA UMBERTO I

VIA PALERMO

Cliffs

3

VIEW OF PALERMO

5

Piazza
Vittorio
Emanuele

4

VIA

i

A

T

TOUR BEGINS

Piazza
Gugliemo II

BACK SIDE TOWERS VIEW

VIA VENEZIANO

VIA ROMA

B

C

CATHEDRAL

WG

CLOISTER

VIA ARCIVESCOVADO

1

VIA TORRES

TOUR ENDS

SP-69

2

BELVEDERE TERRACE VIEW

N

VIA CAPPUCCINI PALERMO

VIA SOLDANO

100 Meters

100 Yards

STAIRS UP TO TOWN

WG

T
Torres
P

PARKING LOT

Eateries
- **1** Antica Pizzeria Guglielmo
- **2** Antica Forneria Tusa
- **3** Caffè Savoia
- **4** Ciambra Restaurant
- **5** Pink Panther Gelateria

To Palermo
via SS-186
by car

VIA IGNAZIO FLORIO

About a mile after crossing over the E-90 ring road, bear left at the intersection with SP-69, continuing on SS-186 (ignore the sign that indicates you should go right for Monreale). After about 1.5 miles, turn right onto Via Ferrata. Follow it slightly left and uphill, then hook right onto Via Ignazio Florio. At the end of Via Ignazio Florio, pull into the big pay parking lot. From this lot, steps lead up to the town, and taxis offer a €2 shuttle service to Monreale's main square, Piazza Vittorio Emanuele.

Eateries in Monreale

The following spots make for a nice lunch or snack break. For locations, see the "Monreale Town" map.

$$ Antica Pizzeria Guglielmo: Enjoy fine pizza and outdoor seating on the square facing the church (daily 7:00-24:00, Piazza Guglielmo II 2, tel. 091-640-3442).

$ Antica Forneria Tusa: Pizza and other Sicilian baked goods provide a quick carryout bite (daily 8:00-20:00, with your back to the cathedral facade, go up the stairs and straight ahead on Via Roma for about five minutes—it's on the left at Via Pietro Novelli 25).

$ Caffè Savoia: This café serves fresh sandwiches with wines by the glass, just downhill from the cathedral (daily 6:30-22:00, Via d'Acquisto 23, tel. 091-640-3827).

$$$ Ciambra: Heading downhill toward grand views over Palermo, their classy dining room is nice for an upscale meal (Wed-Mon 11:00-23:30, closed Tue, Via d'Acquisto 18, tel. 091-640-6717).

Pink Panther Gelateria: Among the enticing *gelaterie* clustered near the cathedral, this is my favorite (Piazza Vittorio Emanuele 1, where Via Palermo meets the square).

MONREALE

PLANNING YOUR TIME

Though Monreale is just 30 minutes from downtown Palermo, morning traffic can be bad; visiting around lunchtime is often a better bet (I'd aim to arrive at 11:30 or so). If you arrive close to the midday closure time (see hours below), visit the cloister first, grab some lunch, and see the cathedral when it reopens. Avoid Sundays, when the cathedral is closed most of the morning and the cloister is closed in the afternoon. There's nothing of importance to see in the town other than the amazing cathedral.

ORIENTATION TO MONREALE

Cost: The **cathedral** is free to enter; other parts of the complex charge admission; I'd pay for the **cloisters** (€6) and skip the rest.

Overachievers can climb up on to the **roof terraces** (closed in bad weather), tour a ho-hum **Diocesan Museum** in the south transept, or check out some royal tombs and an ornate chapel in the **north transept**. It's €2.50 to enter one of these sights, €4 for two, and €6 for all three.

Hours: The cathedral is open Mon-Sat 8:30-12:45 & 14:00-16:45, Sun 8:00-9:15 & 14:30-16:45; in winter (Nov-March) all closing times are 15 minutes earlier. The cloister is open Mon-Sat 9:00-19:00, Sun until 13:30. Add-on sights (roof terraces,

Diocesan Museum, north transept) have similar hours to the cathedral.

Information: Mobile 327-351-0886, www.monrealeduomo.it.

Dress Code: Knees and shoulders must be covered; a disposable cover-up can be purchased at the door.

Visitor Information: A helpful TI is on Monreale's main square (daily 8:00-16:00, Piazza Vittorio Emanuele 2). The gift shop to the left of the cathedral entry sells a detailed map of the mosaics. A printable key to the mosaics and capitals is available at www.seepalermo.com.

Tours: Pick up the fine and thorough **audioguide** to the right of the cathedral entry (€5, 45 minutes, must leave ID, return audioguide 30 minutes before closing).

Length of This Tour: Allow 1.5 hours.

Services: At the cathedral, a good pay WC is within the Diocesan Museum. In town you'll find WCs in cafés near the church, on Piazza Guglielmo II, and Piazza Vittorio Emanuele; there's also a pay WC at the stairway near the parking lot.

Tip: Bring small binoculars to help make out mosaic details.

Starring: A cathedral with 68,000 square feet of glittering golden mosaics and a peaceful cloister with carved column capitals.

◯ SELF-GUIDED TOUR

Begin on Piazza Guglielmo II, in front of the main church doors, facing the two towers. Monreale Cathedral was built on this hilltop by the young king of Sicily, William II. For such an elaborate building, construction was completed very quickly: King William II was in a hurry to finish and show up the cathedral down in Palermo (see the "Dueling Cathedrals" sidebar, earlier).

EXTERIOR
❶ Main Facade

If you didn't already know this was a church, you might mistake it for a fortress. This Norman style of church is called *ecclesia munita* ("church-fortress")—it's both a place of worship and a last line of defense. Two mighty square **towers** frame the facade. The one on the left was never completed, and sports slit windows at the bottom and crenellations at the top.

Between the towers, a Neoclassical **portico** was added in 1770 to protect the main bronze doors—and to help the church look a little less like a fort. The **doors,** completed in 1186, were

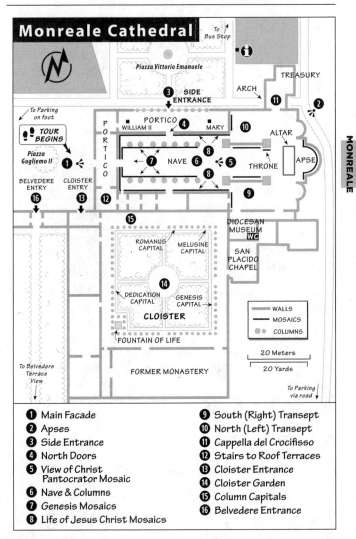

Monreale Cathedral

To Bus Stop

Piazza Vittorio Emanuele

3 SIDE ENTRANCE

TREASURY

ARCH

11

2

To Parking on foot

TOUR BEGINS

Piazza Guglielmo II **1**

PORTICO

PORTICO WILLIAM II **4** MARY

10

ALTAR

8

NAVE **6** **5**

7

THRONE

APSE

8

9

BELVEDERE ENTRY **16**

CLOISTER ENTRY **13**

12

15

DIOCESAN MUSEUM WC

SAN PLACIDO CHAPEL

ROMANUS CAPITAL   MELUSINE CAPITAL

14

DEDICATION CAPITAL   GENESIS CAPITAL

CLOISTER

FOUNTAIN OF LIFE

WALLS
MOSAICS
COLUMNS

20 Meters
20 Yards

To Belvedere Terrace View

FORMER MONASTERY

To Parking via road

MONREALE

- **1** Main Facade
- **2** Apses
- **3** Side Entrance
- **4** North Doors
- **5** View of Christ Pantocrator Mosaic
- **6** Nave & Columns
- **7** Genesis Mosaics
- **8** Life of Jesus Christ Mosaics
- **9** South (Right) Transept
- **10** North (Left) Transept
- **11** Cappella del Crocifisso
- **12** Stairs to Roof Terraces
- **13** Cloister Entrance
- **14** Cloister Garden
- **15** Column Capitals
- **16** Belvedere Entrance

made by Bonanno Pisano, architect of the Leaning Tower of Pisa. Luckily, Pisano was a better sculptor than architect. His doors were cutting-edge for the period (and Italian-made at a time when most similar doors were still being imported from Byzantium). They feature 46 panels with lions and griffons at the bottom, Old Testament scenes on the lower bands, New Testament scenes on the upper bands, and the Virgin Mary and Christ at the top. Remember these scenes, the bronze relief technique, and the storytelling of these panels; we'll compare them to another set of doors in a few minutes. The doors have inscriptions in Vulgar Latin—a progenitor of Romance languages, including Sicilian.

• *Walk along the left side of the cathedral, pass underneath the arch, turn right, and look up at the cathedral's back side. The three cylindrical projections you see are the...*

❷ Apses

Notice the fine series of interlacing Gothic arches of different heights on these towers. Set into the limestone is intricate black lava-stone inlay work, a fusion of Arab and Norman styles. We'll see more of this lava inlay in the cloister. Although this building is not exactly Gothic, but rather a combination of architectural styles, compare this to other well-known cathedrals being built in the 1100s. Construction of Paris' Notre-Dame  began only a few years before, and the Duomo of Pisa, which has a similar design, was being finished around the same time. Each of those buildings took over 100 years to complete. Thanks to Norman wealth and a political desire to finish quickly, Monreale took only 15 years—resulting in an unusually cohesive architectural style for a structure of its size.

• *Retrace your steps back to the portico along Piazza Vittorio Emanuele. Enter the portico through the iron fence. You're looking at the...*

❸ Side Entrance

Look left and right. You're in the middle of a *Sacra Conversazione* ("holy conversation") between two modern bronze statues. These were made in 1997 by Arnaldo Pomodoro, the sculptor who donated the *Sphere in the Sphere* to the Vatican Museums in Rome. The "holy conversation" was a typical way to imagine interactions with God and the saints in medieval and Renaissance art. In this case, William II (on your right) is humbly offering the church of Monreale to Mary (on your left)...and you are invited to witness the donation.

❹ North Doors

The side entrance bronze doors in front of you—while only a decade older than the front entrance doors we saw moments ago—

clearly date from a less artistically advanced age. These doors were made in
the traditional Byzantine style, with
28 panels representing the lives of
saints and the evangelists. Each panel
shows a single, static figure, typical of
Byzantine art. Compare these doors
with the pair we saw earlier: The art
of the east, represented here, remains
rooted in ancient tradition (Orthodox
means no change—intentionally not
evolving with the times), while the art
of the west, on the other doors, begins
its slow march toward the realism and
humanism of the Renaissance.

MONREALE

• *Enter the church and walk straight ahead to the center of the nave, then
turn left to face the altar. Spin around to take it all in.*

INTERIOR

This imposing basilica, at 335 feet long by 130 feet wide, is slathered with over 68,000 square feet of golden **mosaics**—a third more
than at St. Mark's Basilica in Venice. While this is a fine example
of the interplay between architecture and visual art, it's also the
perfect illustration of something uniquely Sicilian: the fusion between classical, Byzantine, Arab, and Norman craftsmanship. Although each glass tile contains a layer of gold thinner than a sheet
of paper, it's estimated that the walls of this cathedral hold about
two tons of gold.

The Byzantines perfected the gold background effect by sand-
wiching pieces of gold leaf between glass. The surfaces of the tiles
were purposely cut unevenly to capture light and give off a shim-
mering effect, helping to light thick-walled, small-windowed,
lantern-lit Byzantine churches, and creating a golden glow that
symbolized the divine light of heaven (for more on mosaics, see the
sidebar on page 228).

The **roof** above you, with gilded and painted trusses, is not the
original, but an exact copy. The cathedral was hit by lightning in
1811, and the original roof burned.

The **floor** is original and was added to over time. The oldest
portions are found in the sanctuary, while the remainder took 300
years to complete. Floors like this—made using marble scavenged
from ancient buildings—were common in this time period. Marble
often cracked as it was being removed, leaving small pieces like
these for patchwork floors. Notice the large red porphyry and colored marble disks. These are ancient columns that have been recycled—sliced like salami.

• *Face the altar. Focus on the top mosaic above the altar in the central apse.*

❺ View of Christ Pantocrator Mosaic

Christ Pantocrator ("All Ruling") is shown in the typical style of the Eastern Orthodox Church, with his right hand raised in the classical gesture of Byzantine blessing. Each finger represents a letter: The straight finger is the letter I, the crossed fingers make an X, and the two curved fingers are for two Cs—that's IC XC, the first and last Greek letters for the name Jesus Christ. The mosaic's dimensions are impressive—the right hand alone is

over six feet long. Christ is a benevolent, welcoming, yet gigantic figure, with flowing hair and beard. With outstretched arms, he seems to embrace you and everyone else in the cathedral at once. In his left hand he nimbly holds the Gospel, open to John 8:12, which

reads (in both medieval Latin and Greek), "I am the light of the world. Whoever follows me shall not walk in darkness."

Seated beneath Christ is the **Virgin Enthroned with Child,** flanked by Greek letters spelling out *panakrontas* ("all-immaculate"). Mary is dressed like a Byzantine empress, draped in heavy, colorful clothes, and surrounded by heavenly gold skies. To either side are the archangels Gabriel and Michael and the apostles.

Below Mary, a row of saints flanks the window. The second saint on the right, in green vestments, is the earliest representation anywhere of **St. Thomas Becket.** Martyred on December 29, 1170 in Canterbury, England, Becket was sainted just one year before the construction of this cathedral began. Becket was a friend of William II's mother, Margaret of Navarre, and supported her while she ran the kingdom during William's childhood. (Ironically, seven years after Becket's murder, William II married

Joan of England, daughter of Henry II—the man who ordered Becket's assassination.)
• *Turn around to look at the columns.*

❻ Nave and Columns

Notice the ancient Roman columns dividing the central nave from the two side aisles. These monolithic columns and their fine Corinthian capitals are unusually well-preserved and certainly recycled—probably taken from an ancient Roman temple. (Look for faces surrounded by cornucopias in the centers of some of the capitals—portraits of Rome's pagan goddesses.) The columns were shipped here from Rome—a gift from Pope Lucius III, who was happy to support and affirm Norman (Western and Christian) control of Sicily. This was a challenging time for the pope: The Great Schism had split Christendom between the Orthodox east and the Catholic west, and the Church faced ongoing threats from Islam (including the Arabs who controlled Sicily before the Normans arrived). And then—just when you thought things couldn't get worse—some smug archbishop in Palermo has the nerve to challenge papal authority by building a cathedral! Pope Lucius was more than willing to help King William II build his rival cathedral.
• *Look high above the arches, to the mosaics between the windows.*

❼ Genesis Mosaics

The story of Genesis runs like a filmstrip around the top of the nave. Start in the upper-right corner, closest to the altar, and work your way clockwise from there, reading each scene in order—just as illiterate medieval peasants would have done. (It can be easier to see the details of each scene from the opposite side of the nave.)

• *To the left of the first window is...*

    Creation of Skies and Earth: Notice the stylized face with flowing hair and beard that fuse into the flowing waters.
• *The next mosaic is between the first two windows; the series continues along the south wall toward the portico from there.*

    Let There Be Light: God, seated comfortably on a giant bouncy ball, creates a fireball of light, from which the angels emerge.

    Separation of Waters: In the circle over his head, God separates the waters. One will be the sea, and the other will be the sky.

    Creation of the Earth: God commands the earth to rise from the sea. Some unusual trees grow.

Creation of the Planets: God grabs a planet, finds a clear shot, and goes in for the dunk.

Creation of Birds and Sea Creatures: The sea at God's feet teems with fish, and the mountain displays a variety of birds, including a flying white dove (symbol of the Holy Spirit), a peacock, a common crane, and a spotted owl.

Creation of Land Animals and Man: Using a very long straw, God breathes life into Adam, who gestures back at his father and seems to say, "Thanks, Dad, now can I have 20 bucks and the keys to the car?"

And on the Seventh Day: God rested. He clearly needs it—he looks like a dazed tourist at the end of a hot day of looking at mosaics.

Garden of Eden: God shows Adam the Tree of Wisdom.

• *Continue to the short wall over the main entry (portico).*

Creation of Woman: While Adam lazily plays with the grass, God lifts Eve out of his rib.

Introduction of Adam and Eve: God escorts Eve by the hand to meet her new beau. Adam points at God, asking if he's sure this is a good idea.

• *Turn to face the long wall on the right to continue the story.*

Eve Tempted by the Serpent: Eve chats with the serpent, who insists that everyone else is doing it.

Original Sin: Eve takes a bite of the apple of knowledge and hands one to Adam. The malicious reptile, after inviting in innocent Eve, seems to stick his tongue out at her.

God Confronts Adam and Eve: God gestures toward the pair, who have now covered their nakedness with large fig leaves, and asks who's to blame. Adam points to Eve, Eve points to the snake, and the snake looks back at God, closing the circle of blame—proving that some things are eternal.

Adam and Eve Cast Out of Paradise: A fiery seraphim and the archangel Michael force the pair out of paradise and into some fluffy fur coats.

Adam and Eve Suffer: Adam works the land while Eve laments her fate. Cradling a spindle with her right hand—procrastinating in her new work-to-live lifestyle—she realizes that maybe ignorance was bliss.

Cain and Abel: The narrative shifts as the next three panels tell the story of Cain killing Abel, then Cain being killed by their other brother, Lamech. Notice how profusely Abel's blood gushes out of his mortally wounded forehead.

• *Turn back to where you started. In the lower band beneath the Creation, find more scenes from the Old Testament...*

Noah's Ark: Notice Noah's tools for this building project. You'll roughly see how ships were built at the time of this church's construction. The type of saw shown was used in Sicily until the 20th century.

Loading the Animals: While the people wait patiently inside, Noah loads the uncooperative animals.

The Flood: Noah reaches out to the white dove carrying back an olive branch, a clear sign that waters have receded. Meanwhile, a crow feasts on a floating corpse.

Unloading the Animals: Now that the waters have receded, Noah carefully unloads the still skeptical animals while the people again wait patiently.

If you're familiar with the Old Testament, quiz yourself and try to pick out a few more scenes. The most notable are the construction of the Tower of Babel, the destruction of Sodom (look for Lot's wife shown as a pillar of salt), the sacrifice of Abraham, and Jacob's Ladder.

• *Now, beneath the arches in the side aisles, find the...*

❽ Life of Jesus Christ Mosaics

On the right side aisle are depictions of Christ healing the sick and performing other miracles. Under the Noah's Ark panel, find the Healing of the Possessed Woman. Next is the Healing of the Leper (the fellow covered with open wounds). At the end of this wall is the Multiplication of the Loaves and Fishes. Christ's story continues along the opposite wall (look for Mary Magdalene Washing Jesus' Feet at the end just before the transept).

• *Now, facing the altar, walk to the right side of the nave, and up a few steps into the...*

❾ South (Right) Transept

The large stone coffins are **royal tombs.** The red porphyry tomb is that of William I. Long and cylindrical, it was carved out of an ancient Roman column. The white marble tomb is for William

II, who built this church. These tombs were originally covered with red porphyry canopies *(baldacchini)*, like the royal tombs in Palermo's cathedral.

• *Walk beyond the tombs and climb a few steps, then turn left and look across the altar.*

The **throne** at the side of the altar is where the king sat for Mass. Notice that it's higher than the archbishop's throne on the opposite side. Above the king's throne, a mosaic shows the king,

dressed in the precious gem-covered robes of a Byzantine emperor, being crowned directly by God. After his power struggle with the archbishop of Palermo, William II needed to reinforce who was boss. This cathedral and this throne sent a clear message.

• *You've seen the most interesting parts of the cathedral interior. To see a bit more, you can pay to enter the Diocesan Museum (enter through the south transept, good WC near entry). Or, circle around to the other side of the altar and pay to enter the (skippable)...*

❿ North (Left) Transept

Along the outer (left) wall of the north transept are the **tombs** of Margaret of Navarre, mother of William II, and of his two brothers. There's also a sarcophagus containing the heart and internal organs of King Louis IX of France. Also known as St. Louis, he died—probably of dysentery—in 1270 while on crusade in Tunisia. While his body eventually made it back to France, his internal organs stayed in Sicily, which was part of his brother's kingdom at the time.

Also found here is the ⓫ **Cappella del Crocifisso,** a frothy Baroque chapel from the 1700s that contrasts sharply with the rest of the church's interior.

• *Before leaving the church, consider climbing the ⓬ narrow stairs to the roof terraces to enjoy a view of the cloister and the surrounding coun-*

tryside. With your back to the altar, the stairway entrance is in the far left corner.

When you're ready to continue on to the cloister, exit the cathedral and turn left, then left again, to return to Piazza Guglielmo II, where we started. The ⓭ *cloister entry is the doorway straight ahead.*

CLOISTER

This cloister was the main outdoor space for the Benedictine monks, who would have rarely ventured out of the monastery. Imagine the

monks pacing the square path, deep in prayer. In the past, the center of the cloister would have been a lush garden, probably used to grow produce for the brothers.

• *Enter the cloister, buy a ticket, and walk straight ahead. You're on the north side of the cloister. Halfway down, find an opening between the columns. Step into the garden and walk toward the center to get oriented.*

⓮ Cloister Garden

The garden is divided into quadrants, each with a different tree planted in its center: date palm, fig, olive, and pomegranate. These

are the four species described both in the Bible and in the Quran. The arcade is a perfect square of 154 feet, with 26 arches per side. The 228 twin columns are made of Carrara marble from Tuscany. The Moorish influence can be seen in the shafts of the columns, which are decorated either with carved arabesque motifs or with golden mosaics inlaid in geometrical patterns.

• *Return to the north side and look at the...*

⓯ Column Capitals

The artistic highlight of the cloister are the capitals atop each column. Each one is an individual artwork, made by several teams of craftsmen. The capitals vary in complexity and style, some with abstract designs and others with intricate scenes from mythology or the Bible.

On the walls opposite the colonnade, patterns are inlaid with black stone. The monks who came to establish this monastery were transferred from near Mount Vesuvius (near Naples on the mainland). As they left their homeland, they knew they would probably not return, so they brought chunks of lava with them—to have a bit of home built into the new monastery.

• *Turn your attention to the columns. We'll circle the cloister clockwise (starting at the north side, where you entered). While it's fun to simply pick out your own favorite details as we go, I'll point out a few capitals worthy of your attention. The best way to track them down is to count columns (starting with the one next to the gap you used to enter the garden).*

North Side: The fifth column after the gap has a capital with a Roman phrase carved into its base: *EGO ROMANVS FILIVS CONSTANTINVS MARMVRARIVS* ("This is Romanus, son of Constantinus the marble carver"). In the 12th century, artists were normally humble craftsmen, and it was uncommon for them to sign their work. As this was an important piece, the best available artists were commissioned and given freedom to carve with artistic license.

Skip one column and stop in front of the seventh, where you'll find the story of Samson *(SANSON)* carved on all four sides.

Skip two more columns, stopping in front of the 10th, to find the cruel, vivid scene of the **Massacre of the Innocents.**

Skip one column and stop in front of the 12th, where you may recognize an international logo: Melusine, also known as the **Starbucks Mermaid.** Melusine was a mermaid who fell in love with a human and married him. She could not reveal her true nature, but needed to bathe and change into a fish once a week. She told her husband not to follow her, but one day, curiosity got the best of him and he discovered her secret. A furious Melusine told him that because he hadn't trusted her, she had to leave him. This may seem a strange topic in a monastery, but the message was clear to the brothers: You need faith and trust to be close to God. On the four corners of the same capital are symbols of the four evangelists: eagle (John), angel (Matthew), winged lion (Mark), and oxen (Luke).

East Side: Soon you'll reach the first corner of the cloister. The corner columns, in groups of four, are decorated with floral motifs. On this corner capital are stories from the **Life of the Virgin Mary.** Find these scenes: the journey of the Three Kings, the presentation of the gifts, the Annunciation, and the Nativity.

Now continue down the east side of the cloister. After the gap halfway down, find the sixth column, with scenes from Genesis, including **Adam, Eve, Cain,** and **Abel.**

South Side: Head to the corner of the cloister, and turn to walk along the south side. Three columns before the gap on the south side, find a column carved with scenes of **winemaking.** Now carry on to the fountain in the corner. Just before it, the last column shows armored **Norman knights** with long shields, sword-fighting against Arabs brandishing sabers.

In the corner is the **Fountain of Life**—strategically located for monks to wash up before entering the dining hall next door.

In the center, the fountain is a stylized palm tree trunk. The pressurized water streams at the top imitate the shape of palm fronds, a watery tree. The stylized palm tree motif is repeated all over the cathedral walls, as a symbol of life, rebirth, martyrdom, and purification. In the Middle Ages, religion was considered a lush oasis of spirituality in the arid desert of mortal sins.

Pause at the corner, where the capitals show scenes from the **life of infant Christ** and the **mission of the apostles.**

West Side: After the fountain enclosure, head to the fifth column—the one that's been highly polished, so it's white and gleaming. This is the **dedication capital:** King William II holds a model of the church, offering it to Mary.

Before exiting, take a moment to savor the spirit of the cloister. The word "cloister" comes from the word "enclosed"—a protected paradise for reaching a higher state of spirituality. Pace the cloister as the monks would do. Meditate. Find the tranquility.

• *Return to Piazza Guglielmo II, where you entered the cloister, and take a last look at the cathedral.*

Consider all of the things you've just seen: Norman towers, a

Latin basilica floor plan, Arab arches and abstract geometric patterns, Byzantine mosaics, and columns and capitals both sacred and profane. You are admiring the apex of Norman "syncretism"—the Sicilian Normans' unique knack for creating a balanced fusion of styles, cultures, and traditions. Understanding this ability to gracefully merge conflicting ideas and cultural symbols is key to appreciating not just Monreale, but Sicily in general. Go in peace.

• *From the southwest corner of Piazza Guglielmo II, an archway leads through a series of courtyards to the ❶❻ belvedere for a view over the landscape below.*

When you're ready to head back to Palermo, taxis wait in Piazza Vittorio Emanuele, and buses departs from the bottom of Via d'Acquisito, at the roundabout.

CEFALÙ

An hour east of Palermo sits the salty fishing village of Cefalù (cheh-fah-LOO). Tucked under the towering rock· called La Rocca, Cefalù entices with narrow lanes, medieval charm, and an imposing Norman cathedral. These days, Cefalù is a popular beach destination, but it still has the feel of an old Sicilian fishing hub. While fishing may not be the main industry anymore, Cefalù's creaky character, stretches of wide sandy beach, and parade of shops and restaurants make this a popular, laid-back tourist resort. If you're going to settle in for a beach break anywhere in Sicily, I'd do it here for a night—or two.

PLANNING YOUR TIME

With few major sights, Cefalù makes an easy day trip from Palermo (about an hour by train or car). Or, for an easygoing start to a Sicilian trip, consider heading here directly from the Palermo airport (about 1.5 hours by car).

With one day in Cefalù, start early with a hike to the summit of La Rocca for expansive views. Then descend into town, where you can follow my self-guided walk, visiting Cefalù Cathedral along the way, and tour the local museum (Museo Mandralisca). Or simply enjoy a bit of beach time. If you're spending the night, finish your day with a *passeggiata* and a candlelit seafood dinner on the harbor.

Orientation to Cefalù

Cefalù (pop. 14,000) is wedged between its Gibraltar-like mountain and a long stretch of sandy beach. At the north end of town, the historic center is a grid of narrow, pedestrian-only streets. The town's spine is Corso Ruggero, which runs past Cefalù's main landmark—its Norman-style cathedral—and the central Piazza del Duomo. The old town stretches south to Piazza Garibaldi, where the modern city begins. The train station marks the southern city limits.

Tourist Information: The TI has little to offer (very sporadic hours—likely Mon-Fri 9:00-13:00, closed Sat-Sun, Corso Ruggero 79, tel. 0921-421-050).

Arrival in Cefalù: Trains from Palermo and Messina arrive at the Cefalù train station, about a 15-minute walk south of the old town center and beach (about €10 by taxi). To walk into town, exit the station, turn right onto Via Antonio Gramsci, jog left onto Via Aldo Moro, cross Via Roma, then bear right onto Via Matteotti to continue to Piazza Garibaldi. From here, the beach is downhill to the left, and the old town is straight ahead, down the pedestrianized Corso Ruggero.

Drivers arrive in Cefalù in the new town on SS-113, near the train station. The no-traffic zone begins at Piazza Garibaldi, but you have several parking options. For cheap long-term parking, there's a garage next to the train station (€5/day). Pay parking is also available along the waterfront promenade, Lungomare Giardina, either on the street (€0.80/hour within blue lines) or at the huge gravel parking lot just south of the waterfront Hotel Riva del Sole (€6/12 hours)—near the start of my self-guided city walk.

Helpful Hints: Taxis line up at the train station and along the beach near Piazza Cristoforo Colombo (taxi tel. 0921-422-554). On Saturday mornings off-season, a **market** selling household goods pops up along the waterfront near Hotel Riva del Sole.

Cefalù Town Walk

Get to know this old Sicilian fishing village by following this 45-minute self-guided walk from the beach, out to the pier, and through some of Cefalù's most characteristic alleyways and piazzas. You'll end at the cathedral on grand Piazza del Duomo.

• *Start your walk on the beach promenade opposite the recommended Al Gabbiano restaurant. Have a seat on the round planter bench and gaze out at the...*

Sand and Sea

Look out at the sea and ponder the sailors from all over the Medi-

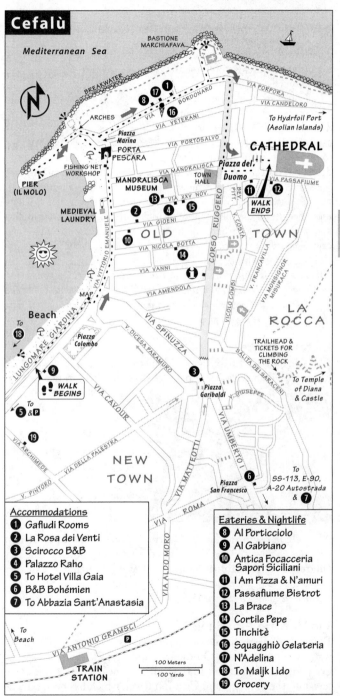

Cefalù

Mediterranean Sea

BASTIONE MARCHIAFAVA

VIA PORPORA

VIA CANDELORO

BREAKWATER

BORDONARO

ARCHES

VIA VETERANI

VIA PORTOSALVO

To Hydrofoil Port (Aeolian Islands)

Piazza Marina

PORTA PESCARA

CATHEDRAL

Piazza del Duomo

FISHING NET WORKSHOP

PIER (IL MOLO)

VIA MANDRALISCA

MANDRALISCA MUSEUM

TOWN HALL

VIA PASSAFIUME

WALK ENDS

BEV. PITT.

V. COSTA

MEDIEVAL LAUNDRY

VIA XXV NOV.

CORSO RUGGERO

OLD

VIA GIOENI

TOWN

V. FRANCAVILLA

VIA NICOLA BOTTA

VICOLO COMBI

V. MONSIGNOR MISURACA

VIA VANNI

LA ROCCA

VIA AMENDOLA

Beach

To

MAP

VIA VITTORIO EMANUELE

LUNGOMARE GIARDINA

VIA SPINUZZA

TRAILHEAD & TICKETS FOR CLIMBING THE ROCK

SALITA DEI SARACENI

To Temple of Diana & Castle

Piazza Colombo

V. DISCESA PARAMURO

WALK BEGINS

To &P

Piazza Garibaldi

G. GIUSEPPE

VIA CAVOUR

VIA UMBERTO I

VIA ARCHIMEDE

VIA DELLA PALESTRA

NEW TOWN

To SS-113, E-90, A-20 Autostrada &

V. PINTORO

VIA MATTEOTTI

Piazza San Francesco

VIA ROMA

VIA ANTONIO GRAMSCI

VIA ALDO MORO

TRAIN STATION

To Beach

P

100 Meters
100 Yards

Accommodations
1 Gafludi Rooms
2 La Rosa dei Venti
3 Scirocco B&B
4 Palazzo Raho
5 To Hotel Villa Gaia
6 B&B Bohémien
7 To Abbazia Sant'Anastasia

Eateries & Nightlife
8 Al Porticciolo
9 Al Gabbiano
10 Antica Focacceria Sapori Siciliani
11 I Am Pizza & N'amuri
12 Passafiume Bistrot
13 La Brace
14 Cortile Pepe
15 Tinchitè
16 Squagghiò Gelateria
17 N'Adelina
18 To Maljk Lido
19 Grocery

CEFALÙ

terranean who landed on this beach throughout history: ancient Greeks, shipwrecked Normans...and pirates looking for an easy target.

Look to the right for a classic view of Cefalù. The sun-drenched buildings that face the sandy harbor—the oldest part of town—were built into a curved defensive wall protecting the knot of streets inland. You can still see surviving stretches of the wall at the base of these buildings.

This sandy beach is one of the best in northern Sicily, where most beaches are either pebbly or rocky. The water here is shallow and warm. If you're here in the summer, listen for the sing-song cry: *"Coc-co! Coc-co bello!"*—the sales pitch of coconut vendors patrolling the beach.

• *Walk along the promenade toward the historic center. On your right, you'll pass the parklike Piazza Cristoforo Colombo. Continue to the end of the promenade, where you'll find a big city map fastened to the battered wall. Use it to get oriented to the...*

Historic Center

The old city is a stack of tight, neatly gridded lanes. It was laid out like many Arab cities, with parallel streets aligned to take advan-

tage of wind patterns and enhance air circulation—a kind of early air-conditioning. Most of the apartment dwellers along these lanes still hang laundry off their balconies to let the wind do the drying.

Just to the right of the city map, a small, brown *Porta Ossuna* sign marks the location of one of the original four city gates. Now all but one are gone—each torn down as the city outgrew its ancient dimensions. (We'll walk through the lone surviving gate, Porta Pescara, later on this walk.)

• *Continue along on charming...*

Via Vittorio Emanuele

Enjoy strolling this street for a few blocks. You'll pass a series of water-view restaurants. On the left, at #55, notice the massive old **grapevine** growing through the wall over the door. This thick vine taps into the underground Cefalino River, which has been providing spring water to Cefalù since ancient times...and still does. In fact, this source of fresh water was one of the attributes that originally attracted Greek settlers to Cefalù.

For another look at how locals have harnessed their river, walk a few feet farther and go through the gate on the left. Steps lead

down to a **medieval laundry** *(lavatorio medievale)*. The smaller square pools were for scrubbing, and the wedge-shaped stones functioned as washboards. Water flowing from the stream to the little taps on the left created a rinsing zone, with the water passing into successive pools. Dirty water was continuously flushed from the basins out to sea. Women had few public social spaces in medieval times, so the laundry would have been a natural gathering place. Imagine the cacophony in this little courtyard: kids running around, and women chatting while doing their washing. Believe it or not, this public laundry was used well into the 1970s.

Back on the street, continue the way you were headed. At #83 (on the left), you'll find a **fishing net workshop.** Pop in and examine the fine craftsmanship of the handmade traps and fishnets—some now creatively made into light fixtures.

• *Continue to #105, on the left, and turn into the archway.*

Porta Pescara

Through this archway you'll find one of the prettiest views of the harbor. This is the last remaining gate of the old city—the Fisherman's Gate. Until the end of the 20th century, Cefalù's main industry was fishing, and this is where the catch of the day would be hauled in to market.

These days, the gate preserves the memory of the town's fishy past with a small **clubhouse** (inside the gate, on the right). The wives of a few local fishermen meet here every Tuesday to embroider and weave scraps of fishing net with colorful fabrics to make clothing and scarves. They are the few women keeping this art form alive in Cefalù. Even if the club is closed, you can admire their work through the windows. On the wall is a portrait

of "Il Presidente" Antonino Brocato, the former head of the local fishermen's union who spent his life fishing the seas around Cefalù.
• *Continue through the Porta Pescara.*

You'll emerge at the harbor. Walk a few steps to the right, where, behind a gate, you'll see a small display of traditional fishing gear. Notice the floating ring with the fat wick—a primitive lantern used to attract octopi and anchovies at night.
• *Go down the steps onto the beach, and wander out along...*

The Pier (Il Molo)

Strolling Cefalù's long breakwater pier rewards you with grand views of the town and beach. This is the old port of Cefalù, also known as *il porticciolo* ("the little port"). The harbor in front was the center of the fishing business for generations—but it's mostly quiet today, now that a modern port occupies the other side of La Rocca.

Facing town, look up to La Rocca looming overhead. It's worth the steep hike up La Rocca for its gobsmacking views (for details, see the listing under "Sights in Cefalù," later). Notice the crenellated wall that runs along the lower, flat layer of rock—offering strategic protection to the town below. The rock also shields the city center from strong winds. The summit is capped by the ruins of a Norman castle, and the hillside is home to an ancient Greek temple.
• *Follow the pier back toward town, circling around to the little square called...*

Piazza Marina

If this square seems familiar, it's because it appears in the final scene of the classic 1988 movie *Cinema Paradiso* (in the Italian drama, flickering images are projected on the blank wall facing the sea). Some of the movie about a small-town projectionist-turned-filmmaker was filmed here in Cefalù. This piazza is *the* place to be at sunset for a romantic picnic on its benches. The two archways facing the sea lead to a rocky coastal path that skirts the north coast and leads out to the lighthouse on the other side of La Rocca.
• *With your back to the harbor, keep left to walk up the gentle slope of Via Bordonaro. This street is popular for its wine bars and restaurants with seaside terraces. If you're in the mood for gelato, stop at **Squagghiò** (on the right at #69) and try their signature flavor—a combination of almond, sour cherry, and pistachio.*

After two blocks, turn left onto narrow Piazza Francesco Crispi

CEFALÙ

and head toward the water. Climb the staircase on the right up to the view terrace called...

Bastione Marchiafava

This terrace, part of a 17th-century fortification, takes in commanding views over the Tyrrhenian Sea. On a clear day, the archipelago of the Aeolian Islands is visible on your right. You can also see Cefalù's lighthouse perched on the point just below La Rocca.

The basin in the center of the terrace was used as a fountain. The decorative lions on its pedestal are in the Arab-Norman style, suggesting it could have been from the 1100s. The lion was the symbol of the Norman King Roger II, who commissioned the cathedral and intended to make Cefalù the capital of his kingdom. Inside the cathedral you'll find a basin with a similar motif, used as a baptismal font.

• *Backtrack to Via Bordonaro and continue uphill. Take the first right onto Cefalù's bustling Corso Ruggero (my favorite place for a predinner passeggiata). A few blocks up, on the left, is...*

Piazza del Duomo

This central piazza is Cefalù's living room. Surrounded by palm trees, bars, and restaurants, this is the heart of the city—and it's always alive.

The focal point is the blocky Cefalù Cathedral. Its imposing scale dominates the town, as if on a stage with a rocky backdrop. Opposite the cathedral, the former Convent of St. Catherine has been converted into a stark white, minimalist **Town Hall**—with the flags of Sicily, Italy, and Europe flying under its concave eaves.

Find a seat and enjoy the scene from a bench at the bottom of the square or from a table at one of the restaurant patios—perfect for nursing a *granita* or a glass of wine. Take time here to do some people-watching as the locals go about their day.

• *Our walk is finished. From here, you could tour the cathedral, then explore the town or hit the beach. To the right of the cathedral, Via*

Bevilacqua Pittore (next to the Duomo Ristorante–Pizzeria) leads to the trailhead for the hike up La Rocca.

Sights in Cefalù

▲▲Cefalù Cathedral (Cattedrale di Cefalù)

Despite its lazy beach-town ambience, Cefalù has one of Sicily's most interesting cathedrals—a classic Norman fortified church, with stout towers, narrow windows, and zipper-toothed crenellations. The stern-looking church (built between 1131 and 1240) hides an elegant surprise inside: a monumental, glittering mosaic of Christ Pantocrator, considered the most elegant in Sicily.

Cost and Hours: Free, daily 9:00-18:30, shorter hours and closed midday Nov-March, tel. 0921-922-021, http://cattedraledicefalu.com.

Background: In 1131, Norman King Roger II was returning from Salerno when a violent storm caused his ship to run aground in the shallow waters off Cefalù—but he survived unharmed. To thank God for his survival, Roger commissioned this massive cathedral. His motives for the project were also political: He intended to make Cefalù his capital city. The Normans may have conquered Sicily, but fusing cultures on the island proved a challenge. Palermo was the Norman stronghold, but Byzantine Taormina remained sympathetic to the Greek Orthodox religion. By relocating his government to Cefalù, strategically located between the two centers of power, Roger would have asserted control over the entire island. But the king died before he could bring his government here, and the Norman capital remained in Palermo. Nonetheless, Roger left Cefalù with the beginnings of this oversized cathedral, which by the 13th century had become a grand monument to the capital that never was.

Visiting the Cathedral: The **exterior** is a textbook example of an *ecclesia munita*, a church-fortress. Notice the crenellations on top of the towers and, lower, the slit windows for archers' arrows (typical features of castles built in France around the same time). Imagine soldiers patrolling outside on the upper gallery while the sounds of Mass drifted out to the piazza. Decorations on the facade are few—most are the simple, geometric, zigzag patterns typical of Norman churches in France and England.

Inside the church, over the altar, the glittering mosaic of Christ Pantocrator ("All Ruling") makes eye contact and invites you to come closer. The cathedral's apse and choir are wallpapered with golden Byzantine-style mosaics (some of which predate those at Monreale), but the rest of the church was left unfinished. After Roger died, his successor focused his energy on projects in Palermo instead.

The long stone **nave** is characteristic of Norman simplicity, with ancient columns and capitals—scavenged from pagan Roman temples—supporting a parade of arches. High in the transept, pointed arch windows hint at the new Gothic style emerging farther north. What makes the architecture here special is the fusion of French-Norman style and North African-Arab

style. The Normans may have pushed Arab rule out of Sicily, but Arab citizens remained. Arab craftsmen working on the cathedral used their traditional design and engineering, which you can see in the high, near-horseshoe arches springing from the ancient Roman columns. This variety of architectural styles—Norman towers, Roman columns, Arab arches, and Byzantine mosaics—makes Cefalù Cathedral a unique, multicultural work of art.

The most recent addition to this patchwork interior is the collection of modern **stained-glass windows,** completed in 2003. They were installed with much controversy due to their stark contrast with the surrounding medieval architecture. The windows' abstract style makes it difficult to make out the biblical scenes, but you can give it a try: The panes in the central nave represent scenes from the Book of Genesis. Over the entry door, the large and colorful pane divided in four sections depicts the Last Judgement. In the aisles are panes inspired by the lives of St. Peter (left aisle) and St. Paul (right aisle).

Now turn your attention to the cathedral's mosaic masterpiece: At the apse, **Christ Pantocrator** watches over the faithful with his

refined and elongated features, soft skin tones, and expressive eyes. The Bible he holds is open to John 8:12, with the first page written in Greek (εἴμαι το φως του κόσμου; "I am the light of the world"). Below Christ, Mary greets you like a Byzantine empress, flanked by angels. In the lower registers, the Twelve Apostles complete the scene.

This cathedral, its mosaics, and Palermo's Palatine Chapel (with a similar Christ Pantocrator mosaic) were all initiated by King Roger II in the early 1100s. At Monreale Cathedral, however, constructed in the late 1100s by Roger's grandson, we see an important shift: The Christ Pantocrator there holds a Bible with the first page written in Latin. This may seem a small detail, but the change in language parallels a major cultural shift away from Byzantine Greek Christianity and toward the Latin church.

Nearby: The skippable **cloister** is next to the cathedral—enter on the left as you face the cathedral's main stairs. It's ringed by columns with carved capitals, similar to those at Monreale, although most of these are worn down to almost nothing.

▲Mandralisca Museum (Museo Mandralisca)

Cefalù's only museum hosts a delightful and impressive array of art that spans centuries. The collection, with minimal English information, fills a former nobleman's townhouse.

Cost and Hours: €6, daily 9:00-19:00—July-Aug until 23:00, Via Mandralisca 13, tel. 0921-421-547, www.fondazionemandralisca.it.

Visiting the Museum: The most interesting section is up on the first floor, with a humble (but beautifully displayed) painting gallery. In a darkened room at the end of this hall is the highlight: *Portrait of a Man* (c. 1465), by Sicily's most famous Renaissance artist, Antonello da Messina (for more on Messina, see the sidebar). The subject looks out slyly with an impish smirk in a three-quarter view. The juxtaposition of the dark background  and brightly lit facial features demonstrates the then-developing technique called *chiaroscuro*, which literally means "light/dark." In the same room is *St. John the Baptist* by late-Renaissance Florentine painter Giovanni Antonio Sogliani.

A few steps up is the archaeology section, with a select assortment of Greek and Roman artifacts, including some of Sicily's best-preserved kraters (wine-mixing urns). The most prized one shows men at a marketplace chopping tuna, something that was a regular activity here in Cefalù from antiquity until very recently.

On the second floor is a collection of ancient coins, an extensive seashell collection, furniture, more paintings, and taxidermied local wildlife—mostly birds.

Antonello da Messina (c. 1430-1479)

The Renaissance didn't thrive in Sicily the way it did in the rest of Italy—so Sicily has few famous artists from the period. The one great exception is Antonello da Messina. A native of Messina, on Sicily's northeast coast, he studied in the court of the king of Naples and later in Milan, and he's thought to have learned the detailed techniques of Netherlandish oil painting from another court artist. Antonello also spent time in Venice, and some sources credit him with introducing oil painting to that city (it's more likely that he showed the Venetians how to make better use of the medium). The altarpiece Antonello painted there for the Church of San Cassiano, with its incipient mastery of perspective, would influence Giovanni Bellini and other Venetian masters. Antonello's portraits are prized for their detailed and expressive faces, and of his remaining works, *Portrait of a Man* (in Cefalù's Mandralisca Museum) is the most intriguing and irreverent.

CEFALÙ

▲▲La Rocca

High above Cefalù soars a mighty rock, La Rocca, crowned at 885 feet by the ruins of a Norman castle. If you're up for a sturdy hike to grand views, summiting the rock is worth the effort. Or, go halfway up to a Greek temple dedicated to Diana, where you'll get the best views of the town below.

Cost and Hours: €4, daily 9:00-20:00, Nov-Feb until 17:00, last entry one hour before closing. Exit times are strictly enforced—the only way out after the gates are locked is to call the police.

Planning Your Hike: It's best to go early or late in the day to avoid the midday heat. Give yourself plenty of time. People in great shape need at least two hours round-trip, not including time to linger and enjoy the views. For a shorter, easier hike, you'll find good city views halfway up, just below the Temple of Diana. Fit hikers should allow at least an hour round-trip for this option.

Summiting La Rocca: The route up is on the zigzagging path called Salita dei Saraceni, which you can find by following brown *Tempio di Diana* signs in the center of the old town. The most straightforward route heads straight up from Piazza Garibaldi (on Via Giuseppe Fiore—find the signed steps tucked between two buildings), or head up from Corso Ruggero on little Vicolo

Saraceni. From Piazza del Duomo, follow narrow Via Bevilacqua Pittore up.

Once you reach the **trailhead,** you'll buy a ticket and go through a turnstile. Confirm what time you'll need to be back down. Then wind your way steeply up well-marked stone steps and gravel paths, passing agave, cactus, and wildflowers. At the rock's plateau, you'll step through a stout stone gateway (with a door that locks at closing time). Just above that, signs point to your two options: left to the archaeological site, or right to the *castello*/castle.

I'd head left to the best views first, while you're still fresh. This route takes you on a trail above the ruins of the Church of Sant'Anna—a small, single-nave chapel from the ninth or 10th century—a few brick ovens, and more building ruins (likely medieval military barracks). You'll then reach the ruins of the **Temple of Diana.** This fourth-century BC temple was built by an indigenous tribe before the arrival of the Greeks in Cefalù. Early settlers strategically built on this rock rather than on the less defensible harbor below. The megalithic temple was made with large, stout blocks of local stone—while there's not much left to see today, the structure is evocative. From the temple, head down to the crenellated wall just below for stunning views over Cefalù's old and new towns and the nearby coastline.

To conquer the summit, head back past the Temple of Diana and follow signs to the *castello*. Here the trail becomes even steeper and the footing more challenging (a mix of rock and dirt). At the top, you'll find the ruins of a Norman **castle** from the time of King Roger II. From what's left—a few stretches of crenellated wall—you can see over the back side of La Rocca, with distant views of the Aeolian Islands, and even Mount Etna.

From the castle, you could head back down the way you came or, to enjoy more scenery, turn your hike into a loop: Continue along the ridge toward the mainland, where you'll reach additional ruined fortifications. From there, hike steeply back down to the main gate.

Beaches

Cefalù has one of the largest sandy beaches in northern Sicily. Beach season starts after Easter and ends in October, depending on the weather. High season is in August, when Italian tourists flood the beach during Ferragosto, the August 15 national holiday.

Sicilian Beach Tips

Italians take their beach vacations seriously. While it's possible to flop a towel down on any stretch of empty beach, spending the money to go to the *spiaggia* like an Italian is a fun experience. Shop around and find the location and amenities that suit you.

All along the beach, seasonal restaurants and cabanas rent handy *lettini* (lounge chairs) sprawled along the prime real estate. (Vendors rent their stretch of beach from the city and charge admission.) A typical *lettino* with shade costs €10-25 per day. Lifeguards and attendants generally keep an eye on your things (so you're paying for more than just the chair). If you go late in the day, negotiate your chair price.

Some beach properties *(lidi)* also have changing rooms, toilets, restaurants, and cocktail bars with service to your chair. Many hotels have beach chairs reserved for their guests—ask your hotel before heading to the beach. Then settle in and listen for the call of the coconut vendors that roam the waterfront.

CEFALÙ

For an easy spot with a decent handy restaurant, try the beach at **Lido Eolo** resort, in front of the recommended Villa Gaia Hotel (daily 8:00-19:00, Lungomare Giuseppe Giardina 133, mobile 388-143-2801). Locals prefer the quieter, far end of  the beach, away from the historic center (about a 15-minute walk south).

Nightlife in Cefalù

The early evening action is centered on Piazza del Duomo and along Corso Ruggero. Locals come out for their evening *passeggiata*, kids play, and teenagers flirt. The bar scene on Via Bordonaro gets lively at dinnertime, and in summer the fun continues until late. **N'Adelina** (at #56) serves artisanal beer and gourmet panini, offering a nice hangout vibe but no sea views.

Disco: In the summer, the *lidi* (beach resorts) are at the center of evening fun. **Maljk Lido** hosts DJs and offers *apericena* deals—an *aperitivo* with generous snacks (open late May-Sept, Lungomare Giardina, tel. 0921-420-205).

Sleeping in Cefalù

There are no big hotels in the historic area—only B&Bs—so if you need comforts like elevators and parking, plan to stay near the train station or along the beach. Prices soar in August, peaking around the Ferragosto holiday on August 15. Many B&Bs close from November through March.

OLD CENTER

$$$ Gafludi Rooms, right in the thick of the action on Via Bordonaro, offers 12 rooms with a funky, artsy vibe and a welcoming rooftop terrace. Some rooms have sea views (hotel was formerly known as Al Saraceno, air-con, free shuttle to parking lot near the modern hydrofoil port on the opposite side of La Rocca, Via Bordonaro 48, tel. 0921-422-639, www.alsaracenocefalu.it, gafludirooms@gmail.com).

$$$ La Rosa dei Venti has seven small apartments in the center of town. The modern, minimalist units have small living rooms, itty-bitty kitchens, and not much character (air-con, no breakfast, Via Gioeni 82, tel. 0921-92-33-86, www.rosadeiventicefalu.com, info@rosadeiventicefalu.com, Fabrizia).

$$ Scirocco B&B overlooks Piazza Garibaldi, with four tidy rooms in several shades of purple. While the rooms are simple and the stairs never end, the panoramic terrace floating above the city is magical (air-con, Piazza Garibaldi 8, mobile 392-644-4131, www.sciroccobeb.it, sciroccobeb@gmail.com, spunky Nicole).

$ Palazzo Raho, well located on a side street in the historic center, has seven stately rooms tastefully decorated in pastel hues (family rooms, air-con, tel. 0921-571-227, Via XXV Novembre 47, www.palazzoraho.it, info@palazzoraho.it, Herman).

ALONG THE BEACH

$$ Hotel Villa Gaia is a family-run budget pick facing the beach about a 10-minute walk from the historic center. Its 15 rooms are basic and homey compared to the resort-like hotels surrounding it, but the place is far enough from the beach scene to be relatively quiet (air-con, elevator, easy free parking, free beach chairs for guests, Via Maestro Pintorno 101, tel. 0921-420-992, www.villagaiahotel.it, info@villagaiahotel.it).

OTHER ACCOMMODATIONS

In the New Town: Slightly out of the tourist fray, **$$ B&B Bohémien** occupies a modern building with four large, airy rooms and a good- quality, locally-sourced breakfast (air-con, Via Umberto I 15c, mobile 349-799-0538, www.bohemienbeb.it, booking@bohemienbeb.it, Mari).

Near Cefalù: About a 20-minute drive from Cefalù, **$$$ Abbazia Sant'Anastasia** is a peaceful hotel and winery within the walls of a medieval abbey. The property is set high above the sea among expansive vineyards, so while the rooms are nothing special, the pretty views and lovely pool area make it a nice alternative to busy Cefalù (family rooms, air-con, elevator, good restaurant and wines, near Castelbuono at Contrada Sant'Anastasia, off SS-286—follow the signs, tel. 0921-67-22-33, www.abbaziasantanastasia.com, relais@abbaziasantanastasia.com).

Eating in Cefalù

Cefalù is a touristy town filled with touristy restaurants. You'll pay a little more here—especially if you want to eat with a sea view or on Piazza del Duomo. Still, the seafood is enticing, and the service is generally good.

Supermarket: FoodSicily Market is the most central grocery (daily 8:00-21:00, Via Archimede 9).

DINING WITH A SEA VIEW

If you're going to eat with a sea view anywhere in Sicily, make it here in Cefalù. Anticipating a warm evening, I'd take a few min-

utes at lunch to find a place that feels right and make a reservation for dinner. The beach promenade just south of the old center has a few options, but I prefer the places on Via Bordonaro (most have view terraces), where you'll see lots of high-end choices mixed in with more rustic options. Simpler restaurants have antipasto buffet spreads with stools facing the sea; fancier places have terraces built out over the rocky shore (look for *terrazza sul mare*). Peasants grab a bite to go and picnic on the beach, either at the west end of town or on a bench at Piazza Marina.

$$$ Al Porticciolo is *the* place for a traditional and fancy seafood dinner on Via Bordonaro. Nicola, Sauro, and Paolo take pride in their fish and meat dishes. The romantic seaside terrace is swoon-worthy at sunset (free welcome drink with this book, reservations smart, Thu-Tue 12:00-15:00 & 19:00-24:00, closed Wed, Via Bordonaro 66, tel. 0921-921-981, www.alporticcioloristorante.com).

$$ Al Gabbiano is a popular choice among the several restaurants offering relaxing views along the beach. They serve pizza and fish in a vast interior, with a large covered terrace and beach-front seating (daily 12:00-24:00, Lungomare Giardina 17, tel. 0921-421-495).

$ Antica Focacceria Sapori Siciliani, steps from the sand in the old town, sells pizza and street food, including *arancini* and pasta dishes. Grab your lunch or dinner here for a picnic on the beach (Wed-Mon 10:30-15:30 & 17:30-21:30, closed Tue, Via Gioeni 87, tel. 0921-820-393).

ON AND NEAR PIAZZA DEL DUOMO

The most central place in town is filled with tables, umbrellas, and people enjoying the delightful vibe. A meal here, while touristy, leaves you with fine memories. Your options range from the basic bars to the more elegant pizzerias—but most are essentially inter-changeable (all are typically open long hours daily in peak season).

$ I Am Pizza serves cheap and basic pizzas, pastas, and sand-wiches, with lots of outdoor tables; it's attached to the higher-end **$$ N'amuri,** with a pricier menu and the same setting.

$$$ Passafiume Bistrot flanks the cathedral with a dozen tables in a cozy space, plus a few outdoor tables. Francesco offers a small menu of creative cuisine and intriguing daily specials. Lino the bartender mixes up a range of fanciful drinks, including an orange flower gin-and-tonic (daily 11:00-15:00 & 18:00-24:00, closed Tue off-season, Via Passafiume 6, tel. 0921-820-404).

OTHER OPTIONS IN THE OLD TOWN

$$ La Brace, with a stylish red dining room reminiscent of a Pari-sian bistro, serves Sicilian dishes with French and Dutch influences. The menu is fresh and seasonal: If the daily catch isn't quality, you won't see it on the menu (open for dinner Tue-Sun 20:00-23:00, closed Mon, Via XXV Novembre 10, tel. 0921-423-570).

$$$$ Cortile Pepe is a good choice for a stylish splurge in Cefalù. Rather than big, sloppy, tourist-pleasing plates of pasta and fish (as is often the local standard), here you'll enjoy delicately crafted, high-end Sicilian cooking. The interior is sophisticated and minimalist, and there are a few breezy tables out front (daily 12:00-15:00 & 19:00-24:00, Via Nicola Botta 15, tel. 0921-421-630).

$$ Tinchitè has a modern dining room and a long string of outdoor tables across the street. The portions are large, and meat is their specialty (daily 12:00-15:00 & 19:00-24:00, Via XXV No-vembre 37, tel. 0921-421-164).

Cefalù Connections

From Cefalù by Train to: Palermo (hourly, 1 hour), **Messina** (hourly, 2 hours), **Rome** (4/day, 10-12 hours). To **Taormina, Catania, Siracusa,** or other east coast destinations, you'll connect through Messina or Palermo.

Route Tips for Drivers: Palermo is an easy, one-hour drive west on highway E-90. To reach **Catania** (2.5 hours), leave Cefalù in the direction of Palermo, then turn south on speedy A-19 to Catania. For **Agrigento** (2.5 hours), head west on E-90, then take A-19 toward Catania. At Caltanissetta, follow signs to *Agrigento* and head south on SS-640.

To reach **Taormina** (3 hours), head east out of Cefalù, following the seafront road before twisting up, up, up to get on the E-90 highway eastbound at Pollina-Castelbuono (toward Messina). Follow this highway along the coast, taking in the scenery of the Madonie Mountains, the Aeolian Islands, and the Strait of Messina. At Messina, head south on SS-114 to Taormina.

CEFALÙ

TRAPANI & THE WEST COAST

Trapani • Erice • Egadi Islands • Mozia Island • Segesta • Selinunte

Sicily's west coast has a different flavor than the rest of the island. For one thing, it's a bit rainier—and therefore greener—than other parts of Sicily. Geographically and culturally, it's Sicily's closest point to Africa (Marsala is 90 miles from the northeast coast of Tunisia). The cuisine of the west coast region feels exotic and vaguely African—this is the place to try couscous with fish broth.

The region is anchored by the port of Trapani, a salty, workaday town with a pleasant historic center that's perfectly situated for exploring the region. Trapani is about 65 miles, or 1.5 hours by car, from Palermo. Several worthwhile stops are within easy striking distance: the skyscraping hill town of Erice, the charming Egadi Islands just offshore, and the salt flats and scant Carthaginian ruins at Mozia Island. Temple lovers can choose between the ancient temple-and-theater ensemble at Segesta or the Greek ruins at Selinunte (both farther afield, but you can hit them on the way in or out of the region).

A visit to this charming and untouristed region nicely rounds out your look at Sicily.

PLANNING YOUR TIME

Trapani has no essential sights other than the enjoyable town itself—which can be experienced in a couple of hours in the early evening. But its good range of hotels and restaurants makes it an ideal home base. To thoroughly visit everything in this chapter, I'd spend two nights in Trapani. If driving from Palermo, see Segesta on the way in, enjoy an easy evening in Trapani, side-trip to Mozia and the salt flats the next morning, then spend the late afternoon

Trapani Day Trips at a Glance

▲**Erice** Misty and atmospheric hilltop town with grand views and a renowned bakery, just a quick cable-car ride away from Trapani. See page 157.

▲**Favignana and the Egadi Islands** Peaceful escape 30 minutes by boat from Trapani's port. Favignana, the easiest to reach, hosts a good museum about the region's once-thriving tuna industry. See page 168.

▲**Mozia Island** Private island with a smattering of Carthaginian ruins and lots of nature, 10 minutes by boat from a dock 30 minutes south of Trapani and easy to combine with a salt flat visit (see next). See page 172.

▲▲**Salt Flat Experiences** Along the coast between Trapani and Marsala, salt flats worked in traditional methods complemented by a visit to a salt museum: Choose from the Museum of Salt, 20 minutes from downtown Trapani, or Saline della Laguna, next to the boat dock for Mozia Island. See page 179.

▲▲**Segesta** Ancient site with beautifully preserved theater, unfinished Greek temple, and city ruins (halfway between Palermo and Trapani). See page 181.

▲▲**Selinunte** Picturesque toppled Greek city with a trio of temples, a 1.5-hour drive south of Trapani (on the way to Agrigento). See page 184.

and early evening in Erice. With an extra day, hydrofoils can take you to the Egadi Islands (Favignana is the best quick look), or you can drive south to visit the Greek site of Selinunte. Selinunte also makes a natural stop on the way between Trapani and Agrigento.

Trapani

Dramatically stretching out into the sea, Trapani (TRAH-pah-nee) sits on a long, curved promontory at the western tip of the triangle that is Sicily. The city's shape resembles a hook, and legend has it that the land was formed when Demeter dropped her scythe in grief as she heard that her daughter, Persephone, had been kidnapped by the king of the underworld.

While Trapani is a sprawling city of 70,000 people (the largest in western Sicily), visitors focus on the lively, characteristic streets of the historic district—at the far end of the peninsula. Light on sightseeing, Trapani is a pedestrian-friendly delight with plenty of handy accommodations and fun places to eat, and offers a chance to get to know a workaday Sicilian port town with a charming historic quarter.

Orientation to Trapani

The old town center lies west of the Villa Margherita public gardens, surrounding the elegant pedestrian street of Via Garibaldi. The area around the intersection of the two main shopping streets, Via Torrearsa and Corso Vittorio Emanuele, is considered the heart of the old town. The functional, modern part of the city spreads east along Via Giovanni Battista Fardella for two miles, toward Erice.

TOURIST INFORMATION

The TI has info on Trapani and the west coast (Mon-Fri 9:00-14:00, Mon and Thu also 14:30-17:30, Sat 10:00-13:00, closed Sun, shorter hours off-season, Palazzo Cavarretta, Via Torrearsa, mobile 340-2427-212, www.trapaniwelcome.it).

ARRIVAL IN TRAPANI

By Bus: Buses from Palermo arrive next to the hydrofoil terminal, along the south side of the peninsula on Via Ammiraglio Staiti. To reach the town center from here, walk a couple of blocks toward the tip of the peninsula, then turn right (inland) on the Via Torrearsa shopping street. Buses from Agrigento arrive at the bus station in the new town, just south of the train station.

By Car: From the autostrada, drivers will arrive near the port on the south side of town. But most parking opportunities line the north coast. To get there, follow the one-way, clockwise loop through town—first driving along the port and past the ferry terminal, then turning inland at Via Duca D'Aosta, and looping back through town on Corso Vittorio Emanuele, then Via Libertà. Following the flow of traffic, you'll hit the north shore at the decorative Piazza Mercato del Pesce colonnade, then drive along the embankment road, Lungomare Dante Alighieri. You'll see lots of pay-and-display spots along here (indicated by blue lines, enforced 8:00-13:00 & 15:00-20:00, pay at coin-op machines, prepayment for the next day is OK). For free parking, continue along Lungomare Dante Alighieri all the way to the big parking lot at Piazza Vittorio Emanuele. Additional pay-and-display spaces can be found in the historic center, including at Piazza Garibaldi and along the port.

HELPFUL HINTS

Tap Water Warning: Due to old pipes, it's not advisable to drink the tap water in Trapani. Stock up on bottled water.

Laundry: Trapani's new town—a longish walk from the historic center—has several good launderettes, including the self-service **La Casa del Pulito** (daily 7:00-24:00, Via Vito Carrera 5, mobile 327-005-2420).

Thursday Morning Market: Trapani's weekly market near the port sells a little of everything—it's like a mobile Walmart (Thu 8:00-14:00, free shuttle bus #2 from intercity bus stop at port along Via Ammiraglio Staiti; drivers can park in lot off Via Isola Zavorra—head east on Via Illio; lot is just past the roundabout where you turn right onto Via Isola Zavorra).

Car Rental: Avis rents cars from a location near the port (Mon-Fri 9:00-13:00 & 15:30-19:00, closed Sat-Sun, Via Avvocato Giuseppe Palmeri 3, tel. 0923-872-848).

Travel Agency: Egatour sells bus tickets for long-distance trips. They also offer day tours to the salt flats and Egadi Islands (€30 salt flats tour offered daily, office open daily 5:30-20:00, Via Ammiraglio Staiti 13—across from the bus stop at the hydrofoil port, tel. 092-321-754, www.egatourviaggi.it, info@egatourviaggi.it).

Local Guides: Azzurra Cusenza guides in Trapani and the surrounding areas. She has a gentle way and an interest in archaeology on the island of Mozia (€60/hour, 2-hour minimum, mobile 340-252-7728, azzurra.cusenza@virgilio.it). **Elena Rutkowska Buscemi** puts her heart into shedding light on the mysteries of the Carthaginian civilization, and guides all over western Sicily (€150/4 hours, €250/8 hours, mobile 355-656-6132, rutkowska.elena@gmail.com).

Private Driver: Michelangelo Marchingiglio, a reliable English-speaking driver and guide, has an eight-seat van for short city trips or longer excursions in the countryside, such as Selinunte (guided driving—€250/4 hours, €350/day; driving only—€160/4 hours, €200/day; more for areas outside western Sicily, mobile 335-822-5215, info@michaelangelotransfer.it).

GETTING AROUND TRAPANI

Trapani's historic center is walkable, and buses can help you reach outlying sights. Bus tickets are available at tobacco shops and newsstands (€1.20/90 minutes, €1.40 if purchased on board). A custodian on each bus helps with tickets, answers questions, and will show you your stop. The bus stop at Via Giovanni Battista Fardella 14, one block east of the Villa Margherita public gardens, serves the Erice cable car (buses #21 and #23 to Cableway stop) and the Pepoli Museum (buses #25, #28, and #30 to Museo stop). Long-

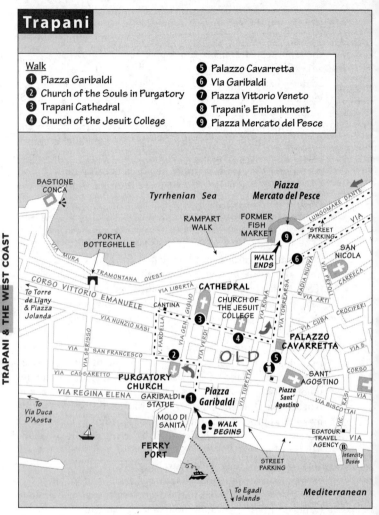

Trapani

Walk
1. Piazza Garibaldi
2. Church of the Souls in Purgatory
3. Trapani Cathedral
4. Church of the Jesuit College
5. Palazzo Cavarretta
6. Via Garibaldi
7. Piazza Vittorio Veneto
8. Trapani's Embankment
9. Piazza Mercato del Pesce

distance buses depart from the bus station on Piazza Montalto and from near the port.

Trapani Town Walk

This one-hour walk will take you from the port, through the historic center, to part of the modern town, and finish at the old fish market. It's ideal in the early evening, just before sunset—when the shops and churches are still open, and people are beginning to come out and stroll. To trace the route of this walk, see the "Trapani" map above.

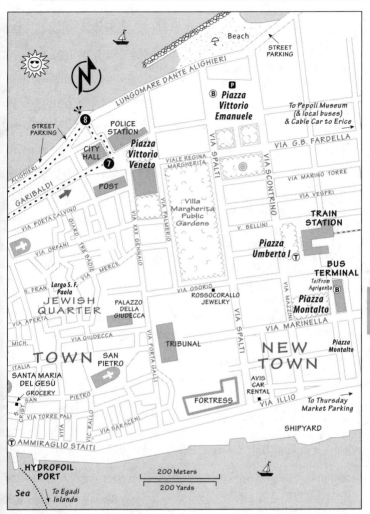

• *Start in Piazza Garibaldi, facing the busy port area, on the south shore of Trapani's peninsula.*

❶ Piazza Garibaldi

The statue on the big pillar is **Giuseppe Garibaldi**—Italy's most famous and colorful revolutionary. Before becoming the leader of the military arm of the unification of the country, he was a jack-of-all-trades and an adventurer who lived in the US and South America. Standing here, he looks toward Marsala, where he landed with his troops in 1860 to begin the Risorgimento, that long and complicated political march that eventually led to unification and the establishment of modern Italy in 1861.

Along the waterfront is Trapani's hard-working port area. You'll see pleasure craft, public boats, and military ships. A few blocks to the left is the departure point for speedy hydrofoils to the Egadi Islands, just offshore (the best one is Favignana, described later in this chapter).

• *Back to back with Garibaldi, take the street ahead on the left, Via Verdi, and head away from the water. After two short blocks, turn left at the green pharmacy sign and walk to the...*

❷ Church of the Souls in Purgatory (Chiesa delle Anime Sante del Purgatorio)

This Baroque church has an interior that's unexceptional—except for the 20 sculpture groups you'll find displayed around its nave. These sculptures—illustrating the story of the Passion of Christ, collectively called *i Misteri*—play an integral role in Trapani's unique Easter celebrations.

Cost and Hours: Leave the suggested €1 donation or languish in *purgatorio*, Mon-Sat 7:30-12:00 & 16:00-19:00, Sun from 10:00, Via San Francesco 33, www.chiesamisteri.it).

Background: Every year on Good Friday, at 14:00, each of the church's statue groups are carried out on the backs of one to two dozen strong men, accompanied by a band playing Sicilian funeral dirges. The scenes make their way through town with a swaying and rhythmic gait. Participants are draped with jewelry, coral (symbolizing blood), flowers, and lights. The whole city turns out in mourning clothes to participate in the

symbolic funeral for Christ. This particular Easter tradition is not native to Sicily, but was brought by Spanish occupiers. Processions like this are common in Sicily—but this one lasts a full 24 hours.

Dating from the early 17th to 18th century, the statue groups are made of wood, cork, and other lightweight materials. The figures' dramatic drapery is made using fabric dipped in glue and plaster, and then molded and dried. Some of the characters are portraits of actual locals, and the role of the Roman centurions is played by Spanish soldiers (who were to Sicily what the Romans were to the Jews 2,000 years ago). Many of the villains—such as Pontius Pilate—are depicted as Ottomans.

Sicily: Jumping-Off Point for Conquest

For thousands of years, Sicily's excellent ports and central location have made it the perfect place to grab a foothold on the path to conquering other parts of the Mediterranean—which explains why the island has been conquered so many times by so many cultures. In ancient times, it was an ideal trade outpost, providing a connection between North Africa and Northern Europe. Successive invaders enjoyed control of the shipping lanes around the island, controlling Mediterranean trade. And on the western tip of the island, near Trapani, the revolutionary Giuseppe Garibaldi and his thousand men landed in 1860 to start the reunification of Italy. Garibaldi captured the island, then continued on a march toward Rome and the final goal of establishing an Italian state.

In 1943, the Allies used a similar strategy to retake Europe from the Nazis. Operation Husky landed hundreds of thousands of troops on Sicily's southern shore in the first major offensive by the Allies, allowing them to use the island as a base of operations in the Mediterranean. (For more on Sicily in World War II, see page 396.)

More recently, Sicily has been used as a strategic, protected airbase with quick access to Europe and North Africa. The United States maintains a naval air station at Sigonella in southeastern Sicily, and NATO forces use the Birgi airport in Trapani for missions to Africa and the Middle East.

Among those in the long chain of sojourners using Sicily as a bridge to Europe are immigrants from Africa, escaping dire consequences by rafting over to Sicilian shores. Most of these refugees use Sicily as a transition point for reaching more prosperous countries in northern Europe. Once registered with refugee status, they are allowed to move freely throughout the European Union.

TRAPANI & THE WEST COAST

Visiting the Church: Entering the church, turn right and follow the story of the Passion (signs in English describe each scene). Local guilds sponsor and maintain each statue group, and have the honor of carrying their ensemble through the city every year on Good Friday; each base is decorated with the symbol of its sponsoring guild. (A video of the Good Friday procession may be playing in the left transept.)

As plain as the church interior is, notice that the left transept is particularly austere. In 1940, Trapani was the first Italian city bombed by the Allies (French bombers based in Tunisia)—who hit this church. Luckily, at the time, the *Misteri* were housed elsewhere.

• *Exit the church and turn left. At the first intersection, turn right up Via*

Generale Enrico Fardella. Go two blocks, then turn right again on Corso Vittorio Emanuele—the lively central spine of the old town.

Immediately on your left, at #46, you'll find an old-fashioned cantina, **Tenute Adragna.** *Gregorio entertains a very local crowd here, selling red* (rosso) *wine right out of the big casks as well as chilled white* (bianco) *wine—just request sweet* (dolce) *or dry* (secco). *Pop in for a glass and make a memory.*

A block farther along Corso Vittorio Emanuele, on the left, you'll find the...

❸ Trapani Cathedral (Cattedrale di Trapani)

It's hard to get a good vantage point to take in this cathedral, which sits right on the main street rather than on a spacious piazza. Before entering (daily 8:00-12:00 & 16:00-20:00), check out the modern iron-and-bronze gate. On the right side of the gate, notice the grill—the symbol of St. Lawrence, the church's patron saint, who was martyred by being grilled alive.

The Baroque/Neoclassical interior wrestles with the vintage-1950s white marble canopy and altar. The left transept has a statue of the protector of sailors—the Madonna of Trapani—whom you'll see all over the city (you can spot her by her ornate crown). This particular Madonna is new, made from a scan of an older original and cut by lasers. The most precious work in the church is found in the fifth chapel on the right: a crucifixion painting attributed to Anthony Van Dyck.

• *Head back out onto the main street and turn left. Two blocks up the street, the second ornate building on the left side of the street is the...*

❹ Church of the Jesuit College (Chiesa del Collegio dei Gesuiti)

This Jesuit church and convent has a fluffy pink Baroque interior. On the right side you'll find yet another statue of the Madonna of Trapani (gotta keep those sailors safe). Notice the statues in the upper niches—the fronts of their bodies have been shorn off. It seems that these saints went out of style and were hidden behind drywall for years (Mon-Sat 9:00-12:00 & 16:00-20:00, unpredictable Sun hours).

• *Exit the church and turn left. The street dead-ends at...*

❺ Palazzo Cavarretta

This centerpiece of historic Trapani was used until the 1920s as the

TRAPANI & THE WEST COAST

Town Hall. Imagine the towns-folk gathering before its ornate balcony for grand pronounce-ments. This end of Corso Vittorio Emanuele was the closest thing old Trapani had to an official gathering place. The palazzo's government days are over, so now it mostly hosts exhibits. At the top of the facade, you'll see a clock and a calendar. Below them are St. John the Baptist, St. Albert, and in the center—you guessed it—the Madonna of Trapani. Three flags wave over the entrance: the red-and-yellow Sicilian flag, the blue EU flag, and—above all, at the very top of the building—the green, white, and red Italian flag.

• *Turn left at Palazzo Cavarretta and head toward the arcade of Piazza Mercato del Pesce. Our walk will end there. But first, we'll take a peek at the modern side of Trapani. A block before the big arcade, turn right and head down the grand pedestrian boulevard called...*

❻ Via Garibaldi

In the evening, Via Garibaldi is a great street to join the Trapani *passeggiata* (Corso Vittorio Emanuele and Via Torrearsa are even better). Sicilians love socializing, and the evening stroll is a precious opportunity to meet friends, window-shop, and get some fresh air before dinner.

We'll stroll the length of Via Garibaldi. Along the way, you'll pass former noble palaces, such as the big, hulking building on the left at the start of the street (at #7)—Palazzo Burgio (now Banco di Sicilia). The nearby salt flats made a few elite Trapani families rich, and they flaunted their wealth by building fancy palaces along this main street. As you continue down the street, you'll notice that some of these fancy townhouses came with faux-historical flourishes: The palace at #40, on the right, has Venetian Gothic balconies, even though it was built in the 1800s, well after the decline of Venice.

Notice the window displays. At #42 (on the right), the Sicilia Bedda shop shows off local produce and lots of gifty edibles, like jams and honey from local farms. At #60 (on the right), Gral café is the local hotspot for taking in soccer games on an outdoor big screen. Farther along, at #77 (left), you'll see red flags marked CGIL. This is the headquarters for one of Italy's labor unions. And just a few doors down, after the church, teens often loiter in front of #83, the high school. Sicilian kids choose their high school a bit like Americans choose colleges, based on areas of study such as arts or engineering. The students at this *liceo* are studying science.

As you walk, you'll also pass a few stretches of single-story buildings on the right. Trapani was badly bombed during World War II due to its important port, and some areas were never fully rebuilt. At #122, in the second stretch of these buildings, the original lower floor is being used for a small fruit shop—but the upper floors are only a jagged edge of broken stone.

• *When the street ends, you'll pop out into a big modern square...*

❼ Piazza Vittorio Veneto (Piazza Municipio)

This piazza marks the end of the old town and the start of the new. The broad boulevard stretching ahead of you is Via Giovanni Battista Fardella, which runs two miles to the cable-car station for Erice. On the left side of the square are the City Hall *(municipio)* and the police station *(questura)*. On the right, the yellow building is marked *Posta* and *Telegrafi*—the post and telegraph office from 1927, a lovely example of the Liberty Style

(what Italians call Art Nouveau). If it's open, step up to the door and admire the fine ironwork. Inside, the ceiling is a stained-glass work of art. Italian post offices are for more than sending mail: This is where people pay bills and parking tickets, receive pensions, and deal with bureaucracy.

• *Leave the piazza by walking toward the water, between the City Hall and the police station. Cross the street and walk straight up to the railing along...*

❽ Trapani's Embankment (Lungomare Dante Alighieri)

From here, you can see almost the entire city of Trapani. Looking right, you'll see the looming mountain, Monte San Giuliano, capped by Erice—accessible via cable car, and a great side-trip destination (described later in this chapter). Trapani is a city of 70,000 but looks much bigger. That's because Erice blends into Trapani, with an additional 26,000 people living at the foot of the mountain, plus 230 full-time residents in the medieval village at the top. The two cities form a larger municipality and share services. For instance, the public transit company is managed

Trapani's Coral Business

Coral was one of Trapani's major industries from the 16th to 19th century. Believed to have protective powers, it was used for jewelry, decorative arts, and clothing. In Greek mythology, coral represents the blood of the monster Medusa, who turned anyone who viewed her hideous face into stone. When she was beheaded by Perseus, her blood hit the seawater and petrified into coral. From the Middle Ages through Baroque times, coral took on a religious meaning as a symbol of the blood of Christ, and was worn as jewelry by women and children to protect them from danger. In the area around Naples, coral was fashioned into "horns"—a fertility symbol that also had protective powers. Today's Sicilians consider coral good luck, worn as protection from the curse of the evil eye. With so many ancient cultures intersecting in Sicily, this kind of cross-cultural mixing of symbols is common.

Coral reefs between Sicily and Tunisia were harvested for generations, until the supply was depleted. Coral is no longer harvested in Sicily, but some artisans remain—making jewelry out of antique coral, coral paste, or even a salt paste dyed to look like coral. In Trapani, Platimiro Fiorenza is one of the last artists working in coral, a profession handed down from his father. His shop, Rossocorallo, sells antique and modern coral jewelry (just south of the Villa Margherita public gardens at Via Osorio 36; for location, see the "Trapani" map, earlier).

by Trapani but also serves Erice. The local hospital is in the jurisdiction of Erice, so all citizens of Trapani are technically born in Erice...but everyone ends their days in Trapani, as the public cemetery is here.

Now turn left; from this vantage you'll see how the historic center of Trapani is squeezed onto a long peninsula curving out into the Mediterranean. The waters off Trapani are quiet these days, but this area used to pulse with fishermen. Tuna fishing and coral collection were big industries, powering the local economy. Both have been curtailed, sending the economy of Trapani in a tailspin. These days, tourism is a new solution for job creation.

• *Stroll with the water on your right, enjoying the humid sea breeze for a few blocks. Stop when you reach the big, arcaded semicircular structure.*

❾ Piazza Mercato del Pesce

This elegant seaside arcade was the site of the old fish market and the center of the local agricultural economy. But much of the old town was cleaned up and renovated in 2005, and the daily market (along with its fishy, smelly transactions) was relocated to the far-western tip of the city. These days, the arcade is occasionally used

for special events. In the center of the piazza, the statue of Venus is a reminder that Trapani was originally the port of the town of Erice, where the goddess was deeply venerated as a protector of sailors. Hmm...haven't we heard that story before?

• *Our walk is over. We're just a few steps from the start of the lively Via Garibaldi* passeggiata *zone, where we strolled earlier. But if it's late afternoon, continue your walk straight along the seafront promenade. This is the spot to be at dusk to view Trapani's impressive sunset. If you continue walking, you'll eventually wind your way to the Torre di Ligny, the westernmost edge of Trapani, with views over the Egadi Islands.*

Sights in Trapani

Pepoli Museum (Museo Regionale Agostino Pepoli)

Trapani's art museum, housed in a former Carmelite monastery two miles west of the town center, is home to an eclectic assortment that includes the personal collection of Agostino Pepoli, a merchant who made a fortune in the salt industry. Modest and distant from the historic center, it's skippable for most visitors, but worth a stop for drivers.

Cost and Hours: €6, Tue-Sat 9:00-17:30, Sun until 12:30, closed Mon, Via Conte Agostino Pepoli 180; take bus #25, #28, or #30 to Museo stop; tel. 0923-553-269, www.regione.sicilia.it/bbccaa/museopepoli/museopepoli.html.

Visiting the Museum: On the ground floor, to the right as you enter, you'll find Renaissance sculptures. The Renaissance never really took off in Sicily, but the Gagini and Laurana families were some of the few locals working in that style. To the left of the entry, a room displays artifacts from revolutionary Giuseppe Garibaldi's landing near Marsala. You'll see a giant flag from his ship, *Il Lombardo;* a uniform from his troops, nicknamed "The Red Shirts"; and an actual guillotine, complete with elevated platform and trapdoor. Upstairs, the painting gallery houses a work thought to be by Titian, *St. Francis with Stigmata.* The collection also includes ceramics, nativity scenes, and elaborate clothing and jewelry made with local coral carved by monks.

Sleeping in Trapani

$$$ Residenza La Gancia fills the old monastery of Santa Caterina with 20 comfortable, near business-class rooms with interesting architectural details. Their top-floor view terrace is a sunny and cheery breakfast room—a nice place to sunbathe, and a fine spot to watch the sunset (air-con, elevator, small gym, Piazza Mercato del Pesce, tel. 0923-438-060, www.lagancia.com, booking@lagancia.com, Nino).

$$$ Gaura Apartments, run by La Gancia, offers 11 seaview apartments, all beautifully designed for maximum efficiency. Their penthouse apartment has a private terrace with a 360-degree view (air-con, elevator, kitchen corner, no breakfast, Via Mura di Tramontana, mobile 347-296-3479, www.gauraapartments.com, info@gauraapartments.com, Rosanna).

$$$ Hotel San Michele, hidden in the tangle of streets, rents 42 modern, bright rooms in blue tones clustered around a cozy inner courtyard that feels like an exotic retreat (Via San Michele 16, tel. 0923-23470, www.sanmicheletp.it, info@sanmicheletp.it, Fabrizio).

$$ Hotel Trapani In has 10 tight, modern rooms shoehorned into a small building near the port (Vicolo dei Pescatori 10, tel. 0923-20119, www.hoteltrapaniin.it, info@hoteltrapaniin.it, Stefania).

$$ Central Gallery Rooms is an apartment hotel with spacious rooms and simple kitchens, located in a gracious palazzo (Via Giuseppe Garibaldi 67, tel. 0923-198-6559, www.centralgalleryrooms.com, centralgalleryrooms@gmail.com).

$ Hotel Moderno has 30 budget rooms clustered around a quiet inner courtyard on a side street. The hotel lacks services, but the rooms are tidy, and just as the name suggests, modern (no breakfast, air-con, elevator, Via Tenente Genovese 20, tel. 0923-21247, www.hotelmoderno.trapani.it, info@hotelmoderno.trapani.it, Nicola).

$ B&B Alla Marina is the home of Goffredo Adragna, whose family owns the local cantina on the main street. The top floor used to be his grandmother's apartment, and has been carefully converted into a B&B, preserving the character of the past. The five rooms share a cozy common space with a view of the port (air-con, elevator, Viale Regina Elena 4, tel. 0923-21153, www.bballamarina.it, info@bballamarina.it).

$ Albergo Maccotta is a simple, family-run 24-room hotel on a quiet lane in the old center. While it has almost no character, it's clean, well run, and a fine value for a budget room (air-con, Via degli Argentieri 4, tel. 0923-28418, www.albergomaccotta.it, albergomaccotta@virgilio.it, Antonio).

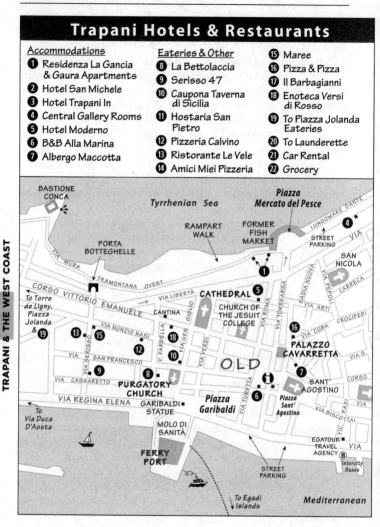

Trapani Hotels & Restaurants

Accommodations
1. Residenza La Gancia & Gaura Apartments
2. Hotel San Michele
3. Hotel Trapani In
4. Central Gallery Rooms
5. Hotel Moderno
6. B&B Alla Marina
7. Albergo Maccotta

Eateries & Other
8. La Bettolaccia
9. Serisso 47
10. Caupona Taverna di Sicilia
11. Hostaria San Pietro
12. Pizzeria Calvino
13. Ristorante Le Vele
14. Amici Miei Pizzeria
15. Maree
16. Pizza & Pizza
17. Il Barbagianni
18. Enoteca Versi di Rosso
19. To Piazza Jolanda Eateries
20. To Launderette
21. Car Rental
22. Grocery

TRAPANI & THE WEST COAST

Eating in Trapani

Trapani is the best place to try Sicilian couscous—traditionally served with a side of fish broth to ladle over it. The town's other specialty is pizza, with crispy crust and lots of cheese, cut into bite-size pieces. Trapani's restaurants sometimes close spontaneously from October through Easter and during bad weather.

IN THE HISTORIC CENTER

$$$ **La Bettolaccia** is a snazzy but unpretentious space tucked deep in the back streets of the old town. They have helpful service

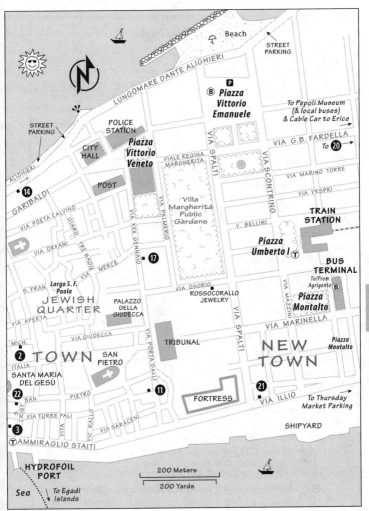

and a tempting menu, including the best fish couscous in town, and a good selection of wines (Mon-Fri 13:00-15:00 & 20:00-23:00, dinner only on Sat, closed Sun, Via Generale Enrico Fardella 23, tel. 0923-25932, Francesco).

$$$ Serisso 47 is a solid option for a romantic, dressy dinner under vaulted ceilings and flower-bedecked branches. Their wine list pairs well with chef Gaetano's thoughtful, gourmet preparations (Tue-Sun 12:30-14:30 & 19:30-22:30, closed Mon, Via Serisso 47, tel. 0923-26113).

$$$ Caupona Taverna di Sicilia, with a "slow food" approach, is a popular spot for locals to gather for big dinners, offering a seasonal menu at reasonable prices. Try their giant cannoli

Marsala Wine

In 1773, John Woodhouse, a cloth merchant from Liverpool, came to western Sicily in search of *barilla*—a salt-resistant plant used in the production of soda ash (a key ingredient in washing powder). In Marsala, he tried a local wine known as *vino perpetuo* ("everlasting wine"). The wine had been aged for decades in wooden barrels in which a fraction of wine was evaporated, and new wine continuously added.

Woodhouse grasped the sales potential of this wine as a competitor for Portuguese Madeira, which was very popular in England. He shipped 8,000 gallons from Marsala to Liverpool; to keep it from spoiling, he added brandy to the oak casks. When the wine arrived, it had taken on a new flavor, which became instantly successful in England. Later, when Madeira wine became scarce due to the Napoleonic Wars, Woodhouse signed an agreement with Lord Horatio Nelson to supply the British Navy with his fortified Marsala wine. Marsala took off after that, becoming a major business in Sicily.

Several other English families followed Woodhouse, including the Whitakers, and the Marsala wine trade created strong financial ties between England and Sicily. (The Whitakers wound up purchasing the island now called Mozia as a retreat—you'll learn more about them if you visit there.)

Marsala wine is a blend with 15-20 percent alcohol, made with a combination of grapes typically including inzolia, catarratto, grillo, and damaschino. There are three colors: amber, ruby, and gold, each of which has its own flavor. While sweet Marsala wine is best known, it also can be dry or semidry. Longer aging creates more depth of flavor—and increases the price. "Fine" Marsala is the cheapest, typically sold as a cooking wine. "Superior" is aged 2 years, "superior reserve" is aged 4 years, "virgin" is aged 5 years, and "virgin reserve," 10 years. Marsala wine became the first DOC *(denominazione di origine controllata)* wine in Italy, meaning that it is given a governmental seal of approval and must be grown in the Marsala region.

Marsala Winery Tour: Cantine Florio is a modern facility near Marsala, about 20 miles south of Trapani on the way to Selinunte, where you can see the winemaking process and learn about their company's history (€13, includes tour and tastes of four wines, reservations required, Mon-Fri 9:00-18:00, Sat until 13:00, closed Sun, Via Florio 1, Marsala, tel. 0923-781-305, www.duca.it, hospitality@duca.it).

Wine Bar in Trapani: Enoteca Versi di Rosso is a good spot to try local Marsala wine, paired with a cheese platter (daily 18:30-23:00, closed Jan, Corso Vittorio Emanuele 63, tel. 0923-27985, Marco).

from the nearby town of Napola (Wed-Mon 12:30-14:30 & 19:30-23:00, closed Tue, Via S. Francesco d'Assisi 32, tel. 0923-546-618, Claudio).

$$ Hostaria San Pietro is a family-run osteria near the port. Its one long room feels tucked away from all the tourists and is filled with locals enjoying the catch of the day (Thu-Tue 12:00-15:00 & 20:00-23:00, closed Wed, Largo Porta Galli, mobile 339-719-8193, Tonino).

$$ Pizzeria Calvino serves precut pizza in a funky building that served as a WWII bordello (look for peephole slits in the walls). The best pizza in town comes with snappy service—typical of proud Italian pizzerias—and the wait can be long. It's smart to reserve in person one hour before opening (Wed-Mon 19:00-23:00, closed Tue, Via Nunzio Nasi 71, tel. 0923-21464).

$$ Ristorante Le Vele has a warm and spacious interior, and is often full of chatty locals enjoying cheesy pizza and good pastas. They open before other restaurants, so it works well for an early dinner (daily 18:30-23:00 except closed Mon off-season, Via Serisso 18, tel. 0923-29743).

$$ Amici Miei Pizzeria is a big, clattery warehouse of dining along the waterfront, with a movie theme. The menu is mostly pizzas, with a few pastas and main courses mixed in. They have an outdoor terrace just across the street from the seawall—making this a great place for pizza with a sea view (daily 12:00-15:00 & 19:30-23:30, Lungomare Dante Alighieri 30, tel. 0923-25907).

$ Maree is a good budget choice, serving deep-fried calamari and other seafood in paper cones. Grab a cone to go, or sit on a stool at the counter (Mon-Sat 9:00-22:00, closed Sun, Via Serisso 15, mobile 334-780-6869).

$ Pizza & Pizza is a humble self-serve joint offering perhaps the cheapest sit-down meal in town right in the old center (a block behind Palazzo Cavarretta). The food is very basic (pizza, grilled sandwiches, microwaved plates of tired vegetables, plastic glasses of wine). Get it to go, or to eat in its sterile, brightly lit interior (Tue-Fri 10:00-14:30 & 17:00-24:00, Sat-Sun 17:00-24:00 only, closed Mon, Piazza Notai, mobile 331-890-8988).

Craft Beer and Pub Grub: $ Il Barbagianni, near the Villa Margherita public gardens at the edge of the new town, is a fun place to experiment with Italian craft beers. They have microbrews both on tap and by the bottle, along with burgers and sandwiches, in an easygoing, modern atmosphere (Tue-Sun 19:00-24:00, closed Mon, Via XXX Gennaio 15, mobile 339-393-6060).

Wine Bar: Enoteca Versi di Rosso has a long list of local wines and light meals to match. Marco and his staff know their wines and can suggest something to suit your tastes (daily 18:30-23:00, closed Jan, Corso Vittorio Emanuele 63, tel. 0923-27985).

Supermarket: A handy **Crai** supermarket is in the tangle of streets behind the hydrofoil port (Mon-Sat 8:00-13:45 & 16:30-20:30, closed Sun, Via San Pietro 30).

ON AND NEAR PIAZZA JOLANDA

For a more local side of Trapani, walk west about eight minutes along the seawall, then take the steps that angle down to the left and continue a block to Piazza Jolanda. This very Trapanese parking-lot square is ringed by restaurants where locals outnumber tourists.

$$ Santa Chiara 19 is a cozy, charming hole-in-the-wall serving reasonably priced local fare—mostly fish and seafood—to a younger-skewing crowd (Tue-Sun 12:30-14:30 & 20:00-22:30, Piazza Jolanda, mobile 329-702-0827).

$$ Antichi Sapori, in the middle of the square, has a longer menu, a rustic interior under vaults, and a huge enclosed terrace (Wed-Mon 12:30-14:30 & 19:30-23:00, closed Tue, Corso Vittorio Emanuele 191, tel. 0923-22866).

$$$ Salamureci, just a block away, is excellent, with quality local fare (including higher-end options such as seafood couscous and sea urchin), a welcoming dining room, and deliberate service (daily 12:30-14:30 & 19:00-23:00, Piazza Generale Scio 17, tel. 0923-21728).

Trapani Connections

BY PLANE

Trapani's **Birgi airport** is a 15-minute drive south of the city. Buses wait just outside of the arrivals hall (hourly, 30 minutes). Taxis connect the airport and downtown Trapani (€30 fixed rate). Trapani's airport has few connections—you're more likely to use Palermo's, a 1.5-hour drive away.

BY PUBLIC TRANSPORTATION

Most buses leave from the port, near the hydrofoil docks and across the street from the Egatour travel agency, at Via Staiti 13. Note that bus companies vary by destination, and few buses run on Sundays. Tickets are available at Egatour (daily 5:30-20:00, tel. 092-321-754). Agrigento and Segesta buses depart from the bus station in Piazza Montalto (tickets sold at Bar Barraco, Via Virgilio 9).

From Trapani by Bus to: Birgi airport (hourly, 30 minutes, Salemi, www.autoservizisalemi.it), **Erice** (5/day, 1 hour, AST, http://www.aziendasicilianatrasporti.it—note that cable car takes just 10 minutes and is more enjoyable), **Segesta** (3/day, 50 minutes, Tarantola Bus, no website—get schedule locally), **Palermo** (hourly, 2 hours, Segesta Autolinee, www.segesta.it), **Palermo**

airport (every 2 hours, 2 hours, Segesta Autolinee, www.segesta. it), **Agrigento** (3/day, 3.5 hours, Salvatore Lumia Bus, www. autolineelumia.it).

By Train to: Marsala (hourly, 30 minutes).

ROUTE TIPS FOR DRIVERS

To reach points south (such as **Selinunte** and **Agrigento**), hop on the autostrada east toward Palermo; soon after passing the Segesta turnoff, take the fork to the right toward *Mazara del Vallo* (autostrada E-90). This zips you south; exit at the olive-growing town of Castelvetrano; soon after is the turnoff for the Selinunte ancient ruins. To proceed to Agrigento, you'll turn east onto SS-115 (blue signs for *Agrigento*). You'll drive across long viaducts over bursting farm fields, then pass through the midsize town of Menfi; soon after, the landscape changes to rocky peaks, and you approach Agrigento. The drive from Trapani to Agrigento takes about 2.5 hours; Selinunte is a little over halfway.

Day Trips from Trapani

From your home base of Trapani, any of the destinations in this section make a fine day trip. To help decide which to visit, see "Planning Your Time," earlier.

Erice

Atop a dramatic mountain overlooking the sea sits Erice (EH-ree-cheh), an ancient village often cloaked in sea mist, worth ▲. Erice is little and quite touristy. But its unusual church, grand views from its castle, easy proximity to Trapani (reachable in 10 minutes by cable car), and delicious sweets make the town a worthwhile 2-3 hour visit. Romantics like to spend the night—enjoying the spooky atmosphere as the tourists roll out and the mountain mist rolls in.

TRAPANI & THE WEST COAST

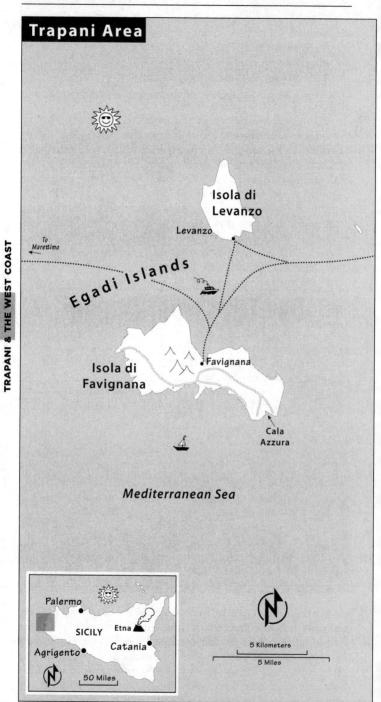

TRAPANI & THE WEST COAST

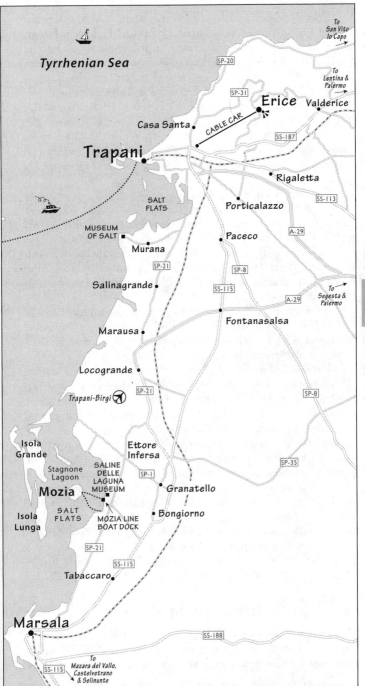

Erice's original settlers were the Elymians, who arrived around 1200 BC from Asia Minor. Unfortunately, little is known about them; they were displaced by the Carthaginians, and later by the Romans. But we do know that all of these ancient cultures worshipped a similar goddess—one related to fertility. The Romans called her Venus Erycina, after Eryx, the ancient city name.

The cliff-capping position of Erice made it a desirable and defensible place to live in the Middle Ages; under the Normans, the city grew to the boundaries you see today. While the village these days is small compared to sprawling Trapani below, it was the opposite in the past: Erice was a thriving city and Trapani simply its port.

Getting to Erice: While you can drive to Erice, it's easiest to take the **cable car** (€9 round-trip, Tue-Sun 9:00-20:00, Mon from 13:00, runs later in summer, closed Nov-March and during high winds, 10-minute ride, departs from station about 6 miles from central Trapani). The cable car drops you a short walk below Erice's main gate (Porta Trapani). Cross the street and walk through the archway on the right, or follow the road around to the right to reach the center of town.

To reach the cable car station in Trapani, you can take **bus** #21 or #23 from Via Giovanni Battista Fardella 14 (every 30 minutes, 15-minute ride). Bus #21 stops directly in front of the station, while #23 stops just around the corner on Via Cosenza.

Drivers can park in the lots in front of the cable car station (€1.50/3 hours). Or, if you enjoy white-knuckle drives, you can twist up the extremely scenic road from Trapani (SP-31, about 30-40 minutes)—less advisable in summer, when the road can be clogged and parking lots full. Once up top, follow signs for *Porta Trapani*, where you'll find a small pay lot; there are also a few spots at the far end of town, near the Castle of Venus. (You'll see other parking lots around town, but I find these the easiest.) The easier approach is simply to park at the lower cable car station and ride up. Since the cable car station is where the switchback road begins, you can decide when you get there. If you're arriving from the autostrada rather than Trapani, exit following signs for *Val d'Erice*.

Tourist Information: A small info kiosk is near the entrance to the city walls, across from the cable car station (daily 10:00-17:00, closed Nov-March, tel. 0915-752-177, www.prolocoerice.it).

Erice Town Walk

This walk introduces you to Erice in about an hour. It begins by sneaking around the back streets—to show you a slice of Erice most tourists miss—then plunges you right back down its touristy main drag to where you started. In this hilly burg, expect lots of up and down.

• *Begin your walk at the simple archway in the stone wall just above the gondola station and parking lot.*

❶ Porta Trapani

This gate, at the western end of the triangular city, is one of the two entrances to the old city of Erice. Examine the lower, larger stones of the walls: These come from the time when the city was allied with the Carthaginians. The city later came under Norman rule, and the walls were fortified (the smaller stones date from this period). While the population in the past reached about 12,000, the city currently has only a few hundred year-round residents...and one priest.

• *Pass through the gate, take the first left, and walk toward the tower.*

❷ Chiesa Madre

The church is called Chiesa Madre—"mother church." Notice that it stands at the town entrance, rather than in the central piazza. The town's cult of Venus was strong, and its temple dedicated to the goddess could be seen for miles around. (We'll see the site

of that temple later.) When paganism fell out of favor, this church—dedicated to a similar female divinity—was built on the opposite side of town, as a counterpoint to Venus.

Approach the church. Notice the large **covered porch.** Called the *gibbena,* this area was reserved for those who were not penitent (they were not allowed to enter the church).

Buy a ticket at the bell tower, then step inside the church (€2.50, daily 10:00-18:00; they also sell a handy town map). The unusual, undulating, stuccoed **ceiling** isn't as old as it seems. While the exterior of the church dates from the 1300s, the interior collapsed

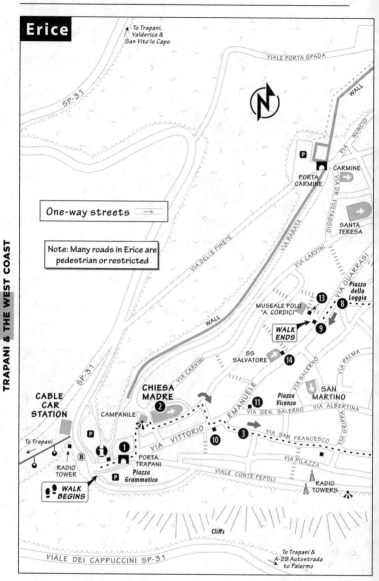

in the late 1800s and was rebuilt in a fanciful Neo-Gothic/Neo-Arabic fusion.

Step up to the **family crest** in the center of the floor. It represents the House of Aragon from Spain, with red-and-yellow stripes. This church was built by the king of Spain, who also happened to rule Sicily at the time.

Turn to the left aisle and find the third chapel. The painting of the **Madonna of Custonaci** is a town treasure. Notice it's set

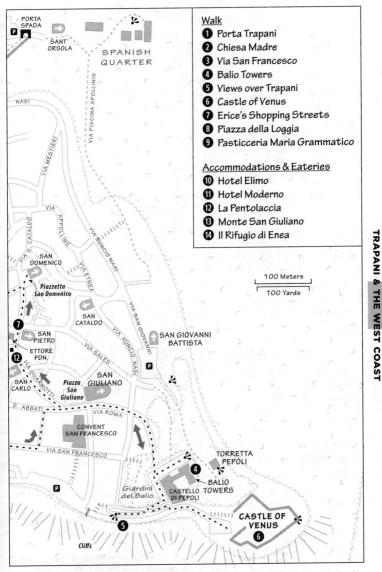

in a special frame that can be carried on processions through the streets—during which townspeople ask for the Madonna's assistance. Just beyond, in the same aisle, find the plaque on the wall that lists the dates of processions held in times of desperate need: rain *(pioggia)*, war *(guerra)*, locusts *(cavallette)*, earthquake *(terremoto)*, and so on *(idem* means "dittos"). These parades were originally held at random in times of need, but the custom grew so popular it became an annual event each August.

To see a more austere original bit of the church from before the reconstruction—with simple stone arches and plain white vaults—go to the last large chapel on the left, which also houses the **treasury.** The Renaissance-era **main altarpiece,** a cascade of marble, is another piece from the older church.

• *Exit and turn left to walk alongside the church building. The nine crosses along the outer church wall are said to be recycled pieces from the original temple of Venus. Reaching the end of the church, continue uphill a few more paces and take the first right; after that, a quick left and a quick right will bring you to...*

❸ Via San Francesco

Follow this quiet lane several blocks gently uphill, nearly to the far end of town. The homes on this residential lane may look plain, but the austerity on the outside is an Arab-Sicilian tradition meant to hide the treasures inside. Look through the gates as you pass, and you'll see that many homes here have fine little courtyards.

Many of the houses here are not inhabited. Erice has become depopulated in recent years, with locals preferring to live down below in the modern suburbs of Trapani. Erice can be cold and windy in the winter, often wrapped in thick, misty clouds, so homes up here are now primarily used as summer retreats.

Continue your stroll, enjoying peekaboo views over the valley on your right. Pay attention on the left (between #80 and #82) for a classic example of a *venula*—a passageway barely wide enough for a person. Erice has many of these passages, which were intended to provide ventilation for the homes around them.

• *Squeeze your way up to the top of this long, skinny venula. When you reach the end, turn right and carry on straight ahead, past the pinkish church, and up the lane until it dead-ends at a wall. Follow the ramp on your right, then curl your way up into the park, Giardino del Balio. Head for the tall, blocky, crenellated towers.*

❹ Balio Towers (Torri del Balio)

These towers still stand from the original medieval castle, some of which was torn down in the 19th century. The rest was refur-

bished as a classy retreat for the Pepoli clan. Salt was a valuable commodity in the past, and the Pepoli family made a fortune at the nearby salt flats in the 19th century. They restored part of the castle to live in and became patrons of the arts (their collection became the foundation of the Pepoli Museum in Trapani).

TRAPANI & THE WEST COAST

Go to the left end of the towers and find the adorable little crenellated **lookout terrace.** Peer between the rocky teeth, over sweeping views of the Sicilian coastline, fertile farmlands, otherworldly Monte Cofano rocketing up at the far end of the bay, and—at your feet—the fanciful little tower called Torretta Pepoli, which was built as the library for the Pepoli family complex.

• *Facing the blocky towers, turn right and walk straight ahead through the gardens until you hit a railing with a fantastico view over the Trapani area. Turn right and walk about 50 yards for the best view (near the drink bar).*

❺ Views Over Trapani

This stunning view suggests why Erice was such a strategic location for centuries. Looking out to sea, you can see hook-shaped

Trapani pointing out toward the Egadi Islands. The island on the left, Favignana, is easy to visit by hydrofoil from Trapani. Notice the modern, concrete, high-rise sprawl between Trapani and Erice's mountain.

Just left of Trapani are the salt pans that put this region on the map economically, and are still fun to visit. Now turn to see the historic castle perched on the hill beside you.

• *This is the...*

❻ Castle of Venus (Castello di Venere)

This rambling, cliff-capping complex is a Norman castle with layers of ruins inside. There are no real exhibits, but scrambling over

its ruins can provide a fun king-of-the-castle experience (€4, daily 10:00-18:00, Nov-March until 13:30).

Whether or not you decide to visit, survey the castle from afar and consider its epic story. This began as a temple to the Phoenician goddess Astarte, built in the seventh century BC, and was later converted into a Roman temple to Venus Erycina. Venus, the goddess of love—like Astarte before her—was important to sailors. Making a sacrifice to her could assure smoother seas: Venus had the power to send Cupid to plant an arrow in the heart of the sea god Neptune, enrapturing him so that the seas stayed peaceful. The sailors came up with a creative way of, ahem, "venerating" the goddess—by paying a visit to the *ierodulai* (priestesses) in this temple. (Today the word *iarusa* means "prostitute" in Sicilian.) This "sacred prostitution" kept the sailors safe...or so they told their wives.

Whatever may have happened on the top of Mount Eryx, there is a special feeling up here—something mystical in the mists that often cover the city.

• *Go back through the park to Via Roma, and retrace your steps down past the pinkish church. Just past the church, where the road forks, bear right to find...*

❼ Erice's Shopping Streets

After enjoying sleepy back streets and communing with the town goddess, we've finally found our way to Erice's tourist gauntlet. While some shops seem tacky, their wares go way back. The tapestries with the zigzag pattern are unique to Erice. The frugal women of Erice used to recycle clothing and fabric scraps, weaving strips together to make sturdy floor coverings. These days, the woven rag rugs are made into artful purses and

tapestries. Some of the shops in Erice have looms; ask for a demo if you see one.

Continue straight as Via Roma turns into Via Guarnotti. At #26 (on the left, just before the overhead passage), you'll pass the Ettore Majorana Foundation, an important conference center and think tank for physicists, established here by a Trapani-born physics professor in 1963.

Walk farther, until you reach the tiny square of Piazzetta San Domenico, one of the loveliest in Erice. Take a look down little Via Antonio Cordici, which veers off from where you enter the square. Some of the shops along the left side of this street (at #22, #10, and #6) show the city's ancient roots: The arrangement of the shop door connected to a window was typical of shops in ancient Carthage.

• *Via Antonio Cordici leads you right into the main square...*

❽ Piazza della Loggia

The lack of real services on this square—banks, markets, or pharmacies—is a reminder that Erice is mostly a tourist spot these days, though there is a sleepy Town Hall and lonely ATM. Even so, the square is a pleasant place for a drink at an outdoor table, if the weather is fine. Hang on, though—you're just steps away from the sweetest part of Erice.

• *Walk straight to the bottom of the square, then turn left down Via Vittorio Emanuele, which is lined with several recommended restaurants. But first, ruin your appetite by dropping in at #14...*

❾ Pasticceria Maria Grammatico

Maria's bakery is an Erice institution, and her almond-based sweets have become famous in Italy. As a child in the 1950s, Maria was sent to live in a convent, where she learned baking techniques from the nuns. She worked long hours in the kitchens, crushing almonds by hand and producing sweets to sell. When she was old enough to leave, she took the recipes she'd learned and opened her own pastry shop—a rare thing for a woman to do at the time. Specialties include *tette delle monache* ("nuns' breasts"), *genovesi* (pastries with custard or ricotta filling), and fresh cannoli. Maria and her assistants can assemble a sampler tray of indulgent sweets if you can't decide where to start (daily 9:00-23:00).

• *Your Erice walk is finished. Use your sugar high to continue downhill a few more blocks on Via Vittorio Emanuele. You'll wind up at the Porta Trapani, right where we began.*

Sleeping and Eating in Erice

Sleeping: Erice is jammed with day-trippers in high season, but spending the night on the mountain—when it's quiet and you have the place to yourself—can be unforgettable. Particularly off-season, evening mists swirl, providing a romantic atmosphere, just as Venus would have wanted.

$$ Hotel Elimo offers 21 old-fashioned rooms in a noble palazzo at the bottom of the main drag (air-con except in 3 economy rooms, elevator, terrace, Via Vittorio Emanuele 75, tel. 0923-869-377, www.hotelelimo.it, info@hotelelimo.it, Floriana).

$ Hotel Moderno was "modern" a few decades ago...probably. Today, its 26 rooms retain a 1970's patina and the same bargain prices in high season (air-con, elevator, terrace, Via Vittorio Emanuele 67, tel. 0923-869-300, www.hotelmodernoerice.it, info@hotelmodernoerice.it).

Eating: Since Erice caters to tourists, its restaurants do, too. Choose wisely. Many restaurants close from November through Easter.

$$ La Pentolaccia, in a 17th-century convent where cloistered nuns used to make sweets, serves a specialty of fish ravioli with swordfish, caper, mint, and eggplant sauce (Wed-Mon 12:00-15:00 & 19:00-22:00, closed Tue, Via Gian Filippo Guarnotta 17, tel. 0923-869-099).

$$$ Monte San Giuliano makes earthy plates such as *fettuccine ai profumi di bosco*—fettucine perfumed by the forest (Tue-Sun 12:15-14:30 & 19:30-21:00, closed Mon, Vicolo San Rocco 7, tel. 0923-869-595).

$ Il Rifugio di Enea offers basic coffee and snacks—handy for a light lunch. They also have a sit-down restaurant area with table service and higher prices. This is an unusual Erice eatery that's open all year (daily 7:00-19:30, Via Vittorio Emanuele 28, tel. 0923-869-142).

Favignana and the Egadi Islands

Just a half hour by boat from Trapani, the quiet Egadi (EH-gah-dee) Islands are a peaceful escape. The trio of islets—Marettimo, Levanzo, and ▲ Favignana—have ancient roots. This was the site of a pivotal naval battle between the Romans and Carthaginians in 241 BC; the Romans prevailed and crushed the Carthaginian fleet, claiming victory in the First Punic War. More recently, the sleepy islands were bases for lucrative tuna fishing. Favignana (fah-veen-YAH-nah) is the easiest to reach and has a fun-to-explore town, a good museum about the local fishing industry, and a few nice beaches reachable by bike. It makes a fun half-day getaway from Trapani.

GETTING THERE

The Liberty Lines **hydrofoil** departs Trapani from the dock on Via Staiti (avoid the larger ferries from the ferry terminal nearby—they take much longer). It's best to buy a one-way ticket and purchase your return on the island; otherwise, you're tied to a departure time (€13 one-way, hourly, 30 minutes, last boat in each direction around 20:00, www.libertylines.it). On Favignana, the boat docks at the small harbor, just in front of the town.

Tuna Fishing

Fishing has always been important in western Sicily, and the sea's top prize used to be bluefin tuna. There were 21 *tonnare*

(tuna canneries) in the province of Trapani at the end of the 1800s, packing high-quality tuna in olive oil for export. Trapani depended heavily on the tuna business for decades.

It all came to an end in the 1980s, when Japanese fishermen came to the Mediterranean and began tracking and netting schools of tuna in the open seas using sophisticated technologies. Their methods took not only the mature tuna but also young offspring. Few fish reached the traditional nets of Trapanese fishermen, and the local tuna fishery collapsed. Florio, the last remaining cannery on Favignana (once known as the Queen of the *tonnara*), closed for good in 2007. The large, ancient cannery warehouses dotting the coast were left idle and empty; some have lately gained new life as hotels and museums (Florio is now a museum).

Tuna is still occasionally caught by local fishermen—especially in May and June, when the tuna migrate past Sicily. Fresh-caught tuna is now considered a delicacy and is very expensive. There is just one remaining cannery in Trapani, processing tuna from other places.

VISITING FAVIGNANA

When you get off the boat, notice the humble fishing fleet of blue-and-white dinghies. Nearby are piles of nets and canopy-covered, stainless-steel fish-processing tables. Now pan to the right, where—across the harbor—you'll see a sprawling industrial facility, with smokestacks and big "garage doors" for boats, from the heyday of Favignana's commercial fisheries. This is now the fine Stabilimento Florio museum. For more on the rise—and fall—of the local tuna industry, see the sidebar.

Towering high above the old factory is the nearly perfect, conical-shaped Mount Santa Caterina. A fortress has stood atop this imposing spot since at least the ninth century; the version you see today was cobbled together under Spanish rule, in the late 15th century.

• *Now continue up the ramp into town.*

Bike Rental: You'll run into a long, orange building with a row of handy rental shops, where you can rent a **bike** or a scooter. If you're spending more than a couple of hours on the island, a bike is a great way to get beyond the main town. (The going rate for a day's bike rental is €5; electric bikes cost more; ask for a helmet; try Noleggio Campo, Scalo San Leonardo 3, tel. 0923-921-599.) The island is dotted with ancient stone quarries and ringed by scenic cliffs and small beaches. Riding from town out to the Cala Azzurra—a beautiful beachy bay at the southeast corner of the island (follow the brown signs on Via Frascia)—takes about 30 minutes, and gives a quick overview of the island. The ride is mostly flat and easy.

• *After the bike-rental shops, turn right and head into town.*

Palazzo Florio and TI: The grand building you'll pass on the right is the Palazzo Florio, built by Ignazio Florio—a wealthy industrialist who bought the entire island (and its fishing rights) in the late 19th century. Today, the palazzo is a civic building that houses the TI (daily 9:30-16:30, closed Nov-March, tel. 0923-925-443).

Piazza Europa and Piazza Madrice: After passing the palazzo, bear left to pop into the inviting Piazza Europa (with the recommended **U Coppu** eatery). At the end of the square, turn up Via Vittorio Emanuele, which takes you up the heart of Favignana's charming, mostly pedestrianized town center, culminating at the main square, Piazza Madrice. Check out the little **Capricci del Tonno** shop, selling old-school tins of tuna—which used to be the island's lifeblood (it's on the corner where you enter the square).

Stabilimento Florio: The only real "sight" in town, this museum housed in a former tuna processing plant is worth ▲. While

it can be difficult for non-Italian speakers to appreciate, it offers a well-presented peek into an old industrial complex (€6; daily July-Sept 10:00-13:30 & 17:00-23:30, June and Oct 10:00-17:00, mid-April-May 10:00-14:00, weekends only in early April, closed Nov-March, mobile 324-563-1991; it's on the harbor, a 10-minute walk from the hydrofoil dock—follow brown *Stabilimento Florio* signs). Your visit includes a tour, but it's usually in Italian only (call ahead to request an English tour).

Even without a guide, the history is powerful. The first exhibit (straight ahead from the entrance) explains the warships of the Carthaginians and Romans, who fought the Battle of the Egadi Islands in 241 BC, which ended the First Punic War. You'll see third-century BC bronze rams that were attached to the bows of these ships, and piles of amphorae, the ancient vessels used for transporting olives and liquids.

Then explore the old fishing factory (to the right as you enter).

Salt Harvesting

Carthaginians began harvesting salt in the area south of modern Trapani in the eighth century BC. They used the salt to cure the fish they caught, mostly tuna. Salt remained a precious resource for more than three millennia—highly valued for its ability to preserve food (in an age before refrigeration). Throughout Europe, salt was worth its weight in gold. The ancient Romans paid their workers a *salario* (from *sale,* the Latin word for "salt"). To this day, when a Sicilian thinks something is too expensive, she might say, "salato!" (meaning salted).

Salt was also an important export, traded as far away as Norway for preserving cod *(bacalau)* for long sea voyages. The Norwegians sent back boatloads of the preserved cod, explaining why that cold-water fish is oddly popular in Sicily and the rest of Italy. Salt continued as an important commodity through the late 19th century, when the Trapani area alone had about 40 salt flats. Nowadays, competition with mass-produced rock salt has reduced the number of active salt flats to fewer than 10.

The Trapani area is ideal for salt harvesting because of its breezy yet sunny climate and its very shallow, smooth, clay-lined sea bed. Ocean water is moved through progressively shallower man-made pools over the course of the summer to evaporate the water and filter out impurities. The color of water in the basins—from blue to orange to pink to milky white—varies based on the depth and the salt concentration. The pink color results when the water becomes so concentrated with salt that the only thing surviving in it is an algae that produces beta carotene. Shrimp eating the algae are consumed by flamingos, making them pink.

The antique windmills scattered in the flats—a unique feature of Trapani salt harvesting—powered an Archimedes screw that moved water from the sea into the starting basin. Wind power also drove the grindstones that reduced the coarse, chunky salt into a more useable powder.

Salt is harvested from June to September. While most production is now mechanized, the best-quality salt is harvested by hand—a labor-intensive practice. Imagine shoveling heavy loads of salt, in blazing heat, with the sun reflecting like a mirror off the water and salt. The salt is stacked in elongated pyramids to dry, and covered over the winter with terra-cotta roof tiles to protect it from rain. The following spring, the previous season's harvest is ground, packaged, and shipped.

Traditional sea salt went through hard times, but it's newly en vogue with cooks and foodies. Most lucrative is *fiore di sale* (better known by its French name, *fleur de sel*). This is the first salt skimmed off the basin in July.

You'll see the cannery *(casa dell'olio)*, where tin cans are neatly lined up on stone tables, and an industrial-sized row of giant kettles, heated by three smokestacks. (Tuna must be cooked before it's canned, and then the cans are heated to complete the preservation process.) A large, darkened hall has video clips of local old-timers describing the old fishing industry (unfortunately, in untranslated Italian). The visit culminates in a giant hall with three dry docks, where you can see giant old wooden boats pulled up on ramps. Illustrations show how the nets could be spread out in this huge hall, and how they were used to block off the mouth of the bay and funnel tuna toward the fishermen's waiting boats.

Eating on Favignana: Prices are much higher here than in Trapani, but it's fun to have lunch on the island. For a fine fish meal, **$$$$ Quello che C'e C'e** has a friendly feel and good pasta in the town center (daily 12:00-15:00 & 20:00-24:00, from main drag head right down Via Garibaldi to #38, tel. 0923-921-480). A bit more affordable is **$$ Il Pakkaro,** an unpretentious pasta shop tucked around the right side of the town church (daily 11:00-15:30 & 18:00-23:00, Piazza Madrice 26, mobile 328-061-3380). For a quick bite on the go, try **$ U Coppu,** near the port; they have deep-fried seafood, sandwiches, and other street food (daily 11:00-22:00, Piazza Europa 33, mobile 388-388-9958).

Mozia Island and Salt Flats

The little island of Mozia, south of Trapani, once supported an ancient trading post, one of the few Carthaginian settlements (i.e., Palermo) on Sicily's west side. A town with defensive walls and a port prospered there for centuries—until the Greeks sacked it in 397 BC. Now privately owned, pleasant Mozia (MAHT-zee-yah) is today little more than a picnic destination—but it's also home to a worthwhile small museum of Greek, Carthaginian, and Roman artifacts. And the salt flats *(saline)* in the shallow lagoon between the island and the mainland are some of Europe's oldest in continuous operation.

Planning Your Time: Mozia pairs perfectly with a trip to the salt flats. The island and the attraction called Saline della Laguna are about 30 minutes south of Trapani and can easily be combined in a day trip—the boat for the island departs directly adjacent to the old windmill at Saline della Laguna. Those with less time should choose the Museum of Salt, just 20 minutes from downtown Trapani.

MOZIA ISLAND

Here, nature, birds, vineyards, archaeological digs of Carthaginian ruins, and a few fine ancient artifacts peacefully coexist. As ancient sites go, there's very little to see. But the boat ride to the island—through salt flats and the Stagnone lagoon marine park—is enjoyable, and the small museum is engaging. For those with an appetite to learn more about the Carthaginians, the trip to Mozia is worth ▲ and a few hours.

Getting There: Two different companies run boats to the island. I prefer the handy **Mozia Line,** which departs right from the windmill. The trip is quick (10 minutes), mellow, and scenic, though it can be canceled in bad weather (€5 round-trip, daily 9:15-18:30, Nov-March 9:00-14:00, runs about every 30 minutes; €10 one-hour lagoon tour also available, mobile 339-490-4090, www. mozialine.com, Mario). Note that the Mozia Line ticket desk shares a kiosk with the Saline della Laguna.

To reach the boat dock by **car** from Trapani, leave town heading south on SP-21, following signs for *Marsala* and *Birgi* (Trapani's airport). After passing the airport and going through the village of Ettore Infersa, follow brown roundabout signs to *Mozia* and *Riserva Naturale dello Stagnone.* When you hit the T-intersection at the shoreline, turn left and drive toward the salt flats; watch for pay parking on the right, near the windmill.

Without a car, you can take a **tour** from Trapani or hire your own **driver;** I like working with Michelangelo Marchingiglio (€80 round-trip transfer, €160 half-day guided tour of salt flats and Mozia, for contact information and tour details, see "Helpful Hints" at the beginning of this chapter).

Island/Museum Cost and Hours: €9 covers your admission to the island and the museum, which is open daily 9:30-13:30 & 14:30-18:30, Nov-March 9:00-15:00, tel. 0923-712-598, www. fondazionewhitaker.it.

Tip: Mozia is often full of mosquitoes. Buy bug repellent at a pharmacy before your visit.

Eating: The big **$$ Mamma Caura** restaurant, overflowing with blue tables along the boat dock at the mainland, has pricey cocktails and decent, basic food with a great view over the salt pans. Over on Mozia Island, there's a fine little **$ café** with good sand-

TRAPANI & THE WEST COAST

wiches and pleasant, shady seating. Both are open basically whenever the boats are running.

Background

In the middle of the lagoon called Stagnone, Mozia is a private island purchased by Joseph "Pip" Whitaker in the late 19th century. Whitaker was part of a wealthy English family that had come to Sicily to make their fortune in the Marsala wine business (for more on that industry, see the "Marsala Wine" sidebar, earlier). Like other upper-class men of the time, he collected art and studied ancient cultures. Whitaker had an interest in archaeology, and suspected that there were ruins of a lost Phoenician city hidden underground. He initiated archaeological digs and—sure enough—unearthed the Carthaginian colony of Motya. A gratified Whitaker rechristened the island with its historical name, Mozia.

❍ Self-Guided Tour

Enjoy the boat ride over—first you'll cut through the middle of the salt pans, then ply the lagoon's shallow waters...just a few feet deep. Notice the captain sighting poles to navigate around rocks. The island is tiny—less than a quarter of a square mile; you can walk from one end to the other in about 15 minutes.

• *As you exit the boat, walk uphill toward the ticket booth. Just past that, you'll reach some information boards. WCs are to the left; beyond the information boards, you'll find a café, and past that, the entrance to the...*

Whitaker Museum

This modest museum displays artifacts from the Whitaker archaeological digs on the island as well as from the area between Trapani Birgi (near the airport) and Marsala. Archaeology wasn't carried out in a professional, systematic way in Sicily until the 1920s; wealthy nobles studied ancient history for fun and did their own excavations as a hobby. Since Whitaker owned the island, he excavated as he pleased—and collected his finds into this homemade museum.

As you enter, grab a flyer with a map and basic information on the sights around the island. Enter the room on the left, and you'll see an aerial photo of Mozia and a model of the Kothon, a sacred rectangular pool. (We'll see this later.) To the right is a small model of the North Gate of ancient Motya under siege. This gate—with its tall towers—suggests how the wall of the city might have looked.

Proceeding through the museum, you'll reach the exquisite (and mysterious) **Youth of Motya,** from the fifth century BC. His identity is unknown, his posture enigmatic. Is he a role model of Greek beauty and harmony striking a pose? Is he a charioteer on parade after winning the Olympics? Is he a portrait of a long-forgotten VIP? What is known is that it's a Greek statue, found in a Carthaginian city, which means it was either purchased by a rich merchant or brought back from the conquest of a Greek city. The youth is well traveled, most recently to Los Angeles, where the Getty Center restored him and added this base.

In the next room, pause at the glass case in the middle. The **seashells** displayed here contain a pigment used to dye textiles that made the Carthaginians famous in ancient times. To make just one gram of the precious purple pigment, 10,000 shells were needed—making the dye as valuable as gold. That's why purple was the color of emperors and kings in ancient times: It was so expensive that only the ruling class could afford it.

Continue into the room with a wall of **funeral stones.** These limestone steles were found in the tophet (necropolis), in the eastern part of Mozia. The slabs have symbols and writing in Phoenician.

Find the terra-cotta **mask** in the glass case on the opposite side of the room. It has sorrowful eyes, but cheerful cheeks. Carthaginians are thought to have made human sacrifices—particularly of infants—to their gods in times of crisis. Because this mask was found in the tophet, a possible place of sacrifice, it's tempting to think it depicts the Carthaginians' attitude toward human sacrifice: a smile for the good the offering might bring, but tears of sadness at the same time. But like so many ancient ways, it is difficult to recapture what motivated the practice.

Now head in the direction the mask is looking. Pause at the partition with photographs of the **Whitaker family.** Look for Pip Whitaker and his two daughters, Norina and Delia. Norina married General Antonino di Giorgio, minister of war under Benito Mussolini. Be-

The Carthaginians

The history of the Carthaginians—the great enemy of the Sicilian Greeks and the Romans—is not well known because they were erased from history by their conquerors, leaving nothing written in their own words. But here are a few things we do know.

The Carthaginians were successors of the seafaring Phoenicians (themselves originally from today's Syria and Lebanon). The Phoenicians were great traders; their name roughly means "the purple people," as they were known for trading rare purple cloth. Around 1000 BC, the Phoenicians colonized modern-day Tunisia, founding a "New City"—Kart Hadascht (Carthage), which became a major trading center in the Mediterranean. From then on, history refers to them as the Carthaginians.

Their talented craftsmen specialized in textiles, jewelry, ivory, glazed majolica tiles, and glass. To trade their goods, talented Carthaginian navigators founded colonies all around the western Mediterranean, establishing a network of trading outposts every 25 nautical miles—the distance they could sail in a single day. They settled as far south as the Atlantic coast of Africa, in modern-day Mauritania. In order to keep track of their business records, they invented a phonetic alphabet with 22 letters.

In the eighth century BC, the Carthaginians arrived in Sicily and established a colony in Motya (Mozia)—just 24 hours of navigation from Carthage. They later founded another port on the north side of the island, Panormus (Palermo). Sicily became a pivotal hub for Carthaginian trade between North Africa, East Spain, Sardinia, Corsica, and West Italy.

Around the same time, the ancient Greeks also began to colonize the western side of Sicily (establishing their first colony in 734 BC—for details, see "The Greeks in Sicily," on page 285). The Carthaginians fought against their Greek neighbors for control of the island and the sea. They raided towns from their home base

fore she died in 1971, Delia left instructions for the creation of the Fondazione Whitaker—a nonprofit foundation for the preservation and maintenance of Mozia, and for the promotion of research on the Carthaginian civilization.

Continue into the room on the other side of the partition, the **Pip Whitaker Room.** Everything here has been left as Pip planned, labeled with tags in his handwriting. In the first half of the room there are findings from Lilibeo: vases, terra-cotta statuettes, lamps, tiny glass jars, and containers. In the middle of the room is a sculpture of two lions attacking a bull, with fragments of the island's fortifications. In the far end of the room are fishing hooks, earrings, arrowheads in bronze, loom weights, and ostrich eggs used in burial rituals.

• *Exiting the museum, head straight down to a tree-shaded area with* at Mozia, eventually establishing dominance over western Sicily. The Greeks took revenge by brutally sacking the large city of Selinunte in 409 BC, and Akragas (Agrigento) in 403 BC—bringing forces of 100,000 men, incredible armies for the time.

A new power rising in the Mediterranean would be Carthage's greatest rival—the Romans. Three Punic Wars ("punic" coming from "Phoenician") pitted the two great powers in a war of attrition (264-146 BC). The most famous conflict featured the Carthaginian general Hannibal, who marched against Rome with his army, mounted on elephants, traveling from Spain over the Alps.

Ultimately, Rome prevailed. Even though Carthage had been defeated, Roman Senator Cato the Elder took to ending all of his public orations with an appeal: *Carthago delenda est*—"Carthage must be deleted." And so it was. The Romans set about erasing the existence of Carthaginian culture—destroying their cities and wiping out their history. The only accounts of the Carthaginians are written not by their own scribes, but by their Greek and Roman contemporaries. These accounts portray the Carthaginians as rootless pirates, and as people who engaged in human sacrifice, possibly involving children.

The complete truth of Carthaginian civilization may never be fully understood. The Phoenicians are credited with inventing the alphabet, but other than funeral inscriptions, there's nothing that records their grand past. We have no names of Carthaginian philosophers, writers, or historians to remember. When visiting the archaeological area of Carthage, only Roman ruins are left—built over the remains of the razed city. Considering how very few remnants of the ancient Carthaginians survive, even the traces at the archaeological site of Mozia become remarkable.

TRAPANI & THE WEST COAST

benches. Just past this, turn right and follow the path to the next stop (watch for the sign to Casa dei Mosaici, Casermetta, *and* Kothon*). Soon you'll reach a large ruined area on your left.*

House of the Mosaics (Casa dei Mosaici)

Survey these ruins to spot scant mosaics made with black and white pebbles. The mosaics depict animals, including lions, bulls, and a lion jumping on a bull. The complex mosaics of the Roman Empire have their roots in this simple type of stonework using cheap materials. This ruin was once a wealthy home with an enclosed courtyard.

• *Now head down to the water and continue along the peaceful southern shore of the island, with the lagoon on your left. As you stroll, you'll notice the city of Marsala coming into view on the horizon. Stay on the waterfront path, and pause when you reach the ruins on your right.*

Barracks (Casermetta)

These ruins were probably military barracks or a watchtower, originally built near one of the towers of the walls. The island was heavily fortified with high walls and surrounded by a shallow lagoon. The Carthaginians had settlements within a day's sailing time, and any call for help could be answered quickly. The people must have felt very safe here, but the city came to a terrible end. The Syracusans surprised

them with an attack using mobile towers, allowing the troops to easily scale the walls. While the fight raged, the call for help was answered, but reinforcements were blocked by a Syracusan fleet waiting in the open sea. Nobody arrived to save the citizens of Mozia, and the city was mercilessly crushed. Notice the red marks on the stones of this tower—likely scorch marks left from the destruction of the city. The men who suffered the most were Greeks living in Mozia, and who were considered to be traitors to their culture.

• *Continue along the coastal trail. Gradually, to the right of Marsala, the long, skinny island called Isola Lunga comes into view. Mozia is just one of three islands in the lagoon; Isola Lunga acts as a barrier island, separating the open sea from brackish waters.*

Pause when you reach the big, rectangular pool on your right.

Kothon

This pool was originally thought to be a dry dock for ships. But a few years ago, the University of Rome excavated and drained the pool. They discovered that spring water was continuously refilling it, and they found a stone pedestal with fragments of feet that corresponded to a statue of a god unearthed nearby. This, along with recently excavated circular walls, made archaeologists change their minds: Now they believe the pool was used

for sacred bathing and religious rituals.

• *Circle all the way around the pool, cross the metal bridge, and head back toward the museum. Once you get there, if you're tired (and tired of sun and/or mosquitoes), you can grab a bite at the café or hop on the boat back to the mainland.*

But if you're intrigued by the Carthaginians and want to see more, extend your visit by about 20-30 minutes by walking to the island's north shore to see a few more ruins.

Optional Detour: North Shore

Back at the museum area, bear left and find the trail leading to the north gate (watch for the sign to *Porta Nord*). This takes you about 10 minutes across the middle of the island, through serene vineyards.

You'll pop out at the **tophet**—the necropolis, where the funeral steles we saw in the museum were found. Turn right and continue along the north shore path (with the water on your left). On a sunny, windy day, you might see lots of kite-flyers and kite-surfers frolicking in the bay at the end of Isola Lunga. You may hear fighter jets screaming overhead: The nearby Birgi airport is used by NATO planes.

After a few minutes, you'll pass more ruins on your right, and finally approach the twin, stubby bases of what was the **North Gate** of the island, with ruins of shops and a main street. This is where the Youth of Motya sculpture was found in 1979. At the shoreline, you'll find traces of a submerged road, which used to pass from the island to the mainland.

From here, continue strolling with the water on your left. This path will take you all the way back to the boat dock in just a few minutes, and along the way you'll see more fragments of the mighty **wall** that once defended Mozia.

As you walk, ponder this: Mozia is an area of 110 acres, but only a quarter of it has been excavated. Imagine what else could be found. For now, the Whitaker foundation has planted some vineyards in the empty fields, allowing new vines to grow alongside the ruins.

SALT FLAT EXPERIENCES

Salt flats sprawl for several miles between Trapani and Marsala; you may see workers tending the salt pans in the shallow lagoon dotted with windmills. While visiting the salt flats, watch for flamingos, herons, egrets, and cormorant—the area is a protected reserve for the many bird species that migrate between Africa and

Europe. For more on this industry, see the "Salt Harvesting"
sidebar, earlier.

Salt Flat Options: There
are two opportunities to get an
up-close look at the salt pans, to
learn about the salt-harvesting
process, and to walk through a
windmill. As these two experiences (both worth ▲▲) are re-
dundant, choose just one: The better of the two, the Museum of
Salt, is close to Trapani—just a 20-minute drive from downtown.
The other salt sight—Saline della Laguna—is about 30 minutes
farther from Trapani, but it's convenient for those going to Mozia
Island.

Museum of Salt (Museo del Sale): This fun little exhibit
comes with a personal touch, since it's part of a family-owned salt-
harvesting facility that goes back for generations. Under a classic old windmill, you'll peruse a three-room museum displaying
traditional salt-harvesting tools. The displays are brought to life
on the 20-minute tour—guided by family members—that tells the
fascinating story with a sense of humor. At the end of the tour, you
can climb up onto the rooftop for a closer look at the 600-year-old
windmill, the salt flats, and the old town of Trapani and Erice's
mountain on the horizon (€3 includes tour, which runs with demand, €1 extra to walk through the working salt pans out back,
daily 9:30-19:00, Via Chiusa in Nubia Paceco, mobile 320-657-
5455, www.museodelsale.it). They also have a **$$** trattoria on-site
(closed Mon except in July-Aug).

Getting There: Head south from Trapani's port on SP-21,
and watch for the turnoff on the right to *Nubia*, then follow brown
Museo del Sale signs.

Saline della Laguna: Compared to the Salt Museum, this is
a more touristy experience, less personal, and more than double
the cost, but it's on the way if you're going to Mozia Island. Your
visit includes an interesting 10-minute film that explains the en-
tire salt-harvesting process. Afterward, you'll explore skimpy ex-
hibits with traditional tools and a few touchscreens, then walk up
the tight, stone spiral stairs to the terrace with the windmill (€7,
daily 9:00-19:00, until 20:30 in summer, can be closed Jan-Feb,
tel. 0923-733-003, www.salinedellalaguna.it). They also organize
guided one-hour visits to the salt flats (€15, in English and Italian,
April-Oct usually daily at 12:00 and 17:00, more in summer.

Getting There: Follow the directions for Mozia Island, earlier.

Ancient Sites in Western Sicily

While Agrigento's Valley of the Temples (see page 196) takes top billing in this part of Sicily, Segesta and Selinunte round out your look at ancient temples on the west side of the island. Segesta makes a good stop between Palermo and Trapani, while a Selinunte visit works well between Trapani and Agrigento.

Segesta

TRAPANI & THE WEST COAST

Just off the freeway halfway between Palermo and Trapani, an ancient theater perches atop a hill with a temple in the valley below. This is the ancient city of Segesta...or what's left of it (worth ▲▲). The theater with its lovely views and the unfinished temple are good places to contemplate the rise and fall of civilizations.

Segesta (seh-JESS-tah) was a city of the mysterious Elymians, people from Asia Minor who settled here, at Erice, and around the tip of western Sicily. The Greeks thought they were colonists from Troy. We don't know much about them, as their language has never been deciphered, but we do know that they intermingled with Greeks and adopted their culture. Segesta played an important role in the Peloponnesian War, and their diplomatic flirtation with Athens contributed to the eventual decline of the great Greek city-state. More on that later...

GETTING THERE

Segesta is about a one-hour drive from Palermo. Coming from there on the A-29 expressway, take the right fork for Trapani and the Birgi airport. A few miles later, be ready for the Segesta exit—it's immediately after a long tunnel, on the right. Exiting here (from either direction), turn right at the roundabout, toward *Segesta Stazione*. (While the site itself is in the opposite direction, you'll park offsite.) Soon after the roundabout, watch on the left for the Segesta parking lot on the hill. Pay at the kiosk and keep your

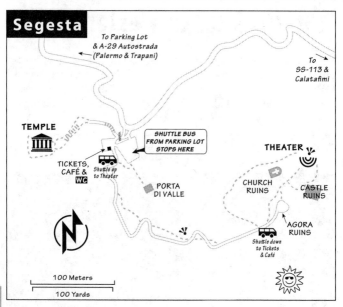

receipt; it serves as your ticket for the parking shuttle to the site entrance (www.segestaparking.com).

ORIENTATION TO SEGESTA

Cost and Hours: €6, daily 9:00-19:30, Oct and March until 18:30, Nov-Feb until 17:00, last entry one hour before closing, tel. 0924-952-356.

Sun Warning: Bring sun protection, as the Segesta site has very little shade.

Services: Near the parking lot are the ticket office, some gift shops, a nice café, vending machines, and WCs. Another, more basic café and WCs are at the site itself.

Shuttle Bus to Theater: Within the site, a shuttle bus runs from the ticket/temple area most of the way up the hill to the theater (€1.50, about 4/hour or with demand, 5 minutes, pay on board). You can ride the bus down, too, but it's a very scenic walk...and much easier downhill.

VISITING THE SITE

The visit to the site is in two parts: the temple and the theater (keep your entry ticket handy, as you'll need to show it at both areas). The temple is a short but steep 10-minute walk from the parking lot (trail begins directly across from the café). The theater is a long, steep, 30-minute uphill hike (about three-quarters of a mile, plus 500 feet of elevation gain; road leads up to the left as you face the café). If you don't want to walk, take the shuttle bus (described earlier).

It makes sense to start with the temple, then head up to the theater for the grand finale. But if the theater bus is leaving soon, you might as well hop on.

Temple

This temple is a beautifully preserved example of Doric Greek architecture, spanning 6 columns by 14 columns. At 69 feet by 183

feet, it is a petite temple for the Greek world of the time. It was built about 420 BC, roughly 25 years after the Parthenon in Athens, and possibly with the help of a Greek architect.

But the temple was never finished. Typically, the columns are made of round, stacked stones connected with pins, and would be fluted after construction to make each column look like one smooth piece. But these columns were never fluted. And the temple is missing other important features as well: It has no cella (the central room used for worship), no roof, and no altar in front.

Historians are unclear as to why the temple was left unfinished, although a common story has emerged: Around 450 BC, Segesta sought an alliance with Athens against their enemies in Seliente. The Segestans were not particularly powerful, so to impress the Athenians, they built this Greek-style temple. It can almost be seen as a stage set rather than a temple—made to impress visiting dignitaries. Once the Athenians signed the pact, the Segestans never bothered to finish the temple's construction. But Segesta's plan failed—Athenian troops never arrived, and the enormous Greek fleet went instead to Syracuse (and was destroyed—eventually leading to the decline of Athens...but that's a story for another guidebook).

Theater

Segesta's small theater has been restored. But its seats, in a concentric semicircle, have many of the original stones. Where you see the view, there would have been a backdrop—the *scena*. Imagine the plays produced here—

both tragedies and comedies. Greek plays were not all blood and pathos...they even had fart jokes, which suggests that some comedy is timeless.

The genius of this theater is the acoustics. Hams enjoy taking the stage and trying it out: Walk to the floor of the theater, to the line of marble in the ground where the stage would have been. Find the center of the theater and take a big step forward. Say something. Sing something. Move around a little until you find the right spot. When you've found the focal point, you'll know it—you'll hear your own voice in your head as if you were wearing headphones. The Greeks used geometry and architecture to create ideal acoustics, so that every seat could hear perfectly, and the actors didn't need to strain their voices. If you're in the focal point, people in the cheap seats can even hear you whisper.

In the hilltop area around the theater, you'll find other ruins from the ancient city, marked by informative plaques in English. For example, the large area where the shuttle bus turns around was the agora. However, these ruins are extremely scant, as the city was built over by the Arabs and Normans before being abandoned 700 years ago.

From the theater, you could ride the shuttle bus back down to the entrance. But consider hiking down the hill (carefully stick to the road, as the gravel paths are slippery). You'll be rewarded with ever-changing views of the temple, framed by flowers and trees. In this setting, you can almost imagine what ancient Sicily looked like.

Selinunte

Near the southwestern tip of Sicily, ▲▲ Selinunte, a once-thriving Greek settlement, lies in ruins like a crushed pile of Legos. The city once covered 250 acres, making the archaeological park a large, picturesque spot. Today it's an evocative collection of temples—one reconstructed, another partially intact, and the rest a pile of toppled columns—spread over two different areas.

GETTING THERE

Selinunte is located on the southwestern coast, about an hour's drive from Trapani, or a 1.5-hour drive from Agrigento. From Trapani, take the main highway, SS-113, back toward Palermo. Just past Segesta, follow signs south to *Mazara del Vallo* on A-29. Exit the highway at Castelvetrano, take a left from the offramp, then the next left, following brown signs to *Selinunte*. The archaeological park is about 20 minutes down the road; park at the main entrance at the concrete roundabout on the right.

PLANNING YOUR TIME

The site has two major sections, on adjacent hilltops overlooking the sea: the temples in the Eastern Agora (Agorà Orientale; also called the Eastern Hill or Collina Orientale), and the Acropolis. On a quick visit, the Eastern Agora temples are the priority—you can see them in about an hour. With another hour, drive over to the Acropolis as well. A third area—the Malophoros—is skippable.

Note that Selinunte sits just a 20-minute drive from the town of Castelvetrano, which is synonymous with its famous, plump olives. While you might be tempted to explore the town, don't bother—it's pretty much the pits, and might crush your romantic affection for its famous product.

ORIENTATION TO SELINUNTE

Cost and Hours: €6, daily 9:00-19:00, Nov-Feb until 17:00, March until 18:00, last entry one hour before closing, tel. 0924-46251, en.visitselinunte.com.

Getting Around the Site: Just inside the ticket building, you'll see signs for a private, pricey shuttle service (€3 to the temples, €6 to the Acropolis area). Skip this, and just drive yourself between the two different areas, both of which have free parking lots. After seeing the Eastern Agora, get in your car, turn left as you face the ticket building, show your ticket at the little kiosk, and drive down the service road to park at the Acropolis area.

Services: Within the site, WCs are in the house just to the right of Temple E.

Eating Nearby (and at the beach): A few scruffy, touristy cafés face the parking lot; more are on nearby streets. In the warmer months, it's worth venturing to the nearby beachfront village of Selinunte, with a fun strip of eateries (to get there, turn right at the roundabout when you exit the archaeological site; where the road seems to dead-end, turn sharply left/downhill). The most appealing of these is the first one you'll reach: **$$ Lido Zabbara** offers a lunch buffet with a tempting table of regional specialties, plus other basic light meals à la carte. It's a rustic, boardwalky spot overlooking a private beach where you can pay to rent an umbrella and chairs, and swim with a temple view (buffet available March-Oct daily 11:30-16:30, beach open May-Oct, tel. 0924-46194).

BACKGROUND

Selinunte was established in 628 BC as a colony of Megara Hyblea, a Greek city on the eastern coast of Sicily. For two centuries, Selinunte grew and prospered. But this expansion caused friction with the city on its northern border, Segesta—an Elymian city under the protection of Carthage.

The Greeks on the east and south coasts and the Carthaginians in the west were in constant conflict, fighting over control of Sicily. In 480 BC, the Sicilian Greeks—led by the tyrant of Syracuse—won a massive battle against the Carthaginians at Himera. The Segestans lost their powerful ally and needed a new protector. They called out to mighty Athens, the enemy of Sparta and Syracuse.

In 413 BC, the Athenians sent an expedition to battle Syracuse and lost. Four years later, the Carthaginians invaded in full force, and, after a nine-day siege, defeated Selinunte before help could arrive from Syracuse. The city was almost totally destroyed, but the Carthaginians decided to move in, inhabiting the Acropolis and setting up temples to their own gods.

Two centuries later, the Romans conquered Sicily, setting the stage for a new conflict with Carthage. The remaining Carthaginians at Selinunte moved to their stronghold at Lilibeum (modern Marsala), and Selinunte was abandoned for good.

VISITING THE SITE

Begin at the trio of temples of the Eastern Agora—which is the first zone you'll reach as you drive in. After buying your ticket, go out back and head for the big temple. While there are a few information boards posted around the site, most visitors simply treat Selinunte as one big toppled-column photo op.

Eastern Agora

The first temple you reach is the remarkably big and intact **Temple E.** There's just one problem: It's not original. This temple was reassembled in the 1950s—a practice that archaeologists today would never consider. (Reconstructing a temple willy-nilly and moving blocks around can change the interpretation of the site.)

On the other hand, this is one of the few Greek temples in Sicily you can actually enter. Climb up the steps and walk around the interior. The peristyle (outer line of columns) is fairly intact, but the inner sanctum (cella) is just a footprint. (For more on the layout of a Greek temple, see the sidebar on page 389.)

Just beyond is **Temple F,** about the same size but still mostly ruined, with a half-dozen stubby columns poking up. A stroll around this temple offers a good look at toppled columns—like great towers of checkers knocked over by a giant toddler. You can see clearly the indentation in the center of each drum, where it was attached to the next one with pegs.

Next up is **Temple G,** a massive pile of monumental rubble. This was once set to be among the largest temples ever constructed in the Greek world. Measuring over 300 feet long and 150 feet wide, it would have been as tall as a modern 10-story building. Only one lonely column remains standing. The temple, which should have been similar in size to the Temple of Olympian Zeus at Agrigento, was never completed. A nearby quarry, the Cava di Cusa, still holds cut blocks, waiting for delivery to the temple. It's worth walking all the way around Temple G, noticing the massive circumference of its toppled column drums compared to Temple F—big temple, big columns.

The building between Temple G and the sea houses a modest **archaeological museum,** called Baglio Florio. Displaying only scant artifacts, it's skippable; most of the best finds are on display at Palermo's Salinas Regional Archaeological Museum (see page 59).

Looking out to sea, you'll spot a ruined colonnade on the adjacent hilltop—our next stop.

• *Head back to the entrance building, hop in your car, and drive over to the second area of Selinunte, the...*

Acropolis

Above the sea, to the west of the temples, is the city center at the Acropolis. Approaching from the parking lot, you'll huff up a ramp around the stout city walls of this fully enclosed, well-fortified city.

Circling around back,

TRAPANI & THE WEST COAST

climb up the stone stairs toward the still-standing colonnade of the Acropolis' centerpiece, **Temple C**—what's left of a temple to Apollo. Loop around this structure, surrounded by toppled columns and the remains of other temples.

Even more interesting, perhaps, are the foundations of **shops and homes** that surround the Temple C ruins. Explore, imagining what it was like when this was a thriving city. From the stony footprints, try to mentally resurrect the rubble: people scurrying to and fro, shopkeepers calling out their wares, and so on. A few doorstep mosaics still survive, which would have indicated what each shop sold (as you face Temple C from the top of the steps, find one of these down the "street" on your left, roped off).

The wide "street" that leads back to the left of the Temple C ruins leads through a part of the Acropolis that's unexcavated and overgrown with bushes—but you can clearly see where the city blocks once stood. At the end of this drag, you'll come to the stout ruins of the city's **North Gate.**

AGRIGENTO & THE VALLEY OF THE TEMPLES

Of all the ancient sites in Sicily, the string of Greek temples on the southwest coast at Agrigento is the most impressive. In the fifth century BC, Agrigento had a population of 200,000 and was the third largest city in the Greek world (after Athens and Syracuse). To realize that 2,500 years ago two of the top three cities in the Greek world were in Sicily is another reminder of the often-underestimated importance of this island in ancient times.

Today, the modern city of Agrigento (pop. 60,000) fills a hillside above the Valley of the Temples—an ensemble of ancient temples unlike anything you'll see elsewhere. You'll enjoy a long, scenic downhill stroll, with stops at some of the best surviving buildings from antiquity. And a fine museum filled with artifacts offers a glimpse into the culture of ancient Agrigento.

PLANNING YOUR TIME

Agrigento is worth a full day for visiting its cliff-hanging temples and museum. While most tourists come just for a few hours to see the ancient site, those who stay the night can also enjoy the modern city's historic center or surrounding countryside. A good plan is to arrive by midday, tour the museum, then see the temples (as it's cooling off and getting less crowded; the temples are floodlit after dark). If you're overnighting here,

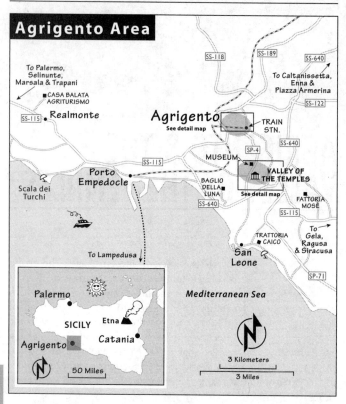

Agrigento Area

To Palermo,
Selinunte,
Marsala & Trapani

CASA BALATA
AGRITURISMO

SS-115   Realmonte

To Caltanissetta,
Enna &
Piazza Armerina

SS-118   SS-189   SS-640

SS-122

Agrigento
See detail map

TRAIN
STN.

MUSEUM   SP-4   SS-640

SS-115

Porto
Empedocle

Scala dei
Turchi

BAGLIO
DELLA
LUNA
See detail map

VALLEY OF
THE TEMPLES

FATTORIA
MOSÈ

SS-640

SS-115

To
Gela,
Ragusa
& Siracusa

TRATTORIA
CAICO

To Lampedusa

San
Leone

SP-71

Mediterranean Sea

Palermo

SICILY

Agrigento

Etna

Catania

50 Miles

3 Kilometers

3 Miles

enjoy the *passeggiata* in the town center (see my "Agrigento Town Walk"), then settle into a countryside hotel before heading out the next morning.

For strategies on visiting the museum and temples, see "Valley of the Temples," later.

Orientation to Agrigento

The city of Agrigento stretches east-west along a hillside, with the historical core in the center. In the middle—where you'll arrive by train, bus, or car—you'll find a tidy little park with a TI kiosk (near Piazza Vittorio Emanuele). The main drag—Via Atenea—leads from here toward the Arabesque neighborhood up the hill known as the Kasbah.

But the main reason for your visit is about a mile and a half to the south, where the Valley of the Temples Archaeological Park runs along a ridge, with the Temple of Juno on the high, east end and the Temple of Castor and Pollux on the low, west end. The

Pietro Griffo Archaeological Museum and most recommended hotels are in the countryside between the city and the temples.

TOURIST INFORMATION

In town, there's an unreliable tourist information kiosk not far from the train station, in the park at the end of Via Atenea (unpredictable hours, theoretically daily 9:00-19:00). A seasonal TI may be open at the Valley of the Temples' Porto V entrance.

ARRIVAL IN AGRIGENTO

For directions on continuing to the Valley of the Temples from Agrigento by taxi or city bus, see "Valley of the Temples—Getting There," later.

By Train: Trains from Palermo arrive at Agrigento Centrale station, a block below the city center (and about 1.5 miles above the temples). The historical center is a five-minute walk: Turn left (uphill) at the stoplight in front of the station, then bear left through the park (with the TI) to find the main drag, Via Atenea.

By Bus: The main bus terminal is at Piazzale Rosselli, on the "back side" of the city's ridge. It's a five-minute walk to the historical center: Walk between the round fascist-era post office and the Cine Astor, carry on uphill to the park, and turn right to find Via Atenea.

By Car: Drivers should head first to the temples and museum (see "Valley of the Temples—Getting There," later). After your visit, to reach Agrigento's town center from the temple area, follow the road up past the archaeological museum and parking lot, taking the right fork for *Centro* onto Via Passeggiata Archeologica. Passing ancient ruins and winding up the hill, this road becomes Via Francesco Crispi, which leads to the train station. Take a right in front of the train station to find pay parking lots just past the park at the entrance to town (on Piazzale Vittorio Emanuele). Another parking lot lies beyond the train station, on Via Empedocle.

Tours in Agrigento

Local Guide

Michele Gallo is a scholar of archaeology and leads an excellent tour of the temples and the museum. For those with more time, he offers tours covering topics such as World War II or Sicilian authors, including one for fans of Andrea Camilleri's Inspector Montalbano mysteries (€60/hour, 2-hour minimum, mobile 360-397-930, www.sicilytravel.net, gallotourguide@gmail.com).

Sicilian Writers

The area around Agrigento, on the southern coast of Sicily, has produced some of the best Italian authors of the 20th century. Their writings explore different aspects of the Sicilian experience, but all agree that, in Sicily, everything is either comedy or tragedy (and often both).

Luigi Pirandello (1867-1936), from Agrigento, won the Nobel Prize in literature in 1934. He wrote about the human condition and the absurdity of it all. His most famous work, the play *Six Characters in Search of an Author,* premiered in 1921 and became a classic of absurdist theater.

Leonardo Sciascia (1921-1989), from Racalmuto, focused on the political and social situation in Sicily in the mid-1900s. His 1961 novella *The Day of the Owl* is a mesmerizing account of the Mafia's hold over Sicilian village life.

Andrea Camilleri (b. 1925), from Porto Empedocle, created the character of Inspector Montalbano—a modern Sicilian version of Sherlock Holmes. His popular mystery series chronicles the detective's adventures in solving crimes while painting a picture of the quirks of Sicilian culture. For more on the series, see page 261.

Local Drivers

Carmelo Patti drives in the Agrigento area, and can take up to four people (€145/half-day—4 hours, €165/full day—7 hours, tel. 0922-31222, mobile 348-017-8474, info@pattibus.it).

Lillo Amato is another reliable driver in the Agrigento area (€145/half-day by car for 1-4 people or by minivan for 4-8; €165/full day by car—€185 by minivan); he also does airport transfers to any Sicilian airport for a flat fee (€150 for up to 4 people, €200 for up to 8, mobile 335-661-8345, amalillo@libero.it, www.autoserviziamato.it).

Agrigento Town Walk

After your Valley of the Temples visit, if time allows, let curiosity lure you into town for this half-hour stroll. The majority of people who visit the magnificent temples near Agrigento never bother to set foot in the modern city. While understandable, that's unfortunate. Those who do take a look find a pleasant

workaday town—worth ▲—crammed with enticing eateries and a main drag that's well suited for a *passeggiata.*

• *From the train station or nearby parking lots, head through the little park and turn onto Via Atenea, stopping at the...*

Porta di Ponte Gate: The Porta di Ponte is the gateway to a fun-to-stroll section of Via Atenea, lined with shops and tempting eateries. Stairstep lanes lure you up and down off this artery. Before passing through, look above at the niche on the left side of the street, and notice the carving of three telamon giants, like the ones at the Temple of Olympian Zeus in the archaeological park. This is the symbol of the city of Agrigento.

• *Now walk down Via Atenea a couple of blocks into town, watching on the right for...*

Pasticceria Infurna: This classic shop (at #96) serves an excellent selection of pastries and unique sweets, such as almond "shells" stuffed with pistachio paste. Everything's made in the shop at this family-run spot, and they have good gelato in summer.

• *Continuing along Via Atenea, you'll soon come to a pair of...*

Side-by-Side Churches: On the right is the clunky brick front of **Santa Rosalia,** whose Baroque facade was taken down in 1951 for repairs. The pieces were numbered for reassembly and...disappeared—possibly decorating a local convent's garden. The citizens are petitioning the city to reconstruct it, but no luck yet. Right next door is **San Lorenzo,** a "Purgatorio" church where the faithful come to pray their naughty relatives out of purgatory.

• *A little farther down Via Atenea, where the street bends, watch for the small triangular square on the right (home to the popular Cantiere 12.25 cocktail bar). At the back of the square you'll see colorfully painted stairs luring you up...*

Via Neve: *Neve* means "snow" in Italian, and this street was once where ice collected in the nearby mountains was sold. The ice sellers have since been replaced with artists—take a quick detour up the steps to enjoy the street-art scene.

• *Back on Via Atenea, you'll soon come to a frilly gray building with a bell tower and clock (on the left). This is the Neo-Gothic **chamber of commerce**, from 1871, which replaced an earlier City Hall building. Walk a little farther until you reach...*

Piazza Pirandello: This piazza marks the end of Via Atenea. Here you could stop for coffee and a sweet at the recommended Café Concordia—try their "ricottamisu," a delightful Sicilian take

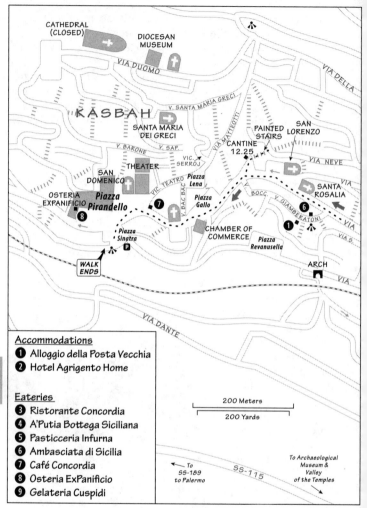

AGRIGENTO

on tiramisu. Then walk downhill two minutes more to **Piazza Sinatra** and a terrace with a grand view overlooking the valley and the sea beyond. If you're in the mood for gourmet fare, sit down for a meal at the recommended Osteria ExPanificio.

• *Our walk is finished. But to explore farther, you could hike 10 more minutes to the upper end of town. From Piazza Pirandello, walk up the right side of the ivy-draped theater (Teatro Pirandello) and climb the stairs leading up into the...*

Kasbah Neighborhood: In this tight, tangled, Arab-style neighborhood you'll find the cathedral (usually closed to the public) and the **Santa Maria dei Greci** church (free, Tue-Sun 10:00-13:30 & 15:30-19:00, closed Mon, mornings only in winter). This

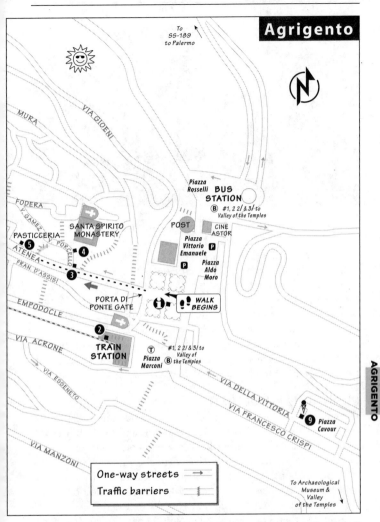

humble 12th-century church was built over the ruins of a Greek temple, which you can see through the glass panes in the floor. On the right are stone seats, where, back in the Middle Ages, cadavers were placed and drained of blood as part of a preservation process.

Exiting the church, find a passage on the right. You can see the steps of the temple, used as a foundation for the church. The structure was about the same size as the Temple of Concordia in the Valley of the Temples. Ponder the fact that the original ancient city stretched from the top of this hill all the way out to the valley—with even more temples that are now long gone.

Valley of the Temples

The Greeks began colonizing Sicily's eastern coast in the eighth century BC. About 150 years later, the now-Sicilian Greeks (Siceliots) established a colony here, calling it Akragas, which quickly became one of their wealthiest city-states. They displayed their prowess by building 15 grand temples in under 80 years, rivaling the great temples of Greece itself. Imagine the *"bella figura"* (grand impression) this must have made on sailors from all corners of the Mediterranean as they approached by sea. A destination for young aristocrats on their "Grand Tour" of continental Europe in the 18th century, this ancient ensemble inspired painters and poets of the Romantic Age—and has inspired visitors ever since.

PLANNING YOUR VISIT

A complete visit here has two main parts, about a half-mile apart: the **Pietro Griffo Archaeological Museum** and the **Valley of the Temples Archaeological Park.** Allow about one hour for the museum, and two hours for the archaeological park.

From May through September, it's best to see the archaeological park's temples early or late and visit the air-conditioned museum during the blazing midday. It works well to do the museum after lunch, then head to the archeological park in late afternoon. In the peak of summer (mid-July-mid-Sept), consider visiting in the relative cool of the evening (the temples are open late into the night, and romantically illuminated).

How to structure your visit also depends on your transportation. For drivers, the best plan is to see the archaeological museum first (setting the stage for the temples) and then visit the temple site. By bus/taxi, it's better to see the temples first, then the museum (note closing times). For details, see "Getting There," next.

With More Time: Consider a visit to the Kolymbethra Gardens (near the western downhill end of the temple ridge).

GETTING THERE

The Valley of the Temples sits between the modern city of Agrigento and the coastline. (The moniker is something of a misnomer—although downhill from the city center, the temples sit along a ridge rather than in a "valley.") The museum is in the countryside between the temples and the modern city.

When planning your arrival, note that there are two entrances to the archaeological park: The **Temple of Juno** entrance is at the eastern end, at the top of the hill; the **Porta V** (a.k.a. Porta Quinta) entrance is at the lower western end. You can exit from either entry. You can also exit in the middle, between the **Temple of Zeus** and the **Temple of Hercules**—across from Bar Ristoro, souvenir stands, and a stop for buses returning to town (and the archaeological museum).

By Car: To reach the temples and museum directly from Trapani and points west, as you approach on coastal road SS-115, you'll pass through congested Porto Empedocle. On the far side of Porto Empedocle, when the road forks, bear left to stay on the main road, signed *Caltanissetta, Palermo,* and *Siracusa*—don't turn off to the right for *Agrigento.* Continue on SS-115/SS-640 for about three miles, and then take the exit to Agrigento. (If coming across the middle of the island from Palermo and points north, follow signs to *Valle dei Templi* to reach this same exit).

Once on this road, you'll soon hit a big roundabout. For the **museum,** continue straight through the roundabout, following blue signs to *Agrigento.* You'll drive through the temple area and under a pedestrian bridge, then pass the museum (the easy-to-miss parking lot entrance is next to the gas station, beyond the museum on Via Passeggiata Archeologica). Parking is €3.

Or, if you're heading to the **temples,** at the roundabout take the third exit (heading west), following signs to *Villaseta* and *Giardino della Kolymbethra.* Look for the blue *P* signs to reach the **Porta V** parking lot and entrance. While it's possible to park at the Temple of Juno entrance, by parking here at Porta V (€3.50), you can take a shared shuttle taxi up to the **Temple of Juno** entrance (€3/person, find the taxi shelter and ask for a ride, 5-minute trip), explore the site on a gentle downhill walk, and finish back at your car.

By Taxi, Bus, or a Combo: City buses and taxis connect Agrigento's bus and train stations to the temples and museum. The best plan is to ride ten minutes by **taxi** (€10-15—be clear on the price before you get in; Agrigento Taxi Coop, mobile 327-496-4365) or **bus #2/** (€1.20, €3.40/24 hours, about hourly) to the convenient **Temple of Juno** entrance, at the uphill end of the temple site, which allows for an easy, downhill visit.

AGRIGENTO

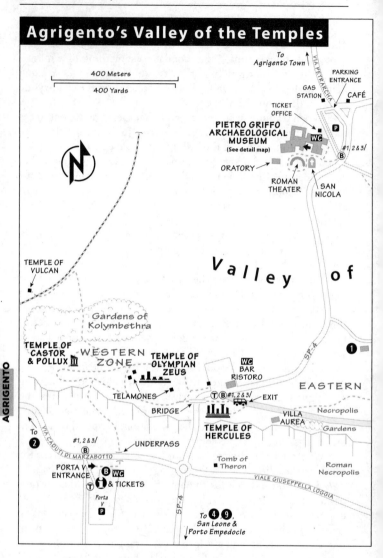

Agrigento's Valley of the Temples

AGRIGENTO

To continue from the temple sites to the **museum,** you can grab a **taxi** at the lower Porta V entrance or exit at the Temple of Hercules (across from Bar Ristoro) to catch any **bus** heading toward town (bus #1, #2, or #3/—tell the driver you want to get off at the museum). You can also walk: From the Hercules exit, the museum is 10-15 minutes away on foot; head uphill to the right.

After your museum visit, you can catch any of these buses back to the bus and train stations. Taxis don't wait at the museum or the park.

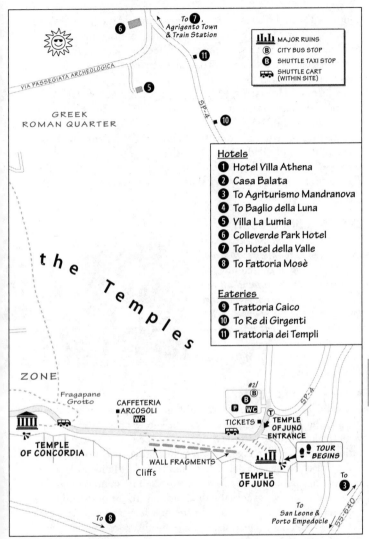

AGRIGENTO

PIETRO GRIFFO ARCHAEOLOGICAL MUSEUM

Built within the arches of a 14th-century Cistercian monastery, this ▲ museum (Museo Archeologico Regionale Pietro Griffo) helps visitors envision the civilization that created the Valley of the Temples. While 900,000 people visit the archaeological site annually, too few take advantage of the museum, which helps bring the temples to life. Its central room is built around a telamon, a stone giant from the Temple of Olympian Zeus. The well-designed collection covers about 2,000 years of life on the shores of the Agrigento area. You'll see vases from Greek settlers of the sixth to third century BC, providing a fascinating glimpse into the fun and frolic of ancient times. With so many great Greek works found in Agrigento, it's clear that this important and wealthy city traded extensively with the wider Greek world.

Cost and Hours: €8, €13.50 combo-ticket with Valley of the Temples Archaeological Park, Mon-Sat 9:00-19:30, Sun 9:00-13:30, tel. 0922-401-565.

Eating: Just uphill from the museum, **$ La Promenade** offers a cold case of salads and pasta dishes—just point to assemble a plate—as well as sandwiches and desserts (open long hours daily). For more (and better) eateries a short drive away, see the "Eating in Agrigento" section, later.

❂ Self-Guided Tour

• Approaching the museum, purchase tickets at the kiosk to the right of the gate. Follow museo *signs on elevated walkways around an excavated theater—setting the stage for the artifacts you're about to see. Once inside, head left into the exhibit.*

The one-way loop begins with Greek artifacts.

❶ Mycenaean Objects

Long before the temples were built in Agrigento, earlier Greek people, the Mycenaeans, landed on the shores of Sicily and traded with the local tribes. (The Mycenaeans seemed as ancient and mysterious to the Golden Age Greeks as Socrates and Plato are to us.) This part of Sicily had deposits of sulfur and bitumen, a key waterproofing ingredient the Mycenaeans used in shipbuilding. The Mycenaean culture eventually died out, but traces of its influence were left on the local style of art. The first few cases display terracotta vessels, bronze spearheads, and—in the third display case—a *fibula* (safety pin) from more than 3,000 years ago.

Farther along is a replica of a **gold Patera dish.** Wine was drunk from shallow dishes like this in ancient times.

Continue around to the right, and in the second case, look for the **Triskeles Bowl.** This was made in the seventh

Pietro Griffo Archaeological Museum

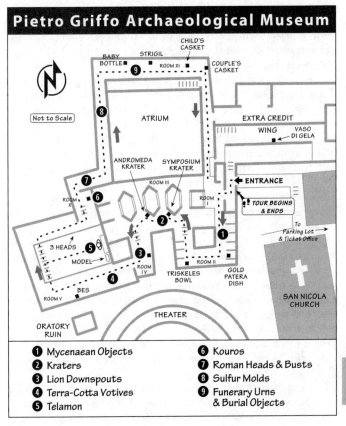

Not to Scale

- **1** Mycenaean Objects
- **2** Kraters
- **3** Lion Downspouts
- **4** Terra-Cotta Votives
- **5** Telamon
- **6** Kouros
- **7** Roman Heads & Busts
- **8** Sulfur Molds
- **9** Funerary Urns & Burial Objects

AGRIGENTO

century BC, and is decorated with the earliest representation of the three-legged symbol of Sicily, the Trinacria. The three legs likely represent the tips of the triangular island, and the face in the center is often identified as Medusa, possibly an allegory for Mount Etna—Medusa turned people into stone, while Etna created new stone. The symbol has been used on Sicilian flags since 1282. (For more about the Trinacria, see the sidebar on page 55).

· *Go up the stairs to a room with display cases featuring a variety of...*

❷ Kraters

These Greek terra-cotta urns were used as mixing bowls for wine. Greeks brewed up strong wine, and before serving it, mixed it with water in a krater. Depending on the time of day (or how drunk

partygoers were), the host could secretly mix more water into the wine to keep their guests' alcohol intake under control. Most of the kraters are decorated with scenes of fun-loving parties or wine-themed antics.

Examine the kraters in the first case at the top of the stairs. These are the earliest in the collection, typical of the sixth century BC, with black figures on a red background. Later, in the fifth century BC, artists realized that if they reversed the technique—black backgrounds with figures in the red clay color—they could add more detail, movement, and skin tone to the figures.

In the lower-right corner of the second case, find the krater with a scene of a **symposium** (circle around the case to see both sides). While to us "symposium" means a meeting for discussion, the original Greek word, *sumpótēs,* meant "drink together"—a drinking party for men. Around back, find the female figure, playing a flute. The women featured in these scenes, called *hetairai,* were typically professional "entertainers" rather than partygoers. Similar to Japanese geishas, these women were educated in music and conversation, and artists such as Praxiteles used them as models. This krater shows a symposium nearing the end. When the wine was almost gone, the men would use the last drops for a target practice game called *kottabos.* They would flick drops of wine at a target, and the man who got closest won a night with the lady in the scene. Some of the other kraters in these cases have similar symposium scenes.

In the fourth case of this section, look for the krater with a wide white band, with lower handles. This is one of two known ancient Greek vessels made from kaolin, a white clay used in making fine porcelain china. The illustration shows lovestruck Perseus liberating a handcuffed (and exasperated) Andromeda.

Stroll around to admire the variety of scenes and patterns on the kraters. Notice that some kraters devote more space to abstract patterns and less to decorative scenes. As time passed, Greek pottery was made in larger quantities, and it was quicker and cheaper to decorate them in bold patterns.

Outside the nearby windows are terra-cotta amphorae, containers used to ship wine and olive oil. They were made long and slender, with a pointed bottom, so they could be sunk into the sand lining the cargo holds of ancient ships, preventing tilting and spilling. Amphorae and their contents would have been the typical Sicilian commodities traded to Greece for fine pottery like you see here.

• *Down the steps from the krater collection are...*

❸ Lion Downspouts

The cat faces hissing at you as you walk by were not just a decoration for the temples, but served a practical purpose. These downspouts drained the temple roofs and also warded off curses (similar to the French gargoyles on churches). Imagine these lions peering down at you in their original state, with brightly painted faces and gleaming white teeth.

• *The next hall is lined with several cases displaying...*

❹ Terra-Cotta Votives

These terra-cotta figures, in a variety of shapes and sizes, are votives—figures offered to the gods to ask for protection, healing, or the granting of a wish. Votives were made from various materials: marble or bronze for wealthy people, cheap terra-cotta for everyone else. They were sold in shops near the temples and brought to the altars, then left as an offering. The terra-cotta figures were produced in large quantities by using molds (some of which are displayed here). Women are common devotional figures, and a

worshipper could buy a figure of the specific goddess from whom they were asking help.

About three-quarters of the way down, at hip level, look for the mischievous, squatting creature. This little guy is Bes, a home protector and an ancient version of the common garden gnome. He was probably situated near the entry to the house, and was believed to look out for all that was good in the home. He was also a protector of women and childbirth, which probably explains his funny posture.

• *Dominating this room—on the wall over your right shoulder—is the gigantic...*

❺ Telamon (Stone Giant)

The centerpiece of the museum is the larger-than-life figure of the telamon, a unique feature of the massive Temple of Olympian Zeus. This is the most complete survivor, and one of many that stood between its towering pillars.

• *Walk down the stairs to see him up close.*

On the right is a cork model of the temple where the telamon once stood. This was the largest Doric temple ever constructed in the Greek world—as tall as a modern 10-story building. Imagine the overall scale of it, covering 370 feet in length—something, it must have seemed to the ancients, that only the gods could create.

This telamon was just one of 38 sandstone figures that decorated the sides of the supersized temple. The telamon has small feet

compared with the rest of his body, but if you kneel down below him and look up, you can understand why: He would have been displayed about 40 feet up, putting his small feet into proportion with his massive torso.

On the left, you'll see three heads from other telamon figures. Each reveals a different ethnicity. The Greek world was international, spread over three continents, and these figures represented the extent of the known world. Notice the white plaster on the face on the left. The golden sandstone of the telamon was covered in plaster and then painted, to make the creature more realistic.

• Sit and admire the telamon, or take a WC break at the nearby restrooms. When you're ready, go up the staircase and make your way around (past more cases of fragments) to the white statue opposite where you entered.

❻ Kouros (Young Boy)

The Greeks were philosophers and mathematicians, and this body is an example of their attention to the proportions of the ideal body. The Romans were obsessed with Greek works, and reproduced them many times for their villas—so most marble sculptures you see in museums are Roman copies of Greek originals. This sculpture is precious because it is an original work from Greece, in the stiff "Severe" style influenced by Egyptian sculpture. It was found, with its legs shattered, at the bottom of a cistern—likely thrown away by Roman-era looters who regarded it as rather plain.

• Continue past the kouros, turning right down the hallway, and into a section of Roman-era artifacts found in Agrigento.

❼ Roman Heads and Busts

Greek Sicily ended around 200 BC, with the defeat of Siracusa. After that, all of Sicily became a Roman colony, and art drifted toward the new Roman style. Here you'll find a row of three Roman sculptures. Notice that the second one has a head that's not permanently attached to its shoulders. The Romans were practical: Generals and emperors came, saw, conquered...and went. So, instead of creating new sculptures from scratch,

AGRIGENTO

only the heads were replaced—like ancient Photoshopping. This head, with its curly hair and beard, may depict Hadrian (the emperor who walled off Scotland)—or may be a later VIP who simply imitated Hadrian's style.

• *Continue down the hallway with a wall of windows. On the right side, near the end of the corridor, examine the...*

❽ Sulfur Molds

These terra-cotta sulfur molds, hanging on a rack, are imprinted with letters in reverse. The inscription identified the *manceps*—the manager who ran the sulfur mine for the imperial family. Sulfur was a valuable commodity used in ancient times for agriculture, medicine, wine production, and religious ceremonies. Sulfur mining around Agrigento helped the area flourish, and supplied the world market up to the 20th century.

• *The next hall is lined with several cases of...*

❾ Funerary Urns and Burial Objects

In Greek and Roman times, it was common for people to be buried with objects that held personal significance: women with jewelry or household objects, men with tools of their trade, warriors with armor, and children with toys.

In the third "room" of cases, find the curved metal object. This is a **strigil,** used in the baths as an exfoliator and commonly buried with men. Look to the left and find the small **terra-cotta donkey,** an ancient baby bottle. The donkey's fat body was easy for an infant to grip, the tail was the spout, and a small bead inside regulated the milk flow.

In the next "room," on the top shelf of the middle case, find two small bronze snakes curled up. These were decorations for women's hair, like ponytail holders. The small pots on either side would have held beauty products.

Notice the caskets lining the hall. Near the end of the hall (in the final "room" of cases) is an elaborately carved **small casket**—

made for a wealthy family's child. Walk around the casket, and you'll see the story of the child's life. On one short end, the scene shows the baby being picked up while an exhausted mother looks on. On the opposite end, baby gets his first driving lesson from his dad and the used-sheep salesman. On the front—angled upward—the boy lies dying, with his sorrowful mother cupping his

AGRIGENTO

chin. This was not an uncommon scene—infant mortality in the ancient world was more than 50 percent.

Compare this elegant example to the simpler **casket fragment** on the wall at the far end of the hall (with the wavy lines). A couple would have shared this casket; the gesture of the woman's hand suggests they were married. The faces on such mass-produced caskets would have been blank when purchased. A sculptor could later personalize the scene with the features of the deceased. This was an economical solution for middle-class Romans.

• *Continue down the hallway to the exit. Along the way, the (skippable) final rooms contain vases, plates, helmets, chest plates, and spearheads of Greek hoplite soldiers, and the **Vaso di Gela**, the largest Greek krater found in Sicily.*

For tips on linking the museum to the archaeological park, or returning to Agrigento, see "Getting There," earlier.

VALLEY OF THE TEMPLES ARCHAEOLOGICAL PARK

A stroll through the ▲▲▲ Valley of the Temples is one of the great travel experiences of the Mediterranean. Along with the temples at Paestum, these are the best-preserved Greek temples in Italy—on par with anything you might find in Greece. Some are partially rebuilt, others are in poetic ruins, and one survives in pristine condition. Thirty thousand Carthaginian slaves built these temples during the fifth century BC. Each of the 15 Doric-style temples honored a different god. Because the various protections offered by these gods complemented each other, Agrigento had ancient visitors' religious needs fully covered. While most of the temples have been lost to time and recycling, the few that survive give a sense of the scale of ancient Agrigento and the importance of Magna Graecia ("Great Greece"), as the Greek colonies throughout the Mediterranean were known.

Cost and Hours: €10, €13.50 combo-ticket with museum or €15 with Kolymbethra Gardens (no combo-ticket for all three sights); daily 8:30-20:00, mid-July-mid-Sept usually open Mon-Fri until 23:00 and Sat-Sun until 24:00, last entry one hour before closing.

Information: Tel. 0922-621-611, www.parcovalledeitempli.it.

Tours: Consider Michele Gallo (see "Tours in Agrigento," earlier), or an **audioguide** (€5, rent at Porta V entrance before taking shuttle taxi to the top of the site, leave photo ID, return it to the same office). Local private guides hang around the entrance.

Kolymbethra Gardens: €6, see combo-ticket details above, daily 9:30-17:30, later in summer.

Visitor Services: There's a seasonal **TI** hut at the entrance to the Porta V parking lot (daily 9:00-13:00, closed Nov-March). **WCs** are at both entrances (Porta V and Temple of Juno) and at Caffeteria Arcosoli.

Getting Around the Valley of the Temples: Within the archaeological park, a shuttle cart is available to connect the temples if needed (May-Oct, 4/hour, €3 one-way). Note that this is different from the shuttle taxi service between the entrances.

Eating: $ Caffeteria Arcosoli sells convenient (if overpriced) sandwiches, coffee, snacks, and gelato inside the park, between the temples of Juno and Concordia. **$ Bar Ristoro,** at the exit near the Temple of Hercules, has a wider selection. Basic snack stands cluster just outside the Porta V entrance/exit. For more options (farther from the temples), see "Eating in Agrigento," later.

◑ Self-Guided Tour

• *We'll start our tour at the eastern end—at the Temple of Juno entrance—and end at the western end, a short walk from the Porta V entrance and Temple of Hercules exit (for tips, see the "Getting There" section, earlier). To trace this route, see the map on page 198. After the turnstile, head up the hill to the left to the temple, the...*

Temple of Juno (Tempio di Giunone)

Circle around to the left (east) side, which was the temple's entrance. From this windswept perch, survey the landscape of Agri-

gento. Rolling hills covered in almond, fig, agave, and cactus tumble into the aquamarine sea. Imagine this site 2,500 years ago when the temples were shiny and new—a line of mighty structures displaying the power of Greek culture.

Built in 460 BC, with 34 columns (6 on each short side and 13 on each long side), the Temple of Juno was still intact in 1500, then crumbled due to earthquakes. In 1787, a local nobleman, inspired by the Enlightenment and the Neoclassical interest in antiquities, reassembled 30 columns and placed capitals atop 16. While this temple is named for Juno, it is not certain which god was worshipped here. (Its name, and those of the other temples here, are just a guess.)

This temple provides a fine opportunity for an architectural review: All Greek temples face east. (For reference, the modern city of Agrigento is north, and the sea is south.) Of the various temple designs, the most common is the peripteral style, with **columns** around the perimeter and on a stepped base. Within the colonnade

AGRIGENTO

is the inner **cella,** a room that enclosed the statue of the divinity. On the eastern side, out front, a raised **altar** was used for sacrificial ceremonies performed in public. Rites were celebrated at dawn, when the temple door would be open to allow the first sunbeams to light the statue of the god/goddess inside. Originally, simple **statues** of the gods were placed on the exterior altar, but as the statues became more elaborate and precious, they were moved inside the cella for protection. (For more on how Greek temples were laid out, see the sidebar on page 389.)

Move for a better look at the southeastern corner of the temple, and search for remnants of white plaster. Sicily has no marble, so its temples were built with sandstone. While sandstone is easier to quarry, it doesn't weather well. To prevent erosion from the sea winds (and imitate the look of marble), the stone was coated in plaster.

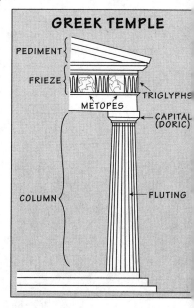

Imagine the process: The stone was quarried in a nearby hill (you can see the quarry if you look inland toward the modern city). Each stone was cut to a prescribed dimension, as if part of a big jigsaw puzzle. Then the stones were rolled on a ramp over logs to the construction site. The massive slabs were hoisted up using pulleys powered by slaves on treadmills, and lowered into place.

Columns were built with drums stacked atop each other, held in place by wooden pegs. Once assembled, they were fluted with elegant vertical grooves to hide the fact that they were not one giant monolith.

Finally, after applying the finely carved decorations, the temple was coated in plaster and painted in bold colors—very different from the classical white that we associate with ancient temples (or, in this case, golden yellow).

• *Now begin the half-mile walk downhill. As you stroll, notice the almond and olive groves, interspersed with silver-gray and green agave, prickly pear, and myrtle. These species are common in the Mediterranean, and grow well with little water. Several large olive trees dot the landscape, some more than 600 years old.*

On your left, keep an eye out for several fragments of an...

Ancient Wall

The ruins of city walls on your left are from about 500 BC. Nearly seven miles of walls, with nine gates, protected the thriving city

of 40,000. Ancient Akragas was large by the standard of the times; its agora (marketplace) was virtually the same size as the great market square of Athens. The ancient city spread from the temples across to where the modern city rises. Work near the museum continues to unearth the city's remains. The most recent find, right next to the museum, is a theater.

The city wall is punctuated by occasional niches. In Christian times, this wall was used for burials, which were not allowed inside the city. The niches, now eroded, have become peek-a-boo windows with sea views.

• *Keep following the path. On your right is Caffetteria Arcosoli, with WCs and overpriced snacks. Soon you approach the...*

Temple of Concordia (Tempio della Concordia)

Built in 435 BC, this is one of the best-preserved Greek temples in the world. Dedicated to an unknown god, archaeologists agreed that it should be called "Concordia" after an inscription found nearby.

In ancient Greece, pagan rites were performed outside the temple, where the worshippers gathered around the altar. Only priests were allowed inside the temple itself, in

the cella. The enclosed space of the cella was called *fanum* and the area out front was called *profanum*, so anyone outside of the sacred space was considered "profane."

After Byzantine Emperor Theodosius declared an end to pagan religions in 597, many Greek temples were converted into Christian churches—including this one, which became the church of Sts. Peter and Paul. The altar was moved indoors, the entrance was moved to the west side, and the temple was remodeled to create a large gathering space for the congregation. Gaps between the columns were filled in and the cella opened up, with arches carved into its solid walls. The finished space had a central nave and two side aisles (which became the common design of most churches).

AGRIGENTO

The temple was used as a church for almost 1,200 years. In 1788, at the peak of Neoclassical fashion (think Napoleon and Josephine), the building was stripped back to its original state and became appreciated as an ancient site.

This is the finest of the Agrigento temples and a great opportunity to understand and appreciate the sophistication of the ancient temple builders. The Greeks understood that viewing architecture from a distance would distort the proportion and symmetry, so they used optical illusion to correct the perspective.

A GREEK TEMPLE

AS IT APPEARS

AS IT WAS BUILT

AS IT WOULD LOOK WITHOUT OPTICAL CORRECTIONS

Facing the temple, notice the columns on the sides—they slant very slightly inward. If not for this design, from a distance the two perfectly parallel columns would appear to lean out. The slant is nearly imperceptible, but if you were to extend the two corner columns up one mile, they would actually touch. Another challenge was the base. If built perfectly horizontal, the long base line would appear to sag in the middle. To compensate for this distortion, the stepped base actually bows up slightly in the middle—and you see a straight line.

• *Continue downhill past a garden and modern building on your left,* **Villa Aurea.** *This was the home of Alexander Hardcastle (1872-1933), an English nobleman who developed a passion for archaeology after visiting the temples. He moved to the site and poured his personal wealth into the reconstruction of the temples.*

The villa often hosts contemporary art exhibits. If its gardens are open, you can detour through them to see entrances of the Christian necropolis or **ipogei,** *caves used for Christian burial.*

Just after the villa, angle left to reach the...

Temple of Hercules (Tempio di Ercole)

This was one of the final temples erected here, and the only one not built by slaves. Most of the temple collapsed over time, but one stubborn column—on the northwest side—has stood proudly for

2,500 years. The other eight assembled columns were put back together in the 1920s by Hardcastle. He became such a local personality that when he died he was buried in a tomb on the hill, with a small window looking out over his beloved temple.

• *Walk toward the temple, then along its left side. At the far end, the path cuts through a pile of rubble. As you squeeze through, notice that some of the columns (and some toppled columns nearby) still have a thick layer of white plaster.*

Continue downhill, across the modern bridge, to the...

Temple of Olympian Zeus (Tempio di Zeus Olimpico)

The struggle between the Greeks and the Carthaginians for control of Sicily culminated in 480 BC at the Battle of Himera (near Cefalú, on Sicily's northern side). To thank the gods for the victory that led to Greek prosperity, this grand temple was built for Zeus, the king of the gods. Longer than a football field and taller than a 10-story building (185 feet wide, 370 feet long, and 108 feet tall), it was the largest Doric temple in the ancient world. A person could have hidden in one of the flutes of the massive columns, and the roof tiles were the size of pizza boxes.

The sacrificial altar in front of the temple's east end (which you approach first) was 40 by 180 feet, bigger than the footprint of the

other temples. It had space to sacrifice hundreds of animals at once, with a few thousand worshippers gathered all around, waiting for a citywide barbecue after the slaughter.

This temple's architectural plan was unique. Rather than a line of open columns surrounding the cella, the temple had a solid outer wall with interlinked columns, which gave it the appearance of a massive block. The inner cella was roofless. The weight of the stone was immense, and underground foundations were built to disperse the load—something rarely seen in Greek temples. At most temples, the entrance door was centered beneath the facade, but here, due to the odd number of columns, the temple had twin entrances, one on either end.

Today, only 5 percent of the temple's original building material remains. The temple collapsed in 1401 and was almost com-

AGRIGENTO

pletely recycled into other structures. As late as 1751, stones from the ruins were used by the Spanish to build a pier at the nearby town of Porto Empedocle.

• *Angle to the right, and curl your way back "inside" the temple ruins.*

One of the defining features of the Temple of Olympian Zeus was its decoration. High above the ground, 38 giant telamon fig-

ures held up the massive roof. Imagine looking up at their toes, 40 feet above your head, between the towering pillars of the temple. The scant remains of three of these giants lie scattered around the site, like dissolving sugar-cube corpses. "Inside" the temple is a copy of the most intact giant (the original is now displayed in the archaeological museum; see page 203). Keep an eye out for other telamon parts around the site.

As you head back out to the path, you'll see a giant column capital. The enormous scale of this temple is hard to grasp.

• *Reemerging at the path, carry on downhill and over a field of rubble to the...*

Temple of Castor and Pollux (Tempio di Castore e Polluce)

Four lonely columns mark the final temple on our walk in the park. Not considered historically accurate, this imagined reconstruction

consists of random pieces put together like Lego blocks. These days, archaeologists would never reconstruct a temple in this manner, which muddles the history of the building. Keeping the stones in a jumble on the ground is preferable.

Before you leave, take a moment to sit and admire the landscape around you. Great civilizations rise, then disappear, leaving only traces of their former glory. Wandering through the plain of evocative rubble, you can only marvel at how wealthy and developed this mysterious Greek world was 2,500 years ago. Meanwhile, modern Agrigento perches on the ridge in front of you. Life goes on.

• *Our tour is over. If you have energy, you can extend your visit in the lovely **Kolymbethra Gardens** (described next—look for the entrance im-*

AGRIGENTO

mediately to the right as you face the Temple of Castor and Pollux). The Temple of Vulcan beyond is skippable.

*From here, **drivers** returning to their cars at Porta V have a short downhill walk: Near the Temple of Castor and Pollux, look for the ramp that leads down to Parcheggio Porta V. You'll walk through an olive grove and an underpass, and pop out at some WCs a short walk from the parking lot. **Taxis** also wait in the parking lot.*

*To catch the city **bus** to the archaeological museum or back to the city center, you'll find buses #1, #2, or #3/ at the exit near the Temple of Hercules.*

Kolymbethra Gardens

This ravine alongside the temples was a water reservoir in Greek times, then later drained by Arabs and turned into a lush garden. The natural abundance of water and wind-sheltered position create an ideal microclimate for cultivation of plants and vegetables. Recently restored, and worth ▲ for horticulturists, the gardens have a fragrant collection of 13 varieties of citrus (including orange, mandarin, lemon, tangerine, and citron) as well as almond and olive trees, all irrigated with ingenious water channels. A wander through the gardens' fragrant, shady paths is a peaceful treat at the end of a walk through the valley.

Sleeping in and near Agrigento

For visitors with a car, the best hotel strategy is to stay close to the temples, preferably with a view, or in a countryside retreat. Most of these hotels are between the train station and the temples. Non-drivers (or those who enjoy hanging out in a lively city) can sleep in the modern town of Agrigento.

IN THE COUNTRYSIDE, NEAR THE TEMPLES

For the locations of these hotels, see the "Agrigento's Valley of the Temples" map, earlier. All offer parking.

$$$$ Hotel Villa Athena sits in a prized position, right in the middle of the archaeological park a few steps from the temples. The hotel is luxurious, with attentive staff, 27 marbled rooms with outrageous views—and prices to match (private entrance to the temples, air-con, elevator, view restaurant, Via Passeggiata Archeologica 33, tel. 0922-596-288, www.hotelvillaathena.it, reservations@hotelvillaathena.it, Claudia).

$$$$ Casa Balata, a luxurious *agriturismo* retreat, perches on a quiet, rocky ridge with grand views about a 20-minute drive from the temples. The giant house has four rooms with all the modern comforts, a saltwater swimming pool, manicured gardens, great dinners, and sharp Daniela at the helm. If you want to splurge in stony elegance away from the chaos of Sicily, do it here (Contrada Rina Cannameli 47, mobile 328-823-5157, www.casabalata.it, casabalata.ag@gmail.com). It's not well-signed and very tricky to find, even with GPS—ask for directions.

$$$ Agriturismo Mandranova, 20 minutes east of Agrigento, produces almonds and olive oil on their large working farm. Twelve posh rooms are housed in a cluster of elegantly restored farm buildings, and four country-style rooms fill a former train station (upscale dinner-€35, SS-115 at signpost 216, Palma di Montechiaro, mobile 393-986-2169, www.mandranova.com, info@mandranova.com, hardworking Silvia).

$$$ Baglio della Luna, a manor house with a courtyard and an old Spanish watchtower, is a peaceful escape. The panoramic views of the temples in the distance and the well-manicured garden offset the 23 dank and dark rooms (air-con, Via Serafino Amabile Guastella 1c, tel. 0922-511-061, www.bagliodellaluna.com, info@bagliodellaluna.com, Felicia).

$$ Villa La Lumia, set in a countryside villa, is one of the few guesthouses inside the archaeological park. Their rooms are cozy, with view terraces overlooking the temples; it's a short walk from the archaeological museum (air-con, Via Passeggiata Archeologica 19, mobile 320-632-5568, www.villalalumia.com, info@villalalumia.com).

$$ Colleverde Park Hotel offers 48 rooms with a whiff of 1980s style and is popular with big tour groups. The shady gardens with a temple view are ideal for contemplating Greek philosophy while sipping cold *limoncello* (air-con, elevator, Via Panoramica dei Templi, tel. 0922-29555, www.colleverdehotel.it, mail@colleverdehotel.it).

$$ Hotel della Valle may be big and impersonal, but the business-class rooms are comfortable, and the pool surrounded by a garden may be just the thing on a hot day (air-con, elevator, spa, Via Ugo La Malfa 3, tel. 0922-26966, www.hoteldellavalle.ag.it, prenotazioni@hoteldellavalle.ag.it).

$$ Fattoria Mosè, an *agriturismo,* is a working farm on a hill overlooking a valley surrounded by ancient olive trees and animals. Hardworking Chiara multitasks the farm work while cooking. Four old-fashioned rooms cluster around homey common spaces in the main building, with six apartments in an annex (home-cooked dinner-€28, Via Mattia Pascal 4a, tel. 0922-606-165, www.fattoriamose.com, info@fattoriamose.com).

IN AGRIGENTO TOWN

For the locations of these hotels, see the "Agrigento" map, earlier.

$ Alloggio della Posta Vecchia is a funky B&B over an art-house theater. The five rooms have frescoed ceilings and antique furniture; guests often include artists performing at the theater (Via Giambertoni 19, tel. 0922-660-179, www. alloggiodellapostavecchia.com, alloggiodellapostavecchia@gmail. com, Angela).

$ Hotel Agrigento Home has a handy solution for those arriving by train: The hotel is built into a part of the station, facing the tracks. The 12 mod rooms are like tiny futuristic apartments (air-con, parking, Stazione Centrale, tel. 0922-556-386, www. hotelagrigentohome.it, info@hotelagrigentohome.it, Valeria).

Eating in Agrigento

IN THE TOWN CENTER

These places are all either along or near Via Atenea. For locations, see the "Agrigento" map, earlier.

$$ Ristorante Concordia, off Via Atenea, is a bustling spot for a family dinner serving home-style Sicilian favorites. Arrive early or reserve—it's popular with locals and tourists alike (Tue-Sat 12:00-15:00 & 19:00-22:30, Sun-Mon dinner only, Via Porcello 8, tel. 0922-22668).

$ A' Putia Bottega Siciliana is a casual modern place for a drink and light meal a few steps uphill from Via Atenea (just above Ristorante Concordia). They have a large selection of beer and wine, with meat-and-cheese platters to match in a chatty, hip setting (daily 12:30-14:30 & 18:30-23:00, Via Porcello 18, tel. 0922-20743).

$ Pasticceria Infurna offers an excellent selection of pastries and unique marzipan sweets and pistachio treats. Davide and his family make everything on-site, and change the front display depending on the season—chocolates in winter and gelato in summer (daily 7:30-24:00, Via Atenea 96, tel. 0922-595-959).

$$ Ambasciata di Sicilia, just off Via Atenea on the downhill side, is a cliffside restaurant with expansive views over the valley that are best in daylight. The menu features fish, served in hearty portions. The *menu del giorno* is posted at the door (Thu-Tue 12:00-15:00 & 19:00-22:30, closed Wed, Via Giambertoni 2, tel. 0922-20526).

$ Café Concordia dishes up traditional Sicilian treats, plus a delightful version of tiramisu called "ricottamisu" (Tue-Sun 6:00-22:00, closed Mon, Piazza Pirandello 36, tel. 0922-25894).

$$ Osteria ExPanificio is a bakery-turned-gourmet restaurant showcasing seasonal ingredients, such as risotto with cantaloupe and smoked cured ham in summer. Eat in their cozy interior, decorated with baking implements, or in the breezy square out front (daily 12:30-14:30 & 19:30-22:30, Piazzetta Sinatra 16, tel. 0922-595-399).

For Dessert: Locals are more than happy to walk a few minutes beyond the train station on the level, esplanade-like Viale della Vittoria to reach **Gelateria Cuspidi,** allegedly the best gelato in the region—it's flavorful and decadent. An interesting beer place is next door.

NEAR THE TEMPLES

For locations, see the "Agrigento's Valley of the Temples" map, earlier.

$$$ Trattoria Caico is a local favorite for an elegant fish dinner in the hopping beachside district of San Leone, about a 10-minute drive from Agrigento. Wine connoisseur Marco and his wife Patrizia preside over the cramped dining room and can help you select the perfect Sicilian wine to complement the catch of the day (Wed-Mon 12:00-15:00 & 19:30-23:00, closed Tue, Via Nettuno 35, San Leone, tel. 0922-412-788).

$$$ Re di Girgenti offers elegantly composed cuisine in a hip-feeling atmosphere, with stellar views of the temples from their roadside terrace. It feels like a sophisticated escape (reservations smart, Wed-Mon 12:30-14:30 & 19:30-22:30, closed Tue, Via Panoramica Valle dei Templi 51, tel. 0922-401-388, www.ilredigirgenti.it).

$$ Trattoria dei Templi, on a busy strip just above the temples, has a lovely, modern, comfortable ambience. The fare is traditional Sicilian fish and pasta dishes with new and interesting twists (Mon-Sat 12:30-15:30 & 19:30-23:00, closed Sun, Via Panoramica Valle dei Templi 15, tel. 0922-403-110).

Agrigento Connections

BY PUBLIC TRANSPORTATION

Three bus operators serve Agrigento: **Cuffaro** (www.cuffaro.info), **SAIS Trasporti** (www.saistrasporti.it), and **Salvatore Lumia** (www.autolineelumia.it).

From Agrigento by Bus to: Palermo (7/day, fewer on weekends and holidays, 2 hours, Cuffaro), **Catania** (hourly, 3 hours, SAIS), **Trapani** (3/day, 3.5 hours, Salvatore Lumia), **Trapani Birgi Airport** (2/day, 3 hours, Lumia).

From Agrigento by Train to: Palermo (hourly, 2 hours).

ROUTE TIPS FOR DRIVERS

To reach **Trapani** or the **Palermo airport,** follow the coastal road west toward Mazara del Vallo, then take the fast E-90 north toward Alcamo—this allows you to bypass central Palermo traffic.

The highway heading north from Agrigento connects to the main Palermo-Catania autostrada, A-19, a few miles north of Caltanissetta—watch for green signs. To reach the **Villa Romana del Casale,** at Caltanissetta follow signs for *Pietraperzia,* then *Barrafranca,* then follow the brown signs to *Villa del Casale* (2 hours).

If you're headed to **Siracusa**—and not stopping at Villa Romana del Casale—it's possible to take the scenic coastal route (SS-115) by way of Gela, but you'll save at least a half-hour by cutting north to the A-19 autostrada and Catania, then south along the east coast (on A-18, 2.5 hours total).

To reach **Ragusa** (again, if you're not visiting Villa Romana del Casale), follow the SS-115 coastal road toward Gela. This road is one of the most scenic on the island; be sure to notice the WWII bunkers in the hills between Agrigento and Gela. Continue through Vittoria and look for the turnoff to Ragusa just past Comiso.

AGRIGENTO

VILLA ROMANA DEL CASALE

Tucked away in what seems like the middle of Sicily's nowhere is one of the world's finest remnants of the Roman Empire. In about AD 300, when Rome was falling and elites were inclined to build their fabulous palaces away from impending chaos, a rich and powerful Roman built a sprawling villa here and ornamented it with 37,000 square feet of exquisite mosaics. The villa owner's identity remains uncertain, but based on the mosaic themes, one theory is that the Roman was a senator—and an importer of exotic animals. Today, this villa offers an intimate peek into the lifestyle of ancient Rome's upper crust.

Villa Romana del Casale is special, as it's one of few surviving Roman sites in Sicily. Although Sicily was the first Roman province outside the Italian peninsula, little of that past remains, as centuries of invaders looted, destroyed, or recycled the works of the civilizations that came before them. Yet Villa del Casale's floors—the largest collection of Roman floor mosaics ever found in situ—survived, probably because of the villa's remote countryside location. And, thanks to a landslide that sealed off the area in the 1300s, the site remained hidden from looters and plunderers for 600 years. When the villa was excavated in the 1930s, society was ready to appreciate ancient treasures, and the site was protected and restored for visitors. Touring the villa, you'll enjoy some of the best-preserved and most playful mosaics in the Mediterranean. The illustrations are simply a delight.

GETTING THERE
Villa Romana del Casale is nestled in a valley about three miles southwest of the nearest town, Piazza Armerina.

Piazza Armerina Area

By Bus: While not ideal, it is possible to visit the site without a car. Buses run to Piazza Armerina from **Palermo** (5/day Mon-Fri, less on Sat, not workable on Sun, 2 hours, SAIS, www.saisautolinee. it) and **Catania** (5/day, 2 hours, Etna Trasporti, www.interbus.it). Confirm schedules both ways before you commit.

Getting Between Piazza Armerina and the Villa: Buses arrive in Piazza Armerina on the square called Piazza Marescalchi (a.k.a. "Piazza Stazione"), just north of the old town center. From that square, **local buses** called "Villabus" depart sporadically to Villa del Casale, dropping off passengers along the road above the site (generally 5/day both ways, 20 minutes, €1.10, €1.30 if bought on board; scheduled departures from Piazza Armerina at 9:00, 11:00, and 12:00; from the site at 11:30, 12:30, 15:30, and 16:30).

You can also take a **taxi** to Villa del Casale (about 15 minutes). Taxis wait near where intercity buses arrive, at the corner of Piazza Marescalchi and Via Generale Muscarà. If no taxi is waiting, ask the staff at one of the bars on the square to call one for you. To return to the bus stop, ask the villa's parking-lot attendant to call a taxi.

Local **drivers** Roberto Sapone and Giuseppe Lazzara offer transfers to Villa del Casale (€5/person, €10 minimum; Roberto also available for longer trips and full-day excursions, mobile 329-291-1435, robertosapone@hotmail.com; Giuseppe's mobile 333-202-7822).

By Car: The villa is a much more efficient stop for drivers (about two hours from Siracusa, Ragusa, or Agrigento). To reach the villa from the main Palermo-Catania autostrada (A-19), head south near Enna in the direction of Caltagirone and Gela. Follow signs to *Piazza Armerina*, then look for brown signs pointing to *Villa Romana del Casale*. (If you're coming from Agrigento, see the "Route Tips for Drivers" at the end of that chapter.)

Villa Parking: Take a ticket as you enter the large parking lot at the villa; pay at the kiosk or nearby machines before you leave. To reach the villa from the parking lot, you'll walk about five minutes through a gauntlet of cafés and souvenir shops, then up the hill to the WCs and ticket desk.

Returning to Ragusa or Siracusa: To Ragusa, drive south in the direction of Caltagirone. For Siracusa, it's best to return north to the A-19 autostrada, head toward Catania, then go south along the coast.

PLANNING YOUR TIME

The speedy tourist can tackle Villa Romana del Casale as a strategic strike midway between Agrigento and Siracusa or Ragusa. To work a dose of hill towns, farm country, and wineries into your itinerary, stay in an *agriturismo*.

The actual visit takes about an hour, mostly walking along three-foot-wide metal catwalks, which are designed to let visitors peer down at the precious mosaics without disturbing them. The villa is under a modern roof that protects sightseers from the brutal midday sun, though that's the most crowded time to visit.

ORIENTATION TO VILLA ROMANA DEL CASALE

Cost: €10, €14 combo-ticket with nearby site of Morgantina and museum in Aidone (described later).

Hours: Daily 9:00-19:00, Fri-Sun until 23:30 in July-Aug; Nov-March daily until 17:00, last entry one hour before closing.

Information: Tel. 0935-68-0036, www.villaromanadelcasale.it.

Crowd-Beating Tips: From mid-May to late September, visit before 10:00 or after 16:00 to avoid the crowds on the narrow catwalks (worst at midday). Outside of these peak months, crowds are usually no problem. If you find a bottleneck on the catwalks, use the Italian word *permesso* (pehr-MEH-soh) to ask other visitors to let you squeeze by.

Visitor Information: Good, English-language info boards are posted throughout the site.

Tours: For a **guided tour,** local private guides hang around near the parking lot, waiting to be hired. A two-hour tour costs €120. I'd skip the €5 **audioguide** that's advertised near the cafeteria.

Length of This Tour: One hour.

Services: Pay WCs are uphill to the left from the parking lot; free WCs are at the bar near the entrance. There are no toilets inside the site.

Eating: A cluster of cafés sits at the edge of the parking lot. I like **$ Siciliamo Café** (look for orange *BAR* sign). They sell good sandwiches, sweets, coffee, and *granita,* and have a few outdoor tables (daily 9:00-19:00, closed Nov-March). The **$ cafeteria** facing the ticket booth is dreary and overpriced, but convenient.

Starring: Elaborate and colorful mosaic floors with scenes of exotic beasts, wild parties, and the first bikinis.

◒ SELF-GUIDED TOUR

• Just past the ticket booth, follow the path leading down to the site, and pause when you reach the arch on your left. Take a moment to get oriented with this book's map, which helps you pinpoint where to stop for each description.

Now turn your attention to the...

❶ Aqueduct

Masters of engineering, the Romans channeled water from the nearby Gela River into the villa with two aqueducts. The one on your left fed the baths, while the other served household needs.

Following the path downhill, on your left you'll pass the three furnaces of the baths (complete with their ranks of small terra-cotta steam pipes).

VILLA CASALE

• *Rather than enter the site here, continue on the main stone pathway and circle around to the...*

❷ Monumental Entrance

Stand just outside of the patio surrounded by columns—which was the villa's "front door." Before you enter, imagine these ruined

stumps extending up into a colorful triumphal arch. The villa was the centerpiece of a larger estate *(latifundium)*—a sprawling complex made up of living quarters, entertainment spaces, baths, and warehouses.

This landlocked villa, sitting on a hillside surrounded by thick woods, may seem randomly located. But it was strategically situated between Sicily's coasts and the two most important cities at the time, Akragas (Agrigento) and Katane (Catania). Some scholars theorize that the villa's owner was involved in the trade of exotic animals from North Africa and the Middle East. With access to ports, the location would have been practical for a trader in the ancient "stock" market, moving goods from the far reaches of the empire back to Rome.

From this grand entrance, a wall of frescoes on your right welcomed visitors. While it's mostly gone now, you might be able to make out the faded fragments of a horse. Walk toward the entrance and notice the fresco fragment ahead (immediately right of the entry) that looks a bit like a vertical shish kebab. The Roman Empire was divided into four parts and ruled by four "tetrarchs"; this staff *(signum)* represented the tetrarchs who ruled the declining empire when this estate was built. This political symbol at the door announced the owner's importance and alliances.

Imagine approaching the entrance after a long, dusty journey on horseback. Just to the left is a trough decorated with mosaics of birds and foliage, where the horses could have a much-appreciated drink.

• *Now step inside.*

❸ Entry Hall

Just inside the wall, a small pool in the floor (at the base of the pillar) served to clean smelly feet, and the adjacent basin to refresh a dirty face.

Look around: You're standing in the entry hall, a semicircular covered portico supported by columns. In the middle, the *impluvium*, a basin where the roof drained, was a typical feature of entry halls in Roman homes. From this space, guests could spin off into different directions: the bath, the toilets, or the main house.

• *Head straight, into the small covered area, then angle left into the outdoor area. Straight ahead are the...*

❹ Baths *(Thermae)*

Romans bathed like we take coffee breaks. Baths were a daily social event—a ritual for the hygiene-obsessed ancients. Without soap, they used hot water to get clean. The bath process was similar to what you'd find in a fancy spa today. Bathers would go from room to room, slowly heating their bodies and opening pores in preparation for a massage and scrubbing.

From this point, you can see the **tepidarium,** a warm room with a double floor and double walls, and the **caldarium** beyond, where the sauna and the hot pools were.

Look through the opening to the right of the tepidarium. This was the **massage room.** On the floor, you'll see a mosaic of the masseuses ready to welcome you. The bracelets on their right ankles might indicate that they were slaves. The slaves would provide an aromatic-oil massage, and then clean the oil off with a strigil—a curved metal scraper that would remove dead skin, dirt, and body hair all at the same time. The process left Romans generally hairless. Imagine their surprise when they met hairy invaders with beards (*barba* in Italian), whom they called...Barbarians. The mosaic floors served a practical purpose, providing a nonslip surface to walk on.

• *Just to the right is the...*

❺ Frigidarium

The final bathing step: a cold-water shock to close pores in the cold room *(frigidarium)*. Immediately in front of you is a deep water soaking pool that held tepid water. Beyond is a circulation space with a floor mosaic of sea gods. In the far wall, you can see an opening where cold water gushed out of the aqueduct into a frigid pool.

Take a moment to consider the excavations here. When the villa was discovered, the floors were preserved, but the roof and most of the walls had been destroyed by landslides and eroded by time. During the restoration (completed in 2012), archaeologists and architects took pains to enclose the mosaics to protect them from the elements. Using wood, plasterboard, and steel, the grand

VILLA CASALE

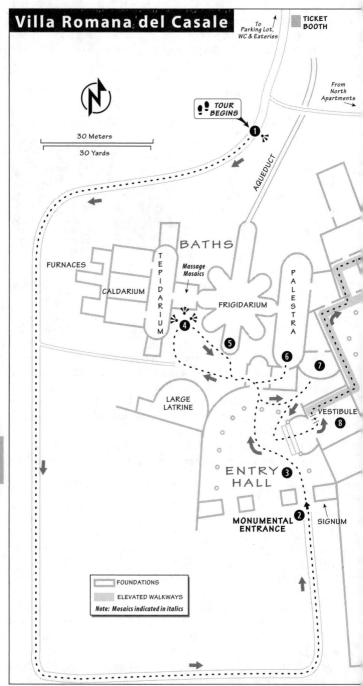

Villa Romana del Casale

TICKET BOOTH

To Parking Lot, WC & Eateries

From North Apartments

TOUR BEGINS

1

30 Meters

30 Yards

AQUEDUCT

BATHS

FURNACES

CALDARIUM

TEPIDARIUM

Massage Mosaics

FRIGIDARIUM

PALESTRA

4

5

6

7

LARGE LATRINE

VESTIBULE

8

ENTRY HALL

3

MONUMENTAL ENTRANCE

2

SIGNUM

FOUNDATIONS

ELEVATED WALKWAYS

Note: Mosaics indicated in italics

VILLA CASALE

1. Aqueduct
2. Monumental Entrance
3. Entry Hall
4. Baths
5. Frigidarium
6. Palestra
7. Small Toilet
8. Adventus Vestibule
9. Peristyle Courtyard
10. Hall of the Small Hunt
11. Ambulatory of the Great Hunt
12. The Gymnasts
13. Elliptical Peristyle & Triclinium
14. Master's Southern Apartments
15. Master's Northern Apartments
16. Basilica

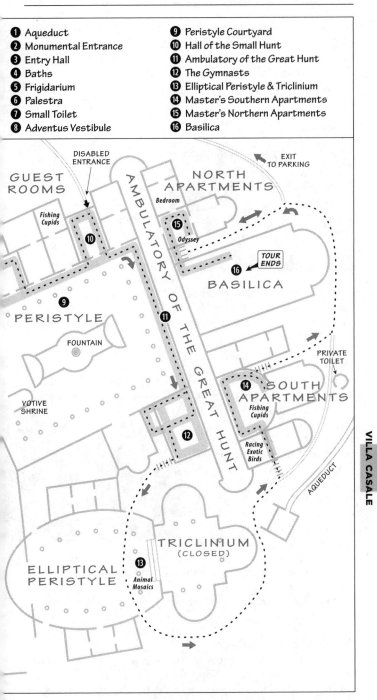

VILLA CASALE

space of the original villa was re-created—but with the ambience of a barn rather than a palace. Traces of ugly 1970s construction (with its sweat-inducing fiberglass and aluminum roofs) still remain at the frigidarium, the palestra, and the triclinium.

• *Walk back up the way you entered, then proceed straight ahead to see the...*

❻ Palestra

Exercise was a part of the bath experience in Roman times, and this room served as a home gym. The shape of the room is similar to a chariot racetrack *(circus)*, perhaps providing competitive inspiration to the athletes. The mosaic floors show teams with different colors racing around a central spine, much like the Circus Maximus in Rome, à la *Ben-Hur*.

• *Head back up into the entry hall, then go left, into the little gap between the buildings.*

❼ Small Toilet

Imagine a whole team of athletes taking a communal bathroom break in this bathroom next to the gym—which could explain why Sicilians do not have a word for "privacy" (they just use ours, and roll the *r*). Rather than flipping through a magazine on the throne, Sicilian ancients communally viewed a mosaic conversation piece—the animal race scene on the floor—while sitting cheek-to-cheek. A steady stream of water meant things

were constantly flushing. And although the hygiene-conscious Romans didn't have toilet paper, they did have sticks equipped with a sponge at the end.

• *Return one more time to the entry hall, and U-turn left, entering the covered area.*

❽ Adventus Vestibule

After cleaning up at the baths, a visitor was ready to meet the family. This grand vestibule is where the owner of the villa welcomed guests. Study what little remains of the mosaic. From the top of the metal staircase, you can look down to see how this mosaic is like a welcome mat: The noble family entourage awaits the arriving owner with ceremonial togas, laurel crowns, and a candelabrum.

• *Turn left and continue around the catwalk, peering down into the large space just beyond, in the center of the villa.*

❾ Peristyle Courtyard

Roman villas were typically built as enclosed compounds facing an inner courtyard, a *peristylium*, with a fountain surrounded by a lush garden.

Some of the columns surrounding the peristyle are restored originals, some are reconstructed, and a few are still intact—either marble (with veins) or one-piece granite. All the capitals are original, in the Corinthian style (the Roman favorite).

The exotic animal heads in the floor design ringing the peristyle may have served as a catalog, illustrating which type of animals the villa owner sold.

Facing the inner courtyard are many rooms. As you continue from here, you'll pass over a series of service and guest rooms with floor mosaics showing scenes of daily life. While I point out and describe my favorite scenes, take your time to enjoy the villa in general. It's mostly a one-way path (you'll go with the flow of the crowds). If a scene catches your interest, you'll generally find it described in English on a nearby info post. As a rule of thumb, rooms with geometric patterns rather than lively scenes were less important service rooms.

• *Near the far end of this side of the peristyle, pause at the...*

❿ Hall of the Small Hunt

A guest entering the villa would have been escorted to this side of the house, with a cluster of rooms facing the courtyard. This room,

featuring a hunting scene, could have been the dining room. The floor mosaic depicts Roman techniques for capturing game; you can read it like a comic strip. Start on the bottom, where the hunt is in progress. In the middle, the hunters gather for an al fresco Thanksgiving dinner to

Roman Mosaics

Mosaics were a common way to cover floors in ancient Greece and Rome, particularly where they could add traction to the floors in wet areas such as baths. Ancient Romans also paved walls and ceilings with mosaics. The Romans learned their techniques from the Greeks: The earliest mosaics were made with pebbles pressed into wet plaster, and initially were simple designs with geometric patterns. Later, as the art form advanced, they used finer materials, such as marble tiles, colored glass, or semiprecious stones. The Romans had the advantage of a large empire, so they could import stones of almost every color—giving their patterns more subtlety and their portraits more realism.

Mosaic tiles used in ancient times were usually about the size of a fingernail, but could be as small as a pinhead. The Romans became masters of micromosaics, using such tiny pieces that the images look like photographs. Mosaics are one of the finest art forms from ancient times because they're durable and their colors don't deteriorate as paint does on statues or frescoes.

This art form didn't die with the fall of Rome in the fifth century. It continued on in the Byzantine Empire, with craftsmen creating mosaics like the ones in Hagia Sophia in Istanbul, St. Mark's Basilica in Venice, Monreale Cathedral near Palermo, and many fine examples in Ravenna (in northern Italy)—all made centuries after the end of ancient Rome.

VILLA CASALE

enjoy their catch. The actual giving of thanks takes place a level up, where the hunters burn incense for Diana, the goddess of the hunt.

Notice the fresco fragments on the walls. The Romans had a decorating style that we might consider busy and over-the-top. Elaborate floors competed with Technicolor wall paintings, fancy furniture, and knickknacks.

As you circle the room, glance down to the left at the floor with cupids (putti) fishing. This likely was a room for children. The "V" symbols on their heads are a mystery.

• Circling around, at the far end of the peristyle, pass over the long...

⓫ Ambulatory of the Great Hunt

This grand hall, the artistic highlight of the villa, showcases a 200-foot-long hunting scene possibly depicting the owner's business in action. You'll see ostriches, cheetahs, lions, elephants, camels, deer, rhinoceroses, fish, and many other species. As you stroll the length of this scene, note how the highly detailed animals are laid out—west to east—like a map from Morocco to India. Stop and admire the accuracy of the animal bodies. The skin of the elephant looks scored and rough to the touch. The hunters demonstrate their creative techniques for capturing prey without killing them (leaving that work to the gladiators). The boat with

waterproof boxes shows how Roman fishermen transported exotic fish for aquariums. Note the interesting clothing worn by the Romans from different parts of the empire, like an ancient fashion show.

• *Your tour of this long scene continues after a fun little detour. Follow the catwalks up a ramp, then look down to see...*

⓬ The Gymnasts

There really is nothing new under the sun—apparently, women in bikinis were popular even 2,000 years ago. While these figures

are commonly called "the bikini girls," in reality they are serious athletes—lifting weights, running, and playing the first known game of beach volleyball. Notice the realistic action poses and elegant hairstyles. The winner sports a palm frond (a symbol of victory) and a crown of roses. The woman on the far left in the golden gown is suffering an unfortunate wardrobe malfunction.

In the top left corner, underneath the "bikini girls" mosaic, you'll see a fragment of the older floor mosaic with geometric patterns. Even the Romans enjoyed remodeling and home improvement, changing decor over time.

• *After the gymnasts, you'll reach the far end of the Ambulatory of the Great Hunt.*

End of the Hunt

Notice the tiger licking her cub. This is possibly illustrating a trick that hunters used to confuse and distract the animal: A mirrored orb fooled the tiger into thinking she sees her baby, but actually showed her own reflection. Immediately behind the tiger, as we approach unknown territories, mythological figures appear. Notice the griffin hunched over a box. After the capture of so many animals, the final scene turns the tables on the human captors. You can barely make out a frightened human face peering out from inside the box (next to the griffin's paw). The hunt has been reversed, and the hunter has become the prey.

• *Stepping outside, go down some stairs to reach the...*

⓭ Elliptical Peristyle and Triclinium

Watch your step. This is the only section of the mosaic you can walk on. Along the flat side, find the lizard and the jackalope among the curly vines. The building on your left is the great dining hall, or triclinium (closed for restoration). Here, the owner would have hosted lavish banquets with guests comfortably lounging on couches *(triclinia)* while eating, vomiting, and eating again. Its mosaic floors feature scenes from the "12 Labors of Hercules."

• *Continue around the far end of the triclinium, and go in the door marked...*

⓮ Master's Southern Apartments

Based on its playful mosaics, this series of rooms may have been the apartments of the villa owner's children. Apparently, ancient Roman rich kids had some interesting hobbies—such as drag-racing chariots, pulled by exotic birds.

In the semicircular room nearby, chubby fishing cupids are pulling in today's catch. This space was a peaceful circulation hub for the private portions of the house, with a cool, burbling fountain coordinating with mosaics of aquatic scenes.

• *There are a few more mosaics at this end to peruse, before you are routed back outside. As you exit, notice the small, octagonal foundation (on your right) of the private toilet for the owners, just steps from the master bedroom.*

Turn left and follow signs back inside, to the...

⓯ Master's Northern Apartments

As these rooms were the living quarters for the owner of the villa, the majority have fine mosaics. Take your time to enjoy each one.

As you enter, you'll find a famous episode from Homer's *Odyssey*. The Cyclopes were described by Homer as one-eyed giants living in caves up on Mount Etna. Although Polyphemus, depicted here, has three eyes, those extra eyes don't seem to help. Mischievous Ulysses still tricks him with a cup of "grape juice." (Never trust Greeks bearing gifts...)

Over in the next room, the private bedroom of the *dominus* and his *domina*, there's a full moon, and things are getting steamy...
• *Ahem! It's time to discreetly go back out the way you entered, then continue straight ahead, into the...*

⓰ Basilica

We usually think of a basilica as a Christian church. But the term dates from centuries before Christ: For the Romans, a basilica was

a grand public meeting place, such as a hall of justice. And the Romans copied the basilica type of building straight from the Greeks. For the Greeks, it was the formal hall where the governor *(basileus)* ran the administration of the territories.

Seated on the throne just below the apse of this hall, a wooden coffered ceiling overhead (like the replica you see today), the owner of this villa would have formally received guests and potential customers, and managed the estate. This is the only room without any mosaics. Instead, the floors are covered in exotic and precious marble slabs that would have continued onto the walls. Since this was where business deals were struck, the intent of this room's decor was to impress and intimidate visitors.

And even today, with little more than its original footprint and 34,999,291 mosaic chips (I counted them myself) decorating

VILLA CASALE

Antiquity Smuggling

Museums around the world display Greek Sicilian works, bought on the open market. Although legally any ancient artifacts of value found on private property belong to the Italian government—and it is a crime to remove them—pieces slip through the cracks with alarming regularity. Many of Sicily's archaeological sites are poorly guarded, lacking funds for proper maintenance. Grave robbers have been known to hop over fences and dig up precious works at night. Statues are purposely smashed and transported as rubble, then reassembled outside of Italy at black market warehouses.

Although Italy has made a major effort to stop the theft—tasking a special police force with tracking and recovering stolen works—it's a challenge, especially when art dealers sell artifacts to prestigious museums, sometimes for millions of dollars.

For instance, in the 1980s, the J. Paul Getty Museum of Los Angeles purchased the seven-foot-tall *Venus of Malibu* for $18 million from an unscrupulous art dealer. The piece turned out to have been stolen from the Morgantina archaeological site, near Aidone. (One of the most heavily looted archaeological sites in Italy, it has lost unknown treasures to thieves.) The Italian government pursued the return of the goddess, and the Getty eventually signed an agreement in 2007 to return a number of works to Italy—including the statue that has since been rechristened *Goddess of Morgantina* (now in the Aidone Archaeological Museum—see the listing on the next page).

The looting continues, however. Major theft rings have been broken up as recently as 2017. The Italian government has a long way to go if they are ever to recover all of their looted art.

its many rooms, Villa del Casale—1,700 years later—may not intimidate, but it certainly impresses.

• *Our tour is finished. Head back outside and follow signs to the exit.*

SIGHTS NEAR VILLA ROMANA DEL CASALE
Piazza Armerina Town

The nearest town to Villa Romana del Casale—about a 15-minute drive away—is Piazza Armerina (pop. 20,000). This hill town, clustered along a ridge that runs roughly east-west, is crowned by a Baroque cathedral with a colorful tile dome. While there were settlements in the area for centuries, the city on the hill was started by the Normans in the 12th century, and most of the village that you see today was built from the 12th to 17th century.

There are few notable sights in Piazza Armerina, but a half hour's climb up the narrow streets to the cathedral will take you through charming medieval back alleys of this workaday Sicilian village. At the top of town, you'll find a Spanish castle, a cathedral and its museum, and some views over the city. Drivers looking for views can follow the windy, uphill Via Giovanni Verga to the terrace near the sports stadium (Campo Sportivo).

Archaeological Sites near Aidone

For most visitors, seeing Villa Romana del Casale is plenty. But archaeology completists may want to drive about 30 minutes east to the pleasant, sleepy hill town of Aidone, with a small museum, and about 15 minutes farther to the (scant) ruins of another ancient site, Morgantina, with an interesting main square and views.

Aidone Archaeological Museum: This small museum, filling a former monastery, houses an interesting collection of Greek and Roman artifacts found at the Morgan-  tina archaeological area. The star of the museum is the *Goddess of Morgantina*— formerly known as the *Venus of Malibu* (see sidebar for details). This famous limestone-and-marble statue, dating from 425-500 BC, is incomplete— missing her hair and arms. You'll also see several other finds from Morgantina, and artifacts on loan from the Metropolitan Museum of Art in New York City (€6, €10 combo-ticket with Morgantina site, €14 combo-ticket for both plus Villa del Casale, daily 9:00-18:30, Largo Torres Trupia 1, Aidone, tel. 0935-87307).

Morgantina: This archaeological site, just east of Aidone, has the remains of an ancient Sicel city that was later conquered by the Greeks and Romans. This is where the *Venus* was originally found. There isn't much left, but it's interesting for its main square (agora) and sweeping territorial views (€6, see combo-ticket options above, daily 9:00-17:00, Nov-March until 16:00, tel. 0935-87955).

SLEEPING NEAR VILLA ROMANA DEL CASALE

See the "Piazza Armerina Area" map for locations.

$$ Agriturismo Masseria Bannata, near Piazza Armerina, sits tucked into the side of a hill along the road north out of town. Signora Nietta has thoughtfully restored the six rooms on her family farm—some of them former chicken coops and feeding troughs—with quirky antiques and an eye for modern Italian design (family rooms, closed Nov-March, Contrada Bannata, on SS-117 at km 41, mobile 328-298-8448, www.agriturismobannata.com, info@agriturismobannata.it).

$ Casa del Poeta, run by Masseria Bannata, is a former hunting lodge near Lake Pergusa, a half hour north of Piazza Armerina. The four rooms are artsy and modern, with a poetry theme—the poem of the day is available at the front desk (air-con, Via Diana, Pergusa, mobile 328-298-8448, www.lacasadelpoetaenna.com, info@lacasadelpoeta.it).

$ Torre di Renda, a country hotel and restaurant clinging to a cliff overlooking Piazza Armerina, rents 20 rooms with simple, modern charm set inside an old farmhouse (air-con, pool in summer, C. da Torre di Renda, tel. 0935-680-0208, www.torrerenda. it, info@torrerenda.it). Their restaurant serves up quality food with a grand view.

$ Gigliotto, an *agriturismo* farm hotel, is also a winery just off the highway south of Piazza Armerina. Both the property and farm have an antique feel. Although it's big and attracts groups for lunch, the views are postcard worthy and it's open for drop-in visits year-round (wine tastings-€10 and up, good restaurant, on SS-117 at km 60, San Michele di Ganzaria, mobile 337-889-052, www. gigliotto.com, gigliotto@gigliotto.com).

EATING NEAR VILLA ROMANA DEL CASALE

In addition to the places right at the villa itself, consider driving to this more appealing countryside choice. **$$$ Ristorante al Fogher** sits in a little cottage under the freeway a few miles north of Piazza Armerina. Chef Angelo Treno uses quality local ingredients and creates modern dishes from old recipes. The €30 fixed-price lunch, a gourmet steal, includes wine (Tue-Sat 12:30-14:30 & 19:00-22:00, Sun 12:30-14:30, closed Mon, reserve for dinner, Viale Conte Ruggero—SS-117, tel. 0935-684-123, https://alfogher. sicilia.restaurant).

VILLA CASALE

RAGUSA &
THE SOUTHEAST

Ragusa • Southeast Countryside Drive • Noto

Sicily's southeast is charming, prosperous, and uncrowded—an ideal place for in-the-know travelers to relax for a day or two. With rolling green hills and low, stacked-stone walls, it looks almost like Ireland. Soaring hill towns (Ragusa) have their counterpoint in valley villages (Scicli). Small hamlets cluster along the sea, some with sunny beaches.

The fate of the entire region was altered by one massive event: the catastrophic earthquake of 1693. Villages with 2,000 years of history were flattened in an instant, and later rebuilt in the Baroque style that was all the rage at the time. The town of Noto, reconstructed after the quake, is the jewel in the crown of Sicilian Baroque.

This region is one of Sicily's quietest and least touristed corners. Exploring here, you'll enjoy relatively affluent country towns and a relaxed pace. Ragusa—an easy-to-like hill town with a stunning setting—is an ideal home base, with more than its share of good hotel and restaurant options.

PLANNING YOUR TIME

Ragusa can be seen in a day, but its lovely, quiet nature—combined with the option to visit nearby villages—makes it an ideal spot to linger for a couple of days.

Day 1: Explore Ragusa, starting with the steep climb from the lower town (Ragusa Ibla) to the upper town (Ragusa Superiore). Then head back to the lower town for your reward: a fancy lunch at the elegant Duomo restaurant. In the afternoon, follow my Ragusa Ibla Walk, tour some interesting interiors (Palazzo Arezzo di Trifiletti and/or the Open Doors tour), drop in on vespers at the

Church of San Giuseppe (Mon-Sat at 17:30), and do a *granita* tasting at Caffetteria Donnafugata.

Day 2: Follow my Southeast Countryside loop drive, stopping for lunch on the coast. If you plan to see Donnafugata Castle on a day when it closes earlier in the afternoon, you could do the drive in reverse to arrive there first. Finish your day with a relaxing dinner in Ragusa Ibla.

Ragusa

Built along a steep promontory, and surrounded by a verdant gorge, Ragusa is a pleasant, sleepy place to catch your breath on a busy  Sicily itinerary. It feels off the beaten path—a peaceful eddy all its own. It's low impact...except for the wear and tear on your knees, negotiating its steep cityscape.

In fact, Ragusa (pop. 76,000) isn't a single town. It's two towns—each with its own character—connected by a wandering staircase. The original city, Ragusa Ibla, is on the smaller, lower hill. Ancient "Hybla" was almost entirely destroyed by the 1693 earthquake. Most of the town's wealthier families decided that it wasn't worth the effort to rebuild their broken homes, and relocated to the higher hill and plain above. There they built Ragusa Superiore, anchored by a new, earthquake-fortified cathedral, with a grid street plan and room for expansion. Meanwhile, Ragusa Ibla was slowly rebuilt—in part by the people who could not afford to start over—keeping its medieval character of winding lanes and homes burrowed into the rock.

Today, the upper town bustles with modern shops and services, while the lower town is sleepy and residential, with pretty churches and great restaurants. Together, they make a perfect home base for your southeast Sicily visit.

Getting There: Ragusa is in a remote area of southeast Sicily without major highways or direct routes, which means it takes a bit of time to get there. From Agrigento, the coastal route (SS-115) is best, cutting up near Gela (2.5 hours). From Siracusa, head south on E-45 past Avola, then head west through Noto and Modica—both great on-the-way stops (1.5 hours).

Orientation to Ragusa

Ragusa's two towns are set on adjacent hills: the lower, ancient city of Ragusa Ibla and the upper, modern town of Ragusa Superiore. Most visitors concentrate their time in Ragusa Ibla (and should), but Ragusa Superiore can be worth a quick look.

The two hills are connected by a lower saddle of land, marked by Piazza della Repubblica (with a TI and near a free parking lot). From here, a scenic and strenuous stair-and-hill climb heads up to Ragusa Superiore.

The heart of Ragusa Superiore is the Cathedral of San Giovanni Battista, surrounded by cafés, eateries, and elegant shopping streets. The smaller, more modest center of Ibla is the piazza of the Cathedral of San Giorgio, from which Corso XXV Aprile runs down to the Ibleo public gardens at the bottom edge of town. You can walk from one end of Ragusa Ibla to the other in about 15 minutes.

No matter where you walk, in either part of Ragusa, count on hills and stairs...everywhere.

TOURIST INFORMATION

Each part of town has a TI. In Ragusa Ibla, you'll find the TI on Piazza della Repubblica, just next to the Purgatorio Church (TI open Mon-Fri 9:00-19:00, Sat-Sun until 14:00, mobile 366-874-2621). In Ragusa Superiore, the TI faces the cathedral on Piazza San Giovanni (same hours, tel. 0932-684-780).

ARRIVAL IN RAGUSA

By Car: There are two free options for parking in Ragusa Ibla. For most visitors, the best spot is the large main lot just below Piazza della Repubblica, a manageable uphill walk (enter the lot from Via Avvocato Giovanni Ottaviano, the road that hugs the southern edge of Ragusa Ibla). There's also a free lot at the eastern end of Ragusa Ibla, near the Ibleo public gardens.

If you're heading for Ragusa Superiore, there's an easy pay parking garage under the post office (enter on Corso Italia). If you park here, consider visiting Ragusa in reverse, walking downhill from Superiore to Ibla—and then ride bus #11 back uphill to your car (the bus stops on Corso Italia near the post office). Throughout Ragusa, street parking within white lines is always free; blue lines require a pay-and-display ticket.

By Bus or Train: Long-distance buses and trains arrive on the southern outskirts of Ragusa Superiore, a long walk from the cathedral and town center (15 minutes from the train station, 25 minutes from the bus station, gently downhill)—and too far from Ragusa Ibla to attempt on foot with luggage.

You have two main options for reaching Ragusa Ibla (and most of my recommended accommodations): You can hop in a **taxi** and pay the fixed rate of €10. Or you can take **bus #11** (on Sundays, bus #1), which departs from the bus terminal on Via Zama (bus stop right out front) and from near the train station on Piazza del Popolo. (To reach the bus stop from the train station, exit and bear left toward the little park with a modern obelisk; the bus leaves across the street—downhill—from the obelisk. There's no bus stop sign.) Bus #33 is also an option and leaves from the same points. See below for route and fare info.

GETTING AROUND RAGUSA

By Bus: Ragusa's public buses help connect its two towns, though the schedule is unpredictable and the stops can be tricky to find. Bus #11 (Mon-Sat) or #1 (Sun) begins in Ragusa Superiore at the bus terminal, then stops near the train station before winding steeply down the switchbacks to Piazza della Repubblica. From there, it loops around the base of Ragusa Ibla's ridge (stopping at the main parking lot below Piazza della Repubblica), then climbs up to the end of the line, in front of the Ibleo public gardens (total trip is just 15 minutes; buses leave roughly 2-3/hour). Bus #33 runs

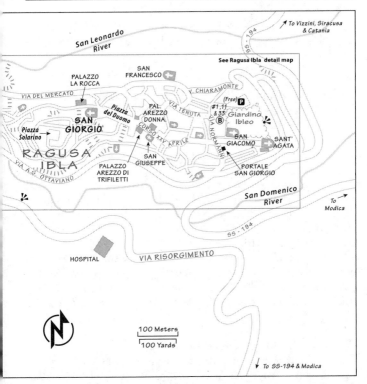

a similar route, but doesn't always go up to the gardens in Ibla—ask before you board. Tickets cost €1.20, whether you buy them on the bus or at a tobacco shop.

By Taxi: Taxis charge a fixed rate of €10 to travel between Ragusa Ibla and Ragusa Superiore. You may find them waiting in Ragusa Superiore at Piazza Zama and Piazza Libertà, or in Ragusa Ibla at Piazza Giovan Battista Hodierna at the entrance to the Ibleo public gardens. If you can't find one, call 0932-1832, or go into any bar and ask them to call for you.

HELPFUL HINTS

Market: The weekly market takes place on Wednesday (roughly 8:00-14:00) on the outskirts of town in the parking lot at the football stadium, Stadio A. Campo.

Festivals: San Giorgio, the patron saint of Ibla, is celebrated with processions at the end of May or in early June.

Local Guide: Francesca Giovatto is an effervescent Ragusan who delights in showing the beauty of her city and region to visitors (€180/half-day, mobile 339-137-5952, francescagiovatto@ virgilio.it).

Open Doors Tour (A Porte Aperte): This innovative, intimate,

50-minute tour gets you inside three spaces that are usually off-limits to the general public: the little theater inside the Palazzo Arezzo di Donnafugata; the Circolo di Conversazione private club; and the private garden of yet another palazzo (€10, tours offered 2-3/week with demand, reserve ahead and meet your guide at Via del Convento 13, mobile 366-194-177, aporteaperte@gmail.com). This tour works well in conjunction with a visit to the Palazzo Arezzo di Trifiletti.

Ragusa Ibla Walk

This walk takes you along the spine of the ancient city of Ragusa, from the cliff-hanging Ibleo public gardens to the cathedral square. While you could walk through the center of Ibla in 15 minutes, this stroll will take 30 minutes at a leisurely pace—longer if you visit the palace or church interiors.

• We'll begin at the ceremonial stone gateway of the Giardino Ibleo, Ragusa's public gardens. To get to the starting point, you can ride bus #11 (or, on Sundays, bus #1) from the train station, bus station, or Piazza della Repubblica to the end of the line. Or you can simply walk downhill the length of Ragusa Ibla, to its eastern tip.

❶ Public Garden (Giardino Ibleo)

Step through the gateway and go for a little stroll clockwise through this delightful ▲▲ public park. The main path—lined with stout

palm trees—feels at once elegant and well used. Notice the Ragusans hanging out on benches, playing with their kids, catching up with neighbors, and so on.

As you walk, you'll pass a church on the left and come upon a convent (now a hotel). Nearing the end of the path, bear left to reach a grand terrace offering a fine overlook into the ravine below. It's easy to imagine why a town would be built in this well-protected, strategic location.

• Head back out the way you came in. From the garden gate, turn left and walk downhill about 30 yards. On your left, tucked back from the street, notice the...

❷ Portale San Giorgio

Ragusa Ibla was a thriving city in the Middle Ages. But the 1693 earthquake virtually flattened the town—causing the townspeople to rebuild on the higher, flatter hilltop of Ragusa Superiore. The Gothic church that stood here from the mid-1300s collapsed in the quake, and this doorway is all that's left. It's among the oldest surviving architecture in Ragusa Ibla. Notice the lunette over the doorway: It's decorated with a sculpted relief of St. George (San Giorgio) slaying the dragon.

• *Backtrack up to the garden gate. With the garden at your back, walk straight ahead, through the piazza, and up...*

❸ Corso XXV Aprile

This is the main street of Ragusa Ibla, and it's filled with small shops, restaurants, and *gelaterie*. Walk up a few short blocks, and jog left with the street. On your right, just after the jog, look for #41, with a door (usually open) at the base of a tower. Peeking in here, you'll see a candlelit shrine to the Virgin Mary. This tiny chapel is attached to the Church of Santa Maria Maddalena. Ragusans drop in as they pass by to pay their respects; some even cross themselves as they walk by on the street.

• *At the top of Corso XXV Aprile, you pop out at the square called...*

❹ Piazza Pola

To your left is the Baroque **Church of San Giuseppe,** with its elaborate convex facade. Built in the late 18th century, this church

serves a convent of cloistered Benedictine nuns whose once-large community has dwindled to only eight elderly nuns. You can join them in their lovely, small church for the saying of the rosary and the singing of vespers (Mon-Sat at 17:30).

For a look at some interesting shops, take a little detour down ❺ **Via Orfanotrofio** (the street to the right as you enter Piazza Pola from Corso XXV Aprile). After a block, bear left at the fork, and look on the left for **Cinabro Carrettieri** (#22). Signor Biagio does traditional Sicilian artwork, including cart painting—check out his decorated Fiat 500. Next door, **Lucernaio** is a microbrew pub, serving an assortment of Italian craft beers on tap or by the bottle. And across the street, the recommended **I Banchi**—owned by a local celebrity chef—has a bakery selling high-end snacks and desserts to go, plus a sit-down restaurant in back.

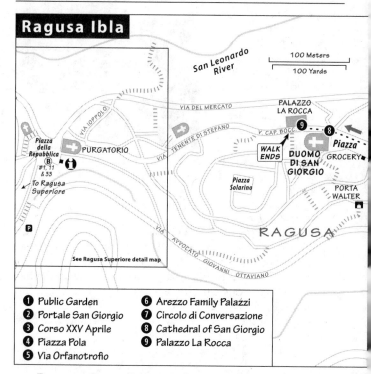

Ragusa Ibla

1 Public Garden
2 Portale San Giorgio
3 Corso XXV Aprile
4 Piazza Pola
5 Via Orfanotrofio
6 Arezzo Family Palazzi
7 Circolo di Conversazione
8 Cathedral of San Giorgio
9 Palazzo La Rocca

Return to Piazza Pola, and if you're in the mood for a snack break, check out the recommended **Caffetteria Donnafugata,** on the corner of the square. Grab a seat at a streetside table, and ask for a tasting of three types of *granite.*

• *Now continue uphill on Corso XXV Aprile, which becomes pedestrian-only. Stop at #9, on the right.*

6 Arezzo Family Palazzi

On opposite sides of the street, you'll see two palaces belonging to different members of the Arezzo family. These longtime aristocrats have been in Sicily since the 12th century, and in Ragusa since the late 1700s. Keep an eye out for their coat of arms, decorated with four hedgehogs.

The larger palace on the right (at #9)—**Palazzo Arezzo di Donnafugata**—is owned by the branch of the family that built the countryside Donnafugata Castle and its extensive gardens (see the "Southeast Countryside Drive," later in this chapter). This town palace has its own small, private theater, which was originally accessed only from the palace ballroom. But a later owner opened the theater to the public, converting former warehouse and storage areas into a foyer and lounges. The theater is adorably tiny, with just 98 seats, and regularly hosts classical concerts (schedules posted on

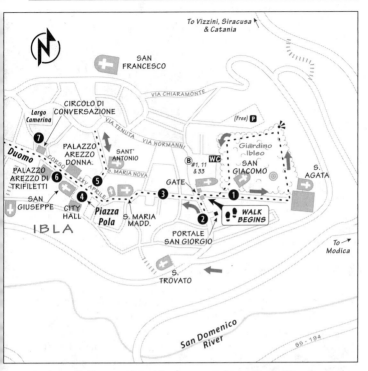

signboard). For a peek inside, you can join an Open Doors tour (see "Helpful Hints," earlier).

On the other side of the street (at #4) is the **Palazzo Arezzo di Trifiletti,** worth ▲. Members of the Arezzo family have lived in this beautiful Baroque palace since the mid-19th century. The current owner enjoys leading 30-minute English tours of his home, offering a unique behind-the-scenes glimpse of historic and contemporary Italian aristocratic life (€5, reserve ahead by email or phone, mobile 339-400-0013, www.palazzoarezzo.it, eventipalazzoarezzo@gmail.com).

• At the next corner, admire the short but stately building on the right.

❼ Circolo di Conversazione

Resembling a Greek temple, this "Conversation Circle" was founded in the mid-1800s by 18 elite local families as a private social club. Here they could enjoy each other's company without mixing with the rabble. A bit like a Lions Club, upper-class professional men gathered here for generations, and still do today, to chat in a fancy meeting room with velvet drapes and cushy chairs. Women were finally admitted in 1973 (they have their own room). The building's facade almost feels like a stage

set—designed specifically to evoke the classical "look" that was all the rage among Grand Tour travelers. It's not open to the public, but you can get a look at the convivial meeting rooms and the grand ballroom, with red-silk walls and a frescoed ceiling, on an Open Doors tour (see "Helpful Hints," earlier).

• *Continue ahead to the long, sloping main square, crowned by the...*

❽ Cathedral of San Giorgio (Duomo di San Giorgio)

The centerpiece of Ragusa Ibla, this church was designed by the local architect Rosario Gagliardi, who kept busy after the earth-

quake designing churches for Ragusa Ibla, Modica, and his hometown of Noto. He admired the Baroque facades of churches in the German Rococo style, with a tall, central bell tower, and used optical illusions to add interest to his designs. For example, notice how the church's entry staircase veers to the left. To make sure that both the dome and the bell tower would be visible from the piazza, Gagliardi slightly skewed the orientation of the church so that it's not strictly aligned with the square. Find the repeating motif

of Saint George—San Giorgio—on a horse slaying a dragon in the exterior decoration: on the sides of the facade, on the stained-glass window, and even on the wrought-iron gate that surrounds the steps. At night, the church is floodlit, enhancing its Baroque drama.

To visit the interior, walk along the right side of the church to find a smaller, separate staircase that leads to the entrance (free, daily 10:00-12:30 & 16:00-19:00, tel. 0932-220-085).

• *Continue alongside the church on Via Capitano Bocchieri to #33 (on the right).*

❾ Palazzo La Rocca

Look up at the balconies on this late Baroque palazzo. Peering down at you are masks, animals, and cherubs. Take a moment to identify some of the characters: musicians playing flute and lyre, a couple in an awkward embrace, a man with a barrel of wine, and Tom Petty. Many of the Baroque *palazzi* of Ragusa have these creative flourishes.

Turn back the way you came to enjoy a picture-perfect view of the dome of San Giorgio. The church's architect wanted you not only to see the dome from the front, but also to view it from the back side, so he carefully framed it here in this streetscape. This kind of dramatic staging is a typical, playful feature of Baroque architecture here in southeastern Sicily, taking inspiration from nature to give movement and interest to buildings. It's like a cross between architecture and opera—have fun with it.

• *Your stroll is over. From here, you can relax over a lavish lunch at the fancy, recommended Duomo restaurant (inside the Palazzo La Rocca).*

Or, if you're feeling energetic, you can tackle a strenuous uphill climb to glorious views and the upper, modern part of the city. Continue along Via Capitano Bocchieri and work your way down to Piazza della Repubblica, in the little saddle between the two towns. That's where the next walk begins.

Hill Climb to Ragusa Superiore

The best sight in Ragusa is the city itself. To get a sweeping panoramic view, tackle the ▲▲ scenic stair-and-hill climb between the upper and lower towns. It's a sweaty calf-buster, but you'll be rewarded with pretty alleyways, stately *palazzi,* and colorful churches. (Entry is free to the several churches on this walk; most are closed at lunchtime.)

A total of 248 steps—and an uphill walk—connect Ibla's Piazza della Repubblica to the Cathedral of San Giovanni Battista. Those who are fit can make the trek in about 20 minutes. With a slow pace and time for photo ops, allow at least 45 minutes. Taking this climb at sunrise or sunset is a treat for photographers.

• *Start in Piazza della Repubblica, the little square (with a TI) that sits in the gap between the upper and lower towns. This point is on the western edge of Ragusa Ibla; a short uphill walk from the parking lot on*

Via Avvocato Giovanni Ottaviano (take the stairs up and head beyond the tall red hotel); and right next to the stop for bus #11.

❶ Piazza della Repubblica

Face the **Purgatorio Church** (Chiesa delle Anime Sante del Purgatorio), which overlooks this piazza. Above the entrance door, notice the inscription MISE-REMI-NI-MEI ("pity me"), carved just below poor souls writhing in flames. The concept of purgatory—the stopping-off point for unforgiven souls on the way to heaven—gained attention during the Counter-Reformation, and churches like this focused on departed loved ones who might need extra prayers to be purified of leftover sins. Purgatory churches are common in Sicily, but not found in mainland Italy.

Turning your back on purgatory, turn right and walk about 30 yards to the base of the stairway signed *Salita Commendatore*. High on the corner above the stairs, find the monk holding a pole. This marks one end of **Palazzo Cosentini,** a noble 18th-century palazzo that—like many in Ragusa—has intricate wrought-iron balconies supported by elaborately carved decorations. Check out the supports on the upper level, which are in the shape of the grotesque figures traditionally thought to keep the evil eye away. Take a walk to the other end of the pale pink facade, enjoying the fanciful characters, including a "flashy" woman at the very end.

• *It's time to climb. Head up the stairs under the monk.*

❷ Stair Climb (Salita Commendatore)

Several stairs up, you reach a wide landing. On the right is the **Church of Santa Maria dell'Itria,** built in the early 17th century by the Knights of Malta. Its beautiful bell tower is tiled with blue majolica and floral motifs. (Keep in mind that you can duck into any open church for a bit of cool shade and a jolt of Baroque.)

Climbing the steps to the next landing, you'll find another Baroque gem, **Palazzo della Cancelleria,** with an unusually narrow facade and tunnel staircase passing through it.

• *Continue straight, up and up, passing beneath two modern roads. Just after the second underpass, follow the steps on the left. Cross the street to get your first glimpse back toward Ragusa Ibla, with the spire of Santa Maria dell'Itria on the left.*

But we're not done climbing: Turn your back to the view and take the steps to the left, near where you just exited. You'll walk up, hugging the fronts of houses (and gasping at the grand views), then take the steps under the archway on your right—where you'll find your reward: a magnificent view of Ibla. This is also the location of a special church...

❸ Church of Santa Maria delle Scale (Chiesa di Santa Maria delle Scale)

This church dedicated to "Saint Mary of the Stairs" is the only one in Ragusa that predates the massive earthquake. It's partially re-

modeled in Baroque style, but not because of earthquake damage. The church was enlarged in the 1700s, when a population boom demanded more worship space. These days, many churches, including some on this walk, have barely enough attendance to keep the doors open. In Italy, only about one-third of the population attends Mass regularly. Like many others on the island, this church still maintains a small but aging parish.

If it's open, step inside, and look for fragments of the original church. A portal on the right side of the nave (straight ahead as you enter) is in the Catalan-Gothic style, from the period of Bourbon (Spanish) rule. Its elaborate carvings, like much of medieval church decoration, were once brightly painted (look closely to see remains of pigment). In the right aisle, find the exquisite 1538 terra-cotta relief depicting the Dormition of the Virgin.

• *Facing the church, take the steps to the right.*

As you ascend, you leave medieval Ragusa behind. Stop for a minute and look at the view over Ragusa Ibla framed by the church

bell tower. Virtually everything you see was built after the 1693 earthquake, which so devastated the town that many people gave up and started over on the higher land here, with room for growth, a breeze, and no more dank houses. The population in Ibla dwindled, as most chose to move to the new town.

• *At the top of the steps, you'll find a level street. Follow it to the left, then bear right onto Via 24 Maggio. You're now at the...*

❹ Edge of Ragusa Superiore

The new, post-quake town of Ragusa, built in the 1700s, begins here. Both sides of the street are lined with large townhouses—a

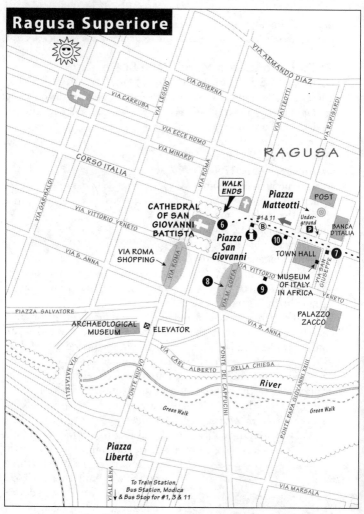

popular new style of home being constructed all over Europe at the time. Large families needed large homes. Even now, many still live with multiple generations under one roof. You'll find grandparents hanging the laundry out the window while grandkids play on the sidewalk.

Enjoy the relaxed vibe as you stroll uphill to the center, bearing right to stay on Corso Italia. Ragusa is a prosperous town and always has been. There's a feeling here that's different from other parts of Sicily. The streets are tidy, everyone knows everyone, kids wander freely, and doors are often left unlocked. The people take pride in their city and are curious about visitors. Be sure to say "*Salve!*" to greet residents as you pass.

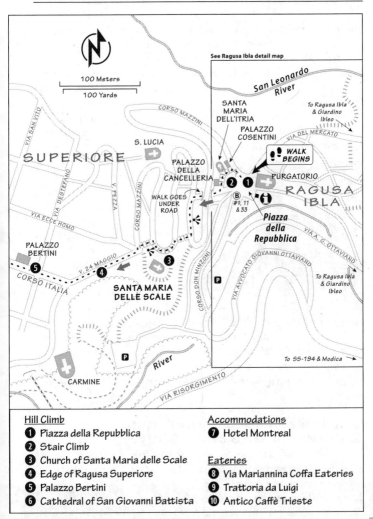

See Ragusa Ibla detail map

Hill Climb

1. Piazza della Repubblica
2. Stair Climb
3. Church of Santa Maria delle Scale
4. Edge of Ragusa Superiore
5. Palazzo Bertini
6. Cathedral of San Giovanni Battista

Accommodations

7. Hotel Montreal

Eateries

8. Via Mariannina Coffa Eateries
9. Trattoria da Luigi
10. Antico Caffè Trieste

As you walk up Corso Italia, townhouses give way to larger *palazzi* and modern apartment buildings. A few short blocks up

on the right, you'll arrive at the 18th-century **5 Palazzo Bertini,** with its three curious *mascheroni* (masks) peering down at you. Its balconies used to be street-level doorways (before the roadway was lowered), and those faces once greeted visitors entering the palace. Each face is said to represent a type of power. On

RAGUSA & THE SOUTHEAST

the left, the grotesque caricature with a turban and a gnarled nose represents the power of money. The face in the center, wearing a plumed hat, is calm and sure, representing the power of nobility. And the grizzled face on the right is a reminder that the poor have perhaps the most daunting power of all: the power of nothing to lose.

Ahead on the left, you'll see the Town Hall—marked with the flags of Sicily, Italy, and the European Union. In the basement (enter on Via San Giuseppe, the street to the left) is the curious

little Museum of Italy in Africa, worth a visit at the end of this walk (free, described under "Sights in Ragusa").

Across the street, the square called Piazza Matteotti is surrounded by examples of bombastic, fascist architecture from

the Mussolini era. The main post office sits in the square like a cathedral of civil service, and just to the right is the even more fascist Banca d'Italia building. The monument on the left side of the square honors postal workers who gave their lives for Italy.

• *Continuing uphill, the recommended Antico Caffè Trieste (on your right) is handy for a drink or treat. Just beyond, you'll reach your final destination...*

❻ Cathedral of San Giovanni Battista (Cattedrale di San Giovanni Battista)

This church dedicated to St. John the Baptist dominates Ragusa Superiore. Surrounded by lively cafés and shopping streets, it's the centerpiece of everyday life. It was built to replace the city's original cathedral in Ragusa Ibla, which was destroyed by the earthquake. To accommodate for the hilly terrain, this replacement was built on a unique platform that creates two piazzas, one in front of the church and one a level below, with cafés and shops tucked into its base.

From the piazza in front, notice a couple of details. The bell tower is rather squat, relatively short, and with thick walls. And on either end of the facade, the walls slope, as if this were a fortified bastion. After the quake, church architects were taking no chances;

they overengineered the building inside and out with massive columns and thick outer walls.

• *Our hill climb is finished. (Phew!) Settle in with a drink at one of the cafés on the piazza or choose one of the good restaurants nearby (see "Eating in Ragusa," later). Behind the church, you'll find Via Roma—the city's mostly pedestrianized shopping street.*

When you're ready to return to Ragusa Ibla, you could either retrace your steps (trust me: the walk is much easier downhill), hop in a taxi, or ride bus #11 (#1 on Sun; bus stop is at Corso Italia 26, near the TI).

Sights in Ragusa

Ragusa itself and its wealth of Baroque architecture are the main attractions in town (described in the "Ragusa Ibla Walk" and "Hill Climb to Ragusa Superiore," earlier). But two free little museums provide some historical context for other periods of the town's history.

Museum of Italy in Africa (Museo Civico L'Italia in Africa)

Under the Town Hall is a tiny museum dedicated to an odd chapter in Italian history: the colonization of Africa from 1885 to 1960. Italians were encouraged (especially under fascism) to move to the brave new world in Africa, receiving land in payment. This little-known story is described by a quirky private collection of uniforms from the colonization of Libya, Somalia, Ethiopia, and Eritrea. Signor Mario Nobile has a great passion for the subject and has spent years assembling this rare collection. He shares his knowledge kindly in Italian, occasionally with an exuberant assistant who speaks some English. This gives an interesting insight into a period of Italian (and African) history that is relatively unknown.

Cost and Hours: Free, generally Mon-Fri 9:00-13:00, Tue and Thu also 15:00-17:00, closed Sat-Sun, try knocking anytime to see if someone is there, signing the guestbook will make Signor Mario's day, go down the street on the left side of the Town Hall—Via San Giuseppe 3, tel. 0932-676-111.

Ragusa Archaeological Museum (Museo Archeologico Ibleo)

Tucked under the center of Ragusa Superiore, this dusty little museum displays a mish-mash of ancient artifacts from the surrounding province. While there are no English descriptions, you'll find Roman mosaics, Greek helmets, devotional objects from early Sicel culture, and rare drinking glasses. It's skippable unless you're an archaeology enthusiast.

Cost and Hours: Free, but you'll be asked to sign the guestbook, Mon-Sat 9:00-18:30, closed Sun, Via Natelelli 11, tel. 0932-622-963.

Getting There: It's under a bridge, a five-minute walk down Via Roma behind the cathedral. Follow Via Roma (left, with the cathedral behind you) until you nearly reach the bridge—look for the free elevator on your right. Ride it down, turn right, circle around the car wash, and find the door to the museum.

Sleeping in Ragusa

RAGUSA IBLA

Most visitors sleep in Ragusa Ibla, the charming lower town. Drivers usually find it's easiest to park at the free lot below Piazza della Repubblica, then walk up to Ibla—though some listings are closer to the parking lot near the Ibleo gardens, at the east end of town. Ask your host for advice. Note that many old Ragusa

buildings are burrowed into cliffs, which means they can be a bit dank and musty inside.

$$$ San Giorgio Palace Hotel is dug into the side of Ragusa Ibla, with rooms stacked vertically from the road up to the old town. Their 32 rooms are sleek and Italian-modern—some higher rooms have views over the valley and others, lower down, have tidy garden patios. An internal elevator makes the trip from valley floor to the city a snap (RS%, air-con, elevator, parking, Via Avvocato G. Ottaviano, tel. 0932-686-983, www.sangiorgiopalacehotel.it, info@sangiorgiopalacehotel.it, Ivan).

$$$ Hotel Antico Convento, sitting within the peaceful Ibleo gardens, is a remodeled medieval convent with a hotel, restaurant, and cooking school. It has 16 spartan rooms furnished with holy elegance and nun-sized doorways (air-con, elevator, parking pass provided, Viale Margherita 41, tel. 0932-686-750, www.anticoconventoibla.it, info@anticoconventoibla.it, Barbara).

$$ Epoca Camere con Stile, with four elegant rooms in a lovely palazzo, perfectly combines a family home with modern style. Each room is furnished with period furniture belonging to the family that's lived here for generations. Beautiful, clean, and personal, it has a quiet courtyard and sun terrace (air-con, free loaner electric bikes, Via Orfanotrofio 43, mobile 347-549-3584, www.epoca-ibla.it, info@epoca-ibla.it, Costanza).

$$ Giardino sul Duomo has 15 tidy, modern rooms at the tippy top of town, thoughtfully managed by Michele. Their quiet communal garden floats above the city, with a stellar view of Ibla and Superiore, and boasts the only swimming pool in the center (family rooms, air-con, parking nearby, Via Capitano Bocchieri 24 but enter at Via Dottor Solarino, tel. 0932-682-157, www.giardinosulduomo.it, info@giardinosulduomo.it).

$$ Hotel dell'Orologio is an *albergo diffuso* of 24 rooms—some in a main building and the rest scattered over a few blocks of the chaotic medieval core. Rooms vary from apartments with terraces to actual caves burrowed into the cliff—choose your room on their website (air-con, lots of stairs, Via Ioppolo 12, tel. 0932-228-386, www.hoteldellorologio.com, info@hoteldellorologio.com, Giorgio).

$ B&B L'Orto Sul Tetto feels like your Italian *nonna's* house, strewn with books, old furniture, and embroidered curtains. The three rooms fill a vertical townhouse, with a cute garden on the roof (air-con, communal fridge, Via T. Distefano 56, tel. 0932-247-785, www.lortosultetto.it, info@lortusultetto.it, Paolo). They also rent two modern apartments nearby.

$ B&B Terrazza dei Sogni has spare, super-clean Ikea-modern rooms in a lively area near the Ibleo public gardens. The terrace on the roof, perfect at sunset, has sun chairs and lovely views of the city (air-con, street parking nearby, Vico Domenico Morelli 8, mobile 333-493-9521, www.terrazzadeisogni.it, info@terrazzadeisogni.it).

$ Il Barocco rents 17 brightly colored rooms with old-fashioned furnishings. Although they don't have views, there's an inviting patio and the location is convenient (air-con, elevator, Via Santa Maria la Nuova 1, tel. 0932-663-105, www.ilbarocco.it, info@ilbarocco.it).

RAGUSA SUPERIORE

While the upper town isn't as characteristic as Ibla, it's got easy parking and is closer to the train and bus stations.

$$ Hotel Montreal is a perfectly located family-run place, just steps downhill from the cathedral, facing the main post office. Their 50 rooms are standard business class, with a 1980s hunter-green look (air-con, elevator, pay parking garage, Via San Giuseppe 14, tel. 0932-621-133, www.montrealhotel.it, info@montrealhotel.it).

Eating in Ragusa

RAGUSA IBLA

The old town is the place to dine in Ragusa. It's crammed with appealing eateries, ranging from traditional to trendy.

$$$$ Duomo is *the* place for top-end elegance in Ragusa. Chef Ciccio Sultano is a local celebrity, with a reputation for creative and beautifully presented cuisine. While the dinner tasting

Ragusa Ibla Hotels & Restaurants

San Leonardo River

100 Meters
100 Yards

VIA DEL MERCATO

VIA IOPPOLO

PURGATORIO

Piazza della Repubblica
#1, 11 & 33
To Ragusa Superiore

VIA TENENTE DI STEFANO

Piazza Solarina

PALAZZO LA ROCCA

V. CAP. BOCC.

DUOMO DI SAN GIORGIO

Piazza

PORTA WALTER

RAGUSA

VIA AVVOCATO GIOVANNI OTTAVIANO

Accommodations

1. San Giorgio Palace Hotel
2. Hotel Antico Convento
3. Epoca Camere con Stile
4. Giardino sul Duomo
5. Hotel dell'Orologio
6. B&B L'Orto Sul Tetto
7. B&B Terrazza dei Sogni
8. Il Barocco Rooms

menus start at €135, there's usually a lunch deal for €59—including two glasses of wine (Tue-Sat 12:30-14:00 & 19:30-22:30, Mon 19:30-22:30 only, closed Sun, reservations required, Via Capitano Bocchieri 31, tel. 0932-651-265).

$$$ I Banchi is a food emporium combining a slick boutique restaurant and an upscale bakery (it's owned by Chef Sultano from Duomo). Up front is a dessert case and a bakery counter. For a full meal, settle in at a table out on the sidewalk or under classy white vaults; they have a tempting à la carte menu as well as expensive fixed-price meals (daily 8:00-24:00, meals served 12:30-15:00 & 19:30-23:00, Via Orfanotrofio 39, tel. 0932-655-000).

$$ Il Barocco has a long list of affordable pizzas, as well as a full menu of *primi, secondi,* and shareable antipasto platters, with ample outdoor seating (Thu-Tue 12:30-14:30 & 19:30-23:30, closed Wed, Via Orfanotrofio 27, tel. 0932-652-397).

$ Trattoria La Bettola is a charming time warp, with lace curtains, checkered tablecloths, and nostalgic music. The homey atmosphere comes with antique prices, which is why their nine tables fill fast. If you're looking for local Ragusan cuisine, skip it—the menu is a generic list of crowd-pleasing pan-Italian clas-

RAGUSA & THE SOUTHEAST

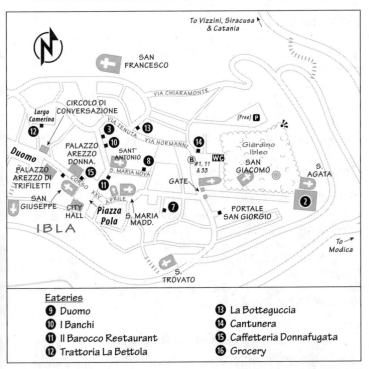

Eateries

9 Duomo
10 I Banchi
11 Il Barocco Restaurant
12 Trattoria La Bettola

13 La Botteguccia
14 Cantunera
15 Caffetteria Donnafugata
16 Grocery

sics (Tue-Sat 19:30-23:00, Sun 12:30-14:30 & 19:30-23:00, closed Mon, Largo Camerina 7, tel. 0932-653-394).

$ La Botteguccia sells custom-made *panini* in their small corner deli near the Ibleo public gardens (Mon-Sat 7:30-15:30 & 16:30-20:00, closed Sun, Via Caporale Bellini 2, mobile 330-678-596).

$ Cantunera makes street food such as piping-hot *arancini* with tasty fillings or *crispelle*—fried dough stuffed with anchovies, cheese, or other savories. They have a selection of Sicilian microbrews, and a few indoor and outdoor tables. Or get your food to go, and enjoy it in the sunny piazza out front or on a bench in the nearby Ibleo gardens (Wed-Mon 11:30-15:00 & 18:00-23:00, closed Tue, Largo San Domenico 18, tel. 0932-185-7234).

$ Caffetteria Donnafugata serves up coffee, pastries, *granita*, and savory snacks with streetside seating. Ask for a sampler tasting of three *granita* flavors and a giant brioche for dipping (€5)—easily enough for two people (daily 7:00-24:00, Corso XXV Aprile 29, tel. 0932-653-399).

Supermarket: A tiny **Despar** grocery can be found in Ibla at Piazza Duomo 6 (Mon-Sat 7:30-13:30 & 17:00-20:00, closed Sun).

RAGUSA & THE SOUTHEAST

RAGUSA SUPERIORE

Don't go out of your way to dine in Ragusa Superiore. But if you need a spot to eat after a strenuous hill climb, these choices are close to the cathedral. For locations, see the "Ragusa Superiore" map, earlier.

Via Mariannina Coffa, the street leading downhill from the cathedral square, is lined with enticing, modern eateries with outdoor terraces. You'll find a creative pizzeria (**$$** Konza), Japanese/sushi (**$** Toshi), and a microbrew taproom (**$$** Yblon), as well as more traditional bars and *trattorie*. It's sleepy at lunch (when many places are closed), but it's a great place to browse if you find yourself here at dinnertime.

$$ Trattoria da Luigi, a block from the cathedral square, has a cozy, modern interior and a short and sweet menu with affordable prices (Fri-Wed 12:00-14:30 & 19:00-22:30, closed Thu, Corso Vittorio Veneto 96, tel. 0932-624-016).

$ Antico Caffè Trieste has been caffeinating the locals for a hundred years. They serve light lunches, but I'd take one of each from the sweet case (Mon-Sat 6:30-20:30, closed Sun, Corso Italia 76, tel. 0932-621-061, Gianni).

Ragusa Connections

Unless otherwise noted, Interbus provides bus service to and from Ragusa (www.interbus.it).

From Ragusa by Bus to: Catania (hourly, 2 hours), **Palermo** (4/day, 4 hours, AST, www.aziendasicilianatrasporti.it), **Taormina** (hourly, 3.5 hours, change in Catania), **Modica** (hourly, 25 minutes), **Scicli** (5/day, 1.5 hours, change in Modica), **Noto** (8/day, 2.25 hours). Most connections to other points in Sicily require a change in Catania.

By Train to: Siracusa (4/day, 2 hours).

Southeast Countryside Drive

RAGUSA LOOP

Sicily's southeast is a prosperous, mostly rural area with a relaxed vibe. Destroyed by the 1693 earthquake and reborn in Baroque style, the region's architecture is a festival of curlicue facades and undulating interiors, with a harmony not seen in other parts of the island. This lovely area and its trail of Baroque villages is worth ▲—or even more, for Sicily aficionados who enjoy country joyrides. The beloved Italian TV show featuring the exploits of Inspector Montalbano was filmed in this area, making it particularly enjoyable for fans.

Using Ragusa as a home base, this loop drive links up a quartet of delightful stops—enough to fill a leisurely day, and still make it back home to Ragusa in time for a nap, *passeggiata,* and dinner. The highlights include a large valley town known for its chocolate factories (Modica); a smaller valley village with an interesting church and fun-to-stroll pedestrian zone (Scicli); a humble beachfront fishing village (Donnalucata); and, for those with more time and an appetite for aristocratic Italian lifestyles, the quirky country manor house of Donnafugata.

Planning Your Drive: The four stops on this drive (Modica, Scicli, Donnalucata, and Donnafugata Castle)—plus Ragusa— form a handy loop, each one spaced about 20 to 30 minutes apart. Without stops, plan on two hours of driving (50 miles). An easy day plan is to leave Ragusa at 9:30, stop in Modica to poke around and sample chocolates, then push on for lunch in either charming Scicli or coastal Donnalucata before touring Donnafugata Castle and its aristocratic country gardens.

Your main decision is whether to visit **Donnafugata Castle,** which keeps irregular hours. On Tuesday, Saturday, and Sunday, when the castle is open until 16:30 (last entrance 16:00), you can do the drive as outlined below and end at the castle. On other days, reverse the route to do the castle first—or skip the castle entirely (while worthwhile, it's not a must—read the description and decide).

From Ragusa to Modica

• *From Ragusa's lower parking lot, head right on Via Avvocato Giovanni Ottaviano and follow signs to* Modica *(on SS-115); you'll twist up switchbacks, then drive about 20 minutes through a lunar landscape above a dramatic, rocky ravine. As you approach Modica, follow signs for* centro storico *and park along the main street (see tips later).*

▲Modica

The city of Modica (pop. 54,000) fills a river valley a short drive from Ragusa. Although slightly smaller than Ragusa, the way it's

Southeast Countryside Drive

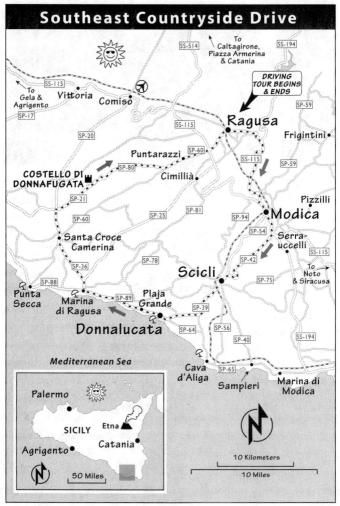

situated—a wall of Baroque clambering up the steep cliffs of a ravine—makes it appear large and impressive.

While the city itself is appealing to stroll, visitors flock to Modica primarily to sample the local specialty, *cioccolato di Modica*. Sicily was under Spanish rule just as explorers were returning from the New World with exotic new foods, including tomatoes, corn...and cocoa beans. Modica mastered this new ingredient, crushing it on basalt plates *(metates)* and adding local sugar, creating an early version of chocolate bars. No visit to the town is complete without sampling the crunchy texture and bittersweet taste of this old-style chocolate.

Orientation to Modica: Modica climbs up the hills on either side of its main street, Corso Umberto I. On a quick visit it's best to skip the upper town (Modica Alta) to focus on the lower town in the valley (Modica Bassa). Look for pay-and-display **parking** along Corso Umberto I (marked with blue lines); there's easy free parking in a lot as you first arrive in town, about a five-minute

walk from the center. The **TI,** right along the main street near the lower cathedral, has a map of interesting sights in the vicinity (Mon-Sat 9:00-13:00 & 15:00-19:00, closed Sun, Corso Umberto 141, mobile 346-6558-227).

Visiting Modica: The lower town's main landmark is the **Cathedral of San Pietro,** with a grand staircase out front and a frilly interior.

But the main attraction is chocolate. Across from San Pietro, down a little alley, you'll find **Antica Dolceria Bonajuto,** the old-

est and most famous chocolate producer in town. Inside their old-time, wood-paneled shop, browse the glass cases, and—just inside the entrance, on the floor—see the traditional grinding stone that was used to crush cocoa beans. The bustling kitchen in back turns out molten hot chocolate by the cup, as well as fancy local pastries. On the counter, a chocolate sample buffet lets you compare flavors—orange, spicy pepper, cinnamon, and about a dozen others. Try each one—after all, they don't add any fat to this style of chocolate, so it's practically a health food (daily 9:00-20:30, Corso Umberto I 159, tel. 0932-941-225, www.bonajuto.it).

Other chocolate shops line the main drag. Or, for something different, you can walk five minutes to the sweet **Museum of Old Tools** (Museo degli Arnesi di Una Volta), dedicated to preserving tools and household items from the past. Each little display features an old Sicilian trade: shoemaker, pharmacist, tailor. The passionate custodians will demonstrate how some of the antique items work (€2.50, Tue-Sun 10:00-13:00 & 16:00-19:00, Mon by appointment, Piazza Matteotti, mobile 366-102-3458, www. gliarnesidiunavolta.it). To get there, turn your back to the cathedral, turn left, and walk to Piazza Matteotti. The museum is on the left in the inner courtyard of the big building that dominates the square.

With more time, you can hike 10 minutes (or drive 3 minutes) uphill to Modica's other cathedral, the even more striking **Cathedral of San Giorgio.** If it looks familiar, it's because the same architect designed the Cathedral of San Giorgio in Ragusa Ibla. Inside you'll enjoy another grand Baroque space with massive stone columns.

Eating in Modica: $$ Osteria dei Sapori Perduti serves up hearty bowls of pasta in a red-checkered tablecloth atmosphere, with a few sidewalk tables. It's about a five-minute walk from the lower cathedral, and just below the upper cathedral (Wed-Mon 12:00-15:00 & 19:30-24:00, closed Tue, Corso Umberto I 228, tel. 0932-944-247, Federica).

• *When you're ready to move on, take the scenic route to Scicli: Follow Corso Umberto I south to the main roundabout and take the third exit, toward Pozzallo (ignore the first exit that's signed for* Scicli*). Stay to the right to join Via Nazionale, which eventually puts you on road SP-42 (following signs to* Scicli*).*

The final approach to Scicli is down a dramatic series of switchbacks, revealing more and more of the valley-filling town and the caves and walls high on the cliffs above it. Dropping down to the main road, turn right onto Corso Umberto I to head into town, following signs for cen-tro. *A series of sharp left turns leads you to the elongated main square, Piazza Italia, where you can look for street parking.*

▲Scicli

Scicli (SHEEK-lee, pop. 27,000)—also rebuilt after the earthquake of 1693—has small-town charm and a Baroque face. The

hills surrounding the village are not just picturesque—they're pockmarked with caves where townspeople lived until the 20th century. While there are no big-league sights here, Scicli is an enjoyable place to simply stroll, with a fine little pedestrian zone and a church with a fascinating statue and story.

Orientation to Scicli: There's no big parking lot in the center; look for pay-and-display parking (marked with blue lines) either

Inspector Montalbano Mysteries

For fans of fictional Sicilian detective Inspector Montalbano, the areas around Agrigento, Ragusa, and Scicli might feel familiar. The engaging mystery novels by Sicilian author Andrea Camilleri (1925-) have been translated into English and also inspired a popular TV series filmed in south and southeast Sicily.

In the books and show, police precinct chief Salvo Montalbano solves crimes large and small while navigating the everyday realities of Sicilian life. He runs into prostitution, drug crime, the Mafia, and murder, but he also deals with stubborn colleagues, nosy neighbors, and his on-again, off-again northern Italian girlfriend, Livia. Montalbano operates with panache, spot-on intuition, and a wicked sense of humor. Sicilian to the core, he always has time—even in the midst of an intense investigation—to savor a wonderful Sicilian meal, preferably in silence. The plots are creative and ingenious but, above all, shine a light on the unique character of Sicilian culture.

Camilleri is arguably Sicily's most famous living writer and has penned more than 20 books following Montalbano's adventures. Camilleri was a screenwriter and worked in television before he started writing the series in his 60s. Now in his 90s, despite failing eyesight, he is still turning out novels set in and around his home town of Porto Empedocle (near Agrigento).

The popular TV series, *Inspector Montalbano,* is now in its twelfth season in Italy and distributed worldwide. It's even spawned a spinoff prequel, *The Young Montalbano.* Fans flock to the locations seen in the television series, including the Town Hall in Scicli (his office), Ragusa Ibla (Vigàta, where the detective works), Punta Secca (Marinella, his seaside home), Sampieri (coastal beach), and Donnafugata Castle (the lair of a mafioso nemesis).

along Piazza Italia, or just beyond it, along Via Nazionale. The pedestrian zone, Via Francesco M. Penna, is just a few short blocks away.

Visiting Scicli: Begin on the tree-lined **Piazza Italia.** Look up to the cliffs that hem in the town, and you'll see caves and walls embedded in the volcanic rock (called tuff, or *tufo*). The archaeological areas between Modica (Cava d'Ispica) and Scicli (Chiafura) are sprinkled with caves with a long history of human habitation (some as far back as the Bronze Age). Because tuff (volcanic ash that has compacted into rock) is easy to carve, these cliffs are ideal for burrowing into, with the added benefit that the caves stay cool in summer and warm in winter. In the past, caves were used for dwellings, and some functioned as burial tombs. The caves surrounding Scicli were inhabited from the Byzantine era (5th century) until the 1950s, when the last residents moved out. These days, some of the caves are used for *presepe* displays (nativity scenes) during Christmastime.

On top of the cliffs sits the Castelluccio, which roughly translates to "big and broken-down castle." This fortification was central to the defense of this region until the earthquake, when it was damaged and abandoned.

On the main square, butted up against an eyesore modern building, is Scicli's main church, **Chiesa Madre di San Ignazio**

de Loyola (free, daily 8:00-12:00 & 15:00-18:30). Inside, on the left aisle, look for the side chapel with a fascinating statue called the Madonna delle Milizie. The Virgin Mary is depicted as a warrior-queen, sitting on a rearing white horse and brandishing a sword. According to local legend, in 1091, this "Militarized Madonna" appeared to help the Normans fight off the Saracens (North African Muslims). The statue is flanked by two paintings showing the Madonna riding into battle.

According to legend, the Normans and Saracens battled on the coast near here in 1091. Europe was under continued attack by the Ottoman Empire from the 16th to 18th century—so this statue and paintings served as emotion-stoking religious propaganda. Notice that the Madonna's horse simultaneously tramples two different types of heathens: a dark-skinned African and a lighter-skinned Turk. If this strikes you as culturally insensitive—and it should—skip a visit here on the last Saturday in May, when this statue is paraded around town in an annual mock battle that commemorates the Virgin's appearance to

the Normans. For the festivities, some locals dress up as, ahem, Saracens. The chatty custodian, who speaks only Italian (and doesn't care that you don't), loves to point out details of the statue: The Madonna is depicted not as a standard-issue brunette, but with decidedly jet-black hair—like a good Sicilian. And the horse's belly is made with a wine barrel.

Exit the church to the left, and go left around the corner onto Via Nazionale. Walk two short blocks until you reach (on the left) the town's pedestrian zone, **Via Francesco M. Penna,** lined by stately civic buildings and fine churches. The start of this area is marked by a dignified municipal building and—attached to that—the lovely San Giovanni Evangelista church. Stop in to see its bright-blue-accented interior. Even in this land of dazzling Baroque, it's like stepping into a Fabergé egg.

As you stroll along Via Francesco M. Penna, you'll pass nice restaurants, trendy bars, and boutiques. Appreciate the frilly stone-and-metal balconies that jut out overhead. A couple of blocks down on the right, at #24, step into an antique *farmacia* (pharmacy) to appreciate displays of pill bottles and tonics from a different time. Just beyond at #34, Palazzo Spadaro offers tours of its lovely period interior, used in the *Inspector Montalbano* TV series as the detective's office. At the end of the street, the deconsecrated church of Saint Teresa has an interesting display of detached frescoes in a fluffy Baroque interior.

Eating in Scicli: $$ Baqqalà serves up all fish, all the time, on its charming little urban terrace a two-minute walk from the pedestrian zone (Thu-Tue 12:30-14:30 & 20:00-22:30, closed Wed, Piazza Ficili 3, tel. 0932-931-028). With Via Francesco M. Penna at your back, cross Via Nazionale and bear right, then look for the restaurant on your left.

• *To get back on the road, from Piazza Italia, drive south on Corso Giuseppe Garibaldi to SP-39, following signs for* Donnalucata. *The streets in central Donnalucata form a one-way loop; ideally drive along the loop closer to the water (Via Pirandello/Via Sanremo) and look for free street parking. You'll find pay lots a bit farther out.*

Donnalucata

This little fishing village/beach resort is a scenic spot to take a lunch break and walk on the sand. This was the site of the 1091

battle between the Normans and the Saracens, when the Madonna legendarily appeared in battle armor to lead the Normans to victory (a moment commemorated by the statue we just saw in Scicli). A monument to the battle eventually became the bell tower of the Church of Santa Caterina da Siena—and a village grew around it. Today the pretty little church (about two blocks north of the beach) has a simple, contemporary interior with recent gilded mosaics.

Once in town, there's not much to do other than walk the beach—which is short but broad, protected by a stout breakwater—stroll the concrete waterfront promenade, and enjoy a seafood lunch.

RAGUSA & THE SOUTHEAST

Eating in Donnalucata: Two appealing places serve up fish and seafood just a block off the waterfront promenade, at the west end of town nearest the beach. **$$$ Ristorante Mezzaparola** is popular, with a long list of changing specials and a glassed-in terrace (Thu-Tue 12:30-14:30 & 19:30-22:30, closed Wed, Via Martiri d'Ungheria 2, tel. 0932-937-474). Next door, **$$$ Brise Ristorantico** feels simpler, with a cute interior and a fine terrace; they serve lunch only on the weekend (Wed-Mon 19:30-22:30, Fri-Sun also open 12:00-14:30, closed Tue, Via Luigi Pirandello 45, mobile 393-898-0467).

• *To continue to Donnafugata Castle, head west on the waterfront Viale della Repubblica (SP-89), following signs for Marina di Ragusa. As you approach this large beach resort, you'll pass through three roundabouts (follow signs for* Ragusa*) before turning left on SP-36 toward Santa Croce Camerina. After going around that town, follow signs to* Comiso, *and turn right at the brown signs for* Castello di Donnafugata.

Donnafugata Castle (Castello di Donnafugata)

Originally a farmhouse, this property was transformed in the 19th century into a Neo-Gothic castle by Baron Corrado Arezzo de Spuches, a journalist and influ-

ential politician of his day (he had enough clout to deviate train tracks to pass closer to his property). Corrado enjoyed traveling abroad and brought home architectural ideas to incorporate into his fanciful palace. What he created is a textbook example of the mix-and-match Historicism of the Romantic Age. It's a big, blocky house, anchored by medieval-style, round, crenellated towers, with faux-Venetian Gothic window frames. While Europe has plenty of country estates that are more impressive and more enjoyable to tour (this barely cracks the top 50), they're relatively rare in Sicily, making this a unique opportunity to get a taste of rural aristocratic life.

Cost and Hours: €6, Tue and Sat-Sun 9:00-13:00 & 14:30-16:30, Wed-Fri 9:00-13:00 only, closed Mon, parking-€2, tel. 0932-619-333.

Eating: The stable yard in front of the castle has several cafés.

Visiting the Castle: You'll tour 20 rooms, each with high ceilings, frescoes, silk-clad walls, and bright, cheery colors. First you'll see the grand public rooms, then the much more understated private quarters. A collection of period clothing displayed in several rooms helps tell the story of the castle and the bygone times of the Sicilian aristocracy. In the Coat of Arms Hall, get a good look at the Arezzo family's seal: a shield with four hedgehogs. In Sicilian dialect, a hedgehog is *rizzo*, which sounds like Arezzo.

After exiting the interior, angle through the courtyard to another turnstile that leads out to 20 acres of gardens, with a stone maze, a temple, and a grotto. You'll find a scrubby mix of vegetation: giant banyan trees, lavender and rosemary shrubs, and palm trees. Also look for the steps up to the terrace and turrets in front of the house, offering a good view of the eclectic architecture.

By the way, the name "Donnafugata"—meaning "fleeing woman"—connects the castle to a famous story of a queen who escaped from an aged suitor who had imprisoned her. While it's fun to imagine that story at this romantic site, it actually happened at a different castle near Palermo.

• *Leaving Donnafugata, you'll turn left and follow signs to return to Ragusa. The rolling countryside, striped with stone-walled farms, is worth slowing down for. Linger, take pictures of the cows, and enjoy your drive in this beautiful, green part of the island.*

Noto

RAGUSA & THE SOUTHEAST

Nicknamed "the Garden in Stone," Noto (pop. 24,000, 20 miles southwest of Siracusa) may well be Sicily's most pristine small city. It's the capital of Sicilian Baroque. Like neighboring cities, the ancient Noto Antica was destroyed with the earthquake of 1693. Besides some sections of town walls, little of the old city remains. Rather than rebuild in the same spot, residents moved five miles to

Noto

200 Meters
200 Yards

SAN DOMENICO

WALK ENDS

MONTEVERGINI

PALAZZO NICOLACI

Piazza XVI Maggio

CORSO

SAN NICOLÒ

VIA CAVOUR

SAN FRANCESCO

Piazza San Francesco all'Immacolata

To Siracusa via SP-115 & A-45

TEATRO TINA DI LORENZO

SAN CARLO

WC

Piazza Municipo

VITTORIO

STADIUM

VIA NAPOLI

To Modica & Ragusa via SS-115

CITY HALL

VIA DUCEZIO

PORTA REALE

WALK BEGINS

EMANUELE

Villa Comunale

STATUE

VIA AURISPA

VIA ROMA (SS-115)

VIA MAIORE

VIA PIOLA

VIA PRINCIPE (SS-115)

To Train Station

To Siracusa via SS-115 & E-45

Eateries
1 Caffè Sicilia
2 Caffè Costanzo
3 Sabbinirica
4 Ristorante Marpessa

the south. Starting with this blank slate, they designed the town in one fell swoop and built it according to a master plan—something rarely seen in Sicily before that time. The new city was planned on a regular grid with wide, straight streets and large squares. These gracious spaces were also functional: In case of another major earthquake, townspeople could easily find safe areas to gather. This new approach to urban planning and the unity of its single architectural style make Noto a visually striking place. A stroll through its elegant piazzas is like being immersed in a giant sculpture.

Tourist Information: The TI is right along the main street, a few steps from the cathedral (daily 10:00-20:00, later in Aug, until 18:00 off-season, Corso Vittorio Emanuele 135, mobile 339-481-6218.

Getting There: For drivers coming from Siracusa, follow E-45 south toward Avola and take the Noto exit. From Ragusa, it's an hour drive on country roads.

Arrival in Noto: The entrance of the town (and the start of my self-guided walk) is on its south side, at the ceremonial gateway called Porta Reale. Buses arrive just in front of the gate at the park. Drivers can find parking in two side-by-side pay lots just a block up the hill from Porta Reale, at the corner of Via Cavour and Via Fabrizi.

Noto Town Walk

This short walk is a straight shot through the heart of Noto. Along the way, you'll pass through the town's three main piazzas, designed as part of the rebuilt city. You can walk from one end to the other in 10 minutes if you don't stop—but you'll want to allow 30 minutes or more, especially if you plan to sample the town's gelato.
• *Start just outside the city on the south side, where a monumental gate faces the city park.*

Porta Reale

This royal gate welcomes you with the three symbols of the town: in the top center, a pelican (symbol of dedication to Ferdinand II, the Spanish/Bourbon king when the gate was built in 1838); on the left, a tower (symbol of strength); and on the right, a *cirneco* dog (an ancient local breed, representing fidelity—faith).
• *Walk through the gate and along...*

Corso Vittorio Emanuele

The architects who planned the new city after the great earthquake laid out a main axis that leads through three elegant piazzas—each one an outdoor living room. This traffic-free artery is a showcase of churches and monuments, but it's also alive with street vendors with carts, shops, cafés, and world-famous *gelaterie*. While it may seem like the main street in any Sicilian town, pay attention to the harmonious architecture. The buildings are all the same color and style, and are built on a similar scale. What sets Noto apart is the harmony of its design. As you walk, feel the flow from building to building.

In any other city in Sicily, you'll rarely find a grid of streets, much less any street that's straight for more than a few blocks. While the Romans appreciated the concept of urban planning, this wisdom was lost to the ages until the Renaissance. In Sicily, it was finally reapplied right here in Noto. For example, the city's main thoroughfare is rotated approximately 20 degrees from the east-west axis—an idea that originally came from the Roman architect and philosopher Vitruvius.
• *A few steps take you into Noto's first square...*

Piazza San Francesco all'Immacolata

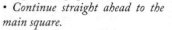

This unique, split-level square is divided in two: a lower square around a fountain, and an upper square around the statue of the Immacolata, the Virgin Mary. The wide staircase leading up to the Church of San Francesco unifies the two, creating a pleasant gathering space.

• *Continue straight ahead to the main square.*

Piazza Municipio

The oversized cathedral square, with its gracious steps creating a hangout zone for locals, is the centerpiece of the city.

The **Cathedral of San Nicolò** was nearly destroyed in 1996, when its dome collapsed due to lack of maintenance. The ensuing scandal focused a spotlight on the need to preserve the city, and funds were raised to reconstruct the church, which reopened with a shiny new dome in 2007.

Hike up the stairs and step inside (free, daily 8:00-12:30 & 15:30-19:00). You'll know immediately that this is a very new

church, with stark and noticeably modern decor. As you enter, on the left in the first niche is a model of the damaged church after the collapse. At the base of the nearby pillar, look for the modern cross (marked *Croce Lignea*), made with pieces of wood from the shipwrecked boats of African refugees. (Other, similar crosses are displayed around the church.) The stained-glass windows in the central nave are recent, featuring a mix of older and newer saints. Walk up to the front of the church, before the main altar, and look up. Under the cupola, the Virgin Mary leads apostles and local saints to the skies, with the four evangelists on the tops of the pillars just below.

As you exit the church, you're facing yet another beautiful

building, Noto's **City Hall** (Palazzo Ducezio), with a convex facade supported by twenty columned arches. The building is named for Ducezio, an ancient king of the Sicels, who founded the city and was one of the last to resist the Greek invader/colonizers of the island. Most of the building is off-limits to the public but you can pay a few euros to step into its Hall of Mirrors (Salone degli Specchi), with a ceiling fresco celebrating Ducezio (I'd skip it).

• *You're just a few steps from two opportunities to sample Noto's famous...*

Gelato

Noto recently gained some renown for its gelato artistry. **Caffè Sicilia**—a block past the cathedral, on the left at #125—prides itself on sourcing ingredients locally (closed Mon, Corso Vittorio Emanuele 125). Besides gelato, they make a wide range of Sicilian desserts. Is it the best in town? Only one way to find out...

To comparison-shop, head to **Caffè Costanzo,** another excellent *pasticceria* and *gelateria.* It's less famous, less crowded, and some believe better. You'll find it just downhill from the cathedral, at the bottom of the square on the right side of City Hall (Thu-Tue 7:30-24:00, closed Wed and Nov, Via Silvio Spaventa 7). Their almond *granita* is delicious.

• *Just across from Caffè Sicilia is the street called...*

Via Corrado Nicolaci

On the third weekend of May, this street is transformed into a floral tapestry, decorated with millions of flower petals as part of

a competition called Infiorata di Noto. Each participant is assigned a portion of the street on which to create a floral mosaic. Walk along the street to find photos of previous competitions.

On the left side of the street is the aristocratic townhouse called **Palazzo Nicolaci.** Its exterior demonstrates the delightfully whimsical decoration common to Sicily's Baroque architecture: You'll see carved lions, seahorses, and sirens (thought to protect households against *u malocchiu*—the evil eye). You can tour 10 opulent rooms of this townhouse, with colorfully tiled floors, antique furniture, chandeliers, frescoed ceilings, and balconies with sweeping views over the city (€4, daily 10:00-19:00, possibly later in summer, shorter hours off-season, mobile 320-113-2936).

At the very top of Via Nicolaci, the street ends with the concave facade of the **Church of Montevergini.** If it's open, duck in to see a few costumes and banners used by the historical guilds of Noto for special occasions, such as Easter celebrations.

• *Return to Corso Vittorio Emanuele.*

Across from the bottom of Via Nicolaci is the **Church of San Carlo.** For a few euros, you can climb its 50 tiny and steep steps to a terrace with sprawling views down to the Ionian Sea. Also on the terrace is a chunk of the old church's bell tower and bells.

• *Continue on the Corso. At #93, on the left, you'll find* **$ Sabbinirica,** *a popular deli/sandwich shop with indoor and outdoor seating. This is a great (if slow) spot to get a top-quality sandwich, made with local produce (daily 10:00-22:00, closed Sun afternoon).*

Corso Vittorio Emanuele terminates at Noto's final square...

Piazza XVI Maggio

This is the third and final "outdoor room" in the town plan of Noto.

On the right is the **Church of San Domenico,** where the main architect of Noto, Rosario Gagliardi, is buried. If it's open, take a moment to go inside—in the left aisle a 10-minute video loop shows the stunning collapse of the dome of San Nicolò in 1996. Custodians are there to discuss the restoration and collect donations for necessary renovations.

Opposite the church is the small but charming **Teatro Tina di Lorenzo,** built by the local nobility in 1870. Originally it had neither

a royal box nor seats for commoners—just room for aristocrats. Commoners were welcome inside only if they were willing to stand. (More seats were added in 1920.) The theater—which still hosts performances from November through May—was rechristened for a beloved actress who lived in Noto at the turn of the 20th century. It's worth paying the small fee to step inside and see the beautiful interior (€2, daily 10:00-13:30 & 15:00-17:30). Considering that the Baroque style is architectural theater, what more fitting way to end this walk than with a visit to a real theater?

Back out on the square, take a moment to appreciate the city as a whole. Unlike much of Sicily, with its jumble of styles from different periods, Noto is planned, with streets and buildings well thought out. It's a snapshot in time of architectural innovation in action.

• *Our walk is finished. Head back the way you came, perhaps brows-ing for lunch. One nearby handy spot is **Ristorante Marpessa**, with a nice outdoor terrace; as you face the theater, it's at the left end of the parking-lot square, tucked down the little alley (Tue-Sun 7:30-22:00, closed Mon, Vico Carrozzieri 10, tel. 0931-835-225).*

Noto Connections

Two bus operators serve Noto: **AST** (www.aziendasicilianatrasporti. it) and **Interbus** (www.interbus.it).

From Noto by Bus to: Ragusa (8/day, 2.25 hours, AST), **Sir-acusa** (6/day, 1 hour, Interbus), **Catania** (7/day, 1.5 hours, Inter-bus).

From Noto by Train to: Siracusa (4/day, 30 minutes).

SIRACUSA

The bustling seafront city of Siracusa (sih-rah-KOOH-zah) mingles big-league ancient history, a charming old town squeezed onto an island, lively restaurants and hip bars, and equal parts serious sightseeing and lazy vacationing. All around, it's one of Sicily's most pleasing destinations.

Ancient Syracuse was a huge power in the Greek world—for a time even eclipsing its rival city-state, Athens; today, a rich trove of Greek (and Roman) ruins hint at the glory of what was one of the most important cities of Magna Graecia. The medieval-era town came tumbling down in the catastrophic earthquake of 1693, and was rebuilt in the Baroque fashion of the time.

The modern mainland city of Siracusa (pop. 125,000) huddles around its expansive bay, as if protecting the little island of Ortigia like a jewel. The once-fortified Ortigia (or-TEE-jah) is the ancient birthplace and contemporary heart of the city, with meandering lanes of eroding palaces and ruins side-by-side with hipster wine bars. Just a generation ago, Ortigia was mostly deserted. But in the last decade or two, a new affluence has swept the island neighborhood, giving it a bohemian and trendy energy that fills it with joy. Happily, Siracusa is increasingly accessible to visitors but not overrun with crowds.

There are some major sights in the modern, mainland part of town: ancient ruins, an archaeological museum, catacombs, and a modern church. But spend most of your time in the fascinating historic quarter filling the island of Ortigia. With its colorful market, lively main square, funky back alleys, and breezy sea views, Ortigia is, for me, the most enjoyable urban environment anywhere in Sicily.

PLANNING YOUR TIME

Siracusa demands at least one full day: a half-day for the important ancient sites on the mainland, and a half-day to explore the island of Ortigia. Allow two nights to really savor the town.

Ideally, visit the ancient sites when they first open to avoid tour groups and the midday heat. Ortigia is most enjoyable late in the afternoon and in the evening. With two days, devote one full day to just poking around Ortigia.

Here's an ambitious full-day plan:

8:30	Hit the Neapolis Archaeological Park when it opens
10:00	Visit the Paolo Orsi Archaeological Museum
11:00	Tour the modern church across the street, and/or the nearby catacombs
12:00	Head over to the island of Ortigia to browse the market and grab lunch
13:30	Follow my "Ortigia Walk," dropping into sights that interest you
17:00	Take in a puppet show
19:00	Stroll the harbor promenade
20:00	Dinner in Ortigia

Orientation to Siracusa

Siracusa is made up of two parts: the drab, modern mainland city and the small, historic island of Ortigia at the center of the harbor. The mainland and Ortigia are connected by a pair of bridges: Ponte Santa Lucia and the older, stone Ponte Umberto I.

Focus your visit on charming **Ortigia.** The main spine of the old town runs from the Temple of Apollo down Corso Giacomo Matteotti to Piazza Archimede, then to Piazza Duomo by way of Via Roma. The centerpiece of Ortigia is its lovely cathedral, surrounded by one of Sicily's finest squares.

The only reason to go to the **mainland** is to visit the Neapolis Archaeological Park, the nearby Paolo Orsi Archaeological Museum, and the catacombs, all to the northwest of Ortigia.

TOURIST INFORMATION

Siracusa has two TIs, both near the cathedral in Ortigia. Each one is only marginally helpful and keeps unpredictable hours, but they're good for city maps and other brochures (Via Roma 31, Mon-Wed 7:30-17:00, Thu-Fri until 14:00, closed Sat-Sun, tel. 0931-65201; Via Maestranza 33, Mon-Fri 8:30-13:30, closed Sat-Sun, tel. 0921-464-255; www.siracusaturismo.net).

SIRACUSA

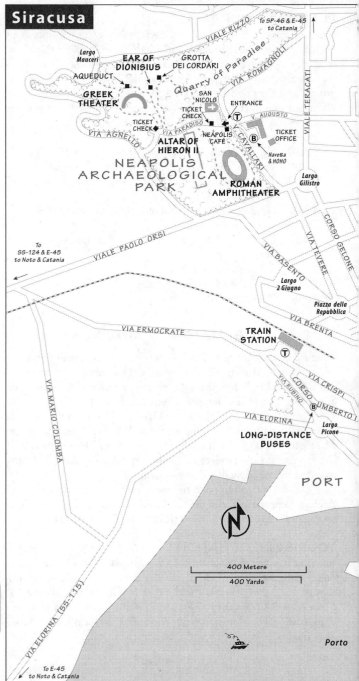

Siracusa

VIALE RIZZO

To SP-46 & E-45
to Catania

Largo
Mauceri

EAR OF
DIONISIUS

GROTTA
DEI CORDARI

VIA ROMAGNOLI

AQUEDUCT

Quarry of Paradise

VIALE TERACATI

GREEK
THEATER

SAN
NICOLO

ENTRANCE

V. AUGUSTO

TICKET
CHECK

NEAPOLIS
CAFÉ

TICKET
OFFICE

TICKET
CHECK

VIA PARADISO

CAVALLARI

Navetta
& HOHO

VIA AGNELLO

ALTAR OF
HIERON II

Largo
Gilistro

NEAPOLIS
ARCHAEOLOGICAL
PARK

ROMAN
AMPHITHEATER

CORSO GELONE

VIA TEVERE

To
SS-124 & E-45
to Noto & Catania

VIALE PAOLO ORSI

VIA BASENTO

Largo
2 Giugno

Piazza della
Repubblica

VIA ERMOCRATE

VIA BRENTA

TRAIN
STATION

VIA CRISPI

VIA RUBINO

CORSO UMBERTO I

VIA MARIO COLOMBA

VIA ELORINA

Largo
Picone

LONG-DISTANCE
BUSES

PORT

N

400 Meters

400 Yards

VIA ELORINA (SS-115)

To E-45
to Noto & Catania

Porto

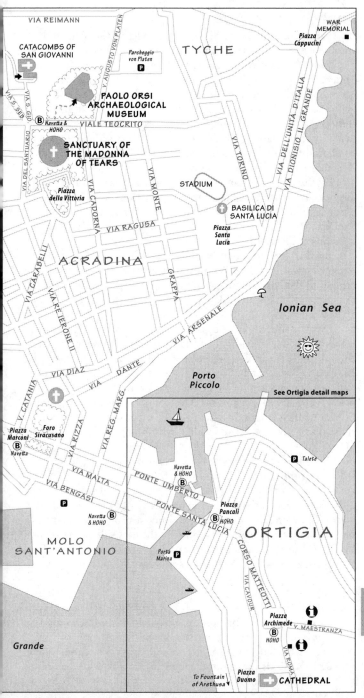

ARRIVAL IN SIRACUSA

By Train: Trains arrive at Siracusa Centrale on the mainland. If you're staying in Ortigia, it's worth investing €10 or so for a **taxi** (they wait in front of the station). It's a 15-minute **walk** to the bridges that connect the mainland to Ortigia, then another 5- to 15-minute walk depending on your accommodations. You can also get to Ortigia by **bus** from nearby Piazza Marconi. Exit the train station to the left, then immediately bear right onto Corso Umberto I. Continue walking for five minutes to Piazza Marconi, where you'll find the stop for the small electric *navetta* bus (for details, see "Getting Around Siracusa," later).

By Bus: Long-distance buses, including buses from Catania's airport, arrive one block from the train station along Corso Umberto I. From here, it's 15-minute **walk** to Ortigia (follow Corso Umberto I, which leads straight to its bridge). Or you can catch the local **bus** at Piazza Marconi (see above).

By Car: Approaching Siracusa, you'll be funneled into the narrow end of the city's peninsula, eventually reaching the twin bridges to Ortigia. Before you get there, decide whether you want to drive and park on the island, or stow your car on the mainland and walk across.

If you're sleeping in Ortigia, your hotel can likely register your car for the "ZTL" zone (limited traffic zone; begins when you cross either bridge, generally in effect weeknights after 20:00, Sat after 16:00, and Sun after 11:00), and can give you advice about where to park—the Parcheggio Talete garage is likely the best option (see below). Otherwise, park in the **Molo Sant'Antonio lot** (€1/hour, €10/24 hours; to enter drive up to gate—a camera records your license plate; pay on exit) and walk across the Ponte Santa Lucia to Ortigia.

The most straightforward long-term pay parking in Ortigia is **Parcheggio Talete** (€10/24 hours; access is outside the "ZTL" zone). For short-term parking, there's also a small pay lot to the right as you enter the island, along the harbor at **Porta Marina** (€2/hour). There are also many free, unlimited-time parking spaces, mostly along the embankment road on the east side of the island. Be careful to park only in spaces with white lines—yellow lines are for locals only (and towing cars is a favorite sport of the *vigili* in Ortigia).

HELPFUL HINTS

Tap Water Warning: Because of old pipes, it's not advisable to drink the tap water in Siracusa. Buy bottled water.

Market: A bustling food market fills Ortigia's **Via Emmanuele de Benedictis,** next to the Temple of Apollo (Mon-Sat 7:00-14:00, closed Sun).

Laundry: Wash & Dry Siracusa offers self-service laundry on the mainland, a block from the Umberto I bridge to Ortigia (Mon-Fri 8:30-13:30 & 15:30-20:00, Sat until 13:30, closed Sun, Corso Umberto I 13, mobile 327-540-6891).

Spelling: Siracusa is also known internationally as "Syracuse" and Ortigia is often spelled "Ortygia" in English. I've used the Sicilian spellings, unless referring to the ancient city of Syracuse.

GETTING AROUND SIRACUSA

By Bus: Small electric buses *(navetta)* connect Ortigia and sights on the mainland (€1; ticket good for 90 minutes, buy from machine on board or at a tobacco shop before boarding; runs roughly every 15 Sicilian minutes). The bus makes a loop around the periphery of Ortigia, then heads inland and along the coast. It then stops near the Paolo Orsi Archaeological Museum, Catacombs of San Giovanni, and Sanctuary of the Madonna of Tears. The bus then continues to the Neapolis Archaeological Park, down to Piazza Marconi (the closest stop to the train and long-distance bus stations), and then to Molo Sant'Antonio before crossing back to Ortigia.

By Hop-on, Hop-off Bus Tour: The **Siracusa Open Tour** is unusually cheap and handy for reaching the mainland sights, and makes many of the same stops as the local bus. You can catch it in Ortigia (at Piazza Archimede, and at the main parking lot, Parcheggio Talete) and ride it to the sights on the mainland, then back to Ortigia. Hop on at any stop and pay the driver for an all-day ticket. The headphone commentary is paltry, but think of this as affordable round-trip transportation to the mainland sights (€5, daily 9:00-19:00, 2-3/hour, less frequent off-season, tel. 0931-959-912, www.siracusaopentour.com).

Tip for Reaching Mainland Sights: The unpredictable *navetta* and the affordable hop-on, hop-off bus use the same stops. Because of this, the easiest plan is to simply take whichever one comes first. The handiest place to do this is across Ponte Umberto I from Ortigia.

By Taxi: From Ortigia to the mainland sights, a taxi for up to four costs €10; catch one at Piazza Pancali, in front of the Temple of Apollo. At the Neapolis Archaeological Park, taxis wait across the street from the entrance for the return ride. For private drivers, see "Tours in Siracusa," next.

Tours in Siracusa

Local Guides

Liliana Rainieri offers private tours of Siracusa and the surrounding areas toward Ragusa (€130/3 hours, €200/full day, mobile

Siracusa at a Glance

In Ortigia

▲▲**Siracusa Cathedral** Eclectic cathedral mirrors the patchwork of civilizations that built Siracusa. **Hours:** Mon-Sat 9:00-18:30, July-Aug until 19:00, Oct-March until 17:30, closed Sun except for Mass. See page 290.

▲**Catacombs of San Filippo Apostolo** Catacombs linking a crypt, WWII air-raid shelter, and Jewish bath. **Hours:** Mon-Sat 10:00-12:30 & 15:00-17:00, closed Sun and Nov-March. See page 292.

In Mainland Siracusa

▲▲**Neapolis Archaeological Park** Remains from the ancient Greek city-state, plus a Roman theater. **Hours:** Daily 8:30-19:30, off-season closes one hour before sunset. See page 293.

▲▲**Paolo Orsi Archaeological Museum** One of Sicily's top archaeology museums, with artifacts from prehistory to the Roman era. **Hours:** Tue-Sat 9:00-19:00, Sun until 14:00, closed Mon. See page 298.

▲**Sanctuary of the Madonna of Tears** Unexpectedly modern church dedicated to a weeping Madonna. **Hours:** Mon-Sat 7:00-13:00 & 15:00-20:00, Sun until 21:00. See page 297.

▲**Catacombs of San Giovanni** Best catacombs in Siracusa, below a ruined church. **Hours:** Daily 9:30-12:30 & 14:30-18:30, closed Mon Nov-Feb, closed Jan. See page 301.

333-125-6596, www.lilianarainieri.altervista.org, liliana.rainieri@gmail.com).

Eva Greco also leads private tours of Siracusa and nearby destinations (€160/half-day, mobile 338-755-8537, evatour@libero.it).

Paolo Gallo can drive and guide you anywhere in southeast Sicily and beyond (€210/half-day, €320/full day, up to 4 people, mobile 338-529-6915, www.sunnysicily.com, info.sunnysicily@gmail.com).

Private Driver

Salvatore Giurdanella drives within Siracusa and can connect to Catania or other cities in the region (one-way to Neapolis Archaeological Park—€10/up to 4 people, €20/up to 8 people; to Catania airport—€60/up to 4, €80/up to 8; to Taormina—€110/up to 4, €150/up to 8, mobile 339-221-8690).

Boat Tours

Blu Marlin offers fun boat tours around Ortigia or along the mainland coast to see dramatic rock formations and small grottos (each tour €10, 50 minutes; €15 for combined 1.5-hour tour; English commentary; departs when a group forms). In summer, the boat stops in scenic spots for passengers to take a quick dip. Kindly Carmelo and Ornella use glass-bottom boats in summer, and can also do tours off-season if you book in advance (info desk at Porta Marina, Ortigia, mobile 347-659-6900, merlino.carmelo@alice.it).

Ortigia Walk

This hour-long walk leads you around the island of Ortigia, the heart of old Siracusa. You'll start at the historical beginning—the ancient Greek Temple of Apollo—then ramble through the side streets, unravel the architectural knot of the cathedral, and finish at a viewpoint on the far side of the island. From there, the island's other sights are within a few minutes' walk. This walk works well anytime; it's cool and mellow in the late afternoon, but note that the market will be dead then.

· *Begin on the mainland side of the bridges that lead to Ortigia (not far from the Molo Sant'Antonio parking lot and bus stop). Look for the giant anchor marking Ponte Santa Lucia (the bridge on the right) and cross partway over, pausing at the high point of the bridge for a look around.*

❶ Santa Lucia Bridge Spin-Tour

Two bridges link the mainland of Siracusa with the island of Ortigia. You're standing on Ponte Santa Lucia, named for the city's most famous saint (more on her later).

Face the mainland. This modern part of Siracusa was built after the unification of Italy in the late 1800s, with a grid plan in the Liberty Style (Italy's version of Art Nouveau). Look left to find the big military-looking building, which houses the coast guard.

Spinning clockwise, look on the little piazza between the two bridges for the golden statue of ancient Syracuse's most famous resident: the third-century BC mathematician/physicist/genius, **Archimedes** (see sidebar, later).

The older, stone bridge just behind Archimedes—**Ponte Umberto I**—was built to celebrate the Risorgimento (unification of

Ortigia Walk

Porto Piccolo

OLD POST (HOTEL)

To Mainland Siracusa

Navetta
HOHO

ARCHIMEDES STATUE

PONTE UMBERTO I

PONTE S. LUCIA

WALK BEGINS

Piazza Cesare Battista

Lungomare Vittorini

P Talete

WC

Via Vittorio Veneto

HOHO

Largo XXV Luglio

De Benedictis

MARKET

Piazza Pancali

HOHO

TEMPLE OF APOLLO

Largo Graziella

NEO-VENETIAN BLDG.

Via Regalibera

SAN PAOLO

VIOLA CAFÉ

Via Savoia

Corso Matteotti

CARMINE

Via Mirabella

SAN FILIPPO NERI

Via Vittorio Veneto

Via De Tolomei

HOHO

Marina P

BLUE MARLIN TICKETS

PORTA MARINA

Via Cavour

Via Dione

Piazza Archimede

PALAZZO MONTALTO

Via Gargallo

IMMACO-LATA

MOLO ZANAGORA

Foro Vittorio Emanuele II

V. Ruggero

PASS. ARETUSA

Andolina

FASCIST BLDG.

HOHO

V. MAESTRANZA

PUPPET THEATER

SAN FILIPPO APOSTOLO

PAPYRUS MUSEUM

Largo Amedeo

PALAZZO BENEVENTANO

JESUIT CHURCH

CITY HALL

Piazza Minerva

JEWISH

SAN GIOVANNI BATTISTA

Porto Grande

Piazza Duomo

CATHEDRAL

ARCH-BISHOP'S PALACE

Via San Giuseppe

PUPPET MUSEUM

FORT

PALAZZO BORGIA DEL CASALE

VIA PICERALI

SANTA LUCIA

Via Roma

SAN GIUSEPPE

QUARTER

Via Nizza

Via Eolo

Largo Aretusa

WALK ENDS

FOUNTAIN OF ARETHUSA

V. CAPODIECI

BELLOMO GALLERY

V. PRIV.

D'ORTIGIA

STA. TERESA

Via Salomone

Lungomare Alfeo

Lungomare Maniace

Ionian Sea

Piazza Federico di Svevia

CASTELLO MANIACE

200 Meters
200 Yards

N

Walking Tour

1 Spin-Tour from Santa Lucia Bridge
2 Piazza Pancali
3 Temple of Apollo
4 Ortigia Market
5 Corso Matteotti
6 Via Cavour
7 Siracusa Cathedral
8 Piazza Duomo
9 Fountain of Arethusa
10 Viewpoint Over the Bay

Shopping

11 Via Cavour
12 Baco
13 Ebano
14 Galleria Bellomo
15 Giacomo Lo Presti

Italy), circa 1870. The little electric public bus *(navetta)* leaves from that bridge's far end.

The stately former **post office,** in the distance behind Archimedes, is an example of the bold infrastructure erected by Mussolini and his fascist regime.

Now spin right and face the end of the bridge and Ortigia. The **Neo-Venetian building** on the right side of the bridge, with Gothic windows and a red hue, is a souvenir of the Romantic movement of the late 19th century.

The **harbor** all around you is now home to a few fishing and sightseeing boats. But take a moment to look out and admire the bay where the ancient Greek Syracusans were able to chain off their harbor and trap enemy fleets. We'll get a better look at the full scope of this bay at the end of this walk.

Cross to the end of the bridge, turn left, and walk along the embankment. Lashed to a lamppost on your left is a kayak-polo net—a reminder that Italy won the sport's world championship right here in 2016.

• *When you reach the Umberto I bridge, turn right and jog slightly uphill to the leafy...*

❷ Piazza Pancali

This lively square—which feels more like a stunted boulevard—is where the gritty mainland meets the dreamy old town of Ortigia. The handy hop-on, hop-off bus stops here, offering an easy connection to the mainland sights (see "Getting Around Siracusa," earlier.)

Consider hydrating at the **drink kiosk** in the meridian, with lots of fresh-squeezed juice options. For something simple yet refreshing, try a *seltz*—fresh-squeezed lemon, fizzy water, and a pinch of salt. For added sweetness, get it *con sciroppo* (with flavored syrups like tangerine).

A few steps farther uphill on the right is a **signboard** labeled *Avvisi Funebri.* Posted here are funeral notices with public invitations. Ortigia is a tight-knit community, and the entire neighborhood is welcome to attend memorial services.

• *Walk to the top of the block and cross the street to a big open-air archaeological site. Walk around the left side of the site, pausing just before the little clump of palm trees, and look across the field of rubble.*

SIRACUSA

Archimedes (c. 287-212 BC)

During ancient Syracuse's heyday as a leading city-state of the Greek world, no native son was more distinguished or influential than the scientist and mathematician Archimedes.

Some of Archimedes' inventions are still in use today—most notably the Archimedes screw, or screw pump. This simple yet ingenious device (essentially a very large screw set inside a cylinder) makes it possible to move water upward, against gravity—useful for pumping out the hold of a ship or for digging holes and draining water all at once.

Archimedes was well known for his brilliance in his time. Celebrated for great works of naval engineering that protected ancient Syracuse, he is said to have set fire to an entire Roman fleet with mirrors reflecting sunbeams. Archimedes famously discovered a way to measure the density of precious metals with water displacement while in a bathtub, and in his excitement ran through the city naked, yelling, "Eureka" ("I've found it"). He also wrote the mathematical law of the lever, prompting his other famous quote: "Give me a place to stand and I will move the Earth."

Perhaps Archimedes' most advanced work was in the field of calculus, developing methods to determine area and volume. His calculation of the ratio of a circle's circumference to its diameter is known today as the Archimedes' Constant—or π. Legend tells that a symbol of his work—a sphere and cylinder of the same height and diameter—was carved on his tomb, although it has never been found.

The Romans would have liked to put Archimedes' genius to use. When they finally conquered Syracuse, they ordered his capture, unharmed. Unfortunately, a Roman legionary encountered the scientist, who was so deep in thought about mathematics he ignored the soldier. The soldier, infuriated, killed Archimedes for his insolence.

Today, Archimedes is immortalized in Ortigia with a memorial statue on Ponte Umberto I and a piazza in the heart of the island. Locals call him *il genio*—the genius.

❸ Temple of Apollo

To the left of the wall, look for the two standing columns with the oversized capitals. These are the remains of the first Doric stone temple in Sicily, from about 580 BC. Notice the huge footprint of the temple. A long stretch of wall from the inner room (the cella) still stands. Short and stocky, this is one of

SIRACUSA

the earliest stone temples, and predates the Parthenon in Athens by 130 years.

The surviving columns are short and fat, and closely spaced together. Each column is hewn from a single piece of stone, which is rare. (Later, to allow taller columns—and work with smaller and easier-to-move chunks of stone—columns would be made by stacking round drums connected by pins.) As builders became more sophisticated, the temples grew taller—with slender, refined columns spaced farther apart—and included more detailed decoration. Everywhere you step in Ortigia, ancient history lies just underfoot.

• *With the temple ruins on your right, walk a few more steps up along the fence, then turn left on Via Emmanuele de Benedictis. You've entered the...*

❹ Ortigia Street Market

This street hosts a lively market (Mon-Sat 7:00-14:00, closed Sun). If you're here when it's in action, venture three blocks down this

main drag, then back up. Fish and produce are at the far end. At 13:00, the activity begins to die down, and by 14:00, the market is gone...not a trace. This used to be a purely local scene, with lots of greengrocers. The big building on the left as you enter was the market hall. But today's locals are more likely to

do their shopping at suburban supermarkets. There aren't enough vendors to justify opening the market hall, and the outdoor stalls cater mostly to tourists.

There are lots of places along here to grab a meal or snack—either a fancy sit-down restaurant or a quick bite of street food. It's fun to comparison-shop these places for lunch; some are also open for dinner (see "Eating in Siracusa," later).

• *Returning to the Temple of Apollo, circle all the way around to the far side of the square for a closer look at the temple columns. Then carry on straight ahead, away from the square, pausing at the start of the big, modern street...*

❺ Corso Giacomo Matteotti

The broadest boulevard in Ortigia was cut through the existing buildings by Mussolini in the 1920s with no regard for what was there before, as fascist dictators are wont to do. This grand avenue has bold features—notice the stern balconies and cold uniformity, in keeping with fascist ideology. Originally named Via del Littorio—a fascist reference to banner carriers in ancient Rome—the street was later renamed for the Italian patriot and freedom fighter Giacomo Matteotti, who was killed by Mussolini in 1924. Notice also the name of the square you just left: Largo XXV Luglio—July 25, the date Mussolini was deposed and arrested in 1943.

Walk 50 yards uphill on Corso Giacomo Matteotti to the round, Art Deco café on the right (near the green pharmacy cross). The **Viola Café**, with its striking fascist design, has been a popular local meeting spot since the 1920s.

• *Circle around the right side of Viola Café and head up the more characteristic Via Cavour. This narrow, colorful, restaurant-and-shop-crammed lane leads directly to the cathedral.*

❻ Via Cavour

Stroll up Via Cavour, enjoying the renewed energy of old Siracusa. Survey boutiques, window-shop restaurants for your next meal, and

notice the trendiness. Until the early 2000s, Ortigia was run down and seedy. Since then, a new interest in the island has started a regeneration and a surge in tourism.

Notice the long and narrow side lanes. Stop at an intersection and look up at the balconies probably festooned with laundry—reminders that this is still a real neighborhood.

Via Cavour becomes increasingly more characteristic a couple of blocks in. As you stroll, drop into some of the fun shops. The Fish House gallery (at #29, on the right) sells all manner of fishy decor. Just beyond, the Olive Food and Wine shop (#27) carries a variety of Sicilian olives, olive oil, wine, jams, and other gifty edibles. Farther up, Tami' (#13) is a design shop with a mix of Sicilian and international wares; their outpost for bags and sunglasses is across the street (#14). Near the top of the street, the recommended Osteria la Gazza Ladra (#8, on the left) is a great spot for dinner, while Bel Bon, a few doors up at #2, is a popular choice for gelato.

From the *gelateria*, turn left and detour 50 yards to **Piazza Archimede** for a look at its fountain, dedicated to Artemis the huntress. As you enter the square, notice that the building straight ahead still sports its fascist-themed reliefs, celebrating employment. The Italians lifted their fascist dictator Mussolini to power in 1922 in part because he promised good jobs. Each of these panels portrays a noble livelihood.

Return to Via Cavour, turn left, and carry on as you were (the street's name changes to Via Landolina). On the right is the **Jesuit Church**—so crowded by the buildings that it's hard to appreciate

The Greeks in Sicily

Sicily is perhaps the most important place outside Greece when it comes to ancient Greek history. Ancient Syracuse

briefly eclipsed Athens as the leading city-state of the civilization. Many scholars maintain that the best-preserved ancient Greek buildings are not in Greece, but in Italy.

As Greece rose from 800 to 400 BC, its population exploded nearly tenfold, forcing a "Go west, young man" mentality. The Greek version of manifest destiny began in Sicily, familiar to the Greeks because their Mycenaean ancestors had traded with local tribes.

The first expedition of settlers landed in 734 BC near modern Taormina, and named their colony Naxos, after the Aegean island. Settlers from the Greek port of Corinth arrived in 732 BC and founded ancient Syracuse. Greek colonists soon flooded Sicily's shores, settling primarily in the east (closer to Greece) and on the southern coast (good trade routes). Sicily benefited greatly from access to markets in southern Italy, Africa, and Rome, and soon became an important part of the Magna Graecia ("Great Greece") empire.

Most Greek cities in Sicily had a theater, a market square, and temples built to mimic those at home. While all ethnically Greek, the colonial cities were not ruled by an overarching Greek government. Each colony had its own leadership, and rivalries imported from home kept the colonies in a state of constant discord and war. The Carthaginians (a.k.a. Phoenicians) controlled western Sicily from their base on Mozia island (see "The Carthaginians" sidebar on page 176). In a pivotal 480 BC battle, forces from Syracuse and Agrigento held off a Carthaginian invasion, securing (partial) Greek control of Sicily, and spurring the rise of Athens—which now feared Carthage less.

Greek settlements in eastern Sicily, however, continued to squabble with the Carthaginians. They sought help from mighty Athens, and the Athenians answered the call—by invading the island in 413 BC. They sent 100 ships and 10,000 soldiers, but having underestimated their Sicilian cousins, the Athenian fleet was destroyed in Syracuse's harbor in a dramatic naval battle (bringing the Second Peloponnesian War to an end). Empowered Syracuse eclipsed Athens on the world stage, kicking off Sicily's own ancient Golden Age.

Then came the Romans. Sicily was one of Rome's first conquests (third century BC). Over the course of three Punic Wars (264-146 BC), Rome finally succeeded in defeating the troublesome Carthaginians, all but wiping their civilization from record. The Roman conquest of Sicily also marked the end of ancient Greek Sicily.

SIRACUSA

its ornate facade...for that reason, the Jesuits never finished construction.

• *The street empties out into Piazza Duomo. On the left side of the square is the glorious...*

❼ Siracusa Cathedral

Siracusa's cathedral (Duomo di Siracusa) is a fine example of the city's 2,500 years of cultural influences: from Greek to Byzantine, to Arab, Norman, and Baroque.

The **facade** of the cathedral, from around 1750, is inspired by the great Baroque churches of Rome, but amped up with a Sicilian razzle-dazzle. Baroque architecture typically features lots of decoration in different planes, creating dramatic light and dark contrast. The apostles Peter (with his key) and Paul (with his sword) greet you at street level, while Mary hovers high above, in the middle. To the right of Mary is Santa Lucia, the famous local saint who is celebrated throughout Europe with a festival of lights (see the sidebar, later). The cathedral interior holds some of her relics (and is worth touring later—for details see the listing under "Sights in Siracusa").

But the surprise of this church is revealed on its side. Walk around the left side and look at the puzzle of stones that make up the **outer walls.** The church is like Sicily itself: a layer cake of civilizations. Studying the side of the church reveals the highlights of Sicilian history.

The structure was originally an ancient Greek temple, with 6 columns at the front and back, and 14 columns on the sides. It was built here at the highest point on the island to honor Athena, the goddess of war, after the defeat of Carthage in 480 BC. The original temple's steps are still visible along the base.

In AD 535, under Byzantine rule, the temple was converted into a church. To create solid walls, the Byzantines simply filled in the spaces between the still-standing columns. Looking up, you can still see much of the ancient Doric **colonnade** built right into the church. Then, in 827, the Arabs crossed over from North Africa and turned the church into a mosque.

Centuries later, the Normans conquered Sicily in a relatively short time (1060-1090). As they were busy conquering and converting new territories to Christianity, they had to economize on time and workforce. In their haste, they built a combo fortress/church (notice the **crenellations** they added along the top). The great quake of 1693 knocked down the Norman fortress-style facade and severely damaged the cathedral. It was later repaired (look at the columns farther away and note how the wall becomes thicker), and the facade was rebuilt in supercharged Baroque, making this cathedral a patchwork of the highlights of Sicilian architecture.

• *Look around and take in the...*

❽ Piazza Duomo

This "square" serves as a delightful stage upon which the story of this community plays out. Designed in a graceful semicircle (a charming Baroque trick to heighten the community-theater feel), this is the living room of the island. Those who lived here in the 1990s remember when the facade of the cathedral was blackened by time, and the square was littered with cars and surrounded by dreary and depressed lanes. Now it's one of the most pleasant piazzas in Sicily.

The black lines in the pavement show where the earliest pre-Greek temple stood, built in the ninth century BC here on the

highest point of the island. Looking back to where you entered the square, you'll see two grand buildings. On the right is the **City Hall,** festooned with the flags of Sicily, Italy, and the EU. The bottom floor is a rare building that predates 1693; the upper floor—like most of post-quake southeastern Sicily—is Baroque.

Across from City Hall, on the left, is the grandiose townhouse of the noble **Beneventano** family. Study the powerful symmetry of the imposing Baroque facade, with the family crest (two dancing wild boars) above the massive door. If the door is open, peek inside at the intriguing inner courtyard. Sometimes the shutters upstairs are open, affording an enticing peek at a glorious ceiling fresco.

Now turn to face the bottom of the square, and start walking in that direction. First you'll pass the **archbishop's palace** (on the left, adjoining the cathedral). At the end of that building is the entrance to a vast **WWII-era bomb shelter** dug deep beneath this square (€5 to enter including a tour, but there's little to see other than big caves and zigzag tunnels).

At the far end of the square is the Rococo facade marking the **Church of Santa Lucia alla Badia.** If it's open, step inside (free, Tue-Sun 11:00-16:00, closed Mon). In the otherwise empty interior, hanging over the main altar is a precious Caravaggio painting, *The Burial of Santa Lucia* (1608). In Caravaggio's typical chiaroscuro style (with a deep contrast between light and dark), we see Lucia's

Santa Lucia

The patron saint of Siracusa, Lucia (Italians say loo-CHEE-yah) was born here in AD 283, a time of Roman rule. She was a Christian during Diocletian's persecution of Christians, making her an oppressed minority.

Lucia's wealthy family had promised her in marriage to a non-Christian suitor. When her mother fell ill, Lucia brought her to visit the tomb of St. Agatha of Catania. During this visit, her mother was miraculously healed, and Lucia had a vision of St. Agatha. The young woman was so inspired that she canceled her impending nuptials and gave her dowry to the poor.

Lucia's angered fiancé alerted the authorities, and she was arrested and sentenced to a brothel. She refused to go. When the guards tried to physically remove her, they found that she could not be moved at all—not by pushing or pulling, nor even when she was harnessed to a team of oxen. They tried to burn her, but the wood refused to light. Some versions of the story say that they gouged out her eyes. Finally, they killed Lucia by stabbing her through the neck.

Lucia was buried in Siracusa, where her body remained for almost 700 years. In the meantime, she became one of the most widely popular of the early martyred saints. In the Middle Ages, during the Byzantine control of Siracusa, Lucia's bones were brought to the capital of Constantinople (today's Istanbul). The Venetian fleet sacked Constantinople in 1204 and brought most of those relics back to Venice—where they remain today. Siracusa's cathedral also has several relics of the beloved saint, including a piece of her arm and finger bones, which are venerated and paraded through town on holy days.

In art, Santa Lucia is often represented as a beautiful, fair-skinned young lady—usually carrying her eyeballs on a plate. Thanks to the story of her blinding—and the root of her name (*lux*, Latin for "light")—Lucia is the patron saint of the blind.

Devotion to Santa Lucia extends far beyond Sicilian shores. Because of her associations with light—and the proximity of her feast day (December 13) to the winter solstice—Santa Lucia Day is often a festive celebration of light. In Scandinavian lands, schoolchildren parade through the streets, clad in white, carrying candles, and singing: "Sa-ahn-tah-ah Loo-oo-chee-ee-yah! San-TAH loo-chee-ee-yah!"

body lying supine on the floor. A Christian in the fiercely anti-Christian age of the Roman emperor Diocletian, Lucia rejected an arranged marriage, donated her wealth to the poor, and pledged herself to pious chastity. She was sentenced to a brothel, and the two burly brutes in the foreground have attempted to physically carry her away—but Lucia cannot be moved (for more on Lucia, see the sidebar).

As dark and moody as his paintings, Caravaggio was quarrelsome and violent. He'd had great success as a painter in Rome, but fled the city after accidentally killing a man in a bar. He bounced from Naples to Malta to Sicily, where he spent a year. This commission (arranged by a friend) helped him get back on his feet for a while.

• *Exiting the church, turn left and left again. Continue downhill a couple more blocks, looking up to notice the fine wrought-iron balconies (dating from the Spanish occupation), then angle right to reach the bay. Belly up to the railing overlooking a big pit filled with a pond and some plants.*

❾ Fountain of Arethusa

Most locals don't even know the formal name for this structure (Fonte Aretusa), which they call "fountain of the ducks." You'll see

papyrus here. Siracusa has a long tradition of making papyrus (in the style of the ancient Egyptians). A local artist, Flavia, still makes it in the traditional way just a half-block from here (at Via Capodieci 47), and there's a papyrus museum a few minutes' walk away (at Via Nizza 14).

While just a pretty water feature today, this fountain is a big deal historically. This was the original freshwater spring that made the island a desirable place for settlement when the Greeks arrived in the eighth century BC from Corinth. The homesick Greeks convinced themselves that the freshwater spring was connected to Greece by an underground river. Whether true or not, this spot was ideal: a big natural harbor, an easy-to-defend island, and plenty of fresh water bubbling up.

In more modern times, Jewish artisans used the fountain water to power nearby tanneries (the old Jewish quarter—called Giudecca—runs from here inland). When the Jews were expelled in 1493 by Sicily's Spanish overlords, the fountain became the community laundry, which it remained until the 1800s.

• *Walk 50 yards to the right, out to the far end of a paved terrace. As you walk, you'll pass over a spiral painted in the pavement...a nod to hometown genius Archimedes and his hydraulic screw.*

❿ Viewpoint Over the Bay

Here, at the end of your town walk, you can survey Siracusa's sweeping bay. This bay was a natural refuge, attracting sailors and traders since the time when the ancient Greeks arrived. Far to the left is the town fortress, reached by a pleasant harborside walk. Far to the right is the modern city (on the mainland), marked by the pointy peak of the modern Sanctuary of the Madonna of Tears, a church built in the 1950s to celebrate the miracle of the weeping Virgin Mary. The most important archaeological site in town—the Neapolis Archaeological Park—is near that church (see "Sights in Siracusa," later).

Ponder this: You are standing at one of Europe's most southern points. And, had you stood here in 413 BC, in the middle of the Second Peloponnesian War, you would have had front-row seats to perhaps the most pivotal naval battle in Greek history—the Battle of Syracuse, which ended in the total defeat of the Athenian fleet.

• *Our walk is finished. Within a few minutes from here are several more sights: The **Bellomo Palace Gallery** is the town's top art gallery; just beyond that are the **Puppet Museum** and **Puppet Theater**. And there's much to be seen on the mainland, too (to get there from here, head back to Piazza Archimede to catch the hop-on, hop-off bus). All of these sights are described in the next section.*

Sights in Siracusa

IN ORTIGIA

My self-guided town walk, earlier, connects several of Ortigia's top sights—including the cathedral.

▲▲Siracusa Cathedral (Duomo di Siracusa)

Siracusa's cathedral is a delightful and engaging potpourri of the civilizations that have called Ortigia—and Sicily—home. The exterior (including the stately Baroque facade, and the ancient exo-skeletal columns around the side) is described earlier, in the self-guided walk. The interior is well worth a visit for its surprising integration of architectural styles.

Cost and Hours: €2, Mon-Sat 9:00-18:30, July-Aug until 19:00, Oct-March until 17:30, closed Sun except for Mass, tel. 0931-179-103.

Visiting the Cathedral: As you enter, walk straight ahead down the left aisle, along a row of original 2,500-year-old Doric columns. (You can also see these columns from the outside.) Notice how the sixth column (on the left as you enter) nearly wobbled off its perch with the great shake of 1693.

Now cross into the main aisle, in the center of the nave, and look up. Take it all in. High above, the lettering marks the top of the original Doric temple's inner cella wall, to which

SIRACUSA

the Byzantines added arches in the sixth century. The ancient roof would have been wooden, just like today. There's no transept, because the original temple didn't have one; you are essentially experiencing the harmonious architectural proportions of the Greeks. The inlaid marble floor dates from the 1500s, when Siracusa was under Spanish rule.

Now head over to the right aisle, which is lined with chapels that take their dimensions from the spacing of the ancient columns. (The one exception is the later Chapel of the Crucifix, to the right of the main altar, which has more cohesive Baroque dimensions; it's dedicated to a 13th-century Byzantine-style crucifix.) Look high above at the fine workmanship of the exquisitely preserved capitals from ancient times. About halfway along, the Baroque decor of the Chapel of the Blessed Sacrament is more typically flamboyant than the rest of the otherwise tame interior.

Just past it, look for the chapel with a reliquary containing the venerated relics of Santa Lucia—this town's most revered patron saint (see the sidebar, earlier). Another chapel holds the tunic, veil, and shoes of the saint. And near the exit, a tiny room shows footage of the church's Santa Lucia statue on its twice-annual procession through town.

Bellomo Palace Gallery (Galleria Regionale di Palazzo Bellomo)

This museum fills the first floor of a noble mansion with paintings (15th-18th century), folk art, and religious artifacts. The gallery offers very little written English information, but the €3 audioguide helps you delve into the collection.

Cost and Hours: €8, €13.50 combo-ticket with Neapolis Archaeological Park or Paolo Orsi Archaeological Museum, Tue-Sat 9:00-19:00, Sun until 13:30, closed Mon, Via Capodieci 16, tel. 0931-69511.

Visiting the Museum: The ground floor displays exquisite 15th-century altarpieces and stone carvings from churches. From the courtyard—with a collection of horse carriages—you can climb up the stone staircase and loop around the upper level, starting with the 18th-century, wood-carved relief map of Ortigia.

The collection's prized possession is **Antonello da Messina's** *Annunciation* (1474). After a trip to the Italian mainland, Antonello brought to Sicily the technique of painting with oil, a mastery of depth, and a passion for detail he's thought to have picked up from

SIRACUSA

Flemish painters that he met in his travels. Like Netherlandish painters of the age, Antonello has created a real world in which his subjects live: Mary inhabits an authentic room with characteristic windows and ceiling beams, and the plant in a vase at the foot of her desk is as detailed as the subjects' faces. Appreciate the peaceful, enigmatic smile on Mary's face as she's greeted by the angel, arms crossed over her heart. Outside the window, a shooting star streaks the sky...and then appears *inside* the window, in the form of a ghostly dove—the Holy Spirit—heading straight for Mary (for more on Antonello, see page 131).

▲Catacombs of San Filippo Apostolo (Catacombe di San Filippo Apostolo)

For a handy catacombs experience right in Ortigia, stop by the Church of San Filippo Apostolo. The concise, free tour (required) uncovers three floors of history—digging deep below the marble paving stones of the present-day church.

Cost and Hours: Free but donations appreciated, Mon-Sat 10:00-12:30 & 15:00-17:00, closed Sun and Nov-March, 15-minute tours depart every 30 minutes, Piazza San Filippo, mobile 380-522-7021.

Visiting the Church: Your guide takes you steeply down the stairs, going deeper and deeper through three underground levels (ending 60 feet below the surface). First is the circa-1700 church crypt, with tombs of aristocrats. Below that is a limestone cave, in use since ancient Greek times. From here, tunnels burrow under the churches and squares of old Ortigia. During World War II, this space was converted into an air-raid shelter; your guide will point out faint illustrations of Allied and Axis bomber planes and parachutes on the wall. Finally, you'll descend a spiral staircase to a natural spring, which was used as a purification bath *(mikveh)* by the local Jewish community going back to the 1200s. (The surrounding neighborhood, Giudecca, was the old Jewish quarter.) Heading back up all those stairs and squinting in the sunlight, you'll have a new appreciation for all that lies underfoot in Ortigia.

Puppet Museum (Museo dei Pupi)

Members of the Mauceri family—who also operate nearly nightly puppet shows at their nearby theater (described later, under "Entertainment in Siracusa")—have been puppeteers for three generations. You can see their collection of traditional Sicilian puppets from past shows in a small museum, lovingly displayed and curated.

SIRACUSA

Cost and Hours: €3, €10 combo-ticket includes performance at nearby Puppet Theater; open Mon-Sat 11:00-13:00 & 15:00-18:00, closed Sun; corner of Via della Giudecca Piazza San Giuseppe, tel. 0931-199-5531, www.teatrodeipupisiracusa.it.

IN MAINLAND SIRACUSA

Ancient Syracuse quickly outgrew the footprint of little Ortigia island and stretched out onto the mainland, and some impressive remains can be found about 1.5 miles from Ortigia at the Neapolis Archaeological Park. Three other interesting sights—the Paolo Orsi Archaeological Museum, the modern Sanctuary of the Madonna of Tears, and the evocative Catacombs of San Giovanni—are an unappealing 10-minute walk east of the archaeological park along Viale Teocrito.

It's quick and easy to get from Ortigia to the mainland sights by bus (10 minutes) or taxi (5 minutes); for details see "Getting Around Siracusa," earlier. By foot, it's a 30-minute walk through dreary urban sprawl.

Because getting from Ortigia to these sights requires some effort, plan to visit all that interests you here in one go. If you're getting an early start, do the archaeological park first, then walk back to the Viale Teocrito sights. If you link the sights by bus, visit the Viale Teocrito sights first.

▲▲Neapolis Archaeological Park (Parco Archeologico della Neapolis)

At its peak in the fifth century BC, the city-state of Syracuse was the dominant military and economic power in the Greek world, with a population that rivaled Athens in size. While this city is long gone, wandering through its remains in this vast archeological park gives you a sense of ancient Syracuse's immensity and power. You'll see a big Greek theater, the remains of a water system, the footprint of a sacrificial altar, a (later) Roman amphitheater, and the immense quarry where thousands of slaves cut the stone that made it all. For an overview, see the "Siracusa" map at the beginning of this chapter.

Cost and Hours: €10, €13.50 combo-ticket with Paolo Orsi Archaeological Museum or Ortigia's Bellomo Palace Gallery, free first Sun of month; daily 8:30-19:30, off-season closes one hour before sunset, last entry 1.5 hours before closing; tel. 0931-66206. In summer (mid-May-mid-July) the Greek theater hosts open-air performances and closes earlier.

Getting In: The main ticket office is at the entrance to the park, but if there's a line, you can buy tickets across the street in the office at the bus parking lot. Keep your ticket handy—you'll need to show it to enter different parts of the park.

Eating: A variety of cheap cafés cluster around the bus parking lot and near the site entrance. The most appealing choice is the **$$ Neapolis Café** just inside the main entrance, with light food and drinks overlooking the ruins.

◐ Self-Guided Tour: Once inside the complex, a long, paved lane leads downhill toward the huge Greek theater. As you walk, on your left you'll pass a Roman amphitheater (which we'll see last), a café, and WCs. On your right is the lush vegetation of a huge ancient quarry-turned-garden.

• *Near the bottom of the lane on the left, stop at the green railing and ponder the remains of the...*

Altar of Hieron II (Ara di Ierone II): Dating from the third century BC, this is the longest altar ever built in the Greek world.

Scratch that: It wasn't built—it was chiseled, creating a mammoth monolithic altar. As long as a stadium, the altar was dedicated to Zeus, and was used once a year for a grand festival that featured the sacrifice of 450 oxen (followed by the ancient world's longest lineup for barbecue). Sicilian Greeks had the habit of supersizing everything they built, making sure their new community was more impressive than the homeland they left behind. Ancient Syracuse became, for 300 years, the pinnacle of Greek civilization in the Mediterranean world.

• *At the bottom of the paved lane, take a right, following signs to* Teatro Greco. *For the best overview, take the stairs to the right just after the ticket check, and climb to the terrace atop the seats (a fairly steep 5-minute hike).*

Greek Theater (Teatro Greco): The most important ancient monument here dates from 500 BC, back when a theater functioned like a church, teaching moral and religious principles. Most of the seats are carved directly from stone—etched into the hillside. (As this theater had an original seating capacity of 15,000, archaeologists derive that the total population of ancient Syracuse would have been 150,000.) Of course, there was no amplification, so acoustics were important. A back wall helped to reflect the sound. The terrace above and behind the seats functioned as a grand lobby for the thousands attending performances; it was covered by a wooden roof and decorated with fine statues of heroes and gods filling the niches.

The theater is still in use today, performing shows Greeks would have seen. If you're here during the summer outdoor theater season (mid-May-mid-July), you'll see protective wooden seats cov-

ering the original stone.
Consider attending a per-
formance—it's a magi-
cal experience for those
who love ancient history,
outdoor theater, or rowdy
Sicilian school groups (in
summer, box offices are
near the ticket checkers;
for details, see "Entertain-
ment in Siracusa," later). Like theatergoers then and now, appreciate the grand view over Siracusa and its bay from the top of the
theater.

• *Tucked along the very top of the theater's seats (listen for the waterfall)*
is the...

Aqueduct (Acquedotto): The waterfall *(nymphaeum)* is part of
an aqueduct carved from the rock, allowing water to flow about
15 miles from a mountain spring into the city. Get up close and
inspect the engineering. Imagine this cavern, decorated with statues of nymphs, gushing with life-giving water. When the Roman
Empire fell in the fifth century, the theater was abandoned. The
tower to the left was built centuries later as a watchtower when the
site was recycled...into a grain mill.

• *Head back down to where you entered. As you walk, check out the over-*
view of the vast, lush quarry on your left—our next stop. Back at the
ticket checker, head left and climb down the stairs, following signs to
Orecchio di Dionisio, *then* Latomia del Paradiso. *Walk through the*
jungle of vegetation that now fills the quarry. You'll pass through an
arch, then pause when you see a stony pinnacle sticking up amid the trees.

Quarry of Paradise (Latomia del Paradiso): When marveling
at the wonder of ancient temples and theaters, it's easy to forget
that their construction was made possible by slaves, who quarried,
carried, and laid the stones until they died. Those slaves were often
prisoners of war: About 7,000 Athenians were consigned to this
quarry after being soundly defeated in the Second Peloponnesian
War. The one tower of stone still standing amid the vast green zone
was a pillar supporting the roof of a giant cavern, which collapsed
with the earthquake. Today this verdant "Garden of Paradise" (an
ironic name once you know its history) is overgrown with acanthus
(whose jagged foliage inspired the Corinthian capital), oleander,
bay leaf, bamboo, wild oranges, and mulberry.

• *Follow the path deep into the jungle. Soon you'll hit a cliff face, where*
you'll see a tall, narrow cave.

Ear of Dionysius (Orecchio di Dionisio): This cave was named
for the city's ancient dictator. It's said that the tyrannical ruler of
Syracuse would sit at the top of the cave and use its acoustics to

eavesdrop on the slaves below—often his political enemies.

See the chisel marks wallpapering the cave and imagine how blocks of stone were cut, over the generations, from the top down. Wooden pegs were placed in grooves carved a few inches deep then moistened with water. The pressure of the expanding wood would crack the stone into blocks.

Walk deeper in and clap or sing a few bars, sampling the acoustics. (Beware of the pigeons above you who call this cave home.)

• *Climb back out of the quarry the way you came in. Then hike up the paved lane (back past the Altar of Hieron II) toward the entry. Before you reach it, watch for the path on the right leading downhill to the...*

Roman Amphitheater (Anfiteatro Romano): The Romans may have conquered ancient Syracuse in 212 BC, but ultimately

they were conquered by Greek culture. This amphitheater, dating from the first century AD, is a fine example of Roman engineering. While Greeks would build into an existing hill, a Roman theater is generally freestanding. The Romans put two theaters together and called it an amphitheater (from *amph*, "double"). While Greek tragedies had their share of implied violence, those scenes always happened offstage. By contrast, the Romans shamelessly incorporated actual blood and gore into their entertainment. The amphitheater floor was layered with sand to soak up the blood. ("Arena" comes from the Latin word for sand.) Look for the archway, under which the losers of battle would be carted away.

For the best view, circle above to the upper level. The lane is lined by stone sarcophagi, from a Greek necropolis discovered during the excavation of a nearby modern road. From above the theater, you can see a small pool in the center, which was likely used for gladiator fights using aquatic animals.

• *As you leave the amphitheater and head for the exit, notice the small Romanesque church on the left.*

Church of San Nicolò: The Normans invaded Sicily and ruled the island from 1060 to 1198, making their mark with a lot of fine Norman (Romanesque) architecture. This church of San Nicolò, from the 11th century, sits atop Piscina Romana, a first-century Roman cistern.

Look toward the spire of the modern church, the Sanctuary of the Madonna of Tears (described next). When that church was started in the 1960s, layers and layers of Greek and Roman ruins were found. An entire ancient city lies beneath your feet...from here to the harbor at Ortigia.

Other Mainland Sights

These three sights cluster within a few minutes' walk of the stop for the hop-on, hop-off bus and *navetta* on Viale Teocrito. For locations see the "Siracusa" map near the beginning of this chapter.

▲Sanctuary of the Madonna of Tears (Santuario della Madonna delle Lacrime)

This giant, conical pilgrimage church rises like a massive spaceship in the middle of modern Siracusa—visible from just about every point in the city. The

church was built to commemorate a 1953 miracle and is supposedly shaped like a teardrop *(lacrima)*. To me this modern church looks more like a supersized lampshade...or like someone dropped a waffle cone, gelato-side down. It's worth stepping inside to appreciate the building's unusual architecture and the reverence with which the faithful venerate the miraculous Madonna.

Cost and Hours: Free, Mon-Sat 7:00-13:00 & 15:00-20:00, Sun until 21:00, Via del Sanctuario 33, www.madonnadellelacrime. it.

Background: In 1953, in the home of a humble Siracusa couple, a simple bas-relief of the Virgin Mary began weeping...and didn't stop for three days. The wife had been ill and had lost her vision, but suddenly regained her sight as tears flowed down the Madonna's cheeks. Vatican investigators verified that the tears were, indeed, human and authenticated the miracle. The couple's house was suddenly on the pilgrimage trail, and the sculpture became the centerpiece of this striking, French-designed church, completed decades later.

Visiting the Church: At first, the **interior** has a stark and gloomy bomb-shelter ambience. But give it a chance to speak to you—it's really a sculpture of light, changing throughout the day. The entire top of the structure sits on 22 steel discs that keep the cone secure in an earthquake. Look up as you enter and see how the slits in the concrete cone create a halo of light.

The focal point of the church—near the main altar—is the case displaying the little **Madonna.** The inexpensive plaster sculpture is a stark contrast to the massive marble altar that protects it and the giant structure of the church. Go closer to the altar and wonder, how could liquid have flowed from this bust? The unlikely, modest miracle happened at a time of turmoil in post-WWII Sicily, and was an inspiration to the people of Siracusa. A **reliquary** holding the original tears cried by the Madonna in 1953 is often displayed here in the sanctuary, or in the crypt below.

Also in the **crypt,** you'll see the small ruins of Roman houses found during the church construction. Straight ahead from the altar and below is the **Museum Ex Voto,** which displays items given in thanks for miracles performed. You'll see artificial limbs, wedding dresses, crutches, and countless silver plaques shaped like the subject of the miracle. As you face the altar, at 10 o'clock find the model of the church made entirely out of matches.

▲▲Paolo Orsi Archaeological Museum
(Museo Archeologico Regionale Paolo Orsi)

Considered one of the finest archaeology museums in Sicily, this collection spans from prehistory to Roman times with artifacts from eastern Sicily. Filling a bewilderingly laid-out facility in a lush park, the museum can be challenging to visit. But its highlights paint a vivid picture of ancient Syracuse and the rest of Sicily in antiquity. You'll see classical sculpture, everyday items, and an exquisitely carved, early Christian sarcophagus from the nearby Catacombs of San Giovanni.

Cost and Hours: €10, €13.50 combo-ticket with Neapolis Archaeological Park or Ortigia's Bellomo Palace Gallery; Tue-Sat 9:00-19:00, Sun until 14:00, closed Mon, last entry one hour before closing; coin collection closes at 13:30, Wed until 17:30; Viale Teocrito 66, tel. 0931-489-511.

Visiting the Museum: From Viale Teocrito, enter the park and make your way to the blocky modern building at its center.

Inside, pick up a floor plan

and wrap your head around the unusual layout: The two-floor museum is shaped like a honeycomb, with sectors based on topic. We'll progress through the wings chronologically (they're lettered from A to D), but each wing is a maze in itself, and artifacts are crammed into overloaded glass cases. Just explore, go with the flow, and expect to get lost, then found, again and again. If you focus on the highlights below—usually marked with large signs—you'll be rewarded.

• *Head downstairs to the surprisingly engaging...*

Coin and Jewelry Collection: Inside a heavily fortified vault, display cases show off the coinage of various invaders, empires, and kingdoms that have ruled Sicily, as well as other civilizations the Sicilians have traded with. The coins are remarkably detailed (use the magnifying glasses to examine them) and well described in English. Surveying the coins from the ancient Greek era, notice how each city-state embossed its coins with its own unique symbology. For example, ancient Syracuse's coins typically had a chariot on the "tails" side and a profile of Artemis on the "heads" side.

• *Back upstairs, turn left from the ticket desk and circle around the rooms on this floor, starting with...*

Prehistory (Sector A): In this section you'll find pottery and bones, including the skeletons of a pair of **dwarf elephants,** which were once found on the island. Notice that, with the sinus cavity exposed, the elephant skull looks like a fearsome one-eyed monster. Some believe these remains could be the origin of the Cyclops myth.

Ancient Syracuse (Sector B): Running down a long corridor around an inner courtyard with trees, these rooms display the richest part of the collection—artifacts from the Greek era.

Here you'll find room after room of artifacts from ancient Ortigia, the settlement of Megara Hyblaea, a few miles up the coast, and other Greek colonies in eastern Sicily. Look for the headless **Kouros di Megara** (550 BC, from Naxos in Greece's Cycladic islands). It would take a couple of hundred years before this stiff Archaic sculptural style would relax into the realistic Classical style that Greek art is known for. This figure was found in the necropolis outside town. Kouros ("young boy") statues like this are common finds, but this one is unique, as it was used as a funerary monument. The inscription on his right leg identifies him as "Sombrotidas, son of Mandrokles, doctor."

To go on a scavenger hunt, survey the glass cases in the central section of the sector. Look for #79—a tiny, stylized **bronze horse** from ancient Corinth (c. 710 BC) that was found in a necropolis and has become a symbol of both the museum and the city. Near the end of Sector B are architectural fragments, such as drain spouts (some are shaped like lion heads and some are painted). Ancient Greek culture was Technicolor—notice fragments of painted decoration, and brightly painted statues and terra-cotta figures.

Syracuse Territory and Other Greek City-States (Sector C): Continue around to see pottery, architectural fragments, votives, spearheads, kraters (large vessels used to dilute wine), and so on—organized by the colonies where the items were found. Find *Dea di Grammichele*, a seated terra-cotta votive with an enigmatic, Archaic smile (4th-5th century BC).

• *From Sector C, find the stairs up to the second floor—passing from BC to AD.*

Sarcophagus of Adelphia/Hellenistic and Roman Collection (Sector D): This area is divided into two parts. First, near the top of the stairs, find the room devoted to the breathtaking **Sarcophagus of Adelphia** (late 4th century AD), from the nearby Catacombs of San Giovanni. Its incredibly detailed Old and New

Testament scenes are worth lingering over. The inscription tells us it was carved for Adelphia, whom you can see in the center, alongside her husband, within a scallop-shell frame. We don't know exactly who she was, but based on the quality of her monument, she was likely the wife of a very powerful man, or perhaps a relative of the emperor. This carving was created just after the time of Constantine, when Rome became Christian, making it an unusual piece; the figures are clumsy, signaling the beginning of the slow decline of Roman art.

Finally, circle around the upper floor to find the **Hellenistic and Roman** sculpture collection, proudly featuring Priapus (the god of fertility) at the entry. Farther in—deep in a maze of classical sculpture—find the famous **Venus Landolina,** a headless second-century-AD Roman copy of a second-century-BC Greek original. Roman sculptors were technically proficient, but lacked the artistic mastery of their Greek predecessors—so replicas like this were common. Although headless, this Venus is regarded for her beauty.

▲Catacombs of San Giovanni
(Catacombe di San Giovanni)

Below the ruins of the abandoned church of San Giovanni (which collapsed in the 1693 earthquake) are hidden tombs of Christians

from the fourth century AD. Carved into the limestone, the catacombs are a complex network of large underground chambers organized into streets. Some tombs are simple niches, others have large arches with fresco fragments, and others are carved out of old Roman cisterns. While this sounds spooky, most tombs are empty and the long galleries of spacious, elegant rotundas make these catacombs less claustrophobic than some. On a visit here, you'll also see the ruins of the aboveground church and the early-Christian underground church of San Marciano—Siracusa's *other* patron saint—decorated with evocative Byzantine-style frescoes.

Cost and Hours: €8, required 30-minute guided tours leave sporadically; open daily 9:30-12:30 & 14:30-18:30, closed Mon Nov-Feb, closed Jan; Largo San Marciano 3, tel. 0931-64694, info@kairos-web.com.

Shopping in Siracusa

Ortigia has an artsy soul. In recent years, artists and craftsmen have taken over dilapidated buildings and turned them into workshops for handmade goods. Artists without shops often set up card tables along Via Landolina, Via Picherali, and Via Roma. For locations, see the "Ortigia Walk" map, earlier.

Via Cavour, described in more detail on my self-guided "Ortigia Walk" (earlier), is lined with shops and is a handy place to browse.

Baco sells creative, handmade jewelry, all crafted in this small shop by owners Marco and Simona. You can hang around and watch them work (daily 10:30-20:30, shorter hours July-Aug and off-season, closed Jan-Feb, Via Roma 101, mobile 366-176-6111).

Ebano offers handmade leather bags made with mixed recycled materials, including waterproof canvas and tires (daily 11:00-20:00, Via Roma 154, mobile 324-605-9099, Giuliana).

At **Galleria Bellomo,** Flavia Massara paints on papyrus paper, which she also makes in the traditional way in her shop. Ask her for a demo (Mon-Sat 10:30-13:30 & 17:00-19:30, closed Sun, Via Capodieci 47, mobile 0931-61340, www.bellomogallery.com).

Giacomo Lo Presti is a workaholic ceramist, making original creations with Sicilian themes in a hole-in-the-wall studio (Mon-Sat 9:00-12:30 & 16:00-20:30, closed Sun, Via Dione 62, mobile 339-213-4086).

Entertainment in Siracusa

▲Puppet Theater (Teatro dei Pupi)

This charming 80-seat theater is run by the hardworking Mauceri family, who have a passion for this traditional art. Along with live performances, they also run the small Puppet Museum a few short blocks away (see "Sights in Siracusa," earlier). On most evenings, they perform an episode of a traditional saga, recounting the adventures of Charlemagne and the French knights. The stories are like old-time serial melodramas of good versus evil, with superhero characters that captivate children. The play is in Italian, but they provide an English synopsis. While the storylines can be complex, the presentation and effects are entertaining beyond any language barrier. The puppets, their shiny armor and helmets, props, scenery, and sets are all lovingly crafted with traditional methods by family members, who also perform live vocals and sound effects.

Cost and Hours: €8.50, €10 combo-ticket includes nearby Puppet Museum; schedule inconsistent but typically 6 days/week (closed either Sun, Wed, or Fri), May-June at 16:30, July-Aug at 18:00 and/or 21:00, March-April and Sept-Oct at 17:00, closed Nov-Feb; tickets available one hour before show time, €1 extra to reserve ahead, reservations smart July-Aug; €2 tour of workshop and backstage available; Via della Giudecca 22, tel. 0931-465-540, www.teatrodeipupisiracusa.it.

Greek Theater in a Greek Theater

The Greek theater in the Neapolis Archaeological Park hosts a drama festival every summer, presenting famous Greek plays in Italian. Popular and lively, this is a fun way to experience an ancient site being used for its intended purpose. The cheapest seats are usually occupied by noisy student groups, so it's worth paying extra for a better seat. Performances typically begin in bright sunshine and end after sunset—be prepared for all the elements (from €15, mid-May-mid-July, tel. 0931-487-200, www.indafondazione.org/en).

Sicilian Puppets

To understand puppets in Sicily, you have to start during the Middle Ages, when epic literary cycles were common, told by traveling troubadours recounting great adventures in faraway lands. Each country had its own version: In France, the stories were of Charlemagne and his knights; in England, King Arthur and the Knights of the Round Table; and in Arabia, the folk tales from the *One Thousand and One Nights.*

In Italy in the 1500s, writers Ludovico Ariosto and Torquato Tasso recorded the French stories of Charlemagne and his chivalrous knights, writing the poems *Orlando Furioso* and *Gerusalemme Liberata.* In the 1860s, a poem called *The History of the French Knights* compiled earlier stories, and was turned into traveling puppet shows in Naples and Sicily. Generations of *pupari,* or puppeteers, wrote their own plays and performed them in squares across southern Italy. Traditionally, the music was performed live by musicians, then later by a cylinder piano.

Puppets—*pupi* (POO-pee) in Italian—are heavier than marionettes and moved by one central rod in the head and

another controlling the right hand (used for sword fights). A string moves the less-mobile left arm. Sword fights are synchronized with wooden shoes worn by the puppeteers, who rhythmically tap the floor. Usually there are two puppeteers on an elevated backstage, but some shows require up to four. The stage and scenery are designed with optical illusions to make the puppets look much larger than they are. Nowadays, most music and sound effects are recordings, but voices of characters and some sound effects, like thunder or drums, are performed live. Building a puppet from scratch requires at least a full month of work, using wood, metal, fabric, and pigments.

The traditional main characters are the French knights Orlando (a.k.a. Roland) and his cousin, Rinaldo. Female characters are Angelica, a pagan princess from faraway Catai, and the sweet Fiordiligi. Each character has unique features to make them easily recognizable: Orlando has red plumage and shiny armor with an eagle on his chest plate and helmet. Blue-eyed, fair-haired Rinaldo has yellow plumage and a lion on his shield and helmet. Princess Angelica has big green eyes and a sultry voice, and is usually involved in some sort of love triangle. Fiordiligi has dark hair, a simple dark dress, and no makeup. The fight scenes are the highlight of every play, sometimes involving dragons or giants, often resulting in a decapitation, and always with a high body count.

Sleeping in Siracusa

All of my accommodations in Siracusa are in Ortigia. There's little reason to sleep on the charmless mainland.

$$$$ Algilà Ortigia Charme Hotel fills two buildings near the water, tastefully renovated with all the luxuries. Their rooms are sophisticated and modern while maintaining the elegance of the historic palaces they occupy. Although pricey, this can be a worthy splurge—or a bargain off-season (air-con, elevator, Via Vittorio Veneto 93, tel. 0931-465-186, www.algila.it, info@algila.it).

$$$$ Charme Hotel Henry's House is less hotel and more cozy home of a quirky art collector. Its 14 rooms cluster around a common seaview terrace, each decorated with funky antique furniture and modern art (air-con, elevator to some rooms, pay parking, Via del Castello Maniace 68, tel. 0931-21361, www.hotelhenryshouse.com, info@hotel3h.com, Tony).

$$$$ Hotel Livingston sits atop a cliff at the edge of the island, overlooking the sea. The 17 rooms have a regal feel, with elegant furniture and brocade fabric on the walls. While not all rooms have a sea view, the rooftop view terrace is a fine place for breakfast (air-con, elevator, spa, valet parking, Via Nizza 17, tel. 0931-463-830, www.livingstonhotel.it, booking@livingstonhotel.it, Annamaria).

$$$ Domus Mariae Benessere is a convent, spa, and hotel all in one. Their rooms are plush, if small. The sisters are often found gliding along the hallways and offer Mass once a week (air-con, elevator, Via Vittorio Veneto 89, tel. 0931-64475, www.domusmariaebenessere.com, info@domusmariaebenessere.com, Luisa).

$$$ Allegroitalia is bright and modern, with 28 apartments in a rambling old palace. The rooms are spacious, each with a small kitchen, dining area, and coffeemaker (air-con, elevator, no breakfast, tel. 0931-179-8050, Via G.B. Alagona 55, www.allegroitalia.it, info@allegroitalia.it, bubbly Domenico).

$$ Hotel Gargallo has 18 tidy, pastel rooms in the bustling center of Ortigia. While the hotel feels tight, the quality is high for the price (air-con, Via Tommaso Gargallo 58, tel. 0931-464-938, www.hotelssiracusa.com, info@hotelgargallo.it).

$$ Lemóni Suite has 10 modern rooms with shipshape attention to detail; it feels like you're on a yacht docked in the Ortigia marina (air-con, Via Tommaso Gargallo 52, tel. 0931-21559, www.lemonisiracusa.com, booking@lemonisiracusa.com, Marcello).

$$ Residence dei Baroni, on the far side of Ortigia, is a good budget bet, especially for families. All 20 rooms have small kitchens, and some have loft bedrooms and small seaview windows (air-con, family rooms, Via Largo della Gancia 32, tel.

Ortigia Hotels & Restaurants

Accommodations

1 Algilà Ortigia Charme Hotel
2 Charme Hotel Henry's House
3 Hotel Livingston
4 Domus Mariae Benessere
5 Allegroitalia
6 Hotel Gargallo
7 Lemóni Suite
8 Residence dei Baroni
9 B&B Vittoria

Eateries & Other

10 Ristorante Don Camillo
11 Le Vin de l'Assassin
12 Osteria da Seby
13 Osteria la Gazza Ladra
14 Castello Fiorentino Pizzeria
15 Solaria Enoteca & Salumeria Roma Grocery
16 Schiticchio Pizzeria
17 Antica Giudecca
18 Le Comari Inn
19 Moon
20 Piazza Duomo Eateries
21 Via Emmanuele de Benedictis Eateries
22 Harbor Promenade Eateries
23 Gusto Ortigia Market

SIRACUSA

0931-67363, www.residencedeibaroni.com, info.residenceortigia@
kiwibeachresorts.it, Adna).

$ B&B Vittoria, warmly run by mother-and-son team Sim-
onetta and Fabrizio, is a budget gem, with six simple rooms. The
common area feels like your Sicilian aunt's house, and a courtyard terrace offers a quiet spot to relax (air-con, family rooms, Via
Vincenzo Mirabella 18, tel. 0931-462-119, www.vittoriaflorio.it,
mail@vittoriaflorio.it). They also offer two small apartments.

Eating in Siracusa

All of my recommended eateries are in Ortigia. On the mainland,
there are a few cheap cafés at the Neapolis Archaeological Park, but
for a quality meal, stick to this charming island.

$$$$ Ristorante Don Camillo is a local institution, serving fine cuisine since 1985 in a vaulted dining room. Their €50-
60 tasting *menus* are a worthwhile splurge (Mon-Sat 12:30-14:30
& 20:00-22:30, closed Sun, Via della Maestranza 96, tel. 0931-
67133).

$$$ Le Vin de l'Assassin has an interesting French-Sicilian
fusion menu, using local products with French preparations. The
dining room is colorful, artsy, and chic, and the outdoor seat-
ing—on a characteristic lane—is appealing (Tue-Sun 19:00-22:00,
closed Mon, reservations smart, Via Roma 115, tel. 0931-66159).

$$$ Osteria da Seby is a white-tablecloth sort of place, where
Seby and his crew serve a seafood-focused menu. While a bit old
school and well-discovered by tourists, this is a reliable choice for
a fancy fish dinner (Tue-Sun 10:00-15:00 & 19:00-23:00, closed
Mon, Via Vincenzo Mirabella 21, tel. 0931-181-5619)

$$ Osteria la Gazza Ladra is a tiny hole-in-the-wall place
that serves fresh home-cooking following family recipes. Come
early for a glass of wine (open for drinks only at 17:30)—but re-
serve a spot for dinner, as there are only a dozen small tables. Try to
snag one outdoors along the tightest, most appealing stretch of Via
Cavour (food served Tue-Sun 19:30-22:30, closed Mon, cash only,
Via Cavour 8, mobile 340-060-2428, www.gazzaladrasiracusa.
com, Marcello).

$$ Castello Fiorentino Pizzeria serves up big wood-fired
pizzas down a tight alley behind the cathedral. Choose between
a streetside table or the traditional dining room (Tue-Sun 12:00-
24:00, closed Mon, Via del Crocifisso 6, tel. 0931-21097).

$$ Solaria Enoteca, in an old-fashioned wine library, is run
by Gianfilippo and Elisa. Ask for a €15 tasting that includes bread,
cheese, and olives, paired with three glasses of wine (Mon-Sat
11:30-14:30 & 18:00-24:00, closed Sun, Via Roma 86, tel. 0931-
463-007).

$ Schiticchio Pizzeria—a modern-feeling spot along atmospheric Via Cavour—has pizza and a range of good beers. They specialize in enormous burgers made with local ingredients, served on a cutting board with a knife...you'll need it (Thu-Tue 12:30-15:00 & 19:30-23:00, closed Wed, Via Cavour 30, mobile 331-334-3721).

$ Antica Giudecca, near the Puppet Theater, is a neighborhood hangout with zero pretense. They sell pizza by the slice, calzone, *arancini,* and other *tavola calda* (buffet spread) items, all churned out nonstop by Signora Lucia and her husband. While most locals stop here for carryout, you can sit at one of the humble tables (Mon-Sat 7:00-14:00 & 18:00-22:00, closed Sun, Via della Giudecca 28, tel. 0931-449-152).

Vegetarian: A couple of very different vegetarian eateries sit a few blocks apart. **$$ Le Comari Inn** offers appealing vegetarian variations on traditional Sicilian dishes, with outdoor seating on a charming square facing a church (Thu-Sun and Mon-Tue 19:00-23:00, Sun also 11:00-15:00, closed Wed, Piazza San Giuseppe 8, tel. 0931-24833). **$$ Moon** is a wildly creative eatery (its name stands for "Move Ortigia Out of Normality") with a big, minimalist, trendy interior and inviting outdoor tables. They serve up ambitious, hit-or-miss vegan food, with a fusion approach that incorporates Asian and African elements (Wed-Mon 19:00-23:00, Sun also 12:30-15:00, closed Tue, reservations smart, Via Roma 112, tel. 0931-449-516, www.moonortigia.com).

Eating on Piazza Duomo: The glorious town living room that surrounds Ortigia's cathedral is one of Sicily's most inviting public spaces. A few eateries face this elegant square and are ideal for a scenic lunch or a romantic evening drink. While food may be better in back-street restaurants, this location is hard to resist, and prices are reasonable. Both of these **$$** places are open long hours daily: **La Volpe e l'Uva** has Sicilian-style pizzas, big salads, and pastas (at #20, tel. 0931-66029), while **Gran Caffè del Duomo** has a predictable menu of pastas, pizzas, main courses, and its own gelato counter (at #18, tel. 0931-21544).

Market Eateries Along Via Emmanuele de Benedictis: The main drag of Ortigia's outdoor market—which extends just off the Temple of Apollo, near Piazza Pancali—is a fun place to browse for a meal (they're all open at lunch, and about half are open for dinner; everything is closed Sun). Options range from sit-down *trattorie,* to high-end fish restaurants, to cheap-and-cheery fried street food. There's also a pair of popular **$** deli/sandwich shops at the far end (**Caseificio Borderi** and its neighbor **La Salumeria Fratelli Burgio**) that are touristy but good for grabbing a sandwich to go.

Strolling, Drinking, and Dining Along the Harbor: From the Fountain of Arethusa, you can stroll down to a delightful promenade that runs south along Ortigia's dreamy seafront—with views over the nearly 360-degree harbor. You'll pass a stretch of interchangeably romantic and overpriced **$$$** fish restaurants—popular for a pricey meal or (better) a €5 predinner cocktail. The food is forgettable, but the views are not. If you continue south, at the quieter far end the recommended **Charme Hotel Henry's House** has an inviting **$$** bar with two levels of outdoor seating and an aging-hippie ambience (drinks and light food).

Groceries: Run by cheery Jennifer, **Salumeria Roma** is a simple grocery store buried deep in the heart of Ortigia, where you can get a made-to-order sandwich for just a few euros (Mon-Sat 7:30-14:00 & 16:30-20:30, closed Sun, Via Roma 102). **Gusto Ortigia Market** is centrally located and has a wine shop and deli (daily 7:30-21:00, Via della Maestranza 80).

Siracusa Connections

BY PUBLIC TRANSPORTATION

Unless otherwise noted, buses are operated by Etna (bus info: mobile 331-687-7678, www.etnatrasporti.it).

From Siracusa by Bus to: Noto (6/day, 1 hour, Interbus, www.interbus.it), **Catania** (6/day, 1.5 hours), **Palermo** (2/day, 3.5 hours), **Taormina** (1/day, 2.5 hours).

From Siracusa by Train to: Noto (4/day, 30 minutes), **Catania** (9/day, 1.5 hours), **Taormina** (7/day, 2 hours), **Ragusa** (4/day, 2 hours), **Cefalù** (6/day, 5 hours, change in Messina), **Rome** (5/day, 11 hours).

ROUTE TIPS FOR DRIVERS

Siracusa is well connected to the rest of Sicily by the speedy E-45 expressway, which zips south to Noto in about 45 minutes, or north to Catania in about an hour. If you're connecting Siracusa to Ragusa, be sure to pause in Noto—it's a perfect lunch or gelato stop (see the Ragusa chapter).

CATANIA

Sitting at the foot of Mount Etna on the eastern shore of Sicily, the island's second largest city is an urban hub in a beautiful setting. Mamma Etna steams and sputters above, while the city below is made of her ashes: Most historic buildings are built with a black lava stone trimmed in white, giving the city a reverse-negative look.

With its handy airport and easy connections to sights on Sicily's eastern shores (Taormina, Mount Etna, Siracusa), many visitors simply pass through Catania en route to its more glamorous neighbors. But, while it's admittedly rough around the edges, those who spend some time in Catania will find a surprisingly genteel main square, wonderfully chaotic fish market, hidden Roman theater, and fascinating WWII museum.

Catania was one of the first Greek settlements, and came to prominence in Roman times, when it was likely the largest Roman city in Sicily. It had two large theaters and a smaller odeum, as well a stadium only slightly smaller than the Circus Maximus in Rome. But time, invasion, and modern sprawl erased much of the ancient city, and today, only scattered remnants can be found.

What remains of Catania from the Middle Ages is also scant. In 1693, an eruption of Mount Etna was followed by a major earthquake, destroying the city. It was rebuilt in Baroque style, following the architectural trend coming out of Rome. Later, in World War II, Catania was hit hard again, and some neighborhoods still bear the scars of war—with crumbling buildings and ugly, hastily built postwar apartments. But these days the city is on the rise, and new initiatives are remaking the center into a lively, youthful hotspot.

I wouldn't go out of my way to visit Catania—but I wouldn't go out of my way to avoid it, either. While less appealing than some other Sicilian destinations, Catania warrants a half-day look. The city rewards travelers who enjoy the gritty energy of urban Sicily, and it can be a handy home base for those relying on public transportation.

PLANNING YOUR TIME

Catania's airport makes it a common arrival or departure point on a Sicilian trip. The city is also a hub for trains and buses serving eastern Sicily. For a half-day of good sightseeing, follow my self-guided walk through town (including a visit to the cathedral, a walk through the fish market, and a peek at the Roman theater), then ride the Metro out to the city's fine WWII museum. Lovers of Sicilian Baroque will want to tour the frilly Palazzo Biscari—a noble palace with a charming owner (reservations required; details under "Sights in Catania," later).

Strategic travelers without a car can use Catania as a home base for exploring Mount Etna, Taormina, and Siracusa—all well connected from Catania by public transportation.

Orientation to Catania

Catania (pop. 315,000) sprawls from the base of Mount Etna to the Ionian Sea. The main axis for visitors runs north from Porta Uzeda near the fish market, through Piazza del Duomo (past the cathedral) to Via Etnea, the main shopping street. Pedestrian-only Via Etnea stretches from Piazza Università, through Piazza Stesicoro (with a handy Metro stop), and on to the public gardens at Villa Bellini. With the exception of the WWII museum (near the train station), the main sights are within a couple of blocks of this axis.

TOURIST INFORMATION

The TI faces the side of the cathedral (Mon-Sat 8:00-19:00, Sun 8:30-13:30, Via Vittorio Emanuele 172, tel. 095-742-5573). There's also a branch at the airport.

ARRIVAL IN CATANIA

By Train: Trains from Palermo, Messina, and Siracusa arrive at Catania Centrale train station, near the port. You'll exit toward a chaotic, giant roundabout called Piazza Giovanni XXIII.

Taxis are just to the right (look for the orange *TAXI* sign, figure about €8-10 to the city center), and local bus stops line up directly ahead. It's a dreary 15-minute walk to Via Etnea in the heart of the city (cross the piazza and turn left, following Corso Martiri della Libertà to Piazza Stesicoro).

It's easier and more appealing to hop on the **Metro**—the Giovanni XXIII station is directly in front of the train station (look for the red M signs). Buy a €1 ticket at the machine and take the train just one stop to Stesicoro, the end of the line (2-4/hour depending on time of day). You'll pop out at Piazza Stesicoro, in the middle of town. Also note that the WWII museum is a five-minute walk away (head straight out of the train station, bear right along the busy road past the Metro entrances, and you'll find the museum in the Ciminiere industrial-mod complex on the right).

By Bus: Intercity buses use the central bus station, across the piazza from the train station, behind the Metro stop. From here, the **Metro** is the easiest way into town (see above). For details on connecting in Catania (en route from Palermo to Ragusa or Taormina), see "Catania Connections" at the end of this chapter.

By Car: Drivers will find it easiest to aim for the train station or port, thereby avoiding the congested center. The easiest parking for a short visit is near Porta Uzeda, at Parking Borsellino (€1/hour, just off the roundabout at Via Jonica). If you're staying overnight, ask your hotel about the best place to park. Lock your vehicle and put your belongings in the trunk, out of sight.

By Plane: See "Catania Connections" at the end of this chapter.

HELPFUL HINTS

Safety: The areas I've described in this chapter get a fair amount of tourist traffic and are safe to explore. However, the center of Catania has some rougher neighborhoods that might not feel entirely safe, especially after dark. Since the city is quickly gentrifying and the character of neighborhoods can change fast, get advice from your hotelier about areas to avoid. In general, after dark it's best to stick to well-lit major thoroughfares.

Laundry: A handy self-service laundry is **Hydro Wash,** at the north end of Via Etnea (daily 8:30-24:00, Via Etnea 648, mobile 340-262-6351). **La Lavandaia** is between the town center and the train station (daily from 8:30, Piazza Vittorio Emanuele-Ettore Majorana 28, mobile 393-948-930).

Festivals: Every February 3-5, the festival celebrating the patron of the city, **Sant'Agata,** fills the streets for three days of madness with processions, oversized candles, and fireworks. (See the "Festival of Sant'Agata" sidebar, later, for details.)

Markets: Catania has two lively markets, both busy Mon-Sat 8:00-14:00 (closed Sun). The **fish market** *(piscaria)* by Porta Uzeda, in the heart of the city near the cathedral and main square, sells fish, meat, cheese, veggies, and more. A bit farther north, the **Fera 'o Luni** market at Piazza Carlo Alberto has clothes

CATANIA

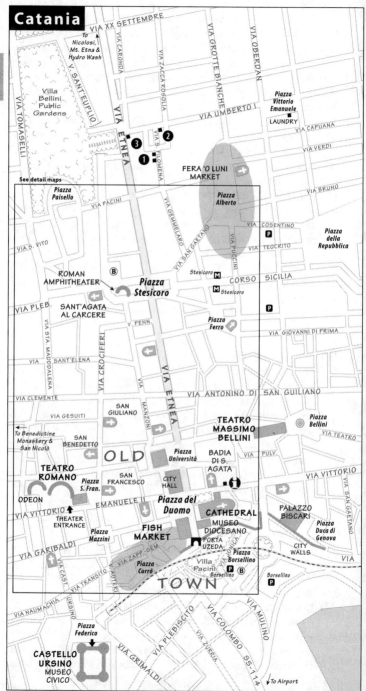

Catania

VIA XX SETTEMBRE

To Nicolosi,
Mt. Etna &
Hydro Wash

Villa
Bellini
Public
Gardens

See detail maps

❸ ❷ ❶

FERA 'O LUNI
MARKET

Piazza
Alberto

Piazza
Vittorio
Emanuele

LAUNDRY

Piazza
della
Repubblica

Piazza
Paisello

VIA PACINI

ROMAN
AMPHITHEATER

Piazza
Stesicoro

SANT'AGATA
AL CARCERE

Stesicoro

CORSO SICILIA

Stesicoro

SANT'ELENA

Piazza
Ferro

VIA GIOVANNI DI PRIMA

VIA CLEMENTE

VIA ANTONINO DI SAN GUILIANO

SAN
GIULIANO

TEATRO
MASSIMO
BELLINI

Piazza
Bellini

To Benedictine
Monastery &
San Nicolò

SAN
BENEDETTO

OLD

Piazza
Università

BADIA
DI S.
AGATA

TEATRO
ROMANO

SAN
FRANCESCO

CITY
HALL

ODEON

EMANUELE II

Piazza del
Duomo

PALAZZO
BISCARI

Piazza
Duca di
Genova

Piazza
S. Fran.

CATHEDRAL

MUSEO
DIOCESANO

CITY
WALLS

THEATER
ENTRANCE

FISH
MARKET

PORTA
UZEDA

Piazza
Mazzini

Villa
Pacini

Piazza
Borsellino

Piazza
Currò

Borsellino

Borsellino

TOWN

VIA NAUMACHIA

Piazza
Federico

CASTELLO
URSINO

MUSEO
CIVICO

VIA GRIMALDI

VIA PLEBISCITO

VIA ZURRIA

VIA COLOMBO SS-114

To Airport

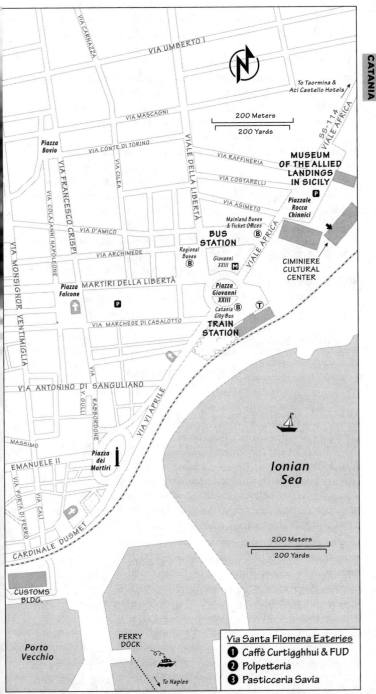

CATANIA

Via Santa Filomena Eateries
1 Caffè Curtigghhui & FUD
2 Polpetteria
3 Pasticceria Savia

CATANIA

and household goods in addition to foods (just off Via Etnea at Piazza Stesicoro). Watch your valuables in both markets.

GETTING AROUND CATANIA

By Public Transportation: Catania's concise **Metro** system caters mostly to suburban commuters, but tourists will find it's a cheap (€1/ride, €2/day) and easy way to connect the train station (Giovanni XXIII stop) to downtown (Stesicoro stop).

Catania's network of public **bus** lines (run by AMT, one ticket good for 90 minutes, sold at newsstands and tobacco shops but not on board) seems always in flux. On a short visit to the areas I describe, I'd stick to the Metro, walking, and occasional taxis, with one exception: It can be handy to hop on a bus (likely line #BRT1, but look for others) to travel up and down Via Etnea (www.amt.ct.it).

By Taxi: Taxis wait at orange-signed taxi stands. Use only official taxis, and ask for an estimated price before you get in. Always use the meter unless you have agreed to a fixed price (tel. 0953-30966, www.radiotaxicatania.org).

By Private Car: Giuseppe Leotta offers transfers and day trips from Catania (€65 transfer, €120 for 4 hours, more for larger cars, mobile 366-438-1797, www.luxurycarservices.it, info@luxurycarservices.it).

Tours in Catania

Local Guide

Diana Mazza comes from a family of Sicilian guides and does Taormina and Siracusa walking tours as well (€60/hour, 2-hour minimum, mobile 347-126-4530, trinacria2000@hotmail.com).

Food Tours

Streaty Food Tours runs fun market tours that include a historical background of the city with bites along the way. They take you places you'd probably not go on your own (€39, Mon-Sat at 10:30, 3 hours, www.streaty.com, info@streaty.com).

Bus Tours

Two competing bus companies line up alongside the cathedral, offering both Catania tours and excursions to Mount Etna. Yellow **Katane Live** buses have three options: a hop-on, hop-off city loop (€5, daily 9:00-20:00, off-season until 19:00, hourly, 1 hour), a coastal tour to Aci Castello (€15, 4/day, 2 hours), and a tour to Rifugio Sapienza on Mount Etna (€30, daily at 10:00, www.katanelive.com). Red **Tourist Service** hop-on, hop-off buses leave more frequently, make a city loop, and then go along the coast, with a break at Aci Trezza (€15, daily 9:30-19:00, hourly, 1.5 hours);

they also operate a tourist train (€5 loop around the city center) and bus tours to Mount Etna (€35, daily at 11:30, return at 17:30, www. touristservice2006.com).

Catania City Walk

At first glance, Catania can feel a little intimidating and rough around the edges. But this 1.5-hour walk through its historic heart can help you get comfortable with the city's lively and warm soul.

• *Begin your walk outside the city walls at the Porta Uzeda, just south of Piazza del Duomo. Stand facing the gate, with the railroad trestle and the park at your back.*

❶ City Walls

In the 1500s, during the time of Spanish rule, Catania's defenses were fortified with sloping black lava walls. These stout walls are

a symbol of the city's resilience; even after the 1693 earthquake, they remained intact. Where you are standing used to be water, and the city gate of **Porta Uzeda** was literally a port where boats unloaded their cargo. The bad smell of the port offended the noses of the nobles and the clergy living in palaces attached

to the walls, so the port was filled in and the harbor moved eastward.

Looking to the left, you can see the **fish market** and produce stalls spilling out under the train bridge. (We'll enter the fish market later from the other side.) If you see smoke in that direction, it's usually vendors roasting stuffed artichokes or peppers.

Immediately left of the gate, **Café Etoile d'Or** can power you up for this walk with a coffee, pastry, or a frosty almond *granita* and brioche (daily, Viale Cardinale Dusmet 7).

• *Pass through Porta Uzeda and walk to the square (Piazza del Duomo). On your right is the fancy facade of the...*

❷ Catania Cathedral (Cattedrale di Sant'Agata)

As you approach the cathedral, you'll walk along a row of buildings displaying the defining building material of Catania: black **lava stone** (basalt) with white trim (limestone). Catania is a child of Mount Etna, which, if it's clear, you can see up the broad main street ahead, Via Etnea.

The cathedral is dedicated to **Sant'Agata** (or *A Santuzza* as the locals call her in adoration), the patron saint of the city. She is cel-

CATANIA

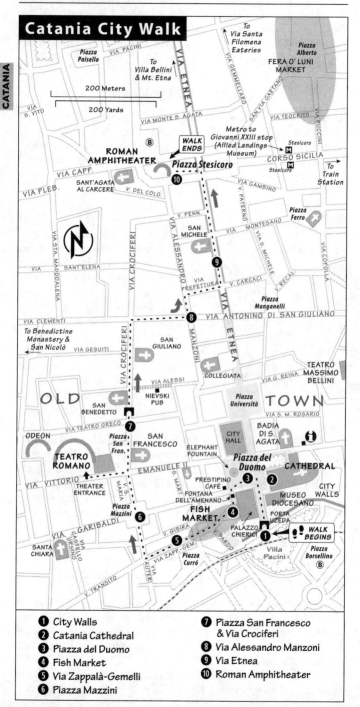

Catania City Walk

1. City Walls
2. Catania Cathedral
3. Piazza del Duomo
4. Fish Market
5. Via Zappalà-Gemelli
6. Piazza Mazzini
7. Piazza San Francesco & Via Crociferi
8. Via Alessandro Manzoni
9. Via Etnea
10. Roman Amphitheater

ebrated during an annual February festival with a wild procession through the city. (For more on Sant'Agata, see the sidebar.)

This church sits over the ruins of an ancient Roman bath and was originally a Norman cathedral-fortress (you can see the surviving Norman apses around the back side of the church, at Via Vittorio Emanuele II #159). But most of the church came tumbling down in the 1693 earthquake and was rebuilt in the Baroque style. The columns decorating the facade were originally from Roman buildings in Catania, then repurposed as the columns for the nave of the church, and finally salvaged for the facade after the church collapsed.

Step **inside** (free, Tue 9:30-12:30, Wed-Sat 9:30-12:30 & 16:00-18:00, Sun 9:00-12:30 & 19:00-20:30, closed Mon). Look for the sunken column bases from the old church, and compare them to the thick columns alongside. After the earthquake, the new church was overbuilt for added stability. Ahead at the altar, you can see the difference between the new, light Baroque nave and the old, heavy Norman apses with small windows. The reliquary of Sant'Agata is to the right of the altar, near the glass casket of Cardinal Dusmet, a beloved local priest known for his devotion to the poor.

The sacristy, in the left transept, contains a fresco that captures the close and, at times, dangerous relationship between Catania and Mount Etna. In 1669, a new vent opened on Etna and erupted for four long months—creating two craters that became known as the Monti della Ruina, "Mountains of Ruin." The initial lava flow destroyed several towns as it worked its way 10 miles south to Catania. After five weeks, the lava finally reached the stout city walls—which thankfully held, diverting the flow as it coursed around the town for another seven weeks. Catania was mostly unharmed, even as the lava flow extended the nearby coastline into the sea. The fresco, made not long after by an eyewitness, shows people boarding boats to escape the eruption, while practical women hang their laundry near the hot lava to dry.

• *Exit the cathedral and walk to the center of the piazza, near the elephant fountain.*

❸ Piazza del Duomo

This main square is the heart of Catania. The little **elephant** in the center is the symbol of the city—a Roman sculpture in lava stone with an Egyptian obelisk on its back.

. From here, do a quick spin tour of the square. Starting with the cathedral and turning left, you'll see the big, stone dome of the church of **Sant'Agata alla Badia.** You can climb 170 steps to the rooftop terrace at the base of the dome for a grand view of the city and its smoldering volcano (€3, same hours as cathedral).

Looking farther left, you'll see the beginning of Catania's main shopping street, **Via Etnea.** With limited traffic, this is an enjoyable artery to stroll and a lively spot in the evening. Just a block up the street is the pleasant Piazza Università, with the headquarters of the historic University of Catania.

To the left of Via Etnea is Catania's **City Hall.** If you're curious about the city's Sant'Agata celebrations, pop inside the doorway, where a video loop shows footage of the annual event.

Opposite the cathedral, the square buzzes with shops and cafés. The recommended **Prestipino** is a classic spot for a special pastry, *minnuzze di Sant'Agata*, "breasts of St. Agatha": small, rounded cakes topped with a cherry to look like...well, breasts. (See the "Festival of Sant'Agata" sidebar for the story.)

Tucked back in the corner by all those cafés is the shiny white **Fontana dell'Amenano.** At this fountain, you can get a peek at the underground Amenano River (which once ran above ground through Catania). This also serves as a gateway to the lively fish market.

As you continue circling left, the black building trimmed with white limestone is **Palazzo dei Chierici,** once a seminary and now a municipal building (when Mussolini visited Catania in 1937, he addressed a crowd from its balcony). Finally, just to the right of the cathedral entrance is the **Diocesan Museum.** Its ecclesiastical art collection is skippable; the highlight is the heavy float used for the celebrations of Sant'Agata (Mon-Fri 9:00-14:00, Tue and Thu 15:00-18:00, Sat 9:00-13:00, Via Etnea 8, tel. 095-281-635, www.museodiocesanocatania.com). Skip the rooftop access available here—the views are better at Sant'Agata alla Badia (described above).

• *Now cross the square diagonally to the Amenano fountain. There, squeeze through the passageway and go down the steps to the sunken*

Festival of Sant'Agata

A third-century Christian martyr, Sant'Agata (Saint Agatha) is one of the most venerated saints in Sicily and southern Italy. Tradition says that when she was tortured for her faith, Agata's breasts were cut off, which is why she's usually portrayed holding a plate with breasts on it. The patron saint of breast cancer, wet nurses, fire, and eruptions, she has many devoted followers.

The festival of Sant'Agata, held each February 3-5, is one of the largest religious celebrations in Italy. In Catania, more than 100,000 people attend, filling the historic center for three days of intense religious worship. Devotees gather dressed in white robes, gloves, and black hats, and are often escorted by their families. During the procession, it's a great honor to pull the float carrying the relics of Sant'Agata, even for a few minutes. It can be dangerous, too, as the float weighs three tons and is moved by a crowd of men. Oversized candles accompany the float, coating the city streets in a thick layer of wax. Smaller floats provided by historic guilds follow Agata's relics through the streets. The procession runs along Via Crociferi, and when it passes at dawn near the Benedictine convent, nuns gather on the bridge overhead to sing. The festival culminates in a fireworks display over the city. Every year on August 17, a smaller version of the procession takes place to commemorate the retrieval of Agata's bones from Constantinople in 1126.

To better understand the fervor of this religious celebration, visit the courtyard of the City Hall, where you can watch a video of previous years' celebrations. In the courtyard are two carriages used by the mayor and city authorities to open the festivities. The Museo Diocesiano (next to the cathedral) houses the main Sant'Agata float, and the Church of San Francesco at the end of Via Crociferi has a collection of the smaller floats used during the procession.

Any time of year you can stop into a café in Catania to try *minnuzze di Sant'Agata* ("breasts of St. Agatha"). These rounded cakes, filled with ricotta, covered in icing and marzipan, and topped with cherries, represent the severed breasts of the city's beloved saint.

plaza—if it's earlier in the day (and not Sunday), you'll find a noisy jumble of shoppers and makeshift sales kiosks at the...

❹ Fish Market *(Piscaria)*

Starting in the early hours of the morning (until closing at 14:00), this fish market is one of the noisiest—you can hear the commotion from blocks around as the fishmongers shout and sing like auctioneers at a county fair. Fishermen have sold their catches here for over a thousand years. Their sing-song vocalization comes from an Arab tradition, as the market was likely established under Arab rule. Walk down and take a lap around the tables, admiring the wide variety of fish, from swordfish to eel to translucent heaps of baby fish used to make fish patties.

For an in-depth tour of the fish market, see page 322.

• *After exploring the lower area of the fish market, head back up to street level and, for more market activity, stroll down Via Zappalà-Gemelli (go left from the top of the stairs).*

For a shorter walk, you could go to the far end of Piazza del Duomo and head left on Via Vittorio Emanuele II to Piazza San Francesco. You'll rejoin the walk at stop #7.

❺ Via Zappalà-Gemelli

Along this street are market stalls and shops tempting you with very affordable produce, meat, and cheeses. This is the real deal, a thriving market where locals shop every day except Sunday. Thirty years ago, this was the only way to shop, as there were no supermarkets. *Fare la spesa* (doing the shopping) took hours, as each item had its own store: butcher, baker, pasta shop, and so on. The Sicilian way of life has become more contemporary, with big box stores and shopping malls popping up where citrus groves used to be. But this market is one of the few that staunchly hangs on, with a real, untouristy vibrancy that few other Italian markets can match.

Walk a long block, passing more cheese shops and fruit vendors. Try *fichi d'india* (prickly pears), which are loved by the locals. Get the precut ones, and don't try to peel them yourself—or you'll be pulling little spines out of your fingers for the rest of your trip.

• *You'll come to a little piazza with a white church on your left. Keep going straight, then take the next right onto Via Auteri. Two short blocks ahead, you'll find...*

❻ Piazza Mazzini

After the 1693 earthquake, the city was not just rebuilt, but also redesigned. Palaces rose on long, straight streets, and public piazzas like this one were constructed. The new geometric design served two purposes: to organize the city and make it more gra-

cious, and to provide open spaces where it would be safe to gather during a major earthquake. The portico of the piazza, meant to house a marketplace, has ancient Roman marble columns recycled from a church that collapsed in the earthquake.

• *Walk straight up to the next square...*

❼ Piazza San Francesco and Via Crociferi

As you cross Via Vittorio Emanuele, look to your left. About a block up on the right (at #266), the surprising **Roman Theater** hides behind a plain gray facade (worth visiting, and described under "Sights in Catania," later).

But here on the piazza, on your right, is the **Church of San Francesco.** If it's open, go in and you'll find some of the floats *(candelore)* used for the Sant'Agata procession. Each of the city's guilds has a float that they bring out only for the big celebration.

The street in front of the church (with the archway) is **Via Crociferi,** one of the prettiest in Catania and home to a cluster of lovely Baroque churches, palaces, and convents. If you find the doors of the churches open, go in for a look. The archway itself is connected to a convent of cloistered nuns, where the procession of Sant'Agata ends.

Walk up Via Crociferi, and under the archway. If you're in need of refreshment, take the staircase on the right down to the colorful communist-themed pub, **Nievski,** on the landing below. Or pop into the small grocery at Via Crociferi 24 for a salad and sandwich.

• *Continue a long block on Via Crociferi, then turn right on the downhill, stepped, tree-lined Via Antonino Di Sangiuliano. Then take the next left on Via Alessandro Manzoni.*

❽ Via Alessandro Manzoni

All along this street, you'll find *mercerie*—stores selling fabric, yarn, and costumes. In medieval times, each street had shops specializing in similar services, such as shoemaking or stocking making. Catania still maintains many of the traditions that other Italian cities abandoned long ago, including this one.

• *After one short block, turn right on Via Prefettura, then left onto...*

❾ Via Etnea

The main shopping street of Catania is always hopping. It's become mostly pedestrianized in recent years and has an elegant feel, with long views toward the cathedral in one direction, and Mount Etna in the other.

Stroll up the street for a few minutes. Soon you'll reach the long, rectangular Piazza Stesicoro, bordered by Baroque palaces. On the left side of the square, in the middle of the circus of whizzing Vespas and speeding cars, are ruins of the ancient ❿ **Roman Amphitheater,** excavated in the 18th century. Built with black lava stone, it may have seated 15,000 spectators. Catania, positioned between Africa and Rome, was along the trade route for wild game. Animal shipments often stopped in Catania, and likely weak or dying animals were used in games here.

• *Our walk is finished, but there's more to explore. Here are some options:*

For some more market action, exit Piazza Stesicoro to the left on Via Etnea, then right on Via Pacini, to the **Fera 'o Luni street market** *(closed after 14:00 and Sun).*

If you'd like to zip out to Catania's ▲▲ **WWII museum,** *ride the Metro: Find the red* M *signs at the opposite end of Piazza Stesicoro from the amphitheater ruins (along Corso Sicilia), buy a €1 ticket at the machine, and take the Metro just one stop to the Giovanni XXIII station. It's about a five-minute walk from there (see the listing under "Sights in Catania," later).*

Or, to extend your stroll, continue straight up Via Etnea, browsing the shops until you reach the entrance to the public gardens at **Villa Bellini,** *about a 10-minute walk. If you're ready for gelato, the recommended Pasticceria Savia is on the right side of Via Etnea (at #302), just across the street from the gardens.*

For eating options, the charming **Via Santa Filomena**—*with some recommended eateries—is five minutes away (see the "Catania" map, earlier).*

Sights in Catania

▲▲Fish Market Scavenger Hunt

Exploring a traditional street market—like Catania's fish market *(piscaria)* near Piazza del Duomo—is one of the liveliest, most genuinely local experiences you can have in Sicily. Shoppers have been wandering these market stalls for centuries, gathering the freshest ingredients for family feasts. From the cacophonous sing-song of the fishmongers to the billowing smoke of grilling vegetables, this is Sicilian life at its least polished.

Dive into the action and toss aside your inhibitions (or fear of mysterious animal parts). Talk to the locals as best as you can: Ask for un *assaggio* (oon ah-SAH-joh)—a sample of whatever looks interesting. If you can't identify something, ask *"Che cos'e?"* (kay-kos-AY). Give each travel partner €5 and see what they come back with for an impromptu picnic.

Sicilian culture insists that you try to negotiate—it's considered a little pathetic to pay full price. Try saying, *"Ma è troppo caro"* (it's too expensive)—or, with a smile, *"Sconto?"* (discount?). If that doesn't work, offer to buy two items...if they'll give you a price break. The seller could refuse—but negotiating is an authentic market experience. Don't be shy and don't let language hold you back. Locals will appreciate your enthusiasm and interaction.

When to Go: The market is open Mon-Sat 8:00-14:00 (closed Sun) but is most fun in the morning. Watch your step—or you'll be slopping through bloody fish guts and gills.

Fish of All Shapes and Sizes: Start just off Piazza del Duomo at the Amenano fountain, and head down the stairs into Piazza di Benedetto—the beating heart of the fish-vending action. The selection changes every day and with the season. You might find seasonal specialties such as *spatola* (ribbon fish), *tonno* (tuna), *pesce spada* (swordfish), *neonato* (baby fish), *masculini* (small and lean anchovies), and so on. And there will be things you've never seen before. Early morning is best for variety and quality.

The vendors sing, yell, and chatter like auctioneers to get the attention of buyers. Ask someone to translate what the vendors are saying. Sometimes they're not just commenting on the fish but also on the people passing by...including tourists.

Walk through the tunnel ahead to find the frozen fish section—cheaper and more convenient, but not for gourmets. Go through the arch on the right, and the fresh fish sections begin once again. Look for vendors selling little bites, such as anchovies on toast.

When you reach the petite Piazza Pardo, look for a kiosk where local shoppers refresh themselves with a brew called *seltz e limone* (*seltz,* for short)—fresh-squeezed lemon juice with seltzer water. They'll ask you *"sale?"* (SAH-lay?) to see if you want salt added. (It may sound strange, but a little salt makes this brew exceptionally thirst-quenching.)

Turn toward the train bridge at the end of the piazza, and you'll see a barbecue roasting artichokes or peppers (just follow the smoke). If stuffed artichokes are in season, buy one to share—this is a truly local treat.

Meats, Cheese, and Produce: Continuing up Via Pardo, you'll find butchers selling all kinds of cuts—from snout to tail and everything in between. Farther along are fruits, veggies, and dry goods, including the precious *pistacchio di Bronte*—the nuts the locals call "green gold."

At the corner of Via Pardo and Via Gisira, admire the *formaggi e salumi* (cheese and cold cuts) shop. Buy a few *etti* (1 *etto* = 3.5 ounces) of whatever looks good—perhaps *pecorino stagionato* (aged pecorino cheese)—and sample their delicious *olive condite* (dressed olives).

From here, continue down Via Pardo for more meats, some housewares, and produce. Count the types of citrus you pass—Sicily produces the largest variety in Italy. In May and June, look for yellow *nespole* (loquats), a popular fruit treat. At the end of summer, you'll find another Sicilian favorite, *fichi d'india* (prickly pears). Let the vendor peel them for you or you'll be in for a prickly surprise. Locals like them chilled.

Café Break: At the end of the market stalls on Via Pardo, you'll hit the intersection with Via Garibaldi. Turn right and head back toward Piazza del Duomo and the cathedral. On the left corner of the square, look for Prestipino Café (at Piazza del Duomo 9), and grab a seat at a shady table. This venerable watering hole sells coffee and street food day and night. Belly up to the bar and chat with the barman, order a *granita* and brioche or a *cipollina*—one of many savory pastries this classic café offers.

▲Roman Theater and Odeum (Teatro Romano e Odeon)

There are plenty of ancient theaters in Sicily, but none is as surprising as this Roman one, which hides behind a plain, run-down facade. From the street, you'd never guess that an ancient theater has been incorporated into the newer surrounding buildings—structures that were lived in until the 1950s. Thought to be a Greek theater that was rebuilt in Roman times, this venue could have held up to 7,000 people. Head all the way to the top

of the theater for great views of the seats and surrounding buildings, and to visit the small museum of artifacts found on-site (follow signs for *Casa Liberti*). The water in the orchestra pit comes from the underground Amenano River, which seeped into the theater as the ruins settled. Behind the Roman Theater, be sure to visit the smaller odeum, a more intimate performance space.

Cost and Hours: €6, daily 9:00-19:00, off-season until 17:00, WCs, Via Vittorio Emanuele II 266, tel. 095-715-0508.

▲Palazzo Biscari

Taking up several city blocks near the cathedral, the sprawling Palazzo Biscari clings to the city wall like a Baroque barnacle. Built after the 1693 earthquake, this extravagant example of Sicilian Baroque is said to have 700 rooms. Live-in Prince Ruggero Moncada welcomes you to his over-the-top palazzo and tells the history of his family with passion and a sparkling sense of humor. His home is filled with portraits of his ancestors, all of whom he brings to life with colorful stories of the good, bad, and ugly. You'll see a string of state rooms, including a lavish ballroom and staircase that are reminiscent of Versailles. Of the private noble palaces to visit in Sicily, this is the most impressive and probably the most fun.

Cost and Hours: €10 donation requested, tours offered most days 9:00-17:00, email in advance to join a group for a one-hour tour. If the prince has no scheduled tours, you may be able to book a private tour (minimum 4 people or €40, Via Museo Biscari 16, tel. 095-715-2508, mobile 320-211-4802, www.palazzobiscari.com, info@palazzobiscari.com).

▲Benedictine Monastery and Church (Monastero e Chiesa dei Benedettini di San Nicolò l'Arena)

Tucked in the corner of the noisy city, this historic monastery and church complex seem a world apart—with quiet courtyards, gardens, and students from the University of Catania (which owns it) shuttling between classes. The outer courtyard, corridors, and back garden of the sprawling grounds are free to visit, and wandering the maze of halls is delightful. For a full experience, join a 1.5-hour guided tour.

Cost and Hours: Church—usually free, open Mon-Sat 9:00-13:00, closed Sun; monastery grounds—free, Mon-Fri 8:00-20:00, Sat 9:00-14:00, closed Sun; monastery guided tour—€7, on the hour daily 9:00-17:00 (Aug 11:00-18:00), at least one tour daily in English (usually around lunchtime), call to confirm times; tel. 095-710-2767, mobile 334-924-2464, www.monasterodeibenedettini.it.

Getting There: It's a 10-minute walk west of the city center. Take Via Gesuiti Clementi.

Background: The Benedictine order has had a presence on Mount Etna for centuries, and moved to Catania in 1558. After the 1693 earthquake destroyed their monastery, it was rebuilt here on 10 acres—making it one of the largest such complexes in Europe. After the reunification of Italy, the state took control of the complex and repurposed it as a military hospital. Finally, in 1977 it was given to the University of Catania, and today students here study liberal arts, philosophy, archaeology, history, and foreign languages.

Visiting the Monastery: The guided tour includes two exquisite **cloisters:** the Chiostro di Levante, with an elaborately decorated coffeehouse, and the Chiostro di Ponente, with a Renaissance colonnade and fountain. Also on the tour are the Museo della Fabbrica, where you'll see an ancient Roman house with mosaics, and the monastery kitchen (built atop a lava flow), refectory, lecture hall, and fine library. The enormous **church** attached to the monastery—with its imposing, clearly unfinished facade—is the largest

CATANIA

in Sicily and yet only half the size originally intended. Construction began in the late 1600s but was interrupted by an eruption of Mount Etna and the earthquake, which made the heavy structure unstable and impossible to complete. Inside, on the floor, a meridian runs almost the entire width of the church, providing a daily calendar lit by a sunbeam.

▲▲Museum of the Allied Landings in Sicily (Museo Storico dello Sbarco in Sicilia—1943)

Italy has few museums about World War II, but this well-presented exhibit helps remedy that. It focuses on Operation Husky, the 1943 Allied fight to gain a foothold in Italy through Sicily. While viewed from a distinctly Italian perspective (and without English explanations), the powerful exhibits speak for themselves as they tell the story of life before, during, and after the invasion. The museum's outlying location at Le Ciminiere (a former sulphur refinery) makes it optional for most, but it's well worth the trip for anyone interested in World War II.

Cost and Hours: €4, Tue-Sun 9:00-17:00, last entry 2 hours before closing, closed Mon, Piazzale Rocco Chinnici, tel. 095-401-1929. Consider the companion book for English explanations (€6).

Getting There: The museum is located outside the city center just past the Catania Centrale train station, in the Ciminiere cultural center. From downtown, either take a taxi (about €8) or ride the Metro (€1) one stop from the Piazza Stesicoro station to the Giovanni XXIII station, where you'll exit into the tumultuous scene in front of Catania Centrale. Put the train station and port at your back, and angle to the right up the busy street (Viale Africa) toward the old smokestacks. The museum is well signed within this converted industrial-mod complex.

Background: Sicily saw lots of action in World War II. American, British, and Canadian forces under the command of U.S. General George Patton and British General Bernard Montgomery invaded Sicily from Africa, landing at Gela and Siracusa on July 9, 1943. They fought a hard and bloody campaign against the Axis forces, and in just 38 days they'd taken all of Sicily—and were ready to cross over to the mainland to work

their way up the Italian peninsula. (For more on World War II in Sicily, see the "Sicily Goes to War" sidebar on page 396.)

Visiting the Museum: You'll begin by viewing a 12-minute film (with English subtitles) that sets the stage for Italy's role in World War II, and the inception of Operation Husky. Then you'll step into a re-created Mussolini-era Sicilian piazza with fascist flags and slogans (*credere, obbedire, combattere*—"believe, obey, fight"). Poke into shops, read the latest newspaper headlines, and peer into a typical home. With the sound of approaching aircraft, run for cover in an air-raid shelter *(rifugio)*—where you'll experience a simulated air raid, with shaking walls, screaming, and flashing lights. When the coast is clear, you'll step out to find the aftermath of the bombing—the same piazza is in rubble. A video screen shows historical footage of destroyed Sicilian cities.

From there, you'll follow a one-way route through a roughly chronological explanation of the Sicilian campaign. On the first floor, you'll see maps and models illustrating the Allied landings, then walk through display cases with original uniforms, weapons, and personal items from the Axis and Allied forces. At the end of the first floor is a pillbox bunker with mannequin soldiers operating a machine gun.

The top-floor exhibits outline more specifics from the landings and show off more weapons. And you'll see life-size wax figures of Roosevelt, Churchill, Mussolini, Hitler, and King Victor Emmanuel III. The exhibit ends with the memorial to the unknown soldier, commemorating the 14,864 fallen troops of the Sicilian landing.

Back down on the main floor, you'll find a case with WWII uniforms donated by visitors, an engine from a German Junkers Ju 88 bomber, a wheel from an American B-25 bomber, torpedoes, artillery, and miniature models. Before exiting, walk through the evocative collection of black-and-white photographs of soldiers in Sicily, taken by American war journalist Phil Stern.

More Sights in Catania

With extra time in Catania, you could consider visiting these sights, though they are near rather rough neighborhoods that make some visitors uncomfortable. For locations, see the "Catania" map, earlier.

CATANIA

Civic Museum (Museo Civico)

This eclectic city history exhibit fills the **Castello Ursino,** a 13th-century fortress that's one of the few Catanian structures to survive the 1693 earthquake. The archaeological collection of the Biscari family is housed here, along with paintings, sculpture, and a coin collection.

Cost and Hours: €6, daily 9:00-19:00, about a 10-minute walk from the fish market at Piazza Federico di Svevi, tel. 095-345-830).

Teatro Massimo Bellini

A few blocks east of Via Etnea, this fine opera house looms over an elegant square (close to streets often busy with sex workers, though the area is quickly gentrifying). While tours of the interior are sporadic, music lovers can try to catch a performance (Via Giuseppe Perrotta 12, tel. 095-730-6111, www.  teatromassimobellini.it). During the day, the Comis Café—facing the theater on the piazza—is a fun place to nurse a gelato or *granita*.

Sleeping in Catania

Catania is busier, crazier, and less accustomed to tourism than other cities in Sicily. It's well worth the money to stay in a comfortable hotel in a better part of town. Stick close to Via Etnea or within a block of the cathedral—where you'll find my recommended hotels. If you have a car, consider the seafront places I list north of the city, in the village of Aci Castello.

IN THE CITY

$$$$ Asmundo di Gisira is like sleeping in a contemporary art installation with an Andy Warhol vibe. Each of the six rooms mixes funky furniture with huge pieces of art, such as a 10-foot-high flamingo (air-con, elevator, terrace, solarium, Via Gisira 40, tel. 095-097-8894, www.asmundodigisira.com, info@asmundodigisira.com).

$$$$ Duomo Suites & Spa, in a tight, vertical building, has 12 colorful rooms—each with movie quotes from famous Sicilian films on the walls—along with bold colors and graphic art (air-con, elevator, terrace bar, parking, Via Garibaldi 23, tel. 095-288-3731, www.duomosuitesespa.it, info@duomosuitesespa.it).

$$$ Manganelli Palace, on the fourth floor of Palazzo Man-

Catania Center Hotels & Restaurants

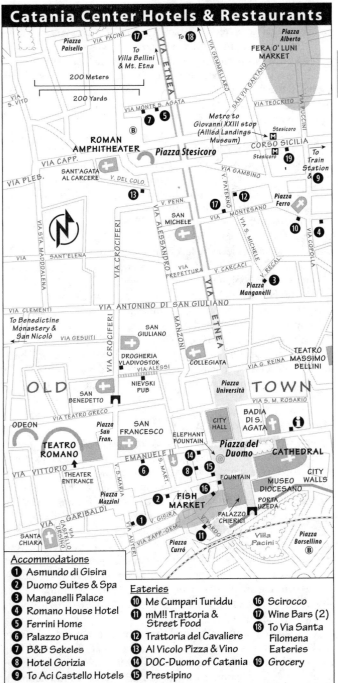

Piazza Paisello

VIA PACINI

To Villa Bellini & Mt. Etna

To 18

Piazza Alberto

FERA O' LUNI MARKET

VIA GERMANELLO

VIA ETNEA

200 Meters
200 Yards

VIA S. VITO

VIA MONTE S. AGATA

SAN VIA GAETANO

VIA TEOCRITO

VIA PUCCINI

ROMAN AMPHITHEATER

Piazza Stesicoro

Metro to Giovanni XXIII stop (Allied Landings Museum)

Stesicoro

CORSO SICILIA

Stesicoro

To Train Station &

VIA CAPP.

VIA PLEB.

SANT'AGATA AL CARCERE

V. DEL COLO.

VIA GAMBINO

Piazza Ferro

VIA COPOLLA

VIA STA. MADDALENA

VIA CROCIFERI

VIA ALESSANDRO

SAN MICHELE

V. PENN.

V. PATERNO

VIA MONTESANO

VIA S. MICHELE

Y. RECAL.

Piazza Manganelli

SANT'ELENA

VIA PREFETTURA

VIA CARCACI

VIA CLEMENTI

VIA ANTONINO DI SAN GIULIANO

To Benedictine Monastery & San Nicolò

VIA GESUITI

SAN GIULIANO

MANZONI

VIA ETNEA

TEATRO MASSIMO BELLINI

VIA CROCIFERI

DROGHERIA VLADIVOSTOK

VIA ALESSI

COLLEGIATA

VIA G. REINA

OLD

NIEVSKI PUB

SAN BENEDETTO

Piazza Università

TOWN

VIA S. M. ROSARIO

ODEON

VIA TEATRO GRECO

Piazza San Fran.

SAN FRANCESCO

BADIA DI S. AGATA

TEATRO ROMANO

THEATER ENTRANCE

ELEPHANT FOUNTAIN

EMANUELE II

V. MARI

CITY HALL

Piazza del Duomo

CATHEDRAL

VIA VITTORIO

V. S. MARIA

CITY WALLS

Piazza Mazzini

FOUNTAIN

MUSEO DIOCESANO

FISH MARKET

PALAZZO CHIERICI

PORTA UZEDA

VIA GARIBALDI

V. GISIRA

VIALE CASTELLO URSINO

SANTA CHIARA

VIA AUTERI

VIA ZAPP-GEM.

Piazza Currò

Villa Pacini

Piazza Borsellino

Accommodations

1. Asmundo di Gisira
2. Duomo Suites & Spa
3. Manganelli Palace
4. Romano House Hotel
5. Ferrini Home
6. Palazzo Bruca
7. B&B Sekeles
8. Hotel Gorizia
9. To Aci Castello Hotels

Eateries

10. Me Cumpari Turiddu
11. mM!! Trattoria & Street Food
12. Trattoria del Cavaliere
13. Al Vicolo Pizza & Vino
14. DOC-Duomo of Catania
15. Prestipino
16. Scirocco
17. Wine Bars (2)
18. To Via Santa Filomena Eateries
19. Grocery

CATANIA

ganelli, has a palatial air with 20 aristocratic rooms and a private sun terrace (air-con, elevator, parking, Via Recalcaccia 2, tel. 095-715-1842, www.manganellipalace.it, info@manganellipalace.it).

$$$ Romano House Hotel is a starkly modern hotel in the shell of an old palace a couple of blocks from Via Etnea, with comfy rooms and echoey public spaces (air-con, elevator, Via Giovanni di Prima 20, tel. 095-352-0611, www.romanohouse.it, info@romanohouse.it).

$$ Ferrini Home enjoys a central location just steps from the action on Via Etnea, but far enough away to be peaceful. Their small apartments, with kitchenettes and contemporary decor, work well for families or longer stays (air-con, Via Monte Sant'Agata 5, tel. 095-093-2592, www.ferrinihome.com, info@ferrinihome.it).

$ Palazzo Bruca has eight thoughtfully furnished, good-value rooms and three apartments hidden in a palace with a large courtyard. Some rooms have a view of the Baroque churches on Via Croficeri (air-con, elevator, secure on-site pay parking, Via Vittorio Emanuele II 201, tel. 095-594-4908, www.brucaroomhotelcatania.it, info@brucaroomhotelcatania.it, Lavignia).

$ B&B Sekeles has five bright, shabby-chic rooms, just off Via Etnea, which share a peaceful rooftop terrace. Each has a small balcony and comes with thoughtful extras (air-con, Via Monte Sant'Agata 15, mobile 346-634-9162, bbsekeles@libero.it).

$ Hotel Gorizia, a basic family-run hotel, has seven cheap and cheery rooms decorated in sunny yellow a block from Piazza del Duomo (air-con, elevator, Via Spadaro Grassi 8, tel. 095-715-0528).

NEAR CATANIA, IN ACI CASTELLO

Drivers who want to avoid Catania traffic can consider a cluster of seafront hotels with parking near the village of Aci Castello, a few miles north of town. Leave your car at the hotel and connect to town on bus #534 (to Catania's train station and Via Etnea, hourly, 40 minutes), or a sightseeing bus (see "Tours in Catania," earlier). From here, the airport is a 30-minute drive (without traffic).

$$$ Grand Hotel Baia Verde, a massive old-time resort, spreads out along the rocky coast. Their 147 rooms range from standard business class to plush and romantic suites. The dated public spaces open onto lovely sea views with sprawling grounds and a tempting swimming pool (air-con, elevator, parking garage, Via Angelo Musco 8/10, tel. 095-491-522, www.baiaverde.it, baiaverde@baiaverde.it).

$$ Zeus Residence Hotel has small, generic apartments stacked up along the water and around a small courtyard. Their 14 rooms have views of the sea and old lava flows surrounding the hotel (air-con, elevator, parking, sun terrace, Via Antonello da

Messina 8, tel. 095-711-1320, www.zeusresidencehotel.it, info@
zeusresidencehotel.it, Diego).

$ Villa Ortensia B&B has the feeling of a cozy relative's
house on the sea. Their seven rooms are decorated with antiques,
family photos, and flowery touches. The terrace and lush garden are
fine spots to enjoy a warm Sicilian evening (air-con, Via Antonello
da Messina 93, mobile 346-688-6040, www.bbvillaortensia.it,
bbvillaortensia@gmail.com, Ermina).

Eating in Catania

Youthful and always busy, Catania has a thriving dining scene. I've
focused my listings on and just off the central spine of Via Etnea,
where most visitors spend their time.

$$$ Me Cumpari Turiddu mixes a nostalgic theme with a
hipster atmosphere. Owner Roberta once was a lawyer in Milan,
but seeing *Cinema Paradiso* inspired her to return to Sicily to follow
her dream of opening a restaurant. Tucked a couple of blocks off
Via Etnea, this place is bright and sophisticated (daily 10:30-24:00,
Piazza Turi Ferro 36, tel. 095-715-0142).

$$$ mM!! Trattoria serves *delizioso* fresh fish right in the
heart of the fish market (Mon-Sat 12:00-14:30 & 19:30-23:00,
closed Sun, Via Pardo 34, mobile 349-722-9801). Next door,
$$ mM!! Street Food makes tuna hamburgers, *panini* with tuna
sausage, *coppo fritto,* and *sarde beccafico,* matched by microbrews or
local wine (Mon-Sat 12:30-15:30 & 18:00-23:00, closed Sun, Via
Pardo 26, tel. 095-348-897).

$$ Trattoria del Cavaliere reflects Catania's affection for
carne di cavallo—horse meat. (Even Garibaldi was advised to leave
his horses outside the city.) Adventurous eaters enjoy atmosphere
and service as old-school as the food; their large outdoor terrace
faces a functional apartment block (daily 10:00-15:00 & 19:00-
24:00, Via Paternò 11, tel. 095-310-491).

$$ Al Vicolo Pizza & Vino serves enormous pizzas and over-
sized antipasto platters to hungry locals, with outdoor tables on a
traffic-free street a block off Via Etnea (daily 19:30-24:00, Via del
Colosseo 5, tel. 095-836-0730, www.alvicolopizzaevino.it).

$ DOC-Duomo of Catania, just steps off Piazza del Duomo,
offers one of the best values in town—an all-you-can-eat €9 buffet
that includes a glass of wine (available most days). The €15 option
includes a generous platter of cold cuts (reservation required at din-
ner, Tue-Sun 12:00-24:00, closed Mon, Via Vittorio Emanuele II
171, mobile 340-992-6331, www.duomoofcatania.it, Giuseppe).

$ Prestipino, a deceptively tiny shop, makes quality fare—
from salty street-food snacks to decadent sweets—for takeaway
or to eat at stay-awhile tables on Piazza del Duomo. Franca, the

CATANIA

owner, is your long-lost chatty Sicilian auntie (daily 7:00-24:00, Piazza del Duomo 9, tel. 095-320-840, www.prestipinoeventi. com).

$ Scirocco, a hole-in-the-wall overlooking the fish market, turns out €6 fresh fried calamari and fish served in a paper cone. Eat it standing or nibble while you stroll the market (daily 10:30-23:00, Piazza Alonzo di Benedetto 7, tel. 095-836-5148).

Wine Bars: Sicily's top wine-growing area—Etna—is right at Catania's doorstep, and you'll find two popular wine bars in the city center. **$$ Razmataz** is always hopping, with a bustling scene of young backpackers filling a borderline-seedy square; they serve basic food (daily 12:00-16:00 & 19:00-24:00, Via Montesano 17). Those more serious about wine head a few blocks away to **$$ Cru Enoteca,** with a better variety, more knowledgeable staff, and more tranquil, focus-on-the-wines approach; they also have boards of local meats, cheeses, and other nibbles to complement the wines (Tue-Sun 17:00-24:00, closed Mon, just a few steps off Via Etnea at Via Pacini 8, mobile 393-920-3936).

Supermarket: A relatively large **Simply** grocery store is near the Stesicoro Metro stop, just off of Via Etnea (daily 8:30-20:30, Corso Sicilia 50, tel. 095-326-099).

On or near Via Santa Filomena

This fun little street, tucked a long block off the top of Via Etnea (a 10-15 minute walk from the cathedral area), is lined with appeal-

ing eateries with al fresco tables tumbling out onto the cobbles. It's a great street to simply stroll for a place that looks good—but here are some of my favorites. For locations, see the "Catania" map, earlier.

$$ Caffè Curtigghiu fills fast on summer nights. In Sicilian dialect, *curtigghiu* means "courtyard" but also "gossip"—chef Emanuela encourages you to turn off your phone and chat. The menu mixes Roman, Eastern Sicilian, and Jewish dishes (Mon-Sat 18:30-24:00, Sun from 12:00, Via Santa Filomena 43, mobile 329-221-8331). They also have a **$$ bistro** next door, with a more affordable street-food menu.

$$ FUD is the upscale Italian idea of what a burger should be: quality ingredients prepared well and presented artfully. In addition to beef, chicken, and pork, you could try a donkey, buffalo, or horse burger—all washed down with a high-end craft beer (daily 12:30-24:00, Via Santa Filomena 35, tel. 095-715-3518, www.fud.it).

$$ Polpetteria pleases meat lovers, with a long menu of meatballs *(polpette)* created using different meats, spices, and preparations. They also have lots of pizzas and ample outdoor seating (long hours daily, Via Santa Filomena 48, tel. 095-715-9433).

Gelato: Pasticceria Savia, a block off Via Santa Filomena, is the local favorite for gelato, *granite,* and a wide variety of delectable treats. Enjoy yours at a table out front, on a bench along nearby Via Etnea, or in the Villa Bellini park just across the street (Tue-Sun 6:00-22:00, closed Mon, Via Etnea 302, tel. 095-322-335).

Catania Connections

BY PLANE

Catania's Fontanarossa Airport, located three miles south of the city, is small but busy. You'll get a great view of Mount Etna as you take off or land (airport code: CTA, tel. 095-281-170, www.aeroporto.catania.it).

Connecting the Airport and City Center: For the short drive into the city, **taxis** wait right outside the terminal (€19, confirm price before departing).

The **Alibus airport shuttle bus** does a central city loop (€4, buy on board with cash or credit card, exit terminal to the right to find waiting buses, runs every 25 minutes, daily 4:40-24:00; stops at Via Etnea, Piazza del Duomo, and the train station—see website for route map; www.amt.ct.it).

Connecting the Airport and Other Destinations: Long-distance buses line up near the terminal (exit to the right, ticket kiosks on sidewalk). You'll find direct buses to **Taormina** (hourly, 1.5 hours), **Agrigento** (hourly, 3 hours), and **Palermo** (hourly, 3 hours). See "By Bus," below, for bus company details.

BY TRAIN

Catania is the main transportation hub for the eastern half of the island. Catania Centrale train station links the train system from Messina to Siracusa, but bus connections are often more reliable (see next).

From Catania by Train to: Taormina (hourly, 1 hour), **Messina** (hourly, 2 hours), **Siracusa** (9/day, 1.5 hours), **Palermo** (6/day, 3 hours), **Naples** (3/day, 8 hours), **Rome** (4/day, 11 hours).

BY BUS

Across the piazza from the Catania Centrale train station are two large bus lots. The main lot, for destinations across Sicily, is at the intersection of Viale della Liberta and Via Archimede. Buses from Palermo arrive at this lot; connecting buses to Ragusa, Siracusa, and Taormina depart from the same place. Ticket offices for all long-distance buses are in a secondary lot across the street, on Via D'Amico (buses running to the mainland use this lot).

Palermo and Agrigento are served by **Sais Autolinee** (Via D'Amico 181, www.saisautolinee.it). Rifugio Sapienza is served by **AST** (www.aziendasicilianatrasporti.it). All other destinations are served by **Etna Trasporti** (Via D'Amico 187, www.interbus.it).

From Catania by Bus to: Rifugio Sapienza on Mount Etna (bus #607, 1/day, 2 hours), **Taormina** (hourly, 1.5 hours), **Siracusa** (6/day, 1.5 hours), **Ragusa** (hourly, 2 hours), Piazza Armerina near **Villa Romana del Casale** (7/day, 1.5 hours), **Agrigento** (hourly, 3 hours), **Palermo** (hourly, 3 hours), **Naples** (1/day, 8.5 hours), **Rome** (1/day, 10.5 hours).

MOUNT ETNA

Mount Etna Volcano Visit • Mount Etna Wine Country

Mount Etna, Europe's most active volcano, presides over her island like Mount Fuji presides over Japan. Mount Etna dominates the skyline of the east coast of Sicily, soaring to almost 11,000 feet. The area around the mountain is diverse, with the busy city of Catania nestled into her southern flank, wineries dotting the north and the east slopes, quiet countryside dotted with pistachio groves to the west, and the jagged cliffs of Taormina just up the coast. The natural beauty of the region, the varied climate, and Etna's habit of frequent huffing and puffing make it one of the top sights in Sicily.

For the traveler, there are two reasons to visit Mount Etna: to experience the volcanic landscape (and perhaps even summit the rumbling giant); and to experience the wonderful wine country that those volcanic conditions sustain. Depending on your time and interests, you can choose to do one or the other, or a little of both.

PLANNING YOUR TIME

Mount Etna and its wine country are close to both Catania and Taormina—in just over an hour from either place, you can be climbing on volcanic craters at altitude or sipping local vintages of Etna wine. But because the volcano sights and the best wine area are on different sides of the mountain (on the south slope and north slope, respectively), combining them into one day is ambitious.

Volcano Sights: To experience the high-mountain volcanic side of Etna, you'll head for a base camp called Rifugio Sapienza, on Etna's south flank (facing Catania). Driving there takes roughly an hour from Catania or Taormina. Once there, activities range

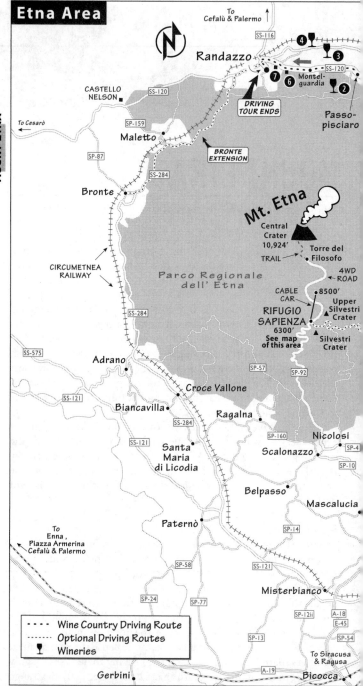

Etna Area

To Cefalù & Palermo

SS-116

Randazzo

4

3

SS-120

Montelguardia

7

6

2

Passo-pisciaro

CASTELLO NELSON

SS-120

To Cesarò

SP-159

Maletto

DRIVING TOUR ENDS

BRONTE EXTENSION

SP-87

SS-284

Bronte

Mt. Etna

Central Crater 10,924'

Torre del Filosofo

TRAIL

4WD ROAD

CIRCUMETNEA RAILWAY

Parco Regionale dell' Etna

CABLE CAR

8500'

Upper Silvestri Crater

RIFUGIO SAPIENZA 6300'
See map of this area

Silvestri Crater

SS-284

SS-575

Adrano

SP-57

SP-92

Croce Vallone

SS-121

Biancavilla

SS-284

Ragalna

SP-160

Nicolosi

SP-4

Scalonazzo

SP-10

SP-121

Santa Maria di Licodia

Belpasso

Mascalucia

To Enna, Piazza Armerina Cefalù & Palermo

Paternò

SP-14

SS-121

SP-58

Misterbianco

SP-24

SP-77

A-18

SP-12ii

E-45

SP-13

SP-54

To Siracusa & Ragusa

A-19

Gerbini

Bicocca

- - - - Wine Country Driving Route
- - - - - Optional Driving Routes
🍷 Wineries

MOUNT ETNA

MOUNT ETNA

SS-185

Castiglione di Sicilia

Francavilla di Sicilia

To Messina & Cefalù (via Autostrada)

A-18 E-45

Gola di Alcantara

SP-89

SP-7

SS-185

Castelmola

Solicchiata

Alcantara River

Mazzarò

"QUOTA MILLE"

❶ Linguaglossa

To Autostrada

Taormina

Piedimonte Etneo

SS-120

Ponte Boria

Giardini-Naxos

NAXOS

SP-59

Presa

FIUMEFREDDO EXIT

A-18 E-45

Nunziata

Fondachello

SS-114

Fornazzo

Sant' Alfio

Riposto

Milo

Giarre

SP-173

SP-59

SP-118

DRIVING TOUR BEGINS

SP-92

Zafferana Etnea

Santa Venerina

Praiola

Cozzarelle

SP-4i

Linera

Pozzillo

SP-174

Fleri

Stazzo

SP-141

BENANTI

❺

SP-115

SP-173

Pedara

Acireale

SP-43

To Naples ↗

Viagrande

SP-8

San Giovanni La Punta

A-18

SS-114

Capo Mulini

SP-42

Gravina

SP-41

Aci Trezza

Canalicchio

Aci Castello

SP-10

SS-114

Catania

SP-53

Fontanarossa

Golfo di Catania

Wineries
❶ Tenuta di Fessina
❷ Planeta Feudo di Mezzo
❸ Filippo Grasso
❹ Romeo del Castello
❺ Benanti

Other
❻ Ristorante Veneziano
❼ Parcostatella Agriturismo

10 Kilometers

10 Miles

Palermo

SICILY

Etna

Agrigento

Catania

50 Miles

from a quick-but-rewarding hike around low-lying craters (allow an hour) to heading up to the summit via cable car, 4x4 bus, or with a hiking expedition (allow several hours).

If you're going to the summit, it's best to get an early start. The peak is most likely to be clear first thing in the morning (winter skies can be clearest); as the day goes on, evaporating moisture tends to cling to Etna, often socking it in by midmorning. And the Rifugio Sapienza base camp tends to get quite crowded as the day goes on, peaking around midday. The first cable car heads up at 9:00—try to be on it. If you're going higher on Etna, be aware that the last summit hike departs at 10:30; for the crater walk at 9,800 feet, arrive at least two hours before the cable car stops running (last ascent at 16:15 April-Nov).

Wine Country: You'll find quality wineries on Etna's easy-to-reach eastern and southeastern slopes (facing the sea), and on its northern slope (facing the Nebrodi mountain range). I particularly enjoy the northern slope, which is more scenic, less trampled by day trippers, and comes with its own dreamy culture. You could do a strategic strike at one winery, or settle in for a full day of scenery, wine tastings, and stay-awhile meals at destination restaurants. Spending the night is a good option for wine lovers or anyone who enjoys lingering in the countryside.

Note that nearly all of Etna's wineries expect you to call at least a day ahead to arrange a tour and tasting—you can't drop in spontaneously. While this may seem like a hassle, it's well worth it for the personal attention you'll receive and the authenticity of the experience.

The Whole Shebang: Energetic, ambitious travelers who get a very early start can try to squeeze both Etna experiences into one long day (side-tripping from Catania or Taormina, or en route between those destinations)

    8:00 Hit the road (or start earlier)

    9:00 Arrive at Rifugio Sapienza, take cable car and 4x4 bus to 9,800 feet, and walk around the crater

  12:00 Descend, hop in your car, drive around to the north slope wine country

  13:30 Lunch in wine country

  15:00 Wine tastings, scenic drives, exploring villages

  17:00 Depart wine country

18:30ish   Arrive back at your home base (or settle in for a
           memorable dinner in wine country and drive home
           late)

Note that this plan assumes good enough weather (and fitness) to warrant the trip up to Etna. If you just do the easy hike at the Silvestri craters (accessible from the Rifugio Sapienza parking lot), you can get a later start and/or make your way to wine country earlier. Those going all the way to the top of Mount Etna will need to save the wineries for another day.

WINE COUNTRY ACCOMMODATIONS

The north slope of Mount Etna is a tempting place to spend the night—particularly for those who want to settle in for more wine, more scenery, or both. Several wineries also rent rooms; here are two good choices. For locations, see the "Etna Area" map.

$$$$ Tenuta di Fessina, a recommended winery, is a plush choice—filling its picture-perfect railroad-depot compound with seven rustic-elegant rooms, all appointed for maximum comfort (just outside Linguaglossa at Contrada Rovittello, tel. 094-239-5300, www.tenutadifessina.com, hospitality@tenutadifessina.com). This also works for nondrivers, as the Circumetnea train stops just 50 yards away.

$ Parcostatella is a rustic farmhouse off the main road near Randazzo. The rooms are classic Sicilian country, with knotty pine paneling and tile floors. You'll eat your breakfast where the cows used to munch (Via Montelaguardia 2, Randazzo, tel. 095-92-036, www.parcostatella.com, info@parcostatella.com).

Mount Etna Volcano Visit

You can spot Mount Etna from virtually anywhere in eastern Sicily—especially from Taormina or Catania. But for a closer look, drive up twisty mountain roads over a volcanic landscape to the

base camp at Rifugio Sapienza, a small settlement at about 6,300 feet, on Etna's south side. From here, you'll have a front-row seat overlooking the volcanic landscape and access to a number of ways to experience the mountain.

Rifugio Sapienza Base Camp

The outpost at Rifugio Sapienza (6,300 feet)—tucked in a bald, volcanic landscape—is the base for all Etna excursions. Clustered together are the base station of the *funivia* (cable car), a hotel, and the Guide Alpine Etna Sud office (where you can book excursions to the very top); a five-minute walk away you'll find the Silvestri craters. A few shops and eateries sprawl in the area between these two points.

ORIENTATION TO RIFUGIO SAPIENZA

Information: You can check the current status of the volcano at www.vulcani.ingv.it; weather information by elevation is available at www.mountain-forecast.com. Parco dell'Etna info tel. 095-821-111, www.rifugiosapienza. com.

Extreme Weather Warning: Even though the mountain is on a Mediterranean island, the weather at the top is alpine. Things change fast. Rain clouds are attracted to Etna like a magnet—and once they gather, they tend to stay put. Fierce winds can pick up without warning. The cable car doesn't run in strong winds, and excursions are cancelled in bad weather. Use common sense and ask before venturing out if you're unsure of the conditions. From November through March, the mountain can have deep snow even at lower levels.

What to Wear and Bring: Even if you just plan to stroll on the lower-lying Silvestri craters, wear solid shoes with good tread, as there are no groomed trails. Dress in layers; a waterproof jacket is always a good idea. The upper cable car station is at 8,500 feet, and the air is thin—so it's colder, and you'll tire more easily. If you don't have a heavy coat or boots, you can usually rent them at the upper cable car station for a few euros. If you're summiting Etna, bring a hat, gloves, and warm jacket—even in August (also bring a packed lunch—you'll get a B.Y.O. lunch break at the summit). Hiking poles are a good idea for longer walks. On windy days, hikers will want sunglasses to protect eyes from blowing ash.

Mount Etna

Mount Etna, at 10,924 feet, is Sicily's grand summit. The mountain started as an underwater volcano—half a million years ago, its summit was below sea level. Today its exact height varies depending on what Europe's most active volcano has been up to lately.

Geologically speaking, Sicily is located atop the slow-motion collision of the Eurasian and African tectonic plates. The force of that collision created the mountainous spines of mainland Italy and Sicily. And fissures between the plates, where magma escapes, created and feeds numerous volcanoes—including Vesuvius, Stromboli, and Etna.

Etna itself is not a single volcano. It is made up of hundreds of craters scattered all over its flanks. With a circumference of roughly 100 miles, Mount Etna at its base covers an area comparable in size to London. From that broad footing, it slopes up gently—and then, at the top, points up steeply. It's classified as a stratovolcano, along with its explosive cousins Vesuvius (in mainland Italy), Krakatoa (in Indonesia), and Mount Saint Helens (in Washington state).

Etna is called a "gentle giant" because the mountain typically just spews ash and occasionally oozes thick, slow-moving lava. Even though the probability of a sudden violent eruption is low, the mountain is always active. Up to several hundred metric tons of vapor spew from the top craters every day. It's not unusual for the "black snow" of Etna to blanket much of the island.

While in recent years, most volcanic activity at Mount Etna has occurred at the summit, historically numerous "flank"  eruptions occurred farther down the mountainside. As a result, more than 300 small so-called lateral craters dot the volcano. Flank eruptions at lower elevations can be hazardous to the belt of towns that circles the mountain (at about 2,000 feet above sea level). Etna rarely kills anyone, but if a side vent eruption persists, the lava flow can swallow a small town within a few days.

Destructive as she can be, Mount Etna is also a major reason that the small island of Sicily can support so many people. The volcanic soil is particularly fertile, perfect for growing nearly everything—especially grapes. And in the seas around Sicily, Etna's ash fertilizes the phytoplankton—creating an underwater layer of "soil" that supports abundant sea life.

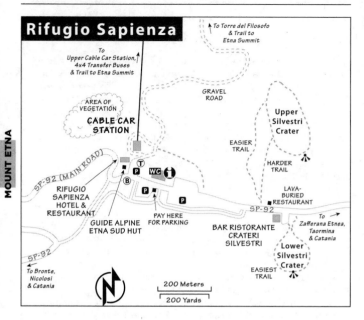

Rifugio Sapienza

To Torre del Filosofo & Trail to Etna Summit

To Upper Cable Car Station, 4x4 Transfer Buses & Trail to Etna Summit

GRAVEL ROAD

AREA OF VEGETATION

CABLE CAR STATION

Upper Silvestri Crater

EASIER TRAIL

HARDER TRAIL

SP-92 (MAIN ROAD)

RIFUGIO SAPIENZA HOTEL & RESTAURANT

LAVA-BURIED RESTAURANT

SP-92

GUIDE ALPINE ETNA SUD HUT

PAY HERE FOR PARKING

BAR RISTORANTE CRATERI SILVESTRI

To Zafferana Etnea, Taormina & Catania

Lower Silvestri Crater

SP-92

To Bronte, Nicolosi & Catania

EASIEST TRAIL

MOUNT ETNA

200 Meters
200 Yards

Eating: The area near the lower cable car station has a variety of basic **$ snack stands** offering a quick bite. For something a little better, head to one of the restaurants, such as **$$ Rifugio Sapienza,** right next to the cable car station. Closer to the Silvestri craters, **$ Bar Ristorante Crateri Silvestri** is a busy spot with a coffee bar, good snacks, and overcrowded WCs. Their restaurant has outdoor seating with views of the craters (daily 8:00-20:00).

Sleeping: $ Rifugio Sapienza offers 24 simple, alpine-style rooms next to the cable car station (cable car discount for guests, tel. 095-915-321, www.rifugiosapienza.com, info@rifugiosapienza. com).

GETTING THERE

By Car: The winding drive up to Rifugio Sapienza can be approached from two sides. From Catania, follow signs to *Gravina,* pass the town of Mascalucia, and continue to Nicolosi, which is the southern gateway to the mountain. From the north (Taormina or Messina), exit the E-45 highway at Giarre, heading toward Santa Venerina and then Zafferana Etnea. From Nicolosi or Zafferana Etnea, follow brown *Etna Sud* signs to reach Rifugio Sapienza. Parking is available at several lots near the cable car, and near the Silvestri craters. Spaces with white lines are free, though a "custodian" may ask for a donation to watch your car (€2 is enough). Spaces with blue lines are pay-and-display; the visitor info office

Mount Etna in Myth

The ancients relied on myths to explain powerful natural phenomena, such as lightning or storms—or volcanoes. The Aegean Greeks who arrived in Sicily knew of the massive eruption at Santorini from folk legend, but Mount Etna's ongoing belching and rumbling were something new.

The Greeks came to identify Mount Etna, with its fiery eruptions, as the subterranean workshop of Hephaestus, god of fire and the maker of Zeus' thunderbolts. And the Greeks saw the volcano as home to other mythological creatures. The Cyclops—one-eyed giants—lived in caves on the slopes of Etna, and the large rock formations off the coast near Catania (at Aci Trezza) were the work of the Cyclops Polyphemus, who threw stones from the mountain while Ulysses and his crew fled the island. Typhon, a monster confined under the volcano by Zeus, caused tremors whenever he turned over; his unhappy gasps were said to make the volcano erupt.

and a souvenir shop facing the lot sell parking passes (€1.20/hour, €6/day).

By Public Transit: Each morning at 8:15, long-distance bus #607 departs from Catania's central bus station (across from the train station) to Rifugio Sapienza. This is the only public bus connection to Etna. Arrive at the station early to buy your tickets at the ticket kiosk and to find your bus, which stops on Via D'Amico. The bus takes two hours and includes a pit stop partway up, in Nicolosi; the return bus departs at 16:30 (€6.60 round-trip, AST, www.aziendasicilianatrasporti.it).

By Excursion Bus: See "Tours of Mount Etna," below.

By Taxi: A taxi from the center of Catania, while expensive, works for a short visit to the Silvestri craters. Try to negotiate a set price in writing before departing. A round-trip visit, with an hour at the craters, should take about three hours at €40 per hour. You can also use a taxi for longer excursions up the mountain—but remember that the meter is ticking the whole time.

By Private Driver: Giuseppe Leotta can take you to the volcano in style (€65 one-way transfer, €120 for 4 hours, more for larger cars, mobile 366-438-1797, www.luxurycarservices.it, info@luxurycarservices.it).

TOURS OF MOUNT ETNA

Because there's only a single public bus per day, plenty of tour companies offer Etna excursions. These range from no-frills day tours to specialized trekking trips with alpine guides.

Tourist Service buses (with recorded commentary) run to Etna from Catania, taking a short break in Nicolosi before stopping at Rifugio Sapienza for three hours, arriving back in Catania at 17:30 (€35, departs daily at 11:30 from Piazza del Duomo, also stops at the train station and Piazza Stesicoro, www.touristservice2006. com).

Katane Live offers a similar tour from Catania (€30, departs daily at 10:00 from Catania cathedral; stops in Nicolosi, Rifugio Sapienza, and Zafferana Etnea; www.katanelive.com).

SAT offers a basic Etna tour from Taormina to Rifugio Sapienza; you'll have free time to take the cable car or explore the Silvestri craters (€35, daily April-Oct, fewer off-season, reserve at least one day ahead, tel. 0942-24653, www.satexcursions.it, info@ satexcursions.it).

Etna Finder offers more excursion options, some in 4x4 vehicles with driver-guides that take you on a bumpy ride to remote parts of the mountain. Their service is professional and personal, with small groups and good explanations (from €55, includes pick-up and drop-off at hotel, €160 all-day excursion to the summit, mobile 393-910-8061, www.etnafinder.com, info@etnafinder.com).

Mount Etna Activities

SILVESTRI CRATER HIKES

For an easy, quick, and free look at a volcanic landscape, choose one of these two hikes around the extinct craters at the eastern end of Rifugio Sapienza. Both craters are readily accessible, and either can be seen in less than an hour: The lower crater is an easy walk with little elevation gain; the upper crater is a steep climb with fewer people and better views. If you don't have the time or money to ascend the mountain by cable car, a hike around the Silvestri craters offers a satisfying Etna visit.

▲▲Lower Silvestri Crater (Easy)

On the left side of the Bar Ristorante Crateri Silvestri, a small trail leads up a short hill to the lip of the crater. This inactive crater, only 400 feet in diameter, is the result of a massive 1892 eruption.

Circle around the lip of the crater. About halfway around, turn back to face the mountain above you. Looming on the right is the climbable upper Silvestri crater (described next). Just to the left, notice how the cable car basically follows the path of a 2001-2002 eruption (it was rebuilt shortly thereafter). Notice the green "island" at the top of the ridge that was not wiped out by the lava flow. This is called a *dagala*—from the Arabic "touched by Allah." Look down into the crater at your feet, where visitors have followed the old custom of stacking rocks into little towers.

Now turn 180 degrees, and face out toward the sea, taking a few steps for a better look over the entire valley. Visually trace the coastline to see the city of Catania, which starts at the cor-

ner of its big bay and sprawls up its valley. On the horizon, look for other small craters. Mentally connect these and the one you're standing on—forming a chain of vents that line up along the same fault. A vein of magma (super-heated molten rock) occasionally pushes through to the surface. You're seeing the evidence that

Etna is not just one big crater, but a cluster of hundreds of craters like this one—some dating back thousands of years, and some growing and changing right now.

▲▲Upper Silvestri Crater (Moderately Strenuous)

Just uphill from the lower crater, you'll see intrepid hikers summiting this much steeper option. The trail begins on the left side of Bar La Capannina. As you begin the ascent, notice that the

restaurant is surrounded by lava—all the way up to the roof. Major eruptions and lava flows in 2001 and 2002 destroyed parts of the tourism infrastructure here, including the cable car. The lava passed around this restaurant but didn't destroy it; the owner

says the buried window was "kissed by the lava flow."

Choose your path up—the one that swings left is easier, while the right fork is steeper and (for those in shape) faster, but the lava fragments underfoot (called *lapilli*) can be slippery at an incline. Notice the color of the various lava fields—compare the darker stone around the bases of the posts supporting the cable car to the lighter-colored stone on which you are standing, which is over 120 years old. (For more on how to read geology into the various landscapes of Etna, see the sidebar.) Look around—from this perch, flows are visible from different centuries, like an open history book.

Lava Rock

While visiting Etna—whether at high or low elevations—take a moment to appreciate the unique volcanic rock that makes up this giant, steaming mountain.

As Etna's lava flows slowly cool, they gradually solidify into a basaltic stone. The base color is dark, dense, and gray. Eruptions of the last century are richer in iron than those of the past—which you'll notice in the rusty, reddish tone of the lava stones. Mixed in are shades of yellow (indicating the presence of sulfur) and even broken slabs of lemony sandstone—pushed all the way up from the sea bed as Etna rose. You'll also see piles and piles of scree—small pebbles at the base of an eroded incline.

Large chunks of stone scattered around a crater are called "lava bombs"— masses of incandescent lava that shoot out of the crater during an eruption like a giant hairball.

Underfoot, the two main types of volcanic terrain have names of Hawaiian origin. Most of the Etna landscape consists of sharp, jagged *ah-ah*—named for the feeling of walking on the sharp rocks without shoes. The compact basaltic lava that looks like smooth layers of frozen liquid is called *pahoehoe*: This lava is made for walking.

On the drive up the mountain, you'll notice as the climate and the terrain changes—from subtropical near the bottom, to alpine near the top. Watch for lava tubes—natural tunnels that run under the volcanic rock. Historically, Sicilians used the tubes for storing ice. In the winter, they'd shovel snow into the caves and layer it with fern leaves to make it easier to divide into large chunks of ice. The high elevation and natural volcanic insulation kept the ice frozen through the summer—when it could be chopped up and taken down to towns along the coast, for preserving fish and making *granita*. Watch out too for the spiny golden barrel cactus that grows on Etna's slopes—locally called *cuscino di suocera* ("mother-in-law's cushion").

At the top of the upper crater, look down on the lower Silvestri crater, to see its almost perfect cone shape.

GOING HIGHER ON MOUNT ETNA

Rifugio Sapienza is the jumping-off point for trips higher on Mount Etna. There are three stages: A cable car takes you to 8,500 feet; from there you can go by 4x4 bus to a crater at 9,800 feet; and from there you can hike to the 10,800-foot summit. Go up as far as you like, depending on conditions and how much time and money you have.

On its own, the cable car is probably the least satisfying as a standalone experience, leaving you with a "halfway there" feeling. For a more complete Etna visit, continue to a higher crater in the 4x4 bus (the best choice for most travelers, including families); sturdy travelers can hike all the way to the summit. Summit trips are best from June to October, when there's no snow; the cable car and 4x4 bus run year-round.

▲Cable Car *(Funivia)* to 8,500 Feet

The continually moving cable car whisks you partway up the side of the mountain in about 10 minutes. You can do the ride up and

back, with a quick walk up top, in less than an hour. There's not much to see at the upper station—some basic eateries, tacky souvenir stands, and WCs—but you can scramble around on the rocky terrain, looking for different types of volcanic rock. A little pinnacle a few minutes' walk above the station offers nice views down over the valley, and a good look at smooth fields of cooled lava *(sciara)*. You can follow the 4x4 switchbacks up the hill for a ways (toward Torre del Filosofo), but note that hiking above 8,900 feet (2,700 meters) without an alpine guide is forbidden.

Cost and Hours: €30 round-trip, daily April-Nov 9:00-16:15—this is the last ascent, Dec-March 9:00-15:45, tel. 095-914-141, www.funiviaetna.com.

▲▲4x4 Bus and Crater Walk at 9,800 Feet

This option offers maximum volcano thrills with minimum time and exertion (allow 2-3 hours round-trip from the lower cable car

station). You'll ride up the cable car, then hop on a 4x4 shuttle bus that takes you on a rough, rocky road to a crater formed during the 2002 eruption. An alpine guide will explain the geology while leading you on an easy, 45-minute walk around the crater's rim. From there, you'll be able to see the summit steaming just above. Take a moment to dig your hands into the soil and feel the heat of an active volcano.

Cost and Hours: €64 round-trip—includes €30 for cable car, €25 for 4x4 shuttle, and mandatory €9 guiding fee; ask for the "volcano excursion" at the lower cable car station; last departure two hours before the cable car closes—best to arrive by 13:30.

▲▲Guided Hike to the Summit at 10,800 Feet

This true hike up the mountain will take you up trails close to the central crater—making it a good choice for fit travelers with some hiking experience, and plenty of time to devote to the mountain (5-6 hours round-trip). To book this guided excursion, at Rifugio Sapienza, head to the Guide Alpine Etna Sud hut (next to the hotel), then borrow a coat and hiking shoes if needed (included in the price). Hikes depart as groups of 20 form. You'll take

the cable car up to meet a 4x4 bus, then head to the 2002 crater. From there, a long, steep hike up (1,000 feet) leads close to the mountain's summit, where you'll break for lunch. You'll return to the cable car station on foot, taking in more scenery on the way down.

Cost and Hours: €85 includes borrowable coat and hiking boots, bring your own lunch, last hike departs at 10:30 and returns at 16:30 to correspond with public bus and excursions, tel. 095-791-4755, www.etnaguide.eu; also sold as an all-day side trip from Catania through Etna Finder for €160 (see "Tours of Mount Etna," earlier).

Mount Etna Wine Country

While travelers flock to Etna's volcanic sights at Rifugio Sapienza, it'd be a shame to miss its lovely wine country, too. Grapes love this region's climate and unique volcanic soil, and Mount Etna has become synonymous with top-quality wines.

Wineries surround Etna to the east and north, but my favorite wine country anywhere in Sicily is along Etna's north flank, along the 12-mile stretch of rural road between the towns of Linguaglossa and Randazzo (outlined in this chapter's self-guided driving tour). This area boasts beautiful scenery, charming wineries, and world-class wines. Travelers with an affinity for good wine—or even just beautiful landscapes—should devote a half-day to this area; true wine aficionados won't regret spending the night—or

longer (see recommended accommodations near the beginning of this chapter).

Slow Train Around Wine Country: The historic, narrow-gauge **Circumetnea** ("Around Etna") railway begins in Catania (Borgo Station) and trundles around the western and northern sides of Etna—including stops in Randazzo and Linguaglossa—before terminating by the sea, in Riposto. Unfortunately, the train doesn't always run according to schedule (or at all), most of the train cars are old and rickety, and it's a slow journey (2 hours from Catania to Randazzo, then another hour to Riposto). But patient, flexible, and adventurous travelers could find this a memorable way to see the region (about 5/day, details at www.circumetnea.it).

Mount Etna Wineries

Scores of Etna wineries invite travelers for a taste and a tour. Visits usually include a walk through the vineyards, a look at a traditional

palmento wine cellar/press, a tour of the modern production facility, and a representative tasting of their wines. Wineries in Sicily generally require you to book ahead for a tasting; very few do drop-in tastings. Assume a reservation is required unless otherwise noted. For locations, see the "Etna Area" map at the beginning of this chapter.

Wine Tours: Etna Wine School offers educational tours of Etna wine country. Benjamin Spencer and Brittany Carlisi, American wine professionals who moved to Etna to share their love of Sicilian wine, can tailor a day to your interests and level of expertise (€100/person for half-day with 1 winery, €180/person for full day with 2 wineries, minimum 2 people, reserve in advance, can also arrange transportation for €170/half-day, possible to add Mount Etna tour and gastronomic experiences, mobile 347-334-8782, www.etnawineschool.com, info@etnawineschool.com).

NORTH SLOPE WINERIES

Wine lovers find it worth the drive to reach Etna's remote but remarkably scenic north slope. These wineries (and some nearby towns) are generally linked up by the self-guided drive later in this chapter, but be sure to get specific driving directions when you book your tasting.

Tenuta di Fessina has rustic antiques and designer fixtures filling an old 17th-century depot where wine was once processed and loaded onto the train (you'll see the little Circumetnea train trundle through occasionally). Their informative tastings are well run by Jacopo, and each wine is paired with a small plate. At €35 for seven wines, this is the best value for a tasting and light lunch (minimum 2 people, reserve one day in advance, Contrada Rovitello, SS-120, tel. 094-239-5300, www.tenutadifessina.com, fessina@tenutadifessina.com).

Planeta, a large, commercial winery, has estates all over Sicily. **Feudo di Mezzo** is their winery on Mount Etna (above Passopisciaro, halfway up to the upper Quota Mille road). You can choose a simple wine-and-oil tasting or a grand tour of wines from their different estates paired with a full lunch. This is a big winery, with a regular schedule of events, and is the easiest to book on short notice (€10-55 tastings, minimum 2 people, book 2 days in advance, Contrada Sciaranuova, SS-120, Passopisciaro, tel. 0925-195-5460, www.planeta.it, winetour@planeta.it).

Filippo Grasso is a no-frills wine producer with a straightforward attitude. Expressive Mariarita will show you around her

family's vineyard and present some of their excellent, good-value wines in their warehouse. These vineyards are located on one of the most prestigious terroirs on the mountain. Dropping in at this rustic, family-run place is OK—just ring the bell as the locals do, when they come for affordable *vino sfuso* (bulk wine) for just €2 per liter (€25 tasting, light snack included if you reserve ahead, Contrada Calderara, SP-89, mobile 349-759-5056, www.filippograsso.it, info@filippograsso.it).

Romeo del Castello is a family-run estate on a compelling

Etna Wines

Wines have been made in the Mount Etna region since antiquity. But an infestation of phylloxera aphids that damaged Sicilian vines in the late 1800s—combined with depopulation after World War II—caused many wineries to cease operation. In the 1970s and 1980s, new European Union regulations (and funding) benefitted ambitious winemakers who could afford to implement them, while hampering traditional winemakers by prohibiting the use of old wine cellars, called *palmenti*, for crushing and storing grapes. You'll see many abandoned *palmenti* in the Etna region, and some that have been repurposed.

Etna winemaking struggled along until the early 2000s, when a handful of well-established vintners from mainland Italy realized Etna would be as an ideal place to make wine. These pioneers led a renaissance in high-quality Etna wines. Today, wine lovers and critics from around the globe are taking notice of this remote corner of Sicily.

Grape vines thrive in Etna's nutrient-rich volcanic soil. Some vineyards are steeply angled, allowing the vines to catch the sun just so. Etna's north slope—at about 3,300 feet in elevation—means cooler temperatures than elsewhere on the island, causing grapes to ripen very slowly. The black soil retains the heat of the sun, keeping vines warm during particularly cold nights.

Etna wines, distinguished by their strong minerality, include white, rosé, red, and classic-method sparkling wines. Whites typically use the indigenous grape called carricante (meaning "overloaded," for its heavy yield), which results in savory (not fruity) flavors. The dominant red wine grape is nerello mascalese, with a pinot noir-like bouquet that has earned comparisons to Burgundy wines.

Fine Etna wines are expensive by Sicilian standards, but worthwhile when combined with a quality winery visit. Because the rejuvenated Etna winemaking scene is so new, experts are waiting to discover how well these wines will age—suggesting that the intense interest in Etna wines has only just begun.

Etna wine pilgrims should consider Benjamin Spencer's *The New Wines of Mount Etna*, which navigates this fast-evolving scene (Gemelli Press, 2019).

property. The vineyard's young and old vines are separated by a pear orchard. The family lost about 50 acres in a 1981 lava flow, and if you walk the vineyard, you'll come across the 20-foot-high wall of lava where the flow stopped. The tasting room is in their 230-year-old home, decorated with personal mementos and Art Nouveau wallpaper. After a visit with Chiara and her family, you'll see why they call their estate *Allegracore,* "Happy Heart" (€40-50 for tasting and lunch, Contrada Allegracore, SP-89, tel. 095-799-1992, www.romeodelcastello.it, info@romeodelcastello.it).

SOUTHEAST SLOPE WINERY

If you can't make it to the north slope, here's an option that's conveniently located between Catania and the volcanic sights at Rifugio Sapienza.

Benanti, just outside Catania in Viagrande, prides itself on its boutique winery approach, and its popularity with wine critics and

enthusiasts lets it charge more than others. The tour includes a vineyard walk (which climbs an extinct lateral crater) and a visit to their 18th-century *palmento,* as well as a guided tasting (€60 for tour, tasting of 5 wines and lunch; other options available, RS%—20 percent discount, minimum 2 people, reserve at least 5 days in advance, tel. 095-789-0928, www.benanti.it, info@ benanti.it, Bianca).

North Slope Wine Country Drive

The scenic north slope of Mount Etna warrants a drive—even for teetotalers. You'll feel worlds away from the tourist crush at nearby Taormina and Rifugio Sapienza...this is the lovely, rural, time-passed Sicily of romantic travel dreams. Along the way, you'll have several opportunities to visit a winery for a tour and tasting (but book ahead), and some fine opportunities for a memorable meal. This self-guided drive is designed to follow a visit to Mount Etna's volcanic sights, for a jam-packed, showstopper day. It's also possible to only visit the wineries, and/or add a visit to a nutty city (options outlined next). To trace the route of this drive, see the "Etna Area" map at the beginning of this chapter.

Wine and Volcano in One Day: This drive assumes you'll approach the north slope vineyards from the Mount Etna volcanic sights. Altogether it's 1.5 hours of driving (about 40 miles/60 km) to follow the route from the base camp at Rifugio Sapienza to the medieval village of Randazzo (not counting stops). The optional detour to Bronte (to sample pistachio goodies) adds another hour.

Wine-Tasting Only: Those who want a more leisurely day focused on wine can following one of these route options. If coming directly from **Catania,** head straight to Zafferana Etnea: Angle up through small towns, by way of Canalicchio, San Giovanni La Punta, and Fleri—passing the recommended Benanti winery (about 2 hours driving without stops).

If coming from **Taormina,** skip Zafferana Etnea and jump straight ahead to Linguaglossa—to get more quickly to the most beautiful stretch of wine country. Hop on expressway E-45 south, exit at Fiumefreddo, and twist up to Linguaglossa on SS-120 (about 1.5 hours driving without stops).

Bronte Extension: For most visitors, the wine road between Linguaglossa and Randazzo is the best look at this area. But foodies and pistachio addicts with time to spare can extend their trip to Bronte (30 minutes from Randazzo). From here, rather than looping all the way back around Etna, you can go south on SS-284, then SS-121, to head directly back to Catania (about one hour).

From Rifugio Sapienza to Zafferana Etnea
From Rifugio Sapienza, it's 30 minutes to the first stop, the village of Zafferana Etnea.
• *Head east from Rifugio Sapienza, passing the Silvestri craters. You'll drop down on the curvy SP-92 (following Zafferana signs) for 11 miles (18 km). Once in Zafferana, turn left on Via Carso; at the end of the street you'll find the main church and the main square.*

Zafferana Etnea
This town of 10,000 inhabitants is the closest to Etna's summit—which means it often deals with "black snow" from Etna's ash falls. In larger concentrations, the ash can be dangerous, and clean-up crews once bagged it as toxic waste. But now the usefulness of the ash is recognized in creating all kinds of products, including beauty scrubs. Visitors stop in Zafferana to buy honey produced on

the slopes of the mountain, and it's a good place to sample some local sweets. Every weekend in October, the town holds its Ottobrata—the Sicilian version of Oktoberfest. Here you'll find *vino rosso* instead of beer, homemade *salsiccia* instead of wurst, and pistachio-and-mushroom spread instead of kraut.

From the front steps of Zafferana's main church, a long, marbled, tree-lined belvedere reaches out toward the sea, offering inviting cafés, soccer-playing kids, and great views. Look for street parking near the main square—white lines indicate free parking for one hour, but you must set a cardboard clock (or leave a note) with your arrival time on the dashboard.

Sweets in Zafferana Etnea: Donna Peppina's bakery, easy to find right on the main square, serves local pastries and take-away snacks. Try the *siciliana,* a fried dough pocket with or without anchovies, and *sciatore,* a sugar-bomb chocolate-covered cookie that resembles a pair of skis (daily 7:00-24:00, Via Roma 220, tel. 095-708-1410). **Dolceria Salemi,** an unpretentious cookie shop tucked just uphill from the main square, made its name in 1947, when they invented *foglie da té*—a crispy almond cookie shaped like tea leaves (they also come in walnut and pistachio versions). Stop by for a free sample (Tue-Sun 8:30-13:00 & 16:30-20:00, closed Mon, Via Eusebio Longo 28). To find it, with the belvedere at your back, turn left down Via Roma, then take the first right up Via Eusebio Longo; it's a couple of short blocks up, on the right.

From Zafferana Etnea to Linguaglossa

• *Leave Zafferana Etnea heading north on Via Roma (SP-59, tracking signs toward Milo and Linguaglossa) for the 45-minute drive to Linguaglossa.*

This rural road—an appealing, upper alternative to the busy highway in the valley below—follows Etna's lower edge. As you drive through the towns of Milo and Fornazzo, enjoy the lush scenery. The vegetation here is almost subtropical in comparison to the barren, dry, rocky landscape of Etna's north and west slopes (where we're headed).

Keep an eye on your right for grand vistas; in some places, it's possible to see the toe of Italy and—on a clear day—even the Bay of Siracusa.

Dropping down into Linguaglossa, you'll cross over the 1895 narrow-gauge train tracks that once carried casks of wine to be shipped from the port of Riposto. Today, the Circumetnea ("Around Etna") train, which originates in Catania, allows urbanites a very scenic (and slow) passage through Etna's bucolic wine country.

• *As SP-59 enters Linguaglossa (you'll see a faded Benvenuti sign), take the hairpin right turn onto Via Matteotti. At the end of this street, turn left onto Via Roma (SS-120).*

Linguaglossa

This sweet, inviting village has a funny name: "Tongue Tongue" (*lingua* is tongue in Latin, *glossa* is Greek)—named for a giant lava flow that once licked the town. Notice the stately main street; historically, Linguaglossa was a prosperous burg. As the northern gateway to Etna wine country—and therefore a crossroads for trade—locals developed the gift of gab necessary for lengthy negotiations...perhaps a second meaning behind the town's name. Aside from its chatty natives, Linguaglossa is known for its *salsiccia a punta di coltello*—sausages made with local pork seasoned and chopped with a knife.

Eating in Linguaglossa: $$ Dai Pennisi is the town's most respected butcher shop and also an upscale eatery, where you can choose your meat from the case and wait while they cook it. Watch the local sausage being mixed by hand in a vat behind the counter (open 9:00-23:00; restaurant open 12:30-15:00 & 19:30-23:00, closed Sun night and all day Mon; Via Umberto 10, tel. 095-643-160, Mariaconcetta).

Between Linguaglossa and Randazzo

• *From Linguaglossa, carry on west on SS-120 toward Randazzo (9 miles/15 km). You'll roughly follow the route of that 1895 Circumetnea railway. Note that the recommended* **Tenuta di Fessina** *winery is just 10 minutes outside Linguaglossa.*

This stretch is the gateway to Etna's north slope wine region. You'll pass through some of the loveliest wine country in Sicily as you travel toward Randazzo, and begin to see why so many wineries are taking advantage of the region's ideal volcanic soil.

As you drive, you'll enjoy glimpses of Etna's blackened slope and extinct lateral craters mixed among olive groves and orchards. Keep an eye out for surviving WWII-era turrets—guarding those strategic views. (This area was heavily bombarded.)

As you pass the village of **Solicchiata** (with a recommended eatery—see next page), look for the many *palmenti* that line the

road. A feature of any Etna winery, a *palmento* is the traditional stone cellar where grapes were fermented and pressed—before the EU outlawed them 30 years ago as being unsanitary. In recent years—with the renaissance in Etna wines—they are being restored and often converted into restaurants and tasting rooms.

How to spot a *palmento*: Look for windows with cross-hatching on a building's lower level. How many *palmenti* can you count?

You'll soon reach the humble town of **Passopisciaro**, a working-class hub for local vintners; you may see winemakers socializing in the shade of the trees on the main square.

• *Just beyond Passopisciaro, the turnoff to the recommended **Planeta** winery is on the left (uphill). Beyond that, on the right, watch for the sign and turnoff to reach the endearingly humble **Filippo Grasso** winery. If you haven't booked a tasting in advance, this is the one spot that typically welcomes drop-ins...if they're home.*

As you continue along road SS-120, occasionally you'll see side roads leading up (on your left) to the upper road around the base of Etna—called *"Quota Mille"* ("Altitude 1,000"—for its height above sea level). Wilder and poorly signed, this alternate route runs parallel to the road you're following, with even better views of the petrified lava flows and northeast Sicily. Hardy travelers might consider returning on this upper road on their way back to civilization at the end of this drive. (But watch out for wildlife—cows and deer use this road, too.)

Just after the little town of Montelaguardia, you'll pass one of those *Quota Mille* signs—your signal to keep an eye out on the left for a 1981 lava flow. Look uphill to see the lava that coursed downhill; on the right, watch for a house that was swept away—except for one wall that still stands.

Eating Between Linguaglossa and Randazzo: The village of Solicchiata is home to **$$ Cave Ox**, a well-respected restaurant with a simple menu (pizzas and a few regional standards) and one of the region's best wine lists (closed Tue, at #159 on the main road).

On the outskirts of Randazzo, **$$$ Ristorante Veneziano** is a local favorite for a special-occasion splurge. While the restaurant is rooted in tradition, Chef Giuseppe prides himself on his modern preparation and technique. The space is casual and the menu features local specialties like Nebrodi pork and pasta with seasonal sauces, all served with Etna wines. The cuisine is high-end, the setting is unpretentious, and the remote location keeps prices reasonable (Tue-Sun 12:30-15:00 & 19:30-22:30, closed Mon, reservations smart on weekends, just east of Randazzo on SS-120, tel. 095-799-1353, www.ristoranteveneziano.it). Don't confuse this restaurant—which is right along the main road—with a different Veneziano, which you may see signposted at Parco Statella Agriturismo, nearby.

• *Next up is the turnoff for another wine-tasting experience (for those who have reserved), the recommended **Romeo del Castello** winery (from SS-120, before entering the town of Randazzo, take a hard right turn onto SP-89 just after passing the Lidl supermarket). Otherwise, continue straight on to...*

Randazzo

Randazzo (pop. 11,000)—the de facto capital of Etna's northern wine country—is a city made of the mountain. The medieval core of the town, as well as its main church and bell tower, are all built with black lava stone (basalt). You'll see basalt carved like fine marble, framing windows and decorating buildings. A wander through this very untouristy town takes you back to the late Middle Ages.

The city historically had three separate communities—Greeks, Latins, and Lombards (people from northern Italy)—each with different traditions and languages. Each neighborhood had its own church: San Nicola for the Greeks, Santa Maria for the Latins, and San Martino for the Lombards. The churches are a patchwork of architectural styles, but they all feature blocks of the local Etna basalt.

Randazzo has the largest market in the area, filling the streets on Sunday mornings with vendors, selling food, clothes, and household goods.

Eating in Randazzo: $$ San Giorgio e Il Drago sits deep in the town, tucked back by a deserted monastery. Inside it's a cozy, classic trattoria that's ideal for a home-cooked Sicilian meal (if you peek in the kitchen, you may see Mamma rolling pasta). The *antipasti* are especially tempting, along with a good range of pasta dishes (Wed-Mon 12:30-14:30 & 15:00-24:00, closed Tue, Piazza San Giorgio 28, Randazzo, tel. 095-923-972).

$ Macelleria Sparta is a meat-and-cheese shop in the heart of town. Nunzio makes his own cheeses from sheep's milk and proudly displays beautiful lumps of pecorino and baked ricotta. For a few euros, he'll dish up a sampler platter of his cheeses and some of the house salami (Wed-Mon 12:30-14:30 & 19:30-22:30, closed Tue, Via Umberto 117, tel. 095-921045).

$$ Agora Enoteca will transport you back in time with its medieval tavern interior. Their antipasto platter is a parade of interesting nibbles, and the main dishes use local Etna products (Thu-Tue 12:00-15:00 & 19:30-23:00, closed Wed, Via Fisauli 7, mobile 329-072-5005).

Wine Shop: Il Buongustaio dell'Etna, in the heart of Randazzo, is a well-stocked wine shop and bar that also serves local snacks. While there's a bit of a language barrier, this is a great chance to peruse wines and select a glass without scheduling a winery visit (daily 9:00-23:00, Via Umberto 8, mobile 320-976-0623).

• *For most travelers, Randazzo is the natural end point of the Etna wine country drive. Retrace your steps toward Linguaglossa (or, if you're adventurous, take the upper Quota Mille road), then drop down to the E-45 expressway (from the town of Ponte Boria). Once on the E-45, it's just 20 minutes north to Taormina, or 30 minutes south to Catania.*

But if you'd like to explore further, consider extending your drive about 30 minutes southwest—beyond wine country and into pistachio country.

Optional Extension: Bronte and Pistachio Country

• *To reach Bronte from Randazzo, continue west on SP-120; about a half-mile out of town, take the left fork to continue south on SS-284, marked for* Maletto *and* Bronte.

In this area, farms dot the slopes of Etna, with some vineyards, olive groves, and wild fig trees. In spring and early summer, you'll likely see bright-yellow scotch broom—the first plant that populates a volcanic lava flow. After Maletto, you'll notice the landscape changing—becoming barren, with grand views of the mountain on the left. Soon you'll see pistachio groves and almond trees, and arrive in Bronte.

Visiting Bronte: This somewhat drab city (pop. 19,000) is the main population center for the west and north slopes of Etna—so close that it was named for one of the Cyclops thought to live inside the volcano (see the "Mount Etna in Myth" sidebar, earlier). Among travelers, it's famous as the center of production for high-quality pistachios—the town is surrounded by gnarled groves of ancient pistachio trees. While there's not much to see, Bronte pleases pistachio pilgrims with some delicious eating options.

Little Bronte produces less than one percent of the world's pistachios. The combination of volcanic soil, a biennial harvest (to protect the trees), and natural irrigation produces smaller nuts than the more typical varieties from California, Iran, and Turkey. But Bronte pistachios have an intense color and taste that makes them sought after (and expensive) in the culinary market. Sicilians prize them so much that they've protected their nuts with a special DOP label, a sort of trademark for Italian foods.

By the way, the town is associated with England's greatest naval hero, Admiral Horatio Nelson. Some land in this area was turned into a duchy in 1799 and given to Nelson as thanks for the role he played in restoring King Ferdinand of the Kingdom of the Two Sicilies to his throne. Nelson intended to use his new castle (a former abbey nicknamed Castello Nelson) as a summer home, and even had an English garden planted—but died before he ever saw it. While the castle, a short drive from Bronte, is likely closed to the public for restoration, it may reopen to visitors (ask locally). The town's name is also linked to the English literary Bronte family. Patrick Bronte—father of Charlotte, Emily and Anne—so admired Nelson that he is said to have adapted the spelling of his own name from Brunty to Bronte in recognition of the admiral's duchy.

Eating in Bronte: If you want to try some of the town's "green gold," head to one of two places at the far end of town (along SS-284, on the right): **$ Il Pistacchio** has a helpful owner, Alfio, who offers samples of pistachio products, including pastes and liquors. Ask to see samples of pistachios from other countries to understand the difference (Mon-Fri 9:00-19:00, ring to be let in, Viale Catania 62, tel. 095-692-946, ilpistacchio.it).

$ Life Caffè, closer to town, is an unpretentious roadside café serving up good coffee, pastries, and gelato, all made with Bronte's signature pistachios. Try an *arancino* rice ball stuffed with pistachio pesto, prosciutto, and béchamel (always open, Viale Catania 10, tel. 095-692-252).

• *After Bronte, you can head back the way you came, via Randazzo and Linguaglossa, to the E-45 expressway. Or, if you're headed south to Catania, consider a more direct route around the back side of Etna: Simply carry on south from Bronte on SS-284, then follow SS-121 to Catania (about one hour).*

MOUNT ETNA

TAORMINA

Clinging to a seaside cliff within view of smoldering Mount Etna, Taormina is Sicily's classic resort town. Saturated with languid echoes of 19th-century Grand Tour elegance, this tidy town has a too-perfect feel, but starry-eyed cruise ship visitors and honeymooners don't seem to notice. Taormina is a good place to take a breather from sightseeing and relax, sip a glass of sparkling Mount Etna wine, and watch the crowds waltz by. Taormina may seem overly touristy...but after dark, when the town turns into one sprawling, posh cocktail party, you really won't mind.

Taormina makes a workable springboard for day trips to Mount Etna, Catania, the Aeolian Islands, and even to Siracu-

sa, Ragusa, or Villa Romana del Casale. It's a good alternative to gritty, intense Catania, and is within an hour's drive of Catania's international airport. While some see Taormina as a high-end "vacation from your vacation," for a more authentically Sicilian beach break, I prefer Cefalù.

PLANNING YOUR TIME

Taormina has only one important sight, its Greek-Roman Theater, and a single day is plenty to experience the town. You can see everything there is to see in one simple stroll.

Regardless of the length of your visit, begin with my self-guided walk through town to get your bearings, then hike up to the Greek-Roman Theater. With that, your sightseeing obligations are satisfied. Then simply enjoy the town and its views, or consider an easy excursion: Ride the gondola down to Isola Bella and its beach, take the bus (or drive) up to Castelmola's scenic perch above town, or side-trip into the Mount Etna wine region (described in the previous chapter).

Orientation to Taormina

Taormina (pop. 11,000) sits halfway up the side of Mount Tauro, overlooking the Ionian Sea. While the townscape is steep (expect lots of stairs and hills), most of the action is clustered around the level main drag of Corso Umberto. This street stretches between the two city gates, Porta Catania (west end of town) and Porta Messina (east end of town). You can walk the entire length of Corso Umberto in about 10 minutes (or, since you're on vacation, stroll it in about 15 to 20 minutes).

The streets that tumble downhill below Corso Umberto are filled with hotels, colorful shops, and a public garden with views. High above Taormina is the scenic village of Castelmola; far below (accessed by gondola) is the pebbly beach at Isola Bella. Most public transit stops just outside Porta Messina.

TOURIST INFORMATION

The helpful TI is located near the Greek-Roman Theater, inside Palazzo Corvaja (Mon-Fri 8:30-14:15 & 15:30-19:00, closed Sat-Sun, Piazza Santa Caterina, tel. 0942-23243).

ARRIVAL IN TAORMINA

By Train: Trains arrive at the Taormina-Giardini train station below town. Two different buses can take you to the Porta Mes-

sina area (destination posted in bus windshields): The bright blue Interbus goes to the Via Pirandello bus terminal (€1.90, hourly, 8-minute uphill walk to Porta Messina); the local orange ASM bus (*linea verde*—green line) goes to Piazza San Pancrazio, the local bus hub just outside Porta Messina (€1.10, every 1.5

hours). Taxis wait just outside the train station (€15 fixed fare to most hotels, confirm price).

By Bus: Most intercity buses arrive at the bus terminal/parking lot on Via Pirandello, downhill from Porta Messina (to get into

Greater Taormina

.5 Kilometer

1/2 Mile

To Messina & Cefalù

To Savoca, Forza d'Agrò, Mazzeo and Letojanni Beaches

Taormina Exits

A-18 E-45

River

SP-10

Castelmola

VIA GARIPOLI

Ionian Sea

SS-114

VIA DA VINCI

MADONNA DELLA ROCCA

AUTOSTRADA TUNNELS

San Pancrazio

Lumbi

GONDOLA

PORTA MESSINA

MAZZARÒ

TAORMINA

Main Bus Terminal

Porta Catania

CORSO UMBERTO

GREEK-ROMAN THEATER

Beach

A-18 E-45

PORTA CATANIA

See detail map

Isola Bella

Cliffs

VIA PIRANDELLO

To Catania & Siracusa

SS-114

TAORMINA-GIARDINI TRAIN STATION

VIA CROCEFISSO

To Giardini Naxos & Catania

TAORMINA

town, hike left uphill about 8 minutes). A few intercity buses stop at Piazza San Pancrazio, outside Porta Messina.

By Car: No cars are allowed in Taormina's old center, and the city is surrounded by a confusing one-way loop road that twists back on itself again and again. Approaching town on the E-45 expressway from Catania and the south, take the Taormina exit (be ready for it, just after a long tunnel). Continue straight, following signs to *Taormina/Castelmola*. You'll then twist along a serpentine road up into town...stay the course. Check with your hotel before you arrive—some have on-site or valet parking, and some may encourage you to drop off your bag before driving to one of Taormina's two parking garages.

The garages, at opposite ends of town, are signposted along the road into town; signs show the number of available spaces (roughly €2/hour, €15-17/24 hours). **Parcheggio Porta Catania,** a five-minute uphill walk to Porta Catania at the western end of town, is convenient to most accommodations. **Parcheggio Lumbi** is handier for places at the east end of town (a provided shuttle bus takes you to Piazza San Pancrazio—the bus hub just outside Porta

Messina). To return to your car, look for the *servizio navetta* sign and shuttle kiosk in the middle of the road 50 yards in front of Porta Messina, where you can "call" the shuttle.

By Plane: The nearest international airport is at Catania (code: CTA, described on page 333), 40 miles from Taormina and about a one-hour drive in good traffic. Taxis from Catania airport to Taormina run about €80. Airport buses connect Catania with Taormina's bus terminal (€8.20, hourly, 1.5 hours, buses and ticket kiosks are to the right from terminal exit, Interbus/Etna Bus, www.interbus.it).

HELPFUL HINTS

Markets: On Wednesdays, Taormina's street market bustles from 8:00 to 13:00 along Via Von Gloden and Piazza Wolfgang Goethe (on the way up to Castelmola—about 10 minutes uphill from Piazza Duomo).

Laundry: Laundry Center has self-service machines and full-service wash (Mon-Sat 9:00-14:00, closed Sun, longer hours in summer, just off Corso Umberto at Salita Santippo 16, mobile 346-174-6282).

Festivals: In April, Taormina hosts a balcony-decorating competition: **Vetrine e Balconi in Fiore** ("windows and balconies in bloom"). In preparation, from late March onward, residents ornament their town with flowers and colorful decorations. In summer (late June/early July), Taormina hosts an important **film festival** with showings at the Greek theater (the theater also hosts famous musicians throughout the summer). Every July 9, locals honor their patron saint, **San Pancrazio,** with religious processions throughout the city.

GETTING AROUND TAORMINA

By Bus: Local buses are operated by two companies: ASM (orange buses) and Interbus (blue buses).

ASM buses have limited frequency but can be useful for reaching sights outside the city center (€1.10/ride—pay driver, tel. 0942-683-800, www.taorminaservizipubblici.it). The ASM bus hub is at Piazza San Pancrazio, just outside Porta Messina; look for the blue *fermata* sign on the left (on a building), just beyond and across from the taxi stand. Line names are displayed on bus windshields. The most useful is the **green line** *(linea verde)*, which goes down to Isola Bella and the train station, and up to the Sanctuary of Madonna della Rocca (runs about every 1.5 hours). (To reach Isola Bella, it's faster and more fun to ride the gondola—see "Sights in Taormina," later.) The **red line** *(circolare rossa)* does a loop around Taormina every 45 minutes (stopping at a few handy places, including Via Leonardo da Vinci and Porta Catania). The **blue line** *(linea blu/*

beachbus) heads to beaches north of town, at Mazzeo and Letojanni (6/day).

Interbus (which also operates the local hop-on, hop-off bus) runs several bright blue local lines throughout Taormina and to a few destinations beyond. It's best to catch these at the intercity bus terminal on Via Pirandello. Stops include the Taormina-Giardini train station and the villages of Castelmola and Giardini Naxos. Confirm at the ticket desk which line to take, then look for your destination posted on the bus windshield (€1.90, hourly, buy tickets at the bus terminal office).

By Taxi: There's a taxi stand on Piazza Vittorio Emanuele, near Palazzo Corvaja and the TI; taxis also wait just outside Porta Messina and Porta Catania. Drivers offer a few fixed-price trips, such as a Castelmola village excursion (see Castelmola listing in "Sights in Taormina," later).

Tours in Taormina

Local Guides

Franco D'Angelo does an interesting walk through Taormina's back streets and lesser-known corners (€60/hour, 2-hour minimum, mobile 349-283-1679, franz.tourguide@gmail.com).

Tommaso Pante is based in nearby Milazzo, on the north coast, and leads tours of Taormina, Messina, and the Aeolian Islands (€60/hour, 2-hour minimum, mobile 347-185-6950, www.sunway.it, tpante@gmail.com).

Driver: Sebi Melita, an English-speaking driver, offers regional day trips and transfers (4-hour excursion to Etna or Siracusa—€200, Catania airport transfer—€80, transfer from Messina cruise port for up to 8 people—€80-110, mobile 346-371-8757, www.sicilywithsebastian.com, info@sicilywithsebastian.com).

Bus Tours

Details for the following buses are always in flux—confirm everything locally (look for brochures or ticket sellers). All three typically depart from the bus terminal on Via Pirandello; Interbus and SAT routes also use the Piazza San Pancrazio stop near Porta Messina (more convenient to the town center, but the bus stop area can be congested and confusing). Sightseeing buses typically stop running off-season.

Interbus runs a hop-on, hop-off bus with a €13 one-day ticket that covers three different loops. The most useful is line A, which stops at the train station, beaches, and Castelmola (hourly). Lines B (to Alcantara Gorge) and C (to the *Godfather* towns of Savoca and Forza d'Agrò) head farther out of town (tel. 0942-625-301, www.interbus.it).

City by See runs a pricey open-top bus loop tour that connects Taormina with Castelmola and Isola Bella (hourly, €20/24 hours, tel. 090-213-5672, www.citybysee.com).

SAT offers a "Taormina Hop-On" route that stops at most points of interest, including the Sanctuary of Madonna della Rocca, Castelmola, Isola Bella, and Giardini Naxos (hourly, €10 one-way ticket; €20/day hop-on, hop-off access; tel. 0942-24653, www.taorminahop.it).

Excursions from Taormina
SAT offers a rotating schedule of day trips to Mount Etna, the Aeolian Islands, and other destinations across Sicily. Using Taormina as a home base, you could see Sicily by doing a few of these tours and skip renting a car (€35 basic Etna tour, €70 Aeolian Islands tour, reserve at least 24 hours in advance, check the latest schedule online or at their office at Corso Umberto 73, tel. 0942-24653, www.satexcursions.it, info@satexcursions.it).

Taormina Town Walk

This lazy, self-guided walk will take you along Taormina's convivial Corso Umberto, through grand Piazza IX Aprile, and to the doorstep of the impressive Greek-Roman Theater—connecting all of the town's important landmarks and best panoramic views. Along the way, we'll squeeze in a little town history.

• *Begin at the west end of town, just outside Porta Catania, on the little square called Piazza Sant'Antonio Abate.*

❶ Porta Catania
The road you're standing on was once a major thoroughfare that connected the larger cities of Catania and Messina.

Walk a few steps downhill to the small park with several huge palm trees and look out over the water. What a lovely location for a town! This area was first populated by the Sicels—an ancient people who predated the island's Greek colonizers by hundreds of years. When Greek seafarers arrived around 734 BC, they founded Naxos—the little village you see clinging to the peninsula below, and the oldest known Greek settlement on Sicily (today called Giardini Naxos). Those first settlers likely came from the Greek island of—wait for it—Naxos. At the time, ancient Greece was overcrowded, and many city-states chose to send citizens out to find fortune and more fertile land in the west. The colonists who came to the east coast of Sicily brought more than just Greek culture: They also brought rivalries from their home cities and were at near-constant war with their neighbors in Sicily. In 403 BC, the powerful Greek city of Siracusa crushed little Naxos, sending the

Taormina Town Walk

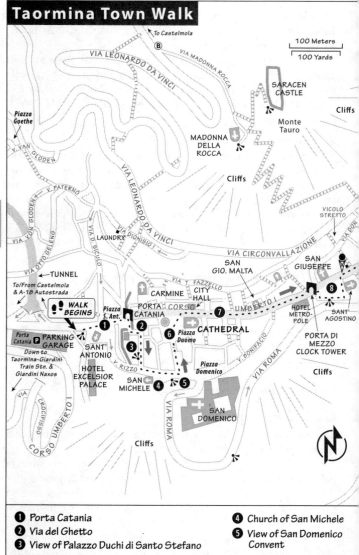

1 Porta Catania
2 Via del Ghetto
3 View of Palazzo Duchi di Santo Stefano

4 Church of San Michele
5 View of San Domenico Convent

survivors to seek shelter on higher ground. They established a more defensible hillside city called Tauromenion, "the mountain shaped like a bull."

Notice that Taormina has two parts: the Greek city, which runs from the Greek-Roman Theater to the clock tower *(torre dell'orologio)* on Piazza IX Aprile, and the medieval Norman city that stretches from there to Porta Catania. We'll enter through the

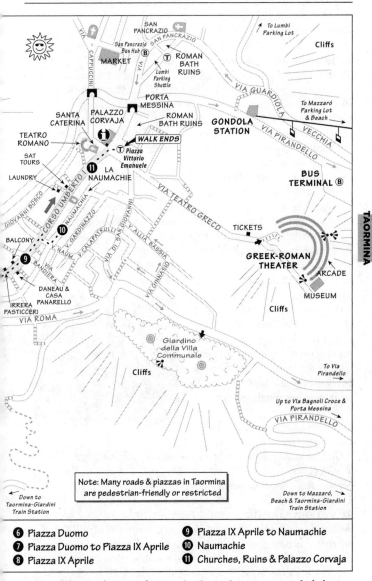

6 Piazza Duomo

7 Piazza Duomo to Piazza IX Aprile

8 Piazza IX Aprile

9 Piazza IX Aprile to Naumachie

10 Naumachie

11 Churches, Ruins & Palazzo Corvaja

newer (Norman) part of town, built as the city expanded during the Middle Ages.

As you look out from the viewpoint, on your left is the **Hotel Excelsior Palace,** a reminder of another important epoch in the town's history. Some 2,500 years after the Greeks arrived here, Taormina became an important stop on the Grand Tour itineraries of wealthy northern Europeans seeking out great artifacts of the ancient world (see the sidebar). German author Johann Wolfgang

Goethe arrived in 1786 and praised Taormina in his writing; a century later, Friedrich Nietzsche authored his seminal *Thus Spoke Zarathustra* (introducing his notion that "God is dead") right here. Taormina's legacy as a major hotspot for high-end tourism left it with many grand hotels; this one was a later addition, built in 1904 in the Neo-Moorish style, but it still evokes the elegance of the Grand Tour era. Now pan to the right, where you'll see a huge, concrete square just below you—the rooftop of the big Porta Catania parking garage, which injects a steady flow of latter-day Grand Tourists into town.

Head a few steps back up to the little chapel of **Sant'Antonio Abate,** which faces the square where you began. If it's open, step inside to see a remarkable example of the southern Italian and Sicilian custom of *presepi*—elaborate nativity scenes that sprawl into complete miniature villages. This one, not surprisingly, shows a village set in a dramatic cliff-hanging location.

Exiting the chapel, walk up to the old entry into the city walls. This is **Porta Catania,** which marks the city limits about 500 years ago. Taormina long ago outgrew its fortifications, incorporating the walls into the fabric of the city. Look left, up the street, to see a modern building supported by the town wall. Though the wall looks plain now, parts of it were originally decorated. Step through the gate, then look overhead to see fresco fragments from the ninth century.

• *Once through the gate, take an immediate right and walk along the wall down the lane called Vico de Spuches. Follow it downhill as it bends around and changes names to...*

❷ Via del Ghetto

As the name implies, this area was once Taormina's Jewish quarter, when it was home not only to a synagogue but also to a mosque. Six centuries ago, Christians, Jews, and Muslims lived side-by-side in a tolerant community. But when Sicily's Spanish overlords began pursuing their Inquisition in the 15th century, the era of tolerance ended, and beginning in 1493, all non-Christian communities faced persecution or expulsion. Many Muslims left for North Africa, while the Jewish population either left Sicily or converted to Christianity, taking on new last names to conceal their past.

• *Walking down Via del Ghetto, follow the fenced garden of a fine palace. When you reach the bottom of the street, look up (over your right shoulder) for a great view of...*

The Grand Tour

In the 1500s, the Vatican sponsored excavations throughout Italy to rediscover and inspire interest in Europe's antiquity. By the 17th century, the history of Greece and Rome and their influence across Europe became fashionable topics. This Neo-classic movement flourished well into the 19th century. Young wealthy nobles from England and northern Europe traveled through the Continent, accompanied by a chaperone and guide, to witness the great artistic, architectural, and cultural treasures from past civilizations. For the rich, the Grand Tour was a rite of passage and an extension of one's education; the journey could take from a few months to several years. Travelers would take up residence in cities across Italy, using their days to contemplate art, to paint, and to write. Sicily was an important part of the Grand Tour; explorers here included Oscar Wilde, Richard Strauss, Richard Wagner, Johann Wolfgang Goethe, and Florence Trevelyan, who built the villa on Taormina's Isola Bella. Their travels inspired others to do the same, and many Grand Tour destinations—including Taormina, Sorrento, and Florence—are still top tourism spots today. The romantic accounts of the Grand Tour still linger in the cultural memory of Europe, and modern tourism is a direct consequence of those elegant times.

TAORMINA

❸ Palazzo Duchi di Santo Stefano (Fondazione Mazzullo)

Once the home of a noble family, this palace now houses modern art exhibits. Focus on the building itself and notice the different ar-

chitectural styles on display: The lower floor dates from the 1100s, during a period of Norman rule. The upper floor was added 400 years later in imitation of the earlier style, but with exaggerated Neo-Norman flourishes. You'll see over-the-top window designs: Gothic pointed-arch windows on the upper floor, with six-pointed stars. To finish it off, the roofline is more decorative than defensive, with geometric embellishments made of local lava stone. Notice how the palace also incorporates a stretch of the town wall into its structure.

• *Now, facing the sea, look for the small stone church across the street.*

❹ Church of San Michele (Chiesa di San Michele)

Approaching the church from the side, you'll see that the road covers the bottom part of a doorway on the long side. This illustrates how, as the city grew, the street level changed. Now circle around to the front door to see evidence of the old synagogue: The smaller door to the left was the entry to the *mikvah,* or Jewish ritual bath. After the expulsion of the Jewish community at the end of the 15th century, this building sat unused for 300 years, until it was turned into a church.

• *Now look out to sea. Head to your left, where you have a view of a larger church and bell tower. These are part of the...*

❺ San Domenico Convent
(a.k.a. San Domenico Palace Hotel)

Taormina has always attracted famous visitors, and this one-time convent has been the backdrop for many Italian movies. It also

played host to an infamous visitor: Nazi General Field Marshal Albert Kesselring. He took over this complex as the headquarters for the German command of Sicily in World War II. This part of Taormina was heavily bombed during the Allied

invasion of the island, and much of the area was rebuilt after the war. Today, the rebuilt convent is one of the fanciest hotels in the city, and a fun place to grab an elegant (if overpriced) *aperitivo.*

• *Walk a few steps downhill, keeping an eye on the left for the street marked by a traffic barrier (Via Strabone). Turn up this street, which runs into Taormina's best spot for cheap eats, the recommended Da Cristina pizzeria. Take the stairs up alongside the pizza shop, and you'll pop out at...*

❻ Piazza Duomo

In most Italian cities, the main cathedral sits in the heart of town on the central square, but Taormina's is well off-center, closer to the

western gate. Since this end of town is newer—built during the Middle Ages as Taormina expanded from its original Greek core—it was considered more desirable.

Look up at the small **cathedral** (Duomo). Although it resembles a tiny Norman *ecclesia munita* (church-fortress), it was built in the 13th century—a century after Norman rule. It incorporates several architectural styles, with a blocky exterior, defensive-looking crenellations along the roofline, a delicate rose window, and a Baroque marble-capped doorway (rebuilt in the 17th century). Inside, the central nave is dominated by six monolithic pink marble columns, possibly taken from the Greek-Roman Theater.

The **fountain** in the center of the piazza was built under Spanish rule in 1635. This patchwork of statues is a symbol of ancient Tauromenion: the city on the "bull-shaped mountain." The figure was originally a minotaur (half-man, half-bull), but the front hooves have been chiseled off. The bust of a crowned woman was added on top. She holds two symbols of power: a globe with a cross in one hand, and a scepter in the other. The statue—known by locals as *la sirenetta* ("the little mermaid")—is featured on the town's coat-of-arms.

• *Now let's head along the street running on the left side of the cathedral. This is Taormina's main street,* **Corso Umberto.**

❼ Piazza Duomo to Piazza IX Aprile

Corso Umberto connects Porta Catania (where we began, behind you) to Porta Messina. This street is what put the city on the map,

as it was the only route along the coast in the Middle Ages.

The pink building on the left side of the street (across from the cathedral) is **City Hall.** On the facade, notice three Stars of David. After the bombings of World War II, rubble revealed evidence of the Jewish neighborhood that once thrived here. These stars were added as a memorial to the neighborhood that no longer exists.

Stroll along this strip brimming with some of Sicily's most overpriced souvenirs. Keep an eye out for ceramic "head of the Moor" planters, shaped like the head of a woman or Arab man. For the whole story on these popular (if problematic) Sicilian fixtures, see the sidebar.

A few short blocks down on the right, at #190, notice the wide, low **arch** over the doorway. This is a feature of Catalan-Gothic architecture common from the 13th through 15th century, when Spanish nobles living in Taormina brought architects here to replicate the style of their homeland. Watch for more arches in this style farther along this street (including at #176, #174, and #172).

Across the street and a few steps down, at #185, is the tiny former church of **San Giovanni dei Cavalieri di Malta,** built in 1533. The large blocks at the base of the church were taken from ancient

The Head of the Moor

Across Sicily, you'll find planters on balconies and doorsteps—and in souvenir shops—shaped like two heads: a man with Arab features, and a fair-skinned woman. Several folk tales, dating back a thousand years, attempt to explain the origin of these heads.

In one version, set during the Arab domination of Sicily, a beautiful young lady was watering plants in her garden. An Arab stranger passed her garden, fell in love, and successfully wooed her. His secret, however, was that he was already married back home. When the woman found out, she devised a plan to ensure he could never leave her: She chopped off his head, put it in her garden, and planted seeds of basil in it. She watered it daily with her tears, and the plant grew lush and vigorous. Passersby thought the unusual pot must be the reason for the beautiful plant, so they created "Moor head" planters of their own.

A similar story recounts a love affair between a French noblewoman and an Arab—a forbidden romance in Norman Sicily. After the woman's father discovered their affair, both were decapitated, and their heads were set on the castle walls as a warning.

Origin story aside, the vases became a popular decoration only in the past few decades. As tone-deaf as the caricatured faces seem, Sicilians proudly sell all kinds of souvenirs (including jewelry and clothing) featuring the famous heads.

Greek buildings nearby. Today the building is used as a memorial for the 20th century's world wars. It's occasionally opened by a retired *carabiniere* (police officer).

• *Continue window-shopping along Corso Umberto until you walk through the tall, stone gate (Porta di Mezzo) at the end of the street. You'll emerge at...*

❽ Piazza IX Aprile

This gate marks the end of Taormina's medieval westward "expansion." You're now crossing into the historic core of Greek Tauromenion—the city's living room. This piazza is supposedly named for the day in April 1860 when word arrived in Taormina that Giuseppe Garibaldi had landed across the island at Marsala, with the intent to unify Italy (for more on the Risorgimento, see page 395). The news of the alleged landing ignited a revolt in town against the island's Bourbon rulers. In reality, Garibaldi arrived a month later, on May 9—but the locals proudly named the piazza to commemorate their early revolution.

Walk across the broad, checkerboard view terrace and belly up to the railing. Survey the scene with a quick spin-tour, starting by looking out to sea.

First, look southeast (right), toward Greece. The green promontory at the end of the bay is where those first Greek settlers founded Naxos in the eighth century BC. Farther right, on the horizon, Mount Etna smolders, as she has done for eons.

Now bring your eyes back to the piazza. Just to the right of Mount Etna is the faded red Hotel Metropole, which was a popular spot for poets and artists visiting during the Grand Tour. To the right of the hotel is the Porta di Mezzo gate, topped by the clock tower *(torre dell'orologio)*. The original 16th-century clock was replaced by this one in the 1900s. On the other side of the gate (with tables spilling into the square) is the pricey and venerable Caffé Wunderbar. A staircase to the right of Wunderbar leads up to a sanctuary high above the city, the Madonna della Rocca (you can just barely see its cross poking out above the rocks). Not visible above that is the hilltop village of Castelmola. (Both sights—accessible by hike, car, or bus—are described under "Sights in Taormina," later.)

The Baroque church facing the piazza is dedicated to St. Joseph (San Giuseppe), but it's often called the Purgatory Church. Notice its grim imagery: skull and crossbones over the door and at the peak of the facade, and flames at the base of the steeple. This was the town ossuary and the place to come pray your relatives out of purgatory. Attached to the right is a church-run community center for kids (Salesiani Don Bosco). Across the street to the right of that, jutting out into the square, is another church—though this one has been converted into the town library. Just to the right of the public WC, you can see the top edge of the Greek-Roman Theater. The swath of green below is part of the public gardens. And down at sea level, the rocky point is called Capo Taormina.

• *Return to Corso Umberto and continue in the direction you were headed.*

❾ Piazza IX Aprile to Naumachie

If you're in the mood for a gelato, stop at #135 (**La Gelateria,** on the left) and indulge in a seasonal fruit flavor—or go full Sicilian and have your *brioche con gelato* (gelato on a bun). Next to La Gelateria is Taormina's narrowest street and favorite photo-op, Vicolo Stretto.

Farther down at #123, **Irrera Pasticceri di Sicilia** sells sweets from Messina (daily 9:00-24:00, closed Feb). Try the *nipitiddata* (little pastry baskets filled with dense chocolate, dried figs, and almonds), *pignolata* (fried dough covered with lemon and chocolate glazes), and *pasticciotto* (pastry disks filled with lemon custard and sour cherry or candies).

As you stroll, look up and admire the **balconies** projecting over the street, adorned with cascading plants and flower baskets, including "head of the Moor" planters. This street ramps ups its decorative flair every March and April for the city's annual balcony-decorating competition, when shop owners and residents try to outdo each other with elaborate displays.

The cheerful pink store at #126 is **Daneau,** one of the oldest shops in the city. Signora Adriana's family emigrated from Slovenia to Sicily and has been here for over a hundred years selling Italian pottery and linens.

At #122, the **Casa Panarello** is a charming mix of architectural details, with lanterns, vines, and a clock.

• *Continue a bit farther along Corso Umberto, then turn right on Via Naumachia and walk down the steps on the left to the massive wall, known as Naumachie.*

⑩ Naumachie

This 400-foot-long wall was built by the Romans in the first or second century AD as a supporting structure for a large water reservoir. The word *naumachie* refers to the grand mock naval battles held by the Romans to celebrate their victories at sea. Although this structure would have been large enough to host such reenactments in the reservoir, there's no evidence that any battles were staged here. The wall, uncovered after the WWII bombings of 1943, is now the foundation for modern apartments above. The courtyard before you is covered in basalt slabs and was used as a Roman gymnasium. The 18 niches in the wall were filled with sculptures overlooking the athletes.

• *Retrace your steps back to Corso Umberto and continue to the right.*

⓫ Churches, Ruins, and Palazzo Corvaja

At #42 (on the right) is the facade of the **Church of Santa Maria del Piliere**—or what's left of it. The church was named after Il Piliere, the admiral of Italy for the Knights of Malta. Built around 1530, it still features some original Renaissance details: the portal in pink marble, the wooden door, and the rose window above. It was used as a church until the 1800s but was later repurposed into a cocktail bar and restaurant.

Farther down Corso Umberto, where the street widens, is the **Church of Santa Caterina of Alexandria,** built in the 1600s on top of a small Greek tem-  ple. Inside the church, on the floor on the right side, a glass panel exposes traces of the Greek ruins under- neath. Behind the church (take a left on Via Teatrino Romano) are ruins of a Roman theater, or odeum. The architecture of the odeum is similar to that of the more famous Greek-Roman Theater, but on a smaller scale. This one was covered by a roof and used for more intimate performances.

The large palace to the right of Santa Caterina is the handsome **Palazzo Corvaja.** The Arabs originally built on top of a Roman forum here (10th-11th century) to create a defensive tower (hence the crenellated roof). The Spanish enlarged it during their occupa- tion (15th century), and for a time the Sicilian parliament met here, presided over by the Spanish queen. Today, the palace houses the TI and a museum space for special exhibits.

• *Our walk is finished. You have several options:*

From the little tree- and taxi-lined square adjacent to Palazzo Corvaja, it's a short walk to Taormina's top sight, the **Greek-Roman Theater:** *Go past the trees (on the upper street), following signs to* Teatro Antico *(on Via Teatro Greco); you'll arrive at the theater ticket desk in five minutes.*

The street's lower fork leads steeply downhill on Via Giovanni di Giovanni, past the recommended Bam Bar, to the leafy **public gardens.**

Corso Umberto itself continues straight on to **Porta Messina**—*and just beyond, the handy Piazza San Pancrazio bus stop (see "Getting Around Taormina," earlier). From Porta Messina, the gondola station to access* **Isola Bella** *beach is to the right, down Via Pirandello.*

Or you could simply find an inviting café—perhaps back at glorious Piazza IX Aprile, where you can nurse a cocktail at Wunderbar, and do what the leisure class did in the 19th century: Breathe the perfumed air, marvel at the beauty of Taormina, and reflect on your own Grand Tour around Sicily.

Sights in Taormina

▲▲Greek-Roman Theater (Teatro Antico)

Sicily is home to many Greek theater ruins, but none has a setting quite like Taormina's: hanging off the edge of a cliff with expansive views of Mount Etna and the Ionian Sea. The original theater was built by the Greeks in the third century BC, but much of what is visible today is a Roman remodel—hence its unusual hybrid appearance and name.

Cost and Hours: €10, daily 9:00-19:00, April and early Sept until 18:30, late Sept until 18:00, shorter hours Oct-March, audioguide-€5, Via Teatro Greco 40, tel. 0942-23220.

Crowd-Beating Tips: Cruise crowds flood the theater from roughly 10:00 to 14:00. It's best to go when it opens or in the late afternoon.

Visiting the Theater: For today's visitors, the most striking feature of this theater is how its **stage** frames the view of Mount Etna. Greek theatergoers, however, didn't see that grand vista: They would have looked out upon a solid backdrop. But the theater's scenic location was chosen deliberately. It perfectly combines the four elements important to ancient Greek thought: The theater sits atop a rocky hill (earth), overlooking the sea (water), with a gentle salty breeze (air), and a smoldering volcano in the distance (fire).

The semicircular rows of **seats** are arranged to give everyone an equally good view of the performers and to enhance the acoustics. Greek plays relied on dialogue to create action and tension, and scenes of violence were performed offstage and conveyed only through sound. So it was important that the audience ("those who hear") didn't miss a thing. Look at the red wall on the top level above the seats: **Niches** in this wall held bronze urns, reflecting and amplifying sound.

The Romans had a different idea: The people in the theater were spectators ("those who watch"). The Romans remodeled the theater to suit Roman tastes and accommodate performances with visually captivating action, such as gladiator games. Since the site is bound by rocky cliffs, building a true, round amphitheater was impossible here. Instead, the Romans removed the first 10 rows of seats to create an area large enough for gladiator battles (the large **orchestra** in front of the stage). They also added a wall to protect spectators from the wild beasts used in the games.

Remarkably, the theater is still used today. Every summer, musicians from all over the world perform here, with the spectacular backdrop of the sea, sunset, and Mount Etna.

The small house perched on the hill overlooking the theater hosts a modest **museum** holding artifacts—stone slabs with Greek inscriptions, a few mosaic floor fragments, and a carved, child-sized marble sarcophagus.

The little **terrace** next to the museum boasts the best views over town. The lush public gardens (described next) are just below, inviting you for a shady stroll. Scanning the cliffs above Taormina, notice the three skyscraping landmarks along the peaks above town (from left to right): the Sanctuary of Madonna della Rocca; the Saracen Castle; and the hill town of Castelmola. Each is reachable from Taormina by a very steep but scenic hike—or an easy drive or bus ride.

While you're up here, continue along the **walkway** above the top level of seats—passing a portion of reconstructed arcade, the efficient passageways for entering and leaving this huge theater. Then gaze out over the Ionian Sea. To the north is a string of beach towns, starting with Letojanni.

You can also head down to the **stage level,** where you can walk around the vast vaulted side wings.

Public Gardens (Giardini della Villa Comunale)

This lovely green area, just below the Greek-Roman Theater, was originally the private garden of Florence Trevelyan—a 19th-century English noblewoman who also built a villa on Isola Bella. Lady Trevelyan (1852-1907) fell in love with Sicily while on her Grand Tour and never returned to England. Today her garden and home (see next) are open to the public.

Nicely groomed terraces are sprinkled with statues and fantastical faux-ancient buildings (a uniquely British custom: a gigantic lawn with garden ornaments, called "follies"). Lady Trevelyan was an expert gardener: As on Isola Bella, Lady Trevelyan used this space to cultivate her collection of exotic plants. Green thumbs will delight in exploring the mish-mash of species. As this is the city's main park, you'll find kids playing and families chatting on shady benches, making this an inviting spot for a stroll after a hot hike up to the theater.

Cost and Hours: Free, daily 8:00-20:00, later in summer.

▲Isola Bella Beach and Island

Tucked along the craggy shoreline below Taormina is Isola Bella—a "beautiful island" tethered to its mainland beach by a peb-

TAORMINA

bly isthmus just a couple of feet wide. The now-deserted, skippable villa on the island was built by Lady Florence Trevelyan, who also owned the public gardens (see more about Trevelyan in the gardens listing, earlier).

You can pay to access the island and scramble around its rocky paths, but several buildings and pathways are closed off. I'd come instead for the fun gondola ride down and a scenic swim in the crystal-clear waters (bring water shoes), rather than for the island and villa.

At the beach, you'll find a row of beach bars and restaurants renting chairs and umbrellas. At one end, a narrow, walkable isthmus connects the beach to the tiny Isola Bella islet, bought by Lady Trevelyan in 1890 and left to the city upon her death. While the island is an extremely scenic backdrop, there's not much to see, since all that's left of the villa is a few run-down rooms burrowed into the rock.

Cost and Hours: Beach—free; island access—€4, daily 9:00-19:00, April and early Sept until 18:30, late Sept until 18:00, shorter hours Oct-March, tel. 0942-628-738.

Getting There: ASM's *linea verde* bus (see "Getting Around Taormina," earlier) or the SAT "Taormina Hop On" route (see "Tours in Taormina," earlier) will get you to Isola Bella, but it's more enjoyable to take the **gondola** (€3 one-way, 5-minute ride departs every 15 minutes, daily 8:00-24:00, Mon from 9:00, shorter hours off-season, tel. 0942-681493, www.taorminaservizipubblici.it). The upper gondola station is just outside Porta Messina, about 200 yards ahead (on the left) on Via Pirandello. The gondola takes you to the Mazzaró station at the bottom. From here it's a 10-minute walk to the beach: Head through the parking lot toward the water and turn right onto the main road (Via Nazionale). Continue uphill for about 200 yards; just after rounding the bend, watch for stairs on the left that lead down.

▲Castelmola

High on the rock above Taormina, the small, remarkably scenic village of Castelmola offers commanding views of Mount Etna, Taormina, and the Ionian Sea. With twisting alleyways and medieval charm, Castelmola is understandably touristy, but a delight to wander. If you drive, stop off at the Sanctuary of Madonna della Rocca on your way up (described later).

Getting There: Perhaps the best part of a visit to Castelmola is the journey up—and there are plenty of ways to get here. The local **Interbus** line (hourly from the bus terminal; see "Getting Around Taormina," earlier) and **hop-on, hop-off** buses all stop in Castelmola (see "Tours in Taormina," earlier). Either way, it's about a 15- to 20-minute ride.

The **hike** up is for fit adventurers only. It's less than two miles, but virtually straight up—with an elevation gain of nearly 1,200 feet. Get hiking advice from the Taormina TI, and don't underestimate the Sicilian heat.

Drivers leave town just past the Porta Catania parking garage and follow blue signs to *Castelmola*. As you reach the top of Taormina, be ready to turn left onto Via Leonardo Da Vinci. Partway up on the right, watch for the easy-to-miss sharp turnoff for the Sanctuary of Madonna della Rocca (smart to combine visits). As you enter Castelmola, look for the big pay-and-display garage below the town center. This is your easiest parking option. From here, you'll huff up about 75 steps to the central square, Piazza Sant'Antonio. The town center is a ZTL zone (nonlocal cars are prohibited), although if you continue a little farther on the main road, there's a smaller pay lot under the overpass on the right—just past a ZTL warning sign. You can park in this lot for a few euros without violating the ZTL limits (and you'll save some steps).

Taxis from Taormina offer a flat fee (€40) for a round-trip ride to Castelmona, 30 minutes in the village, and a stop at the Sanctuary of Madonna della Rocca.

Visiting the Village: The main square is elegant **Piazza Sant'Antonio,** laden with black-and-white basalt mosaics. Enjoy exploring the shop- and café-lined streets and strolling past tall, skinny houses with petite balconies and grand views. Directly uphill from the square are the ruins of a Norman castle, with even better views. Just downhill from the square is the small Church of San Giorgio, where a tight spiral staircase (at the back of the church) leads down to a terrace with more views over Taormina.

Or, from Piazza Sant' Antonio, you can head (with your back to the sea) straight along Via Alcide de Gasperi. At the first left (Via Papa Pio IX), look for signs down to **Bar Turrisi**—a town institution famous for its phallic-themed decor. If the decoration is too much for you, for heaven's sake, don't flip through the guestbook. While the sexually charged furnishings may be a gimmick, locals claim there's a story behind them. Supposedly, Castelmola needed 1,000 residents in order to gain independence from Taormina. Determined to achieve their goal, the locals got, ahem, busy, and within a short time, 1,000 Castelmolans declared their autonomy. As the story goes, these phallic symbols are a tribute to Castelmola's civic-minded determination.

Though the bar is as touristy and overpriced as you'd expect, the place is entertaining, its several balconies promise great views, and the unusual "almond wine" *(vino alla mandorla)* is a specialty.

Just below Bar Turrisi is an inviting little piazza (facing the Church of San Nicolò di Bari), ringed by pleasant outdoor eateries.

▲Sanctuary of Madonna della Rocca

Perched on a peak above Taormina is this little church carved into the rock. It offers perhaps even better, less obstructed views over

Taormina than Castelmola. Step into its serene interior, then head out to the terrace and look down over the serpentine, stairstep trail that connects it to Taormina below. Hovering just above on Mount Tauro is Taormina's Saracen Castle (Castello Saraceno, closed to the public). This was likely the site of the acropolis of ancient Tauromenion, though much of what you see today was built in the 10th century under Arab rule (hence the name), with later Norman modifications.

Cost and Hours: Free, hours vary but generally daily 9:30-12:30 & 16:00-19:30, shorter hours off-season, mobile 338-803-3448.

Getting There: Drivers can stop here on their way to or from Castelmola; keep a sharp eye out for the tiny *Via Madonna della Rocca* sign that points to the hairpin turn. Street parking is limited.

The sanctuary is also a stop on the *linea verde* of the local **ASM bus** (see "Getting Around Taormina," earlier) and on the **hop-on, hop-off bus** run by SAT (see "Tours in Taormina," earlier). The **hike** up from Taormina's main square is only about a half-mile, but it's very steep—the elevation gain is more than 500 feet.

Giardini Naxos

The little town of Giardini Naxos runs along a sandy beach popular with sun-worshippers—many of whom have no idea how historic this area is. The very first Greek settlers in Sicily landed here and colonized what they called Naxos in 734 BC.

The city was destroyed 300 years later by neighboring Syracuse. Survivors pursued a safer location, establishing Taormina on the cliff (and displacing the indigenous Sicels). This former settlement is not much but a few scattered ruins, but the small museum and park around it with lovely views of Etna make Giardini Naxos a peaceful getaway from the tourist crowds.

Cost and Hours: Museum and archaeological area—€4, daily 9:00-19:00, shorter hours off-season, Lungomare Schiso, tel. 0942-51001.

Getting There: Take the local Interbus line (direction: Catania/CTA airport, confirm your stop at the ticket desk; see "Getting Around Taormina," earlier). SAT's hop-on, hop-off bus also stops at Piazza Municipio in Giardini Naxos (see "Tours in Taormina," earlier).

Day Trips from Taormina

While these day trips are worth considering if you have several days in Taormina, I wouldn't try to squeeze them in on a short visit.

Aeolian Islands: This stunning little archipelago just northeast of Sicily is made up of seven volcanic islets, each with its own personality. For the most efficient visit, book an excursion package or a tour with a local guide (see "Tours in Taormina," earlier).

Alcantara Gorge: A one-hour drive inland from Taormina (on SS-185), this gorge is popular for hiking and swimming in a flooded volcanic gorge with peculiar rock formations at the foot of Mount Etna. It's also accessible via the Interbus hop-on, hop-off line B (see "Tours in Taormina," earlier).

Filming Locations: Touristy **Savoca** and **Forza d'Agrò,** about 30-40 minutes north (on SS-114), were major filming locations for the *Godfather* series, standing in for the town of "Corleone" on film. Interbus hop-on, hop-off line C stops at both towns.

Beaches: For beaches beyond Isola Bella and Giardini Naxos, head for **Mazzeo** or **Letojanni,** about a 15-minute drive north of Taormina (on SS-114, or on ASM's *linea blu/beachbus*). Some of the best beaches are private; you'll pay €10-20 for a lounge chair.

Sleeping in Taormina

$$$$ The Ashbee fills a historic, cliffside mansion just outside Porta Messina. The property has an air of exclusivity, with jasmine-scented gardens, a grand circular driveway, and a pool with a panoramic view that seems a world away from busy Taormina. The 24 quiet rooms are spacious and come with all the extra touches, making this place perfect for a honeymoon or elegant splurge (good restaurant, air-con, elevator, pay parking, closed Nov-March, Via San

Taormina Hotels & Restaurants

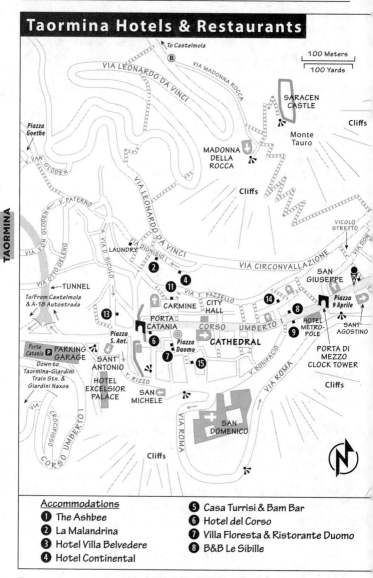

Accommodations

1. The Ashbee
2. La Malandrina
3. Hotel Villa Belvedere
4. Hotel Continental
5. Casa Turrisi & Bam Bar
6. Hotel del Corso
7. Villa Floresta & Ristorante Duomo
8. B&B Le Sibille

Pancrazio 46, tel. 0942-23537, www.theashbeehotel.com, info@ theashbeehotel.com).

$$$$ La Malandrina has six upscale, pastel apartments and two suites with private terraces offering expansive views. The location is central, with a grocery and launderette nearby, but the neighborhood feels quiet (air-con, no elevator, valet parking, Via Dionisio I 2E, tel. 0942-23310, www.lamalandrina.it, info@ lamalandrina.it).

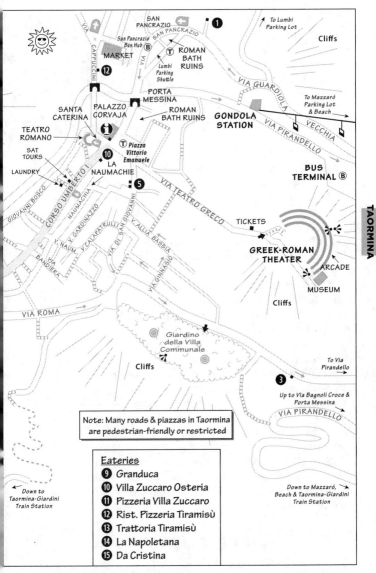

Note: Many roads & piazzas in Taormina are pedestrian-friendly or restricted

Eateries
- ⑨ Granduca
- ⑩ Villa Zuccaro Osteria
- ⑪ Pizzeria Villa Zuccaro
- ⑫ Rist. Pizzeria Tiramisù
- ⑬ Trattoria Tiramisù
- ⑭ La Napoletana
- ⑮ Da Cristina

$$$$ Hotel Villa Belvedere is a large, old-time resort clinging to the edge of Taormina, next to the public gardens. The 55 rooms are simple and comfortable, but the star of the property is the garden and swimming pool with glorious sea views (air-con, elevator, Via Bagnoli Croce 79, tel. 0942-23791, www.villabelvedere. it, info@villabelvedere.it, Valerio).

$$$ Hotel Continental is a big, standard hotel with friendly, professional staff and a terrace that is *indimenticabile* ("unforgettable"—add that word to your Italian vocabulary). It's conveniently located at the top of the steps above Piazza Duomo and Porta Catania. The 34 rooms are clean and modern, most with small patios and some with views. The grand terrace—a delight both early and late—lets you eat breakfast while watching Etna steam (RS%—use code "RICKSTEVES," air-con, elevator, Via Dionisio I 2a, tel. 0942-23805, www. continentaltaormina.com, info@continentaltaormina.com, Stefano).

$$ Casa Turrisi has five good-value, chic, and modern rooms shoehorned into an old house. The location, down a charming street below the tourist action at the Greek-Roman Theater, is central but has a calm neighborhood feel (terrace, Via Giovanni di Giovanni 43, tel. 0942-626-172, www.casaturrisi.com, casaturrisi@gmail. com).

$$ Hotel del Corso, near Porta Catania, is a simple family-run hotel. The 15 rooms are basic but well located, some with small balconies overlooking the garden of Palazzo Duchi di Santo Stefano (RS%, air-con, elevator, Corso Umberto 239, tel. 0942-628-698, www.hoteldelcorsotaormina.com, info@hoteldelcorsotaormina. com, friendly Alex).

$ Villa Floresta is a charming, traditional B&B in a 16th-century Spanish-style house run by Maria and her gregarious father, Ernesto. The four characteristic rooms have small balconies, and share a rooftop terrace accessed through a timbered attic (air-con, Via Damiano Rosso 1, mobile 331-708-0115, www.villafloresta.it, info@villafloresta.it).

$ B&B Le Sibille has four rooms and two apartments on Corso Umberto, just steps away from Piazza IX Aprile—location, location, location (Corso Umberto 187a, mobile 349-726-2862, www.lesibille.net, info@lesibille.net).

Eating in Taormina

$$$ Ristorante Duomo is a little gem with a romantic hidden terrace overlooking Piazza Duomo. Their creative pasta dishes use quality ingredients, and the staff is attentive (daily 12:00-14:30 & 19:00-23:00, Vico degli Ebrei, tel. 0942-625-656).

$$$ Granduca feels a little touristy but is well respected for its traditional Sicilian dishes. The food takes a backseat, however, to the panoramic views from the dining room—some of the best in the city (Wed-Mon 12:00-23:00, closed Tue and Nov-Feb, Corso Umberto 172, tel. 0942-24983).

$$$ **Villa Zuccaro Osteria** is a welcoming restaurant specializing in quality, fresh ingredients. You can dine in the simple modern interior or out on one of their two terraces, one of which has views over the ancient Roman wall known as the Naumachie. Their seafood pastas are inventive, such as the *linguine ai ricci di mare*—linguine with sea urchins (daily 12:00-24:00, Corso Umberto 38, tel. 0942-615-056).

$$ **Pizzeria Villa Zuccaro** is the place for a quality Sicilian-style pizza in a peaceful garden setting. Gabriele, the award-winning pizza chef, proudly fires up crust that's crisp on the outside and soft on the inside (Wed-Mon 12:00-23:00, closed Tue and Nov-Feb, Piazza Carmine 5, tel. 0942-628-018).

$$ **Ristorante Pizzeria Tiramisù** is a local favorite for a traditional Sicilian meal. Set outside the city walls (just uphill from Porta Messina), prices are reasonable and the atmosphere is laid-back. Try their *involtini di pesce spada* (swordfish rolls) or *rigatoni alla Norma*. They take pride in their homemade desserts, as the name of the restaurant implies (reservations smart, daily 12:30-15:00 & 19:30-23:00, Via Cappuccini 1, tel. 0942-24803, www.tiramisutaormina.it).

$$ **Trattoria Tiramisù,** a sister restaurant, serves a similar menu in a cozier space on the opposite end of town. This location, close to Porta Catania, has a few outdoor tables, usually filled with families slurping the *zuppa di pesce*—fish soup (reservations smart, daily 13:00-14:30 & 19:30-23:00, Viale Apollo Arcageta 9, tel. 0942-21172, https://trattoriatiramisu.it/).

$ **La Napoletana** offers a simple menu of salads, beer, and Naples-style pizza. They cook their pies quickly at a high temperature in a state-of-the-art, wood-fired oven—and the result is soft, light, and chewy crust. The outdoor seating fills a small, peaceful square just off Corso Umberto and seems far from the crowds (Thu-Tue 12:00-23:30, closed Wed, Dec-Feb open for dinner only, Piazza Varò, tel. 0942-628-049).

$ **Da Cristina** serves quality takeaway food at low prices. Choose from a dozen kinds of rustic pizza by the slice, *schiacciate* (stuffed pizza), or piping hot *arancini* deep fried on the spot. Cristina's small cafeteria next door offers more selection and basement seating (daily 9:00-23:00, closed Wed off-season, Via Strabone 2, tel. 0942-21171).

$ **Bam Bar** specializes in *granite* and serves a dozen seasonal flavors on a picturesque street near the Greek-Roman Theater.

Try layering two *granita* flavors, top them with *panna* (whipped cream), and eat it all with a warm brioche bun. *Attenzione! Limone* does not go with *cioccolata* (daily 7:00-23:00, closed Mon Sept-June, Via Giovanni di Giovanni 45, tel. 0942-24355).

Taormina Connections

BY PUBLIC TRANSPORTATION

From Taormina by Train to: Palermo (7/day, 4.5 hours, change in Messina), **Aeolian Islands/Milazzo** via Messina (hourly, 1.5 hours, change in Messina), **Cefalù** (9/day, 3-4 hours, change in Messina), **Catania** (hourly, 1 hour), **Siracusa** (7/day, 2 hours).

From Taormina by Bus: Intercity buses are operated by Interbus/Etna Trasporti and usually depart from the bus terminal on Via Pirandello (a few routes depart from nearby Piazza San Pancrazio—confirm when you buy your ticket). Connections include **Messina** (6/day, 1.5 hours), **Catania**'s airport and downtown (hourly, 1.5 hours), **Siracusa** (1/day, 2.5 hours, more with change in Catania), **Palermo** (hourly, 4 hours, Etna Trasporti to Catania, then SAIS to Palermo), **Ragusa** (hourly, 3.5 hours, change in Catania), and **Piazza Armerina** with a stop at **Villa Romana del Casale** (1/day, 3 hours). Bus info: tel. 0942-625-301, www.interbus.it.

ROUTE TIPS FOR DRIVERS

Taormina sits along the E-45 expressway, which follows Sicily's east coast between Catania and Messina.

If you're heading to **Cefalù** (about 3 hours from Taormina), you could zip down to Catania on E-45, then cut through the middle of Sicily on the A-19 expressway. But it's approximately the same amount of time, and far more scenic, to take the northern coastal route: Head north on E-45 toward Messina—with great views over the Strait of Messina. As you pass above Messina, carry on toward Palermo, staying on E-90 past Milazzo and along the north coast—with views of the Aeolian Islands just offshore. Approaching Cefalù, you'll exit at Pollina-Castelbuono, wind down to the seashore, and carry on the rest of the way into town. (Coming from this direction, using the Cefalù exit—farther along—will overshoot your goal and waste some time.)

SICILIAN HISTORY

Three Millennia at a Glance

HISTORY IN A HURRY

Sicily's history is about settlers and invaders. Three thousand years ago, three tribes lived on the island: the Sicels, the Sicani, and the Elymi. They were joined by Phoenicians (Carthaginians) and, starting around 734 BC, by the Greeks. Later, the Romans invaded and defeated the Greeks, and eventually the Carthaginians, establishing Roman rule until the fall of the empire.

Barbarians ruled for a short period, replaced by the Byzantines. The Arabs arrived and modernized the island, bringing an age of prosperity. In 1060, the Normans conquered the island, creating a peaceful Golden Age. After the Norman line ended, the island was ruled by foreign powers from afar—the German Swabians, then the French Angevins, then a centuries-long succession of Spanish rulers. In 1860, Sicily was folded into the new Italian state, but the lack of a stable government gave rise to the Mafia, a problem that persisted through fascism, worsened with World War II, and marked much of the 20th century. The 21st century has seen Sicily in renewal, with cities remodeled and cleaned up, better industry and infrastructure, and a global outlook that welcomes visitors.

PREHISTORIC SICILY
(2000-750 BC)

Ancient Sicily had two native peoples: in the east, the Sicels (or Siculi, for whom the island is named), and in the west, the Sicani (or Sikans). Around 1200 BC, a new group, the Elymi (or Elymians), arrived from Asia Minor (claiming to have escaped from Troy) and settled in the west, scattered on a few fortified hilltop

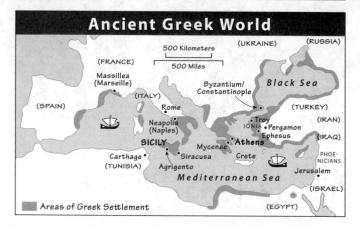

Ancient Greek World

Areas of Greek Settlement

towns. Mycenaeans from Greece also visited the island and traded with the natives.

ANCIENT COLONIES
(734-264 BC)

In their ancient version of "westward expansion," the Greeks began to seek more land and resources. They sent settlers to establish colonies in fertile Sicily—first arriving on the eastern shore, where they established Naxos (734 BC), near present-day Taormina. Collectively, the Greek cities in Sicily were part of Magna Graecia, or "Great Greece" (the southern Italian colonies of Greece) and were eventually ruled as city-states by what the locals considered to be "tyrants"—illegitimate rulers who seized power in popular revolts.

Meanwhile, the Phoenicians and Carthaginians established colonies in the west, at Mozia (south of today's Trapani) and Palermo (around 800 BC). The Greeks and the Carthaginians fought over the fertile island, looking to control its valuable resources and strategic location.

When they weren't fighting the Carthaginians, Greek settlers in Sicily played out the rivalries of their home city-states—jockeying among themselves for control of the island—with Athens occasionally getting drawn into the fray. Ancient Syracuse (today's Siracusa) rose to be the greatest of the Greek cities, surpassing even Athens in power and attracting the great minds of the age—including Plato and, later, Archimedes. But soon, a

A Typical Greek Temple

Greek temples, built to house the cult image of a god, follow the same basic layout, with an inner chamber surrounded by a parade of columns. Important activities mostly took place outside, at an altar in front of the temple doors.

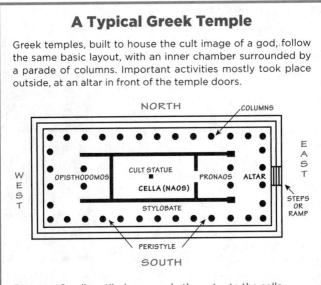

Pronaos: Small vestibule or porch, the entry to the cella

Cella (or naos): The heart of the temple, where the cult image of the god was kept

Opisthodomos: Rear chamber, usually with no access to the cella and sometimes used as a treasury

Peristyle: Colonnade, the columns surrounding the cella

Stylobate: Platform on which the peristyle stands

HISTORY

third power emerging in the Mediterranean set its eyes on Sicily: the Romans.

For more on Sicily's Greek age, see the sidebar on page 285; for the Carthaginians, see page 176.

Sights

- Archaeological Park and Museum of Giardini Naxos (near Taormina)
- Mozia Island (near Trapani)
- Salinas Regional Archaeological Museum (Palermo)
- Segesta
- Selinunte
- Valley of the Temples Archaeological Park and Pietro Griffo Archaeological Museum (Agrigento)
- Neapolis Archaeological Park and Paolo Orsi Archaeological Museum (Siracusa)
- Cathedral of Siracusa

ROMAN DOMINATION
(264 BC-AD 410)

The expanding Roman Republic eventually turned its attention to Sicily, eyeing its strategic location: Conquering Sicily would cripple the Romans' greatest rival—Carthage—and  help them gain control of the Mediterranean. After three long wars where they defeated great Carthaginian generals (such as Hannibal) and conquered powerful Greek colonies (such as Syracuse), Sicily became a Roman province. And Rome became master of the Mediterranean. They called it *Mare Nostrum* ("Our Sea"); soon booty and slaves from vanquished lands poured into the Republic.

The Romans bickered among themselves over their slice of the pie, pitting wealthy landowners (the ruling Senate) against the working class (plebs) and the rebellious slaves (Spartacus' revolt, 73 BC). In the chaos, charismatic generals like Julius Caesar, who could provide wealth and security, tried to seize power as dictators. The republic fell; in its place an empire was formed, with the new emperor, Augustus, establishing a period of peace (Pax Romana) and expansion.

Though Rome conquered Greece, it adopted Greek culture. From hairstyles to statues to temples to the evening's entertainment, Rome was forever "Hellenized," becoming the curators of Greek culture, passing it down to future generations. In some cases, Greek structures in Sicily were retrofitted to Roman specifications, best embodied by the Greek-Roman Theater in Taormina.

In Sicily, large estates were formed and given to Roman patricians. Few survive today, but the Villa Romana del Casale is a particularly well-preserved example. Sicily's forests were sacrificed to supply timber for the Roman fleet, and the island became the breadbasket of the empire, producing grain and little else. The Sicilians were left to farm the land, take on Roman ways, and pay taxes.

Before Christianity was legalized (AD 313), Christians in Sicily were persecuted. This produced two important Christian martyrs who are still highly revered today: Sant'Agata of Catania (see page 319) and Santa Lucia of Siracusa (see page 288).

Sights
- Villa Romana del Casale
- Greek-Roman Theater (Taormina)
- Roman Theater and Odeum (Catania)
- Catacombs of San Giovanni and Church of San Filippo Apostolo (Siracusa)

BARBARIANS AND BYZANTINES
(AD 410-827)

The Visigoths sacked Rome in AD 410—but by then the Roman Empire was already effectively over. Constantine the Great had transferred the center of his new "Byzantine" empire to Constantinople in AD 330. As Rome fell, waves of tribes poured into Italy, and the Vandals took over Sicily. Byzantine Emperor Justinian sent his best general, Belisarius, to reassert control over the island. Belisarius succeeded, and the Byzantines ruled the island for almost 300 years (535-827), with one emperor even choosing to move his capital to Siracusa.

ARAB SICILY
(827-1060)

As Islam expanded beyond the Middle East, Arabs spread throughout North Africa and began trading with Sicily. From nearby Tunisia they conquered the town of Mazara in 827, then Palermo, with its excellent port, and later established a capital there. Arab rule spread across the island, eventually bringing the Greek-Byzantine capital of Siracusa under its control. The Arabs brought mathematics, engineering, and advances in agriculture to the island. Palermo was laid out and developed as the center of the emirate. For more on this period, see the sidebar on page 53.

While little architecture survives from this period, Arab culture still permeates Sicily—perhaps most noticeably in its cuisine

(with its sweet-and-sour *agrodolce* sauces) and in its thriving markets, where vendors still advertise their wares with an almost Arabic-sounding cadence. Arab design and architectural flourishes were also highly influential in Sicily's later Norman period, while major Palermo landmarks like the cathedral and the Norman Palace were built by skilled Arab craftsmen.

Sights

- Ballarò and Capo markets (Palermo)
- Fish market in Catania
- Palermo Cathedral
- Norman Palace (Palermo)
- Kolymbethra Gardens (Agrigento)

Church Architecture

History comes to life when you visit a centuries-old church. Even if you wouldn't know your apse from a hole in the ground, learning a few simple terms will enrich your experience. Note that not every church has every feature, and that a "cathedral" isn't a type of church architecture, but rather a designation for a church that's a governing center for a local bishop.

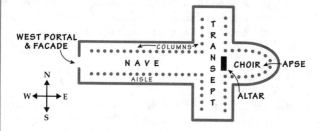

Aisles: The long, generally low-ceilinged arcades that flank the nave.

Altar: The raised area with a ceremonial table (often adorned with candles or a crucifix), where the priest prepares and serves the bread and wine for Communion.

Apse: The space beyond the altar, generally bordered with small chapels.

Barrel Vault: A continuous round-arched ceiling that resembles an extended upside-down U.

Choir: A cozy area, often screened off, located within the church nave and near the high altar, where services are sung in a more intimate setting.

Cloister: A square-shaped series of hallways surrounding an open-air courtyard, traditionally where monks and nuns got fresh air.

Facade: The outer wall of the church's main (west) entrance, viewable from outside and generally highly decorated.

Groin Vault: An arched ceiling formed where two equal barrel vaults meet at right angles. Less common usage: term for a medieval jock strap.

Narthex: The area (portico or foyer) between the main entry and the nave.

Nave: The long, central section of the church (running west to east, from the entrance to the altar) where the congregation stood through the service.

Transept: The north-south part of the church, which crosses (perpendicularly) the east-west nave. In a traditional Latin cross-shaped floor plan, the transept forms the "arms" of the cross.

West Portal: The main entry to the church (on the west end, opposite the main altar).

THE NORMAN KINGDOM OF SICILY
(1060-1189)

Normans—Vikings (Norsemen) who settled in France—went on expeditions to England (Battle of Hastings, 1066) and to southern Italy and Sicily. By 1090, they dominated most of the island, and conquered it from Arab rule (with the support of the pope). Under the first Norman king, Roger II, the island was united. A policy of religious tolerance allowed the kingdom to flourish, taking advantage of each group's skills to create a fusion of styles in art and architecture. Roger's nephew (the last Norman king, William II) turned Sicily into the most prosperous, important kingdom of Europe, building Monreale Cathedral—but he died young and without an heir.

Sights

- Monreale Cathedral (outside Palermo)
- Church of La Martorana (Palermo)
- Cefalù Cathedral
- Palatine Chapel and Norman Palace (Palermo)
- Catania Cathedral

HOLY ROMAN EMPIRE AND FRENCH ANGEVINS
(1189-1282)

After William II's death, Sicily passed from the Normans to their closest relative, the young duke Frederick II of Swabia, who was half German and half Sicilian-Norman. The ambitious new ruler united his kingdoms—becoming Holy Roman Emperor (1220) and adding Jerusalem to boot (1225). He based his court mostly in Sicily and southern Italy; the people loved him because he grew up in Palermo and spoke fluent Sicilian and Arabic (and five other languages). His fans called him "Stupor Mundi" (wonder of the world) for his charisma and freethinking ways, although Pope Gregory IX called him an antichrist and excommunicated him not once but twice. After his death in 1250, a chaotic power grab left the French Angevins holding the throne. Their rule of Sicily was short and ugly, ending with a bloody revolt in 1282.

Sights

- Palazzo Conte Federico (Palermo)
- Castello Ursino (Catania)

HISTORY

Sicilian Emigration

The 19th century saw massive political and social upheaval in Sicily. The Spanish nobility was deposed in the 1860s, when Italy unified, but instability reigned for the remainder of the century.

4. ITALIAN IMMIGRANTS AT ELLIS ISLAND - 1905

Lost baggage is the cause of their worried expressions. At the height of immigration the entire first floor of the administration building was used to store baggage.

Photo-study by Lewis W. Hine

While the south and north of Italy were relatively equal in terms of wealth at the beginning of the 19th century, the fate of the Sicilians changed under Italy's new monarchy. The ruling Savoy family was from Piedmont, in northern Italy. They exploited Sicilian resources and levied high taxes. Sicilian industries such as silk production declined, as the northern king invested in factories closer to home. Sicilians became poorer and disillusioned. At the same time, a pest called phylloxera decimated vineyards and wine-making, and the lucrative sulfur industry collapsed due to competition from the US.

As the economy suffered, desperate peasants looked for better fortunes abroad—some villages in central Sicily were completely abandoned. Men would leave first, establishing themselves in a new home, most returning to bring their families with them. A few started over completely, abandoning their wives and families—and never returning. Historians estimate that between 1880 and 1920, more than a million people left Sicily, many heading for the US (until nativist laws passed in the 1920s made it more difficult to immigrate). Today, more than 20 million people in the United States can claim Sicilian heritage.

Sicilian-Americans looking to connect with their homeland can find traces of their past with some research or the help of a genealogist. Birth certificates or emigration records can offer clues, and travelers can visit any town's City Hall or main church for birth and death records. To get started, check out the Statue of Liberty-Ellis Island Foundation (www.libertyellisfoundation.org) for searchable ship manifests with hometown information. Cognomix—another genealogy site—lets you find the origin and concentrations of Italian families (website mostly in Italian, www.cognomix.it).

SPANISH DOMINATION (1282-1860)

To eject the French, the Sicilians asked the Spanish House of Aragon for help. With the French gone, the Aragon king was free to annex Sicily (and later add southern Italy to his holdings).

In 1469, King Ferdinand II of Aragon (including Sicily) married Queen Isabel of Castile—unifying Spain and pulling Sicily along for the ride. Sicily would remain a Spanish holding for the next 300 years. These so-called Catholic Monarchs lorded over Sicily with a firm grip, bringing the Inquisition and expelling the Arabs and Jews from the island in 1492.

An earthquake in 1693 devastated the southeastern corner of the island, and cities were reborn in the flowery Baroque style imposed by the Counter-Reformation. In general, Sicily's over-the-top Baroque architecture and dramatic religious processions are the most visible legacies of Spanish rule.

Sights

- Quattro Canti and Oratorio of San Lorenzo (Palermo)
- Church of Santa Caterina (Palermo)
- Fountain of Shame (Palermo)
- Church of the Souls in Purgatory (Trapani)
- Noto (near Ragusa)
- Ragusa Ibla
- Palazzo Biscari (Catania)

KINGS AND DICTATORS
(1860-1945)

In 1860, the revolutionary Giuseppe Garibaldi landed on the west coast of Sicily (at Marsala) to begin the Risorgimento—the unification of Italy after centuries of being divided and ruled by foreigners. In the process, Sicily's entrenched noble families lost much of their land, and the aristocratic social order was swept away. The new kingdom of Italy joined Sicily to the mainland under a king from the far north (the Savoy dynasty). As throughout Italy, the Risorgimento came with a boost in local pride, coinciding with the construction of grand opera houses in Palermo and Catania.

But although the Risorgimento was, at first, a positive development for Sicily, the faraway Savoy king both ignored Sicily and southern Italy...and raided their assets. Religious orders were abolished, and private land was turned over to the monarchy. Industry in the north was modernized and developed, while the south was left mostly agricultural. Poor and corrupt management under the new government gave rise to crime syndicates, which later became known as the Mafia. Many Sicilians and other southern Italians

Sicily Goes to War

Sicily did not fare well during World War II under Italy's fascist regime. Dictator Benito Mussolini (r. 1922-1945) sent a lieutenant, Cesare Mori, to curb the Mafia and cruelly establish his supremacy over the island. As the war dragged on, many Sicilian men were conscripted, leaving their families with no one to tend the fields. Bitterness toward the fascist government grew with food rationing, austerity, and Italian defeats in Africa; soon Mussolini's alliance with Hitler turned Sicilians against him.

By July 1943, the island was garrisoned with 70,000 German soldiers and 230,000 Italian troops. Meanwhile, the Allies developed an invasion plan—"Operation Husky"—choosing Sicily as their launch pad for the conquest of Italy.

From the southern beaches, British General Bernard Montgomery pushed north on the eastern shore, while the Americans under General George Patton took a wide sweep to the west, taking Palermo and racing to reach Messina before the British. The starving locals greeted Allied troops with relief and joy. After only 39 days, the entire island was liberated.

The fall of Sicily was the beginning of the end for Mussolini. When Hitler and Mussolini met in the north of Italy to discuss the Sicilian situation, the Allies bombed Rome. As shells began falling just outside the Italian capital, it was finally clear that Mussolini's alliance with Nazi Germany was leading the country to ruin. The Fascist Grand Council dismissed Mussolini, and King Victor Emmanuel III ordered his arrest. The dictator was put under house arrest, but the Germans later freed him, installing him as the leader of the Italian territory they still controlled. Meanwhile, the south was gradually liberated by the Allies.

The Italian government surrendered to the Allies on September 3, 1943. The king fled to Allied-occupied southern Italy, abandoning Rome to Nazi forces, who occupied it for nine terrible months. Italy endured the ravages of war until April 1945, when Mussolini was shot by Italian partisans as he tried to escape to Switzerland. A year later, Italy's monarchy was finally abolished by a vote of the people—even though Sicily voted in favor of keeping it.

HISTORY

chose to seek better fortunes in North and South America (see the sidebar, earlier).

In 1922, Benito Mussolini seized the Italian government, ruling as prime minister, then dictator for the next two decades with the king as a figurehead. Mussolini responded to the Great Depression (1930s) with big public works projects, government investment in industry, and an expanded army. But he also allied his country with Hitler's Nazi regime, drawing an unprepared Italy into World War II (1940; see the sidebar).

In 1943, Sicily took center stage in the war when the Allies invaded the island to free Italy from the Germans. Unfor-

tunately, when it came time to reestablish local Sicilian rule, US forces made the mistake of enlisting help from well-connected Sicilian-American families—and the Mafia filled the vacuum left by Mussolini's strong-arm rule (for more on the Mafia, see page 48).

HISTORY

Sights
- Garibaldi Statue (Trapani)
- Teatro Massimo (Palermo)
- Teatro Massimo Bellini (Catania)
- Museum of the Allied Landings in Sicily (Catania)

MODERN SICILY (1946-TODAY)

At war's end, Italy was physically ruined and extremely poor. The nation rebuilt in the 1950s and 1960s with Marshall Plan aid from the United States. Being a founding member of what would become the European Union was also a boost.

However, the national government remained weak, changing on average once a year, shifting from right to left to centrist coalitions (Italy has had 65 governments since World War II). The country remained sharply divided between the rich industrial north and the poor rural south. Many Sicilian men moved to northern Europe to find work; many others left farms and flocked to the cities.

In Sicily, postwar rebuilding was often quick and dirty, without a master plan and with little concern for the island's historic character. Concrete suburbs and unsightly industrial areas proliferated. Inner cities were left in rubble, and some areas, particularly in Palermo, waited decades for reconstruction.

The flow of reconstruction funds fell into the hands of cor-

HISTORY

Sicily Almanac

Official Name: Regione Sicilia, but locals just call it "Sicilia."

Population: About 5.1 million.

Latitude and Longitude: 37° N and 14° E (latitude similar to San Francisco).

Area: 9,927 square miles, including the three archipelagos of Aeolian islands, Egadi islands, and Pelagie islands, and other minor islands.

Geography: Sicily is shaped like an arrowhead, with its tip pointing west, toward Spain. Seventy miles long and 85 miles wide, with more than 700 miles of coastline, Sicily is the biggest island in the Mediterranean. The terrain is generally mountainous or hilly, with the mountains along the north coast considered a continuation of Italy's Apennine Mountains. The highest point is Mt. Etna (10,924 feet)—the tallest active volcano in Europe. Sicily's central location—just 90 miles from the African coast and two miles from the Italian peninsula—has long made it a natural stepping stone between Africa and Europe.

Biggest Cities: Palermo (the capital, 680,000), Catania (315,000), and Messina (240,000).

Climate: Sicily has a Mediterranean climate, with mild, wet winters and hot, dry summers. Sicily is also affected by sea currents from nearby Africa and often receives strong Saharan winds in summer. In winter, many interior mountain ranges are snowcapped.

Language: The official language is Italian, though most people on the island also speak Sicilian (especially among close friends and

rupt politicians, multinational corporations, and organized crime. Sicilian Mafia influence reached new heights in 1982, with the assassination of Carlo Alberto Dalla Chiesa, a general sent from Rome to deal with the mob problem in Sicily. The Mafia's rise culminated in 1992 with the assassinations of two prestigious anti-Mafia prosecutors—Giovanni Falcone and Paolo Borsellino—who were leading investigations against organized crime. Instead of discouraging prosecution, the tide turned, and hundreds of Mafia bosses were convicted.

After surviving the government-a-year turbulence and Mafia-tainted corruption of the postwar years, Sicily today is more stable and organized. Pollution and corruption are waning, and the 21st century has seen renewed investment in cities across the island. Former slums in Palermo, Catania, and Siracusa now house chic boutiques. Rustic fishing villages are becoming vacation destinations, dusty fields now host wind turbines, and new family). Although it is a Romance language, Sicilian draws heavily from Greek, Arabic, French, and Spanish; the differences are great enough that Italian and Sicilian are not mutually intelligible.

Economy: Sicily's Gross Domestic Product is $105 billion; the GDP per capita is $21,000. About 68 percent of the economy consists of service jobs (especially tourism), eight percent is industry (textiles, construction, chemicals), and four percent is agriculture (fruit, vegetables, olives, wine, fishing). The island has about 860 miles of train lines (mostly government-run and not all connected) and over 450 miles of expressway (autostrada).

Government: Sicily is the largest of Italy's 20 regions, and one of five with semi-autonomous powers, including its own parliament and president. The regional government has the constitutional power to approve laws on education, healthcare, and transportation. Sicily itself is divided into nine provinces (Palermo, Trapani, Agrigento, Caltanissetta, Enna, Ragusa, Siracusa, Catania, and Messina) and 390 "communes," each with a community council and mayor.

Flag: Diagonally divided in red and yellow with the Trinacria symbol in the center (head of a Medusa with three dislocated legs and three ears of wheat). For more on this symbol, see page 55.

Notable Sicilians: Archimedes, Empedocles, Santa Lucia, painter Antonello da Messina, composer Vincenzo Bellini, playwright Luigi Pirandello, painter Renato Guttuso, writer Andrea Camilleri, Italian-American filmmakers Frank Capra and Martin Scorsese—and fictional gangster Vito Corleone.

HISTORY

highways zip across the island. Tourism is a burgeoning industry, with hotel owners jump-starting a revitalized business climate.

As you travel through Sicily today, you'll encounter a fascinating region with a rich history and an up-and-coming economy. While Sicily has been dominated for centuries by invaders, now it's ready for a new wave of foreigners—tourists, travelers, and you—to come and make your own history.

PRACTICALITIES

This chapter covers the practical skills of European travel: how to get tourist information, pay for things, sightsee efficiently, find good-value accommodations, eat affordably but well, use technology wisely, and get between destinations smoothly. For more information on these topics, see www.ricksteves.com/travel-tips.

Tourist Information

Before your trip, scan the website of the Italian national tourist office (www.italia.it) for a wealth of travel information. If you have a specific question, try contacting one of their US offices (New York: Tel. 212/245-5618, newyork@enit.it; Chicago: Tel. 312/644-9335, chicago@enit.it; Los Angeles: Tel. 310/820-1898, losangeles@enit. it). The region of Sicily has its own tourism organization; regional offices are listed on their website (www.visitsicily.info).

In Sicily, a visit to the tourist office (abbreviated **TI** in this book) can be useful or time-wasting, depending on the city. Some TIs are more helpful and informative than others (noted in each chapter). Be aware that office hours and locations often change and that many TIs close on Sundays, holidays, and in winter (Nov-Easter).

Note that TIs are in business to help you enjoy spending money in their town. While this corrupts much of their advice—and you can get plenty of information online—I still make a point to swing by the local TI to confirm sightseeing plans, pick up a city map, and get information on public transit (including bus and train schedules), walking tours, special events, and nightlife. Anticipating a harried front-line staffer, prepare a list of questions and a proposed plan to double-check. While Italian TIs are about half as helpful as those in other countries, their information is twice as important.

Some TIs have information on the entire region, so try to pick up maps and printed information for destinations you'll be visiting later in your trip.

Be wary of travel agencies or special information services that masquerade as TIs but serve fancy hotels and tour companies. They're selling things you don't need.

Travel Tips

Emergency and Medical Help: For any emergency service—ambulance, police, or fire—call **112** from a mobile phone or landline. Operators, who in most countries speak English, will deal with your request or route you to the right emergency service. If you get sick, do as the locals do and go to a pharmacist for advice. Or ask at your hotel for help—they'll know the nearest medical and emergency services.

Theft or Loss: To replace a passport, you'll need to go in person to an embassy (see below). If your credit and debit cards disappear, cancel and replace them (see "Damage Control for Lost Cards" on page 407). File a police report, either on the spot or within a day or two; you'll need it to submit an insurance claim for lost or stolen rail passes or travel gear, and it can help with replacing your passport or credit and debit cards. For more information, see www.ricksteves.com/help.

US Embassies and Consulates: Embassy in Rome—tel. 06-46741 for 24-hour emergency line, tel. 06-4674-2420 for non-emergencies, by appointment only (Via Vittorio Veneto 121). Consulates in Milan—tel. 02-290-351 (Via Principe Amedeo 2/10); Florence—tel. 055-266-951 (Lungarno Vespucci 38); and Naples—tel. 081-583-8111 (Piazza della Repubblica). Consular agency in Palermo—tel. 091-38-5057 (Via Vaccarini 1). For all, see http://it.usembassy.gov.

Canadian Embassies and Consulates: Rome—tel. 06-854-442-911 (Via Zara 30); Milan—tel. 02-626-94238 (Piazza Cavour 3). For both, see www.italy.gc.ca.

Avoiding Theft and Scams: Although violent crime is rare in Sicily, petty theft is common in large cities. With sweet-talking con artists meeting you at the station and well-dressed pickpockets on buses, tourists face a gauntlet of rip-offs. Pickpockets don't want to hurt you—they usually just want your money and gadgets. Green or sloppy tourists are prone to scams.

Thieves strike when you're distracted. Don't trust overly kind strangers. Keep nothing important in your pockets, and be especially careful with expensive cell phones—maintain a firm grip when you're using one. Be on guard at bustling and noisy street markets. Hold your bags in front with your arms over them. The sneakiest thieves pretend to be well-dressed businessmen or tourists wearing fanny packs and toting cameras and even Rick Steves guidebooks. The best deterrent is for you to look confident and aware, not confused and afraid.

Watch out for fast-fingered moms with babies and groups of children picking the pockets and handbags of naive tourists. Be particularly aware of groups of young women who seem to have nothing to do. Pickpockets troll tourist crowds around major sights and at train stations. Watch them target tourists who are overloaded with bags or distracted with their phones.

Scams abound. When paying for something, be aware of how much cash you're handing over, demand clear and itemized bills, and count your change. Don't give your wallet to self-proclaimed "police" who stop you on the street, warn you about counterfeit (or drug) money, and ask to see your cash. If a bank machine eats your ATM card, check for a thin plastic insert with a tongue hanging out (thieves use these devices to extract cards).

If you feel you are being scammed or are in a situation that makes you feel threatened, use your camera to document the incident and call the police immediately. This alone may deter criminal behavior. Don't be scared—just be aware and be smart, and you'll be fine.

Time Zones: Italy, like most of continental Europe, is generally six/nine hours ahead of the East/West Coasts of the US. The exceptions are the beginning and end of Daylight Saving Time: Europe "springs forward" the last Sunday in March (two weeks after most of North America), and "falls back" the last Sunday in October (one week before North America). For a handy time converter, use the world clock app on your mobile phone or download one (see www.timeanddate.com).

Business Hours: Traditionally, Italy used the siesta plan, with people generally working from about 9:00 to 13:00 and from 15:30-16:00 to 19:30-20:00, Monday through Saturday. Siesta hours are no longer required by law, so some shops stay open through lunch or later into the evening, especially larger stores in tourist areas.

Sicily sticks to the old ways more than the mainland, and the siesta is still in effect, even in larger cities, especially during summer. Smaller stores are usually closed on Sunday, and often on Monday. Many businesses close for a couple of weeks around August 15—expect big cities to be empty for most of the month.

Watt's Up? Europe's electrical system is 220 volts, instead of North America's 110 volts. Most newer electronics (such as laptops, smartphones, and hair dryers) convert automatically, so you won't need a converter, but you will need an adapter plug with two round prongs, sold inexpensively at travel stores in the US. Sockets in Italy and Switzerland only accept plugs with slimmer prongs: Don't buy an adapter with the thicker ("Schuko" style) prongs—it won't work. Avoid bringing older appliances that don't automatically convert voltage; instead, buy a cheap replacement in Europe.

Discounts: Discounts for sights are generally not listed in this book. However, seniors (age 65 and over), youths under 18, and students and teachers with proper identification cards (obtain from www.isic.org) can get discounts at many sights—always ask. Italy's national museums generally offer free admission to children under 18, but some discounts are available only for citizens of the European Union (EU).

Tobacco Shops: Known as *tabacchi* (often indicated with a big *T* sign), these Italian-style minimarts are ubiquitous across the country. They're handy places to pay for street parking and purchase such things as batteries, tickets for city buses and subways, and sometimes postage. If you aren't sure where to buy something, a *tabacchi* is a good place to start.

Online Translation Tips: Google's Chrome browser instantly translates websites; Translate.google.com is also handy. The Google Translate app converts spoken English into most European languages (and vice versa) and can also translate text it "reads" with your smartphone's camera.

Money

Here's my basic strategy for using money in Europe:
- Upon arrival, head for a cash machine (ATM) at the airport and withdraw some local currency, using a debit card with low international transaction fees.
- Pay for most purchases with your choice of cash or a credit card. You'll save money by minimizing your credit and debit card exchange fees. The trend is for bigger expenses to be paid by credit card, but cash is still the standby for small purchases and tips.
- Keep your cards and cash safe in a money belt.

Exchange Rate

1 euro (€) = about $1.20

To convert prices in euros to dollars, add about 20 percent: €20 = about $24, €50 = about $60. (Check www.oanda.com for the latest exchange rates.) Just like the dollar, one euro is broken down into 100 cents. Coins range from €0.01 to €2, and bills from €5 to €200 (bills over €50 are rarely used; €500 bills are being phased out).

PLASTIC VERSUS CASH

Although credit cards are widely accepted in Europe, cash is king in Sicily. Carry cash at all times (especially small bills and change), as it's the only way to pay for cheap food, taxis, tips, and local guides. Some businesses (especially smaller ones, such as B&Bs and mom-and-pop cafés and shops) may charge you extra for using a credit card—or might not accept credit cards at all. If you're unsure, especially at restaurants, ask before you sit down: *Carta di credito?* (KAR-tah dee KREH-dee-toh).

When using cash, many businesses will try to avoid taking bills larger than €20, and it can be difficult to get change. Break big bills when you can. Cashiers often demand exact change, and will happily wait for you to search your bag for it. Hoard your coins, especially if you're driving, as you will need them for tolls and parking meters.

I use my credit card to book hotel reservations, to buy advance tickets for events or sights, and to cover larger expenses. It can also be smart to use plastic near the end of your trip, to avoid another visit to the ATM.

WHAT TO BRING

I pack the following and keep it all safe in my money belt.

Debit Card: Use this at ATMs to withdraw local cash.

Credit Card: Handy for bigger transactions (at hotels, shops, restaurants, travel agencies, car-rental agencies, and so on), payment machines, and online purchases.

Backup Card: Some travelers carry a third card (debit or credit; ideally from a different bank), in case one gets lost, demagnetized, eaten by a temperamental machine, or simply doesn't work.

A Stash of Cash: I always carry $100-200 US as a cash back-up. A stash of cash comes in handy for emergencies, such as if your ATM card stops working.

What NOT to Bring: Resist the urge to buy euros before your trip or you'll pay the price in bad stateside exchange rates. Wait until you arrive to withdraw money. I've yet to see a European airport that didn't have plenty of ATMs.

BEFORE YOU GO
Use this pre-trip checklist.

Know your cards. Debit cards from any major US bank will work in any standard European bank's ATM (ideally, use a debit card with a Visa or MasterCard logo). As for credit cards, Visa and MasterCard are universal, American Express is less common, and Discover is unknown in Europe.

Know your PIN. Make sure you know the numeric, four-digit PIN for all of your cards, both debit and credit. Request it if you don't have one and allow time to receive the information by mail.

All credit and debit cards now have chips that authenticate and secure transactions. Europeans insert their chip cards into the payment machine slot, then enter a PIN. American cards should work in most transactions without a PIN—but may not work at self-service machines at train stations, toll booths, gas pumps, or parking lots. I've been inconvenienced a few times by self-service payment machines in Europe that wouldn't accept my card, but it's never caused me serious trouble.

If you're concerned, a few banks, including Andrews Federal Credit Union (www.andrewsfcu.org) and the State Department Federal Credit Union (www.sdfcu.org), offer a chip-and-PIN card that works in almost all payment machines.

Report your travel dates. Let your bank know that you'll be using your debit and credit cards in Europe, and when and where you're headed.

Adjust your ATM withdrawal limit. Find out how much you can take out daily and ask for a higher daily withdrawal limit if you want to get more cash at once. Note that European ATMs will withdraw funds only from checking accounts; you're unlikely to have access to your savings account.

Ask about fees. For any purchase or withdrawal made with a card, you may be charged a currency conversion fee (1-3 percent) and/or a Visa or MasterCard international transaction fee (1 percent). If you're getting a bad deal, consider getting a new debit or credit card. Reputable no-fee cards include those from Capital One, as well as Charles Schwab debit cards. Most credit unions and some airline loyalty cards have low or no international transaction fees.

IN EUROPE
Using Cash Machines
European cash machines have English-language instructions and work just like they do at home—except they spit out local currency

PRACTICALITIES

instead of dollars, calculated at the day's standard bank-to-bank rate.

In most places, ATMs are easy to locate—in Sicily ask for a *bancomat*. When possible, withdraw cash from a bank-run ATM located just outside that bank. Ideally use it during the bank's opening hours so if your card is munched by the machine, you can go inside for help.

If your debit card doesn't work, try a lower amount—your request may have exceeded your withdrawal limit or the ATM's limit. If you still have a problem, try a different ATM or come back later—your bank's network may be temporarily down.

Avoid "independent" ATMs, such as Travelex, Euronet, Moneybox, Cardpoint, and Cashzone. These have high fees, can be less secure than a bank ATM, and may try to trick users with "dynamic currency conversion" (see below).

Exchanging Cash

Avoid exchanging money in Europe; it's a big rip-off. In a pinch, you can always find exchange desks at major train stations or airports—convenient but with crummy rates. Anything over 5 percent for a transaction is piracy. Banks generally do not exchange money unless you have an account with them.

Using Credit Cards

US cards no longer require a signature for verification, but don't be surprised if a European card reader generates a receipt for you to sign. Some card readers will accept your card as is; others may prompt you to enter your PIN (so it's important to know the code for each of your cards). If a cashier is present, you should have no problems.

At self-service payment machines (transit-ticket kiosks, parking, etc.), results are mixed, as US cards may not work in unattended transactions. If your card won't work, look for a cashier who can process your card manually—or pay in cash.

Drivers Beware: Be aware of potential problems using a US credit card to fill up at an unattended gas station, enter a parking garage, or exit a toll road. Carry cash and be prepared to move on to the next gas station if necessary. When approaching a toll plaza, use the "cash" lane.

Dynamic Currency Conversion

If merchants offer to convert your purchase price into dollars (called dynamic currency conversion, or DCC), refuse this "service." You'll pay extra for the expensive convenience of seeing your charge in dollars. If an ATM offers to "lock in" or "guarantee" your conversion rate, choose "proceed without conversion." Other prompts might state, "You can be charged in dollars: Press YES for dollars, NO for euros." Always choose the local currency.

Security Tips

Pickpockets target tourists. Keep your cash, credit cards, and passport secure in your money belt, and carry only a day's spending money in your front pocket or wallet.

Before inserting your card into an ATM, inspect the front. If anything looks crooked, loose, or damaged, it could be a sign of a card-skimming device. When entering your PIN, carefully block other people's view of the keypad.

Don't use a debit card for purchases. Because a debit card pulls funds directly from your bank account, potential charges incurred by a thief will stay on your account while the fraudulent use is investigated by your bank.

To access your accounts online while traveling, be sure to use a secure connection (see the "Tips on Internet Security" sidebar on page 446).

Damage Control for Lost Cards

If you lose your credit or debit card, report the loss immediately to the respective global customer-assistance centers. Call these 24-hour US numbers collect: Visa (tel. 303/967-1096), MasterCard (tel. 636/722-7111), and American Express (tel. 336/393-1111). In Sicily, to make a collect call to the US, dial 800-172-4444. Press zero or stay on the line for an English-speaking operator. European toll-free numbers can be found at the websites for Visa and MasterCard.

You'll need to provide the primary cardholder's identification-verification details (such as birth date, mother's maiden name, or Social Security number). You can generally receive a temporary card within two or three business days in Europe (see www.ricksteves.com/help for more).

If you report your loss within two days, you typically won't be responsible for unauthorized transactions on your account, although many banks charge a liability fee of $50.

TIPPING

Tipping in Sicily isn't as automatic and generous as it is in the US. For special service, tips are appreciated, but not expected. As in the US, the proper amount depends on your resources, tipping philosophy, and the circumstances, but some general guidelines apply.

Restaurants: In Sicily, a service charge *(servizio)* is sometimes built into your check (look at the bill carefully). If it is included, there's no need to leave an extra tip. If it's not included, it's common to leave about €1 per person (a bit more at finer restaurants) or to round up the bill. For more details on restaurant tipping, see page 424.

Taxis: For a typical ride, round up your fare a bit (for instance, if the fare is €4.50, pay €5). If the cabbie hauls your bags and zips you to the airport to help you catch your flight, you might want to toss in a little more. But if you feel like you're being driven in circles or otherwise ripped off, skip the tip.

Services: In general, if someone in the tourism or service industry does a super job for you, a small tip of a euro or two is appropriate...but not required. If you're not sure whether (or how much) to tip, ask a local for advice.

GETTING A VAT REFUND

Wrapped into the purchase price of your Sicilian souvenirs is a Value-Added Tax (VAT) of about 22 percent. You're entitled to get most of that tax back if you purchase more than €155 (about $185) worth of goods at a store that participates in the VAT-refund scheme. Typically, you must ring up the minimum at a single retailer—you can't add up your purchases from various shops to reach the required amount. (If the store ships the goods to your US home, VAT is not assessed on your purchase.)

Getting your refund is straightforward...and worthwhile if you spend a significant amount on souvenirs.

Get the paperwork. Have the merchant completely fill out the necessary refund document. You'll have to present your passport. Get the paperwork done before you leave the store to ensure you'll have everything you need (including your original sales receipt).

Get your stamp at the border or airport. Process your VAT document at your last stop in the European Union (such as at the airport) with the customs agent who deals with VAT refunds. Arrive an additional hour before you need to check in to allow time to find the customs office—and wait. Some customs desks are positioned before airport security; confirm the location before going through security.

It's best to keep your purchases in your carry-on. If your item isn't allowed as carry-on (such as a knife), pack it in your checked bag and alert the check-in agent. You'll be sent (with your tagged bag) to a customs desk outside security; someone will examine your bag, stamp your paperwork, and put your bag on the belt. You're not supposed to use your purchased goods before you leave. If you show up at customs wearing your new Italian leather shoes, officials might look the other way—or deny you a refund.

Collect your refund. You can claim your VAT refund from refund companies, such as Global Blue or Premier Tax Free, with offices at major airports, ports, or border crossings (either before or after security, probably strategically located near a duty-free shop). These services (which extract a 4 percent fee) can refund your money in cash immediately or credit your card (within two billing cycles). Otherwise, mail the stamped refund documents to the address given by the shop where you made your purchase.

CUSTOMS FOR AMERICAN SHOPPERS

You can take home $800 worth of items per person duty-free, once every 31 days. Many processed and packaged foods are allowed, including vacuum-packed cheeses, dried herbs, jams, baked goods, candy, chocolate, oil, vinegar, mustard, and honey. Fresh fruits and vegetables and most meats are not allowed, with exceptions for some canned items. As for alcohol, you can bring in one liter duty-free (it can be packed securely in your checked luggage, along with any other liquid-containing items).

To bring alcohol (or liquid-packed foods) in your carry-on bag on your flight home, buy it at a duty-free shop at the airport. You'll increase your odds of getting it onto a connecting flight if it's packaged in a "STEB"—a secure, tamper-evident bag. But stay away from liquids in opaque, ceramic, or metallic containers, which usually cannot be successfully screened (STEB or no STEB).

For details on allowable goods, customs rules, and duty rates, visit http://help.cbp.gov.

Sightseeing

Sightseeing can be hard work. Use these tips to make your visits to Sicily's finest sights meaningful, fun, efficient, and painless.

MAPS AND NAVIGATION TOOLS

A good map is essential for efficient navigation while sightseeing. The maps in this book are concise and simple, designed to help you locate recommended destinations, sights, and local TIs, where you can pick up more in-depth maps.

You can also use a mapping app on your mobile device. Be aware that pulling up maps or looking up turn-by-turn walking directions on the fly usually requires a data connection: To use this feature, it's smart to get an international data plan. With Google Maps or City Maps 2Go, it's possible to download a map while online, then go offline and navigate without incurring data-roaming charges, though you can't search for an address or get real-time walking directions. A handful of other apps—including Apple Maps, OffMaps, and Navfree—also allow you to use maps offline.

PRACTICALITIES

PLAN AHEAD

Set up an itinerary that allows you to fit in all your must-see sights. For a one-stop look at opening hours, see the "At a Glance" sidebars for Palermo and Siracusa.

Note that hours in Sicily can be unpredictable. I've listed the official opening times, but these can change with the whim of the ticket taker. Hours listed online may be no closer to reality than the ones listed in this book. The only way to be sure of a sight's opening hours is to check locally. Call or drop by and ask: *Aperto oggi?* (ah-PER-toh OH-jee; Are you open today?) and *A che ora chiude?* (ah kay OH-rah kee-OO-day; What time do you close?).

While you won't find the crowds typical in Italy's big, mainland cities, a few of Sicily's major sights—such as Villa Romana del Casale, Taormina's Greek-Roman theater, and the Palatine Chapel in Palermo's Norman Palace—can be very busy at peak times, especially when a cruise ship is in town. Going first thing in the morning or at the end of the day usually makes for a smoother visit. Evening visits (when possible) are usually peaceful, with fewer crowds.

Don't put off visiting a must-see sight—you never know when a place will close unexpectedly for a holiday, strike, or restoration. Many museums are closed or have reduced hours at least a few days a year, especially on holidays such as Christmas, New Year's *(Capodanno),* Italian Liberation Day (April 25), and Labor Day (May 1). During the Feast of the Assumption, a.k.a. Ferragosto (Aug 15), beach destinations are flooded by vacationing Italians. Cities empty out for much of the month of August, and while tourist attractions remain open, shops and restaurants are often closed until September. A list of holidays is in the appendix; check for possible museum closures during your trip. In the off-season (Nov-Easter), most Sicilian sights have limited hours and may be open only in the mornings.

If you plan to hire a local guide, reserve ahead by email. Popular guides can get booked up.

Study up. To get the most out of the self-guided tours and sight descriptions in this book, read them before you visit.

AT SIGHTS

Here's what you can typically expect:

Entering: Be warned that you may not be allowed to enter if you arrive less than 30 to 60 minutes before closing time. And guards start ushering people out well before the actual closing time, so don't save the best for last.

Many sights have a security check. Allow extra time for these lines. Some sights require you to check daypacks and coats. (If you'd rather not check your daypack, try carrying it tucked under your arm like a purse as you enter.)

Photography: If the museum's photo policy isn't clearly posted, ask a guard. Generally, taking photos without a flash or tripod is allowed. Some sights ban selfie sticks; others ban photos altogether.

Temporary Exhibits: Museums may show special exhibits in addition to their permanent collection. Some exhibits are included in the entry price, while others come at an extra cost (which you may have to pay even if you don't want to see the exhibit).

Expect Changes: Artwork can be on tour, on loan, out sick, or shifted at the whim of the curator. Pick up a floor plan as you enter, and ask the museum staff if you can't find a particular item. Say the title or artist's name, or point to the photograph in this book and ask, *Dov'è?* (doh-VEH, meaning Where is?).

Audioguides and Apps: Many sights rent audioguides, with recorded descriptions in English. Many audioguides have a standard output jack, so if you bring your own earbuds, you can often enjoy better sound. To save money, bring a Y-jack and share one audioguide with your travel partner. Museums and sights often offer free apps that you can download to your mobile device (check their websites).

Services: Important sights usually have a reasonably priced on-site café or cafeteria (handy places to rejuvenate during a long visit). The WCs at sights are free and generally clean.

Before Leaving: At the gift shop, scan the postcard rack or thumb through a guidebook to be sure that you haven't overlooked something that you'd like to see. Every sight or museum offers more than what is covered in this book. Use the information in this book as an introduction—not the final word.

FIND RELIGION

Churches offer some amazing art (usually free), a cool respite from heat, and a welcome seat.

A modest dress code—no bare shoulders or shorts for anyone, even kids—is enforced at a handful of major churches, such as the cathedrals in Siracusa and Monreale, but is typically overlooked elsewhere. However, Sicily is more conservative than mainland Italy, and it's best to err on the side of respectful dress at religious sites. If you're caught by surprise, you can improvise, using maps to cover your shoulders and a jacket for your knees. A few major churches let you borrow or buy disposable ponchos to cover up in a pinch. (I wear a super-lightweight pair of long pants rather than shorts for my hot and muggy Italian sightseeing.)

Some churches have coin-operated audioboxes that describe the art and history; just set the dial on English, put in your coins, and listen. Coin boxes near a piece of art illuminate the art (and present a better photo opportunity). I pop in a coin whenever I can. It improves my experience, is a favor to other visitors trying to appreciate a great piece of art in the dark, and is a little contribution to that church and its work. Whenever possible, let there be light.

Sleeping

Extensive and opinionated listings of good-value rooms are a major feature of this book's Sleeping sections. Rather than list accommodations scattered throughout a town, I choose hotels in my favorite neighborhoods that are convenient to your sightseeing.

My recommendations run the gamut, from dorm beds to fancy rooms with all of the comforts. To stay in the countryside, try *agriturismo* farmhouses—I've listed several. I like places that are clean, central, relatively quiet at night, reasonably priced, friendly, small enough to have a hands-on owner or manager, and run with a respect for Italian traditions. I'm more impressed by a handy location and a fun-loving philosophy than flat-screen TVs and a fancy gym. Most of my recommendations fall short of perfection. But if I can find a place with most of these features, it's a keeper.

Book your accommodations as soon as your itinerary is set, especially if you want to stay at one of my top listings or if you'll be traveling during busy times. See the appendix for a list of major holidays and festivals in Sicily.

Some people make reservations as they travel, calling ahead a few days to a week before their arrival. It's best to call hotels at about 9:00 or 10:00, when the receptionist knows which rooms will be available. Some apps—such as HotelTonight—specialize in last-minute rooms, often at business-class hotels in big cities. If you encounter a language barrier, ask the fluent receptionist at your current hotel to call for you.

RATES AND DEALS

I've categorized my recommended accommodations based on price, indicated with a dollar-sign rating (see sidebar). The price ranges suggest an estimated cost for a one-night stay in high season in a standard double room with a private toilet and shower, including breakfast, and assume you're booking directly with the hotel (not through a booking site, which extracts a commission). Room prices can fluctuate significantly with demand and amenities (size, views, room class, and so on), but relative price categories remain constant.

Room rates are especially volatile at larger hotels that use "dynamic pricing" to set rates. Prices can skyrocket during festivals and conventions, while business hotels can have deep discounts on

Sleep Code

Hotels are classified based on the average price of a standard double room with breakfast in high season.

$$$$	**Splurge:** Most rooms over €170
$$$	**Pricier:** €130-170
$$	**Moderate:** €90-130
$	**Budget:** €50-90
¢	**Backpacker:** Under €50
RS%	**Rick Steves discount**

Unless otherwise noted, credit cards are accepted, hotel staff speak basic English, and free Wi-Fi is available. Comparison-shop by checking prices at several hotels (on each hotel's own website, on a booking site, or by email). For the best deal, *book directly with the hotel.*

weekends when demand plummets. Of the many hotels I recommend, it's difficult to say which will be the best value on a given day—until you do your homework. Taxes, which can vary from place to place, are generally insignificant (a dollar or two per person, per night).

Booking Direct: Once your dates are set, compare prices at several hotels. You can do this by checking Hotels.com, Booking.com, and hotel websites. To get the best deal, contact family-run hotels directly by phone or email. When you go direct, the owner avoids the commission paid to booking sites, thereby leaving enough wiggle room to offer you a discount, a nicer room, or a free breakfast (if it's not already included). If you prefer to book online or are considering a hotel chain, it's to your advantage to use the hotel's website.

Getting a Discount: Some hotels extend a discount to those who pay cash or stay longer than three nights. And some accommodations offer a special discount for Rick Steves readers, indicated in this guidebook by the abbreviation **"RS%."** Discounts vary: Ask for details when you reserve. Generally, to qualify for this discount, you must book direct (not through a booking site), mention this book when you reserve, show this book upon arrival, and sometimes pay cash or stay a certain number of nights. In some cases, you may need to enter a discount code (which I've provided in the listing) in the booking form on the hotel's website. Rick Steves discounts apply to readers with either print or digital books. Understandably, discounts do not apply to promotional rates.

It's common for hotels in Sicily to cut their rates by 10-50 percent in the off-season (roughly Nov-mid-March), although prices at hostels and cheaper hotels won't fluctuate much. Haggle if you

Using Online Services to Your Advantage

From booking services to user reviews, online businesses play a greater role in travelers' planning than ever before. Take advantage of their benefits—and be wise to their drawbacks.

Booking Sites

Hotel booking websites, including Priceline's Booking.com and Expedia's Hotels.com, offer one-stop shopping for hotels. While convenient for travelers, they present a real problem for small, independent, family-run hotels. Without a presence on these sites, these hotels become almost invisible. But to be listed, a hotel must pay a sizeable commission...and promise that its own website won't undercut the price on the booking-service site.

Here's the work-around: Use the big sites to research what's out there, then book directly with the hotel by email or phone, in which case hotel owners are free to give you whatever price they like. Ask for a room without the commission markup (or ask for a free breakfast if not included, or a free upgrade). If you do book online, be sure to use the hotel's website. The price will likely be the same as via a booking site, but your money goes to the hotel, not agency commissions.

As a savvy consumer, remember: When you book with an online booking service, you're adding a middleman who takes roughly 20 percent. To support small, family-run hotels whose world is more difficult than ever, book direct.

Short-Term Rental Sites

Rental juggernaut Airbnb (along with other short-term rental sites) allows travelers to rent rooms and apartments directly from locals, often providing more value than a cookie-cutter hotel. Airbnb fans appreciate feeling part of a real neighborhood and getting into a daily routine as "temporary Europeans." Depending on the host, Airbnb can provide an opportunity to get to know a

arrive late in the day during off-season. In sweltering August, room rates are low in the cities but at their highest in beach destinations.

TYPES OF ACCOMMODATIONS
Hotels

Double rooms listed in this book range from about €50 (very simple, toilet and shower down the hall) to €450 (maximum plumbing and more), with most clustered around €120 (with private bathrooms). Prices are higher in big or heavily touristed cities, and lower off the beaten path. Traveling alone can be expensive: A *camera singola* is often only 25 percent less than a *camera doppia*.

Some hotels can add an extra bed (for a small charge) to turn a double into a triple; some offer larger rooms for four or more people local person, while keeping the money spent on your accommodations in the community.

Critics view Airbnb as a threat to "traditional Europe," saying it creates unfair, unqualified competition for established guesthouse owners. In some places, the lucrative Airbnb market has forced traditional guesthouses out of business and is driving property values out of range for locals. Some cities have cracked down, requiring owners to occupy rental properties part of the year (and staging disruptive "inspections" that inconvenience guests).

As a lover of Europe, I share the worry of those who see residents nudged aside by tourists. But as an advocate for travelers, I appreciate the value and cultural intimacy Airbnb provides.

User Reviews

User-generated review sites and apps such as Yelp and TripAdvisor can give you a consensus of opinions about everything from hotels and restaurants to sights and nightlife. If you scan reviews of a restaurant or hotel and see several complaints about noise or a rotten location, you've gained insight that can help in your decision-making.

But as a guidebook writer, my sense is that there is a big difference between the uncurated information on a review site and the vetted listings in a guidebook. A user-generated review is based on the limited experience of one person, who stayed at just one hotel in a given city and ate at a few restaurants there. A guidebook is the work of a trained researcher who forms a well-developed basis for comparison by visiting many restaurants and hotels year after year.

Both types of information have their place, and in many ways, they're complementary. If something is well reviewed in a guidebook and it also gets good online reviews, it's likely a winner.

PRACTICALITIES

(I call these "family rooms" in the listings). If there's space for an extra cot, they'll cram it in for you. In general, a triple room is cheaper than the cost of a double and a single. Three or four people can economize by requesting one big room.

Arrival and Check-In: Hotels and B&Bs are sometimes located on the higher floors of a multipurpose building with a secured door. In that case, look for your hotel's name on the buttons by the main entrance. When you ring the bell, you'll be buzzed in.

Hotel elevators are becoming more common, though some older buildings still lack them. You may have to climb a flight of stairs to reach the elevator (if so, you can ask the front desk for help carrying your bags up). Elevators are typically very small—pack light, or you may need to send your bags up without you.

Making Hotel Reservations

Reserve your rooms as soon as you've pinned down your travel dates. For busy national holidays, it's wise to reserve far in advance (see page 471).

Requesting a Reservation: For family-run hotels, it's generally cheaper to book your room directly via email or a phone call. For business-class hotels, or if you'd rather book online, reserve directly through the hotel's official website (not a booking website). For complicated requests, send an email. Almost all of my recommended hotels take reservations in English.

Here's what the hotelier wants to know:
- Type(s) of rooms you want and size of your party
- Number of nights you'll stay
- Your arrival and departure dates, written European-style as day/month/year (for example, 18/06/20 or 18 June 2020);
- Special requests (en suite bathroom, cheapest room, twin beds vs. double bed, quiet room)
- Applicable discounts (such as a Rick Steves reader discount, cash discount, or promotional rate)

Confirming a Reservation: Most places will request a credit-card number to hold your room. If you're using an online reservation form, look for the *https* or a lock icon at the top of your browser. If you book direct, you can email, call, or fax this information.

Canceling a Reservation: If you must cancel, it's courteous—and smart—to do so with as much notice as possible, especially for smaller family-run places. Cancellation policies can be strict; read

The EU requires that hotels collect your name, nationality, and ID number. When you check in, the receptionist will normally ask for your passport and may keep it for anywhere from a couple of minutes to a couple of hours. (If not comfortable leaving your passport at the desk for a long time, ask when you can pick it up.)

If you're arriving in the morning, your room probably won't be ready. Check your bag safely at the hotel and dive right into sightseeing.

In Your Room: Most hotel rooms have a TV, telephone, and free Wi-Fi (although in old buildings with thick walls, the Wi-Fi signal might be available only in the lobby). Simpler places rarely have a room phone. Pricier hotels usually come with a small fridge stocked with beverages, called a *frigo bar* (FREE-goh bar; pay for what you use).

More pillows and blankets are usually in the closet or available on request. Towels and linens aren't always replaced every day. Some hotels use lightweight "waffle," or very thin, tablecloth-type towels; these take less water and electricity to launder and are preferred by many Italians.

From: rick@ricksteves.com
Sent: Today
To: info@hotelcentral.com
Subject: Reservation request for 19-22 July

Dear Hotel Central,

I would like to stay at your hotel. Please let me know if you have a room available and the price for:
• 2 people
• Double bed and en suite bathroom in a quiet room
• Arriving 19 July, departing 22 July (3 nights)

Thank you!
Rick Steves

the fine print before you book. Many discount deals require pre-payment, with no cancellation refunds.

Reconfirming a Reservation: Always call or email to reconfirm your room reservation a few days in advance. For B&Bs or very small hotels, I call again on my day of arrival to tell my host what time to expect me (especially important if arriving late—after 17:00).

Phoning: For tips on calling hotels overseas, see page 444.

PRACTICALITIES

Nearly all places offer private bathrooms, which have a tub or shower, a toilet, and a bidet (which Italians use for quick sponge baths). The cord over the tub or shower is not a clothesline. You pull it when you've fallen and can't get up.

Double beds are called *matrimoniale*, even though hotels aren't interested in your marital status. Twins are *due letti singoli*. Convents offer cheap accommodation but have more *letti singoli* than *matrimoniali*.

Breakfast and Meals: Italian hotels typically include breakfast in their room prices. If breakfast is optional, you may want to skip it. While convenient, it's usually pricey for what you get: a simple continental buffet with (at its most generous) bread, croissants, ham, cheese, yogurt, and unlimited *caffè latte*. A picnic in your room followed by a coffee at the corner café can be much cheaper.

Hotels in resort areas may charge you for half-pension, called *mezza pensione*, during peak season. Half-pension means that you pay for one meal per day per person (lunch or dinner). If half-pension is required, you can't opt out and pay less. If it's an option, it can be worth considering, especially if they charge less per meal than you've been paying for an average restaurant meal (and provided the chef is good).

Checking Out: While it's customary to pay for your room upon departure, it can be a good idea to settle your bill the day before, when you're not in a hurry and while the manager's in.

Hotelier Help: Hoteliers can be a good source of advice. Most know their city well, and can assist you with everything from public transit and airport connections to finding a good restaurant, the nearest launderette, or a late-night pharmacy.

Hotel Hassles: Even at the best places, mechanical breakdowns occur: Sinks leak, hot water turns cold, toilets may gurgle or smell, the Wi-Fi goes out, or the air-conditioning dies when you need it most. Report your concerns clearly and calmly at the front desk.

If you find that night noise is a problem (if, for instance, your room is over a nightclub or facing a busy street), ask for a quieter room in the back or on an upper floor. To guard against theft in your room, keep valuables out of sight. Some rooms come with a safe, and other hotels have safes at the front desk. I've never bothered using one and, in a lifetime of travel, I've never had anything stolen out of my room.

For more complicated problems, don't expect instant results. Above all, keep a positive attitude. Remember, you're on vacation. If your hotel is a disappointment, spend more time out enjoying the place you came to see.

Bed-and-Breakfasts

B&Bs can offer good-value accommodations in excellent locations. Usually converted family homes or apartments, they can range from humble rooms with communal kitchens to high-end boutique accommodations with extra amenities. Boutique B&Bs can be an especially good option, as they are typically less expensive than a big hotel, but often newer and nicer, with more personal service. Because the B&B scene is constantly changing, it's smart to supplement this book's recommendations with your own research.

Be aware that B&Bs can suffer from absentee management. The proprietors often live off-site (or even in another town) and may be around only when they are expecting guests. Clearly communicate your arrival time, and after checking in, be sure you have your host's telephone number in case you need to reach them.

Short-Term Rentals

A short-term rental—whether an apartment, house, or room in a local's home—is an increasingly popular alternative, especially if you plan to settle in one location for several nights. For stays longer than a few days, you can usually find a rental that's comparable

Keep Cool

If you're visiting Italy in the summer, you'll want an air-conditioned room. Most hotel air-conditioners come with a control stick (like a TV remote; the hotel may require a deposit) that generally has similar symbols and features: fan icon (click to toggle through wind power, from light to gale); louver icon (choose steady airflow or waves); snowflake and sunshine icons (cold air or heat); clock ("O" setting: run X hours before turning off; "I" setting: wait X hours to start); and the temperature control (20 degrees Celsius is comfortable). When you leave your room for the day, turning off the air-conditioning is good form.

to—and even cheaper than—a hotel room with similar amenities. Plus, you'll get a behind-the-scenes peek into how locals live.

Many places require a minimum-night stay and have strict cancellation policies. And you're generally on your own: There's no hotel reception desk, breakfast, or daily cleaning service.

Finding Accommodations: Aggregator websites such as Airbnb, Booking.com, and the HomeAway family of sites (HomeAway, VRBO, and VacationRentals) let you browse properties and correspond directly with European property owners or managers. If you prefer to work from a curated list of accommodations, consider using a rental agency such as InterhomeUSA.com or RentaVilla.com. Agency-represented apartments typically cost more, but this method often offers more help and safeguards than booking direct.

Before you commit, be clear on the location. I like to virtually "explore" the neighborhood using the Street View feature on Google Maps. Also consider the proximity to public transportation, and how well-connected the property is with the rest of the city. Ask about amenities (elevator, air-conditioning, laundry, Wi-Fi, parking, etc.). Reviews from previous guests can help identify trouble spots.

Think about the kind of experience you want: Just a key and an affordable bed...or a chance to get to know a local? There are typically two kinds of hosts: those who want minimal interaction with their guests, and hosts who are friendly and may want to interact with you. Read the promotional text and online reviews to help shape your decision.

Confirming and Paying: Many places require you to pay the entire balance before your trip. It's easiest and safest to pay through the site where you found the listing. Be wary of owners who want to take your transaction offline; this gives you no recourse if things

PRACTICALITIES

go awry. Never agree to wire money (a key indicator of a fraudulent transaction).

Apartments or Houses: If you're staying in one place for four or more nights, it's worth considering an apartment or rental house (shorter stays aren't worth the hassle of arranging key pickup, buying groceries, etc.). Apartment and house rentals can be especially cost-effective for groups and families. European apartments, like hotel rooms, tend to be small by US standards. But they often come with laundry machines and small, equipped kitchens *(cucinetta)*, making it easier and cheaper to dine in.

Rooms in Private Homes: In small towns, there may be few hotels or apartments, but an abundance of Airbnb rentals and some *affittacamere* (rental rooms). These can be anything from a set of keys and a basic bed to a cozy B&B with your own Sicilian grandmother. Renting a room in someone's home is a good option for those traveling alone, as you're more likely to find true single rooms—with just one single bed, and a price to match. Beds range from air-mattress-in-living-room basic to plush-B&B-suite posh. Some places allow you to book for a single night. While you can't expect your host to also be your tour guide—or even to provide you with much info—some may be interested in getting to know the travelers who come through their home.

Other Options: Swapping homes with a local works for people with an appealing place to offer (don't assume where you live is not interesting to Europeans). A good place to start is HomeExchange. To sleep for free, Couchsurfing.com is a vagabond's alternative to Airbnb. It lists millions of outgoing members, who host fellow "surfers" in their homes.

Agriturismi

Agriturismi—working farms that double as countryside B&Bs—began cropping up in the 1980s to allow Italy's small family farms

to survive (as in the US, many have been squeezed out by giant agribusinesses). By renting rooms to travelers, farmers receive generous tax breaks that allow them to remain on their land and continue to grow food crops. These B&Bs make a peaceful home base for those exploring rural Sicily, and are ideal for those traveling by car—especially families.

It's wise to book several months in advance for high season (late May-mid-Oct). July and August are jammed with Italians and other European vacationers; in spring and fall, it's mostly Americans. Weeklong stays (typically Saturday to Saturday) are preferred at busy times, but shorter stays are possible off-season. To sleep cheaper, try early spring and late fall. Most places are closed in winter (about Nov-Easter).

As the name implies, *agriturismi* are in the countryside, although some are located on the outskirts of a large town or city. Most are family-run. *Agriturismi* vary dramatically in quality—some properties are rustic, while others are downright luxurious, offering amenities such as swimming pools and riding stables. The rooms are usually clean and comfortable. Breakfast is often included, and *mezza pensione* (half-pension, which in this case means a home-cooked dinner) might be built into the price whether you want it or not. Most places serve tasty homegrown food; some are vegetarian or organic, others are gourmet. Kitchenettes are often available to cook up your own feast.

To qualify officially as an *agriturismo,* the farm must still generate more money from its farm activities, thereby ensuring that the land is worked and preserved. Some farmhouse B&Bs aren't working farms, but are still fine places to stay. Some travelers who are enticed by romanticized dreams of *agriturismi* are turned off when they arrive to actual farm smells and sounds. These folks would be more comfortable with a countryside B&B or villa that offers a bit more upscale comfort. In this book, I've listed both types of rural accommodations; if you want the real thing, make sure the owners call their place an *agriturismo.*

In addition to my listings, local TIs can give you a list of places in their area. For a sampling, visit www.agriturismoitaly.it or search online for *agriturismo.*

Hostels

A hostel provides cheap beds in dorms where you sleep alongside strangers for about €25-30 per night. Travelers of any age are welcome if they don't mind dorm-style accommodations and meeting other travelers. Most hostels offer kitchen facilities, guest computers, Wi-Fi, and a self-service laundry. Hostels almost always provide bedding, but the towel's up to you (though you can usually rent one for a small fee). Family and private rooms are often available.

Independent hostels tend to be easygoing, colorful, and informal (no membership required; www.hostelworld.com). You may pay slightly less by booking directly with the hostel. **Official hostels** are part of Hostelling International (HI) and share a booking site (www.hihostels.com). HI hostels typically require that you be a member or else pay a bit more per night.

Eating

Italians are masters of the art of fine living. That means eating long and well. Lengthy, multicourse meals and endless hours sitting in outdoor cafés are the norm. Americans eat on their way to an evening event and complain if the check is slow in coming. For Italians, the meal is an end in itself, and only rude waiters rush you.

A highlight of your Sicilian adventure will be the island's cafés, cuisine, and wines. Trust me: This is sightseeing for your palate. Even if you liked dorm food and are sleeping in cheap hotels, your taste buds will relish an occasional first-class splurge. You can eat well without going broke. But be careful: You're just as likely to blow a small fortune on a disappointing meal as you are to dine wonderfully for €25. Rely on my recommendations in the various Eating sections throughout this book.

In general, Italians eat meals a bit later than we do. At 7:00 or 8:00, they have a light breakfast (coffee—usually cappuccino or espresso—and a pastry, often standing up at a café). Lunch (between 13:00 and 15:00) is traditionally the largest meal of the day. Then they eat a late, light dinner (around 20:00-21:30, or maybe earlier in winter). To bridge the gap, people drop into a bar in the late afternoon for a *spuntino* (snack) and aperitif.

RESTAURANT PRICING

I've categorized my recommended eateries based on the average price of a typical main course, indicated with a dollar-sign rating (see sidebar). Obviously, expensive specialties, fine wine, appetizers, and dessert can significantly increase your final bill.

The categories also indicate the personality of a place: **Budget** eateries include street food, takeaway, order-at-the-counter shops, basic cafeterias, and bakeries selling sandwiches. **Moderate** eateries are nice (but not fancy) sit-down restaurants, ideal for a straightforward, fill-the-tank meal. Most of my listings fall in this category—great for a good taste of local cuisine at a reasonable price.

Pricier eateries are a notch up, with more attention paid to the setting, presentation, and (often inventive) cuisine. **Splurge** eateries are dress-up-for-a-special-occasion swanky—typically with an elegant setting, polished service, pricey and intricate cuisine, and an expansive (and expensive) wine list.

BREAKFAST

Italian breakfasts, like Italian bath towels, are small: The basic, traditional version is coffee and a roll with butter and marmalade. In Sicily, pastries dominate the breakfast table, with sweet cakes and cookies in abundance. Many places have yogurt and juice (the deli-

Restaurant Code

Eateries in this book are categorized according to the average cost of a typical main course. Drinks, desserts, and splurge items can raise the price considerably.

$$$$ **Splurge:** Most main courses over €20
$$$ **Pricier:** €15-20
$$ **Moderate:** €10-15
$ **Budget:** Under €10

Pizza by the slice and other takeaway food is **$;** a basic trattoria or sit-down pizzeria is **$$;** a casual but more upscale restaurant is **$$$;** and a swanky splurge is **$$$$.**

cious red orange juice—*spremuta d'arancia rossa*—is made from Sicilian blood oranges), and possibly also cereal, cold cuts and sliced cheese, and eggs (typically hard-boiled; scrambled or fried eggs are less common). Small budget hotels may leave a basic breakfast in your room (stale croissant, roll, jam, yogurt, coffee).

If you want to skip your hotel breakfast, consider browsing for a morning picnic at a local open-air market. Or do as the Italians do: Stop into a bar or café to drink a cappuccino and munch a *cornetto* (croissant) while standing at the bar. While the *cornetto* is the most common pastry, you'll find a range of *pasticcini* (pastries, sometimes called *dolci*—sweets). Look for *treccina* (an 8-shaped pastry, often filled with custard, jam, or chocolate), *sfoglia* (filodough crust that's fruit-filled, like a turnover), or *ciambella* (doughnut filled with custard or chocolate)—or ask about local specialties.

In the hot summer months, many Sicilians opt for *granita* at breakfast time. This frozen slush, made with blended fruit or milk, comes in flavors like coffee, almond, or lemon, and can be topped with whipped cream. To make your order authentic, ask for a warm brioche to dip into your *granita* (or use it as a scoop).

ITALIAN RESTAURANTS

While *ristorante* is self-explanatory, you'll also see other types of Italian eateries. A trattoria and an *osteria* (which can be more casual) are both generally family-owned places serving home-cooked meals, often at moderate prices. A *locanda* is an inn, a *cantina* is a wine cellar, and a *birreria* is a brewpub. *Pizzerie, ros-*

ticcerie (delis), *tavola calda* ("hot table") bars, *enoteche* (wine bars), and other alternatives are explained later.

I look for restaurants that are convenient to your hotel and sightseeing. When restaurant-hunting, choose a spot filled with locals, not the place with the big neon signs boasting, "We speak English and accept credit cards." Restaurants parked on famous squares generally serve bad food at high prices to tourists. Venturing even a block or two off the main drag leads to higher-quality food for less than half the price of the tourist-oriented places. Locals eat better at lower-rent locales. Family-run places operate without hired help and can offer cheaper meals.

Most restaurant kitchens close between their lunch and dinner service. Good restaurants don't reopen for dinner before 19:00. If you arrive at opening time, most restaurants will be empty and available—the main push of customers arrives later. Small restaurants with a full slate of reservations for 20:30 or 21:00 often will accommodate walk-in diners willing to eat a quick, early meal, but you aren't expected to linger.

When you want the bill, mime-scribble on your raised palm or request it: *"Il conto, per favore."* You may have to ask more than once. If you're in a hurry, request the check when you receive the last item you order.

Cover and Tipping

Avoid surprises when eating out by familiarizing yourself with two common Italian restaurant charges: *coperto* and *servizio*. You won't encounter them in all restaurants, but both charges, if assessed, by law must be listed on the menu.

The *coperto* (cover), sometimes called *pane e coperto* (bread and cover), is a minor fee (€1.50-3/person) covering the cost of the typical basket of bread, oil, salt, cutlery, and linens found on your table. It's not negotiable, even if you don't eat the bread. And it's not a tip (it goes to the owner)—think of it as entitling you to use the table for as long as you like.

The *servizio* (a 10- to 15-percent service charge) is similar to the mandatory gratuity that American restaurants often add for groups of six or more. You can consider it a "tourist tax," as you're most likely to encounter it in locations with lots of tourists. Because the service charge is sometimes built into your bill, look carefully at your check to see if you've already paid a tip—don't leave any tip beyond this.

If there is no *servizio* on the bill, a common tip at a simple restaurant or pizzeria is €1 per person at the table (or simply round up the bill). At a finer restaurant, leave a few euros per person. Don't leave the tip on the table; hand it directly to the server to make sure he or she receives it. Be prepared to tip with cash/coins, as credit/debit card receipts won't have a tip line as in the US.

Courses

A full Italian meal consists of multiple courses (all described below). For most travelers, it's simply too much food—and the euros can add up in a hurry. To avoid overeating (and to stretch your budget), share dishes. A good rule of thumb is for each person to order any two courses. For example, a couple can order and share one antipasto, one *primo,* one *secondo,* and one dessert; or two *antipasti* and two *primi;* or whatever combination appeals.

Small groups can mix *antipasti* and *primi* family-style (skipping *secondi*). If you do this right, you can eat well in better places for less than the cost of a tourist *menù* in a cheap place.

Some touristy restaurants serve a *piatto unico,* with smaller portions of each course on one dish (for instance, a meat, starch, and vegetable).

Antipasto: An appetizer such as bruschetta, grilled veggies, deep-fried tasties, thin-sliced meat (prosciutto or carpaccio), or a plate of olives, cold cuts, and cheeses. To get a sampler plate of cold cuts and cheeses in a restaurant, ask for *affettato misto* (mixed cold cuts), *antipasto misto* (cold cuts, cheeses, and marinated vegetables), or *tagliere* (a sampler "board"). This could make a light meal in itself.

Primo piatto: A "first dish" generally consisting of pasta but also rice or soup. If you think of pasta when you think of Italian food, you can dine well here without ever going beyond the *primo.*

Secondo piatto: A "second dish," equivalent to our main course, of meat or fish/seafood. Italians freely admit the *secondo* is the least interesting part of their cuisine.

Contorno: A vegetable side dish may come with the *secondo* but more often must be ordered separately. Typical *contorni* are *insalata mista,* spinach, roasted potatoes, or grilled veggies. This can be an interesting, if overlooked, part of the menu. Vegetarians can skip the *secondo* and order several *contorni* to make a meal.

Dolce: No meal is complete without a sweet. On most menus you'll find typical Italian desserts such as tiramisu and *panna cotta* as well as local favorites. For a rundown of Sicily's dessert specialties, see page 7.

Ordering Tips

Seafood and steak may be sold by weight and priced by the *etto* (100 grams, 3.5 ounces) or the kilo (1,000 grams, 2.2 pounds). The abbreviation *s.q. (secondo quantità)* indicates an item is priced by weight (often used at antipasto buffets). Unless the menu indicates a fillet *(filetto),* fish is usually served whole with the head and tail.

However, you can always ask your server to select a small fish and fillet it for you. Sometimes, especially for steak, restaurants require a minimum order of four or five *etti* (which diners can share). Make sure you're clear on the price before ordering.

Some special dishes come in larger quantities meant to be shared by two people. The shorthand way of showing this on a menu is "X2" (for two), but the price listed could indicate the cost per person.

In a traditional restaurant, if you order a pasta dish and a side salad—but no main course—the server will bring the salad after the pasta (Italians prefer it this way, believing that it enhances digestion). If you want the salad with your pasta, specify *insieme* (een-see-eh-may; together).

Because pasta and bread are both starches, Italians consider them redundant. If you order only a pasta dish, bread may not come with it; you can request it, but you may be charged extra. On the other hand, if you order a vegetable antipasto or a meat *secondo*, bread is often provided to balance the ingredients.

At places with counter service—such as at a bar or a freeway rest-stop diner—you'll order and pay at the *cassa* (cashier). Take your receipt to the counter to claim your food.

Fixed-Price Meals and Ordering à la Carte

You can save by getting a fixed-priced meal, which is frequently exempt from cover and service charges. Avoid the cheapest ones (often called a *menù turistico*). Look instead for a genuine *menù del giorno* (menu of the day), which offers diners a choice of appetizer, main course, and dessert. It's worth paying a little more for an inventive fixed-price meal that shows off the chef's creativity.

While fixed-price meals can be easy and convenient, galloping gourmets prefer to order à la carte with the help of a menu translator. When going to an especially good restaurant with an approachable staff, I like to find out what they're eager to serve. Sometimes I'll simply say, *"Mi faccia felice"* (Make me happy) and set a price limit.

BUDGET EATING

Italy offers many budget options for hungry travelers. Self-service cafeterias offer the basics without add-on charges. Travelers on a hard-core budget equip their room with a pantry stocked at the market (fruits and veggies are remarkably cheap), or pick up a sandwich or *döner kebab*, then dine in at picnic prices. Bars and cafés are

PRACTICALITIES

also good places to grab a meal on the go. In Sicily, cheap and tasty street food can be found in almost every city, either at the markets or in any bar.

Pizzerias

Pizza is cheap and readily available. Stop by a pizza shop for stand-up or takeout (many pizza places sell whole pies meant for one person; *pizza al taglio* means

"by the slice"). Supermarkets usually have a pizza counter too.

Some shops feature *pizza rustica*—thick pizza baked in a large rectangular pan and sold by weight. If you simply ask for a piece, you may wind up with a gigantic slab and be charged top euro. Instead, clearly indicate how much you want: 100 grams, or *un etto*, is a hot and cheap snack; 200 grams, or *due etti*, makes a light meal. Or show the size with your hands—*tanto così* (TAHN-toh koh-ZEE; this much). They'll often helpfully cut it up into smaller pieces. If you want your pizza warm, say *"sì"* when they ask if you want it heated up (*riscaldare;* ree-skahl-DAH-ray). For a rundown of common types of pizza, see that section, later.

Bars/Cafés

Italian "bars" are not taverns, but inexpensive cafés. These neighborhood hangouts serve coffee, mini pizzas *(pizzette)*, sandwiches, and drinks from the cooler. This budget choice is the Italian equivalent of English pub grub.

Many bars are small—if you can't find a table, you'll need to stand or find a ledge to sit on outside. Most charge extra for table service. To get food to go, say, *"da portar via"* (for the road). All bars have a WC *(toilette, bagno)* in the back, and customers—and the discreet public—can use it.

Food: For quick meals, bars usually have trays of cheap, pre-made sandwiches (*panini,* on a baguette; *piadini,* on flatbread; or *tramezzini,* on crustless white bread)—some are delightful grilled. (Others have too much mayo.) In bigger cities, they'll have a variety of salads ready to serve up from under the glass counter. To save time for sightseeing and room for dinner, stop by a bar for a light lunch, such as a ham-and-cheese sandwich (called *toast*); have it grilled twice if you want it really hot.

Prices and Paying: You'll notice a two- or three-tiered pricing system. Drinking a cup of coffee while standing at the bar is cheaper than drinking it at an indoor table (you'll pay still more at an outdoor table). Many places have a *lista dei prezzi* (price list) with two columns—*al bar* and *al tavolo* (table)—posted somewhere by the bar or cash register. If you're on a budget, don't sit down without first checking out the financial consequences. Ask, "Same price if I sit or stand?" by saying, *"Costa uguale al tavolo o al banco?"* (KOH-stah oo-GWAH-lay ahl TAH-voh-loh oh ahl BAHN-koh). Throughout Italy, you can get cheap coffee at the bar of any establishment, no matter how fancy, and pay the same low, government-regulated price (generally a euro or less if you stand).

If the bar isn't busy, you can probably just order and pay when you leave. Otherwise: 1) Decide what you want; 2) find out the price by checking the price list on the wall, the prices posted near the food, or by asking the barista; 3) pay the cashier; and 4) give the receipt to the barista (whose clean fingers handle no dirty euros) and tell him or her what you want.

Ethnic Eateries

A good bet for a cheap, hot meal is a *döner kebab* (Middle Eastern-style rotisserie meat wrapped in pita bread). Look for little hole-in-the-wall kebab shops, where you can get a hearty takeaway dinner—either as a sandwich or a wrap—for about €3. Asian restaurants, although not as common as in northern Europe, can also be a good value.

Tavola Calda Bars and *Rosticcerie*

For a fast and cheap lunch, find an Italian variation on the corner deli: a *rosticceria* (specializing in roasted meats and accompanying *antipasti*) or a *tavola calda* bar (a "hot table" point-and-shoot cafeteria with a buffet spread of meat and vegetables; sometimes called *tavola fredda*, or "cold table," in the north of Italy). For a healthy light meal, ask for a mixed plate of vegetables with a hunk of mozzarella (*piatto misto di verdure con mozzarella;* pee-AH-toh MEE-stoh dee vehr-DOO-ray). Don't be limited by what's displayed. If you'd like a salad with a slice of cantaloupe and a hunk of cheese, they'll whip that up for you in a snap. Belly up to the bar; with a pointing finger, you can assemble a fine meal. If something's a mystery, ask for *un assaggio* (oon ah-SAH-joh) to get a little taste. To have your choices warmed up, ask for them to be heated (*riscaldare;* ree-skahl-DAH-ray).

Wine Bars

Wine bars *(enoteche)* are a popular, fast, and inexpensive option for lunch. Surrounded by the office crowd, you can get a salad, a plate of meats (cold cuts) and cheeses, and a glass of good wine (see blackboards for the day's selection and price per glass). A good *eno-*

teca aims to impress visitors with its wine, and will generally feature excellent-quality ingredients for the simple dishes it offers with the wine (though the prices add up—be careful with your ordering to keep this a budget choice).

Aperitivo Buffets

The Italian term *aperitivo* means a predinner drink, but it's also used to describe their version of what we might call happy hour: a light buffet that many bars serve to customers during the predinner hours (typically around 18:00 or 19:00 until 21:00). The drink itself may not be cheap (typically around €8-12), but bars lay out an enticing array of meats, cheeses, grilled vegetables, and other *antipasti*-type dishes, and you're welcome to nibble to your heart's content while you nurse your drink. While it's intended as an appetizer course before heading out for a full dinner, light eaters could discreetly turn this into a small meal. Bars advertising *"apericena"* (*cena* means dinner) tend to have buffets hearty enough to pass as dinner. Drop by a few bars around this time to scope out their buffets before choosing.

Markets, Groceries, and Delis: Assembling a Picnic

Picnicking saves lots of euros and is a great way to sample regional specialties. A picnic can even be an adventure in high cuisine. Be daring. Try the fresh ricotta, *presto* pesto, shriveled olives, and any regional specialties the locals are excited about.

Markets: For the most colorful experience, gather your ingredients in the morning at a produce market. Towns big and small have markets selling everything imaginable for a fantastic picnic, including cheese, meat, bread, sweets, and prepared foods (Palermo, Catania, and Siracusa have epic markets). You'll often find street-food stalls tucked into the marketplace as well (note that many stalls close in the early afternoon).

Groceries and Delis: Another budget option is to visit a supermarket (look for the Conad, Carrefour, and Co-op chains), *alimentari* (neighborhood grocery), or *salumeria* (delicatessen) to pick up cold cuts, cheeses, and other picnic supplies. Some grocery stores, *salumerie,* and any *paninoteca* or *focacceria* (sandwich shop) can make a sandwich to order. Just point to what you want, and they'll stuff it into a *panino*. Almost every grocery store has a deli case with prepared items like stuffed peppers, lasagna, olives or chicken, all usually sold by weight; if you want it reheated, remember the word *riscaldare* (ree-skahl-DAH-ray). And *rosticcerie* sell cheap food to go—you'll find options such as lasagna, rotisserie chicken, and sides including roasted potatoes and spinach. For more on *salumi* and cheeses, see those sections, later.

Ordering: A typical picnic for two might be fresh rolls, *un etto* (quarter-pound) of cheese, and *un etto* of meat (sometimes ordered by the slice—*fetta*—or piece—

pezzo). For two people, I might get *un etto* of prosciutto and *due pezzi* of bread. Add two tomatoes, three carrots, two apples, yogurt, and a liter box of juice. Total cost: about €10.

If ordering *antipasti* (such as grilled or marinated veggies) at a deli counter, you can ask for *una porzione* in a takeaway container *(contenitore)*. Use gestures to show exactly how much you want. To set a price limit on what you order, say *"Da___euro, per favore."* The word *basta* (BAH-stah; enough) works as a question or as a statement.

Shopkeepers are happy to sell small quantities of produce, but it's customary to let the merchant choose for you. Say *"per oggi"* (pehr OH-jee; for today) and he or she will grab you something ready to eat. To avoid being overcharged, know the cost per kilo, study the weighing procedure, and do the arithmetic. Remember that a kilo is 2.2 pounds.

ITALIAN CUISINE STAPLES

Much of your Italian eating experience will likely involve the big five: pizza, pasta, *salumi*, cheese, and gelato. Here's a rundown on what you might find on menus and in stores. I've included specifics on regional cuisine throughout this book. For more food help, try a menu translator, such as the *Rick Steves Italian Phrase Book & Dictionary*, which has a menu decoder and plenty of useful phrases for navigating the culinary scene.

Pizza

Here are some of the pizzas you might see at restaurants or at a pizzeria. Note that if you ask for pepperoni on your pizza, you'll get *peperoni* (green or red peppers, not sausage); request *diavola*, *salsiccia piccante*, or *salame piccante* instead (the closest thing in Italy to American pepperoni).

Bianca: White pizza with no tomatoes (also called *ciaccina*)

Capricciosa: Prosciutto, mushrooms, olives, and artichokes—literally the chef's "caprice"

Eating with the Seasons

Italian cooks love to serve you fresh produce and seafood at

its tastiest. You'll see Sicily's seasonal specialties displayed in open-air markets throughout the island. To get a plate of the freshest veggies at a fine restaurant, request *"Un piatto di verdure della stagione, per favore."* ("A plate of seasonal vegetables, please."). Italians take fresh, seasonal ingredients so seriously that a restaurant cooking with frozen ingredients *(congelato)* must note it on the menu. Here are a few examples of what's fresh when:

March-May: Calamari, *romanesco* (similar to cauliflower), fava beans, green beans, asparagus, artichokes, wild fennel, citrus

April-June: Asparagus, zucchini flowers, zucchini

May-June: Tuna, mussels, cantaloupe, loquats, strawberries

May-Aug: Eggplant, clams, watermelon, mulberry

July-Sept: Figs, *fichi d'india* (prickly pears), grapes

Oct-Nov: Mushrooms, persimmons, nuts (pistachio, hazelnuts, walnuts)

Nov-Feb: Radicchio, cardoon (wild artichoke), *puntarelle* (chicory shoots)

Funghi: Mushrooms

Margherita: Tomato sauce, mozzarella, and basil—the red, white, and green of the Italian flag

Marinara: Tomato sauce, oregano, garlic, no cheese

Napoletana: Mozzarella, anchovies, and tomato sauce

Ortolana: "Greengrocer-style," with vegetables (also called *vegetariana*)

Quattro formaggi: Four different cheeses

Quattro stagioni: Different toppings on each of the four quarters

Pasta

While we think of pasta as a main dish, in Italy it's considered a *primo piatto*—first course. There are more than 600 varieties of Italian pasta, and each is specifically used to highlight a certain sauce, meat, or regional ingredient. Most pastas in Italy are made fresh.

Italian pasta falls into two broad categories: *pasta lunga* (long pasta) and *pasta corta* (short pasta). *Pasta lunga* can be round, such

Sicilian Food

Like all things Sicilian, the local cuisine resembles Italy's, but it's decidedly its own thing. The Sicilian diet relies on Italian staples such as pastas, olives, savory breads, and tomatoes, but gives them a local twist. The island's warm temperatures and fertile volcanic soil mean that the best possible ingredients are available home-grown in Sicily.

Thanks to centuries of North African and Middle Eastern influences, Sicilian cuisine includes distinctive ingredients such as couscous, almonds, ginger, apricots, cinnamon, and lots of citrus. The Arabs popularized fried foods, which is why so many Sicilian street food classics—and even some pastas—are deep-fried. Sicilian cooking also comes with Greek and Spanish touches. Choosing between fish couscous and spaghetti Bolognese on the same menu, you know you're at a crossroads of cultures.

Sicilian Staples

Seafood is abundant in Sicily: all kinds of fish (swordfish is popular), octopus, squid (cuttlefish), shrimp, and on and on. The real prize is tuna, which is caught wild in the early summer—if it's available fresh, try some. Seafood is commonly served with some combination of pine nuts, pistachios, raisins, and breadcrumbs. Octopus *(polpo)* is often served as a salad with celery and olive oil, or simply boiled, chopped, and accompanied by a wedge of lemon.

Citrus abounds—especially around Etna. Deep-red blood oranges are especially prevalent. Dishes scented with orange and lemon are common, and you'll see tempting juice kiosks offering fresh-squeezed O.J. or a thirst-quenching *seltz*—fresh-squeezed lemon juice, a pinch of salt, and fizzy water (no added sugar).

Pistachios are another Sicilian staple. The best-quality pistachios are grown on the northwestern slopes of Mount Etna, near the town of Bronte. You'll notice pistachios liberally used in cooking (for example, crushed up and sprinkled on pasta).

Oversized **olives** from Castelvetrano are the local answer to Greek Kalamata olives. **Sundried tomatoes** *(pomodori secchi)* are still traditionally made by drying tomatoes on wooden planks on sunny days.

Sicily's **cheese** staple is sheep's-milk ricotta. It's used liberally, including sweetened as a filling for cannoli. Another standby is *pecorino*—a semi-hard sheep's-milk cheese that ages well. Pecorino is common in other parts of Italy; the local version is *pecorino siciliano. Caciocavallo* is the Sicilian version of parme-

PRACTICALITIES

san—a dry, crumbly, salty, grateable cheese. While the name is confusing (*cavallo* means "horse"), it's made of cow's milk that was traditionally hung on a rack—like a horse's saddle—to dry and age.

Street Food

Sicily is Italy's street food mecca. In the hardscrabble markets of Palermo and Catania, locals seek out deep-fried rice balls (*arancine*), chickpea fritters (*panelle*), onion turnovers (*cipollina*), "Sicilian pizza" (*sfincione*), potato croquettes (*cazzilli*), boiled octopus (*polpo bollito*), and the notorious spleen sandwich (*pani ca' meusa*). While these dishes are most authentic in the urban markets of Palermo, Sicilian street food is beginning to appear on menus at sit-down restaurants in other parts of Sicily, and on the mainland as well. For a full primer on street food, see page 94.

Sicilian Specialties

Consider trying one of these regional dishes. For local pasta specialties, see "Sicilian Pasta Dishes."

Caponata: Simple yet luxurious sweet-and-sour eggplant stew, served both hot and cold, as a starter or as a side

Couscous al pesce: Couscous served with a side of fish broth, which you ladle on to taste. Fancier variations are topped with a more elaborate array of shellfish and other seafood (*couscous al mare* or *couscous ai frutti di mare*).

Insalata pantesca: A salad made with tender potatoes, tomatoes, onion, and capers

Insalata siciliana (or *insalata di arance*): A popular springtime salad, both delicious and refreshing, made with juicy chunks of orange, chopped wild fennel, and raw onions. You'll never see this prepared the same way twice.

Nero dei Nebrodi: High-end restaurants brag about their "black pork from Nebrodi"—meat from small free-range black pigs raised in the Nebrodi Mountains of northeast Sicily. The pigs, originally brought here under Spanish rule, are the same breed that produces the most expensive Spanish *ibérico* ham.

Parmigiana di melanzane: Eggplant parmesan—fried eggplant layered with tomato sauce and cheese—is a classic that, Sicilians claim, originated on the island.

Polpette: Meat rolls or meatballs made with mixed meat, fish, or even veggies. Real Sicilian meatballs combine beef, veal, and pork with a bit of fish.

Polpettone: A traditional meatloaf; its core is filled with spinach, carrots, and cheese

Sarde a beccafico: Rolled-up sardines sprinkled with raisins, pine nuts, and breadcrumbs

Sarde beccafico alla Catanese: Breaded and fried sardines

as *capellini* (thin "little hairs"), *vermicelli* ("little worms"), and *bucatini* (long and hollow), or it can be flat, such as *linguine* (narrow "little tongues"), *fettuccine* (wider "small ribbons"), *tagliatelle* (even wider), and *pappardelle* (very wide, best with meat sauces).

The most common *pasta corta* are tubes, such as *penne, rigatoni, ziti, manicotti,* and *cannelloni;* they come either *lisce* (smooth) or *rigate* (grooved—better to catch and cling to sauce). Many short pastas are named for their shapes, such as *conchiglie* (shells), *farfalle* (butterflies), or *cavatappi* (corkscrews).

Here's a list of common pasta toppings and sauces. On a menu, these terms are usually preceded by *alla* (in the style of) or *in* (in):

Aglio e olio: Garlic and olive oil

Amatriciana: Pork cheek, *pecorino* cheese, and tomato

Arrabbiata: "Angry," spicy tomato sauce with chili peppers

Bolognese: Meat and tomato sauce

Boscaiola: Mushrooms and sausage

Burro e salvia: Butter and sage

Cacio e pepe: *Parmigiano* cheese and ground pepper

Carbonara: Bacon, egg, cheese, and pepper

Carrettiera: Spicy and garlicky, with olive oil and little tomatoes

Diavola: "Devil-style," spicy hot

Frutti di mare: Seafood

Genovese: Basil ground with *parmigiano* cheese, garlic, pine nuts, and olive oil; a.k.a. pesto

Gricia: Cured pork cheek and *pecorino romano* cheese

Marinara: Usually tomato, often with garlic and onions, but can also be a seafood sauce ("sailor's style")

Pajata: Calf intestines (also called *pagliata*)

Pescatora: Seafood ("fisherman style")

Pomodoro: Tomato only

Puttanesca: "Harlot-style" tomato sauce with anchovies, olives, and capers

Ragù: Meaty tomato sauce

Scoglio: Mussels, clams, and tomatoes

Sorrentina: "Sorrento-style," with tomatoes, basil, and mozzarella (usually over gnocchi)

Sugo di lepre: Rich sauce made of wild hare

Tartufi: Truffles (also called *tartufate*)

Vongole: Clams and spices

Sicilian Pasta Dishes

Rather than defaulting to the cliched *spaghetti carbonara* or *Bolognese,* try some uniquely Sicilian pasta dishes.

Anelletti al forno: Ring-shaped pasta, originating in Palermo, baked with tomatoes, meat, eggplants, and cheese

Busiate alla Trapanese: A twisty noodle topped with red pesto made from almonds, tomatoes, garlic, and basil

Pasta alla botarga: Dried tuna roe—very salty and very fishy

Pasta alla Norma: Named for an opera by Catania-born composer Vincenzo Bellini, it's made with fried eggplants, tomato sauce, basil, and salted ricotta cheese on top.

Pasta con le sarde: Topped with sardines and anchovies. The similar *pasta alla Palermitana* includes sardines, fennel, pine nuts, and breadcrumbs.

Pasta cu maccu: A stick-to-your-ribs fava-bean stew with pasta— once eaten by famished peasants

Spaghetti ai ricci: Spaghetti topped with sea urchin, a top-end choice for eaters who enjoy a taste of the sea

Salumi

Salumi (cured meats), also called *affettati* (sliced meats), are an Italian staple. While most American cold cuts are cooked, in Italy they're far more commonly cured by air-drying, salting, and smoking. (Don't worry; these so-called "raw" meats are safe to eat, and you can really taste the difference.)

The two most familiar types of *salumi* are *salame* and prosciutto. *Salame* is an air-dried, sometimes-spicy sausage that comes in many varieties. When Italians say *"prosciutto,"* they usually mean *prosciutto crudo*—the raw ham that air-cures on the hock and is then thinly sliced. Produced mainly in the north of Italy, prosciutto can be either *dolce* (sweet) or *salato* (salty). Purists say the best is *prosciutto di Parma.*

Other *salumi* may be less familiar:

Bresaola: Air-cured beef

Capocollo: Peppery pork shoulder (also called *coppa*)

Culatello: High quality, slow-cured prosciutto

Finocchiona: *Salame* with fennel seeds

Lonzino: Cured pork loin

Mortadella: A finely ground pork loaf, similar to our bologna

Pancetta: Salt-cured, peppery pork-belly meat, similar to bacon

Quanciale: Tender pork cheek

Salame di Sant'Olcese: What we'd call "Genoa salami"

Salame piccante: Spicy hot, similar to pepperoni

Speck: Smoked pork shoulder

If you've got a weak stomach, avoid *testa in cassetta* (head-cheese—organs in aspic) and *lampredotto* (cow stomach).

Cheese

When it comes to cheese *(formaggio),* you're probably already familiar with most of these Italian favorites.

Arancina vs. *Arancino*

Sicily's most popular street food is deep-fried rice balls with *ragù* (meat sauce) inside—but what you get varies, depending on where you are on the island. In Palermo and the west, where the rice balls originated in the 10th century, they're called *arancina* (fem., pl. *arancine*). In Catania and the east, they're called *arancino* (masc., pl. *arancini*). Classic western *arancine* are round, flavored with saffron, and contain no tomatoes. Traditional eastern *arancini* are pointy, usually contain tomatoes, but rarely have saffron. The pointed shape resembles the profile of Mount Etna, and the molten *ragù* inside echoes the volcano's hot lava.

In either city, you'll find variations in shapes and fillings. Sometimes the shape indicates what's inside. Look for these at bars and pizza shops: butter and ham (spherical); eggplant (oval, darker crust); pistachio cream (oval); and *alla Palermitana*—with sardines, wild fennel, pine nuts, and pecorino cheese (oval).

No matter which one you pick, watch your language: Never call it *arancino* in the west, or *arancina* in the east. Just... don't.

Asiago: Hard cow cheese that comes either *mezzano* (young, firm, and creamy) or *stravecchio* (aged, pungent, and granular)

Burrata: A creamy mozzarella

Fontina: Semihard, nutty, Gruyère-style mountain cheese

Gorgonzola: Pungent, blue-veined cheese, either *dolce* (creamy) or *stagionato* (aged and hard)

Mascarpone: Sweet, buttery, spreadable dessert cheese

Mozzarella di bufala: Made from the milk of water buffaloes

Parmigiano-reggiano: Hard, crumbly, sharp, aged cow cheese with more nuanced flavor than American parmesan; *grana padano* is a less expensive variation.

Pecorino: Either *fresco* (fresh, soft, and mild) or *stagionato* (aged and sharp, sometimes called *pecorino romano*)

Provolone: Rich, firm, aged cow cheese

Ricotta: Soft, airy cheese made by "recooking" leftover whey

Scamorza: Similar to mozzarella, but often smoked

Gelato

American ice cream and Italian gelato are similar but decidedly not the same. Gelato is denser and creamier (even though it has less butterfat than ice cream), and connoisseurs swear it's more flavorful.

A key to gelato appreciation is sampling liberally and choosing flavors that go well together. At a *gelateria*, ask, as Italians do, for a taste: *"Un assaggio, per favore?"* (oon ah-SAH-joh pehr fah-VOH-ray). You can also ask what flavors go well together: *"Quali gusti stanno bene insieme?"* (KWAH-lee GOO-stee STAH-noh BEH-nay een-see-EH-may).

Most *gelaterie* clearly display prices and sizes. But in the textbook *gelateria* scam, the tourist orders two or three flavors—and the clerk selects a fancy, expensive chocolate-coated waffle cone, piles it high with huge scoops, and cheerfully charges the tourist €10. To avoid rip-offs, point to the price or say what you want—for instance, a €3 cup: *"Una coppetta da tre euro"* (OO-nah koh-PEH-tah dah tray eh-OO-roh).

The best *gelaterie* display signs reading *artiginale, nostra produzione,* or *produzione propia,* indicating that the gelato is made on the premises. Seasonal flavors are also a good sign, as are mellow hues (avoid colors that don't appear in nature). Gelato stored in covered metal tins (rather than white plastic) is more likely to be homemade. Gourmet gelato shops are popping up all over Italy, selling exotic flavors. Unless it's a gelato emergency, avoid the chain called Grom—it's the Starbucks of gelato in Italy.

Gelato variations or alternatives include *sorbetto* (sorbet—made with fruit, but no milk or eggs); *granita* or *grattachecca* (a cup of slushy ice with flavored syrup); and *cremolata* (a gelato-*granita* float).

Classic gelato flavors include:

After Eight: Chocolate and mint
Bacio: Chocolate hazelnut, named for Italy's popular "kiss" candies
Cassata: With dried fruits
Cioccolato: Chocolate
Crema: Vanilla
Croccantino: "Crunchy," with toasted peanut bits
Fior di latte: Sweet milk
Fragola: Strawberry
Macedonia: Mixed fruits
Malaga: Similar to rum raisin
Riso: With actual bits of rice mixed in
Stracciatella: Vanilla with chocolate shreds
Tartufo: Super chocolate
Zabaione: Named for the egg-yolk-and-Marsala wine dessert
Zuppa inglese: Sponge cake, custard, chocolate, and cream

BEVERAGES

Italian bars serve great drinks—hot, cold, sweet, caffeinated, or alcoholic.

Water, Juice, and Cold Drinks

Italians are notorious water snobs. At restaurants, your server just can't understand why you wouldn't want good water to go with your good food. It's customary and never expensive to order a *litro* or *mezzo litro* (half-liter) of bottled water. *Acqua leggermente effervescente* (lightly carbonated water) is a mealtime favorite. Or simply ask for *con gas* if you want fizzy water and *senza gas* if you prefer still water. You can ask for *acqua del rubinetto* (tap water) in restaurants, but your server may give you a funny look. Chilled bottled water—still *(naturale)* or carbonated *(frizzante)*—is sold cheap in stores. Half-liter bottles of mineral water are available everywhere for about €1. (I refill my water bottle with tap water.)

Juice is *succo,* and *spremuta* means freshly squeezed. Order *una spremuta* (don't confuse it with *spumante,* sparkling wine)—it's usually orange juice *(arancia),* and from February through April it's almost always made from Sicilian blood oranges *(arance rosse).* Stands selling *spremuta* are all over the island, and many will mix different juices to make fresh-squeezed concoctions.

In grocery stores, you can get a liter of O.J. for the price of a Coke or coffee. Look for *100% succo* or *senza zucchero* (without sugar) on the label—or be surprised by something diluted and sugary sweet. Hang on to your water bottles. Buy juice in cheap liter boxes, then drink some and store the extra in your water bottle.

Tè freddo (iced tea) is usually from a can—sweetened and flavored with lemon or peach. Lemonade is *limonata.*

Coffee and Other Hot Drinks

The espresso-based style of coffee so popular in the US was born in Italy. If you ask for *"un caffè,"* you'll get a shot of espresso in a little cup—the closest thing to American-style drip coffee is a *caffè americano.* Most Italian coffee drinks begin with espresso, to which they add varying amounts of hot water and/or steamed or foamed milk. Milky drinks, like cappuccino or *caffè latte,* are served to locals before noon and to tourists any time of day (to an Italian, cappuccino is a morning drink; they believe having milk after a big meal or anything with tomato sauce impairs digestion). If they add any milk after lunch, it's just a splash, in a *caffè macchiato.* Italians like their coffee only warm—to get it very hot, request *"Molto caldo, per favore"* (MOHL-toh KAHL-doh pehr fah-VOH-ray). Any coffee drink is available decaffeinated—ask for it *decaffeinato* (deh-kah-fay-NAH-toh).

If you want a hot drink other than coffee, *cioccolato* is hot chocolate, and *tè* is hot tea.

Cappuccino: Espresso with foamed milk on top (*cappuccino freddo* is iced cappuccino)

Caffè latte: Espresso mixed with hot milk, no foam, in a tall glass (ordering just a "latte" gets you only milk)

Caffè macchiato: Espresso "marked" with a splash of milk, in a small cup

Latte macchiato: Layers of hot milk and foam, "marked" by an espresso shot, in a tall glass. Note that if you order simply a *"macchiato,"* you'll probably get a *caffè macchiato.*

Caffè corto/lungo: Concentrated espresso diluted with a tiny bit of hot water, in a small cup

Caffè americano: Espresso diluted with even more hot water, in a larger cup

Caffè corretto: Espresso "corrected" with a shot of liqueur (normally *grappa, amaro,* or *sambuca*)

Marocchino: "Moroccan" coffee with espresso, foamed milk, and cocoa powder; the similar *mocaccino* has chocolate instead of cocoa.

Caffè freddo: Sweet and iced espresso

Caffè hag: Instant decaf

Alcoholic Beverages

Beer: While Italy is traditionally considered wine country, in recent years there's been a huge and passionate growth in the production of craft beer *(birra artigianale).* Even in small towns, you'll see microbreweries slinging their own brews. You'll also find local brews (Peroni and Moretti), as well as imports such as Heineken. Italians drink mainly lager beers. Beer on tap is *alla spina.* Get it *piccola* (33 cl, 11 oz), *media* (50 cl, about a pint), or *grande* (a liter). A *lattina* (lah-TEE-nah) is a can and a *bottiglia* (boh-TEEL-yah) is a bottle.

Cocktails and Spirits: Italians appreciate both *aperitivi* (palate-stimulating cocktails) and *digestivi* (after-dinner drinks designed to aid digestion). Popular *aperitivo* options include Campari (dark-colored bitters with herbs and orange peel), Americano (vermouth with bitters, brandy, and lemon peel), Cynar (bitters flavored with artichoke), and Punt e Mes (sweet red vermouth and red wine). Widely used vermouth brands include Cinzano and Martini.

Digestivo choices are usually either strong herbal bitters or something sweet. Many restaurants have their own secret recipe for a bittersweet herbal brew called *amaro;* popular commercial brands are Fernet Branca and Montenegro. If your tastes run sweeter, try any of these flavored liqueurs: *amaretto* (almond), Frangelico (hazelnut), *limoncello* (lemon), *nocino* (walnut), *sambuca* (anise), or a sweet Marsala wine. *Grappa* is a brandy distilled from grape skins and stems; *stravecchio* is an aged, mellower variation.

Wine: The ancient Greeks who colonized Italy more than 2,000 years ago called it Oenotria—land of the grape. Centuries later, Galileo wrote, "Wine is light held together by water." Wine *(vino)* is certainly a part of the Italian culinary trinity—grape,

PRACTICALITIES

Ordering Wine

To order a glass of red or white wine, say, *"Un bicchiere di vino rosso/bianco."* House wine comes in a carafe; choose from a quarter-liter pitcher (8.5 oz, *un quarto*), half-liter pitcher (17 oz, *un mezzo*), or one-liter pitcher (34 oz, *un litro*). When ordering, have some fun, gesture like a local, and you'll have no problems speaking the language of the *enoteca. Salute!*

English	Italian
wine	*vino* (VEE-noh)
house wine	*vino della casa* (VEE-noh DEH-lah KAH-zah)
glass	*bicchiere* (bee-kee-eh-ray)
bottle	*bottiglia* (boh-TEEL-yah)
carafe	*caraffa* (kah-RAH-fah)
red	*rosso* (ROH-soh)
white	*bianco* (bee-AHN-koh)
rosé	*rosato* (roh-ZAH-toh)
sparkling	*spumante/frizzante* (spoo-MAHN-tay/freed-ZAHN-tay)
dry	*secco* (SEH-koh)
fruity	*fruttato* (froo-TAH-toh)
full-bodied	*corposo/pieno* (kor-POH-zoh/pee-EH-noh)
sweet	*dolce* (DOHL-chay)

olive, and wheat. (I'd add gelato.) Ideal conditions for grapes (warm climate, well-draining soil, and an abundance of hillsides) make the Italian peninsula a paradise for grape growers, winemakers, and wine drinkers.

Even if you're clueless about wine, the information on an Italian wine label can help you choose something decent. Terms you may see on the bottle include *classico* (from a defined, select area), *annata* (year of harvest), *vendemmia* (harvest), and *imbottigliato dal produttore all'origine* (bottled by producers).

In general, Italy designates its wines by one of four official categories:

Vino da Tavola (VDT) is table wine, the lowest grade, made from grapes grown anywhere in Italy. It's often inexpensive, but Italy's wines are so good that, for many people, a basic *vino da tavola* is just fine with a meal. Many restaurants, even modest ones, take pride in their house wine *(vino della casa)*, bottling their own or working with wineries.

Sicilian Wines

Wine has been produced on the shores of Sicily since the time of the Greeks. The island, with a variety of grape-growing areas with differing characteristics, is one of the biggest producers of wine in Italy. While once considered the land of cheap and cheery table wine, you'll now find upscale wineries ranging from big producers like Planeta to small family operations. Some of the grape varieties grown here are common on the mainland, but others, such as the red nerello grape, can be found only in Sicily.

Western Wines: More than half of the vineyards in Sicily are in the relatively small area around Trapani, on the west coast. These wines are inexpensive and generally good; you can buy a decent bottle at a wine shop for less than €10. The common white grape varieties are catarratto, grillo, grecanico, zibibbo, and inzolia. Among the red varieties is perricone.

But western Sicily is best known for its Marsala wine, a fortified wine that earned the first DOC designation (indication of quality) in Italy. Marsala is made with four local grape varieties (grillo, inzolia, catarratto, and damaschino), and comes in sweet, dry, and semidry versions. Most local cooks keep a bottle of Marsala handy—this grade is called "fine" and is only aged one year. The grades (and prices) go up depending on its age, from two to 10 years or more. For more on Marsala wine, see page 154.

Eastern Wines: On this side, wines are grown from the south coast around Ragusa and Noto to the slopes of Mount Etna. Sicily's most famous and plentiful variety, Nero d'Avola, is grown all over the island but originates in the southeastern corner. In recent years the Etna area has become a magnet for boutique producers due to the rich volcanic soil and old vines. Wineries cluster around the north slope, like a Sicilian Napa Valley. Look for the native nerello and carricante varieties here. For more on Etna wines, see page 351.

PRACTICALITIES

Denominazione di Origine Controllata (DOC) meets national standards for high-quality wine. Made from grapes grown in a defined area, it's usually quite affordable and can be surprisingly good. Hundreds of wines have earned the DOC designation.

Denominazione di Origine Controllata e Guarantita (DOCG), the highest grade, meets national standards for the highest-quality wine (made with grapes from a defined area whose quality is "guaranteed"). These wines can be identified by the pink or green label

Hurdling the Language Barrier

Many Sicilians—especially those in the tourist trade and in big cities—speak English. And all Sicilians speak both Italian and Sicilian.

In smaller, nontouristy towns, Sicilian and Italian are the norm. The two languages have a lot in common, but some words are very different. For example, a cup of coffee is *tazzina da caffé* in Italian but *cichira* in Sicilian (likely borrowed from the Portuguese *xicara*).

Sicilian is more than a dialect; it's actually an older language than Italian. It descended from the Latin spoken by Roman conquerors and has elements of Greek, Arabic, French, Catalan, and Spanish—the legacy of years of foreign influence, trade, and occupation. Sicilian is not an active language, as new words are not being created.

During the early 20th century, the government enforced Italian as the national language, bringing Sicilian to the verge of extinction. However, Sicilian is now making a comeback, as it is being reintroduced and taught in schools.

While you can simply communicate with Sicilians in Italian, you will commonly hear them conversing in Sicilian. Like many Italians, Sicilians have an endearing habit of talking to you even if they know you don't speak their language—and yet, thanks to gestures and thoughtfully simplified words, it somehow works. Don't stop them to tell them you don't understand every word—just go along for the ride.

Locals visibly brighten when you know and use some Italian or Sicilian pleasantries. For a list of Italian survival phrases, see the appendix, and for some helpful Sicilian phrases, see next.

on the neck...and the scary price tag on the shelf. They're generally a good bet if you want a quality wine, but you don't know anything else about the winemaker. (*Riserva* indicates a DOC or DOCG wine that's been aged for even longer than required.)

Indicazione Geografica Tipica (IGT) is a broad group of wines that don't meet the standard for DOC or DOCG status, but have been designated as "typical" of a particular region.

Staying Connected

One of the most common questions I hear from travelers is, "How can I stay connected in Europe?" The short answer is: more easily and cheaply than you might think.

The simplest solution is to bring your own device—mobile phone, tablet, or laptop—and use it just as you would at home (following my tips, such as getting an international plan or connecting to free Wi-Fi whenever possible). Another option is to buy a

Note that Italian is pronounced much like English, with a few exceptions, such as: *c* followed by *e* or *i* is pronounced *ch* (to ask, *"Per centro?"*—"To the center?"—you say, pehr CHEHN-troh). In Italian, *ch* followed by *e* or *i* is pronounced like the hard *c* in Chianti (*chiesa*—church—is pronounced kee-AY-zah). Adding a vowel to the English word often gets you close to the Italian one. Give it your best shot. You'll find that doors open more quickly...and with more smiles.

Sicilian for Beginners

English	Italian	Sicilian
Good day.	*Buon giorno.*	*Bon jornu.*
Please.	*Per favore.*	*Pi fauri.*
Thank you.	*Grazie.*	*Ringraziamu.*
Let's go.	*Andiamo.*	*Amuninni.*
How much is it?	*Quanto costa?*	*Quantu soddi?*
It costs too much!	*E' troppo caro!*	*Chi??? Nunzi! Iè troppu caru!*
Where is...?	*Dov'e?*	*Unn'è?*
You are beautiful.	*Tu sei bella.*	*Tu si bedda.*
My grandpa was Sicilian!	*Mio nonno era Siciliano!*	*Me nonnu iera di cà, paesano!*

For more tips on hurdling the language barrier, consider the *Rick Steves Italian Phrase Book* (available at www.ricksteves.com).

European SIM card for your US mobile phone. Or you can use European landlines and computers to connect. Each of these options is described next, and more details are at www.ricksteves.com/phoning. For a very practical one-hour talk covering tech issues for travelers, see www.ricksteves.com/mobile-travel-skills.

USING A MOBILE PHONE IN EUROPE
Here are some budget tips and options.

Sign up for an international plan. To stay connected at a lower cost, sign up for an international service plan through your carrier. Most providers offer a simple bundle that includes calling, messaging, and data. Your normal plan may already include international coverage (T-Mobile's does).

Before your trip, call your provider or check online to confirm that your phone will work in Europe, and research your provider's international rates. Activate the plan a day or two before you leave, then remember to cancel it when your trip's over.

PRACTICALITIES

How to Dial

International Calls

Whether phoning from a US landline or mobile phone, or from a number in another European country, here's how to make an international call. I've used one of my recommended Palermo hotels as an example (tel. 091-616-6881).

Initial Zero: Drop the initial zero from international phone numbers—except when calling Italy.

Mobile Tip: If using a mobile phone, the "+" sign can replace the international access code (for a "+" sign, press and hold "0").

US/Canada to Europe

Dial 011 (US/Canada international access code), country code (39 for Italy), and phone number.

▶ To call the Palermo hotel from home, dial 011-39-091-616-6881.

Country to Country Within Europe

Dial 00 (Europe international access code), country code, and phone number.

▶ To call the Palermo hotel from Germany, dial 00-39-091-616-6881.

Europe to the US/Canada

Dial 00, country code (1 for US/Canada), and phone number.

▶ To call from Europe to my office in Edmonds, Washington, dial 00-1-425-771-8303.

Domestic Calls

To call within Italy (from one Italian landline or mobile phone to another), simply dial the phone number, including the initial 0 if there is one.

▶ To call the Palermo hotel from Rome, dial 091-616-6881.

More Dialing Tips

Italian Phone Numbers: Italian phone numbers vary in length; a hotel can have, say, an eight-digit phone number and a nine-digit fax number. Italy's landlines start with 0; mobile lines start with 3 and cost substantially more to dial.

Use free Wi-Fi whenever possible. Unless you have an unlimited-data plan, you're best off saving most of your online tasks for Wi-Fi. You can access the internet, send texts, and even make voice calls over Wi-Fi.

Most accommodations in Europe offer free Wi-Fi, but some—especially expensive hotels—charge a fee. Many cafés (including Starbucks and McDonald's) have free hotspots for customers; look for signs offering it and ask for the Wi-Fi password when you buy something. You'll also often find Wi-Fi at TIs, city squares, major

Toll and Toll-Free Calls: Italy's toll-free lines, called *numero verde* (green number), begin with 800 or 803. They can be dialed free from Italian phones without using a phone card but don't work from the US. Any Italian phone number that starts with 8 but isn't followed by a 0 is a toll call (generally costing €0.10-0.50/minute). International rates apply to US toll-free numbers dialed from Italy—they're not free.

More Phoning Help: See www.howtocallabroad.com.

European Country Codes		Ireland & N. Ireland	353 / 44
Austria	43	Italy	39
Belgium	32	Latvia	371
Bosnia-Herzegovina	387	Montenegro	382
Croatia	385	Morocco	212
Czech Republic	420	Netherlands	31
Denmark	45	Norway	47
Estonia	372	Poland	48
Finland	358	Portugal	351
France	33	Russia	7
Germany	49	Slovakia	421
Gibraltar	350	Slovenia	386
Great Britain	44	Spain	34
Greece	30	Sweden	46
Hungary	36	Switzerland	41
Iceland	354	Turkey	90

PRACTICALITIES

museums, public-transit hubs, airports, and aboard trains and buses.

Minimize the use of your cellular network. Even with an international data plan, wait until you're on Wi-Fi to Skype, download apps, stream videos, or do other megabyte-greedy tasks. Using a navigation app such as Google Maps over a cellular network can take lots of data, so do this sparingly or use it offline.

Limit automatic updates. By default, your device constantly checks for a data connection and updates apps. It's smart to disable

Tips on Internet Security

Make sure that your device is running the latest versions of its operating system, security software, and apps. Next, ensure that your device and key programs (like email) are password- or passcode-protected. On the road, use only secure, password-protected Wi-Fi hotspots. Ask the hotel or café staff for the specific name of their Wi-Fi network, and make sure you log on to that exact one.

If you must access your financial info online, use a banking app rather than accessing your account via a browser. A cellular connection is more secure than Wi-Fi. Avoid logging onto personal finance sites on a public computer.

Never share your credit-card number (or any other sensitive information) online unless you know that the site is secure. A secure site displays a little padlock icon, and the URL begins with *https* (instead of the usual *http*).

these features so your apps will only update when you're on Wi-Fi. Also change your device's email settings from "auto-retrieve" to "manual" (or from "push" to "fetch").

When you need to get online but can't find Wi-Fi, simply turn on your cellular network just long enough for the task at hand. When you're done, avoid further charges by manually turning off data roaming or cellular data (either works) in your device's Settings menu. Another way to make sure you're not accidentally using data roaming is to put your device in "airplane" mode (which also disables phone calls and texts), and then turn your Wi-Fi back on as needed.

Use Wi-Fi calling and messaging apps. Skype, WhatsApp, FaceTime, and Google Hangouts are great for making free or low-cost calls or sending texts over Wi-Fi. With an app installed on your phone, tablet, or laptop, you can log on to a Wi-Fi network and contact friends or family members who use the same service. If you buy credit in advance, with some of these services you can call or send a text anywhere for just pennies per minute.

Some apps, such as Apple's iMessage, will use the cellular network if Wi-Fi isn't available: To avoid this possibility, turn off the "Send as SMS" feature.

USING A EUROPEAN SIM CARD

With a European SIM card, you get a European mobile number and access to cheaper rates than you'll get through your US carrier. This option works well for those who want to make a lot of local calls, need a local phone number, or want faster connection speeds than their US carrier provides. It's simple: You buy a SIM card in

Europe to replace the SIM card in your "unlocked" US phone or tablet (check with your carrier about unlocking it) or buy a basic cell phone in Italy.

In Italy, tourists should buy SIM cards at mobile-phone shops. You'll be required to register the SIM card with your passport as an antiterrorism measure (which may mean you can't use the phone for the first hour or two). Costing about $5-10, SIM cards usually include about that much prepaid calling credit, with no contract and no commitment. Expect to pay $20-40 more for a SIM card with a gigabyte of data.

There are no roaming charges for EU citizens using a domestic SIM card in other EU countries. Theoretically, providers don't have to offer Americans this "roam-like-at-home" pricing, but most do. To be sure, buy your SIM card at a mobile-phone shop and ask if non-EU citizens also have roam-like-at-home pricing.

In Italy, the major mobile-phone providers are Wind, TIM, Vodafone, and 3 ("Tre"). Certain SIM-card brands—including Lycamobile, which operates in multiple European countries—are reliable and economical. When you run out of credit, you can top it up at newsstands, tobacco shops, mobile-phone stores, or many other businesses (look for your SIM card's logo in the window).

WITHOUT A MOBILE PHONE

It's possible to travel in Europe without a mobile device. You can make calls from your hotel and check email or browse websites using public computers.

Most **hotels** charge a fee for placing calls—ask for rates before you dial. You can use a prepaid international phone card (*carta telefonica prepagata internazionale*—usually available at newsstands, tobacco shops, and train stations) to call out from your hotel. Dial the toll-free access number, enter the card's PIN code, then dial the number.

You'll only see **public pay phones** in a few post offices and train stations. Most don't take coins but instead require insertable phone cards, which you can buy at a newsstand, convenience store, or post office. Except for emergencies, they're not worth the hassle.

Some hotels have **public computers** in their lobbies for guests to use; otherwise you may find them at public libraries (ask your hotelier or the TI for the nearest location). On a European keyboard, use the "Alt Gr" key to the right of the space bar to insert the extra symbol that appears on some keys. If you can't locate a special character (such as @), simply copy and paste it from a web page.

MAIL

You can mail one package per day to yourself worth up to $200 duty-free from Europe to the US (mark it "personal purchases").

PRACTICALITIES

Connecting Sicily with Mainland Italy

If your trip to Sicily is part of a longer European trip, you may want to connect directly to mainland Italy. The easiest and fastest way is to fly to or from Palermo, Catania, or Trapani; flights take 1-2 hours and can be inexpensive if booked in advance (especially for connections to Rome).

Budget travelers and those who enjoy the scenic route can consider linking by ferry, train, or bus. Long-distance buses (cheapest) and trains depart daily to most major cities on the mainland (buses cross the Strait of Messina overnight via ferry while trains have special cars that are loaded onto a ferry and rejoin the tracks on the other side). If taking an overnight train, you can reserve a sleeping car in advance. Long-haul ferries carry both cars and walk-on passengers, and take 8-15 hours to connect Sicilian ports including Palermo and Catania with Naples, Civitavecchia (near Rome), or Livorno (near Florence). The quickest ferry trip is from Messina, on Sicily's northeast coast, to Reggio di Calabria or Villa San Giovanni, at the tip of Italy's boot (30 minutes).

If you're sending a gift to someone, mark it "unsolicited gift." For details, visit www.cbp.gov, select "Travel," and search for "Know Before You Go." The Italian postal service works fine, but for quick transatlantic delivery (in either direction), consider services such as DHL (www.dhl.com).

Transportation

Figuring out how to get around in Europe is one of your biggest trip decisions. **Cars** work well for two or more traveling together (especially families with small kids), those packing heavy, and those delving into the countryside. **Trains** and **buses** are best for solo travelers, blitz tourists, city-to-city travelers, and those who want to leave the driving to others. Smart travelers can use short-hop **flights** within Europe to creatively connect the dots on their itineraries. Just be aware of the potential downside of each option: A car is an expensive headache in any major city; with trains and buses you're at the mercy of a timetable; and flying entails a trek to and from a usually distant airport.

If your itinerary mixes cities and countryside, my advice is to connect cities by train or bus and to explore rural areas by rental car. Arrange to pick up your car in the last big city you'll visit, then use it to lace together small towns and explore the countryside. For more detailed information on transportation throughout Europe, see www.ricksteves.com/transportation.

TRAINS

To travel by train affordably within Sicily, you can simply buy tickets as you go, including online. Note that the Italy rail pass is generally not a good value, but if your travel extends beyond Italy, there are various multicountry rail passes that might be worth checking into. For advice on figuring out the smartest train-ticket or rail-pass options for your trip, visit the Trains & Rail Passes section of my website at www.ricksteves.com/rail.

Note that the train system in Sicily is not extensive and does not connect the entire island. The train line on the west coast, for example, does not connect to any other lines. Most trains are slow, and in some cases, the bus is a better option.

Types of Trains

Trains in Sicily are operated by the state-run **Trenitalia** company (www.trenitalia.com, a.k.a. Ferrovie dello Stato Italiane, abbreviated FS). Since ticket prices depend on the speed of the train, it helps to know the different types of trains: pokey R or REG *(regionali);* medium-speed RV *(regionali veloce),* IR (InterRegio), D *(diretto),* and E *(espresso);* and fast IC (InterCity) and EC (EuroCity). Several types of trains that operate on the mainland do not run in Sicily. These include Trenitalia's high-speed Frecce trains, as well as private Italo trains.

Schedules

Check schedules online at www.trenitalia.it (domestic journeys only); for international trips, use www.bahn.com (Germany's excellent all-Europe schedule website). At the train station, the easiest way to check schedules is at a handy ticket machine. Enter the desired date, time, and destination to see all your options. Printed schedules are also posted at the station (departures—*partenze*—posters are always yellow; see the "Deciphering Italian Train Schedules" sidebar). Trenitalia also has a call center for answering general questions (daily 7:00-24:00, tel. 06-6847-5475).

Point-to-Point Tickets

Train tickets are a good value in Italy. Typical fares are shown on the map on page 457, though ticket prices can vary for the same journey, mainly depending on the time of day, the speed of the train, and advance discounts.

PRACTICALITIES

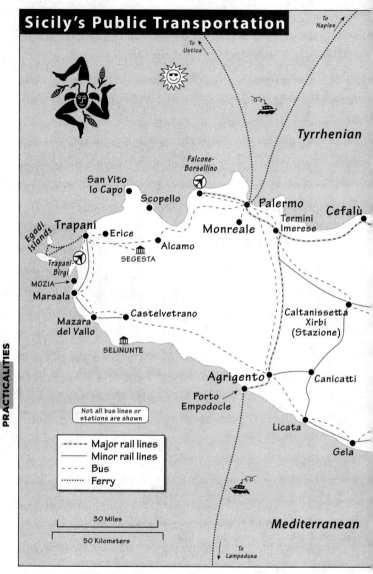

Sicily's Public Transportation

To Naples

To Ustica

Tyrrhenian

Falcone-Borsellino ✈

San Vito lo Capo

Scopello

Palermo

Cefalù

Termini Imerese

Egadi Islands

Trapani

Erice

Monreale

Alcamo

SEGESTA 🏛

Trapani-Birgi ✈

MOZIA →

Marsala

Mazara del Vallo

Castelvetrano

SELINUNTE 🏛

Caltanissetta Xirbi (Stazione)

Agrigento

Canicatti

Porto Empodocle →

Licata

Gela

Not all bus lines or stations are shown

- ∙∙∙∙∙ Major rail lines
- ——— Minor rail lines
- - - - Bus
- ∙∙∙∙∙∙ Ferry

30 Miles

50 Kilometers

Mediterranean

To Lampedusa

PRACTICALITIES

Classes of Service: Trains offer standard first- and second-class seating (with first class costing up to 50 percent more than second). Buying up gives you a little more elbow room, a snack, or perhaps a better chance at seating a group together, if you're buying on short notice.

Advance Discounts: Ticket price levels include Base (full fare, easily changeable or partly refundable before scheduled departure), Economy (one schedule change allowed before depar-

ture, for a fee), and Super Economy (sells out quickly, no refund or exchange). Discounted fares typically sell out several days before departure. Fares labeled *servizi abbonati* are available only for locals with monthly passes—not tourists. Regional trains don't offer advance discounts or seat assignments, so there's little need to buy those tickets in advance.

Age-Based Discounts: Families with young children can get price breaks—kids ages 4 and under travel free; ages 4-11 at

Deciphering Italian Train Schedules

At the station, look for the big yellow posters labeled *Partenze—Departures* (white posters show arrivals). Departures are listed chronologically, hour by hour, showing the trains leaving the station throughout the day.

Reading from the left, the schedule lists the time of departure *(ora)*, the type of train *(treni)*, and service classes offered *(classi servizi)*—first- and second-class cars, dining car, *cuccetta* berths, and, more important, whether you need reservations (usually denoted by an R in a box). All Frecce trains, many EuroCity (EC) and InterCity (IC) trains, and most international trains require reservations.

The next column lists the train's destination *(principali fermate destinazioni)*, often showing intermediate stops (with arrival times in parentheses). Note that your destination may be listed as an intermediate stop. Travelers who read the fine print end up with a far greater choice of trains. You may also see pertinent notes about the train, such as "also stops in..." *(ferma anche a...)*, "doesn't stop in..." *(non ferma a...)*, "stops in every station" *(ferma in tutte le stazioni)*, "delayed..." *(ritardo...)*, and so on.

The last column gives the track *(binario)* the train departs from. Confirm the *binario* with a ticket seller or railway official, the electronic board that lists immediate departures, or monitors on the platform.

For any odd symbols on the poster, look at the key at the end. Some phrasing can be deciphered easily, such as *servizio periodico* (periodic service—doesn't always run). For the trickier ones, ask a local or railway official, or try your *Rick Steves Italian Phrase Book & Dictionary*.

You can also check schedules for trains anywhere in Italy at ticket machines. Enter the date and time of your departure (to or from any Italian station), and view all your options.

half-price. When booking online, be sure to confirm the exact age ranges that qualify for discounts by clicking on the info links. With the "Offerta Familia" discount, families of three to five people with at least one kid (under 12) get 50 percent off the child fare and 20 percent off the adult fare on InterCity night trains. You may also see a "Bimbi Gratis" offer: One child age 5–15 free per adult paying the full base fare. If buying tickets at a counter, ask for the "Offerta

Familia" deal (or, at a ticket machine, choose "Yes" at the "Do you want ticket issue?" prompt, then choose "Familia").

Discounts for youths and seniors require purchase of a separate card (€40 Carta Verde for ages 12-26, €30 Carta Argento for ages 60 and over), but the ticket discount is so minor (10-15 percent respectively for domestic travel), it's not worth it for most.

Buying Tickets: It's easy to buy tickets for **domestic travel** online at www.trenitalia.com. On the website, choose English and be sure to read the pricing info, as many of the cheaper tickets are not refundable or changeable. You can keep the ticket on your mobile device (either as a PDF or in a "ticketless" format with a booking code), or you can print it out.

If you instead go to the train station to buy your ticket, avoid ticket-office lines whenever possible by using the ticket machines in station halls. Pay all ticket costs in the station before you board, or you'll pay a penalty on the train. You'll be able to easily purchase tickets for travel within Italy, make seat reservations, and even book a *cuccetta* (koo-CHEH-tah; overnight berth). If you do use the ticket windows (e.g., to buy international tickets), be sure you're in the correct line. Key terms: *biglietti* (general tickets), *prenotazioni* (reservations), *nazionali* (domestic), and *internazionali*.

Trenitalia's ticket machines (new ones are red, old ones are green-and-white; marked *Trenitalia/Biglietti*) are user-friendly and found in all but the tiniest stations in Italy. You can pay with cash (change given when indicated) or by debit or credit card (even for small amounts, but you may need to enter your PIN). Select English, then your destination. If you don't immediately see the city you're traveling to, keep keying in the spelling until it's listed. You can choose from first- and second-class seats, and request tickets for more than one traveler. Don't select a discount rate without being sure that you meet the criteria (for example, Americans are not eligible for certain EU or resident discounts). Rail-pass holders can use the machines to make seat reservations. If you need to validate your ticket, you can do it in the same machine if you're boarding your train right away.

For longer-haul runs, it can be cheaper to buy Trenitalia tickets in advance. Because most Italian trains run frequently and there's no deadline to buy tickets, you can keep your travel plans flexible by purchasing tickets as you go. (You can buy tickets for several trips at one station when you are ready to commit.) For busy weekend or holiday travel, however, it can be a good idea to buy tickets in advance.

Most **international tickets** can't be bought online or from machines; for these tickets and anything else that requires a real person, you must go to a ticket window at the station. A good alternative, though, is to drop by a local travel agency. Agencies sell

Open or Non-Reserved Ticket—Need to Validate

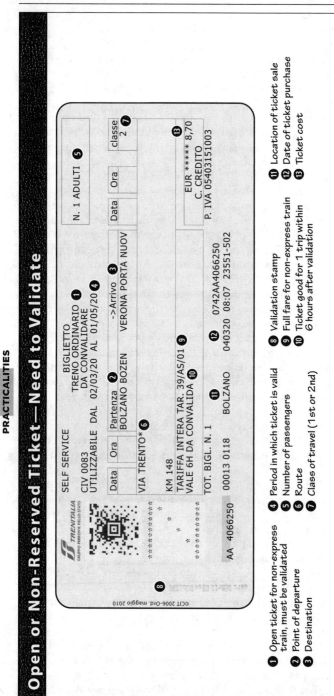

1 Open ticket for non-express train, must be validated
2 Point of departure
3 Destination
4 Period in which ticket is valid
5 Number of passengers
6 Route
7 Class of travel (1st or 2nd)
8 Validation stamp
9 Full fare for non-express train
10 Ticket good for 1 trip within 6 hours after validation
11 Location of ticket sale
12 Date of ticket purchase
13 Ticket cost

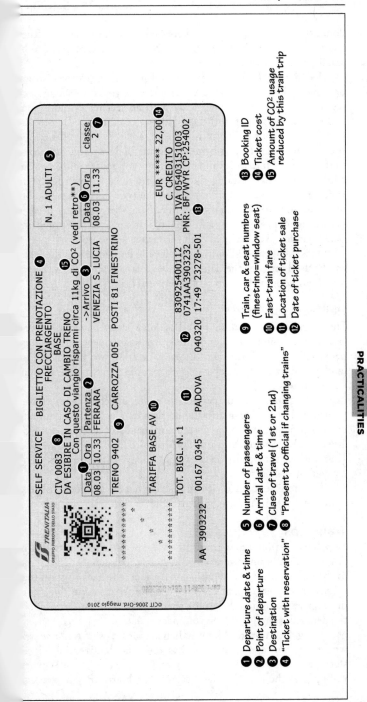

SELF SERVICE   BIGLIETTO CON PRENOTAZIONE ❹
FRECCIARGENTO
BASE
CIV 0083 ❽
DA ESIBIRE IN CASO DI CAMBIO TRENO
Con questo viaggio risparmi circa 11kg di CO_2 (vedi retro**) ❻

N. 1 ADULTI ❺

Data ❶ Ora	Partenza ❷		->Arrivo ❸	Data ❻ Ora	classe ❼
08.03 10.33	FERRARA		VENEZIA S. LUCIA	08.03 11.33	2

TRENO 9402   CARROZZA 005 ❾   POSTI 81 FINESTRINO

TARIFFA BASE AV ❿

TOT. BIGL. N. 1

830925400112
0741AA3903232 ❶❷
040320 17:49 23278-501

EUR ****** 22,00 ❶❹
C. CREDITO
P. IVA 0540315100
PNR: BF7WYR CP:254002 ❶❸

00167 0345   PADOVA ❶❶

AA 3903232

ⒸCIT 2006-Ord. maggio 2010

❶ Departure date & time
❷ Point of departure
❸ Destination
❹ "Ticket with reservation"
❺ Number of passengers
❻ Arrival date & time
❼ Class of travel (1st or 2nd)
❽ "Present to official if changing trains"
❾ Train, car & seat numbers (finestrino=window seat)
❿ Fast-train fare
⓫ Location of ticket sale
⓬ Date of ticket purchase
⓭ Booking ID
⓮ Ticket cost
⓯ Amount of CO_2 usage reduced by this train trip

domestic and international tickets and make reservations. They charge a small fee, but the language barrier (and the lines) can be smaller than at the station's ticket windows.

Validating Tickets: If your ticket includes a seat reservation on a specific train *(biglietto con prenotazione)*, you're all set and can just get on board. An open ticket with no seat reservation (generally for a *regionali* train) must always be validated. Before you board, stamp your ticket (it may say *da convalidare* or *convalida*) in the machine near the platform (usually marked *convalida biglietti* or *vidimazione*). Once you validate a ticket, you must complete your trip within the timeframe shown on the ticket. If you forget to validate your ticket, go right away to the train conductor—before he comes to you—or you'll pay a fine. Note that you don't need to validate a rail pass each time you board (after it's been activated at a ticket window, you write in each travel date as you go).

Tickets purchased online are prevalidated, meaning that they can be used only for the date and time that you select (or within a four-hour window for unreserved regional trains).

Rail Passes

The single-country Eurail Italy Pass may save you money if you take several long train rides or prefer first-class travel, but for most people it's not a good value. In Sicily, no train trip within the island would warrant a rail pass, as it's cheaper to buy point-to-point tickets instead.

Furthermore, a rail pass doesn't offer much hop-on convenience in Italy, since many trains, such as Le Frecce (mainland only), EuroCity, and InterCity, require paid seat reservations (€5-10 each). Most regional trains don't require (or offer) reservations. Reservations for berths on overnight trains cost extra and aren't covered by rail passes.

For more detailed advice on figuring out the smartest rail-pass options for your train trip, visit RickSteves.com/rail.

Train Tips

Seat Reservations: Few trains in Sicily require a seat reservation. A reservation is important only on routes that connect the island to the mainland. If you're taking an unreserved *regionale* train that originates at your departure point (e.g., you're catching the Palermo-Agrigento train in Palermo), arriving at least 15 minutes before the departure time will help you snare a seat.

Baggage Storage: Many Italian stations have *deposito bagagli* where you can safely leave your bag for a standardized but rather steep price (€6/5 hours, €12/12 hours, €17/24 hours, payable when you pick up the bag, double-check closing hours; they may ask to

Rail Pass or Point-to-Point Travel?

Will you be better off buying a rail pass or point-to-point tickets? It pays to know your options and choose what's best for your itinerary.

Rail Passes

A Eurail Italy Pass lets you travel by train in Italy for three to eight days (consecutively or not) within a one-month period. Italy is also covered (along with most of Europe) by the classic Eurail Global Pass. Discounted rates are offered for seniors (age 60 and up) and youths (ages 12-27). Up to two kids (ages 4-11) can travel free with each adult-rate pass (but not with senior rates). All rail passes offer a choice of first or second class for all ages. Rail passes are best purchased outside Europe (through travel agents or Rick Steves' Europe). For more on rail passes, including current prices, go to RickSteves.com/rail.

Point-to-Point Tickets

If you're taking just a couple of train rides, look into buying individual point-to-point tickets, which may save you money over a pass. Use this map to add up approximate pay-as-you-go fares for your itinerary, and compare that to the price of a rail pass. Keep in mind that significant discounts on point-to-point tickets may be available with advance purchase.

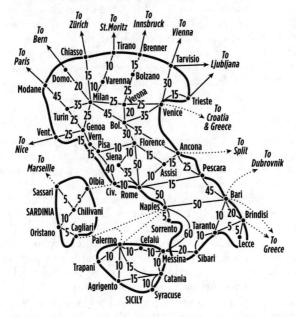

Map shows approximate costs, in USD, for one-way, second-class tickets on faster trains.

photocopy your passport). Due to security concerns, no Italian stations have lockers.

Theft Concerns: In big cities, exercise caution and prudence at train stations to avoid thieves and con artists. Homeless and marginalized people lurk around the station trying to skim tips (or worse) from unsuspecting tourists. If someone helps you to find your train or carry your bags, be aware that they are not an official porter; they are simply hoping for some cash. And if someone other than a uniformed railway employee tries to help you use the ticket machines, politely refuse.

Italian trains are famous for their thieves. Never leave a bag unattended. Police do ride the trains, cutting down on theft. Still, for an overnight trip, I'd feel safe only in a *cuccetta* (a bunk in a special sleeping car with an attendant who keeps track of who comes and goes while you sleep—approximately €40 or more).

Strikes: Strikes, which are common, generally last a day (often a Friday). Train employees will simply explain, *"Sciopero"* (SHOH-peh-roh, strike). But in actuality, a minimum amount of "essential" main-line service is maintained (by law) during strikes. When a strike is pending, travel agencies (and hoteliers) can check to see when the strike goes into effect and which trains will continue to run. Revised schedules may be posted online and in Italian at stations, and station personnel still working can often tell you what trains are expected to run. If I need to get somewhere and know a strike is imminent, I leave early (before the strike, which often begins at 9:00), or I just go to the station with extra patience in tow and hop on anything rolling in the direction I want to go. See www.trenitalia.com, choose English, then "Information and Contacts," and then "In Case of Strike."

BUSES

You can usually get anywhere you want in Sicily by bus, as long as you're not in a hurry and plan ahead using bus schedules (pick up at local TIs or bus stations). For reaching small towns, buses are sometimes the only option if you don't have a car.

Long-distance buses in Sicily are a great alternative to the train. They are usually cheaper, more direct, more frequent, and occasionally (unlike trains) have free Wi-Fi. They're especially useful on routes poorly served by train. Unfortunately, no single bus company handles every Sicilian route. Instead, multiple regional bus companies operate various routes around the island and to the mainland. These include Salemi (www.autoservizisalemi.it), Sais (within Sicily, www.saisautolinee.it) and Sais Trasporti (Sicily and mainland Italy, www.saistrasporti.it), Big Bus (www.bigbus.it), and Interbus/Segesta/Etna Trasporti (www.interbus.it), to name a few. Since websites tend to be in Italian, it's smart to confirm routes and times locally.

Larger towns have a (usually chaotic) long-distance bus station *(stazione degli autobus),* with ticket windows and several stalls (usually labeled *corsia, stallo,* or *binario)*—but to save time, buy your ticket at a travel agent. Smaller towns—where buses are more useful—often have a central bus stop *(fermata),* likely along the main road or on the main square, and maybe several more scattered around town. In small towns, buy bus tickets at newsstands or tobacco shops (with the big *T* signs). When buying your ticket, confirm the departure point *("Dov'è la fermata?").*

Before boarding, confirm the destination with the driver. You are expected to stow big backpacks underneath the bus (open the luggage compartment yourself if it's closed). Upon arrival, double-check that the posted schedule lists your next destination and departure time.

Sundays and holidays are problematic; even from large cities, schedules are sparse, departing buses are jam-packed, and ticket offices are often closed. Plan ahead and buy your ticket in advance. Most travel agencies book bus (and train) tickets for a small fee.

TAXIS AND RIDE-BOOKING SERVICES

Most Italian taxis are reliable and cheap. In many cities, two people can travel short distances by cab for little more than the cost of bus or subway tickets. Ride-booking services such as Uber do not operate in Sicily.

RENTING A CAR

It's cheaper to arrange most car rentals from the US, so research and compare rates before you go. Most of the major US rental agencies (including Avis, Budget, Enterprise, Hertz, and Thrifty) have offices throughout Europe. Also consider the two major Europe-based agencies, Europcar and Sixt. Consolidators such as Auto Europe/Kemwel (www.autoeurope.com—or the sometimes cheaper www.autoeurope.eu) compare rates at several companies to get you the best deal.

Wherever you book, always read the fine print. Ask about add-on charges—such as one-way drop-off fees, airport surcharges, or mandatory insurance policies—that aren't included in the "total price."

Rental Costs and Considerations

Figure on paying roughly $250 for a one-week rental for a basic compact car. Allow extra for supplemental insurance, fuel, tolls, and parking. To save you money on fuel, request a diesel car.

PRACTICALITIES

Manual vs. Automatic: Almost all rental cars in Europe are manual by default—and cars with a stick shift are generally cheaper. If you need an automatic, request one in advance. When selecting a car, don't be tempted by a larger model, as it won't be as maneuverable on narrow, winding roads or when squeezing into tight parking lots.

Age Restrictions: Some rental companies impose minimum and maximum age limits. Young drivers (25 and under) and seniors (69 and up) should check the rental policies and rules section of car rental websites.

Choosing Pick-Up/Drop-off Locations: Always check the hours of the locations you choose: Many rental offices close from midday Saturday until Monday morning and, in smaller towns, at lunchtime. When selecting an office, plug the addresses into a mapping website to confirm the location. A downtown site is generally cheaper—and might seem more convenient than the airport. But pedestrianized and one-way streets can make navigation tricky when returning a car at a big-city office or urban train station. For example, it's far easier to pick up and return a rental car to the Palermo or Catania airport. Both are just outside the city, easy to reach by bus or taxi from the center, and offer quick, easy access to the main highways.

Wherever you select, get precise details on the location and allow ample time to find it. And be aware that some Sicilian cities—including Palermo and Siracusa—have a "ZTL" (limited traffic zone) that's carefully monitored by cameras. If your drop-off point is near this zone, get clear directions on how to get there to avoid getting a big fine.

Have the Right License: If you're renting a car in Sicily, bring your driver's license. You're also technically required to have an International Driving Permit—an official translation of your license (sold at AAA offices for about $20 plus the cost of two passport-type photos; see www.aaa.com). While that's the letter of the law, I generally rent cars without having this permit. How this is enforced varies from country to country: Get advice from your car-rental company.

Picking Up Your Car: Before driving off in your rental car, check it thoroughly and make sure any damage is noted on your rental agreement. Rental agencies in Europe tend to charge for even minor damage, so be sure to mark everything. Find out how your car's gearshift, lights, turn signals, wipers, radio, and fuel cap function, and know what kind of fuel the car takes (diesel vs. unleaded). When you return the car, make sure the agent verifies its condition with you. Some drivers take pictures of the returned vehicle as proof of its condition.

Car Insurance Options

Sicily can be a rough-and-tumble place to drive. Getting a car that's fully insured will save you stress. I pay for complete coverage here, and drive care-free.

When you rent a car in Europe, the price typically includes liability insurance, which covers harm to other cars or motorists—but not the rental car itself. To limit your financial risk in case of damage to the rental, choose one of these options: Buy a Collision Damage Waiver (CDW) with a low or zero deductible from the car-rental company (roughly 30-40 percent extra), get coverage through your credit card (free, but more complicated), or get collision insurance as part of a larger travel-insurance policy.

Basic **CDW** costs $15–30 a day and typically comes with a $1,000-2,000 deductible, reducing but not eliminating your financial responsibility. When you reserve or pick up the car, you'll be offered the chance to "buy down" the deductible to zero (for an additional $10–30/day; this is sometimes called "super CDW" or "zero-deductible coverage").

In Italy, most car-rental companies' rates automatically include CDW coverage. Even if you try to decline CDW when you reserve your car, you may find when you show up at the counter that you must buy it after all (along with mandatory **theft insurance,** about $15–20 a day).

If you opt for **credit-card coverage,** you must decline all coverage offered by the car-rental company—which means they can place a hold on your card for up to the full value of the car. In case of damage, it can be time-consuming to resolve the charges. Before relying on this option, quiz your card company about how it works. Considering the controlled chaos that defines driving in Sicily, I find it is worth the cost to purchase insurance.

For more on car-rental insurance, see www.ricksteves.com/cdw.

Navigation Options

If you'll be navigating using your phone or a GPS unit from home, remember to bring a car charger and device mount.

Be wary of using internet-based maps in Sicily, particularly on country roads. Aside from highways and state roads, routes that appear to be major on an online map can turn into gravel donkey trails quickly. If something doesn't look right, turn around and stop to ask a local. Before setting out, confirm the best route with your hotelier, particularly for farmhouse or countryside lodgings.

Your Mobile Phone: The mapping app on your mobile phone works fine for navigation in Europe, but for real-time turn-by-turn directions and traffic updates, you'll need mobile data access. And driving all day can burn through a lot of very expensive data. The economical work-around is to use map apps that work offline. By downloading in advance from Google Maps, City Maps 2Go, Apple Maps, Here WeGo, or Navmii, you can still have turn-by-turn voice directions and maps that recalibrate even though they're offline.

You must download your maps before you go offline—and it's smart to select large regions. Then turn off your data connection so you're not charged for roaming. Call up the map, enter your destination, and you're on your way. Even if you don't have to pay extra for data roaming, this option is great for navigating in areas with poor connectivity.

GPS Devices: If you want the convenience of a dedicated GPS unit, consider renting one with your car ($10-30/day). These units offer real-time turn-by-turn directions and traffic without the data requirements of an app. The unit may come loaded only with maps for its home country; if you need additional maps, ask. Also make sure your device's language is set to English before you drive off.

A less-expensive option is to bring a GPS device from home. Be sure to buy and install the maps you'll need before your trip.

Maps and Atlases: Even when navigating primarily with a mobile app or GPS, I always make it a point to have a paper map, ideally a big, detailed regional road map (especially in Sicily, where online maps may not have correct information). It's invaluable for getting the big picture, understanding alternate routes, and filling in when my phone runs out of juice. The free maps you get from your car-rental company usually don't have enough detail. It's smart to buy a better map before you go, or pick one up at a Sicilian gas station, bookshop, newsstand, or tourist shop.

DRIVING

Driving in Sicily can be scary—a video game for keeps, and you only get one quarter. Locals drive fast and tailgate as if it were required. They pass where Americans are taught not to—on blind corners and just before tunnels. Roads have narrow shoulders or none at all. Driving in the countryside is less stressful than driving through urban areas or on busy highways, but stay alert. On one-lane roads, larger vehicles have the right of way.

Road Rules: Stay out of restricted traffic zones or you'll risk huge fines. Car traffic is restricted in many city centers, including Palermo and Ortigia (the historic center of Siracusa). Don't drive or park in any area that has a sign reading *Zona Traffico Limitato* (*ZTL,* often shown above a red circle—see image). If you do, your license plate will likely be photographed and a hefty (€80-plus) ticket mailed to your home without your ever having met a cop. Bumbling in and out of these zones can net you multiple fines. If your hotel is within a restricted area, ask your hotelier to direct you to parking outside the zone. (Although your hotelier can register your car as an authorized vehicle permitted to enter the zone, this usually isn't worth the hassle.) If you get a ticket, it could take months to show up (for more about traffic tickets in Italy, see www. bella-toscana.com/traffic_violations_italy.htm).

Even in cities without a ZTL, it's best to stay away from the center, as the historic streets can be narrow and tricky to navigate. The main streets in most Sicilian cities are pedestrian only; look for signs and ask your hotel before driving into the center. If you're uneasy about driving in cities, look for parking lots on the outskirts of town and walk in.

Be aware of typical European road rules; for example, many countries require headlights to be turned on at all times, and nearly all forbid handheld mobile-phone use. Seatbelts are mandatory, and children under age 12 must ride in child-safety or booster seats. In Europe, you're not allowed to turn right on a red light unless a sign or signal specifically authorizes it, and on expressways it's illegal to pass drivers on the right. Ask your car-rental company about these rules, or check the "International Travel" section of the US State Department website (www.travel.state.gov, search for Italy in the "Country Information" box, then click "Travel and Transportation").

Drive Defensively: Italians are aggressive drivers. Turn signals are optional. If a driver is tailgating you on the highway, pull to the side to let them pass, even if that means driving on the shoulder. If you're traveling in the right-hand lane on the highway, keep an eye out for slow-moving cars that appear out of nowhere. Also, if you brake quickly, it's customary to put on your hazard lights to warn the driver behind you. All this is normal for locals, who may colorfully gesture at you. Don't take it personally.

Sicilians don't follow normal right-of-way rules; observe and follow suit. For example, drivers making a left turn onto a busy street will slowly roll their car into oncoming traffic until everyone stops for them. It's best to stop when you see someone doing this. This makes roundabouts particularly challenging—simply forget everything you've learned about who has the right of way, and approach each roundabout as a unique experience. On country roads, you'll occasionally run into a "Sicilian traffic jam" (livestock blocking the road). There's nothing you can do but wait for the shepherd

PRACTICALITIES

PRACTICALITIES

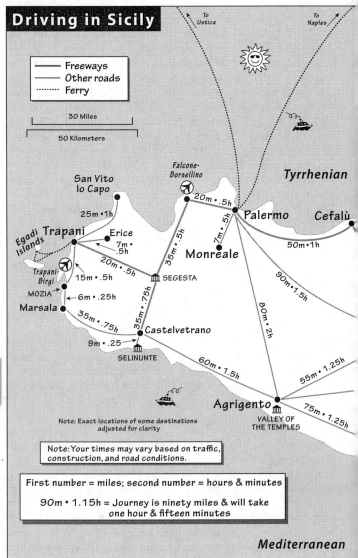

Driving in Sicily

Legend:
— Freeways
— Other roads
······· Ferry

30 Miles

50 Kilometers

To Ustica

To Naples

Tyrrhenian

San Vito lo Capo

Falcone-Borsellino ✈

20m • .5h

Palermo   Cefalù

25m • 1h

Egadi Islands

Trapani   Erice

7m • .5h

7m • .5h

50m • 1h

20m • .5h

35m • .5h

Monreale

Trapani-Birgi ✈

15m • .5h

SEGESTA

90m • 1.5h

MOZIA

6m • .25h

Marsala

35m • .75h

35m • .75h

80m • 2h

Castelvetrano

9m • .25

SELINUNTE

60m • 1.5h

55m • 1.25h

Agrigento

VALLEY OF THE TEMPLES

75m • 1.25h

Note: Exact locations of some destinations adjusted for clarity

Note: Your times may vary based on traffic, construction, and road conditions.

First number = miles; second number = hours & minutes

90m • 1.15h = Journey is ninety miles & will take one hour & fifteen minutes

Mediterranean

to move them along. Feel free to wave at him to make sure he sees you waiting.

Motor scooters are very popular, and scooter drivers often see themselves as exempt from rules that apply to automobiles.

Tolls: You'll pay tolls for some stretches of freeway (autostrada), including from Catania to Messina and Messina to Cefalù (for costs, use the trip-planning tool at www.autostrade.it or search

"European Tolls" on www.theaa.com). When approaching a toll-booth, skip lanes marked *Telepass;* for an attended booth, choose a lane with a sign that shows a hand or coins. Note that although there are toll booths on the autostrada south of Catania, the tolling system itself is not functional.

While I favor freeways because I feel they're safer and less nerve-racking than smaller roads, savvy local drivers know which toll-free *superstradas* are actually faster and more direct than the autostrada (e.g., Palermo to Cefalù). In some cases, if you have some time to spare, smaller roads can be worth the extra hassle—for example, the super-scenic SS-114 running north from Catania along the rocky coastline.

Fuel: Fuel is expensive—often about $6.50 per gallon. Diesel cars are more common in Europe than back home, so be sure you know what type of fuel your car takes before you fill up. Diesel costs less, about $6 per gallon. Gas pumps are color-coded: green for unleaded *(senza piombo)*; black for diesel *(gasolio)*. You'll also see the term *benzina*, which is standard fuel. If you are unsure or need help, stop for full-service gas *(servito)*. To fill up, say *"Pieno"* (pee-EH-noh). Autostrada rest stops can have full or self-service stations (open daily without a siesta break). Many 24-hour stations are entirely automated. Small-town stations are usually cheaper and offer full service but shorter hours.

Signage: Learn the universal road signs (see illustration). Although roads are numbered on maps, actual road signs give just a city name (for example, if you head west from Agrigento, a map would label the road "route S-115"—but the actual road signs read *Porto Empedocle*, the next town along this route). Signs are inconsistent: They may direct you to the nearest big city or simply the next town.

Theft: Cars are routinely vandalized and stolen. Thieves easily recognize rental cars and assume they are filled with a tourist's gear. Be sure all of your valuables are out of sight and locked in the trunk, or even better, with

you or in your room. On any city street or parking lot, "attendants" may tap on your window or approach you after you park (or they may "help" you find a spot). Their self-appointed job is to keep an eye on your car. While you don't have to give them anything, it's a good idea to hand over €1-2.

Parking: White lines generally mean parking is free. Yellow lines mean that parking is reserved for residents only (who have permits). Blue lines mean you'll have to pay—usually around €1 per hour (use machine, leave time-stamped receipt on dashboard). Study the signs. In many cities in Sicily, pay parking is not enforced midday or after dinner, and you'll have the option to prepay for several hours before and after those times. Free zones often have a 30- or 60-minute time limit. Signs showing a street cleaner and a day of the week indicate which day the street is cleaned; there's a €100 tow-fee incentive to learn the days of the week in Italian.

Zona disco has nothing to do with dancing. Italian cars come equipped with a time disc (a cardboard clock), which you can use in a *zona disco*—set the clock to your arrival time and leave it on the dashboard. (If your rental car doesn't come with a *disco*, pick one up at a tobacco shop or just write your arrival time on a piece of paper and place it on the dashboard.) These are generally used in areas where parking is free but has a time limit.

Garages are safe, save time, and help you avoid the stress of parking tickets. Take the parking voucher with you to pay the cashier before you leave.

FLIGHTS

To compare flight costs and times, begin with a travel search engine: Kayak.com is the top site for flights to and within Europe, easy-to-use Google Flights has price alerts, and Skyscanner.com includes many inexpensive flights within Europe.

Flights to Europe: Start looking for international flights about four to six months before your trip, especially for peak-season travel. Depending on your itinerary, it can be efficient and no more expensive to fly into one city and out of another. If your flight requires a connection in Europe, see my hints on navigating Europe's top hub airports at www.ricksteves.com/hub-airports.

Flights Within Europe: Flying between European cities has become surprisingly affordable. Before buying a long-distance train or bus ticket, first check the cost of a flight on one of Europe's airlines, whether a major carrier or a no-frills outfit like Easyjet and Ryanair. Be aware of the potential drawbacks of flying with a discount airline: nonrefundable and nonchangeable tickets, minimal customer service, time-consuming treks to secondary airports, and stingy baggage allowances (also an issue on major airlines). To avoid unpleasant surprises, read the small print about the costs for "extras" such as reserving a seat, checking a bag, or checking in and printing a boarding pass.

Flying to the US and Canada: Because security is extra tight for flights to the US, be sure to give yourself plenty of time at the airport. It's also important to charge your electronic devices before you board because security checks may require you to turn them on (see www.tsa.gov for the latest rules).

Resources from Rick Steves

Begin Your Trip at RickSteves.com

My mobile-friendly **website** is *the* place to explore Europe in preparation for your trip. You'll find thousands of fun articles, videos, and radio interviews; a wealth of money-saving tips for planning your dream trip; travel news dispatches; a video library of my travel talks; my travel blog; my latest guidebook updates (www.ricksteves.com/update); and my free Rick Steves Audio Europe app. You can also follow me on Facebook and Twitter.

Our **Travel Forum** is a well-groomed collection of message boards where our travel-savvy community answers questions and shares their personal travel experiences—and our well-traveled staff chimes in when they can be helpful (www.ricksteves.com/forums).

Our **online Travel Store** offers bags and accessories that I've designed to help you travel smarter and lighter. These include my popular carry-on bags (which I live out of four months a year), money belts, totes, toiletries kits, adapters, guidebooks, and planning maps (www.ricksteves.com/shop).

Our website can also help you find the perfect **rail pass** for your itinerary and your budget, with easy, one-stop shopping for rail passes, seat reservations, and point-to-point tickets (www.ricksteves.com/rail).

Rick Steves' Tours, Guidebooks, TV Shows, and More

Small Group Tours: Want to travel with greater efficiency and less stress? We offer more than 40 itineraries reaching the best destinations in this book...and beyond. Each year about 30,000 travelers join us on about 1,000 Rick Steves bus tours. You'll enjoy great guides and a fun bunch of travel partners (with small groups of 24 to 28 travelers). You'll find European adventures to fit every vacation length. For all the details, and to get our tour catalog, visit www.ricksteves.com/tours or call us at 425/608-4217.

Books: *Rick Steves Sicily* is just one of many books in my series on European travel, which includes country and city guidebooks, Snapshots (excerpted chapters from bigger guides), Pocket guides (full-color little books on big cities), "Best Of" guidebooks (condensed, full-

Rick Steves'
EUROPE
101
History &
Art for the
Traveler

Rick Steves &
Gene Openshaw

PRACTICALITIES

color country guides), and my budget-travel skills handbook, *Rick Steves Europe Through the Back Door.* A more complete list of my titles—including phrase books, cruising guides, and more—appears near the end of this book.

TV Shows and Travel Talks: My public television series, *Rick Steves' Europe,* covers Europe from top to bottom with over 100 half-hour episodes—and we're working on new shows every year (watch full episodes on my website for free). Or, to raise your travel I.Q., check out the video versions of our popular classes (covering most European countries as well as travel skills, packing smart, cruising, tech for travelers, European art, and travel as a political act—www.ricksteves.com/travel-talks).

Radio: My weekly public radio show, *Travel with Rick Steves,* features interviews with travel experts from around the world. It airs on 400 public radio stations across the US, or you can hear it as a podcast. A complete archive of programs is available at www.ricksteves.com/radio.

Audio Tours on My Free App: I've produced dozens of free, self-guided audio tours of the top sights in Europe. For those tours and other audio content, get my free **Rick Steves Audio Europe app,** an extensive online library organized by destination. For more on my app, see page 25.

PRACTICALITIES

APPENDIX

Holidays and Festivals

In deeply Catholic Sicily, a region where everything is either a drama or a comedy, every town has a festival celebrating its patron saint (even more exuberantly than on the mainland). If you happen to be here during a patron saint day, you'll see the town grind to a halt and celebrate with processions, masses, street fairs, festive lights, random fireworks, and devotees hauling huge candles, along with effigies of the saint. Celebrations are open to all, so feel free to jump in.

This list includes selected festivals in Sicily, plus national holidays observed throughout Italy. Many sights and banks close on national holidays—keep this in mind when planning your itinerary. Before planning a trip around a festival, verify the dates with the festival website, TI sites for Italy (www.italia.it) and Sicily (www.visitsicily.info), or my "Upcoming Holidays and Festivals in Italy" web page (www.ricksteves.com/europe/italy/festivals).

In Sicily, hotels get booked up on Easter weekend (Good Friday through Monday), as well as on Liberation Day (April 25) and Labor Day (May 1)—especially when these two holidays fall close to a weekend. In beach destinations, August is flooded with vacationing Italians and Europeans, particularly around the Feast of the Assumption, a.k.a. Ferragosto (Aug 15).

Jan 1	New Year's Day
Jan 6	Epiphany
Jan/Feb	Carnevale celebrations throughout Sicily (feasts and floats)
Feb 3-5	Festa di Sant'Agata, Catania (three days of processions and fireworks)
March/April	Easter weekend (Good Friday-Easter Monday): April 19-22, 2019; April 10-13, 2020; Procession of I Misteri, Trapani (Good Friday)
April 25	Italian Liberation Day
May 1	Labor Day
Late May	Noto Flower Festival (Infiorata di Noto, third weekend in May)
Late May	Festa delle Madonna delle Milizie, Scicli (processions, Norman battle reenactments; last Sat in May)
May/June	Feast Day of Corpus Christi
Late May/ Early June	Feast of San Giorgio, Ragusa Ibla (3-day festival, processions, fireworks)
May-July	Festival del Teatro Greco, Siracusa (Greek plays in the ancient theater)
May-Sept	Palermo festivals (music, food, and arts throughout the summer)
June 2	Anniversary of the Republic
June 24	Feast of St. John the Baptist
Late June	Feast of Sts. Peter and Paul (3-day festival in Modica)
Late June	Taormina Book Festival
Late June/ Early July	Taormina Film Festival (a week of screenings in the Greek theater)
July 9	Feast of San Pancrazio, Taormina
July 10-15	Festa di Santa Rosalia, Palermo (fireworks, large processions)
Early Aug	Feast of San Salvatore, Cefalù
Aug 15	Feast of the Assumption (Ferragosto)
Early Oct	Pistachio Festival, Bronte (town on Mount Etna)
Nov 1	All Saints' Day
Dec 8	Feast of the Immaculate Conception
Dec 13-20	Feast of Santa Lucia, Siracusa (procession of her statue and relics to the cathedral)
Dec 25	Christmas

| **Dec 26** | St. Stephen's Day (visits to living nativity scenes) |

Books and Films

To learn more about Sicily past and present, check out a few of these recommended books and films.

Nonfiction

The Middle Sea: A History of the Mediterranean (John Julius Norwich, 2006). Norwich is a great character and chronicler of Sicily. Here, he explores the connections between countries linked by the sea.

Midnight in Sicily (Peter Robb, 1996). Robb gives a detailed account of Sicily during the height of the Mafia's power, and the ties between organized crime and the Italian government.

On Persephone's Island (Mary Taylor Simeti, 1986). This personal account of an American who marries a Sicilian includes stories about Palermo, their countryside farm, and her Sicilian family.

The Peoples of Sicily: A Multicultural Legacy (Jacquline Alio and Louis Mendola, 2014). Sicily has been a unique, multicultural island for more than a thousand years; this book delves into how that has shaped its history.

Sicily: A Short History (John Julius Norwich, 2015). This readable account, covering 3,000 years of history, clearly sorts out the major events and characters.

Fiction

Day of the Owl (Leonardo Sciascia, 1961). This mystery focuses on the chilling effect the Mafia had on small-town life during the 1960s, when the Mafia's existence as a large-scale crime network was uncertain.

The Godfather (Mario Puzo, 1969). The Corleone family drama unfolds in this classic tale of crime, betrayal, and family honor. Following the success of *The Godfather,* Puzo continued the saga of this Mafia family in several novels, including *The Sicilian.*

The Shape of Water (Andrea Camilleri, 1994). The first in a series of mysteries finds Inspector Salvo Montalbano investigating an embarrassing death and cover-up. This long-standing series is a comedic portrayal of Sicilian life and people, set in the south of the island.

The Sicilian (Mario Puzo, 1984). A continuation of the *Godfather* saga, this story focuses on Salvatore Giuliano, a famous bandit who became a folk hero.

Six Characters in Search of an Author (Luigi Pirandello, 1921). In this intellectual comedy by the Sicilian-born writer, six "unused" characters of an author's imagination demand lines to tell their stories.

Film

Cinema Paradiso (1988). An acclaimed movie director from Rome recalls his childhood in Sicily, where his friendship with projectionist Alfredo introduces him to the passion of his life (Oscar for Best Foreign Language Film).

Divorzio all'Italiana (1961). Marcello Mastroianni plays a married Sicilian baron who falls in love with his young cousin—but divorce is illegal at the time (Oscar for Best Writing, Story and Screenplay).

The Godfather: Part II (1974). The best of the famous trilogy focuses on the tormented early life of Sicilian-born Vito Corleone, establishment of the family business in New York, and the passing of control to his son Michael (six Oscars, including Best Picture).

Il Gattopardo ("The Leopard," 1963). Set during the tumultuous unification of Italy, this Italian *Gone with the Wind* follows the decline of the Sicilian nobility in the 19th century (based on the 1956 novel by Giuseppe Tomasi di Lampedusa).

Il Postino (1994). On a beautiful island, a mailman is introduced to literature by a famous poet. (The movie was filmed in part on one of the Aeolian Islands, off Sicily's north coast.)

Inspector Montalbano (1999). This series (based on the books by Andrea Camilleri) follows a clever police chief inspector in provincial Sicily.

La Terra Trema (1948). This drama from the Giovanni Verga novel *I Malavoglia* is set in a coastal village north of Catania, where entire families of fishermen are at the mercy of greedy wholesalers. Director Luchino Visconti hired local people as actors.

Malèna (2000). Monica Bellucci plays Malèna, a sensual wife living by herself in a closed-minded Sicilian town while her husband is reported dead in World War II.

Salvatore Giuliano (1962). This drama centers around the real-life Robin Hood, who fought against the Italian government for the independence of Sicily—and eventually lost.

Conversions and Climate

Numbers and Stumblers

- Europeans write a few of their numbers differently than we do. 1 = 1, 4 = 4, 7 = 7.
- In Europe, dates appear as day/month/year, so Christmas 2020 is 25/12/20.
- Commas are decimal points and decimals are commas. A dollar and a half is $1,50, one thousand is 1.000, and there are 5.280 feet in a mile.
- When counting with fingers, start with your thumb. If you hold up your first finger to request one item, you'll probably get two.
- What Americans call the second floor of a building is the first floor in Europe.
- On escalators and moving sidewalks, Europeans keep the left "lane" open for passing. Keep to the right.

Metric Conversions

A **kilogram** equals 1,000 grams (about 2.2 pounds). One hundred **grams** (a common unit at markets) is about a quarter-pound. One **liter** is about a quart, or almost four to a gallon.

A **kilometer** is six-tenths of a mile. To convert kilometers to miles, cut the kilometers in half and add back 10 percent of the original (120 km: 60 + 12 = 72 miles). One **meter** is 39 inches—just over a yard.

1 foot = 0.3 meter	1 square yard = 0.8 square meter
1 yard = 0.9 meter	1 square mile = 2.6 square kilometers
1 mile = 1.6 kilometers	1 ounce = 28 grams
1 centimeter = 0.4 inch	1 quart = 0.95 liter
1 meter = 39.4 inches	1 kilogram = 2.2 pounds
1 kilometer = 0.62 mile	32°F = 0°C

APPENDIX

Roman Numerals

In the US, you'll see Roman numerals—which originated in ancient Rome—used for copyright dates, clocks, and the Super Bowl. In Italy, you're likely to observe these numbers chiseled on statues and buildings. If you want to do some numeric detective work, here's how: In Roman numerals, as in ours, the highest numbers (thousands, hundreds) come first, followed by smaller numbers. Many numbers are made by combining numerals into sets: V = 5, so VIII = 8 (5 plus 3). Roman numerals follow a subtraction principle for multiples of fours (4, 40, 400, etc.) and nines (9, 90, 900, etc.). The number 4, for example, is written as IV (1 subtracted from 5), rather than IIII. The number nine is IX (1 subtracted from 10).

Big numbers such as dates can look daunting at first. The easiest way to handle them is to read the numbers in discrete chunks. For example, Michelangelo was born in MCDLXXV. Break it down: M (1,000) + CD (100 subtracted from 500, or 400) + LXX (50 + 10 + 10, or 70) + V (5) = 1475. It was a very good year.

M = 1000	XL = 40
CM = 900	X = 10
D = 500	IX = 9
CD = 400	V = 5
C = 100	IV = 4
XC = 90	I = duh
L = 50	

Clothing Sizes

When shopping for clothing, use these US-to-European comparisons as general guidelines (but note that no conversion is perfect).

Women: For pants and dresses, add 36 in Italy (US 10 = Italian 46). For blouses and sweaters, add 8 for most of Europe (US 32 = European 40). For shoes, add 30-31 (US 7 = European 37/38).

Men: For shirts, multiply by 2 and add about 8 (US 15 = European 38). For jackets and suits, add 10. For shoes, add 32-34.

Children: Clothing is sized by height—in centimeters (2.5 inches = 1 cm), so a US size 8 roughly equates to 132-140. For shoes up to size 13, add 16-18, and for sizes 1 and up, add 30-32.

Sicily's Climate

First line, average daily high; second line, average daily low; third line, average days without rain. For more detailed weather statistics for destinations in this book (as well as the rest of the world), check www.wunderground.com.

J	F	M	A	M	J	J	A	S	O	N	D
Palermo											
59	59	62	67	75	82	87	88	82	76	68	61
50	49	51	55	62	69	74	75	70	64	58	52
8	7	7	6	2	1	1	1	4	6	7	9

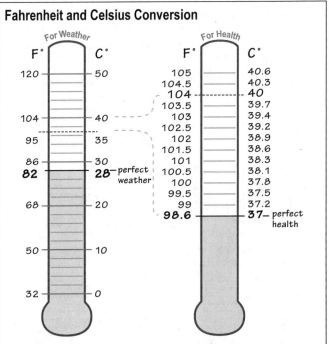

Fahrenheit and Celsius Conversion

Europe takes its temperature using the Celsius scale, while we opt for Fahrenheit. For a rough conversion from Celsius to Fahrenheit, double the number and add 30. For weather, remember that 28°C is 82°F—perfect. For health, 37°C is just right. At a launderette, 30°C is cold, 40°C is warm (usually the default setting), 60°C is hot, and 95°C is boiling. Your air-conditioner should be set at about 20°C.

APPENDIX

Packing Checklist

Whether you're traveling for five days or five weeks, you won't need more than this. Pack light to enjoy the sweet freedom of true mobility.

Clothing

- ❏ 5 shirts: long- & short-sleeve
- ❏ 2 pairs pants (or skirts/capris)
- ❏ 1 pair shorts
- ❏ 5 pairs underwear & socks
- ❏ 1 pair walking shoes
- ❏ Sweater or warm layer
- ❏ Rainproof jacket with hood
- ❏ Tie, scarf, belt, and/or hat
- ❏ Swimsuit
- ❏ Sleepwear/loungewear

Money

- ❏ Debit card(s)
- ❏ Credit card(s)
- ❏ Hard cash (US $100-200)
- ❏ Money belt

Documents

- ❏ Passport
- ❏ Tickets & confirmations: flights, hotels, trains, rail pass, car rental, sight entries
- ❏ Driver's license
- ❏ Student ID, hostel card, etc.
- ❏ Photocopies of important documents
- ❏ Insurance details
- ❏ Guidebooks & maps

Toiletries Kit

- ❏ Basics: soap, shampoo, toothbrush, toothpaste, floss, deodorant, sunscreen, brush/comb, etc.
- ❏ Medicines & vitamins
- ❏ First-aid kit
- ❏ Glasses/contacts/sunglasses
- ❏ Sewing kit
- ❏ Packet of tissues (for WC)
- ❏ Earplugs

Electronics

- ❏ Mobile phone
- ❏ Camera & related gear
- ❏ Tablet/ebook reader/laptop
- ❏ Headphones/earbuds
- ❏ Chargers & batteries
- ❏ Phone car charger & mount (or GPS device)
- ❏ Plug adapters

Miscellaneous

- ❏ Daypack
- ❏ Sealable plastic baggies
- ❏ Laundry supplies: soap, laundry bag, clothesline, spot remover
- ❏ Small umbrella
- ❏ Travel alarm/watch
- ❏ Notepad & pen
- ❏ Journal

Optional Extras

- ❏ Second pair of shoes (flip-flops, sandals, tennis shoes, boots)
- ❏ Travel hairdryer
- ❏ Picnic supplies
- ❏ Water bottle
- ❏ Fold-up tote bag
- ❏ Small flashlight
- ❏ Mini binoculars
- ❏ Small towel or washcloth
- ❏ Inflatable pillow/neck rest
- ❏ Tiny lock
- ❏ Address list (to mail postcards)
- ❏ Extra passport photos

Italian Survival Phrases

English	Italian	Pronunciation
Good day.	*Buon giorno.*	bwohn **jor**-noh
Do you speak English?	*Parla inglese?*	**par**-lah een-**gleh**-zay
Yes. / No.	*Sì. / No.*	see / noh
I (don't) understand.	*(Non) capisco.*	(nohn) kah-**pees**-koh
Please.	*Per favore.*	pehr fah-**voh**-ray
Thank you.	*Grazie.*	**graht**-see-ay
You're welcome.	*Prego.*	**preh**-go
I'm sorry.	*Mi dispiace.*	mee dee-spee-**ah**-chay
Excuse me.	*Mi scusi.*	mee **skoo**-zee
(No) problem.	*(Non) c'è problema.*	(nohn) cheh proh-**bleh**-mah
Good.	*Va bene.*	vah **beh**-nay
Goodbye.	*Arrivederci.*	ah-ree-veh-**dehr**-chee
one / two	*uno / due*	**oo**-noh / **doo**-ay
three / four	*tre / quattro*	tray / **kwah**-troh
five / six	*cinque / sei*	**cheeng**-kway / **seh**-ee
seven / eight	*sette / otto*	**seh**-tay / **oh**-toh
nine / ten	*nove / dieci*	**noh**-vay / dee-**ay**-chee
How much is it?	*Quanto costa?*	**kwahn**-toh **koh**-stah
Write it?	*Me lo scrive?*	may loh **skree**-vay
Is it free?	*È gratis?*	eh **grah**-tees
Is it included?	*È incluso?*	eh een-**kloo**-zoh
Where can I buy / find...?	*Dove posso comprare / trovare...?*	**doh**-vay **poh**-soh kohm-**prah**-ray / troh-**vah**-ray
I'd like / We'd like...	*Vorrei / Vorremmo...*	voh-**reh**-ee / voh-**reh**-moh
...a room.	*...una camera.*	**oo**-nah **kah**-meh-rah
...a ticket to ___.	*...un biglietto per ___.*	oon beel-**yeh**-toh pehr ___
Is it possible?	*È possibile?*	eh poh-**see**-bee-lay
Where is...?	*Dov'è...?*	doh-**veh**
...the train station	*...la stazione*	lah staht-see-**oh**-nay
...the bus station	*...la stazione degli autobus*	lah staht-see-**oh**-nay **dehl**-yee ow-toh-boos
...tourist information	*...informazioni per turisti*	een-for-maht-see-**oh**-nee pehr too-**ree**-stee
...the toilet	*...la toilette*	lah twah-**leh**-tay
men	*uomini / signori*	**woh**-mee-nee / seen-**yoh**-ree
women	*donne / signore*	**doh**-nay / seen-**yoh**-ray
left / right	*sinistra / destra*	see-**nee**-strah / **deh**-strah
straight	*sempre dritto*	**sehm**-pray **dree**-toh
What time does this open / close?	*A che ora apre / chiude?*	ah kay **oh**-rah **ah**-pray / kee-**oo**-day
At what time?	*A che ora?*	ah kay **oh**-rah
Just a moment.	*Un momento.*	oon moh-**mehn**-toh
now / soon / later	*adesso / presto / tardi*	ah-**deh**-soh / **preh**-stoh / **tar**-dee
today / tomorrow	*oggi / domani*	**oh**-jee / doh-**mah**-nee

In an Italian Restaurant

English	Italian	Pronunciation
I'd like...	Vorrei...	voh-**reh**-ee
We'd like...	Vorremmo...	vor-**reh**-moh
...to reserve...	...prenotare...	preh-noh-**tah**-ray
...a table for one / two.	...un tavolo per uno / due.	oon **tah**-voh-loh pehr **oo**-noh / **doo**-ay
Is this seat free?	È libero questo posto?	eh **lee**-beh-roh **kweh**-stoh **poh**-stoh
The menu (in English), please.	Il menù (in inglese), per favore.	eel meh-**noo** (een een-**gleh**-zay) pehr fah-**voh**-ray
service (not) included	servizio (non) incluso	sehr-**veet**-see-oh (nohn) een-**kloo**-zoh
cover charge	pane e coperto	**pah**-nay ay koh-**pehr**-toh
to go	da portar via	dah **por**-tar **vee**-ah
with / without	con / senza	kohn / **sehnt**-sah
and / or	e / o	ay / oh
menu (of the day)	menù (del giorno)	meh-**noo** (dehl **jor**-noh)
specialty of the house	specialità della casa	speh-chah-lee-**tah deh**-lah **kah**-zah
first course (pasta, soup)	primo piatto	**pree**-moh pee-**ah**-toh
main course (meat, fish)	secondo piatto	seh-**kohn**-doh pee-**ah**-toh
side dishes	contorni	kohn-**tor**-nee
bread	pane	**pah**-nay
cheese	formaggio	for-**mah**-joh
sandwich	panino	pah-**nee**-noh
soup	zuppa	**tsoo**-pah
salad	insalata	een-sah-**lah**-tah
meat	carne	**kar**-nay
chicken	pollo	**poh**-loh
fish	pesce	**peh**-shay
seafood	frutti di mare	**froo**-tee dee **mah**-ray
fruit / vegetables	frutta / legumi	**froo**-tah / lay-**goo**-mee
dessert	dolce	**dohl**-chay
tap water	acqua del rubinetto	**ah**-kwah dehl roo-bee-**neh**-toh
mineral water	acqua minerale	**ah**-kwah mee-neh-**rah**-lay
milk	latte	**lah**-tay
(orange) juice	succo (d'arancia)	**soo**-koh (dah-**rahn**-chah)
coffee / tea	caffè / tè	kah-**feh** / teh
wine	vino	**vee**-noh
red / white	rosso / bianco	**roh**-soh / bee-**ahn**-koh
glass / bottle	bicchiere / bottiglia	bee-kee-**eh**-ray / boh-**teel**-yah
beer	birra	**bee**-rah
Cheers!	Cin cin!	cheen cheen
More. / Another.	Di più. / Un altro.	dee pew / oon **ahl**-troh
The same.	Lo stesso.	loh **steh**-soh
The bill, please.	Il conto, per favore.	eel **kohn**-toh pehr fah-**voh**-ray
Do you accept credit cards?	Accettate carte di credito?	ah-cheh-**tah**-tay **kar**-tay dee **kreh**-dee-toh
tip	mancia	**mahn**-chah
Delicious!	Delizioso!	day-leet-see-**oh**-zoh

APPENDIX

For more user-friendly Italian phrases, check out *Rick Steves' Italian Phrase Book & Dictionary* or *Rick Steves' French, Italian, & German Phrase Book*.

INDEX

INDEX

INDEX

MAP INDEX

Explore Europe

At ricksteves.com you can browse through thousands of articles, videos, photos and radio interviews, plus find a wealth of money-saving travel tips for planning your dream trip. And with our mobile-friendly website, you can easily access all this great travel information anywhere you go.

TV Shows

Preview the places you'll visit by watching entire half-hour episodes of Rick Steves' Europe (choose from all 100 shows) on-demand, for free.

ricksteves.com

your travel dreams into affordable reality

Radio Interviews

Enjoy ready access to Rick's vast library of radio interviews covering travel

tips and cultural insights that relate specifically to your Europe travel plans.

Travel Forums

Learn, ask, share! Our online community of savvy travelers is a great resource for first-time travelers to Europe, as well as seasoned pros. You'll find forums on each country, plus travel tips and restaurant/hotel reviews. You can even ask one of our well-traveled staff to chime in with an opinion.

Travel News

Subscribe to our free Travel News e-newsletter, and get monthly updates from Rick on what's happening in Europe.

Audio Europe™

Rick's Free Travel App

Get your FREE **Rick Steves Audio Europe**™ app to enjoy...

- Dozens of self-guided tours of Europe's top museums, sights and historic walks
- Hundreds of tracks filled with cultural insights and sightseeing tips from Rick's radio interviews
- All organized into handy geographic playlists
- For Apple and Android

With Rick whispering in your ear, Europe gets even better.

Find out more at ricksteves.com

Pack Light and Right

*Gear up for your
next adventure at
ricksteves.com*

Light Luggage

Pack light and right
with Rick Steves'
affordable, custom-
designed rolling carry-on
bags, backpacks, day
packs and shoulder bags.

Accessories

From packing cubes to
moneybelts and beyond,
Rick has personally
selected the travel
goodies that will help
your trip
go smoother.

Shop at ricksteves.com

Rick Steves has

Experience maximum Europe

Save time and energy

This guidebook is your independent-travel toolkit. But for all it delivers, it's still up to you to devote the time and energy it takes to manage the preparation and logistics that are essential for a happy trip. If that's a hassle, there's a solution.

Rick Steves Tours

A Rick Steves tour takes you to Europe's most interesting places with great

with minimum stress

guides and small groups of 28 or less. We follow Rick's favorite itineraries, ride in comfy buses, stay in family-run hotels, and bring you intimately close to the Europe you've traveled so far to see. Most importantly, we take away the logistical headaches so you can focus on the fun.

travelers—nearly half of them repeat customers—along with us on four dozen different itineraries, from Ireland to Italy to Athens. Is a Rick Steves tour the right fit for your travel dreams? Find out at ricksteves.com, where you can also request Rick's latest tour catalog. Europe is best experienced with happy travel partners. We hope you can join us.

Join the fun
This year we'll take thousands of free-spirited

See our itineraries at ricksteves.com

BEST OF GUIDES

Full-color guides in an easy-to-scan format. Focused on top sights and experiences in the most popular European destinations

Best of England
Best of Europe
Best of France
Best of Germany
Best of Ireland
Best of Italy
Best of Scotland
Best of Spain

COMPREHENSIVE GUIDES

City, country, and regional guides printed on bible-thin paper. Packed with detailed coverage for a multi-week trip exploring iconic sights and venturing off the beaten path

Amsterdam & the Netherlands
Barcelona
Belgium: Bruges, Brussels, Antwerp & Ghent
Berlin
Budapest
Croatia & Slovenia
Eastern Europe
England
Florence & Tuscany
France
Germany
Great Britain
Greece: Athens & the Peloponnese
Iceland
Ireland
Istanbul
Italy
London
Paris
Portugal
Prague & the Czech Republic
Provence & the French Riviera
Rome
Scandinavia
Scotland
Sicily
Spain
Switzerland
Venice
Vienna, Salzburg & Tirol

HE BEST OF ROME

e, Italy's capital, is studded with
nan remnants and floodlit-fountain
res. From the Vatican to the Colos-
, with crazy traffic in between, Rome
nderful, huge, and exhausting. The
s, the heat, and the weighty history

of the Eternal City where Caesars walked
can make tourists wilt. Recharge by taking siestas, gelato breaks, and after-dark
walks, strolling from one atmospheric
square to another in the refreshing evening air.

l Pantheon—which
t dome until the
y 2,000 years old
over 1,500).

Athens in the Vat-
ies the humanistic
e.

diators fought
other, entertaining

Rome ristorants

Rick Steves books are available from your favorite bookseller.
Many guides are available as ebooks.

Credits

To help research this book, Rick relied on...

CONTRIBUTOR
Cameron Hewitt

Born in Denver and raised in central Ohio, Cameron settled in Seattle in 2000. Ever since, he has spent three months each year in Europe, contributing to guidebooks, tours, radio and television shows, and other media for Rick Steves' Europe, where he serves as content manager. Cameron married his high school sweetheart (and favorite travel partner), Shawna, and enjoys taking pictures, trying new restaurants, and planning his next trip.

Acknowledgments

The authors wish to say *"Grazie"* to the following people for their travel savvy and expertise, which helped shape the first edition of *Rick Steves Sicily:* Michele Gallo, Jackie Alio, Elena Buscemi, Benjamin Spencer, and Boris Behncke. Also thanks to Rainer Metzger for lending us his critical eye and additional Sicily expertise.

Photo Credits

Front Cover: Greek Theater and Mount Etna, Taormina © Antonino Bartuccio/SIME/eStock Photo

Title Page: Ballarò Street Market, Palermo © Dominic Arizona Bonuccelli

Public Domain via Wikimedia Commons: 394, 396

Additional Photography: Dominic Arizona Bonuccelli, Mary Ann Cameron, Alfio Di Mauro, Cameron Hewitt, Sarah Murdoch, Rick Steves, Laura Van Deventer, Andrew Wakeling. Photos are used by permission and are the property of the original copyright owners.

Avalon Travel
Hachette Book Group
1700 Fourth Street
Berkeley, CA 94710

Text © 2019 by Rick Steves' Europe, Inc. All rights reserved.
Maps © 2019 by Rick Steves' Europe, Inc. All rights reserved.

Printed in Canada by Friesens.
First printing April 2019.

ISBN 978-1-64171-102-9
First Edition

For the latest on Rick's talks, guidebooks, tours, public television series, and public radio show, contact Rick Steves' Europe, 130 Fourth Avenue North, Edmonds, WA 98020, 425/771-8303, www.ricksteves.com, rick@ricksteves.com.

Hachette Book Group supports the right to free expression and the value of copyright. The purpose of copyright is to encourage writers and artists to produce the creative works that enrich our culture. The scanning, uploading, and distribution of this book without permission is a theft of the author's intellectual property. If you would like permission to use material from the book (other than for review purposes), please contact permissions@hbgusa.com. Thank you for your support of the author's rights.

The publisher is not responsible for websites (or their content) that are not owned by the publisher.

Rick Steves' Europe
Managing Editor: Jennifer Madison Davis
Assistant Managing Editor: Cathy Lu
Special Publications Manager: Risa Laib
Editors: Glenn Eriksen, Julie Fanselow, Tom Griffin, Suzanne Kotz, Rosie Leutzinger, Jessica Shaw, Carrie Shepherd
Editorial & Production Assistant: Megan Simms
Editorial Intern: Nola Peshkin, Madeline Smith
Contributor: Cameron Hewitt
Graphic Content Director: Sandra Hundacker
Maps & Graphics: David C. Hoerlein, Lauren Mills, Mary Rostad
Digital Asset Coordinator: Orin Dubrow

Avalon Travel
Senior Editor and Series Manager: Madhu Prasher
Editors: Jamie Andrade, Sierra Machado
Copy Editor: Maggie Ryan
Proofreader: Janet Walden
Indexer: Stephen Callahan
Production & Typesetting: Lisi Baldwin, Rue Flaherty, Jane Musser
Cover Design: Kimberly Glyder Design
Maps & Graphics: Kat Bennett, Mike Morgenfeld

Although every effort was made to ensure that the information was correct at the time of going to press, the author and publisher do not assume and hereby disclaim any liability to any party for any loss or damage caused by errors, omissions, overcooked pasta, or any potential travel disruption due to labor or financial difficulty, whether such errors or omissions result from negligence, accident, or any other cause.

COLOR MAPS

Tyrrhenian Sea

To Naples

PALERMO

Cefalù

Trapani ·Erice

Taormina

Randazzo

Egadi Islands ·Mozia

■SEGESTA **Monreale**

Mt. Etna Linguaglossa

RIFUGIO SAPIENZA

Catania

VALLEY OF THE TEMPLES

Piazza Armerina

Ionian Sea

Agrigento

VILLA ROMANA DEL CASALE

SIRACUSA

Ragusa

Noto

50 Miles

Scicli ·Modica

50 Kilometers

Mediterranean Sea

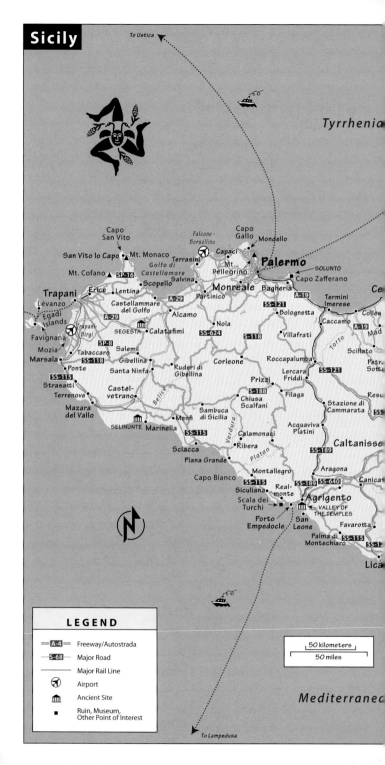

Sicily

To Ustica

Tyrrhenia

Capo San Vito
San Vito lo Capo • Mt. Monaco
Mt. Cofano ▲ SP-16
Trapani
Érice • Lentina
Lévanzo
Egadi Islands
Favignana ✈ Trapani-Birgi
Mozia
Marsala • Tabaccaro
Ponte
Strasatti
Terrenove
Mazara del Vallo

Falcone-Borsellino ✈ • Capaci
Terrasini
Golfo di Castellamare • Salvina
Scopello
Castellammare del Golfo A-29
Alcamo
SEGESTA 🏛 Calatafimi
SP-8
Salemi
Gibellina
Santa Ninfa
Castel-vetrano
Ruderi di Gibellina
Corleone

Capo Gallo • Mondello
Mt. Pellegrino **Palermo**
SOLUNTO
Capo Zafferano
Monreale • Bagheria A-19
SS-121
Partinico Bolognetta
Nola SS-624
Villafrati
S-118
Roccapalumba
Prizzi
S-188
Chiusa Scalfani
Filaga
Lercara Friddi
Stazione di Cammarata

Ce...
Termini Imerese
Caccamo Colles
A-19 Mad
Torto Scillato
Petra Sotta
SS-121
Resu
SS

SELINUNTE 🏛 Marinella
Menfi
Sambuca di Sicilia SS-115
Calamonaci
Sciacca • Ribera
Piana Grande *Verdura* *Platan*
Capo Bianco
Montallegro SS-115
Siculiana Real-monte SS-189 SS-640
Scala dei Turchi
Porto Empedocle • San Leone
Palma di Montechiaro SS-115

Acquaviva Platini
Caltanisse
SS-189
Aragona Canica
Agrigento
🏛 VALLEY OF THE TEMPLES
Favarotta
SS-1
Lica

Belice
Verdura
Platan

LEGEND

═══ A-4 ═══	Freeway/Autostrada
— S-68 —	Major Road
——	Major Rail Line
✈	Airport
🏛	Ancient Site
■	Ruin, Museum, Other Point of Interest

50 kilometers
50 miles

Mediterranea

To Lampedusa

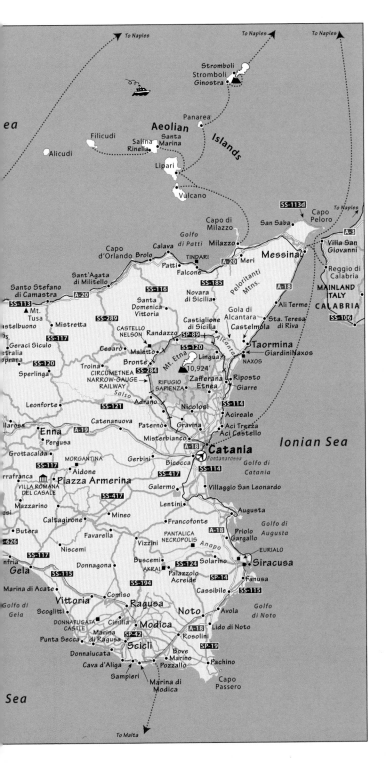

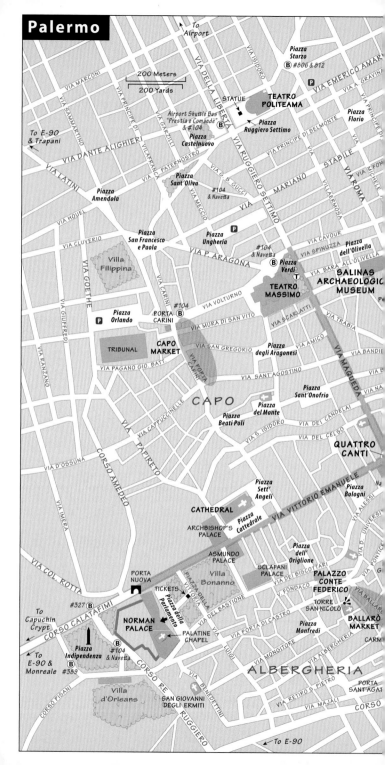

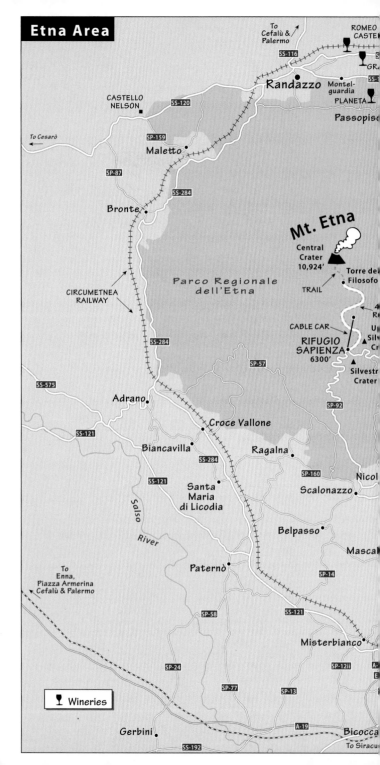